BOTTOM LINE'S

Breakthroughs in Drug-Free Healing

Thousands of the Best Science-Proven Natural Remedies to Curb, Cure and Prevent Common Ailments and Serious Conditions

Bill Gottlieb

Bottom Line
Books
www.BottomLineSecrets.com

To DD, my drug-free darling, for her love, patience and support.

Bottom Line's Breakthroughs in Drug-Free Healing

Thousands of the Best Science-Proven Natural Remedies to Curb, Cure and Prevent Common Ailments and Serious Conditions.

ISBN 0-88723-505-0

10 9 8 7 6 5 4 3 2 1

Bottom Line Books® is a registered trademark of Boardroom Inc.
281 Tresser Blvd., Stamford CT 06901
www.BottomLineSecrets.com

Printed in the United States of America

CONTENTS

▌▌▶ Breakthrough Study   ☀ Resource   ⓘ Product Description

PREFACE
SCIENCE-PROVEN REMEDIES FOR RELIABLE, NATURAL RELIEF

Every year, scientists at universities, research centers and hospitals in the United States and around the world conduct studies showing that drug-free remedies can treat and heal a wide range of health problems, from minor ailments to serious health conditions.

There's just one problem with most of those studies. You rarely ever hear about them!

For example, have you heard that…

• **Eating a daily piece of dark chocolate about the size of a Hershey's kiss** can lower your blood pressure as effectively as drugs.

• **A new super-oil made from avocado and soy** can cut your need for arthritis-relieving painkillers in half.

• **A specially formulated herbal remedy** can help you recover *twice* as fast from the flu, with total relief in just three days.

• **Sprinkling a meal with a deliciously flavored fiber powder** made from the root of a Japanese plant can lower insulin levels by 40%—helping prevent or normalize diabetes. (*"There is nothing as powerful,"* says a university-based diabetes specialist.)

• **A little-known nutritional supplement** can *completely* prevent holiday weight gain (in fact, people who took it actually lost weight).

Yes, those are *scientific findings* from doctors and top health experts—findings that were painstakingly proven, double-checked by peers and then published in medical journals. But those journals aren't sitting next to *Time* and *Newsweek* on the newsstand. They're not even on the coffee table in your doctor's waiting room. No, they're mostly read (and filed away) by medical specialists. Which is why you probably didn't hear about any of those five studies or hundreds like them. Well, no wonder. There's a lot of competition for your attention!

Hit the Mute Button

That's what Marcia Angell, MD, thinks you should do every time there's another TV commercial advertising a prescription drug.

Dr. Angell is a faculty member at Harvard Medical School, former editor-in-chief of the *New England Journal of Medicine* and author of *The Truth About the Drug Companies: How They Deceive Us and What to Do About It* (Random House).

She points out that in a recent four-year period, drug companies *tripled* the amount of money they spent on advertising prescription medications directly to consumers. At the same time, the number of retail prescriptions for drugs nearly doubled. Meanwhile, the number of "adverse effects" from drugs—harm, hospitalization or death—doubled, too! (An expert points out that drugs are the fourth leading cause of death in the United States!)

"Drug companies are primarily marketing machines selling drugs of dubious benefits," says Dr. Angell.

"Drug companies now sponsor almost all research on their own drugs," she continues. "That research is seriously flawed, presenting results that cause both doctors and consumers to believe drugs are a lot better than they are and have fewer side effects than they do."

In fact, while I was writing this book, there was a period of time that I've since dubbed "The Season of Side Effects." *Here's a small sampling of what happened in just four months…*

- **A major cholesterol drug in the pipeline**—in fact, in the midst of the most expensive drug study ever conducted, involving more than 7,000 people—was withdrawn when researchers discovered it *caused* heart attacks, the problem it was meant to solve.

- **The FDA ordered 15 migraine drugs off the market** because they lacked adequate warnings about safety and effectiveness.

- **Drugs used by millions of cancer patients to counter anemia** were found to make cancer worse.

- **Common painkillers such as aspirin, ibuprofen and acetaminophen**—the three most commonly taken drugs in the US—were found to increase the risk of high blood pressure by more than 30%.

- **Drugs for diabetes were found to increase the risk of bone fractures in women.** Ditto for antidepressants.

- **A drug for age-related macular degeneration** was found to increase the risk for stroke.

- **A drug commonly used to treat pneumonia** was linked to severe liver problems.

- **A common anesthetic was found to increase the risk of Alzheimer's disease.**

- **Accidental poisonings from prescription drugs** rose to number two as the cause of unintentional deaths, right behind car accidents.

- **A drug for restless leg syndrome was found to cause compulsive gambling!**

Well, it seems like taking medications is a bit of a gamble, too!

Now, it's not that drugs are bad per se or should never be taken. Far from it.

"There are times when a health problem is so severe or life-threatening that medications are necessary," says Judith Stanton, MD, of the California Healing Institute, in Albany, CA. "For example, if a bladder infection has progressed to the point of a kidney infection, then antibiotics are necessary, as this condition can be dangerous and potentially fatal if not treated."

But, she continues, a drug-free remedy is almost always preferable to a drug—"It's always best to treat any health problem with the most natural method—the method that encourages the body's natural capacity to heal and restores the body's natural balance."

Dr. Stanton also points out the necessity of working *with* your doctor or other qualified health-care professional, whenever you take drug-free remedies. "With any health condition, it's important to work with a health practitioner," she emphasizes. "That individual can help determine the cause of the problem, and the most helpful treatments. The practitioner will also know when an illness is serious and may require drugs or surgery."

The Best Breakthroughs

I'm a health writer and educator, with 30 years of experience, and I've just spent the past year or so finding the *very best* of drug-free breakthroughs, in the massive and comprehensive database of scientific studies maintained by the National Institutes of Health and in many other top medical databases.

I've deeply researched hundreds of diseases and conditions...double-, triple- and quadruple-checked to make sure I'd located each and every drug-free remedy for those problems that had appeared in medical journals in the past couple of years...and then interviewed hundreds of the world's top health experts to put together a collection of the most effective, safest (and often most surprising) of those remedies—the collection you're holding in your hands today.

You see, I just can't stand the idea that people like yourself and your loved ones—people who might have to battle every day against common conditions such as high blood pressure, arthritis, infections, blood sugar problems and overweight—don't have easy access to the best and most recent breakthroughs in the science of natural healing.

And I don't like the idea that your choices for achieving better health are *limited*—that you think you have to take a drug, when there's actually a safer and often more effective alternative. Because if you're like most Americans, you'd rather not take a drug if you don't have to—and, as noted above, with good reason.

Drug-Free Healing, Disease-Free Living

Welcome, then, to *Bottom Line's Breakthroughs in Drug-Free Healing.*

You'll read about the best ways to slow aging...relieve the pain of arthritis...prevent cancer or find natural support...rebalance your blood sugar and defeat diabetes...soothe digestive distress...calm upset emotions...spiff up your eyesight and hearing...relieve pain...reverse heart disease...beat infections...strengthen your memory and avoid Alzheimer's...build better bones...rejuvenate skin...reduce stress and fatigue...and beat the diseases unique to men or to women.

And for each of those areas of concern, you'll find fascinating tales of scientific breakthroughs, and exactly how to use that breakthrough for better health. Share the information and ideas in this book with your doctor, and with the best medical guidance and your own intelligence and insight, enjoy your breakthrough to better health!

Bill Gottlieb
Fall 2008

ABOUT THE AUTHOR

Bill Gottlieb is a health educator, specializing in drug-free remedies. He has written five books, including the best seller, *Alternative Cures* (Rodale), and *The Natural Fat-Loss Pharmacy* (Broadway). His articles on health and healing have appeared in *Bottom Line Personal, Bottom Line Health, Bottom Line Women's Health, Prevention, Men's Health, Health, Natural Healing, Reader's Digest* and many other national periodicals. He is the former editor-in-chief of Rodale Books and Prevention Magazine Health Books. He lives in northern California.

ACKNOWLEDGMENTS

I'd like to thank my editor Karen Daly for her consistent encouragement, flexibility, kindness, judgment and skill. Her support was invaluable. Hearty thanks, too, to my editor, Adrienne Makowski, whose friendly counsel helped keep me on track in the final months of writing this book. An advanced degree of appreciation for Tim McCall, MD, the book's ever-wise medical reviewer. Thanks to Brian Kurtz and Marty Edelston, the executives at Bottom Line who gave the go-ahead for the project. And much gratitude to the other hard workers at Bottom Line Books who helped make this book a reality, especially book designer John Niccolls, Cathy Meyer, Maureen Naccari, Alison Jewett and Giovanni Monsalve. As always, heaps of thanks to my literary agent of 12 years, Christine Tomasino, for her hard and hearted work on my behalf. And, finally, a sincere salute to the hundreds of scientists, doctors and other health professionals whose work was the basis of this book—these dedicated men and women have systematically studied drug-free remedies, with the mission of finding the best ways to prevent and relieve the pain and suffering of their fellow human beings. I am proud and happy to report on their useful findings

AGING & LONGEVITY
HEALTHIER, STRONGER, HAPPIER—AT ANY AGE!

In a not too distant future, more than 70 million Americans will be over 65. And, for those in that age group (or planning to join anytime soon), the good news keeps rolling in. The good news about lifestyle and longevity, that is.

A new study of more than 20,000 people aged 45 to 79 shows that just four everyday habits—eating five servings a day of fruits and vegetables; having a physically active life, whether at work or at play; drinking moderately and not smoking—can extend life by 14 years compared with folks who don't have those habits. You heard right—not one, two, five or 10 years…but *14 years*.

And that study is just one among many reports on scientific breakthroughs that detail the foods, nutritional supplements and types of exercise that can help you live a healthier, longer life.

"By applying what we've learned through scientific research, we will be able to extend our longevity so we can live to what is now considered extreme old age, without disease or decrepitude," says Mark Liponis, MD, corporate medical director of Canyon Ranch health resorts, and author of *UltraLongevity* (Little, Brown).

Ready to start extending your life? Scientists are standing by.

FRUITS AND VEGETABLES FOR A FIT FUTURE

What scares you the *most* about aging?

Maybe it's the thought of *helplessness*—not being able to dress yourself, feed yourself, cook a meal, manage your finances, walk up a flight of stairs…

Well, if you want to take a couple of very important actions to stay as functional as possible for as long as possible—eat a salad, snack on an apple and drink a glass of low-fat milk.

▐▶ *Breakthrough Study*

Researchers at the University of North Carolina at Chapel Hill studied more than 9,000 people aged 45 to 64 for nine years. First, they found out how many daily servings of fruits, vegetables and dairy products they ate. Nine years later, the researchers matched those dietary habits to the participants' ability (or inability) to perform 12 basic daily activities.

Result: Those who ate the fewest daily servings of fruits, vegetables and dairy products were more likely to have the worst levels of daily functioning. *For example, they were…*

• **33% more likely to have impaired "lower-extremity function"** and not be able to walk one-quarter of a mile…walk up 10 steps

THE EIGHT SECRETS OF CENTENARIANS

"Many people believe that the older a person gets, the sicker he or she becomes," says Thomas T. Perls, MD, MPH, director of the New England Centenarian Study at the Boston University School of Medicine. But that's simply not true, he says. His research found that approximately 90% of centenarians are "functionally independent" at the age of 92. How do you survive—and even thrive—into extreme old age? "It's a complex combination of genetics, environment, lifestyle and luck," says Dr. Perls.

When Japanese researchers tried to specify the elements of that complex combination by studying 1,907 centenarians, they found the following factors (some genetic, some environmental, some lifestyle, some luck) were among the most important in whether or not you stay independent into your 9th and 10th decades of life...

• Good eyesight
• Regular exercise
• Ability to chew
• No history of drinking
• No history of severe falls after the age of 95
• Frequent intake of protein
• Living at home
• Waking up in the morning without someone else having to rouse you (the alarm clock is okay)

"A diet that is higher in fruits and vegetables affects more than chronic conditions such as heart disease and cancer," says Denise K. Houston, MS, PhD, RD, the lead researcher for the study published in the *American Journal of Clinical Nutrition*. "It's possible that by eating a healthier diet, you can reduce your likelihood of having functional limitations later in life."

Why it works: The antioxidants in fruits and vegetables help minimize *oxidation*, the rustlike biochemical process that damages tissues—damage that might cause functional limitations, explains Dr. Houston. As for dairy, she points out that it's the main dietary source of calcium and vitamin D, nutrients that can decrease the risk of osteoporosis, broken bones and weakened muscles.

Recommended: Two to 4 daily servings of fruit, 3 to 5 daily servings of vegetables and 2 to 3 daily servings of low-fat dairy products.

Example: A vegetable serving is ½ cup (4 ounces) of vegetables. A fruit serving is one small or medium-size piece of fruit. A dairy serving is one cup (8 ounces) of milk, one cup of yogurt or 1½ ounces of cheese.

without resting...stoop, crouch or kneel...lift or carry something as heavy as 10 pounds.

• **48% more likely to have impaired "activity of daily living"** and not be able to walk from one room to another on the same level; get in or out of bed; eat or drink from a glass; get dressed.

• **36% more likely to have impaired "instrumental activities of daily living"** and not be able to do chores around the house; prepare meals; manage money.

MEDITERRANEAN DIET— LONG LIFE FOR UNCLE SAM

The Mediterranean diet—more vegetables, legumes (beans and peas), fruits, nuts, whole grains and fish; more monounsaturated fat, from foods such as olive oil and avocados; less saturated fat, from meat and dairy products —has been found to extend the life of people in European countries such as Greece and Italy. Well, they're *from* the Mediterranean. The diet suits them. What about us apple pie Americans?

DON'T LIKE OLIVE OIL? DON'T WORRY

For some people, the monounsaturated-rich olive oil that is the centerpiece of the Mediterranean diet is an acquired taste—that they never acquire! Is olive oil a *must* for longer life? Is there a diet *like* the Mediterranean diet, minus the extra-virgin ingredient?

Yes, says an international team of researchers from Greece, France, the Netherlands, Germany, Italy, England and Spain. They analyzed dietary data from nearly 75,000 European men and women who were aged 60 or older when their research began, and who didn't have a history of heart disease, stroke or cancer.

An average of seven years later, those who had eaten a *Modified Mediterranean Diet* had a 14% lower risk of dying than those who didn't, say the researchers, in the journal *Public Health and Nutrition*. What's "modified" about it?

There are still lots of vegetables, fruits and whole grains in the Modified Mediterranean Diet. But the unsaturated fats in the diet are mostly polyunsaturated (from safflower, sesame, soy, corn and sunflower-seed oils, and nuts and seeds), with monounsaturated fats (from olive, canola and peanut oils, and avocados) playing a secondary role. "Intake of monounsaturated fats from olive oil is minimal in the Modified Mediterranean Diet," says Antonia Trichopoulou, MD, PhD, the lead researcher for the study and an associate professor at the University of Athens Medical School.

In other words, you don't have to switch your culinary citizenship to live longer. If you're over 60 and want to eat a diet that extends life, the researchers say to favor a *plant-based diet* that maximizes fruits, vegetables, whole grains, legumes, and nuts and seeds, and minimizes red meat and high-fat dairy products.

⫸ *Breakthrough Study*

Researchers analyzed dietary and longevity data from 215,000 American men and 166,000 American women participating in the National Institutes of Health Diet and Health Study. *They found that men whose diets matched the "Mediterranean dietary pattern" were…*

- **21% less likely to die prematurely of any cause,**
- **22% less likely to die of heart disease** and
- **17% less likely to die of cancer.**

Results for women were 20% less for any cause, 19% less for heart disease and 12% less for cancer.

"These results provide strong evidence for the beneficial effect of higher conformity with the Mediterranean dietary pattern on risk of death in a US population," says Panagiota Mitrou, PhD, a researcher at the government's National Institutes of Health and the lead author of the study in the *Archives of Internal Medicine*. In other words, the Mediterranean diet can extend the life of Uncle Sam (and Aunt Samantha).

☀ *The Sonoma Diet* by Connie Gutterson, RD, PhD (Meredith Books), *The Mediterranean Diet* by Marissa Cloutier, RD, MS (Harper) and *The Miami Mediterranean Diet* by Michael Ozner, MD (Cambridge).

RAISE A GLASS OF WINE TO LONGEVITY!

Do you have a rosy future? You might, if you drink a little rosé.

⫸ *Breakthrough Study*

Researchers at Wageningen University in the Netherlands studied nearly 1,400 Dutch men aged 40 to 60 for 40 years, from 1960 to 2000.

Those who drank ½ glass of wine a day (2½ ounces) lived an average of four years longer than nondrinkers.

In a similar but much larger study, Italian researchers at Catholic University in Rome analyzed data from 34 scientific investigations into alcohol and health, conducted in the US, Europe, Australia, Japan and China, involving more than 1 million people. They found that moderate drinking of *any* kind—wine, beer or liquor—lowered the risk of death by 18%. "People who already consume low to moderate amounts of alcohol should be urged to continue," says Augusto Di Castelnuovo, MS, the lead researcher of the study published in the *Archives of Internal Medicine.*

Why it works: Ethanol—the alcohol in alcoholic drinks—improves three key biomarkers associated with disease prevention and longevity, explains Eric Rimm, ScD, associate professor at the Harvard School of Public Health and a researcher who has extensively studied moderate alcohol consumption and the risk of chronic disease. *Ethanol…*

• **Increases *HDL,*** the "good" cholesterol that carries fat away from the arteries;

• **Lowers *fibrinogen,*** a protein that increases the risk of artery-clogging clots; and

• **Lowers *hemoglobin A1c,*** a biomarker for long-term control of blood sugar.

What to do: If you want to extend your life, consider alcohol as a possible *part* of a healthy lifestyle, says Dr. Rimm.

Best: Studies show that one or two drinks a day, three to seven days a week, is the healthiest pattern, he says.

Example: A drink is 5 ounces of wine, 12 ounces of beer, or 1½ ounces of 80% distilled spirits or liquor, such as whiskey or vodka.

Caution: One or two drinks a day does *not* mean 7 to 14 drinks on Saturday night. Immoderate drinking—binge drinking, or

9 TO 5 UNTIL 95?

Researchers in Israel studied 231 older people, comparing the health of those who had retired at 70 with those who kept working.

Result: The workers were twice as healthy, nearly three times as independent and had double the survival rates.

"Working at age seventy correlates with health, self-sufficiency and longevity," says Robert Hammerman-Rozenberg, MD, at Hadassah-Hebrew University Medical Center, in Jerusalem.

consistently drinking three or more drinks a day—puts you at *higher risk* for heart disease and many other chronic health problems. And…if you're pregnant…if your father or mother suffered from alcoholism…if you're on a blood-thinning medication like warfarin…if you have breast cancer or a family history of the disease…if you're about to drive, operate heavy machinery or do anything that requires normal reaction time—don't drink.

PROTEIN BUILDS OLDER BODIES TOO

Muscle is protein. Kids eat plenty, to fuel growing bodies. Bodybuilders eat plenty, to compete with their pumped-up peers. But while it's well known that older folks *lose* muscle mass, nobody knew if eating more protein-rich food could help create more muscle in the post-60 set. In fact, many thought that older bodies might not have the biochemical wherewithal to turn lean beef into lean body mass.

▏▶ *Breakthrough Study*

Researchers in the Division of Rehabilitation Sciences at the University of Texas Medical Branch (UTMB) in Galveston asked 10 people

with an average age of 41 and 10 people with an average age of 70 to eat a four-ounce patty of lean ground beef. For the next five hours, the researchers took blood and muscle samples that showed whether or not the people in the study were making new muscle.

Both the younger and older groups had a 51% increase in muscle synthesis after eating the beef, report the researchers, in the *American Journal of Clinical Nutrition*.

"This was the first time anybody looked at a real food and its ability to stimulate muscle growth in the young and elderly," says Douglas Paddon-Jones, PhD, lead author of the study and an associate professor at UTMB. "We found aging does *not* impair a person's ability to synthesize muscle protein after eating protein-rich food."

What to do: "The older people in our study had an average of twenty-six pounds less lean muscle mass than the younger people," says Dr. Paddon-Jones. "Sufficient muscle is *fundamental* for the activities of daily living, moving and independence. However, between sixteen and twenty-seven percent of older adults eat less protein than they need. If an elderly person simply increases their protein intake, they might slow down muscle loss."

Recommended: In other research, Dr. Paddon-Jones found that eating a 12-ounce steak—the kind of huge portion you might get at a steakhouse—produces no more protein in the body than eating four ounces. For the most efficient synthesis of muscle from protein in food, he recommends you get protein in smaller portions, throughout the day, and from a variety of sources, including lean beef, chicken, fish, low-fat dairy products, beans and nuts and seeds.

GREEN TEA—TEATIME EXTENDS LIFETIME

Enter the words "green tea" into a database of scientific studies and you'll produce nearly 3,000 entries—study after study (mostly conducted in petri dishes and on laboratory animals) showing that green tea might protect the heart, slow cancer tumor growth, boost the immune system, balance blood sugar and otherwise provide a good cellular buffing.

But those experiments don't tell us if green tea is good for people. That's what a team of Japanese scientists tried to find out, publishing their results in the *Journal of the American Medical Association*.

▐▐▐▶ *Breakthrough Study*

The scientists analyzed diet and health data in more than 40,000 Japanese men and women, aged 40 to 79. Their results were enough to make people who don't drink green tea turn green…with envy.

- **Women and longevity.** Women who drank five or more cups a day of green tea were 23% less likely to die prematurely than those who drank less than one cup a day. Those drinking three to four cups were 18% less likely.

- **Women and heart disease/stroke.** Those who drank five or more cups had a 31% lower risk of dying from heart disease—and a 42% lower risk of dying from a stroke.

- **Men and longevity.** For men, the life-extending effect of green tea was good, though not quite as impressive as for women. (Scientists have yet to find out why.) Men who drank five or more cups of green tea a day were 12% less likely to die than men who drank less than one cup.

- **Men and heart disease/stroke.** Those who drank the most green tea reduced their

risk of dying from a heart attack by 9%—and dying from a stroke by 35%.

Why it works: Green tea is loaded with EGCG (*epigallocatechin gallate*), a powerful anti-oxidant that protects cells from damage.

Important: Green, black and oolong teas are all made from the leaves of the same plant: *Camellia sinensus*. But neither black nor oolong teas (both of which are fermented longer than green tea) reduced the risk of dying.

What to do: "Green tea is good for almost everyone," says Leigh Erin Connealy, MD, MPH, the medical director of the South Coast Medical Center for New Medicine, in Tustin, CA. "I drink a couple of cups of green tea every day. I have my kids drink green tea. I serve green tea in the waiting room." Try getting into the habit yourself, she advises.

Better: For a better-tasting green tea, don't pour boiling water over loose or bagged tea, says Helen Gustafson, author of *The Green Tea User's Manual* (Clarkson Potter). Instead, use water at just below boiling (160 to 190°F). *Her method for a 3- to 4-cup teapot…*

1. Put 3 teaspoons of dry leaf into the infusion basket. (Or use 1 tea bag per cup of water, says Nadine Taylor, RD, MS, author of *Green Tea: The Natural Secret for a Healthier Life,* Kensington.)

2. Cover the tea leaves (or tea bags) with about ½ cup of cold water.

3. Allow the water in your kettle to come to a boil.

4. Pour the hot water into the pot, where it will cool down to produce the appropriate temperature.

5. Wait about two minutes and remove the infusion basket (or tea bags).

WHAT THE *REAL* EXPERTS HAVE TO SAY ABOUT SUCCESSFUL AGING…

Who are the real experts? People who are older, of course! Scientists from the Sam and Rose Stein Institute for Research on Aging, at the University of California, San Diego, conducted face-to-face interviews with 72 people aged 60 to 99, asking them what they thought were the essentials of "successful aging." *The most-mentioned attributes…*

- Positive attitude
- Realistic perspective
- Ability to adapt to change
- A sense of engagement, by pursuing continued stimulation
- Learning
- Feeling a sense of purpose in life
- Being useful to others and society

SUBTRACT CALORIES, ADD YEARS

Take two groups of mice. Let one group eat all it wants (what scientists call *ad libitum*). Put the other group on a calorie-restricted (CR) diet—feeding them only as much nutrient-dense food as needed to stay alive without becoming malnourished. What happens?

The CR mice live 20 to 50% longer than the oldest ad libitum mice!

"Calorie restriction is the only intervention that has consistently been shown to slow aging in mice and rats, as well as in yeast, flies, worms and fish," says John O. Holloszy, MD, professor of medicine at Washington University School of Medicine.

Why does the diet work? Scientists aren't sure but they have lots of theories.

Maybe it reduces *energy expenditure,* the most basic of metabolic processes, thereby reducing *oxidative stress,* the internal rust that

damages and destroys cells. Maybe it improves how cells handle *insulin,* the hormone that controls blood sugar levels—poor insulin regulation ages cells. Maybe it improves the *neuroendocrine system,* the link between body-regulating hormones and the brain. Maybe it simply reduces stress, a known factor in aging. Maybe it's some combination of the above.

But whatever scientific theory about CR and longevity is eventually proven correct, what scientists *can't* prove is whether CR lengthens life in people as it does in animals—they can't take two groups of human babies, put one on a CR diet, allow the other to eat ad libitum and see which group lives longer. (The parents might object, for starters…)

What scientists *can* do, however, is see if adults on a CR diet undergo the same type of changes in the so-called *biomarkers of aging* that occur in CR rodents. If the biomarkers match, perhaps the CR diet might extend *human* life too.

And that's exactly the type of research Dr. Holloszy and his colleagues have conducted.

⮕ *Breakthrough Study*

Dr. Holloszy studied 33 members of the Calorie Restriction Society—people who eat an optimally nutritious diet of approximately 1,800 calories a day, in the belief that it will protect them against disease and extend life. The average age of the people he studied was 51, and they had been eating a CR diet for an average of six years. He compared their biomarkers to the biomarkers of a healthy group of 33 similarly aged people eating a typical American diet, publishing the results in the journal *Experimental Gerontology.* (Dr. Holloszy also had measurements of a few of the biomarkers of those on the CR diet from *before* they started it. Those biomarkers are included below, and you'll note that the CR-dieters weren't superhealthy until *after* they started CR.)

• **Heart and circulation.** The calorie-restricted humans were literally young at heart.

Total cholesterol: 162 after CR (211 before), compared to 202 for those eating the typical American diet.

LDL (bad cholesterol): 86 after CR (124 before), compared to 122 for those eating the American diet.

HDL (good cholesterol): 64 after CR (47 before), compared to 52 for those eating the American diet.

Triglycerides (a potentially heart-harming blood fat): 58 after CR (134 before), compared to 143 for those eating the American diet.

Blood pressure: A remarkable 103/62 after CR (131/82 before), compared to 130/81 for those eating the American diet.

• **Weight and fat.** They were also leaner.

Body mass index (a measure of weight and height to determine body fat): 19.6 after CR (23.7 before), compared to 24.8 for those eating the American diet.

Total body fat: 8.4% after CR, compared to 23.1% for those eating the American diet.

• **Blood sugar.** They had lower levels of blood sugar and insulin, signs of health and resistance to disease—and possible signs of slower aging.

Glucose (blood sugar): 84 after CR, compared to 95 for those eating the American diet.

Insulin (the hormone that regulates blood sugar): 1.5, compared to 7.4 for those eating the American diet.

• **Inflammation.** Those on the CR diet had lower levels of two molecules associated with chronic inflammation, a process linked to many age-related diseases, such as heart disease, stroke, type 2 diabetes, arthritis and Alzheimer's.

7

Tumor necrosis factor: 0.7 after CR, compared to 1.5 for those eating the American diet.

C-reactive protein: 0.2 after CR, compared to 1.1 for those eating the American diet.

• **Thyroid.** The CR group had lower blood levels of a thyroid hormone that helps control metabolic rate.

Theory: The faster your metabolic rate, the faster you age.

Triodothyronine: 74 after CR, compared to 91 for those eating the American diet.

Bottom line: "All of the above effects of CR in humans have also been observed in CR rodents," says Dr. Holloszy.

Other studies conducted by Dr. Holloszy and his colleagues in longevity research, at Tufts University and the Pennington Biomedical Research Center at the University of Louisiana, show that the CR diet also influences the following possible signs of aging in people…

• **Reduces DNA damage.**

Theory: DNA damage not only causes disease but also speeds aging.

• **Lowers daily energy expenditure.**

Theory: The higher the expenditure, the faster you age.

• **Decreases core body temperature.**

Theory: The higher the temperature, the faster you age.

• **Invigorates mitochondria, the structures in cells that generate energy.**

Theory: Mitochondrial failure speeds aging.

• **Increases the youthful elasticity of arteries.**

So while the improvement of longevity biomarkers in people on a CR diet doesn't *prove* that it extends life in humans…it certainly looks like it might!

Option: Obviously, the CR diet isn't for everybody. It requires discipline, a near-constant consideration of foods and nutrients, and the willingness (and willpower) to forgo a range of culinary comforts. But the latest research into CR for people is compelling. The diet is *definitely* healthful—and *might* add years to your life.

☀ *The CR Way: Using the Secrets of Calorie Restriction for a Longer, Healthier Life* (Harper Collins), by Paul McGlothin, vice president for research of the Calorie Restriction Society, and Meredith Averill, society board chair of the Calorie Restriction Society. This is the newest and most accessible book on the topic, filled with inspiration and practical information, including meal plans and recipes, from two of the world's leading advocates and practitioners of the CR diet.

www.calorierestriction.org. Calorie Restriction Society, 187 Ocean Drive, Newport, NC 28570 (800-929-6511); e-mail *president@calorierestriction.org.*

www.livingthecrway.com, the Web site of McGlothin and Averill, where you can inquire about weekend workshops about CR, themed to specific topics, such as heart disease, diabetes and cancer. Phone: 866-894-1812; e-mail *info@livingthecrway.com.*

FEWER VITAMINS, FASTER AGING

What happens when you don't get the vitamins and minerals your body needs?

"Deficiencies can cause DNA damage and cellular aging, and accelerate the aging process," says Bruce Ames, PhD, a professor in the Graduate School Division of Biochemistry and Molecular Biology at the University of California at Berkeley.

Unfortunately, if you're over 50 and *not* taking a vitamin-mineral supplement, it's likely you have one or more deficiencies.

||||▶ *Breakthrough Study*

Scientists in the Food Surveys Research Group at the USDA looked at nutritional data from 4,384 adults aged 51 or older: 1,777 took one or more supplements daily, 428 infrequently and 2,179 didn't take supplements.

Eighty percent or more of those who took supplements met the government's "estimated average requirement" for vitamins A, B-6, B-12, C, E, folate, iron and zinc. Not so for those who didn't use supplements.

"A large proportion of older adults don't consume sufficient amounts of many nutrients from foods alone," says Rhonda Sebastian, the lead researcher for the study published in the *Journal of the American Dietetic Association.* "Supplements improve the nutrient intake of older adults."

What to do: "A multivitamin-mineral supplement is one low-cost way to ensure intake of the Recommended Daily Allowance of micronutrients throughout life," says Dr. Ames.

AGE WELL WITH VITAMIN D

Are you in the dark about the Sunshine Vitamin?

In case you haven't heard the good news, vitamin D (produced in the body when skin is bared to the ultraviolet rays of the sun) isn't just for strong bones anymore. Scientists are finding out that vitamin D might help prevent high blood pressure and heart disease…cancer, including colon, breast and prostate…infections of all kinds…multiple sclerosis…and type 1 diabetes. Now, research is showing that it may also extend life, and keep you strong and on

your feet into your sixties, seventies, eighties and nineties.

||||▶ *Breakthrough Studies*

• **Longer life.** French scientists with the International Agency for Research on Cancer analyzed 18 studies, involving more than 57,000 older adults, in which participants took vitamin D supplements or a placebo. Those who took the vitamin D, with an average dose of 528 IU, had a 7% lower risk of dying.

"The intake of vitamin D from supplements seems to decrease the risk of dying from any cause," says Philippe Autier, MD, the lead author of the study. "If you want to increase your vitamin D intake by taking supplements, it looks like a great idea."

• **Stronger bodies.** Researchers at Wake Forest University School of Medicine in North Carolina studied nearly 1,000 people age 65 and older. Each participated in a physical performance test—of walking speed, the ability to stand up when sitting in a chair and the ability to stay balanced in challenging positions. They were also tested for handgrip strength, a predictor of future disability.

Seventy-five percent of the women and 51% of the men had vitamin D levels that were either "deficient" or "insufficient"—and the lower the levels of vitamin D, the poorer the performance on the test of physical performance and the weaker the handgrip.

"Our study showed a significant relationship between low vitamin D levels in older adults and poorer physical performance," says Denise Houston, PhD, RD, a nutritionist at Wake Forest University School of Medicine in North Carolina and the lead author of the study.

What happens: Vitamin D is necessary for the healthy functioning of muscle cells, and a deficiency of the nutrient causes muscle weakness—particularly in people over 60, who

ANTIOXIDANT SUPPLEMENTS— ARE THEY ANTIAGING?

Antioxidants up death risk! If you were reading the newspaper on the morning of February 27, 2007, you might have seen a headline something like the above, with the article below it reporting that a scientific study published in the prestigious *Journal of the American Medical Association* had concluded that taking antioxidant supplements such as beta carotene, vitamin E and vitamin A *increases* the risk of death by about 5%.

Aren't antioxidant supplements supposed to *extend* your life, by shielding cells from oxidative damage caused by free radical molecules, thereby helping prevent heart disease and cancer? Isn't that the reason an estimated 10 to 20% of Americans take antioxidants?

Well, critics of the study (a so-called "meta-analysis" that looked at the results of 68 other studies on antioxidants, involving more than 232,606 people) quickly chimed in. Many of the analyzed studies involved people taking antioxidant supplements to *treat* heart disease and cancer—an approach proven not to work. The examined research was too diverse—supplement doses too varied, the people taking the supplements too dissimilar—to lump together into one analysis.

"The study does not advance our understanding," says Meir Stampfer, MD, DrPH, professor of nutrition and epidemiology at the Harvard School of Public Health. (Dr. Stampfer also told the Associated Press that he planned to keep taking his vitamins.)

Whom should you believe? And, more important, what should you do?

Don't take an extremely high-dose antioxidant. That's the advice given to his patients by Seth Baum, MD, a cardiologist, director of the Mind Body Medical Institute at the Boca Raton Community Hospital, an affiliate of Beth Israel Deaconess Medical Center of Harvard University, and author of *Age Strong, Live Long* (Desert Spring Press).

"There is a process in the body called an antioxidant 'cascade,' in which antioxidants can become pro-oxidants," he explains. "If you get a lot of one antioxidant and not enough of the others—if you don't get a *balanced* intake—you can end up with an excess of free radicals."

Suggested intake: Dr. Baum recommends his patients take a daily vitamin-mineral supplement with nutrient levels that match the government's Recommended Daily Value (RDV) *and* a low-dose antioxidant. *The amounts of nutrients in the antioxidant...*

• *Vitamin C.* 200 milligrams (mg)

• *Vitamin E.* 150 IU (international units)

• *Lipoic acid.* 25 mg

• *L-carnitine.* 25 mg

• *Coenzyme Q10.* 25 mg

• *Selenium.* 20 micrograms (mcg)

Get the best test for antioxidant status. Blood levels of antioxidants are *not* an indication of whether antioxidants are protecting your cells from oxidation, says Dr. Baum. In fact, high blood levels of a particular antioxidant, such as vitamin C or E, often correlate with *increased* levels of oxidation. If you want to find out if your antioxidant supplement is *really* working, he recommends the Spectrox test, which measures the ability of cells to resist oxidation.

Don't forget about food. "There are many ways to improve your antioxidant function," says Dr. Baum. "Eat plenty of red, yellow and green antioxidant-rich fruits and vegetables—including one ounce a day of dark chocolate, which has more antioxidants than berries. And engage in *moderate* exercise, like brisk walking—exercise that is too vigorous creates oxidation."

ⓘ Spectrox test. SpectraCell Laboratories, 10401 Town Park Drive, Houston, TX 77072 (800-227-5227 or 713-621-3101, fax: 713-621-3234), e-mail *spec1@spectracell.com* or on-line at *www.spectracell.com.*

already have less muscle mass, explains Dr. Houston. Not only that, older adults have a higher risk for vitamin D deficiency because they tend to get out less, and older skin is less efficient at manufacturing vitamin D. They might also get less vitamin D from their diets.

"Higher intake of vitamin D in those over 60 may be needed for the preservation of muscle strength and physical function," says Dr. Houston.

● **Fewer falls.** One hundred twenty-four residents of a nursing home in Boston with an average age of 89 were asked to take either a vitamin D supplement (200 IU, 400 IU, 600 IU or 800 IU) or a placebo for five months. During those five months, 59% of those in the study fell down. But only 20% of the group taking 800 IU of vitamin D fell, compared to 44% to 60% in the other groups. Overall, those taking 800 IU of vitamin were 72% less likely to fall than the others.

"Adequate vitamin D supplementation in elderly nursing-home residents could reduce the number of falls experienced by this high falls risk group," says Kerry Broe, at the Institute for Aging Research, Hebrew SeniorLife, in Boston, and the lead researcher for the study published in the *Journal of the American Geriatrics Society*.

What to do: The current government recommendation for people aged 50 to 69 is a daily intake of 400 IU of vitamin D. For people aged 70 and over, it's 600 IU.

"That's too little for good health, and most people over 60 don't get anywhere near even that amount," says Michael F. Holick, PhD, MD, director of the Vitamin D, Skin and Bone Research Laboratory at Boston University Medical Center and author of *The UV Advantage: The Medical Breakthrough That Shows How to Harness the Power of the Sun for Your Health* (ibooks).

The three best ways to increase blood levels of vitamin D, says Dr. Holick, are to take a vitamin D supplement, eat foods rich in vitamin D and increase sun exposure. *Here are his recommendations…*

● **Supplement.** Taking a daily vitamin D supplement is the easiest and most reliable way to maintain healthy blood levels of vitamin D, says Dr. Holick.

Suggested intake: Take 1,000 IU of vitamin D daily. No particular brand is better than any other. This is the ideal amount for both adults and children.

Important: You may have read about the risk of an overdose of vitamin D. To suffer from an overdose, you need to get more than 10,000 IU a day, every day, for 6 months. That's next to impossible. Not getting *enough* vitamin D is the real risk, says Dr. Holick.

● **Food.** Milk and several other foods are fortified with vitamin D, and fatty fish, such as salmon and mackerel, are good sources.

Red flag #1: A study shows that many cartons of milk contain only 20% of labeled vitamin D levels—because the methodology of adding vitamin D to milk isn't particularly effective. Vitamin D-fortified orange juice, breakfast cereals and bread are more likely to contain the labeled amount.

Red flag #2: Scientists at Boston University Medical Center found that farm-bred salmon have only 25% the vitamin D found in wild salmon, and species of other fatty fish, such as mackerel, vary widely in vitamin D content from fish to fish.

Bottom line: Maximize your dietary intake but also take a supplement, says Dr. Holick.

● **Sun.** Vitamin D from sun exposure is highly variable, depending on the time of the day, the season of the year, the latitude and your skin pigmentation. No general recommendation can assure adequate blood levels of vitamin D. *However, there is a good rule of thumb…*

Recommended: Spend 10 to 15 minutes, 3 to 4 times a week in the sun *without sunscreen* on your arms, legs and hands. After 10 to 15 minutes, apply sunscreen to these areas. Never sun to the point of burning. Always protect your face with sunscreen or a hat.

What most people don't realize: This level of unprotected sun exposure will not increase your risk of skin cancer or wrinkles.

CURING IRON-DEFICIENCY ANEMIA IN OCTOGENARIANS

You're pale, wiped out, short of breath, headachy and weak. No, you're not the newest member of the Bela Lugosi fan club, but something is bothering your blood—iron-deficiency anemia. A lack of the mineral means you can't manufacture enough *hemoglobin,* the oxygen-carrying molecule in red blood cells. You're slowly suffocating from the inside out.

The way to iron out the problem? Iron supplements, of course. But for older people, iron supplements can be hard to stomach…and digest…and defecate, with side effects that can include stomach pain, nausea, vomiting, constipation and black stools. It doesn't have to be that way.

Gerontologists from Israel studied 90 people over the age of 80 with iron-deficiency anemia, dividing them into three treatment groups. Each group received a different daily dose of iron for three months: 15 mg of elemental iron, 50 mg of liquid ferrous gluconate or 150 mg of ferrous calcium citrate.

All three groups had similar and anemia-curing increases in hemoglobin levels. But the groups getting the 50 and 150 mg doses had far more side effects.

"Low-dose iron treatment is effective in elderly patients with iron-deficiency anemia," says Ephraim Rimon, MD, in the *American Journal of Medicine.* "It can replace the commonly used higher doses and can significantly reduce side effects."

If you're over 65 and your doctor has diagnosed iron-deficiency anemia, have a conversation about taking a lower dose of iron.

HMB *STOPS* AGE-RELATED MUSCLE LOSS

The condition called *sarcopenia,* or age-related muscle loss, starts in your mid-30s. By the time you're 50, you're losing 1 to 2% of your muscle mass every year. In your 60s and 70s that slow slide can turn into an avalanche and literally bury you…because not only do the muscles in your arms and legs lose mass, so do the muscles in your diaphragm. That makes coughing more difficult—and increases the risk of death from pneumonia *twenty-fold* compared with older people with a case of sarcopenia that is not as advanced.

The nutrient HMB—short for *hydroxyl methylbutyrate*—can stop sarcopenia in its muscle-mauling tracks.

⫸ *Breakthrough Study*

HMB is a *metabolite,* or breakdown product, of leucine, one of the essential amino acids of protein. As a supplement, it's a favorite of elite athletes and bodybuilders, who use it to add muscle and increase strength. In a study conducted at Iowa State University, scientists evaluated the muscle- and strength-building power of more than 250 nutritional supplements and found that only HMB and creatine actually worked.

Steve L. Nissen, PhD, the world's foremost expert on HMB, led that research. Dr. Nissen wondered if this muscle-building nutrient might also help with sarcopenia. To find out, he asked 120 men and women with an average

INTERESTED IN TESTOSTERONE REPLACEMENT THERAPY? TAKE NOTE OF ESTROGEN REPLACEMENT THERAPY...

Estrogen replacement therapy was touted as a way to ease menopausal symptoms such as hot flashes and protect a woman's heart, bones and brain from aging. Then came the Women's Health Initiative, the largest study ever conducted on the effects of estrogen and other hormone replacement for women—and the finding that treatment with estrogen and other hormones *increased* the risk of heart disease by 29%, *increased* the risk of stroke by 41% and *increased* the risk of breast cancer by 26%.

Enter testosterone, the male hormone that is now widely prescribed for older men to "treat" the symptoms that can accompany an age-related drop in testosterone levels—reduced energy, loss of muscle mass and strength, loss of sex drive and potency and depression. But testosterone replacement therapy is probably a very bad idea.

A study from doctors at the Mayo Clinic, published in the *Mayo Clinic Proceedings,* found that there is no evidence showing testosterone is *not* damaging the heart—a very worrisome finding, given the fact that estrogen causes heart disease. The doctors also found very little evidence showing that testosterone can revive a flagging libido.

"There is no way for physicians to be certain when prescribing testosterone that, on average, it's doing more harm than good," says Victor Montori, MD, lead author of the study. "Researchers should conduct trials measuring the outcomes of testosterone treatment in order to avoid the estrogen disaster." Until then, the old saw applies, better to be safe than sorry.

age of 75 to take a daily HMB supplement for a year, measuring their muscle mass before and after the study.

Result: Muscle loss was virtually halted.

"This is the first time scientific research has demonstrated that sarcopenia can be prevented," says Dr. Nissen.

How it works: Muscle tissue is constantly being made, broken down and remade—and the building material for that metabolic construction project is protein. HMB *increases* the amount of protein your body makes and *decreases* the amount of protein destroyed.

Suggested intake: The people who participated in Dr. Nissen's study on sarcopenia took 3 grams a day. If you're over 200 pounds, try 4 grams, he says. If you weigh less than 120, use 1 or 1.5 grams. He recommends taking it once a day, any time of day.

🛈 Dr. Nissen uses the HMB manufactured by EAS Bodybuilding and Nutrition Supplements.

He says not to use a product that contains HMB and other ingredients. "Stick with the plainest and simplest HMB product. Don't waste your money on unproven ingredients."

SELENIUM—GET A (STRONGER) GRIP

For decades, scientists investigating the trace mineral and antioxidant selenium have touted its antiaging powers, including protection against heart disease, cancer and cataracts. Now they can add protection against weakening muscles to that list.

▐▐▐▶ *Breakthrough Study*

Researchers in Italy tested muscular strength in the hands, knees and hips of 891 people age 65 or older. They found that those with the lowest levels of selenium were twice as likely to have poor muscle strength. *Specifically, they were...*

- **94% more likely to have weak hand muscles (grip),**

- **94% more likely to have weak knee muscles and**

- **69% more likely to have weak hip muscles.**

Low levels of selenium may be one of the reasons for age-related muscle weakness, says Fulvio Lauretani, PhD, one of the authors of the study.

Theory: Selenium is incorporated into molecules called *selenoproteins* that play a role in maintaining muscle strength.

What to do: Increase your dietary intake with selenium-rich foods such as whole-wheat bread (and wheat germ and bran), oats, Swiss chard and Brazil nuts. And don't forget the seafood, such as crab, lobster and oysters.

Suggested intake: In the report in this chapter on antioxidants, on page 10, Dr. Baum recommends an antioxidant supplement that includes 20 mcg of selenium.

FIT FOLKS LIVE LONGER— LOVE HANDLES INCLUDED

Imagine this scenario…

You're over 60. You want to live as long as possible. However, you are told that you must choose between two options for extending life—being thin but out of shape…or being fat but fit.

It's an easy choice, right? Fat is fatal. Or at least that's what we've been told.

▶ Breakthrough Study

Researchers from the University of South Carolina studied scientific data from more than 2,600 adults aged 60 and over who had participated in the 12-year "Aerobics Center Longitudinal Study" at the Cooper Clinic in Dallas, Texas.

The researchers measured the adults' cardiovascular fitness by giving them a treadmill test. They also measured their body mass index (a standard indicator of fatness), their waist size and their percentage of body fat. For the next 12 years, they tracked who died and who didn't. The surprising results, published in the *Journal of the American Medical Association…*

The most significant predictor of who lived and who died wasn't who was fat and who was thin, but who was fit and who was unfit. The least fit (men who couldn't stay on a treadmill longer than 7.8 minutes, and women who couldn't stay on longer than 5.5 minutes) had a death rate *four times higher* than the unfit.

To put it another way, the fittest people in the study—even if they were fat, even if they were extremely obese—lived longer than the least fit.

"Fitness level is a stronger predictor for risk of dying in older adults than overweight or obesity," says Steven N. Blair, PED (Doctor of Physical Education), a professor in the Department of Exercise Science at the University of South Carolina and one of the authors of the study.

What to do: Being physically active doesn't mean you have to go to the gym every day, says Dr. Blair. He recommends walking at a moderate pace for 30 minutes a day, at least five days a week. He also advises you to add other kinds of physical activity to your life, such as gardening, playing with grandchildren or playing golf. And he recommends activities to build muscle strength, such as resistance training.

"It is possible for many older Americans to improve their fitness," he says. "The good news from this study is that you don't have to be *thin* to benefit from being physically active."

EASY STEPS TO YOUNGER ARTERIES

Want your arteries to be 35 years younger in 90 days? Step right this way.

||||➡ *Breakthrough Study*

Researchers at the University of Colorado in Boulder studied 28 healthy men who didn't exercise—13 in their 20s, with an average age of 27; and 15 in their 60s, with an average age of 62.

First, they measured blood flow in the forearms of the men in response to an infusion of *endothelin-1,* a biochemical in arterial cells that helps arteries widen and narrow. The response of the older men was 65% lower than that of the younger men—their arteries were stiff, inelastic, inflexible, *old.*

Next, the researcher put eight of the 15 older men on a daily walking program for 90 days, at the end of which they once again infused all the men with endothelin-1.

The response of the older exercisers had improved by 225% and was comparable to that of the younger men—now, their arteries were supple, elastic, flexible, *young.* And that happened *without* losing weight, shedding fat, or lowering blood pressure. (Needless to say, the arteries of the nonexercising older men stayed about the same.)

What to do: "It's never too late to start exercising," says Christopher A. DeSouza, PhD, one of the authors of the study published in the journal *Hypertension.*

"It's also important to emphasize that these improvements resulted from a *moderate* amount of exercise that most, if not all, middle-aged and older people can perform. Simply go for a moderately brisk walk, for about an hour, at least five days a week."

LONG LIVE THE FIT!

Researchers at the National Cancer Institute analyzed data on physical activity and death rates among more than 250,000 men and women aged 50 to 71. *Compared with inactive people...*

- **Those who got at least 30 minutes of moderate activity** (such as brisk walking) most days of the week were 27% less likely to die.

- **Those who got at least 20 minutes of vigorous activity** (such as jogging, rowing or jump roping) three times a week were 32% less likely to die.

- **Those who got moderate exercise and vigorous activity** were 50% less likely to die.

- **Even smokers who got moderate and vigorous activity** were 52% less likely to die.

- **Even overweight or obese people who got moderate and vigorous activity** were 52% less likely to die.

- **Even people who watched more than 2 hours of television a day** who got moderate and vigorous activity were 50% less likely to die.

- **And even people who got some physical activity,** though less than the moderate level, were 19% less likely to die.
  Notice a trend?

POWER TRAINING THE GOLDEN WAY

Around the age of 50, you start losing muscle mass—and about 15% of your strength per decade!

That's one reason experts on aging and health encourage people over 50 to lift weights, or resistance train, two to three days a week. The goals of resistance training is to slow muscle loss and strengthen aging muscle...to help prevent the falls that flatten

30% of Americans over 65 every year, injuring two million and killing 15,000…and to stop the decline into dependence. But what's the *best* way to resistance train to achieve those goals?

If you go to a gym to learn resistance training—probably the safest and most reliable way—you'll be shown a variety of resistance-training machines that work various parts of your body, such as your arms, legs, hips and back. When you use the machines, you'll be told to push a *heavy* weight—about 75% of the amount of weight you could lift one time (what exercise scientists call 1RM, or one-repetition maximum). And you'll be told to push that weight *slowly,* 8 to 15 times.

Well, resistance-train that way two or three times a week and you'll definitely get stronger. But will you be more *functional*—will that extra strength help you cross a busy intersection before the *Don't Walk* sign starts flashing again…keep your balance if you're jostled… climb stairs…lift and hold your grandchild?

New thinking: New scientific studies show that resistance training to develop muscle power is better for improving everyday functioning than resistance training to develop muscle strength.

What's the difference? Muscle strength is the ability to produce force. Muscle power is the ability to produce force *quickly.*

How do you resistance-train to develop muscle power? By lifting lighter weights at faster speeds, say researchers—a type of resistance training called *power training.*

▶ Breakthrough Study

Researchers from the Veterans Affairs Medical Center in Decatur, GA, and the Department of Exercise Science at the University of Georgia studied 39 men and women, with an average age of 72. For four months, three days a week, one group did "power training" and the other group did standard "strength training."

Both groups performed the same "set" of eight resistance-training exercises—seated row, chest press, triceps extension, leg press, leg extension, seated leg curls, bicep curls and plantar flexion (an exercise for the foot and ankle). Over the first two months of the study, the strength-training group worked up to 80% 1RM. The power-training group stayed at 40% IRM, doing six to eight repetitions as fast as possible.

At the beginning and end of the study, the two groups were tested for their ability to perform 16 everyday tasks that simulated daily activities such as dressing, doing the laundry and carrying groceries (physical function performance). The researchers also measured changes in balance, coordination and endurance. *The results…*

- **Physical function performance.** Those doing power training had a 14% increase…those doing strength training, 4%.

- **Balance and coordination.** Those doing power training had a 17% increase… those doing the strength training, a very slight decrease.

- **Endurance.** Power training led to a 16% increase; strength training, 5%.

"Power training was more effective than strength training for improving physical function in older adults," says Tanya A. Miszko, EdD, the lead researcher of the study published in the *Journal of Gerontology.*

Why it works: Power training affects your *neuromuscular* system—it speeds and synchronizes the action of nerve cells that help control muscles, so that when you "ask" your muscles to move, they move.

What to do: The American College of Sports Medicine recommends this approach to power training for healthy older adults…

THE C-REACTIVE PROTEIN TEST—POTENT PREDICTOR OF HEALTH AND LONGEVITY

C-reactive protein (CRP) is a molecule produced in your body when there's *inflammation*—when the immune system is in overdrive, responding to what it sees as a potential problem.

Because this type of immune activity is often the *first* sign of ill health—the metabolic canary in your body's mine—high levels of CRP are very predictive of all kinds of conditions and diseases, including high blood pressure; stroke; sudden cardiac death; a ruptured blood vessel; atrial fibrillation (irregular heartbeat, which can trigger a heart attack); macular degeneration (a leading cause of blindness); type 2 diabetes; Alzheimer's; colon, prostate and other cancers and recurrence of cancer.

Not surprising, CRP is also predictive of something far more meaningful—whether you're going to live or die in the next couple of years...

Recent finding: A study of nearly 6,000 people who had yearly tests for CRP blood levels showed that...

• Those whose tests went from normal (below 3.0 mg/L) to elevated (above 3.0 mg/L) had nearly a *sevenfold increase in their risk of death,* compared with people with normal tests.

• Among those who had a decrease in CRP, from elevated to normal levels, *the risk of death fell nearly fourfold,* compared with people with elevated levels.

"CRP is the *best* predictor of health and the risk of death ever identified—because immune system hyperactivity and inflammation *precedes* disease," says Dr. Liponis.

Problem: Most doctors are aware of the CRP test but don't order it, says Dr. Liponis. That's because the test doesn't predict any *particular* disease, and because the doctor doesn't know how to lower high CRP levels.

Solution: The health recommendations in this chapter and this book—such as eating healthier, sleeping deeper, exercising more, reducing stress and taking nutritional supplements that boost health—are some of the best ways to lower CRP. And a yearly CRP test is the best way to monitor their effectiveness.

Ask your doctor for the test at your next annual physical exam and yearly thereafter, says Dr. Liponis.

What to look for: Optimal levels are less than 0.7 mg CRP per liter of blood (mg/L), says Dr. Liponis, although 3.0 mg/L and lower is considered normal.

• **One to three sets.** A *set* is one round of all the machines you're using. Try the set described in the study.

• **Light to moderate resistance**, at 40 to 60% of your one-repetition maximum. The study used 40%.

• **Six to ten repetitions.** The study used six to eight.

• **High velocity.** In the study, the researchers instructed participants to push and lower the weights "as fast as you can."

Best: Show these guidelines to a certified instructor at a gym or health club and receive guided, machine-by-machine instruction in power training. And get your doctor's okay before beginning power training or any type of resistance training.

But don't worry, researchers looking at all the studies to date on power training for older people concluded this type of exercise poses a low risk of injury—much less than starting a jogging program, for example.

OPTIMISM—POSITIVELY LONG-LIVED

Do you see that proverbial glass as half-empty or half-full?

Think carefully. Your very life may depend on it.

||||➤ *Breakthrough Study*

Researchers from the Department of Psychiatry and Behavioral Sciences at Duke University Medical School looked at who had died and who hadn't among more than 7,000 men and women who had filled out a standard personality test in the 1960s when they entered college.

Compared with those who were most optimistic, those who were most pessimistic were 42% more likely to have died. (Talk about your self-fulfilling prophecy!)

What happens: Why do optimists outlive pessimists? Perhaps because they're less likely to suffer from depression, which can worsen health, says Beverly H. Brummett, PhD, the lead author of the study published in the *Mayo Clinic Proceedings*. They might also be more likely to live a healthier lifestyle—because they think it will pay off!

What to do: "The difference between an optimist and a pessimist is in their 'explanatory styles'—what they tell themselves about events," says Martin Seligman, PhD, a professor of psychology at the University of Pennsylvania and author of *Learned Optimism: How to Change Your Mind and Your Life* (Vintage).

Optimists tell themselves that bad events are temporary…and that good events have permanent causes.

Pessimists tell themselves that bad events are permanent…and that good events have temporary causes that they can't influence.

"You can build an optimistic explanatory style by recognizing and disputing pessimistic thoughts and beliefs," says Dr. Seligman. *He says to ask yourself these four questions whenever you're thinking pessimistically…*

• **What is the evidence for this belief?** Is your negative belief about an event factually correct? Maybe you think you blew your diet when you went out after work. Count the calories in the nachos, the chicken wings and the light beers. You might find out they came to little more than the dinner you skipped.

• **Is there any less destructive way to look at this?** Most events have many causes, but pessimists latch on to the most permanent. You did poorly on the test—but was it because you are stupid? Perhaps the test was especially hard, the professor was unfair or you were tired.

• **How likely is the worst-case scenario?** Even if your negative beliefs about yourself are true, what are the implications? Your dinner with your spouse was not romantic—but one bad dinner does not mean divorce.

• **Is the situation changeable, and how can I go about changing it?** Is your belief destructive? When your cheat on your diet, the belief "I'm a total glutton" will probably lead you to eat even more. Instead, write down all the ways you can change the event in the future. I'll go for a walk instead of eating…I'll call a friend…I'll eat a lower-calorie alternative.

2

ARTHRITIS
DRUG-FREE RELIEF FOR PAINFUL JOINTS

Forty-six million Americans—about one out of every five adults—have arthritis. Twenty-seven million have osteoarthritis (OA), the wear-and-tear destruction of the cartilage that caps bones and cushions joints. Another 1.3 million have rheumatoid arthritis (RA), an autoimmune disease, with immune cells attacking joints as if they were germs. The remaining millions suffer from any one of about 100 other arthritic conditions, such as gout (caused by sharp-edged uric acid crystals in the joints) or psoriatric arthritis (striking about 10% of people with psoriasis). No matter what type of arthritis you have, you probably *hurt*. Inflamed joints can be painful, stiff and swollen.

Sometimes, relief is risky. There's *acetaminophen*, which can cause liver failure. And there are the nonsteroidal anti-inflammatory drugs (NSAIDs), such as aspirin, ibuprofen and naproxen, which hospitalize more than 100,000 people every year with digestive complications such as bleeding ulcers—and kill 16,000. Then there are the once-praised but now-infamous NSAIDS called COX-2 inhibitors, such as *valdecoxib* (Bextra) and

rofecoxib (Vioxx), which led to an untold number of heart attacks and strokes.

New danger: Research now shows that *ibuprofen* (Advil, Motrin, Nuprin) and *diclofenac* (Voltaren, Cataflam) increase the risk of heart attack and stroke. So does *naproxen* (Aleve, Naprosyn)—although, statistically speaking, not quite as much.

Americans spend more than $75 billion a year on these and other pain-relieving drugs. More than 70% of people with arthritis use nondrug remedies to ease their disease. Problem is there are more than 800 antiarthritis supplements on the market!

Here are the arthritis supplements—and the nondrug therapies—that doctors and scientists say work best.

SOOTHING SUPPLEMENTS

ASU—THE NEW PAIN-RELIEVING SUPER-OIL

ASU is short for *avocado/soybean unsaponifiables*. It's an extract from the oils of those two plants—an extract that can definitely "oil" your stiff, aching joints.

||||➡ *Breakthrough Study*

Researchers in Denmark analyzed data from four studies involving 664 people with osteoarthritis of the knee or the hip who took either ASU or a placebo for three months to a year. Compared to the placebo, ASU was…

- **86% better at reducing pain** and
- **61% better at improving function** in the "activities of daily living," such as carrying groceries, doing the laundry or just walking from room to room.

Those studies also showed ACU could…

Slow the disease. Doctors in France (where ASU is routinely prescribed under the name Piascledine 300) studied 163 arthritis patients who took ASU or a placebo for two years. During that time, those taking the placebo had a 51% loss of joint space in the hip joint—a sign of the erosion of the cushion of cartilage between bones and the relentless progression of arthritis. That's the bad news. The good is those taking ACU had only a 27% loss in joint space.

Reduce the need for painkillers. In a study conducted by doctors in Belgium, 71% of people taking ASU reduced their use of NSAIDs and other painkillers by more than 50%. Only 36% of those taking a placebo achieved the same reduction.

How it works: A researcher at Johns Hopkins University in Baltimore added ACU to a test tube of cartilage cells that had been stimulated to produce a set of *cytokines*, proteins that signal the immune system to launch the inflammatory process (redness, swelling, pain). ASU reduced the level of three key cytokines—cyclooxygenase-2 (COX-2), tumor necrosis factor-alpha (TNF-alpha) and interleukin-1-beta (IL-1beta)—to that of a normal cartilage cell. "These observations provide a scientific rationale for the pain-reducing and anti-inflammatory effects of ASU that are seen in osteoarthritis

patients," says Carmelita G. Frondoza, PhD, in the Department of Orthopedic Surgery.

Suggested intake: 300 milligrams (mg) daily, the amount used in most studies that tested the supplement. Larger amounts (600 mg) didn't produce more pain relief, less inflammation or more mobility.

ⓘ Avosoy, formulated by Jason Theodosakis, MD, coauthor of *The Arthritis Cure* (St. Martin's). Dr. Theodosakis has also formulated an ASU product that includes glucosamine and chondroitin sulfate: Avosoy Complete. (You can read more about these two antiarthritis ingredients on page 21.)

☀ For more information, or to order the product, go to *www.drtheos.com*, 800-311-6883, e-mail *manager@drtheos.com*.

CAT'S CLAW AND MACA— ANCIENT PAIN RELIEF

Cat's claw is a thorny, high-climbing vine that thrives in the Amazon rainforests of Peru; Incan healer-priests used it as a medicine for thousands of years, calling it the "life giving" vine.

Maca is a turniplike root vegetable that grows at high altitudes in the Andes Mountains, eaten by Inca warriors to increase strength and endurance.

What happens when extracts of these two Peruvian super-plants combine into one anti-arthritis supplement?

Life-giving pain relief, flexibility and strength to those aching joints.

||||➡ *Breakthrough Study*

Researchers from hospitals and health centers in Mumbai, India, and from the Albany Medical College in New York, studied 95 people with

THE MEDIA SAID GLUCOSAMINE AND CHONDROITIN SULFATE DON'T WORK (THE MEDIA GOT IT WRONG)

Maybe you're unsure about whether to take a supplement containing the supposed superstars of natural arthritis relief, glucosamine and chondroitin sulfate.

After all, a major study (coauthored by 25 scientists from 19 universities, hospitals and clinics, and costing more than $10 million)—published in the prestigious *New England Journal of Medicine* in 2006—concluded that these natural substances "alone or in combination did not reduce pain effectively" in patients with osteoarthritis of the knee. (The combo *might* work in people with moderate-to-severe knee pain, said the study's authors.)

Headlines blared the painful truth: POPULAR SUPPLEMENT NO BETTER THAN SUGAR PILL.

Those headlines were more fiction than fact, says Jason Theodosakis, MD, a member of the Steering Oversight Committee of the study, an assistant professor at the University of Arizona College of Medicine, and the author of *The Arthritis Cure* (St. Martin's), the book that sparked the huge popularity of glucosamine and chondroitin sulfate.

"I am astounded by the utter simplification contained in the reporting of the study's findings in the media," says Dr. Theodosakis. *He explains...*

The study measured 14 different possible outcomes (such as changes in pain, stiffness, swelling and daily functioning) across three groups: 1) mild/moderate pain, 2) moderate/severe pain and 3) those two groups com-bined. It compared glucosamine, chondroitin sulfate, the arthritis drug Celebrex and a placebo. Compared to the placebo, Celebrex failed to improve 12 of 14 outcomes in groups 2 and 3, and all 14 in group 1.

"In contrast," says Dr. Theodosakis, "in study participants who started with moderate to severe pain—the very people with arthritis who are most likely to miss work or need physical therapy or surgery—the supplements beat out Celebrex in twelve of fourteen outcomes." In fact, he points out, the supplements significantly improved pain and function in 79% of people with moderate to severe pain.

"There have been more than thirty-five positive human studies on glucosamine and/or chondroitin sulfate, and the supplements are approved as over-the-counter or prescription drugs in more than forty countries," says Dr. Theodosakis. "They work."

How they work: Chondroitin sulfate and glucosamine are important factors in the creation, maintenance and repair of cartilage, the cushion between joints. They also alter genetic signaling inside cartilage cells, decreasing the production of molecular factors that inflame and destroy cartilage.

Recommended: Dr. Theodosakis recommends a product with 1,500 mg of glucosamine and 1,200 mg of chondroitin sulfate, taken once a day. If after three months you're not getting sufficient relief, double the dose.

For the best quality, look for glucosamine and chondroitin sulfate that is USP grade and chondroitin that is either porcine- or bovine-derived. (Chondroitin from shark cartilage has too little chondroitin in it; chondroitin from chicken cartilage doesn't work).

mild to moderate osteoarthritis of the knee. They asked them to take one of two supplements for two months—glucosamine sulfate, or a supplement that combined extracts of cat's claw (*Uncaria guianensis*) and maca (*Lepidum meyenii*). Before, during and after the study, the researchers evaluated the participants' pain levels, joint stiffness and ability to perform everyday tasks. *The results...*

• **Less pain.** Within one week, 48% of those taking the cat's claw/maca combo had at least a 20% reduction in pain, as did 47% of those taking glucosamine. By four weeks, those numbers had increased to 81% for the cat's claw/maca group and 75% for the glucosamine group. By the end of the study, there was an overall 62% reduction in pain for those taking cat's claw and maca, and 60% for those taking glucosamine.

● **Less stiffness, more functioning.** After two months, both groups had less stiffness and an increased ability to perform daily functions.

● **Less pain medication.** During the study, both groups took fewer doses of pain medication, with the cat's claw/maca group taking the least. (The researchers note that other studies have shown that cat's claw can block the severe gastrointestinal complications from high doses of NSAIDs. "Not only is cat's claw effective in treating arthritis, it may also limit the side effects of common drug-based approaches to managing arthritis," says Mark Miller, BSc, PhD, a professor at the Center for Cardiovascular Sciences at Albany Medical College and one of the authors of the study.)

The researchers' overall conclusion: "Both a cat's claw/maca combination and glucosamine sulfate provide effective relief of mild to moderate osteoarthritis of the knee." And, says Dr. Miller, "It's likely that the combination of cat's claw, maca *and* glucosamine sulfate might produce even more benefits."

How it works: The extract of cat's claw shuts down genes that tell the body to *break down* cartilage; the extract of maca triggers a cartilage repair factor gene (IGF-1) that boosts the *growth* of cartilage.

"Think of cartilage as a brick wall that has had some bricks knocked out of it," says Dr. Miller. "Cat's claw and maca create new bricks and then call a bricklayer to the site to put the bricks back into the wall."

ℹ The study used a cat's claw/maca product called Reparagen.

Suggested intake: One capsule, three times a day, before meals, for a total of 1,800 mg (1,500

WHEN DRUGS ARE THE RIGHT THING TO DO

"If you have *rheumatoid* arthritis and you are not using a pharmacological therapy to halt the progress of the disease—you're making a mistake," says Dr. Jason Theodosakis, author of *The Arthritis Cure*, which popularized nondrug remedies for osteoarthritis. "The disease is known to progress without DMARDs (disease-modifying antirheumatic drugs) and known to stop with them." DMARDs include about a dozen "immuno-modulatory" drugs—such as *adalimumab* (Humira), *etanercept* (Enbrel) and *leflunomide* (Arava)—that work by calming the immune system.

But for people with osteoarthritis, prescription or over-the-counter drugs should be the treatment of last resort, says Dr. Theodosakis. "These drugs do not halt the progress of the disease and they can have serious side effects."

mg *Lepidium meyenii* root extract [maca], 300 mg *Uncaria guianensis* bark extract [cat's claw]).

☀ *www.reparagen.com*, Park Labs, LLC, Raleigh, NC 27613 (518-330-5651); e-mail *info@ reparagen.com*. In Canada: Cadna Nutritionals, Inc., Toronto, Ontario (800-680-3015).

HYALURONIC ACID LUBRICATES JOINTS

Hyaluronic acid is a substance in synovial fluid, the movement-smoothing, movement-soothing fluid in joints. Hyaluronic acid keeps the liquid viscous and lubricating—but people with osteoarthritis tend to have low levels. Injections of hyaluronic acid are a widely accepted, effective treatment for osteoarthritis. New evidence shows that hyaluronic acid supplements can work too.

||||▶ *Breakthrough Study*

Doctors gave hyaluronic acid supplements or a placebo for eight weeks to 20 people with knee pain from osteoarthritis. At the end of the study, those taking hyaluronic acid had 23% better physical function and 16% fewer symptoms overall. They also had less pain and were more active.

"Daily supplemention with oral hyaluronic acid enhanced the quality of life in people with osteoarthritis of the knee," says Douglas S. Kalman, PhD, RD, director of nutrition and applied clinical research at Miami Research Associates and one of the authors of the study published in *Nutrition Journal*. And, he says, taking the *supplement* can avoid possible problems with repeated *injections* of hyaluronic acid, such as infection at the injection site or discomfort from the shots.

Why it works: The supplement not only replaces the missing hyalurons—it also stimulates the synovial fluid to produce more, says Dr. Kalman.

❶ The study used the product Hyal-Joint. *Suggested intake:* 80 mg a day.

☀ Hyal-Joint is available in Hyal-Joint Hyaluronic Acid Complex, from Country Life, and Hyal-Joint Super Potency Hyaluronic Acid, from Swanson Health Products.

Caution: The supplement is made from chicken combs. If you have an allergy to chickens, turkey or other fowl, do not use it, says Dr. Kalman.

ROSE HIPS FOR RHEUMATOID ARTHRITIS

Roses produce a berrylike fruit called *hips*. They're a traditional, tart ingredient in jams, sauces, puddings and syrups—and, because they're loaded with vitamin C, in nutritional supplements. Now scientists have found a new form and use for rose hips: a powder that can help control both rheumatoid and osteoarthritis.

||||▶ *Breakthrough Study*

Researchers in Denmark and Germany asked 74 women with severe, longstanding (an average of 18 years) rheumatoid arthritis to take either rose hip powder or a placebo for six months.

For those taking rose hips, the ability to perform "activities of daily living" (ADL)—walking down the street, getting dressed, getting in and out of a chair, going shopping—improved by 20 to 25%. And, as a total among all the participants, the number of joints causing pain and discomfort fell by 40%. There was no change in ADL or pain levels among those taking the placebo.

"The trial was more positive than we had ever expected and the findings are incredibly exciting," says Kaj Winther, MD, a doctor at Kolding Hospital in Denmark. "This new evidence shows that the anti-inflammatory and antioxidant compounds in rose hips have quite a wide therapeutic effect. Rose hips could potentially make a huge difference toward improving the lives of people with rheumatoid arthritis."

Also helpful for osteoarthritis: One of the researchers who conducted the study on rheumatoid arthritis—Stefan N. Willich, MD, a professor at the Humboldt University of Berlin—also analyzed data from two studies using rose hip powder for osteoarthritis. In one of the studies, 66% of those taking the powder reported a reduction in pain after three months—compared to 35% taking the placebo. In another, those taking rose hips had a significant reduction in the use of painkillers.

STOP KNEE PAIN BEFORE IT STARTS—EAT MORE FRUIT!

More *fruit*? Yes, say Australian researchers. They recently published the results of a 10-year study of 293 middle-aged men and women (average age of 58) who were free of knee pain when the study began.

First, they analyzed their diets. Ten years later, they conducted MRIs (magnetic resonance imagery) of their knees to see who had developed the type of bone changes that lead to osteoarthritis and who hadn't.

Results: Those with the *highest* intake of fruit and vitamin C (from food only) had the *lowest* incidence of arthritis-causing bone changes.

"The study suggests a beneficial effect of fruit and vitamin C intake in the development of knee osteoarthritis," says Flavia Cicuttini, MD, at Monash University in Melbourne.

Theory: Oxidation is a kind of internal rust caused by many factors, some of which you can avoid (such as smoking) and some of which you can't (such as aging). Oxidation damages the joint. Vitamin C—found abundantly in fruit—is a powerful *antioxidant*.

Fruits richest in vitamin C: Cantaloupe, kiwifruit, oranges, pineapple, pink grapefruit, strawberries.

How it works: Rose hips decrease *inflammation*, says Dr. Winter. His research shows that when people with osteoarthritis take rose hips every day for four weeks, they have lower levels of C-reactive protein, a standard measure of inflammation. "Rose hips might be used as a replacement or supplement for conventional anti-inflammatory drug therapies in people with arthritis," he adds.

In the studies on rheumatoid arthritis and osteoarthritis, the researchers used LitoZin, a rose hip powder specially formulated to maximize and standardize anti-inflammatory factors.

LitoZin is available in the United States as Swanson Ultra LitoZin, *www.swansonvitamins.com* (800-824-4491).

JointVictory, manufactured by Blue Spring, PO Box 57595, Oklahoma City, OK 73157, *www.bluespringwellness.com* (800-350-6545).

Suggested intake: Follow the dosage recommendation on the label.

FISH OIL FOR OCEANIC RELIEF

You have osteoarthritis or rheumatoid arthritis—and your doctor insists that you *need* NSAIDs to counter the pain. After all, your doc knows from medical school that NSAIDs stop the first symptom-producing domino of arthritis from falling—COX, the enzyme that produces arachidonic acid…that synthesizes prostaglandin E2, a hormonelike substance… that triggers inflammation and pain.

Well, if your doc says you need to rely on NSAIDS, tell him there's something not sufficiently fishy about his facts, because fish oil does *exactly the same thing* that NSAIDs do—it blocks COX, says Leslie G. Cleland, MD, one of the world's top experts on fish oil and health, and a doctor in the Rheumatology Unit at the Royal Adelaide Hospital in Australia.

"There is widespread routine prescription of NSAIDs and neglect of fish oil by doctors," says Dr. Cleland. That's because the drug companies have the financial edge, convincing doctors—through aggressive advertising and the statements of paid opinion leaders—that NSAIDs are preferable, and that more evidence is needed before fish oil should be routinely prescribed to arthritis patients.

Well, there's no need for more proof that fish oil works. "The evidence is already ample," says Dr. Cleland. What doctors and their patients really need to know, he says, are ways to maximize the effectiveness of the therapeutic factors in fish oil—the omega-3 fatty acids EPA (*eicosapentaenoic acid*) and DHA (*docosahexaenoic acid*).

▶ *Breakthrough Study*

In the medical journal *Arthritis Research and Therapy*, Dr. Cleland details his perspectives about fish oil and his tips for its effective use.

• **Fish oil is safer than NSAIDs.** Fish oil doesn't cause bleeding ulcers—a side effect from NSAIDs that kills more than 16,000 Americans every year. Fish oil doesn't cause heart attacks as do NSAIDs—and, in fact, may help prevent them. (Remember that *all* NSAIDs can increase the risk of heart disease, not just banned drugs such as Vioxx and Bextra.) Unlike NSAIDs, fish oil doesn't spark the release of inflammation-causing *cytokines*, molecules that may play a role in other inflammation-linked diseases, such as Alzheimer's and type 2 diabetes—and may even damage cartilage, worsening arthritis in the long run.

• **If you take fish oil, you're likely to take fewer NSAIDs.** Studies show that people who regularly use fish oil cut their intake of NSAIDs in half.

• **Fish oil doesn't work in a day.** Fish oil blocks COX *naturally,* says Dr. Cleland—so it takes six to 12 weeks to work. "It is a long-term, not a short-term strategy for the management of arthritis."

• **Eating fish won't work.** It would be impractical for most people to eat the large amounts of fish required to achieve an anti-inflammatory dose of omega-3 fatty acids, he says.

• **Don't take cod liver oil.** "At anti-inflammatory doses, cod liver oil, which is rich in the fat-soluble vitamins A and D, contains more vitamin A than recommended intakes," says Dr. Cleland.

• **Eat a supportive diet.** Omega-6 fatty acids—found in margarine, cooking oils, mayonnaise and nuts—counter the anti-inflammatory power of the omega-3 fatty acids in fish oil. But reducing omega-6 fatty acid intake is simple, says Dr. Cleland—change cooking oils.

Choose cooking oils that are rich in monounsaturated fatty acids, such as olive oil or canola oil–based products, or that are rich in omega-3 fatty acids, such as flaxseed oil or fresh ground flaxseed. Avoid sunflower, cottonseed, peanut and soybean oil products.

• **The best dosage.** Dr. Cleland recommends a daily minimum of 2.7 grams of EPA plus DHA, an amount achieved by nine or more standard fish oil capsules. "People who self-medicate with fish oil generally take one or two capsules daily," he says. "That isn't enough for an anti-inflammatory effect."

Recommended: Try Eskimo 3 brand, says Jacob Teitelbaum, MD, author of *Pain Free 1-2-3!* (McGraw-Hill). "I strongly recommend this brand because it does not contain mercury, lead or other toxins. It is also not rancid and nasty tasting, and is less likely to come back up and repeat on you like many other fish oils." He recommends a dose of ½ to 2 tablespoons daily. "The liquid is cheaper and easier to take than a handful of capsules," he says. You can find Eskimo 3 at *www.enzy.com.*

ℹ️ Nordic Naturals is the brand that proved effective in the most scientific studies, says Harry Preuss, MD, a professor of medicine and physiology at Georgetown University, who conducted extensive research on natural supplements for health and healing. It is also processed for maximum purity and palatability. EPA-containing products in the Nordic Naturals line include Omega-3 and Ultimate Omega, and are widely available.

THE UGH-FREE WAY TO SWALLOW FISH OIL

Fish oil capsules can be expensive, says Dr. Cleland. But many people prefer them to the alternative of fish oil by the spoonful, with its fishy taste and odor. *Here's a technique developed by Dr. Cleland and his colleagues to avoid a French kiss with a fish…*

1. Pour 1 to 2 ounces of juice (orange, tomato, apple or any juice you like) into two small "shot" glasses.

2. Layer the desired dose of fish oil onto the juice in one glass—do not stir.

3. Swallow the juice and fish oil with a single gulp, avoiding contact with the lips (where the fish oil can be tasted).

4. Immediately sip the juice in the other glass slowly through the lips. This will remove any oil from the lips.

   To avoid fishy burps, Dr. Cleland says to take fish oil *immediately* before eating, without any other fluids. "This avoids floating the oil on fluid in the stomach, and helps the fish oil mix with food and pass from the stomach into the intestine."

SAMe—PAIN RELIEF, MINUS SIDE EFFECTS

SAMe is short for *S-Adenosyl methionine*. It's a chemical combo of two building blocks of life—the amino acid *methionine*, which helps synthesize the outer covering of cells; and *adenosine triphosphate*, the super-molecule that stores the energy that cells use to function.

Without SAMe, your body couldn't make DNA, RNA, protein or the neurotransmitters that control brain function…purify blood waste products…or build cartilage.

SAMe was discovered in 1952, and produced as a supplement in the 1970s by Italian scientists. Over the next decade, seven European studies, involving more than 20,000 people with arthritis, showed that SAMe matched NSAIDs for decreasing pain and inflammation, but without a barrage of bothersome side effects. Now, a study shows that SAMe can also match the anti-inflammatory prowess of the new (and infamous) generation of NSAIDs, the COX-2 inhibitors.

⫸ *Breakthrough Study*

Doctors in the Department of Family Medicine and Geriatrics at the University of California, Irvine, Medical Center, asked 56 people with osteoarthritis of the knee to take either celecoxib (Celebrex) or SAMe for two months. For the first month, Celebrex trounced SAMe, producing more pain relief. But by the second month, SAMe had kicked in, and pain reduction was the same in the SAMe and medication groups. Both groups also improved in everyday functioning and in the strength of joints.

"SAMe has a slower onset of action but is as effective as Celebrex in the management of symptoms of knee osteoarthritis—and much safer," says Wadie I. Najm, MD, the lead researcher of the study. He also points out that SAMe can relieve depression, a common problem in people with osteoarthritis. "For that reason, SAMe could be of greater benefit than other natural therapies for arthritis," he says.

Why it works: SAMe speeds up the production of *proteoglycan*, a component of cartilage, explains Sol J. Grazi, MD, an assistant professor at the University of Colorado School of Medicine, and coauthor of *SAMe: The Safe and Natural Way to Combat Depression and Relieve the Pain of Osteoarthritis* (Prima).

Suggested intake: 600 mg, twice a day (1,200), was the amount used in the study.

ℹ️ SAMe supplements are widely available.

Caution: If you decide to use SAMe for long-term pain relief, take a multivitamin supplement containing folic acid, which SAMe can deplete, says Dr. Najm. People with bipolar disorder should not use SAMe.

MSM FOR SEVERE OSTEOARTHRITIS

Perhaps you've heard of DMSO (*dimethyl sulfoxide*). It was first popularized in 1980 on *60 Minutes*. Mike Wallace interviewed a woman who had been in a car accident and developed constant, severe, debilitating neck pain. It was so bad she could hardly get out of bed. Then he interviewed her again—after she began DMSO treatments at the DMSO Clinic at the Oregon Health Sciences University in Portland. Now, she told Wallace, she was pain-free. And free of the need to take pain medication. She was up and about and *very* happy.

DMSO seemed like a miracle—and over the following year, Americans spent about $1 billion on DMSO.

Well, DMSO had its day. Today, you can find bottles of the sulfur-containing stuff mostly on the shelves of mom-and-pop health food stores, where it's still sold as a painkiller. Perhaps its decline in popularity is due to a harmless but unfortunate side effect—people who use it start to emit (and taste) an odor that's been variously described as fishy, oysterlike and/or garlicky. Enter MSM.

MSM (*methylsulfonylmethane*) is what happens to DMSO after it's absorbed by the body—it's a "metabolite" or breakdown product of DMSO, a kind of biochemical progeny. Unlike its parent, however, sulfur-containing MSM doesn't make you stink. Like its parent, MSM is very good at relieving pain.

▌▌▌▶ *Breakthrough Study*

Doctors at the Southwest College of Naturopathic Medicine in Tempe, AZ, asked 50 men and women with osteoarthritis of the knee to take either MSM supplements or a placebo for three months. Compared to the placebo-takers, those taking MSM had "significant decreases in pain and physical function impairment" and "improvement in performing activities of daily living," say the doctors, in the journal *Osteoarthritis and Cartilage.*

How it works: "Sulfur-containing compounds called *glycosaminoglycans* are abundant in the cartilage and synovial fluid of joints," says Stanley W. Jacob, MD, a professor of surgery at

VITAMIN D—YOUR DEFENSE AGAINST ARTHRITIS

Want to prevent rheumatoid arthritis or slow the advance of osteoarthritis? Take a vitamin D supplement. *Consider the evidence...*

• *Lower vitamin D,* faster progression of osteoarthritis. Scientists analyzed a decade of vitamin D levels and knee health in 556 people. Those with the lowest levels of vitamin D intake had *four times* the risk of worsening osteoarthritis of the knee—more loss of cartilage and more bone spurs—than those with the highest intake.

• *Lower vitamin D,* less bone density. Scientists at Boston University measured bone density in people with osteoarthritis of the knee. The lower the blood level of vitamin D, the lower the bone density.

• *Lower vitamin D,* higher risk of rheumatoid arthritis. Researchers at the College of Public Health at the University of Iowa analyzed 11 years of diet and health data for nearly 30,000 women. Those with the highest intake of vitamin D were 33% less likely to develop rheumatoid arthritis.

What happens: Vitamin D strengthens cartilage and delays the growth of bone spurs (slowing osteoarthritis) and helps regulate the immune system (helping to prevent rheumatoid arthritis).

What to do: To find out how to increase vitamin D intake, see page 9 in Chapter 1, "Aging and Longevity."

Oregon Sciences University in Portland, and coauthor of *The Miracle of MSM* (Putnam). "Sulfur levels in arthritic joints are lower than normal. MSM is a sulfur molecule. But we don't know precisely how the sulfur in MSM is utilized by the body to help arthritis."

Recommended for severe cases: "In my experience, MSM is particularly effective for severe, debilitating cases of arthritis," says Dr. Jacob. "It provides significant improvement—less pain, less stiffness and greater mobility."

Suggested intake: 3 grams, twice a day. (6 grams a day.)

ℹ️ MSM supplements are widely available.

GREEN-LIPPED MUSSELS— CLAM UP YOUR PAIN

All over the world, native people use local plants to prevent and treat disease. The coastal-dwelling Maori of New Zealand do the same with local seafood—by eating lots of the abundant and tasty green-lipped mussel (*Perna canaliculus*). Researchers noticed that Maoris living on the coast had far less arthritis than Maoris living in the interior. Perhaps mussels are making the difference.

▶ *Breakthrough Study*

Doctors at the University of Hong Kong asked 80 people with knee osteoarthritis to take either an extract of green-lipped mussel or a placebo for six months.

Results: Those taking the mussel extract had greater decreases in pain and increases in functional ability than those taking the placebo.

Green-lipped mussel extract "may be considered another, safe option in the treatment of osteoarthritis," says Chak S. Lau, MD, a professor in the Department of Medicine at the University of Hong Kong.

COFFEE GOES TOE TO TOE WITH GOUT

Men over 40 who drink the most coffee have the lowest risk of developing gout, the buildup of uric acid crystals that knife into joints. How much lower?

Guys who downed four to five cups a day of caffeinated java had a 40% lower risk, say scientists at the Arthritis Research Center of Canada, in Vancouver, who analyzed 12 years of diet and health data from nearly 46,000 men. At six cups a day, the risk dropped by 60%. (Three cups or less a day only reduced risk by 8%.) For decaf, four-cup-a-day drinkers were 27% less likely to give way to gout.

How does coffee shield against gout? The researchers also analyzed data from nearly 15,000 Americans who participated in the National Health and Nutrition Examination Survey—and found that those who drank the most coffee had the lowest levels of uric acid.

How it works: The mussel contains unique types of omega-3 fatty acids that may block the inflammatory process of arthritis, say Australian researchers.

ℹ️ The study used the product Lyprinol, an extract of the lipid (fat) portion of the mussel.

Suggested intake: Follow the dosage recommendation on the label.

☀️ *www.lyprinolusa.com*, Lyprinol USA, c/o CSC Services of NV, Inc., 502 East John Street, Carson City, NV 89706 (866-393-5558, 480-829-0154), *support@lyprinolusa.com*.

PYCNOGENOL—A BARK THAT'S TOUGH ON ARTHRITIS

In the southwest of France lies the 500,000-acre Landes forest. It is filled with the towering

Maritime Pine, whose bark is the source of *pycnogenol*. Those may be important facts for the geography of your joints.

⫸ *Breakthrough Study*

Doctors asked 35 people with arthritis to take either pycnogenol or a placebo for three months. *Those taking pycnogenol had a…*

- 43% **reduction in pain;**
- 35% **reduction in stiffness;**

THE BEST DIET FOR RHEUMATOID ARTHRITIS

Want to soothe the symptoms of rheumatoid arthritis? Take a cooking class.

Researchers in England divided 130 women with rheumatoid arthritis into two groups—one attended six weeks of weekly, two-hour cooking classes on how to prepare and eat a Mediterranean-type diet, while the other group was given handouts with information about healthy eating.

Six months later, the women who'd taken cooking classes were eating more fruits, vegetables, beans and monounsaturated fat (found in olive oil and avocados), and less saturated fat (found in red meat and milk). They also reported less pain, less early morning stiffness and better overall health. The women who had received the handout didn't make any dietary changes—and didn't feel any better, either.

This type of cooking class might be a "popular, inexpensive and useful addition to other rheumatoid arthritis treatments," says Gayle McKellar, MD, of Glasgow Royal Infirmary, in Scotland.

Helpful: How to find a cooking class? "The best source for cooking schools is *ShawGuides: The Guide to Cooking Schools,* which comes out annually and includes listings for professional and recreational classes in the US," says Kate Heyhoe, editor and cofounder of The Global Gourmet, at *www. globalgourmet.com.* You can find the book at any bookstore, or at *www.shawguides.com.*

- 52% **increase in everyday functioning, such as walking and dressing and**
- 49% **overall improvement in arthritis symptoms.**

They also took fewer medications.

Meanwhile, the placebo group saw little or no improvement in any of those measurements.

"Pycnogenol's natural anti-inflammatory and antioxidant properties were responsible for delivering these excellent results," says Ronald R. Watson, PhD, a professor in the Nutritional Sciences Department at the University of Arizona. *He explains further…*

How it works: "Pycnogenol inhibits COX-1 and COX-2, enzymes that help form prostaglandins, hormonelike substances that increase inflammation," says Dr. Watson. "It also turns down the proinflammatory 'master-switch,' nuclear factor-kappa B."

Suggested intake: The study used 50 mg, three times daily (150 mg).

ⓘ Brands of pycnogenol-containing supplements are widely available.

Caution: Occasionally, pycnogenol may cause minor stomach upset. Take it with food or after meals.

GENTLE MOVES FOR POWERFUL RELIEF

AQUA-EXERCISE—GET THAT BUOYANT FEELING

You're in a soothing envelope of skin-hugging warmth and your body feels light as a leaf. No, you're not dreaming. You're *bobbing*—in a heated pool, doing aqua-exercise, also known as water exercise, or hydrotherapy. And it's H_2Oh-so pain-relieving.

TURMERIC AND ARTHRITIS—CURRY FAVOR WITH YOUR JOINTS

The spicy seasoning turmeric is a second cousin to ginger, a constant in curry powder, a coloring in mustard—and, in India, a natural medicine as common as aspirin, used for its ability to (among other curative talents) relieve pain and minimize inflammation. Western scientists are catching on (or catching up). There are literally hundreds of scientific studies testing whether turmeric (or *curcumin* and other "curcuminoids," the active ingredients in turmeric) can defeat disease. Turmeric vs. cancer. Turmeric vs. Alzheimer's. Turmeric vs. arthritis...

"Turmeric has been used for centuries in the Ayurvedic medicine of India as a treatment for inflammatory disorders, including arthritis," says Janet L. Funk, MD, an assistant professor of Physiological Sciences at the University of Arizona. That's one reason why she and her colleagues decided to test turmeric to see how it might affect laboratory animals with experimentally induced rheumatoid arthritis.

She found that giving turmeric to the animals before arthritis was induced *did* prevent joint inflammation. In science-speak, "Turmeric...demonstrated a profound inhibition of induced-arthritis that is rarely seen..." Turmeric also cut cartilage destruction by 66% and bone destruction by 57%.

Dr. Funk and her colleagues also investigated the mechanism by which turmeric works. In a study published in the journal *Arthritis and Rheumatism*, she showed that turmeric can derail the genetic and molecular momentum of arthritis—the herb influences the action of nuclear factor-kappa B, a so-called "transcription factor" that switches genes on and off—in this case, switching off key inflammatory genes that result in the destruction of cartilage and bone.

Using her animal studies, Dr. Funk estimates that a supplement providing 1.5 grams a day of curcuminoids might be the effective dose for humans—well below the 8 grams a day that other studies have shown is "well-tolerated" and "nontoxic." However, although Dr. Funk points out that many treatments that work on animals have proven to be useful in humans, and says her results are "very promising and exciting," she is *not* encouraging people to use turmeric supplements. "Turmeric might help people with rheumatoid and osteoarthritis," she says, "but more research is needed to reach that conclusion." *But another scientist and herbal expert isn't waiting for more studies to make a practical recommendation...*

What to do: "Curcumin and other curcuminoids in turmeric are first-rate arthritis-alleviating anti-inflammatories," says James A. Duke, PhD, the developer of herbal databases for the USDA and author of *The Green Pharmacy Herbal Handbook* (Rodale) and many other books on herbs.

He provides these dosage options for those interested in using turmeric/curcumin to soothe arthritis. They are roughly equivalent to Dr. Funk's estimate of the effective dose—400 mg of curcumin extract three times a day; 445 mg of a standardized curcumin supplement three times a day; 1 teaspoon to 1 tablespoon of a liquid extract of turmeric divided into several doses over the course of a day or ⅛ to ¼ teaspoon of turmeric tincture three times a day.

Curcumin and turmeric supplements, liquid extracts and tinctures are widely available.

Also try: "I'm all for enjoying turmeric in fabulous food," says Dr. Duke. "One of the most palatable approaches to treating arthritis is with curries—as long as you really load on the turmeric."

⫸ Breakthrough Study

Researchers at the Center for Health Exercise and Sports Medicine at the University of Melbourne, in Australia, divided 71 people with either hip or knee osteoarthritis into two groups—one participated in six weeks of aqua-therapy and one didn't.

Results: After six weeks, the aquatic group had less pain, less joint stiffness, greater physical function, better quality of life and more hip strength. Overall, more than 70% of those in the aquatic group reported less pain and better functioning—compared to 17% in the nonaquatic group. In fact, the benefits were so significant, 60 of the 71 study participants decided to stick with aqua-therapy after the study was over.

What happens: "Three key exercises for arthritis relief—stretching, strengthening and aerobic—can easily be done in water," says Dr. Jason Theodosakis. "Sometimes it's the only way a person with arthritis can exercise without pain."

"Water exercises make the muscles work harder because of the water's increased resistance, but the body's buoyancy diminishes shock and trauma to bones and joints," adds Eugene Zampieron, ND, a naturopathic physician in Woodbury, CT, and coauthor of *Arthritis* (Celestial Arts).

Example: "One of my relatives, who is 64, has suffered for years from knee arthritis that was caused by an injury he sustained in his twenties," says Vijay B. Vad, MD, a professor at Weill Medical College of Cornell University and author of *Arthritis RX* (Gotham Books). "About seven years ago, I convinced him to start aquatherapy, and he now does it five days a week. He claims this one simple activity has kept up his mobility and minimized his pain despite a significantly arthritic knee."

☀ The Arthritis Foundation YMCA Aquatic Program is offered throughout the United States. To find out if there is a program in your area, contact a local YMCA (*www.ymca.net* includes a search feature to find the 20 closest YMCAs by zip code, or call 800- 872-9622) or a local chapter of the Arthritis Foundation (*www.arthritis. org* has a similar search feature to find a local chapter, or call 800-283-7800).

The Aquatic Exercise Association provides a Web site *www.aeawave.com*, where you can download CD-ROMs of "Customized Aqua Exercise Packages," including the *Fluid Flex Stretch and Energize Workout* for people with arthritis, and the *After Hip Replacement Workout.* AEA, PO Box 1609, Nokomis, FL 34274-1609 (888-232-9283, 941-486-8600, or fax 941-486-8820).

Books: *Your Water Workout* by Jane Katz (Broadway), *Water Exercise* by Martha White (Human Kinetics), *Fantastic Water Workouts* by Marybeth Pappas Gaines (Human Kinetics) and *Water Fitness After 40* by Ruth Sova (DSL Ltd.).

ACUPUNCTURE—CHI FOR YOUR KNEE

In Traditional Chinese Medicine (TCM), *chi* is energy, life force, the primal pulse of power flowing in your body. Acupuncture—the insertion of thin, long (and virtually painless) needles on points along invisible tracks of chi called meridians—is a natural way to balance chi, for healing and pain relief. Many researchers now think that acupuncture works to soothe arthritis—a point well taken.

⫸ *Breakthrough Study*

Researchers at the University of Maryland School of Medicine studied 570 patients with osteoarthritis of the knee—giving some patients real acupuncture treatments for knee pain, while others received "sham acupuncture" treatments, in which needles were inserted into nontherapeutic points, or seemed to be inserted but were not.

After 23 sessions over 26 weeks, the real acupuncture group had 40% better daily functioning, a greater increase than the sham group. They also had 25% less pain than the sham group.

"Traditional Chinese acupuncture is safe and effective for reducing pain and improving

SEVEN WAYS TO MAXIMIZE IN-POOL COMFORT AND LONG-TERM PAIN RELIEF

"Working out in water is an *excellent* way for a person with arthritis to decrease pain and increase function-restoring fitness," says Ruth Sova, president of the Aquatic Therapy and Rehab Institute in West Palm Beach, FL. Why? She explains...

"When muscles are more relaxed, stress on the joints is decreased and range of motion is improved. Immersion also increases circulation to the joints. But most important, perhaps, immersion decreases the load and pressure on the joints, which decreases pain tremendously."

There are also psychological benefits, says Sova. "It's horrible to feel that you can't function like you used to, or like other people do. When you get in the water, you can!"

Sova has a few tips for people with arthritis who want to ease into water exercise...

Find the warmest water possible. "Cold water can create more pain, and you don't want that! Ninety-two degrees—skin temperature—is considered *thermoneutral:* You don't chill and you don't overheat. You have to judge what works for you."

If the water is cold... "Wear a neoprene vest, neoprene gloves and neoprene booties. The vest will keep the blood flowing to your arms and legs. The gloves and booties will keep your hands and feet warm."

Don't exercise alone. "If you're in a private pool, be sure you're with someone who can help in an emergency."

Don't bounce right away. "Spend the first ten minutes with simple, walking strides instead of doing any bouncing—even in the water, impact can create physical stress. During those ten minutes gradually increase your stride length and arm swing."

Go for a walk. "Swimming is a great skill but you can't swim on land—walking is what you need to do to function on land. Walk forward and backward and side-to-side, maintaining the most upright alignment possible. Walking in the water will improve your ability to walk on land."

Wiggle a little. "In the water, you often think about moving your shoulders, hips, back and knees—but try to improve your small motor skills, too. Make sure your wrists, fingers, ankles, toes and neck move as far as possible."

Just say no to the noodle. "Be cautious about using equipment that has to be held, such as a noodle or swim bar. Stay away from anything that increases compression on the joints, such as flotation ankle cuffs. You'll do best without any equipment—just by using the buoyancy of the water."

☀ For more information about water exercise and arthritis, see the "Articles of Interest" section of the Web site of the Aquatic Therapy and Rehab Institute, *www.atri.org*. Aquatic Therapy & Rehab Institute, Inc., 13297 Temple Blvd., West Palm Beach, FL 33412 (866-462-2874, 813-949-5821 or fax 561-828-8150); e-mail *atri@atri.org*.

function in patients with symptomatic knee osteoarthritis who are in pain despite therapy with medication," says Brian Berman, MD, in the *Annals of Internal Medicine*.

He points out that the treatment is slow but sure. It took eight weeks to improve function and 14 weeks to improve pain—similar, he says, to slow-acting supplements such as glucosamine, chondroitin sulfate and ASU (all of which are discussed earlier in this chapter).

And he emphasizes the fact that the treatment had no noticeable side effects, unlike the side effects for medications for arthritis that "may rival in severity the arthritis symptoms themselves."

☀ To find an acupuncturist near you, visit the Web site of the National Certification Commission for Acupuncture and Oriental Medicine, *www.nccaom.org*, where you can search for certified acupuncturists by area code or zip code. A similar service is offered at *www.acufinder.com*. Or contact Acufinder.com, 825 College Blvd., Suite 102-211, Oceanside, CA 92057 (760-630-3600).

How they work: "After performing a physical exam—which may involve feeling twelve different pulses that relate to meridians, and looking at your tongue, which, in TCM, reveals where the flow of chi has been disrupted—the acupuncturist will attempt to devise a treatment plan that unblocks your stuck chi," explains Glenn S. Rothfeld, MD, one of the first physicians in the United States trained in acupuncture and coauthor of *Natural Medicine for Arthritis* (Rodale). "Generally, such a plan will involve acupuncture, and might also involve herbal therapy and therapeutic exercises such as chi gong or tai chi."

EXERCISE AWAY STIFFNESS, FATIGUE AND PAIN

"For a long time, doctors believed that exercise *aggravated* or even caused osteoarthritis, and they advised against it," says Dr. Jason Theodosakis. "Perhaps that's one reason why very few osteoarthritis sufferers exercise on a regular basis." But, he says, exercise is one of the best medicines for osteoarthritis, helping to ease symptoms. The newest scientific research shows he's right.

||||➡ *Breakthrough Study*

Researchers at the University of North Carolina at Chapel Hill and the government's Centers for Disease Control and Prevention, in Atlanta,

BEE VENOM—IS IT REAL OR JUST A STING?

Talk about a therapy with a lot of buzz— since the time of Hippocrates, bee stings have been used to treat arthritic joint pain. In 21st-century Korea, bee-venom acupuncture is all the rage, with more than 60 scientific studies testing the therapy. Is all the fuss based on facts? Does bee venom work?

"There is actually some logic to the idea that bee venom could be used to treat arthritis, as it contains several anti-inflammatory chemicals," says Richard Blau, MD, medical director of the Arthritis Institute of Long Island, and author of *Too Young to Feel Old* (Da Capo). "One, called *melitin*, is a hundred times more potent than the steroid cortisone. Another, called *adolpin*, also blocks pain."

However, says Dr. Blau, that doesn't mean you should go out to your local apiary and have your knees coated with bees. Or order your "Starter Bee Venom Kit" via the Internet. (Yes, it's available.) Or let an adventurous acupuncturist try out the technique. ("There is limited evidence demonstrating the efficacy of bee-venom acupuncture in arthritis," say scientists at the College of Korean Medicine, who reviewed all the research on the therapy.)

"The place to study these substances is in controlled clinical trials, where doctors can carefully monitor patients' side effects," says Dr. Blau. In other words, when it comes to bee venom and arthritis, let the buyer bee-ware.

studied 346 people participating in the Arthritis Foundation Exercise Program, at 18 sites around the country. *Compared to when they started the program, people who participated for two months had...*

- **Less pain**
- **Less fatigue**
- **Less stiffness**
- **Better ability to lift objects**
- **Increased strength in arms and legs**

DOES EXERCISE CAUSE OSTEOARTHRITIS?

Can regular exercise *cause* osteoarthritis of the knee, particularly if you're overweight? No, say researchers at Boston University School of Medicine, who analyzed 12 years of data from 1,279 middle-aged and older people. Those who were recreational walkers and joggers had no increased risk of developing OA of the knee. Overweight *was* a risk factor for OA—but being overweight *and* exercising didn't further increase risk. "Physical activity can be done safely without concern that you will develop osteoarthritis as a consequence," says David T. Felson, MD, a professor of medicine and one of the authors of the study, which appeared in *Arthritis Care & Research.*

● **Improved sense that they could manage arthritis**

"If adults with arthritis attend a majority of Arthritis Foundation Exercise Program classes, they can expect improvements in symptoms," says Leigh Callahan, PhD, an associate professor at the Thurston Arthritis Research Center at the University of North Carolina School of Medicine. But, she adds, the study shows that you have to *keep* exercising to hold on to those improvements.

What it does: The program consists of several categories of gentle exercises, performed sitting, standing or on the floor—the type of exercises most important for people with arthritis are range-of-motion, endurance and low-resistance strengthening exercises, along with balance and coordination activities, posture and body mechanics training, breathing exercises and relaxation techniques.

What to do: Contact a local chapter of the Arthritis Foundation to find an Arthritis Foundation Exercise Program near you. The Foundation's Web site, *www.arthritis.org,* has a search feature to help you find a local chapter, or call 800-283-7800.

Best DVDs: *Take Control With Exercise: Based on the Arthritis Foundation Exercise Program* and *Exercise Can Beat Arthritis,* from physical therapist Valerie Sayce.

Best Books: *Exercises for Arthritis* by Erin Rohan O'Driscoll, RN (Hatherleigh), *Arthritis, What Exercises Work* by Dava Sobel and Arthur C. Klein (St. Martin's), *Strong Women and Men Beat Arthritis* by Miriam E. Nelson, PhD (G.P. Putnam).

Self-defense: "Never exercise through joint pain," says Dr. Theodosakis. "Don't overdo—you may injure yourself." (If you experience discomfort more than an hour after exercise, you've probably overdone it, he says.) "And listen to your body. If you feel dizzy or sick to your stomach, if you're short of breath, or if your chest feels pained or tight—stop exercising."

YOGA—RELIEF IS AROUND THE BEND

Maybe you think of yoga as just the *opposite* of an appropriate exercise for somebody with arthritis. After all, aren't the postures and positions of yoga—the curling cobra, the arching cat—for the *flexible?*

Not so, says Timothy McCall, MD, medical editor of *Yoga Journal* and author of *Yoga as Medicine* (Bantam). "There are vigorous styles of yoga—such as Power, Ashtanga and Bikram—that do require flexibility and fitness. But yoga is offered in a wide variety of styles. Yoga poses can be adapted to *any* level of flexibility, including that of someone with arthritis."

In fact, studies now show that practicing yoga can *improve* arthritis…

‖➤ *Breakthrough Study*

Researchers in the Division of Rheumatology at the University of Pennsylvania School of Medicine asked seven people with osteoarthritis of the knee (many of whom were overweight) to participate in an eight-week yoga course.

Results: Eight weeks later, the participants had 47% less pain, 37% less stiffness—and said they felt a lot better. They could also walk nearly 40% faster, probably because they were more flexible, says Sharon L. Kolasinski, MD, one of the doctors who conducted the study.

"This study shows that yoga provides a pain-relieving, function-improving treatment option for overweight, middle-aged people with osteoarthritis who have never practiced yoga before," she says. "Yoga is for everybody, not just people who are already flexible."

What to do: If you're thinking about trying out yoga, Dr. Kolasinski says to find a yoga teacher who has instructed people with arthritis and who can give you a lot of personal attention in class. She also urges you to take it easy.

"Start at a beginner's level and see what you can and can't comfortably do. And as with any exercise program, you can get hurt—so be safe. If you find yourself in pain in any posture, stop it immediately," Dr. Kolasinski says.

Smart idea: She also advises you do yoga *and* other types of exercise. "For a person with osteoarthritis, exercise is absolutely essential for optimal functioning," she says. "But I encourage my patients to do *different* kinds of exercises throughout the week, because no one exercise can improve flexibility, strength and aerobic conditioning. Walk, do some tai chi, do some weight lifting, do some yoga—that way, you're not likely to get bored and you're more likely to keep exercising. It's not about the 'best' exercise for arthritis—it's about the exercise that you're going to *do*."

☀ The Web site of the magazine *Yoga Journal* —*www.yogajournal.com*—has a directory of yoga teachers, with a search function to find teachers and classes in your state. Search the "Teachers and Studios" category, using the keyword "arthritis."

Best Books: *Yoga for Arthritis: The Complete Guide* by Loren Fishman and Ellen Saltonstall (W. W. Norton), and *Arthritis: An American Yoga Association Guide* (Kensington) by Alice Christensen.

Best DVDs: *Yoga for Arthritis* (produced by the Arthritis Foundation, with five people who have arthritis perform the yoga poses), and *Arthritis RX*, a routine that combines yoga, Pilates and physical therapy, created by Vijay B. Vad, MD, a sports medicine physician specializing in nondrug, nonsurgical arthritis therapies.

TAI CHI SOOTHES KNEE PAIN

Tai chi chuan was originally developed in China as a martial art—in fact, the name roughly translates as "supreme ultimate fist." But that smack-down moniker has little to do with the tai chi of today—the slow, gentle, flowing set of movements practiced by people all over the world who want better health, better balance and, for those with arthritis, a better way to relieve arthritis pain.

‖➤ *Breakthrough Studies*

For osteoarthritis: Researchers in the Department of Rehabilitation Sciences at Texas Tech University Health Sciences Center in Lubbock asked 41 people with knee osteoarthritis to participate in a 12-week program of tai chi—six weeks of 40-minute group sessions, three times a week, and six weeks of home-based tai chi practice. Then the participants were

THE LOWDOWN ON HIGH-HEELS AND ARTHRITIS

Physical therapists call it *knee joint torque*—the amount of twist and turn in the knee joint when you walk. The less torque from step to step, they theorize, the less likely it is that you'll develop knee osteoarthritis—or that it will get worse if you have it.

Which is why a team of six curious scientists in the Department of Physical Medicine and Rehabilitation at the University of Virginia asked 29 young women (average age of 26) and 20 older women (average age of 70) to don either flats or shoes with 1½-inch heels and then stroll around their "motion analysis gait laboratory"—where they measured just how much knee-damaging torque those two styles of footwear produced.

Bad news for you Manolo Blahnik fans out there...knee torques of various kinds were, well, pumped up by high heels, from 7 to 19%, in women both young and old.

The study's authors' unfashionable conclusion about 1½-inch (or higher) heels: "Women, particularly those who already have knee osteoarthritis, should be advised against wearing these types of shoes."

asked *not* to practice tai chi for six weeks. A comparison group with osteoarthritis attended 40-minute health lectures three times a week for six weeks.

Results: After 12 weeks, the tai chi participants had less overall knee pain, their "maximum" knee pain was no longer as severe, they were less stiff and they had better physical function (the ability to carry out daily tasks, such as getting dressed and shopping). The comparison group experienced no significant changes.

However: "All improvements disappeared after six weeks of not practicing tai chi," says Jean-Michel Brismée, ScD, one of the researchers who conducted the study. In other words, if you want the pain relief and other benefits to last, tai chi—and don't *untai*.

For rheumatoid arthritis: Researchers at the Tufts-New England Medical Center studied 20 people with rheumatoid arthritis (RA)—10 participated in twice-weekly, one-hour tai chi classes for 12 weeks; 10 attended lectures on nutrition and medical information about RA.

After 12 weeks, five of the people taking tai chi classes had improvements in joint tenderness (20 to 81%), joint swelling (25 to 80%) and the doctor's evaluation of disease activity (44 to 80%). Four of the patients had less pain (20 to 84%), a general improvement in health, as assessed by a questionnaire (71 to 100%) and a decrease in C-reactive protein, a measurement of inflammation (36 to 89%).

"The results suggest that tai chi is a safe and potentially promising complementary therapy for adults with rheumatoid arthritis," says Chenchen Wang, MD, one of the authors of the study.

Why it works: "Tai chi is a perfect exercise for those with arthritis because it involves little impact," says Dr. Eugene Zampieron. "It is gentle and effective in stretching muscles, loosening and lubricating the joints and promoting blood circulation."

He suggests you do exactly what the people with osteoarthritis in the study did. "Learn tai chi in a structured class, which will teach you the fundamentals for exercises that you can eventually do at home."

☀ An instructional video for the tai chi exercises used in the study from Texas Tech University Health Sciences Center is available by contacting the Tai Chi Master (and one of the authors of the study) Dr. Ming Chyu. E-mail *m.chyu@ttu.edu* or call 806-742-3563, x230.

Another instructional DVD is *Tai Chi for Arthritis*, with Dr. Paul Lam, a family physician and tai chi master. To order, and for more information, see *www.taichiforarthritis.com*. The DVD, and a book by Dr. Lam, *Overcoming Arthritis:*

How to Relieve Pain and Restore Mobility Through a Unique Tai Chi Program (DK Adult), are also available at many other Internet and retail outlets where DVDs and books are sold.

The Arthritis Foundation's tai chi program is based on Dr. Lam's. For more information on the Arthritis Foundation tai chi program, and to locate a local chapter of the Arthritis Foundation in order to find a tai chi class near you, see *www.arthritis.org*, or call 800-283-7800.

Also helpful: Another way to find a tai chi class near you is to visit the Web site of the American Tai Chi Association, *www.american taichi.net*, which allows you to search for classes by state, area code and interest, including "Tai Chi for Arthritis." American Tai Chi Association, 2465 J-17 Centreville Road, Suite 150, Herndon, VA 20171; e-mail *contact@americantaichi.net*.

WEIGHT LOSS—POUND FOR POUND PREVENTION

What do top arthritis experts say about weight loss? *They all say the same thing...*

"Obesity is the number one cause of osteoarthritis in women in the United States, and the number two cause—behind previous injuries—in men," says James M. Rippe, MD, associate professor of medicine at Tufts University School of Medicine and author of *The Joint Health Prescription* (Rodale).

"For each additional pound of body weight, three pounds of pressure is added to the knees and six pounds of pressure is added to the hips," says Dr. Eugene Zampieron. "This extra pressure gradually increases the stress on these joints, raising the risk of osteoarthritis later in life."

"Dozens of scientific studies have looked at the relationship between weight and arthritis, and they're all in agreement. If you're overweight, your chances of arthritis of the knee

and hip are much greater than those of someone of normal weight," says Dr. Jason Theodosakis. Here's one of the latest of those studies.

▌▌▌▶ *Breakthrough Study*

Norwegian researchers at the Oslo Orthopedic Center analyzed health data from 1.2 million people. The higher the body mass index—a

---

MAGNETS—AN ATTRACTIVE OPTION FOR PAIN RELIEF?

Two researchers from the Universities of Exeter and Plymouth in England analyzed data from nine studies that looked at whether magnets relieved pain. "There was no significant difference in pain reduction" when magnets were used for foot pain, muscle soreness, back pain or wrist pain, say the researchers, in the *Journal of the Canadian Medical Association*.

However: They couldn't rule out the possibility that magnets might work for *arthritis* pain.

Newest research: Doctors in Devon, England, studied 194 people with osteoarthritis of the hip or knee. Those who wore standard-strength (170–200 mTesla), magnet-containing bracelets for 12 weeks had a 45% greater decrease in pain than those who wore fake, look-alike bracelets.

Other studies from researchers at Harvard Medical School and the University of Texas found magnets in knee wraps reduced pain in people with osteoarthritis of the knee.

Theory: Magnetic fields calm pain fibers or increase circulation.

☀ *www.magnetictherapymagnets.com*, 866-467-6444, Herbal Remedies USA LLC, PO Box 2470, Casper, WY 82602-2470.

Caution: Cardiac pacemakers, defibrillators, insulin pumps and liver infusion pumps are controlled by magnetic fields. If you use any of those devices, don't use magnets for pain relief.

standard measurement of fatness—the greater the chance of hip-replacement surgery for osteo-arthritis of the hip. The fattest men had a 3.4 times greater risk than the thinnest men; the fattest women, a 2.3 greater risk than the thinnest women. The researchers reported their results in the journal *Arthritis and Rheumatism*.

And, in a study from Sweden, men with the highest BMI had a four times higher risk of knee osteoarthritis compared with men with the lowest; women with the highest BMI had a 60% greater risk than women with the lowest.

Latest development: In another study, researchers at Harvard Medical School examined trends in obesity and arthritis among baby boomers (born between 1946 and 1965) and the previous so-called "silent" generation (born 1926 to 1945). Comparing the two generations, they found more baby boomers were more obese at comparable ages. They also found the percentage of arthritis cases caused by obesity rising from 3% in 1971 (when the youngest of the "silent" generation were entering their forties) to 18% in 2002 (as baby boomers entered their forties and fifties).

Good news: Researchers at the Snow Biomechanics Laboratory at Wake Forest University studied 142 overweight, sedentary men and women with knee osteoarthritis—analyzing their knee joints before and after an 18-month weight-loss program. The more weight they lost, the less knee-damaging force to the knee-joint was produced during walking. "Our results indicate that each pound of weight loss will result in a fourfold reduction in the load exerted on the knee per step during daily activities," says Stephen P. Messier, PhD, a professor in the Department of Health and Exercise, and one of the authors of the study. "Over thousands of steps a day, this level of reduction may help relieve knee pain and disability."

What happens: "Increased load on the weight-bearing joints, especially the knees and hips, can cause the cartilage to break down," explains Dr. Theodosakis. He also points out that heavier people are more likely to have arthritis in their fingers and hands. "Perhaps a still-unidentified substance in the blood of the overweight causes cartilage destruction," he says.

What to do: "We can't change our genes, gender or age, but we can certainly reduce our body weight, and that makes hips, ankles, feet and especially knees less prone to the development and progression of arthritis," says Dr. Richard Blau.

For advice on weight loss, see Chapter 14 beginning on page 350.

MINDFULNESS MEDITATION

"Mindfulness is not thinking, interpreting or evaluating," says Mirabai Bush, the executive director of the Center for Contemplative Mind in Society, in Northampton, MA. "It is a non-judgmental quality of mind, which doesn't anticipate the future or reflect on the past. Any activity can be done with mindfulness—talking on the telephone, cleaning your home, driving, working and exercising." Mindfulness can also be done as a form of meditation, she explains—a type of meditation that can help you cope with arthritis.

▶ *Breakthrough Study*

Researchers from the University of Maryland School of Medicine asked 31 people with rheumatoid arthritis to participate in a once-a-week "Mindfulness-Based Stress Reduction" meditation class for eight weeks, followed by a four-month maintenance program during which they refreshed their mindfulness meditation skills; another 32 people with rheumatoid arthritis

THE HELPING HANDS OF MASSAGE

Maybe you think of massage as an unnecessary indulgence—what a person does when he/she wants pampering at a spa. Well, a new survey conducted by the American Massage Therapy Association shows that about one-third of those who get massage do so for *medical* reasons—often to relieve pain. And research from the Institute for Complementary and Alternative Medicine at the University of Medicine and Dentistry of New Jersey, in Newark, and Yale University School of Medicine shows that massage can work to relieve the pain of arthritis...

The study: Sixty-eight people with osteoarthritis of the knee (average age of 70) received either two months of Swedish massage (twice a week for the first month and once a week for the second) or were told that they'd start receiving massage after two months. (Darn!) And, after those two months had passed, those getting massages had less pain, stiffness, better range of motion, better daily functioning and could walk around faster. There was no change in the no-massage group. When the researchers checked two months later—after the study participants *hadn't* been getting massage for two months—they found a lot of the positive changes had persisted.

"This study suggests that massage therapy using Swedish massage is safe and effective for reducing pain and improving function in people with osteoarthritis of the knee," says Adam Perlman, MD, one of the authors of the study. "Current treatment of osteoarthritis with medications is associated with a high rate of adverse affects, such as heart, digestive, kidney and liver problems. The importance of massage as a potential treatment is self-evident."

Why it works: Massage may work to relieve arthritis symptoms by improving circulation, reducing muscle tension and improving flexibility, says Dr. Perlman.

☀ To find a professional massage therapist in your area, you can use the on-line locator service of the American Massage Therapy Association, *www.amtamassage.org/findamassage/locator.aspx*. American Massage Therapy Association, 500 Davis Street, Suite 900, Evanston, IL 60201-4695 (877-905-2700, 847-864-0123, or fax 847-864-1178); e-mail *info@ amtamassage.org.*

were "wait-listed for the program." MBSR also includes gentle hatha yoga exercises.

Results: After six months, the people who were trained in mindfulness meditation had a 35% reduction in psychological distress—the difference between being "extremely distressed" and "a little bit distressed."

Example: The following instruction for mindfulness meditation was adapted from instructions by Steve Smith, an adviser to the Center for Contemplative Mind in Society. The people with rheumatoid arthritis who participated in the study meditated for 45 minutes a day, six days per week.

1. Begin by sitting in a chair, with your back straight. Relax in your sitting posture with a few deep breaths. Allow the body and mind to become utterly relaxed while remaining very alert and attentive to the present moment. Feel the areas in your body that are tense, and the areas that are relaxing. Just let the body follow its own natural patterns. Do not try to force or fix anything.

2. Simply feel the sensations of sitting, sidestepping with your mind the tendency to interpret, to define and think about it. Just let such thoughts and images come and go without being bothered by them.

3. Now, bring your attention to your breathing. Locate the area where the breath is most obvious and let awareness lightly rest there. For some people, it is the sensation of the rising and falling of the abdomen.

For others, it may be the sensations experienced at the nostrils with the inhalation and exhalation.

4. You can use mental labels to guide and sustain attention to the breath—saying "rising/falling" with the rising and falling of the abdomen, or "in/out" with the movement of breath in and out of the nostrils. Let the breath breathe itself without control, direction or force. Feel the full-breath cycle from the beginning through the middle to the end.

5. As soon as you notice the mind wandering off, lost in thought, be aware of that non-judging awareness, and gently connect it again to your breath.

☀ To locate a class in mindfulness-based stress-reduction meditation in your area, visit the Web site of the Center for Mindfulness in Medicine, Health Care, and Society, of the University of Massachusetts Medical School, *www.umassmed.edu/cfm*, which includes a state-by-state directory of instructors and classes throughout the United States.

The mindfulness-meditation used in the study was developed by Jon Kabat-Zinn, PhD, the leading expert on mindfulness-based stress reduction and author of *Full Catastrophe Living: Using the Wisdom of Your Body and Mind to Face Stress, Pain, and Illness* (Delta) and many other books. For mindfulness-based CDs and tapes created by Dr. Zinn, please see the Web site, *www.mindfulnesstapes.com*. You can order the tapes from Stress Reduction Tapes, PO Box 547, Lexington, MA 02420.

Contact information for the Center for Contemplative Mind in Society, *www.contemplativemind.org*, e-mail *info@contemplativemind.org*, The Center for Contemplative Mind in Society, 199 Main Street, Suite 3, Northampton, MA 01060 (413-582-0071, fax 413-582-1330).

AROMATHERAPY—STOP AND SMELL THE ROSEMARY

"The essential oils of aromatherapy can help ease the symptoms of your arthritis, either by reducing inflammation or relieving the stress and tension that trigger and aggravate the pain," says Glen S. Rothfeld, MD, founder and medical director of WholeHealth New England, in Plymouth and Arlington, MA, and coauthor of *Natural Medicine for Arthritis* (Rodale). And that's exactly what a recent study shows.

||||▶ *Breakthrough Study*

Nurses at St. Mary's Hospital in Seoul, Korea, treated 40 people with arthritis with aromatherapy massage. The treatment had a "major effect," they say, significantly reducing pain and depression.

How to use: "To help arthritis, essential oils need to be topically applied," says Jane Buckle, PhD, RN, author of *Clinical Aromatherapy: Essential Oils in Practice* (Churchill Livingston). "Add an essential oil to bathwater," she advises, "or add essential oil to a massage oil, such as almond oil, and massage it into any part of the body that is feeling pain or stress."

Recommended: The essential oil used by the nurses for aromatherapy massage was a blend of two parts lavender, one part marjoram, two parts eucalyptus, one part rosemary and one part peppermint, in a carrier oil of almond (45%), apricot (45%) and jojoba (10%) oil.

ℹ A similar blend for arthritis (containing lavender, marjoram, eucalyptus and rosemary) can be found at *www.essentialblend.com*, Essential Blend, 697 Baker Road, Hudson, WI 54016 (715-220-4527); e-mail *info@essentialblend.com*. They recommend adding 10 to 20 drops to the tub for a relaxing and healing bath, 5 to 10 drops of the oil and 2 tablespoons of water to an aromatherapy diffuser (which can be ordered

LEECHES—A SUPRISINGLY EFFECTIVE THERAPY

Don't expect your doctor to prescribe them anytime soon (or your local pharmacy to stock them), but European physicians are finding out that *leeches*—yes, leeches, the animals detested by Humphrey Bogart in the *African Queen* but prized by natural healers since antiquity for their power to cure blood clots and disinfect wounds—are adept at reducing arthritis pain...

New study: Doctors in Germany studied 51 people with osteoarthritis of the knee, treating 24 with leech therapy ("a single treatment of four to six locally applied leeches"), and 27 with four weeks of daily topical application of the NSAID *diclofenac* (Solaraze, Voltaren Topical). After seven days, those receiving leech therapy had a 64% decrease in pain, while those using diclofenac had a 16% decrease. The people receiving leech therapy also had less stiffness and more ease performing the tasks of daily living, such as getting dressed—benefits that continued for the next three months, until the end of the study.

"Traditional leech therapy seems to be an effective symptomatic treatment for osteoarthritis of the knee," says Andreas Michalsen, MD, in the *Annals of Internal Medicine.* He also notes that it was "safe and well-tolerated."

Theory: Leech saliva contains anti-inflammatory and other active compounds—factors that reduce blood clotting, improve circulation, anesthetize and cut the production of tissue-damaging proteins.

Latest development: The FDA has formally approved the medical leech—*Hirudo medicinalis*—as a "medical device."

☀ *www.leechesusa.com*, Leeches U.S.A. LTD., 300 Shames Drive, Westbury, NY 11590 (800-645-3569, 516-333-2570, fax 516-997-4948); e-mail *info@leechesusa.com.*

there, or through many other outlets specializing in aromatherapy products), or two drops of oil per teaspoon of massage carrier oil.

☀ To find a certified aromatherapist near you, visit *www.naha.org*, The National Association for Holistic Aromatherapy, 3327 W. Indian Trail Road, PMB 144, Spokane, WA 99208 (509-325-3419 or fax 509-325-3479); e-mail *info@naha.org.*

To find a clinical aromatherapist (a health professional trained in using essential oils in a clinical setting, such as a doctor's office or hospital), look for the initials CCAP after his/her name—which means he/she has been formally trained by RJ Buckle Associates, a world-recognized trainer of aromatherapy clinicians. Information: *www.rjbuckle.com*; e-mail *rjbinfo@aol.com.*

PHYSICAL THERAPY—A JOINT EFFORT

They're not personal coaches, anatomy experts or massage therapists—they're more like *all* those health professionals, rolled into one.

"A physical therapist, or PT, is the ideal health-care provider for a person with arthritis," says Maura Daly Iversen, PT, DPT, an assistant professor in medicine at Harvard Medical School and associate director of the graduate programs in physical therapy at MGH Institute of Health Professions, in Charlestown, MA. "The PT is trained to consider all the conditions influencing an arthritis patient and how they impact the way that person functions," she adds. Once the PT has figured out just how your arthritis is affecting *your* body—causing pain and limiting movement—you'll receive a customized program of care to reduce pain, restore function and slow the progress of the disease.

"Physical therapists can join with your physician to help you regain function of an injured joint," adds Dr. James M. Rippe.

"Too often, people think that they can rehabilitate a joint on their own, but don't make this mistake," he advises. "Physical therapists are specifically trained to understand the anatomy of a joint and help with the healing process. They can help you resolve problems with the joint and also build up the muscles around it to encourage a full recovery." In fact, he says, failure to get physical therapy is one of the most common reasons for ongoing joint problems.

Physical therapists use any one or more of a combination of techniques, depending on the patient, says Dr. Iverson. *They include...*

● **Manipulation and massage.** The PT performs passive movements of your limbs and/or massage techniques to extend your range of motion and restore proper movement.

● **Exercise.** The PT designs and helps you implement an exercise program that consists of range-of-motion, strengthening and endurance exercises.

● **Body mechanics training.** The PT teaches you how to walk, sit, stand, lift and reach to diminish the strain on your joints and slow the progress of the disease.

● **Heat therapy.** The PT uses heating pads, warm towels or ultrasound to increase blood flow and relax tissues.

● **Cold therapy.** The PT uses ice packs or ice massage to reduce swelling and pain.

● *TENS* (transcutaneous electrical nerve stimulation). The PT uses a mild electrical current to soothe nerves in the painful area.

● **Assistive device training.** The PT helps you choose and use devices—such as bath stools for the shower, or a long-handled shoehorn—to improve functioning and decrease pain. Assistive devices can also include splints, braces and wraps for protecting joints.

● **Lifestyle training.** The PT gives you advice on when to work and when to rest so as not to worsen your disease by doing too much or too little.

● **Education.** The PT informs you about the disease, so you can understand and manage it better.

☀ You can find a physical therapist near you by using the search function on the Web site of the American Physical Therapy Association, *www.apta.org.* American Physical Therapy Association, 1111 North Fairfax Street, Alexandria, VA 22314-1488 (703-684-2782 or 800-999-2782, TDD 703-683-6748, or fax 703-684-7343).

3

BACK PAIN, HEADACHES & OTHER PAIN PROBLEMS
HOW TO STOP HURTING

 "In recent decades, Americans have been asked to stop smoking and lose weight. Now it's time to focus their efforts on untreated pain."

That's the opinion of B. Todd Sitzman, MD, MPH, director of the American Academy of Pain Medicine and medical director of Advanced Pain Therapy, a pain clinic in Hattiesburg, MS. There are approximately 70 million Americans living with chronic pain (or trying to), with those over 60 aching the most. Unfortunately, much of that pain goes untreated, says Dr. Sitzman. Why?

Doctors have erroneously considered pain an inevitable part of illness and healing. Or they don't want to sentence patients to a lifetime of potentially harmful painkillers. And it's easy to see why not.

You probably don't have to be reminded about the heart-hurting potential of many painkillers—that fact has been a near constant in the news. Experts estimate that the class of drugs known as COX-2 inhibitors, such as *celecoxib* (Celebrex) and *rofecoxib* (Vioxx—taken off the market in 2004), may have caused 100,000 heart attacks and strokes. But COX-2 isn't the only type of painkiller that kills.

Researchers from Harvard Medical School recently found that the near-daily use of aspirin, *ibuprofen* (Advil, Motrin, Nuprin), *acetaminophen* (Tylenol) or *naproxen* (Aleve)—the most commonly used drugs in the United States—can increase the risk of high blood pressure by as much as 48% in men and 80% in women, upping the risk of heart disease and stroke. "These drugs should be used with greater caution," says Elliott M. Antman, MD, of Harvard Medical School, one of the researchers who conducted the study.

Fortunately, painkillers aren't the only way to control pain.

"Start pain treatment with *nonpharmacological* treatments," urges Dr. Antman.

"Nondrug treatments such as exercise, yoga, relaxation techniques and breathing techniques give people more control over their pain compared to just having someone hand them a pill," agrees Guy McCormack, PhD, chairman of the Department of Occupational Therapy and Occupational Sciences at the University of Missouri in Columbia, who conducted a study on the nondrug control of pain.

Here are the very best nondrug breakthroughs for easing your pain.

PAIN IS A BAD IDEA

Chronic pain hurts your *brain,* say scientists from the Feinberg School of Medicine at Northwestern University in Illinois.

Using brain scans, the scientists discovered that chronic pain puts the brain's frontal cortex into overdrive, wearing out brain cells, and causing sleep problems, depression, anxiety, even poor decision-making and concentration.

"This is one more reason why it's essential to control pain," says Dante Chialvo, MD, who led the study.

LOW BACK PAIN

During any three-month period, one out of four Americans has low back pain. Nine out of 10 will experience low back pain at some point in their lives, with 40% having a recurrence within six months and 60% within one year.

What causes all that back-to-back agony? The spine is a stack of bones called *vertebrae,* and between each vertebrae is a fluid-filled disc of cushioning cartilage. In some cases, the discs become *herniated*—from injury, arthritis, or *osteoporosis*—bulging out and pressing on nerves. (This is often the cause of *sciatica,* back pain that extends into the legs.) Or low back muscles can be strained and sprained, with an accompanying ache.

But in most cases of low back pain, doctors never discover the specific cause. They label the perplexing problem *nonspecific low back pain.*

In the last decade, the cost of testing for and treating all that back pain has risen by 65% after adjusting for inflation, say researchers from the University of Wisconsin. But those same researchers, after analyzing nine years of data on more than 3,000 people with spinal problems, say that ever-more expensive diagnostic tests, disc-fusing surgeries and pain-relieving medications aren't providing more improvement in everyday functioning. In short, medical treatments for back pain don't work very well! Spinal surgery, for example, can be particularly pricey—and pointless.

"We may be doing too much back surgery in the United States," says Richard Deyo, MD, a professor at Oregon Health and Science University and an expert in the treatment of low back pain. "Back surgery is not helpful for everyone with low back pain—only those with sciatica, who also have leg pain *with* their back pain, may benefit."

What you may not know: "Patients should understand that even people without back problems and pain often have abnormal MRI scans of the spine, so an abnormality doesn't mean surgery is going to help," says Dr. Deyo. "It's always wise to consider a second opinion when back surgery is recommended."

"There are *many* options for the treatment of low back pain," agrees Amir Qaseem, MD, PhD, MHA, author of new guidelines for treating low back pain from the American Pain Society and the American College of Physicians. "Almost all pain relief medications have risks," he points out. "Patients who prefer not to take medications can benefit from nondrug treatments, such as acupuncture." In fact, acupuncture may double the pain-relieving benefits offered by conventional treatment.

ACUPUNCTURE—BETTER THAN MEDICATION

In Traditional Chinese Medicine (TCM), *chi* is life-energy—the fundamental force of well-being and health. *Acupuncture* is a technique from TCM in which tiny needles are painlessly inserted into specific points said to balance and increase *chi*. And, as a remedy for low back pain, acupuncture is acu-amazing.

▶ *Breakthrough Study*

Researchers in Germany studied 1,162 people with chronic low back pain, dividing them into three groups.

One group received acupuncture—for 30 minutes, two times a week, over five weeks—needles were inserted into specific points on the lower back that acupuncturists say can relieve low back pain.

A second group received the same 10 acupuncture treatments—but the needles were inserted into points on the lower back that aren't specific to back pain.

A third group received conventional therapy—a combination of pain-relieving medications, physical therapy sessions and back exercises.

Result: For the purpose of the study, a 33% improvement in pain and a 12% improvement in functional ability (ease of movement) were considered a "positive response" to treatment.

- **48% of people in the "real" acupuncture group had a positive response**

- **44% in the "fake" acupuncture group had a positive response**

- **27% of those receiving conventional therapy had a positive response**

In other words, acupuncture was nearly twice as effective in relieving pain and improving function as conventional therapy—even acupuncture that wasn't specific to low back pain!

"Acupuncture gives physicians a promising, safe and effective treatment option for chronic low back pain," says Michael Haake, MD, PhD, one of the researchers who conducted the study, which was published in the *Annals of Internal Medicine*. "The improvements in low back pain and function were significant, and lasted long after the completion of the treatment."

How it works: "The superiority of both forms of acupuncture to conventional treatment suggests that there is an underlying mechanism in acupuncture that can help relieve pain," says Dr. Haake. "Acupuncture may act on pain generation, on transmission of pain signals or on the processing of pain signals by the central nervous system. In any case, its mechanism of action is *stronger* than that of conventional therapy."

Other studies on acupuncture and low back pain show the technique can relieve the back pain of pregnancy (60% relief vs. 14%, with no complications or side effects)...cut back-related sick days from work by 30%...and (not surprising) reduce worry about back pain.

Good news: Scientific research shows acupuncture may help relieve the pain of *all* of the conditions discussed in this chapter—not only low back pain, but also neck pain, shoulder pain, headaches, carpal tunnel syndrome, post-surgical pain, temporomandibular joint disorders and fibromyalgia.

What to do: "Look for a practitioner who specializes in chronic pain problems," says Jillian Capodice, LAc, MS, an acupuncturist in private practice in New York City. "Ask your medical doctor and acupuncturist to coordinate their care so that they can implement the treatment plan that works best for you."

☀ To find a qualified acupuncturist near you, visit the Web site of the National Certification Commission for Acupuncture and Oriental Medicine, *www.nccaom.org,* where you can search for certified acupuncturists by area code or zip code. NCCAOM, 76 South Laura Street, Suite 1290, Jacksonville, FL 32202 (904-598-1005; fax 904-598-5001); e-mail: *info@nccaom.org.*

LET DEVIL'S CLAW FIX YOUR ACHING BACK

The seedpod of this desert-growing South African herb curls into two clawlike, barbed extensions—hence the name, devil's claw. But the relief it provides for low back pain is heavenly.

⫸ *Breakthrough Studies*

An international team of researchers from the United States, Canada, Germany and Australia analyzed the results from four studies involving more than 500 people in which an extract of the root of devil's claw (*Harpagophytum procumbens*) was used to treat low back pain.

Result: Overall, devil's claw consistently reduced pain in people having an "acute exacerbation of chronic nonspecific low back pain." (In other words, you're often troubled by low back pain, and now it's *really* bad.)

In fact, one study showed that devil's claw worked just as well for back pain as the pain-killer rofecoxib (Vioxx), a COX-2 inhibitor that was pulled off the market by the manufacturer after studies suggested it posed a risk for heart attack.

And in another study, nine of 51 people with low back pain were *pain free* after taking the herb for three weeks—compared to one of 54 people taking a placebo.

How it works: Devil's claw may slow down the *inflammatory cascade,* the immune-fueled molecular dominos that cause swelling, tenderness and pain. It may also help protect cartilage, the material of spinal discs.

Suggested intake: The studies show that the most effective daily dose is 50 milligrams (mg) of *harpagoside,* the active ingredient of the herb, says Eric Manheimer, MD, clinical professor in the NYU School of Medicine. If you have sciatica—pain radiating into the leg—consider a daily dose of 100 mg. Take the herb for two to three months, with your doctor's approval and supervision.

ℹ Look for a product "standardized" to contain a minimum of 1.2% harpagoside. The product should also state on the label how much harpagoside is in each capsule. For example, devil's claw from the manufacturer Food Science of Vermont is standardized to 5% harpagoside, and each 500-mg capsule contains 25 mg of harpagoside. To get the suggested intake, you would take two to four capsules a day.

Precautions: Devil's claw stimulates stomach acid, so if you've got stomach inflammation (gastritis), or a stomach or duodenal ulcer, you should avoid the herb, says Francis Brinker, ND, a naturopath in the Program for Integrative Medicine at the University of Arizona College of Medicine and author of *Herb Contraindications and Drug Interactions* (Eclectic Medical Publications). And you may want to pass on devil's claw if you're taking warfarin (Coumadin) or any other blood thinner, says Dr. Brinker. There is one reported case of a person taking warfarin who developed a life-threatening bleeding disorder (*purpura*) after starting to take devil's claw.

BACK EXERCISES ARE BAD FOR YOUR BACK

Exercises specifically aimed at relieving low back pain—stretching, bending and strengthening—don't work. In fact, they make pain worse!

That's the startling conclusion of researchers from UCLA and the University of Michigan. But there is a type of exercise that can actually relieve low back pain, they say. In fact, there are dozens of them.

▐▐▐▶ *Breakthrough Study*

For 18 months, the researchers studied 681 people with chronic low back pain. At the beginning and at the end of the study, they measured the severity of the pain, disability caused by the pain and pain-caused emotional upset, such as depression and anxiety (which they dubbed "psychological distress").

They also measured the numbers of hours a week the study participants engaged in "recreational activity"—walking, sports such as tennis, active hobbies such as gardening, and any other type of metabolism-boosting fun.

Finally, the researchers asked the participants whether they had engaged in back exercises—exercises specifically intended to prevent or deal with low back pain, such as backward bends, arching the back and knee lifts.

Result: Compared with those who didn't engage in any recreational activity, those who logged the most hours per week had...

- **38%** *less* **severe low back pain**
- **28%** *less* **average low back pain**
- **52%** *less* **disability from low back pain**
- **40%** *less* **psychological distress from low back pain**

Now here's the big surprise. *Compared with those who never engaged in back exercises, those who did back exercises four to seven days a week had...*

- **212%** *more* **severe low back pain**
- **56%** *more* **average low back pain**
- **49%** *more* **disability from back pain**

The researchers also found that if the pain was severe to begin with, it was very likely that back exercises would make it worse.

(Why back exercises don't work, no one knows. But the International Paris Task Force on Back Pain reviewed 20 studies on back exercises and found "no evidence exists to indicate the effectiveness of specific exercises" on relieving back pain.)

"Individuals with low back pain, rather than being advised to engage in specific back exercises, should instead be encouraged to focus on nonspecific physical activities to help reduce their pain and improve their psychological health," says Eric L. Hurwitz, DC, PhD, who led the study.

What to do: Consider brisk walking for 30 minutes a day, at least six days a week—"a level of walking that we found to be associated with reductions in low back pain, disability and psychological distress," says Dr. Hurwitz.

Or, with your doctor's approval, choose from among these options for recreational exercise...

- **Hike.** Jog. Bike.
- **Do aerobic dancing, water aerobics or step aerobics.**
- **Do yoga or tai chi.**
- **Use a rowing machine, a stair climber or a mini-trampoline.**
- **Square dance, ballroom dance, folk dance or line dance.**
- **Play Ping-Pong, tennis or badminton.**
- **Play golf, wheeling or carrying your clubs.**
- **Swim or snorkel.**
- **Fish, sail or wax your boat.**
- **Garden, rake, plant or mow.**
- **Scrub, sweep, wash, carry out the garbage or carry in the groceries.** (Yes, housework is good for you!)
- **Play with the grandkids or push a stroller.**
- **Paint, caulk or pound some nails.**
- **Fly a kite.** (When it comes to recreational activity, not even the sky's the limit.)

DON'T LET YOUR CAR DRIVE YOUR BACK CRAZY

The odometer in your car is a medical device. Researchers in England found the more miles you drive every year, the higher your risk of developing low back pain! *Others researchers have found…*

• **Driving four or more hours a day** increases the risk of low back pain by 78%.

• **People who drive on the job,** such as taxi cab drivers and police, are at particularly high risk, with more low back pain than people whose jobs involve standing, sitting (not driving) or lifting.

Reason: Prolonged pressure of the upper body on the lumbar (lower) spine while in a slumped position, says Jennifer L. Durkin, PhD, of the Department of Kinesiology at the University of Waterloo, in Canada. Staying in one position for too long also takes its toll, she says.

Fortunately, you can put car-caused back pain in reverse.

▶ *Breakthrough Studies*

Dr. Durkin and a team of researchers tested an in-car electrical massage unit for the lower back to see if it could prevent or ease driving-induced low back pain. In a simulated setting in a laboratory, volunteers were asked to drive for an hour with or without the lumbar massage unit, while the researchers took several measurements.

Result: Those using the massage units had greater blood flow and oxygenation in the muscles of their lower backs and less discomfort, says Dr. Durkin.

In a similar study, another team of Canadian researchers tested a "massaging lumbar support system" in a car, keeping the system turned on one minute for every five minutes of driving. They found a "beneficial effect" on low back muscles compared to no massage. The positive result, they say, "may prove to be extremely important in the quest to combat low back pain caused by automobile seating."

And a study by researchers at the Harvard School of Public Health found that using *any* type of extra lumbar support in the car (massage or not) reduced the risk of back pain among taxi drivers by 47%.

Also helpful: The Harvard researchers found that the *angle* of the seat and back support is crucial in preventing back pain. A seat/backrest (or thigh/back) angle of less than 91 degrees increases the risk of lower back pain *fivefold,* compared to an angle greater than 91 degrees. In other words, keep the seat (thighs) level and the backrest (back) tilted ever-so-slightly back, to form an angle that's "just right" for your back.

ℹ The HoMedics BK-125 Automotive Lumbar 2 Speed Massage Cushion and the MiniMax Lumbar Massager from Brookstone, each cost less than $30. They are available at retail stores and on-line.

FEAR + AVOIDANCE = MORE BACK PAIN

If you're afraid of aggravating a backache, it's likely you'll change the way you move in order to prevent more pain—and likely set yourself up to re-injure your back and develop chronic low back pain! *There's a better way…*

▶ *Breakthrough Study*

Researchers at Ohio State University studied 36 people with recent low back pain, dividing them into two groups—one group that had a lot of fear about aggravating the backache, and one group that was less afraid of re-injury.

Next, the researchers attached muscle sensors to both groups and asked them to perform reaching tasks similar to everyday activities, such as bending to open a mailbox or leaning to ring a doorbell.

Result: Those who feared and avoided pain twisted, bent and made other unusual moves to avoid more pain.

This self-imposed strategy for avoiding pain tends to *weaken* muscles, making them *more* prone to future injury from a sudden movement, says James Thomas, PhD, of the School of Physical Therapy at Ohio University in Athens. And, he says, studies show that people with this "fear-avoidance" response to low back pain tend to experience more pain, not less. And they run a greater risk of developing chronic low back pain. Clearly, fearing and avoiding pain is a bad idea for your bad back.

What to do: "There is no reason to fear or avoid pain during recovery from low back pain," says Steven Z. George, PhD, PT, of the Brooks Center for Rehabilitation Studies at the University of Florida in Gainesville.

"In almost every case of acute low back pain, there's no anatomical reason to be afraid of re-injury. When you fear and avoid the pain, you also fear and avoid the everyday exercise that can help you recover. Which means you're more likely to end up with back pain that *never* goes away."

FISH OIL FOR PAINFUL BACKS AND NECKS

"The use of NSAID medications such as ibuprofen [Advil, Motrin, Nuprin] is a well-established therapy for both acute and chronic nonspecific back and neck pain," says Joseph Charles Maroon, MD, in the Department of Neurological Surgery, University of Pittsburgh Medical Center. "But severe complications are associated with NSAIDs, such as bleeding stomach ulcers, heart attacks and even deaths."

There's a safer, drug-free way to relieve back and neck pain, he says: the omega-3 fatty acids found in fish oil.

▶ *Breakthrough Study*

Dr. Maroon studied 125 patients with back and neck pain who weren't candidates for surgery. They were asked to take daily fish oil supplements with 1,200 mg of the omega-3 essential fatty acids EPA (eicosapentaenoic acid) and DHA (docosahexaenoic acid).

Result: Ten weeks after starting the supplements…

• **59% of the patients had stopped taking NSAID medications for pain**

• **60% said their overall pain was improved**

• **80% were satisfied with their improvement**

• **88% said they would continue to take fish oil**

And unlike NSAIDs, there were *no* significant side effects from the fish oil.

"Ibuprofen and fish oil have the same effect in reducing nonsurgical back or neck pain—and fish oil is safer," says Dr. Maroon.

Suggested intake: A daily dose of 1,200 mg of omega-3 fish oil daily.

ⓘ The study used the Nordic Naturals brand of fish oil. Their Ultimate Omega product contains 650 mg of EPA and 450 mg of DHA, or 1,100 mg. Take it with your doctor's approval and supervision.

LOVING KINDNESS IS KIND TO YOUR BACK

Anger is mad at your lower back.

That's the finding of James W. Carson, PhD, assistant professor in the Comprehensive Pain Center at Oregon Health & Science University, in Portland. The research of Dr. Carson, and his colleagues at the Pain and Palliative Care Program at the Duke University Medical Center in North Carolina, shows that people with chronic back pain who have the most anger also have the most pain, probably because anger translates into tighter muscles. That's why he decided to teach people with low back pain to meditate to decrease anger and increase love and kindness.

▐▐▐▶ *Breakthrough Study*

Forty-three people with chronic low back pain took an eight-week class in loving-kindness meditation or received standard care. (Loving-kindness meditation "has been used for centuries in the Buddhist tradition to develop love, and transform anger into compassion," says Dr. Carson.)

Result: The loving-kindness group "showed significant improvements in pain and psychological distress," he says. And the more they practiced the meditation on any given day, the less pain they experienced that day and the next. There was no change in the group receiving standard care.

Loving-kindness meditation "brought about significant reductions in anger and tension" and "can be beneficial in reducing pain in people with persistent back pain," says Dr. Carson.

Example: A businessman who had described himself as "totally cut-and-dry" in relationship to others remarked near the end of the study, "I never knew it was possible to have such space in my heart for others." A professional woman, who quickly used to lose her temper when dealing with her debilitated mother, said, "When I enter her room now, I can feel myself soften."

What to do: You can do this meditation anytime, anywhere—standing, walking, sitting, or lying down, says the Venerable Bhante Pannyavaro, a Buddhist meditation teacher. Pick a specific person as the "object" of your meditation. It could be someone you love; somebody you know, but don't have positive or negative feelings about, such as a shop clerk; or somebody who you feel has caused you harm.

Here's the process for loving-kindness meditation used by the participants in the study…

a. Recall a time when you felt a very positive feeling of connection with a loved one.

b. Let go of the *content* of this memory while remaining focused on the actual *feelings* of love and kindness triggered by this memory.

c. Use silent mental phrases to direct these positive feelings toward the person on which you're meditating. (It's easiest to start with someone you already love.) Sample phrases include "May this person be at ease." "May this person be content." "May this person be happy." "May this person be safe and secure."

d. At the end of the meditation, simply rest for a minute or two, with your attention focused on any feelings of love generated during the meditation.

e. After a few weeks of daily loving-kindness meditation (10 to 30 minutes a day), begin to direct positive feelings toward a neutral person, such as a postman or store clerk.

f. When you're ready, direct the positive feelings toward a person who harmed you or was a source of difficulty for you in the past and whom you feel you can forgive to some extent—such as a disrespectful former boss, or a dismissive former health care provider.

And don't forget to enjoy the pain-reducing benefits of loving kindness when you're not meditating! "Applying the practice to your daily life is a matter of directing an open, friendly attitude toward everybody you relate to," says Pannyavaro.

☀ The "Metta" section of the Web site *www.buddhanet.net* provides a free course in loving-kindness meditation, by Sujiva, a Buddhist teacher. ("Metta" means "friendliness.")

There are also a number of books about the meditation and a "loving kindness" approach to life. They include *Lovingkindness: The Revolutionary Art of Happiness* by Sharon Salzberg (Shambhala) and *Training the Mind and Cultivating Loving-Kindness* by Chogyam Trungpa (Shambhala).

BACK PAIN AT WORK? USE A HEAT WRAP 9-TO-5

Is your lower back sore after work, maybe because you have to stand all day, sit all day or heft heavy objects? Tomorrow, turn up the heat.

||||➡ *Breakthrough Study*

Researchers in the Department of Health, Safety and the Environment at the Johns Hopkins University School of Medicine studied 43 people who had visited an occupational injury clinic for low back pain. They divided them into two groups. One group received education about back therapy and pain management. The other group received the same education—but also wore a heat wrap for eight hours a day, for three days, a treatment the researchers call *continuous low-level heat wrap therapy* (CLHT).

Result: After one day, the group wearing the heat wraps had a 52% greater reduction in pain intensity and 43% greater improvement in pain relief than the education-only group, says Edward J. Bernacki, MD, who led the study.

After three days, there was a 60% reduction in pain intensity and a 41% improvement in pain relief.

"With recent concerns about the safety of oral pain medications, both patients and physicians are considering alternative treatment options for acute low back pain," says Dr. Bernacki. "The dramatic relief we see in workers using CLHT shows that this therapy is a safe and effective alternative—it has clear benefits for low back pain and plays an important role in pain management."

And heat wraps aren't just an alternative to back *education. They also work better than common medications…*

Researchers in the Department of Physical Medicine and Rehabilitation at the UMDNJ–New Jersey Medical School in Newark studied 371 people with nonspecific low back pain, dividing them into five groups. One group used a heat wrap. One received 1,200 mg a day of ibuprofen (Advil, Motrin, Nuprin). Another group took 4,000 mg a day of acetaminophen (Tylenol). A fourth group took a placebo painkiller. The fifth group wore a heat wrap they thought was the real thing but wasn't.

Compared with the other four groups, those using the real heat wrap had 25% less pain, more flexibility and were better able to perform their daily activities, says Scott F. Nadler, DO, who led the study.

Other studies have found a heat wrap can relieve back pain from arthritis of the spine…reduce postexercise low back pain and stiffness by 50%, when used either before or after exercise…and prevent morning low back stiffness and daytime pain, when worn for eight hours overnight.

Why it works: "A heat wrap goes beyond the simple pain relief provided by over-the-counter pills," says Dr. Nadler. "It increases blood flow to the painful muscles, improving flexibility and mobility.

What to do: Don the heat wrap as soon as you start to experience low back pain. (Or preventively, before or after exercise.) Use it for as many days as necessary, for no more than eight hours in any 24-hour period.

ℹ️ Dr. Nadler recommends the ThermaCare Lower Back and Hip Heat Wrap from Procter & Gamble. "It's the only heat wrap safe for all-day use." (Other wraps can get too hot and cause burns, he says.) The heated discs in the wrap contain iron, salt, sodium thiosulfate, water and activated charcoal, which react with the air to create heat. One drawback is you can't use the wrap twice.

☀️ To learn more about the ThermaCare Heat Wrap, visit *www.thermacare.com,* where you can search for nearby stores carrying the product.

Precaution: If you're 55 or over, use the wrap over clothing and not directly on your skin.

SPINE-SAFE SITTING— ARCH OR SLOUCH?

Back specialists have dubbed the two main types of sitting postures *kyphosed* and *lordosed*.

You're kyphosed when you're slouched— think of a teen on the sofa, hunched over a video game in his lap.

You're lordosed when you're arched— think of a soldier at his desk, shoulders squared, chest high, low back tucked in.

Since prolonged sitting is a major cause of low back pain, those same back specialists have been arguing for decades about which of the two sitting postures is the least likely to produce low back pain.

The comfy, relaxed, semi-sprawled kyphosed style often gets the nod. But the arch is making a comeback.

⫸ *Breakthrough Study*

Researchers from the University of Sydney and Charles Sturt University in Australia reviewed 22 years of studies on seating posture and the health of the low back.

They found that a *sustained slouch* is the most harmful posture. *Slouching…*

- **increases the amount of spine-damaging pressure** inside vertebral discs by 85%;
- **triples the stress on spinal ligaments,** fibrous tissue that connect vertebra to vertebra;
- **causes "creep,"** a gradual deformity in collagen, the protein fibers that maintain the strength of discs and ligaments;
- **flattens the fluid-filled discs,** causing dehydration and degeneration and
- **decreases the activity of the multifidus,** small muscles deep in your lower back that stabilize the spine, shielding it from injury.

And these negative effects persist for up to *seven hours* after you've gotten up from wherever you were slouching.

"In summary, sustained kyphosed sitting postures are unhealthy," says Jennifer Pynt, PhD, one of the researchers. She urges people to maintain a lordosed posture while sitting, "both inside and outside the office."

But isn't slouching, well, *comfortable*? Yes, says Dr. Pynt, "But seated postures perceived as comfortable in the short term may be detrimental in the long term. Sustained kyphosed postures are insidious—they contribute to degeneration, but the pain doesn't occur until the degenerative changes have already occurred."

She points to a study that showed a 51% decrease in days with low back pain among people who maintained a simple, daily regimen

—no kyphosed sitting for at least two hours after getting up in the morning.

What to do: Don't slouch forward, and don't round or hunch your back and shoulders, advises Pamela Adams, DC, a chiropractor and yoga instructor in Larkspur, CA. "You should be conscious of and maintain the curve in the small of your back." In other words, you should be lordosed. And Dr. Adams has a simple secret for staying that way—*lift your breastbone.*

"Pretend that a string is attached to the middle of your chest and is gently pulling your breastbone upward, lengthening the space between your breastbone and your belly button."

Do this breastbone-lifting exercise *whenever* you notice that you are slumping over, she says. And that includes when you're watching TV or working at a laptop, two popular spots for kyphosing.

Red flag: If you've been sitting in a slouch for an hour or more, don't perform any physically demanding tasks for an hour or two after you get up, says Dr. Pynt. Why not? You're more likely to injure your back! "For example, a long period of kyphosed sitting on an airplane or in a car, followed by picking up and carrying heavy luggage, is potentially hazardous to your spine."

BREATH THERAPY— DEEP RELIEF

"Patients suffering from chronic low back pain are often unsatisfied with conventional medical care," says Wolf E. Mehling, MD, of the Osher Center for Integrative Medicine at the University of California, San Francisco. That's why he decided to study an unconventional type of care—*breath therapy*—simple, moment-to-moment, sensory awareness of the breath cycle.

▐▐▐▶ *Breakthrough Study*

Dr. Mehling asked 28 people with chronic back pain to participate in either one of two therapies—15 minutes a day of home back exercises, from physical therapy, "the gold standard treatment" for chronic back pain; or 10 minutes a day of home exercises from breath therapy. At the beginning of the study and two months later, he measured pain levels and ease of movement (function) in both groups.

Result: Seventy-one percent of those in breath therapy had significant pain relief and improvement in function, as compared to 50% in the physical therapy group. The breath therapy group also had more insight into the connection between daily stress and back pain, and felt they had new and improved coping strategies, says Dr. Mehling.

What to do: Breath therapy is based on a three-part process called "Sensation, Presence, Breath"—the sensory and present-time awareness of the inward and outward movements of your breathing, says Juerg Roffler, founder and director of the US Middendorf Institute for Breathexperience, in Berkeley, CA.

"Simply allow your breath to come and go on its own through your body," says Roffler. "Through sensing and participating in experiencing this 'breath moment,' you quickly find ease in your breath and body, with a sense of well-being that draws you away from aches, pains and illness. The power of letting breath come and go is instantly accessible, and available in all situations in your daily life."

Roffler offers these instructions for your first experience of breath therapy…

Natural Breath Exercise: "Choose a quiet place, sitting upright on a stool or an armless chair, preferably with a firm, flat seat. Sit at the front edge of your seat. Place your feet on the floor, and rest your hands on your upper thighs. Let yourself be 'carried'—receive the floor and the chair or stool as a support, rather than sinking into the seat or the ground. Letting yourself be carried creates a particular state of being, facilitating the trust that you can allow breath to come and go on its own.

"Begin your exploration by closing your eyes. Focus inside, bringing your full presence to your breath movement. Without controlling it, let your breath come and go on its own. With neither expectation nor plan, sense how and where your breath is moving you. For the next few minutes, continue to simply sense this movement that breath creates, following its rhythmic coming and going—as it naturally happens."

Practice this technique for five minutes a day.

Why it works: Roffler describes how breath therapy can help relieve the type of tension that can cause and complicate low back pain: "On inhalation, as you allow air to flow in, the body walls expand. As you breathe out, they swing back to their original position. You have a moment of rest, before the next expansion of your organism allows fresh life to come in. Breathing is a constant, rhythmic movement—like the eternal dip and swell of the waves of the ocean. This rhythmic process, which takes place naturally in every living being, is the primal life-giving motion itself. If you breathe naturally, this rhythm moves, integrates and heals you."

The opposite of present-time breathing is stress—and it can create pain, says Roffler. "When we have worries, fears and struggles—either of an external or internal nature—our muscles become tight and inflexible. We become cramped and tense. These states restrict our natural breathing and our harmful to us."

☀ For more information and instruction about breath therapy, including a list of trained breath therapists and their contact information,

INFRARED LIGHT FOR CHRONIC BACK PAIN

Infrared is the invisible wavelength of light that powers night-vision goggles, warming lamps in restaurants and your TV's remote control. *It might also power pain relief for your back...*

Recent finding: Pain specialists in Ontario, Canada, studied 40 people with chronic low back pain that had haunted them for an average of six years. Twenty-one people received infrared therapy for about eight hours a day; while sleeping or during daily activities, they wore a small, portable, battery-powered infrared-emitting unit, embedded into a sturdy lumbar wrap. Another 18 wore the same wrap but the power inside the unit wasn't connected. (Somebody had to be in the placebo group.)

At the beginning of the study and seven weeks later, researchers measured the participants' pain levels on a 1-to-10 scale, with 10 the worst.

- The pain scores in the infrared group fell from 6.9 to 3.0—a 43% drop.
- The pain scores in the placebo group fell from 7.4 to 6.0—a 19% drop.

"The infrared therapy was effective in reducing chronic back pain, and no adverse effects were reported," say the researchers, in the journal *Pain Research Management*. The therapy may work by improving circulation, they say.

ℹ The Lumbar Wrap is manufactured by MSCT Infrared Wraps, in Ontario, Canada, and it was studied by doctors at the Rothbart Centre for Pain Care in Ontario.

If you are interested in obtaining an infrared wrap, contact Rothbart Centre for Pain Care, 5734 Yonge Street, Suite 300, Toronto, Ontario, M2M 4E7 (800-807-0078, 416-512-6407 or fax 416-512-6375); e-mail *reception@rothbart.com* or visit on-line at *www.rothbart.com*.

Use the wrap only with your doctor's approval and supervision.

visit the Web site, *www.breathexperience.com*. The US Middendorf Institute for Breath-experience, 801 Camelia Street, Suite C, Berkeley, CA 94710 (510-981-1710); e-mail *juero@rcn.com*.

BACK PAIN—PROVEN PROFESSIONAL HELP

Wade into the world of professional treatments for back pain and you may find yourself in over your head...and your back! There are so many therapies and therapists to choose from, with each claiming to be effective—maybe even the *most* effective. Which professional treatments *really* provide relief? *Here's what scientists have to say...*

||||➡ *Breakthrough Studies*

● **Chiropractic.** A chiropractor (DC) treats low back pain by using a "spinal manipulation" or "chiropractic adjustment"—a gentle or forceful push to spinal joints that have become restricted in their movement, perhaps because of injury or poor posture. By loosening the joints, the adjustment frees pinched spinal nerves and restores circulation, relieving pain.

Study: Researchers at the UCLA School of Public Health compared chiropractic and medical care for the long-term relief of back pain in 681 people with low back pain. After 18 months, those receiving chiropractic care were 29% more likely to have achieved pain relief and improved functioning. And in a review of 43 studies on chiropractic, researchers at the Northwestern Health Sciences University in Minnesota found the chiropractic worked as well as prescription painkillers in relieving low back pain, and that chiropractors were more effective than physical therapists or general practitioners in providing long-term relief.

☀ You can find a chiropractor in the Yellow Pages, or by using the "Find A Doctor" function at the Web site of the American Chiropractic Association, *www.amerchiro.org*. American Chiropractic Association, 1701 Clarendon Boulevard, Arlington, VA 22209 (703-276-8800 or fax 703-243-2593).

● **Massage.** There are many types of massage, but the most common is Swedish—a gentle gliding and kneading pressure on the muscles, to loosen and relax them.

Study: In an analysis of nine studies on massage and back pain, researchers from England concluded that massage was good for a newly aching back (subacute nonspecific low back pain) but not for a new bout of severe pain (acute nonspecific low back pain). They also found that massage "might be beneficial for patients with chronic nonspecific low back pain." Additionally, the studies showed that massage is more effective at relieving pain than back exercises, supportive corsets or relaxation therapy (such as guided imagery).

☀ To help you find a licensed massage therapist near you, the American Massage Therapy Association (AMTA) provides this Web site, *www.findamassagetherapist.org*. AMTA, 500 Davis Street, Suite 900, Evanston, IL 60201-4695 (877-905-2700, 847-864-0123 or fax 847-864-1178); e-mail *info@amtamassage.org* or visit *www.amtamassage.org*.

● **McKenzie Therapy.** This approach uses a unique and systematic form of diagnosis to precisely classify your back pain—what hurts and why. (Remember, doctors never figure out the cause of most cases of back pain.) A McKenzie therapist then prescribes a customized set of self-help exercises (postural correction, stretching and conditioning) or does hands-on treatments customized to correct the problem.

Study: An analysis of several studies on McKenzie therapy and back pain by researchers at the University of Oregon showed the approach to be uniquely effective for short-term (three months) relief of pain—more effective than NSAIDs, strength training, an educational booklet, back massage, chiropractic or back exercises.

☀ You can locate a McKenzie practitioner using the "Locate a Certified McKenzie Provider" at the organization's Web site, *www.mckenziemdt.org.* Stacey A. Lyon, Executive Director, The McKenzie Institute USA, 126 N. Salina Street, Syracuse, NY 13202-1059 (800-635-8380, 315-471-7612 or fax 315-471-7636); e-mail *info@mckenziemdt.org.*

Book: *Treat Your Own Back* by Robin McKenzie (Optp).

● **Naprapathy.** In this manual therapy, the connective tissue (ligaments, tendons, muscles) of the spine are stretched and manipulated to reduce pain and restore function.

Study: Researchers at the prestigious Karolinska Institute in Sweden studied 409 people with back and neck pain, assigning them either to treatment by a naprapath or to advice and support from a medical doctor. After 12 weeks, 57% of those in the naprapath group said they were "much better," compared to 13% in the medical group. One out of five of those treated by naprapathy had complete resolution of their pain. "Naprapathic manual therapy may be an alternative to consider for patients with back pain," say the researchers, in the *Clinical Journal of Pain.*

☀ To find a licensed naprapathic practitioner, contact the National College of Naprapathic Medicine, 3330 North Milwaukee Avenue, Chicago, IL 60641 (800-262-6620, 773-282-2686); e-mail: *info@naprapathicmedicine.edu* or visit on-line at *www.naprapathicmedicine.edu.*

● **Osteopathy.** Osteopathic physicians (OD) are like an MD *and* DC rolled into one. They use conventional medical treatments such as drugs and surgery for low back pain and spinal manipulation (osteopathic manipulative treatment).

Study: Scientists at the Osteopathic Research Center in Fort Worth, TX, analyzed six studies on osteopathy and back pain, and found the treatment reduced pain by 30% more than other treatments, such as physical therapy and pain medication or placebos.

☀ You can find an osteopath in the Yellow Pages, or by visiting the Web site of the American Osteopathic Association at *www.osteopathic.org,* and using the "Contact Us" function. American Osteopathic Association, 142 East Ontario Street, Chicago, IL 60611 (800-621-1773, 312-202-8000 or fax 312-202-8200); e-mail *info@osteotech.org.*

● **Pilates.** Based on rehabilitation exercises, this fitness technique uses gentle, flowing movements to strengthen and stabilize muscles in the "core" area of the abdomen and along the spine, and to integrate the movements of the pelvis, trunk and shoulders.

Study: Researchers at the School of Rehabilitation Therapy in Ontario, Canada, studied 39 people with chronic low back pain, dividing them into two groups. One group received medical care and one group received Pilates training. After four weeks, the Pilates group had 47% less pain and 38% less functional disability than the group receiving medical care.

☀ You can find a Pilates studio or instructor near you at the Web site *www.pilates.com,* using the "Studio Finder" function. Pilates, 8220 Ferguson Avenue, Sacramento, CA 95828 (800-745-2837); e-mail *info@pilates.com.*

Book: *Pilates for Fragile Backs: Recovering Strength & Flexibility After Surgery, Injury, or Other Back Problems* by Andra Fischgrund Stanton (New Harbinger).

DVD: *Pilates for Lower Back Pain.*

- **Physical therapy.** Physical therapists use a range of techniques to improve back pain, including passive motion of your limbs to extend range of motion, exercise regimens, training in how to sit, stand and walk to prevent and diminish pain, and hot and cold therapy.

Study: In the UCLA study on chiropractic and medical care for low back pain, patients who received medical care *and* physical therapy were 69% more likely to achieve pain relief and improved function than those receiving medical care alone.

You can find a physical therapist near you by using the "Find a PT" function on the Web site of the American Physical Therapy Association, *www.apta.org.* American Physical Therapy Association, 1111 North Fairfax Street, Alexandria, VA 22314-1488 (800-999-2782, 703-684-2782, TDD 703-683-6748 or fax 703-684-7343).

- **Psychological treatment.** Depression, anxiety and frustration often accompany chronic low back pain. That's why it's important to treat your body *and* your mind.

Study: Researchers in the Veterans Administration Connecticut Healthcare System analyzed 22 studies on psychological care for chronic low back pain—studies using cognitive-behavioral therapy, supportive counseling, hypnosis, biofeedback or relaxation. Compared to standard treatments alone, the addition of psychological support lessened pain intensity and disability, and improved overall quality of life. Cognitive-behavioral therapy and biofeedback were the most successful.

"Surgery, opioids, nerve blocks, spinal cord stimulators, implantable drug delivery systems—every one of those particular alternatives for low back pain is much more expensive and has poorer or at best equal outcomes compared to rehabilitation programs that include psychological components," says Dennis Turk, PhD, a professor of anesthesiology and pain research at the University of Washington in Seattle.

To find a biofeedback practitioner, visit the Web site of the Association for Applied Psychophysiology and Biofeedback, *www.aapb. org* and use the "Find a Provider" function. Association for Applied Psychophysiology and Biofeedback, 10200 West 44th Ave, Suite 304, Wheat Ridge, CO 80033 (800-477-8892 or fax 303-422-8894); e-mail *AAPB@resourcenter.com.*

To find a cognitive-behavioral therapist near you, use the "Find A Therapist" feature at *www.abct.org,* the Web site of the Association for Behavioral and Cognitive Therapies, or call the ABCT at 212-647-1890.

To find a supportive psychologist, use the Psychologist Locator function at the Web site of the American Psychological Association (APA) at *www.apa.org* or call the APA's referral service at 800-964-2000.

- **Yoga.** This system of stretching and relaxation postures, breathing exercises and meditation can address many of the possible causes and symptoms of low back pain, including tight and weak muscles, postural problems and stress and emotional distress.

Study: Researchers at the University of Washington, in Seattle, studied 101 people with chronic low back pain, dividing them into three treatment groups. One group took 12 weeks of yoga classes. One group took 12 weeks of exercise classes that emphasized aerobics, strengthening and stretching. And one group was sent a self-help book on back pain (*The Back Pain Helpbook* by James Moore [Da Capo]). Yoga was more effective at relieving pain and reducing disability than either the exercise classes or the book. "Yoga is a safe and effective treatment for chronic back pain," says Karen J. Sherman, PhD, who led the study. "Physicians should encourage their patients to choose yoga instructors who have experience working with individuals with back pain, and who can help them manage the symptom flare-ups that may occur as a result of physical activity."

☀ The Web site of the magazine the *Yoga Journal*—*www.yogajournal.com*—has a directory of yoga teachers, with a search function to find teachers and classes in or near your zip code.

Book: *Cure Back Pain with Yoga* by Loren M. Fishman, MD (Norton).

DVD: *Viniyoga Therapy for the Low Back, Sacrum and Hips.* (This DVD features the therapeutic yoga regimen used in the study by researchers at the University of Washington.)

NECK AND SHOULDER PAIN

Your car was rear ended—and whiplash is flogging your neck and shoulders. That luggage you lugged gave you a crick.

You spent the weekend painting the spare room—and now your swollen, red, inflamed shoulder feels like *it* needs redecorating.

You have a "frozen shoulder"—the body's most mobile joint is painfully stuck in metabolic mud.

You played tennis, served an ace—and tore your rotator cuff, the ring of tendons around the shoulder joint. You'll be finishing the set with the surgeon.

Or you've fractured a shoulder bone or collarbone or vertebrae…dislocated the shoulder joint…pinched a nerve…have arthritis in the cervical vertebrae…have intense stress at work…the list goes on.

Every year, about half of Americans suffer from shoulder and/or neck pain. As you've just read, there are many possible causes.

If the pain isn't severe, resting the injured area and taking an anti-inflammatory supplement (such as fish oil) will help get you through. If the pain is intense or persistent, shoulder aside your busy schedule and consult your doctor—who will try to figure out and treat the cause of your pain, or send you to an orthopedic specialist or physical therapist.

Several breakthrough, drug-free treatments can also help.

STRENGTHEN YOUR NECK, BANISH YOUR NECK PAIN

The level of neck pain in the United States is increasing, running a close second to back pain, say experts. More than half of adults experience neck pain in any six-month period, with nearly half of those reporting persistent problems. Medications can control the pain. But nobody has come up with a way to *cure* it, so that the pain goes away and stays away. Until now.

▐▐▐➡ *Breakthrough Study*

Danish scientists at the National Research Centre for the Working Environment in Copenhagen studied 94 women with chronic neck muscle pain—most of whom spent 80% of their working hours at a computer keyboard (a common cause of neck pain).

The researchers divided the women into three groups. One group received health counseling. One group worked out on a stationary bicycle. And one group was taught a routine of strength-training exercises for neck and shoulder muscles. (Strength training also goes by the names of *resistance training, weight training* and *weight lifting.*) The two exercise groups worked out 20 minutes, three times a week, for 10 weeks.

Result: The group receiving health counseling had no reduction in pain. The bicycle group had a small reduction in neck pain—but only right after exercising. The strength-training group had a significant, week-by-week decrease in neck pain—until their pain was reduced by an average of 79%. In fact, the study showed that as strength *increased* in the trapezius muscle—the big muscle that runs across the shoulders, up the neck and down the middle of the back—pain *decreased*. And pain stayed away after the 10 weeks of training was over.

"Specific strength training of the neck and shoulder muscles is a beneficial treatment in chronic neck muscle pain," says Lars L. Andersen, PhD, who led the study. "Supervised strength training of the painful muscle, three times a week for twenty minutes, should be recommended."

Important: Note that Dr. Andersen says strength training should be supervised. If you want strength training to banish neck pain, you need the guidance of a qualified fitness instructor. The instructor will help you select the right amount of weight for each strength-training exercise, and teach you the proper form of the exercise. Take this book with you to a gym or health club...show the instructor this section (including the strength-training routine below)...and get the guidance and supervision you need.

What to do: In strength training, you exercise specific muscle groups using dumbbells (also called free weights) or various strength-training machines. In this study on neck pain, the participants performed five exercises, using free weights. Each exercise aimed at strengthening the trapezius muscle. *The names of the exercises are...*

1. Shoulder elevation
2. Shoulder abduction
3. Reverse flies
4. One-arm row
5. Upright row

As with typical strength training, the participants started out with a level of weight for each exercise that they could lift 12 times (repetitions) until muscle fatigue prevented them from further repetitions. Gradually, they increased the per-exercise weight level to a dumbbell they could lift 8 times until fatigue.

"The strengthening exercises were performed in a conventional manner," says Dr. Andersen, "raising and lowering a pair of dumbbells in a controlled manner without pause or breaks," with each exercise lasting about 30 seconds.

The participants strength trained for 20 minutes, three times a week. They performed the shoulder elevation exercise (1) at each session, along with two other exercises, alternating the two exercises at each session. (For example, they did exercises 1-2-3 at the first session, 1-4-5 at the second session, 1-2-3 at the third session, et cetera.) At each session, they did three sets of those exercises. (For example, the set of exercises 1-2-3 was done three consecutive times.)

One last thing: Expect some additional pain during the exercises themselves, for about the first five weeks of exercising, says Dr. Andersen. Almost everyone in the study experienced this pain while strength training. But no one was injured...the exercise-related pain eventually went away...and nearly everyone experienced significant daily pain relief.

Warning: People with neck pain from whiplash, arthritis, a severe spinal disorder or with chronic headache did not participate in the study, and should not undertake this regimen, says Dr. Andersen.

FOREARM SUPPORT FOR NECK AND SHOULDER PAIN

People who spend hours on the computer every day often end up with a *repetitive strain injury* that causes shoulder and neck pain. But there's any easy way to prevent or reduce it. Pay attention to your forearms.

‖‖▶ *Breakthrough Study*

For one year, researchers at the University of California, San Francisco, studied 182 people who worked on computers all day. They offered them several ways to cut down on neck and shoulder pain, such as ergonomic training in the least stressful way to sit at a computer, or the use of a trackball instead of a standard mouse.

Result: Only one of the several interventions the researchers offered actually prevented or reduced neck and shoulder pain—the installation of a wide armboard in front of the computer keyboard, to support the forearms. The armboard reduced the risk of neck and shoulder pain by 51%. In those who already had neck and shoulder pain, it cut pain in half.

What to do: Talk to your supervisor about installing forearm support at your computer, and/or install one at home.

❶ The forearm support used in the study was the Morency Rest, which clips on to the front of your desk. It is 11 inches deep, 30 inches wide and has a height of about 1.8 inches.

☀ You can order the Morency Rest on the Internet at *www.morencyrest.com*. R&D Ergonomics Inc., 6 Harvey Brook Drive, Freeport, ME 04032 (800-813-7274 or fax 636-773-0951); e-mail *info@MorencyRest.com*.

Red flag: Don't use a narrow wrist/forearm support. It can cause even *more* pain problems, say the researchers.

WHIPLASH—SHOULD YOU WEAR THAT SOFT COLLAR?

Your car was stopped at the light—but you moved at literally breakneck speed when you were suddenly hit from behind, your head and neck snapping forward and ricocheting backward, traumatizing the ligaments, tendons and muscles in your neck.

Now you've got *whiplash*—your neck is painful and stiff. And while it's likely the pain will go away in a couple of weeks, if it's not treated right it might last for years—or never go away. But what's the best treatment to prevent long-term disability? Is it the standard treatment, wearing a soft cervical collar to immobilize your neck? Maybe not.

‖‖▶ *Breakthrough Study*

Doctors in Germany answered that question by separating 200 whiplash patients into two groups. One group wore the standard soft collar for seven days after the injury; the other group received almost-daily physical therapy (PT) treatments in the two weeks after the injury, including a self-care exercise regimen.

Result: After two weeks, pain intensity was 45% less in those receiving PT. After six months, it was 50% less.

"Compared to standard treatment with a soft collar, a physical therapy regimen that includes active exercises is better for reducing pain after whiplash," say the researchers, in the journal *Pain*.

☀ See page 57 in the "Low Back Pain" section of this chapter for information on how to find a physical therapist near you.

HOW TO THAW A FROZEN SHOULDER

Your shoulder isn't literally frozen, of course. It just feels that way! Doctors call it "adhesive capsulitis" or "shoulder impingement syndrome." First, your shoulder hurts because something in the complex joint is inflamed—muscles, tendons, ligaments and/or *bursa* (a fluid-filled lubricating sac near the joint). Because your shoulder hurts, you move it less. Because you move it less, your shoulder develops scar tissue and loses mobility. Eventually, it becomes frozen. The solution is more motion.

▐▶ *Breakthrough Study*

Researchers in Australia studied 138 people with shoulder pain. Some had advanced to the frozen stage and some hadn't. They divided them into two groups. One group did "range of motion" exercises for five weeks. One group received a shoulder injection of corticosteroids, a powerful anti-inflammatory drug.

Result: Both the range of motion exercises and the shot were equally effective in restoring range of motion, say the researchers, in the *Journal of Rehabilitation Medicine.*

What to do: "Anytime you have shoulder pain, it is good to do stretching exercises to maintain range of motion and prevent a frozen shoulder," says Jacob Teitelbaum, MD, author of *Pain Free 1-2-3* (McGraw-Hill). "When doing range of motion exercises, increase the joint movement up to the point where it causes mild pain, but don't 'push through' pain, as this can further injure the joint." *Dr. Teitelbaum recommends these range of motion exercises…*

1. Use the hand on the noninjured side to lift the hand on the injured side up to the top of a door, so that the hand holds onto the top of the door. Then gently squat down to stretch the shoulder. Hold for 30 seconds.

2. Put the arm of your injured shoulder behind your back from below and use your other hand to pull gently on it and stretch it. Hold for 30 seconds.

3. Put the arm of your injured shoulder over your head, and use your other hand to pull gently on it and stretch it. Hold for 30 seconds.

Do these exercises several times a day.

TENSION AND MIGRAINE HEADACHE

There's thunderclap and cluster, rebound and compression, exercise and ice cream, sex and sinus…

We're talking *headaches*—and specialists have spotted and named 150 different types!

But the two most common types—the chronic headaches that regularly throb the temples and pound the scalps of more than 45 million Americans—are *tension* and *migraine* headaches.

In tension headaches, the muscles in the neck and scalp tighten, triggering pressure and pain on both sides—your head feels a bit like it's in a tightening vise. Tension headaches can last a couple of minutes. Or a couple of appointment-canceling days.

In migraine headaches, blood vessels in the scalp constrict like hundreds of tiny fists, with the intense, throbbing pain typically pummeling only one side of the head. They can settle in for three hours—or three hypersensitive, do-not-disturb days, during which a ray of light can feel like an arrow and a conversation in the next room can sound like a construction site.

How did millions of Americans end up with chronic headaches?

"In the case of chronic tension and migraine headache, it's hard to make an accurate diagnosis," says Alexander Mauskop, MD, director of the New York Headache Center and author of *The Headache Alternative* (Dell). "Headache is a common symptom of many underlying conditions, from muscle tightness and hormonal imbalances to sensitivities to food and other environmental substances."

But no matter the cause, says Dr. Mauskop, "if you suffer from frequent headaches, you have probably become painfully aware of how often modern medicine falls short of giving you what you really need—safe, reliable control over your pain."

Fortunately, he says, "there are alternatives to conventional medicine that can help prevent the headache before treatment is necessary, or provide treatment that is safer, more effective, and in the long run less expensive than drugs."

Starting with "A," for antioxidants.

ANTIOXIDANTS—TREATING UNTREATABLE MIGRAINES

The 11 migraine patients had tried every drug out there for their headaches—beta-blockers,

calcium channel blockers, tricyclic antidepressants, NSAIDs (nonsteroidal anti-inflammatory drugs), even anticonvulsants. None had worked. But researchers had recently discovered that *pro-oxidants* (molecules that *oxidize* cells, triggering a kind of internal rust) can cause an increase in inflammation, swelling and pain sensitivity—and might play a role in producing or worsening migraines. A neurologist wondered if antioxidants could help. The answer was a big relief.

▶ *Breakthrough Study*

Under the direction of Sirichai Chayasirisobhon, MD, in the Department of Neurology at Kaiser Permanente Medical Center in Anaheim, CA, those 11 patients took daily nutritional supplements for 90 days that contained high doses of three antioxidants—pine bark extract (rich in *proanthocyanidins,* a potent antioxidant), vitamin C and vitamin E.

The patients filled out a Migraine Disability Assessment (MIDAS) that measured their ability to function at home, work, school and socially. They also kept diaries, noting the frequency and severity of their migraines.

• **Better functioning.** After taking the supplements, MIDAS scores dropped by 51%. *For example, the 11 people had…*

• 50% fewer days of work or school missed

• 53% fewer days where productivity was cut in half or more

• 51% fewer days where household work wasn't done

• 43% fewer days where social activities were missed

When Dr. Chayasirisobhon examined the data from the nine patients who had benefited the most from the supplements (two didn't get any relief), he found their MIDAS score had dropped by 68%.

• **Fewer headaches.** Among those nine patients, the number of days with a headache fell from an average of 40 out of 90 days, to 18 out of 90 days while taking antioxidants. That's a 56% decrease.

• **Less severe headaches.** Among the nine patients, the average severity of each

headache on a pain scale of 1 to 10 had been 7.2. While taking the supplements, it was 4.8. That's a 33% decrease.

"The antioxidant therapy used in this study may be beneficial in the treatment of migraine, possibly reducing headache frequency and severity," says Dr. Chayasirisobhon, in the journal *Headache*.

Suggested intake: 1,200 mg of pine bark extract, 600 mg vitamin C and 300 IU vitamin E.

ℹ The pine bark extract used in the study was Enzogenol, which is available in retail stores and on the Internet from NOW Foods.

THE WATER CURE

You hear the recommendation quite often; drink eight 8-ounce glasses of water every day. It's supposed to be generally good for your

STOP THE HEADACHE MEDICINE, STOP THE HEADACHES

You frequently take an over-the-counter pain medication for a tension headache or a medication to derail a migraine (such as ergots and triptan drugs). And while they've eased or erased the pain, their daily use has deranged your pain system in such a way that the medications are now *causing* your chronic headaches! Then you take more pills. *And the pain continues...*

Doctors call this a "rebound headache" or a "medication overuse headache" (MOH). Do you have MOH?

If you're using over-the-counter pain medications, ergots or triptans two or three days a week...and if you have migraines or tension headaches (or migraines *and* tension headaches) 15 or more days a month...it's quite possible that you have MOH, says Eric Eross, DO, director of the Headache Institute at the Pain Center of Arizona.

In fact, 80% of the people treated at headache care centers overuse medications, says Fred D. Sheftell, MD, director and cofounder of the New England Center for Headache, in Stamford, CT, and coauthor of *Headache Relief* (Fireside). The number one overused prescription headache medications are *butalbital* compounds such as Fioricet (which contains the barbiturate butalbital, caffeine and acetaminophen).

What's the way out?

"Stopping the culprit medications is the key!" says Dr. Eross. Studies show that stopping the pills will reduce the number of headaches you get by 50% within a month.

See a doctor, get off medications for a while and develop a new treatment plan that doesn't cause even *more* pain. Once you stop the pain relievers, try using the various nondrug strategies outlined in this chapter to cope with the inevitable temporary increase in pain, which may last a few days.

health, right? Well, it might also prevent and treat headaches.

▐▌▌➤ *Breakthrough Studies*

● **Prevention.** Dutch researchers asked people with migraine and tension headaches to drink 48 ounces of water a day; the participants actually managed to quaff about 32 ounces. During the next two weeks, their "total hours of headaches" decreased by 21 hours, and their headache pain was much less.

● **Treatment.** UK researchers from the National Hospital of Neurology and Neurosurgery in London took a survey of nearly 400 people and found that one out of ten suffered from "water-deprivation" headache—an achy headache, made worse by head movement, bending down or walking.

Twenty-two people with water-deprivation headaches said they could get total relief within 30 minutes by drinking one to five cups of water. Eleven people said they got relief within one to three hours by drinking two to four cups of water.

What happens: The UK researchers speculate that the *meninges*—the protective covering of the nervous system—becomes dehydrated, triggering the headache.

What to do: You know! Drink eight 8-ounce glasses of water every day.

TOP THREE REMEDIES FOR TENSION HEADACHES

Tell your doctor you've got chronic tension headaches and you'll probably get a recommendation to use drugs—over-the-counter or prescription pain pills to *treat* the tension headache and possibly another drug such as the tricyclic antidepressant amitriptyline

(Elavil) to *prevent* future tension headaches. There are better, drug-free ways.

▐▌▌➤ *Breakthrough Study*

A decade of scientific research shows that three nondrug approaches can reduce the incidence of chronic tension headaches by 35 to 55%, compared to 33% for drug treatments, says Donald B. Penzien, PhD, of the Head Pain Center in the Department of Psychiatry and Human Behavior at the University of Mississippi, in the journal *Current Pain and Headache Reports*. And nearly four out of five people with chronic headache remain "significantly improved" five years after starting those treatments.

The three treatments are 1) cognitive-behavioral therapy (CBT), 2) biofeedback and 3) relaxation techniques, such as mindfulness-based stress reduction, guided imagery or self-hypnosis.

☀ To find more information on these approaches…

● **CBT,** see page 108 of Chapter 5, "Depression and Other Emotional Downers."

● **Biofeedback,** see page 154 of Chapter 6, "Diabetes and Insulin Resistance."

● **Mindfulness-based stress reduction,** see page 397 of Chapter 16, "Stress, Insomnia and Fatigue."

● **Guided imagery,** see page 393 of Chapter 16.

● **Self-hypnosis,** see page 114 of Chapter 5.

PREVENT MIGRAINES WITH BUTTERBUR

The shrub is called *butterbur* because in the days before refrigeration its huge leaves—three feet in diameter—were used to wrap butter to keep it from melting. An herbal extract from the roots of the plant can melt a migraine.

WHAT TRIGGERS YOUR TENSION HEADACHE?

There are many lifestyle and environmental factors that can trigger tension headaches, says Dr. Donald B. Penzien. Learn to identify and avoid or reduce your triggers, if possible.

The Big Three

- **Stress**—money worries, marriage problems, conflicts at work, et cetera.
- **Too much or too little sleep,** going to bed earlier or later than usual, having an irregular sleep schedule. (Fatigue is one of the biggest causes of tension headaches.)
- **Lack of exercise.** (In some people, exercise can trigger headaches.)

Other Possibilities

- **Skipping meals** or eating too little.
- **Foods and beverages containing the chemical tyramine,** which include caffeine; aged cheeses, such as brie, cheddar and parmesan; alcohol; chocolate; nuts.
- **MSG.** Ingredients that contain MSG include hydrolyzed protein, sodium caseinate, yeast extract, yeast nutrient, maltodextrins, autolyzed yeast, textured protein, calcium caseinate and yeast food.

    Smart idea: To figure out which of those foods might be causing your headache, eliminate all of them and reintroduce them to your diet one at a time, says Lawrence Robbins, MD, director of the Robbins Headache Clinic in Northbrook, IL.

- **Environmental triggers** (it's too hot, cold, bright, noisy, smoky and/or smelly).
- **Sex.**
- **Negative emotions** (anger, anxiety, depression, worry, crying).
- **Eyestrain** (squinting).
- **Poor ergonomic conditions at your computer,** particularly involving the head and neck (your movement is restricted, or you're constantly bending, reaching or straining).
- **Weather changes,** such as excessive heat or humidity.

▶ *Breakthrough Study*

Doctors in the Department of Neurology at Albert Einstein College of Medicine in New York studied 202 patients with migraine, dividing them into three groups. One group took a placebo. One group took 50 mg a day of an extract of butterbur (*Petasites hybridus*). And one group took 75 mg a day.

- **Fewer headaches.** Over the four months of taking the extract, the 75-mg group had an average 58% decrease in migraines. The group taking 50 mg had a 42% decrease, and the group taking the placebo a 26% decrease.

"This level of therapeutic effect is comparable to that achieved by prescription medications," says Richard B. Lipton, MD, who led the study. "Butterbur extract is an effective preventive therapy for migraine."

How it works: "We're not certain about the mechanism of action," says Dr. Lipton. Studies show the extract is anti-inflammatory, and it may relax blood vessels.

Suggested intake: Seventy-five mg a day.

Dr. Lipton emphasizes that the herb is safe—a prescription version of butterbur extract has been available in Germany since 1988 and used by more than 500,000 people. However, parts of the plant *other* than the root may contain carcinogenic compounds, he says. "Don't consume any part of the *Petasites* plant in any form other than that of specific products that have been commercially prepared, with the carcinogens removed."

The butterbur extract, Petadolex, he says is safe. It is available in retails stores, catalogs and on the Internet in products such as Petadolex Pro-Active (Enzymatic Therapy), MigraControl (Source Naturals), MigraSolve (Rainbow Light) and Petadolex (Pure Encapsulations).

TAI CHI FOR TENSION HEADACHES

About four out of five headaches are *tension* headaches, and they're often caused by, well, tension—stress, anxiety, fatigue or anger, says Ryan B. Abbott, at the Center for East-West Medicine at the David Geffen School of Medicine at UCLA. That's why he and his colleagues decided to see if the gentle, flowing, stress-relieving exercises of *tai chi* could help unknot tension headaches.

"Tai chi is a form of traditional Chinese exercise—a 'meditation in motion' that improves health by sharpening mental focus, controlling breathing, increasing coordination and deepening relaxation," says Abbott.

▉▉▶ *Breakthrough Studies*

Forty-seven people with tension headaches were either enrolled in a 15-week program of tai chi instruction or put on a wait-list for the course.

Result: After 15 weeks, those taking tai chi had half the pain from headaches as the group who didn't take tai chi. They also had better daily physical functioning, more' energy and more easeful social interactions.

"As a treatment for headache, tai chi offers several benefits over conventional treatment with medications," says Abbott. He points out that not every person with headaches responds to pain medications...that even among those who respond, there are often accompanying side effects, some of them quite serious...and that medications are expensive.

"Tai chi represents a viable alternative to medication," he says. "But tai chi does more than alleviate pain or provide symptomatic relief. It addresses the underlying cause of the pain of tension headaches—stress. Medications only target the symptoms of stress. When you stop taking the medication, the pain may return. With its emphasis on relaxation, breathing, focus and coordination, tai chi directly affects the stress and tension that contribute to the pain of tension headache."

What to do: The study participants learned the "Yang style" of tai chi, the most popular (and easiest-to-learn) style.

☀ Look in the Yellow Pages or search on the Internet for a tai chi class in your area. The best instructor is usually one with a lot of experience, says Abbott. (The instructor for the study participants had been teaching tai chi for over 20 years.) *Other ways to learn tai chi include...*

DVD: *T'ai Chi for Health: Yang Short Form*, with tai chi master Terence Dunn, is available at retail stores and on the Internet.

Book: *Tai Chi for Health & Vitality: A Comprehensive Guide to the Short Yang Form* by Robert Parry (Hamlyn).

THE HERB THAT PREVENTS A HANGOVER

Seventy-seven percent of people who drink alcohol end up with a hangover at least once a year. For 15%, it's once a month. *Those are expensive drinks...*

The yearly national price tag for immoderate imbibing is $2,000 per adult, or $148 billion a year—because who can go to work (or function if you get there) with a pounding head, shaky hands, dry mouth, upset stomach and feeling about as spry as a bartender's dishrag.

Is there any way to prevent a hangover, besides passing on the next round of piña coladas?

Scientists in the Department of Medicine at Tulane Health Sciences Center in New Orleans think there is.

▶ *Breakthrough Studies*

Led by Jeffrey G. Wiese, MD, the doctors asked 64 healthy, young medical students to attend a barbeque at 6:00 p.m., then drink 5 to 10 drinks (vodka, gin, rum, bourbon, scotch or tequila) from 8 p.m. until midnight. (The scientists didn't have to ask twice.)

Five hours before the scientifically sanctioned party, the volunteers were given either a placebo or an herbal extract of the fruit of the prickly pear cactus (*Opuntia ficus indica*).

Result: Everybody had a hangover the next day, of course. But some got off a little bit easier. *Those who took the prickly pear had…*

- **17% less headache pain**
- **45% less nausea**
- **22% less dry mouth**
- **12% less dizziness**
- **11% less weakness**
- **8% less shakiness**

Overall, the risk of a severe hangover was reduced by 50% among those who took prickly pear.

Why it works: When the body is stressed (and drinking a lot of alcohol is 100 proof stress), it produces *heat shock proteins* that protect cells and speed cellular repair, explains Dr. Wiese. The prickly pear fruit extract may speed up the body's ability to create heat shock proteins.

However: Maybe you're asking yourself, won't an effective antihangover pill *encourage* people to drink more? "Hangover has never been shown to effectively deter alcohol consumption, and no evidence indicates that alleviation of hangover symptoms would result in further consumption," says Dr. Wiese.

ℹ The researchers used a specially formulated and patented prickly pear extract called Tex-OE, found only in HPF Hangover Prevention Formula.

☀ You can find the product on the Internet at *www.hangoverprevention.com*. Nutrimark, LLC, PO Box 346, Cardiff, CA 92007 (800-720-2970); e-mail *service@hangoverprevention.com*.

What to do: Take one dose two hours before drinking—one tablet if you weigh 130 pounds or less; two tablets if you weigh more than 130 pounds.

Trap: High-fiber foods interfere with the action of Tex-OE. Don't drink or eat foods such as fruits, vegetables, beans or whole grains two hours before and two hours after taking the herbal formula.

CoQ10—COMBAT MIGRAINE HEADACHES

Every cell in your body houses hundreds of *mitochondria*, tiny factories that generate ATP (*adenosine triphosphate*), the body's fundamental fuel.

Coenzyme Q10 is like the factory foreman—without this natural substance keeping things in order, mitochondria would have to close up shop.

New thinking: Poorly functioning mitochondria might trigger migraines, says Todd D. Rozen, MD, in the Department of Neurology at the Cleveland Clinic Headache Center. And supplements of coenzyme Q10 might prevent them.

▶ *Breakthrough Studies*

Dr. Rozen and his colleagues studied 31 people with migraines, giving them a daily dose of coenzyme Q10 for three months.

- **Fewer days with migraines.** Sixty-one percent had a 50% or greater reduction in days with migraine headaches; 95% had at least a 25% reduction. (Only two of the patients showed no improvement.) On average, days with migraines decreased from seven to three per month.

• **Fewer migraine attacks.** The number of migraine attacks also decreased, from 4.8 to 2.8 per month.

"There has been a recent explosion in the number of new migraine abortive treatments—drugs that can help stop a migraine once it starts—but safe and effective migraine *preventive* therapies have been lacking," says Dr. Rozen. "Coenzyme Q10 appears to be a good migraine preventive."

Suggested intake: One hundred fifty mg a day.

ⓘ Coenzyme Q10 supplements are widely available at retail stores, from catalogs and on the Internet.

Important: Don't expect immediate results. The study showed coenzyme Q10 takes about four weeks to start working, and produces best results after five to twelve weeks.

Also helpful: A study at the Cincinnati Children's Hospital Medical Center of more than 1,000 children and adolescents with migraines showed that many had low blood levels of coenzyme Q10. When they received coenzyme Q10 supplements (1 to 3 mg per kilogram of body weight, per day), headache frequency was reduced by 35%, and disability from headaches by 52%.

FEVERFEW—STOP AN ATTACK WHEN IT STARTS

In a study published in the journal *Headache*, nearly two-thirds of more than 2,000 people with migraine *didn't* take so-called "aborting medication" for migraines when they thought they *might* be having the early symptoms of a migraine attack. Why not? Because they didn't

want to risk dealing with the medication's side effects, such as nausea, stomach pain, anxiety, fatigue and dizziness.

The frequent result is when the migraine attack changed from "maybe" to "definite," the migraine sufferers ended up with more intense pain…pain that lasted longer…pain that sent them to bed, canceling their activities.

Are you between the rock of a possible migraine attack and the hard place of the side effects of migraine-stopping medication? There's *another* option: An herbal remedy that can stop an incipient migraine attack with few side effects.

◉▶ *Breakthrough Studies*

Roger Cady, MD, and his colleagues at the Headache Care Center in Springfield, MO, studied 29 people with migraines—people who had an average of two to eight migraine attacks per month, with 75% of their attacks worsening from mild to severe.

The migraine sufferers were asked to take an herbal formula containing feverfew and ginger the next time they thought they were getting a migraine. For maximum, speedy absorption, the herbal remedy was a liquid (tincture), with drops taken under the tongue (sublingually).

Result: Two hours after treatment with the herbal formula…

• **14 of the 29 people were pain-free**

• **10 said their headache was mild**

• **Five said their headache had progressed to a moderate level of pain.**

• **No one developed a severe headache.**

Additionally, 55% of those who had started to experience sensitivity to sound (a common feature of a migraine attack) became symptom free, and 53% of those who had started to experience light sensitivity (another common feature) became symptom free.

MAGNESIUM TO THE RESCUE

Doctors in the Department of Neurology at the Health Science Center of the State University of New York gave one gram of intravenous magnesium to 40 people with tension headaches, migraines or super-severe "cluster headaches."

Result: Eighty percent of those receiving intravenous magnesium had *complete elimination* of pain (and migraine symptoms such as light and sound sensitivity) within 15 minutes. In 22 of the 40, there was no recurrence or worsening of pain over the next 24 hours. The doctors also found that those with the lowest blood levels of magnesium at the time of the headache had the best response to the mineral. "Low blood levels of magnesium may cause headache symptoms in susceptible patients," they say.

More evidence: Researchers in Turkey found low magnesium levels in people suffering from "hemodialysis headache" (headache after treatment for chronic kidney failure)...doctors in Italy gave magnesium to nine children and adolescents with tension headaches, reducing symptoms by 70%...doctors in California eased moderate-to-severe migraines in children by giving them magnesium...researchers in New York found that 45% of women with migraine attacks during menstruation had low blood levels of magnesium.

What happens: Constricted blood vessels trigger migraine attacks; magnesium expands blood vessels. "Several studies show that magnesium plays a critical role in blood vessel size," says Dr. Mauskop.

What to do: "Magnesium is probably the single most important nutrient for pain relief," says Dr. Jacob Teitelbaum. "I recommend a daily supplement of 150 to 200 milligrams of magnesium glycinate, the most absorbable form."

Only four people had side effects, and they were very mild (unpleasant taste of the tincture, a short-lasting burning sensation under the tongue).

The herbal formula "was an effective first-line intervention against migraine," says Dr. Cady.

More evidence: In a German study of 170 patients with migraine, a supplement of feverfew extract was three times as effective as a placebo in reducing migraine attacks...French researchers gave an herbal combination including feverfew to 12 people with migraine for 12 weeks, reducing the frequency of attacks by 62% and the severity by 63%.

Why it works: "The effectiveness of feverfew for migraine is attributed to a group of compounds called *sesquiterpene lactones*, which inhibit blood clotting and inflammation and strengthen the tone of blood vessels," says Dr. Alexander Mauskop. "Ginger also reduces the inflammation of blood vessels and the level of biochemicals that cause pain sensitivity. It may also help improve circulation."

The feverfew/ginger supplement used in the study was GelStat Migraine. It is widely available in retail stores, catalogs and on the Internet. Follow the dosage recommendation on the label.

OTHER PAIN PROBLEMS

SURGERY-FREE CARPAL TUNNEL SYNDROME FIX

Tingling and numbness in your fingers and hand. Pain in your wrist, zipping up to the shoulder and zapping down to the palm. Hands so weak you're constantly dropping things.

Those are some of the possible symptoms of *carpal tunnel syndrome*, which can develop from *any* repetitive motion of the wrist—typing, hammering, knitting, playing the piano, waving item after item over the bar code reader at the supermarket checkout.

What happens: The bones of the wrist form a passageway a little wider than a quarter, on the palm side of the hand. It's called the carpal tunnel—and it's well trafficked. Nine tendons pass through, controlling the movement of a couple of fingers. And the *median nerve* traverses the tunnel, bringing sensation to several fingers and movement to some small muscles in the hand. If the area is irritated by repetitive movement…and those nine tendons swell…and the median nerve is squeezed…you can end up with the symptoms of carpal tunnel syndrome.

Surgery to free up the area is an option. But one-third of patients say they have long-term scar discomfort and only poor to fair recovery of hand strength. Fifty-seven percent have a recurrence of their pain, typically beginning two years after the surgery.

Nonsurgical or "conservative" treatments can sometimes help, including anti-inflammatory drugs, a splint to immobilize the wrist at night, acupuncture and stretching and strengthening the wrist and hand.

But if all those conservative methods fail to relieve the pain (and they often do), you still might not have to see the surgeon. There's a new, dramatically effective drug-free treatment for carpal tunnel syndrome, say researchers at the Department of Physical Medicine and Rehabilitation at the Saint Vincent Catholic Medical Centers of New York.

⫸ *Breakthrough Study*

The doctors studied 19 people with carpal tunnel syndrome (CTS) who had tried conservative therapies for four months without getting better.

They had them use a C-TRAC automatic hand-stretching (or hand traction) device for five minutes, three times a day, for four weeks. (More about the device in a moment.) The doctors evaluated them after the four weeks and seven months later.

Result: Their wrists and hands got a lot better…

• **92% less pain.** On a scale of 1 to 10, with 10 the worst, their pain decreased from an average of 8.2 to 0.62.

• **95% less tingling.** Tingling decreased from 8.05 to 0.4.

• **79% less numbness.** Numbness decreased from 8.6 to 1.7.

• **No pain at night.** The average number of times they woke up every night because of CTS symptoms (the number one reason people opt for surgery) fell from 3.0 to 0.

How it works: The pneumatic device (somewhat similar to a blood pressure cuff) wraps around the hand and wrist (with a hole for the thumb), and is inflated. While inflated, the crafty device provides constant, controlled stretching to the *transverse carpal ligament* that roofs the carpal tunnel (and is the tissue that surgeons section to relieve CTS) and to the sheath surrounding the tendons. The effect is it increases the area of the carpal tunnel, taking pressure off the median nerve. In fact, x-rays of people treated with the C-TRAC show a widening of the carpal bones very similar to that of surgery.

"C-TRAC is comparable in effectiveness to splints, injections of corticosteroids and surgery," says Humberto Porrata, MD, who led the study.

What to do: If you've got CTS and are considering surgery, talk to your doctor about whether you should first give C-TRAC a try.

The patients used the device three times daily for five minutes each time—they placed their hand in the device, inflated it for two minutes, deflated it and rested for 1 minute, reinflated it for 2 more minutes, then deflated it and removed it.

To banish symptoms and avoid recurrence, the researchers say to use the device daily for four weeks and then once or twice a month for the next six months.

If your doctor wants to read the study about the device, the citation is Porrata, H., et al. *Journal of Hand Therapy* 20, no. 1 (January–March 2007): 20–27.

☀ You can buy a C-TRAC device at *www.carpaldoctors.com*. Carpal Doctors, LLC, 701 Brickell Ave., Suite 1550, Miami, FL 33131 (866-401-1213); e-mail *info@carpaldoctors.com*.

FOUR WAYS TO EASE POST-OP PAIN

No doubt the surgery would have been horrifically painful if you weren't unconscious the whole time. But now you're awake and you *hurt*. Bad. Painkilling drugs are called for, of course. But sometimes doctors and nurses don't give enough...or you're afraid of getting addicted... or you're concerned about the side effects. Drug-free approaches can help.

▶ *Breakthrough Studies*

• **Deep breathing after coronary bypass.** Researchers at Wright State University in Dayton, OH, found that patients who were given painkillers and taught a slow, deep-breathing technique had less pain than drug-only patients when their chest tubes were removed after coronary bypass surgery.

• **Relaxation tapes after intestinal surgery.** A study of 167 patients by nurses at Case Western Reserve University in Cleveland showed that those who listened to relaxation tapes after intestinal surgery had 16 to 40% less pain right after the operation and three and six days later, compared to people who didn't listen to the tapes.

• **Music after knee or hip replacement surgery.** Nurses at Florida Atlantic University in Boca Raton studied people undergoing hip or knee surgery. They note, "Acute pain and confusion after surgery increase length of stay in the hospital and reduce long-term function." But those who listened to music right after the operation had less pain and confusion and walked sooner.

More evidence: In a review of three studies on music and postoperative pain relief, researchers found that people who listened to music after surgery required 20% less morphine. And in a study of 75 people undergoing a hernia operation, those who listened to music *during* the operation had less pain afterward than those who didn't listen to music.

• **Massage.** Researchers in the VA Ann Arbor Healthcare System in Michigan studied 605 veterans for five days after major surgery, dividing them into three groups—standard care, a daily 20-minute back massage or 20 minutes of daily attention from a massage therapist, without the massage. "Those receiving massage experienced a faster rate of decrease in pain intensity and unpleasantness during the first four postoperative days," says Allison R. Mitchinson, who led the study. "It is time to reintegrate the use of effective and less dangerous approaches than drugs to relieve patient distress."

Problem: "Nondrug strategies are not integrated fully into standard postoperative pain management practices in most hospitals," says Marlene Dufault, PhD, RN, a professor in the College of Nursing at the University of Rhode Island. "Indeed, nondrug methods are underused."

Solution: Before your surgery, talk to your doctors and nurses about your desire to use nondrug pain relief after (or even during) the operation, says Dr. Dufault. Work out a *plan.* It should include nursing care that helps you listen to music you find relaxing and/or guided relaxation tapes in the recovery room and in your hospital room. You can also let nurses know that you want to receive a back massage. (Studies show hand and foot massages also help relieve pain.)

When you pack for the hospital, don't forget to bring a portable listening device and, if it's a CD or tape player, your tapes and/or CDs. An auto-reverse portable tape player with headphones is ideal, say experts from the Guided Imagery Program at the Cleveland Clinic Foundation Heart Center. "Begin listening to the program at any time after your procedure, preferably the morning after your surgery and twice daily during your recovery," they say.

☀ *www.healfaster.com* offers a book and a relaxation CD that has been clinically proven at Harvard Medical School to help reduce the use of pain medications after surgery by 23 to 50%. The author is psychotherapist Peggy Huddleston. Phone 800-726-4173 or 303-487-4440; e-mail *peggy@healfaster.com*.

TEMPOROMANDIBULAR JOINT DISORDERS (TMD)

Ten to 15% of Americans play a leading role in a scary home movie called *Jaw...*

They're the ones with TMD—a disorder of the temporomandibular joint, the ball-and-socket contraption that hooks your lower jawbone (mandible) to the rest of your skull. (The disorder also goes by the acronym TMJ.) *This joint plays a key role in talking, eating and yawning,*

MIRROR THERAPY FOR PHANTOM LIMB PAIN

Ninety percent of people who have a limb amputated have *phantom limb pain*—the amputated arm or leg still hurts! *A mirror may be their best medicine...*

New study: Doctors at Walter Reed Army Medical Center in Washington, DC, studied 18 people with phantom leg pain, dividing them into three groups.

For 15 minutes a day, one group regularly viewed their intact foot in a mirror, while instructed to perform movements with the amputated limb. One group did a similar exercise while looking at a covered mirror. And one group was told to close their eyes and imagine performing movement with the amputated limb.

After one month of treatment, everyone in the mirror group said their pain was better. In the covered mirror group, one person said it was better and three said it was worse. In the imagery group, two said it was better and four said it was worse. When people in the covered mirror group and the imagery group switched to mirror therapy, eight out of nine had a decrease in pain.

What happens: "Pain relief associated with mirror therapy may be due to the activation of 'mirror neurons' in the hemisphere of the brain that is opposite to the amputated limb," says Jack W. Tsao, MD, DPhil, who led the study. But whatever the mechanism, says Dr. Tsao, "mirror therapy may be helpful in alleviating phantom pain in an amputated lower limb."

and when it's not working right there are lots of possible symptoms, including...

• **Pain or tenderness in your jaw,** or achy pain around your ear, or aching anywhere in your face

• **Chewing problems**—you can't chew or it hurts when you do

• **When you open your jaw to talk or chew, it clicks or pops,** or there's a grating sensation

• **Your bite is uncomfortable or uneven**

• **The joint locks,** so it's hard to open or close your mouth

• **You have headaches**

Like many common pain problems, experts aren't really sure what causes TMD. Stress; poor, neck-jutting posture; jaw injury (from something as serious as a car accident or as "minor" as chronic pen chewing)—they're all candidates, along with a long list of other possible culprits.

Therapies for TMD range from jaw surgery to ice packs. What's the best therapy? The cheapest and safest? Read on.

⫸ *Breakthrough Study*

Dentists in the Department of Oral Medicine in the School of Dentistry at the University of Washington in Seattle studied 200 people with TMD, dividing them into three groups.

One group received dentist-prescribed self-care treatment—jaw relaxation exercises, directions not to chew gum or engage in any other type of chronic jaw activity, hot packs on painful areas, advice about the reasonable and effective use of painkillers, gentle jaw stretches and lessons in stress reduction.

One group got the same type of self-care advice, along with an expensive, customized high-tech mouthguard (hard splint), made in a dental laboratory and fitted by the dentist.

And the third group got self-care advice along with an inexpensive soft athletic mouthguard (soft splint), with the dentist supervising the patient's shaping of the splint for his/her own mouth.

Result: After one year, all three groups had similar improvements in pain; range of motion

of their jaw; TMJ clicking and popping sounds and grating; and chewing limitations.

"This study lends support to using the most conservative treatment for TMJ. Patients can be treated successfully with self-care therapies," says Edmund Truelove, DDS, who led the study.

What to do: Talk to your dentist about an appropriate self-care regimen for TMD. You might also want to consider using a soft athletic mouthguard.

ⓘ The mouthguard used in the study was the Form Fit Regular mouthguard from SafeTGard.

☀ *www.safetgard.com.* SafeTGard Inc., PO Box 1468, Golden, CO 80402 (800-356-9026, 303-763-8900) or fax (800-382-6789, 303-763-8071).

Book for self-care: Taking Control of TMJ by Robert O. Uppgaard, DDS (New Harbinger).

FLOAT AWAY FROM FIBROMYALGIA

Fibromyalgia is the twin of chronic fatigue syndrome (CFS). In CFS, you might have near constant, severe fatigue, along with insomnia, memory and concentration problems, digestive upset and frequent infections. In fibromyalgia, you could have all those problems *and* widespread chronic muscle pain and achiness, says Jacob Teitelbaum, MD, medical director of the Fibromyalgia and Fatigue Centers and author of *From Fatigued to Fantastic!* (Avery). "For most people, fibromyalgia and chronic fatigue syndrome are the same illness." (For more remedies for fibromyalgia/chronic fatigue, see page 414 of Chapter 16, "Stress, Insomnia and Fatigue.")

If you're one of the three to six million Americans with fibromyalgia (most of them women), you're looking for ways to ease your symptoms and live a more normal life. You might want to start by heading to the swimming pool.

▶ Breakthrough Studies

Researchers at the University of Toronto looked at seven studies on pool-based exercise and fibromyalgia and found that it was equal to "land-based" aerobic exercise for reducing pain, but did a *better* job improving mood and sleep.

Which isn't that much of a surprise, when you consider another research project on fibromyalgia and exercise conducted by scientists at the Oregon Health & Science University in Portland. They looked at 46 studies on fibromyalgia and exercise, involving more than 3,000 people, and found that *low to moderate intensity exercise* was the most effective at relieving symptoms in people with fibromyalgia. And low-to-moderate aerobic exercise is what pool exercise is all about.

☀ For more information on pool-based exercise, including how to find pool-based exercise programs offered by the YMCA throughout the United States, see page 31 of Chapter 2, "Arthritis."

And there's another way to use the power of water to buoy the health of those with fibromyalgia…

• **Flotation tanks.** Researchers in Sweden studied people with fibromyalgia who regularly relaxed in a light- and soundproof flotation tank filled with buoyant, salty water. They had less pain, better sleep and felt more optimistic and less anxious and depressed. In fact, 22% were *entirely* free of pain after 12 sessions in the tank. "Relaxing in a weightless state in the silent, warm floating tank activates the body's own system for recuperation and healing," says Sven Ake Bood, PhD, who led the study.

☀ For a list of more than 65 sites throughout the United States where you can use floatation tanks, please see the Web site *www.flotation.com*. The site also includes US manufacturers of home floatation tanks and their contact information.Floatation.com, PO Box 2119, Nevada City, CA 95959.

☀ Oasis Relaxation Systems, PO Box 15669, San Diego, CA 92175 (619-265-9391 or fax 619-265-8491); e-mail *info@oasisrelaxation.com* or visit on-line at *www.oasisrelaxation.com*.

LESS MAKEUP, LESS PAIN?

A Swedish researcher noticed that women with fibromyalgia often complained of dry, painful skin, and theorized that cosmetics might have something to do with their pain problem. She asked 48 women with fibromyalgia to reduce their use of cosmetics. "After two years, there was a significant improvement in pain and stiffness, together with improved physical functioning and well-being," says Berit Sverdrup, MD, in the *Journal of Women's Health*. "Cosmetic use may have possible adverse effects on fibromyalgia."

4

CANCER
DEPENDABLE PREVENTION, SYMPTOM-EASING SUPPORT

To predict the likelihood that you'll get cancer—that you'll eventually be among the 1.4 million people diagnosed every year with the disease, or one of the 560,000 a year who die of it—see if you agree with the following three statements...

It seems like everything causes cancer.

There's not much people can do to lower their chances of getting cancer.

There are so many recommendations about preventing cancer that it's hard to know which ones to follow.

If you agreed—you might be more likely to get cancer!

That's the startling finding of researchers from the Harvard School of Public Health and other institutions, who surveyed more than 6,000 Americans. They found that people who agreed with those statements were less likely to practice three health habits that scientists say can help prevent cancer: eating five daily servings of fruits and vegetables, exercising regularly and not smoking.

"Many Americans say, 'Well, there is nothing much you can do about cancer'—and they do nothing about it," says Jeff Niederdeppe, PhD, of the University of Wisconsin, who analyzed the survey results with his colleagues. "The prevalence of fatalistic beliefs about cancer prevention among American adults is a cause for concern," he adds. But there's no reason to be fatalistic.

"Can cancer really be prevented?" asks Michael T. Murray, ND, a naturopathic physician and coauthor of *How to Prevent and Treat Cancer with Natural Medicine* (Riverhead Trade). "Yes—and this is true even if cancer runs in your family. By reducing risk factors such as smoking, and by practicing healthy habits such as eating more fruits and vegetables, you'll greatly reduce your chances of developing the disease."

Here are the top breakthroughs in the practical science of cancer prevention...

PREVENTION

ANTICANCER POWER OF FRUITS AND VEGGIES

Let's cut to the daily chase for an easy and effective way to prevent cancer: People who eat the most fruits and vegetables are 35% less likely to get cancer—any cancer—compared with people who eat the least, say scientists at the Johns Hopkins Bloomberg School of Public Health in Baltimore, in a study published in the *American Journal of Epidemiology*.

Other scientific studies on specific cancers show that people who eat more fruits and vegetables have a lower risk of developing colon cancer (40%)…prostate cancer (50%)…non-Hodgkin's lymphoma (41%)…bladder cancer (49%)…pancreatic cancer (55%)…oral cancer (50%)…stomach cancer (51%)…kidney cancer (40%)…and…well, you get the idea.

Eating more fruits and vegetables has even been shown to lower the risk of dying from a diagnosed cancer—16% lower in people with lung cancer and 44% lower in women with breast cancer who have so-called hormone-positive tumors.

Why are fruits and vegetables so powerfully protective?

They're packed with antioxidants that counter oxidative stress—a kind of internal rust that can damage DNA, triggering cancer. Other compounds in fruits and vegetables activate enzymes that hobble carcinogens…battle proteins that fuel the spread of tumors…turn on cellular signals that tell cancer cells to die or to stop dividing…and probably do a number of other things that scientists haven't figured out yet.

Fruits and vegetables are good, across the cutting board. But some are science-proven superstars.

⫸ *Breakthrough Studies*

• **Apples to prevent breast or colon cancer.** Eating an apple a day may lower cancer risk by up to 42%, say Italian scientists, in the medical journal the *Annals of Oncology*.

In another study, scientists at Cornell University found more than a dozen compounds in apple peels that can slow or kill breast and colon cancer cells in the laboratory.

Recommendation: "To reduce the risk of cancer, eat five to twelve servings of fruits and vegetables a day—including apples," says Rui Hai Liu, MD, PhD, associate professor of food science at Cornell.

• **Avocados to prevent oral cancer.** Compounds in avocados can find and destroy oral cells in a precancerous state, while leaving healthy cells alone, say researchers from Ohio State University.

Useful: The researchers studied Haas avocadoes, the variety commonly found in supermarkets.

• **Black raspberries to prevent esophageal cancer.** Barrett's esophagus afflicts two million Americans and triples or quadruples the risk of esophageal cancer. People with the condition ate one to two ounces of freeze-dried black raspberries every day for six months. At the end of the study, they had lower urinary levels of two biochemicals that indicate cancer-causing oxidative stress, say scientists at the Comprehensive Cancer Center at Ohio State University.

☀ A freeze-dried black raspberry powder is available from: Nutri-Fruit, 7510 SE Altman Road, Gresham, OR 97080 (866-343-7848 or fax 503-663-7095); e-mail: *info@nutrifruit.com* or visit *www.nutrifruit.com* and *www.scenicfruit.com*. Talk to your doctor to see if this product is right for you.

Surprising: In another study at Ohio State, a topical gel made from black raspberries helped slow or stop the growth of oral tumors. "Black raspberries are full of *anthocyanins*, potent antioxidants that give the berries their rich, dark color, and our findings show that these compounds have a role in silencing cancerous cells," says Susan S. Mallery, DDS, PhD, at the university's College of Dentistry. (The gel is being tested in clinical trials.)

• **Blueberry juice to prevent prostate cancer.** The drink Blueberry Punch—a combination of fruit concentrates from blueberry, raspberry and elderberry—slowed the growth of prostate tumors in laboratory animals.

ℹ️ Blueberry Punch is available via the Internet from the Australian firm, Dr. Red Nutraceuticals, at *www.drred.com.au.*

Also helpful: In another study on fruit juice, researchers from UCLA found that 50 men with prostate cancer who drank 8 ounces of pomegranate juice a day had a significant slowing of their disease. "In older men, 65 to 70, who have been treated for prostate cancer, drinking pomegranate juice may help them outlive their risk of dying from the disease," says Allan Pantuck, MD, an associate professor of urology.

• **Broccoli, cauliflower and cabbage to prevent bladder cancer.** People who eat just three servings a month of *cruciferous* vegetables—broccoli, cauliflower and cabbage—reduce their risk of bladder cancer by 40%, say scientists at the Roswell Park Cancer Institute in Buffalo, NY.

Best: Raw vegetables. Cooking destroys 60 to 90% of *isothiocyanates,* a cancer-preventing compound in the vegetables.

Recommended: "*Sulforaphane,* a compound in cruciferous vegetables, may be one of the strongest anticancer fighters we have," says Emily Ho, PhD, an assistant professor at Oregon State University. "I try to eat two servings of cruciferous vegetables a day." And don't forget the sometimes-neglected cruciferous vegetables, Brussels sprouts and bok choy, she adds. Broccoli sprouts also deliver a lot of sulforaphane.

• **Green salads (and gardening!) to prevent lung cancer.** People who eat four or more weekly servings of green salads and work in the garden once or twice a week have a lower risk of lung cancer—64% lower in people who never smoked, 67% lower in people who used to smoke and 71% lower in current smokers.

"This finding is exciting because it is applicable not only to smokers but to the fifteen percent of nonsmokers who develop lung cancer," says Michele R. Forman, PhD, at The University of Texas M. D. Anderson Cancer Center. The most common cause of lung cancer in nonsmokers is secondhand smoke.

• **Onions to prevent pancreatic cancer.** People who eat fruits and veggies rich in antioxidant flavonols—*quercetin,* in yellow onions and apples; *myricetin,* in red onions and berries; *kaempferol,* in spinach and cabbage—have a 22% lower risk of pancreatic cancer, say researchers from America and Germany.

• **Tomatoes (and broccoli) to slow prostate cancer.** A combination of compounds from tomatoes *and* broccoli is more effective in slowing the growth of prostate tumors in laboratory animals than either tomatoes or broccoli alone—and possibly more effective in people than cancer-slowing drugs or surgery, say scientists from the University of Illinois.

Recommended: "Older men with slow-growing prostate cancer should seriously consider altering their diets to include tomatoes and broccoli," says Kirstie Canene-Adams, one of the study's researchers. "To get the effects we found in our study, men could consume daily about one-and-a-half cups of raw broccoli and two-and-a-half cups of fresh tomato, or one cup of tomato sauce or a half cup of tomato paste. I think it's very doable for a man to eat a cup-and-a-half of broccoli per day or put broccoli on a pizza with a half cup of tomato paste."

The study shows it's better to eat tomatoes than to take a tomato-derived lycopene supplement, says John W. Erdman, PhD, another coauthor of the study. (*Lycopene* is the antioxidant in tomatoes that research shows may help to prevent and control prostate cancer.) "And cooked tomatoes may be better than raw tomatoes because the chopping and heating make the cancer-fighting constituents more bio-available." In other words, your body will absorb more of them.

What to do: How many servings of fruits and vegetables do you need to eat every day to better your odds of curtailing cancer? Not as many as you might think…

In a recent study from researchers at the National Cancer Institute, people who ate just six servings a day of fruits and vegetables had a 29% lower risk of head and neck cancer compared to people eating just 1½ servings. In fact, just *one* additional daily serving was shown to lower risk by 6%.

It's not hard to get those fruit and veggie servings, says Steven G. Pratt, MD, coauthor of *SuperFoods Rx* (HarperCollins). "Many people have been discouraged from getting their daily servings of fruits and vegetables, because they believe a serving is a supersize amount of food. But when it comes to fruits and vegetables, getting the optimum number of servings is easy once you understand what a serving size really is—in most cases, about half a cup!"

Specifically, a serving of a fruit or vegetable is…

- **Vegetables…**
  - ½ cup cooked or raw vegetables
  - 1 cup raw greens
  - ½ cup vegetable juice

RED MEAT? DON'T STEAK YOUR LIFE ON IT

When the cartoon character Bart Simpson says, "Don't have a cow, man!"—maybe you should take him literally. And don't have a pig or a sheep, either. *Red meat has been caught red-handed—causing cancer…*

- 43% higher risk of colon cancer. People over 50 who ate the most red meat and processed meat (bacon, red meat sausage, luncheon meats, cold cuts, ham and hot dogs) had a 43% higher risk of colon cancer than people who ate the least, says a study from the International Agency for Research on Cancer, published in the *Journal of the National Cancer Institute.*

  However: Those who ate the most fish had a 58% lower risk of colon cancer than those who ate the least.

- 60% higher risk of breast cancer. Women 65 and older who ate a diet rich in red meat and sweets increased their risk of breast cancer by 60%, says Marilyn Tseng, PhD, from the Fox Chase Cancer Center in Philadelphia.

  However: Women eating a diet rich in vegetables, soy foods and fresh fish had a low incidence of the disease.

- 16% higher risk of lung cancer. In a study of more than 500,000 people aged 50 to 71, those who ate the most red meat had a 16% increased risk of lung cancer, says Amanda Cross, PhD, from the National Cancer Institute. This study showed red meat also increased the risk for cancers of the colon, esophagus and liver.

  Bottom line: "Meat consumption in relation to cancer risk has now been reported in over a hundred studies, from many countries, with diverse diets," says Dr. Cross. In other words, it's nearly a scientific certainty that eating more meat ups your risk for cancer.

  What happens: How does red meat cause cancer? It might be one or more of several factors, say researchers at the National Cancer Institute, such as saturated fat or chemicals in cooked (particularly charred) meat that damage DNA.

  What to do: Have a chicken, man. And some fish.

- **Fruits…**

    - 1 medium-size piece of fruit, such as an orange or an apple

    - ½ cup chopped fruit, including canned or frozen

    - ¼ cup dried fruit, such as 2 table-spoons of raisins or 3 prunes

    - ½ cup fruit juice

Good idea: "The best way to increase your intake of fruits and vegetables is to make sure they're *accessible*," says Joan Salge Blake, RD, clinical assistant professor of nutrition at Boston University and author of *Nutrition & You* (Benjamin Cummings). To do that, she says, buy more *frozen* foods.

"If you go shopping on Saturday, the fresh veggies in your refrigerator are probably gone by Tuesday," she says. "So buy fresh veggies *and* frozen broccoli and green beans—that way, it will be easy to get veggies onto your plate all week. When you buy fruit, buy fresh *and* frozen, such as frozen mango or peach chunks, which you can blend with yogurt for breakfast. Eating frozen vegetables and fruits is fine—and the preparation time is a lot faster than all that chopping and peeling!"

SUNSHINE VITAMIN KEEPS CANCER IN THE DARK

Vitamin D is produced in the skin by sunlight, and scientists used to think that the "sunshine vitamin" was good for one thing and one thing only—to help calcium build bones. But, in 1979, researchers discovered that the surface of every cell is loaded with vitamin D receptors—which means that every cell, not just bone cells, needs the nutrient to function normally. Now, scientists are learning that vitamin D can prevent and fight the biggest cellular abnormality

of them all—cancer. *Specifically, the sunshine vitamin can…*

- **Increase the death rate of cancer cells;**
- **Slow or stop runaway cell growth, the hallmark of cancer;**
- **Reduce blood supply to tumors; and**
- **Stop the spread of cancer beyond the tumor.**

Anticancer power translates into good news for people who get plenty of vitamin D.

⫸ *Breakthrough Studies*

- **Preventing colon cancer.** Researchers at the University of California in San Diego analyzed five studies on colon cancer and vitamin D. People with the highest blood levels of the vitamin had a 50% lower risk of getting the disease, compared to people with the lowest blood levels.

- **Preventing breast cancer.** The same researchers analyzed vitamin D levels and breast cancer rates in 1,760 women. Once again, those with the highest levels of vitamin D had a 50% lower risk.

- **Preventing "aggressive" prostate cancer.** Researchers at Harvard Medical School analyzed data from an 18-year study of nearly 15,000 men. Those with the lowest blood levels of vitamin D had twice the risk of developing the "aggressive" form of prostate cancer that is fast growing and often fatal.

- **Preventing all cancers.** Researchers at Creighton University in Nebraska studied nearly 1,200 postmenopausal women over the age of 55. Those who increased their intake of vitamin D from 400 to 1,000 IU a day had a lower risk of cancer—any kind of cancer—from 40 to 91%, depending on the type of cancer, compared to women who didn't get more vitamin D.

Standout scientific evidence: Researchers looked at the results in another way where blood levels of vitamin D were measured in ng/ml (nanograms per milliliter)—20 ng/ml is the edge of deficiency; 30 to 100 ng/ml is healthy. Among the women in the study, every 25 ng/ml increase in blood levels of vitamin D translated into a decrease of cancer risk by 35%. That's huge!

• **Preventing 185,000 cases of cancer per year with vitamin D.** Overall, statistical analysis shows that increasing blood levels of vitamin D among Americans could result in 185,000 fewer cases of cancer every year and 30,000 fewer deaths, says Michael Holick, MD, PhD, director of the Vitamin D, Skin and Bone Research Laboratory at Boston University Medical Center.

What to do: "Wouldn't it be nice if physicians could recommend something as simple and safe as a daily vitamin to reduce the risk of cancer?" says Sarah-Anne Schumann, MD, in the Department of Family Medicine at the University of Chicago. Now they can, based on the results of the study from Creighton University, which she says should be a "practice changer" for doctors—prompting them to advise their patients to take a supplement of 1,000 IU vitamin D a day.

Why such a seemingly large dose? "Few people get enough vitamin D from diet or sunlight to match the dosage that reduced cancer incidence in this study," Dr. Schumann points out. "And that even includes people who are apparently conscious of their nutritional needs, and take a daily multivitamin, drink a glass of milk a day and eat D-rich salmon at least once a week."

DON'T FORGET THE CALCIUM

Vitamin D is proving to be an anticancer powerhouse. But vitamin D and calcium are a little bit like Fred Astaire and Ginger Rogers, with D taking the "lead," controlling the movement of calcium out of the digestive tract and into the blood. So it wasn't a big surprise to researchers at Harvard Medical School when they found that women who got the highest levels of *both* nutrients had a 39% lower risk of breast cancer, compared to women who got the least. The team of nutrients was particularly protective against the development of fast-growing, "aggressive" breast tumors in premenopausal women.

What to do: For ideas on how to increase both calcium and vitamin D intake with food and nutritional supplements, turn to page 342 in Chapter 13, "Osteoporosis."

GREEN TEA—JAPAN'S ANSWER TO CANCER

"Green tea is a nontoxic cancer preventive for humans. It is nature's remedy." That's the conclusion of four scientists at the Saitama Cancer Center in Japan who have made the study of green tea and cancer their lifework.

Their research shows that drinking 10 four-ounce cups of green tea a day (commonplace among the Japanese) delayed the onset of cancer by seven years in women and three years in men, compared to people drinking three or fewer cups. (Many of the men in their study were smokers, accounting for the lower numbers.)

With green tea's growing popularity worldwide, American researchers are producing similar results.

▷ *Breakthrough Study*

Researchers at the Cancer Center of the University of Minnesota analyzed data from 13 studies on green tea and breast cancer.

Result: Those who drank the most green tea had a 22% lower risk of breast cancer than those who drank the least.

Why it works: Green tea is loaded with EGCG (*epigallocatechin gallate*), a potent, cell-protecting antioxidant. EGCG helps cancel cancer by stopping the action of several "tumor promoters" that trigger the disease, say the Japanese scientists.

What to do: EGCG is the most important anticancer compound in green tea, but not the only one, say the Japanese researchers. "Whole green tea—which also contains the antioxidants ECG and EG—is more effective than EGCG alone for cancer prevention."

Their recommendation: "To prevent cancer, drink forty ounces of green tea a day, or take two point five grams of green tea extract."

Or, they say, you could drink green tea *and* take the extract. For example, 20 ounces a day of green tea and 1.25 grams (1,250 mg) of green tea extract.

ℹ️ Green tea extracts are widely available.

Also helpful: For more information on maximizing your pleasurable intake of green tea, turn to page 5 in Chapter 1, "Aging and Longevity."

SELENIUM SHIELDS AGAINST PROSTATE CANCER

"Selenium is an essential trace mineral like no other," enthuses Margaret Rayman, PhD, an expert in the nutrient. That's because the

RELAX, COFFEE DOESN'T CAUSE CANCER. (AND MIGHT EVEN HELP PREVENT IT)

Americans drink a lot of coffee—well over 400 million cups every day. In fact, we drink more coffee per person than any other nation in the world. But is our love of coffee also the reason why one out of two American men and one out of three American women get cancer?

No way, latte.

Yes, a handful of studies showed a link between coffee and bladder cancer. But when scientists at the prestigious World Cancer Research Fund looked at decades of research on bladder cancer and coffee, they concluded: "The evidence now indicates that coffee is unlikely to have a substantial effect on risk of this cancer."

Another possible cause for concern: A study in 1981 showed that drinking three or more cups of coffee a day might double or triple the risk of pancreatic cancer. But dozens of studies since then haven't confirmed the link, with a team of researchers recently declaring, "A strong association between coffee and pancreatic cancer can now be excluded."

In fact, many studies show coffee may help *prevent* various types of cancer...

• 50% lower risk of colon cancer. In a study of more than 90,000 men and women aged 40 to 69, Japanese scientists found that people who drank three or more cups of coffee a day had half the risk of developing colon cancer than those who didn't drink coffee.

• 41% lower risk of liver cancer. Researchers analyzed 13 studies on liver cancer and found that coffee drinkers had a 41% lower risk than those who never drank coffee.

• 36% lower risk of skin cancer. Scientists at Wayne State University in Michigan found that Caucasian women who drank six or more cups of coffee a day had a 36% lower risk of developing nonmelanoma skin cancer than women who didn't drink coffee.

"For people who like coffee, there is no reason to give it up," says Manami Inoue, MD, PhD, a researcher at the National Cancer Center in Japan who has intensively studied the coffee/cancer link.

Refill anyone?

mineral has been on active duty as an *antioxidant* since oxygen formed on earth. In fact, it's the only trace element important enough to specify in the genetic code—so that bioactive *selenoproteins* are incorporated into every cell, providing protection against the oxidation that can cause genetic damage…and cancer.

▐▶ *Breakthrough Studies*

• **Prostate cancer.** Canadian researchers analyzed 16 studies that looked at selenium and prostate cancer—and found that taking the nutrient lowered risk by 28%.

In another study on selenium and prostate cancer, researchers at the Fred Hutchinson Cancer Center in Seattle found that men with the highest blood levels of selenium had a 39% lower risk (as long as they also took a multivitamin).

• **Colorectal cancer.** Researchers at the Arizona Cancer Center of the University of Arizona analyzed several studies that looked at selenium levels and colorectal cancer and found that those with the highest blood levels of the nutrient had a 34% lower risk of developing the disease.

ASHES TO ASHES

A study that surveyed more than a million people in the United States and Sweden showed that 92% of men and 80% of women who get lung cancer—a disease with 213,000 yearly diagnoses and 160,000 yearly deaths—are or were smokers. The others were probably regularly exposed to secondhand smoke at home or at work, says Heather Wakelee, MD, of Stanford University in California, who led the study.

If you're a smoker—see your doctor about a cessation program. Sure, quitting is hard. But consider the alternative.

• **Esophageal cancer.** People with the precancerous condition Barrett's esophagus *and* low levels of selenium have double or triple the risk of developing esophageal cancer, say researchers at the Fred Hutchinson Cancer Center.

• **Bladder cancer.** Ex-smokers with higher levels of selenium have half the risk of developing bladder cancer, say Dutch researchers.

How it works: Selenoproteins are powerful, DNA-protecting antioxidants. They may also detoxify cancer-causing chemicals, boost immunity, stop cancer cells from multiplying and cut blood supply to tumors, says Gerald F. Combs Jr., PhD, a selenium expert at the government's Grand Forks Human Nutrition Research Center in Nebraska.

Suggested intake: A study in the *Journal of the American Medical Association* showed that supplementing the diet with 200 micrograms (mcg) of selenium might reduce the risk of prostate cancer by 52% and the risk of dying from any cancer by 50%.

In another study of more than 1,300 Americans, taking a selenium supplement of 200 mcg for 10 years reduced overall cancer rates by 41%—and prostate cancer by 71%, esophageal cancer by 67%, colorectal cancer by 62% and lung cancer by 46%.

Best: The most usable forms of supplemental selenium are *selenomethionine* and selenium-rich yeast, says Michael Murry, ND, a naturopath and author of *Encyclopedia of Nutritional Supplements* (Three Rivers Press). Selenium supplements are widely available.

WEIGHT CONTROL SAVES LIVES

Ninety-nine out of 100 Americans don't think being overweight has anything to do with getting cancer, says the American Cancer Society. These individuals couldn't be more wrong—or more at risk...

IIII▶ *Breakthrough Study*

Researchers from the American Cancer Society followed more than 900,000 American men and women for 16 years.

Results: The heaviest men (extremely obese) had a death rate from all cancers that was 52% higher than normal-weight men. The heaviest women had a 62% higher death rate from all cancers compared to normal-weight women.

Scientists use a couple of different terms to define weight levels: *normal, overweight, obese,* and *extremely obese.* Those are determined by body mass index, or BMI, a formula that divides weight by height. So, for example, a 5'10" man would be: *normal* with a BMI of 19 to 24.9 and a weight of 132 to 173 pounds; *overweight* with a BMI of 25 to 29.9 and a weight of 174 to 208 pounds; *obese* with a BMI of 30 to 39.9 and a weight of 209 to 277 pounds; and *extremely obese* with a BMI 40 or over and a weight of 278 pounds or more.

Being overweight also increased the risk of dying from specific cancers—cancer of the esophagus, colon, rectum, liver, gallbladder, pancreas and kidney; non-Hodgkin's lymphoma and multiple myeloma, two blood cancers; for men, cancer of the prostate and stomach; for women, cancer of the breast, uterus, cervix and ovary.

LOWER YOUR BLOOD SUGAR— AND YOUR RISK OF FOUR TYPES OF CANCER

Scientists know that people with type 2 diabetes have a higher risk for several types of cancer—breast, colon, pancreatic, endometrial, liver and kidney. But what about people who *don't* have outright, diagnosable diabetes but *do* have higher-than-normal levels of blood sugar (glucose)—the tens of millions of Americans with the condition called *prediabetes.* (Doctors also call this condition *insulin resistance,* the *metabolic syndrome* or *glucose intolerance.*) Are those people at higher risk, too? *Well, there's no sense giving you a sugarcoated answer...*

New finding: Swedish scientists analyzed 13 years of data on blood sugar levels and cancer from more than 33,000 women and 31,000 men who do not have diabetes.

They found that women with the highest blood sugar levels had a 63 to 75% increased cancer risk, compared to women with the lowest levels.

For women and men, those with the highest blood sugar levels had...

• More than double (249%) the risk of pancreatic cancer

• More than double (216%) the risk of skin cancer (malignant melanoma)

• 86% higher risk of endometrial cancer

• 69% higher risk of urinary tract cancer

"A lifestyle that decreases blood sugar levels may lower cancer risk," says Pär Stattin, MD, PhD, from Umea University in Sweden, one of the study's researchers.

What to do: Please turn to Chapter 6, "Diabetes and Insulin Resistance," to read dozens of great ideas for lowering blood sugar, such as adding more fiber to your diet (choose a powerful and easy-to-digest type), exercising regularly (determine the right amount that does the trick) and taking one or more sugar-lowering supplements (you may be surprised how effective they are).

Bottom line: Twenty percent of cancer deaths in American women and 14% of cancer deaths in American men are caused by being overweight, obese or extremely obese—90,000 preventable deaths a year.

"Overweight and obesity have a very broad impact on cancer across most cancer sites," says Eugenia E. Calle, PhD, who led the study. "That's not something that's really in the consciousness of the American people."

What happens: Being overweight raises the level of estrogen, a risk factor for breast cancer. It causes chronic heartburn, which can lead to esophageal cancer. It generates so-called "growth factors" that tells cancer cells to multiply.

What to do: To lose weight, the American Cancer society recommends the basics: eat five servings a day of low-calorie but filling fruits and vegetables; emphasize whole grains over processed; limit red meat to a few servings per week; and exercise moderately for 30 minutes five days a week or more.

For more ideas about weight loss, turn to Chapter 14, "Overweight: Easy Ways to Shed the Pounds for Good."

EXERCISE—SWEAT AND CANCER DON'T MIX

Take action against cancer. Walk around the block.

⫸ *Breakthrough Study*

Scientists at the University of Southern California analyzed seven years of data from more than 110,000 women, aged 22 to 79.

Results: Women who participated in five or more hours of activity a week (jogging, swimming laps or other aerobic activities that keep your heart hopping) had a 20% lower risk of breast cancer.

"A woman's long-term exercise habits are important in determining her future breast cancer risk," says Leslie Bernstein, PhD, a professor of cancer prevention and the chief researcher on the study.

Why it works: Dr. Bernstein doesn't know for sure. Perhaps it's because exercise lowers estrogen and progesterone levels in the blood; high levels of these hormones are a risk factor. Perhaps it's because exercise lowers insulin, a hormone that boosts estrogen and progesterone. Perhaps it's because exercise helps women maintain weight; extra pounds are a risk factor.

Recommendation: "We recommend women exercise as much as they can each week." However, she says, an earlier study she conducted showed that just 80 minutes of moderate exercise a week reduced breast cancer by 20%, compared to women who didn't exercise. "Any activity is better than none," says Dr. Bernstein.

Any activity could include walking, hiking, jogging, running, calisthenics, aerobic classes, dancing, swimming, bicycling...

Important: Breast cancer isn't the only type of cancer that exercise can outrace. *Studies have found...*

• **Colon cancer.** People with the highest level of exercise had a 20% lower risk, compared to nonexercisers.

• **Lung cancer.** Researchers at the National Cancer Institute found that people who engage in regular physical activity such as brisk walking were 13% less likely to develop cancer.

Exercise scientists writing about cancer in the journal *Medicine and Science in Sports and Exercise* recommend regular (i.e., as often as you can) moderate physical activity to help prevent colon, lung and breast cancer. *Moderate activity is...*

- Walking at a pace of 3 to 4.5 miles an hour on a flat surface
- Bicycling 5 to 9 mph on a flat surface
- Stationary bicycling, using moderate effort
- High-impact aerobics
- Water aerobics
- Using a stair climber at a light-to-moderate pace
- Doubles tennis
- Golf, wheeling or carrying clubs
- Square, folk or ballroom dancing

OLIVE OIL—EXTRA VIRGIN, EXTRA PROTECTION

Why do Italians, Greeks and Spaniards get less colon and breast cancer than northern Europeans? It's probably because they eat the now-famous Mediterranean diet, say scientists. (A study shows that even Americans who eat a "Mediterranean dietary pattern" have a risk of cancer that's up to 17% lower.) But what are the *most* important anticancer factors in that diet? Is it the fish, the fiber, the fruits, the vegetables, the red wine?

Well, some researchers say the "it" in Mediterranean is a food already lauded for helping prevent heart disease—olive oil.

▶ Breakthrough Studies

- **Reducing the risk of colon cancer by 18%.** Italian researchers analyzed eight years of diet and health data from nearly 1,400 men and women. People who used the most olive oil for cooking had a risk of colon cancer that was up to 18% lower than those who used the least.

- **Reducing the risk of breast cancer by 50%.** Researchers analyzing diet and health

HOW CAN A MOP PREVENT CANCER?

The bad news is it's time to clean the house. The good news is you might throw out cancer.

Researchers in England analyzed data from more than 200,000 women in nine European countries. They found that women who did the most housework had the lowest risk of breast cancer—15 or more weekly hours (whew!) of cooking, cleaning, washing and/or childcare reduced risk by 29% in premenopausal women and 19% in postmenopausal women.

Housework works, of course, because it's a type of *physical activity,* say the researchers. But you didn't need a scientist to tell you that.

data from nearly 9,000 women in northern Italy found that those who ate the most olive oil (and raw vegetables) had a 34% lower risk of breast cancer than those eating the least. (Normal-weight woman who ate the most olive oil had a 50% lower risk!)

In another study, researchers from Florence, Italy, looked at mammograms of 2,000 women. They found those with the highest density—a risk factor for breast cancer—also had the lowest intake of olive oil.

And in a study of more than 700 women in the Canary Islands of Spain, those with the highest intake of olive oil had a 27% lower risk of breast cancer than those with the lowest.

How it works: Studies in the laboratory show that olive oil is something like an antidote for the poison of cancer. In one study, extra-virgin olive oil reduced damage to DNA—the key cause of cancer—by 30%.

A study by Italian researchers, published in the *Journal of Nutrition,* showed that olive oil stopped leukemia cells from dividing and killed them. Other research showed that olive oil did

ALCOHOL—MAKE THAT A DOUBLE...EDGED SWORD

It's been linked to greater longevity—and is the brain-numbing cause behind tens of thousands of fatalities, from accidents to homicides. That's alcohol for you. And against you. Delightful and dangerous. Enlivening and deadening.

Well, the link between alcohol *and* cancer is no different. *Alcohol can both prevent and cause the disease, depending on your gender, what you're drinking and how much you drink...*

• **For breast cancer—bad as smoking** or hormone replacement therapy. More than three drinks a day—beer, red wine, white wine or spirits—increases the risk of breast cancer about the same as smoking a pack of cigarettes a day or taking hormone replacement therapy, says Yan Li, MD, PhD, one of a team of researchers who studied more than 70,000 women for 26 years. *Specifically, they found...*

One or two daily drinks was linked to a 10% greater risk of breast cancer, compared to women who averaged less than a drink a day; more than three drinks was linked to a 30% greater risk.

"Our findings provide more evidence for why heavy drinkers should quit or cut down," says Dr. Li.

Definition of a drink: One drink is 4 to 5 ounces of wine, 12 ounces of beer, or 1½ ounces of 80% distilled spirits or liquor, such as whiskey or vodka.

• **For prostate cancer—choose a good red.** Men aged 40 to 64 who drink four or more glasses of red wine a week have half the risk of prostate cancer, say researchers from Fred Hutchinson Cancer Research Center, in Seattle. Beer, liquor and white wine weren't protective.

"It's difficult to recommend any alcohol consumption, given the risks with heavy consumption," says Janet L. Stanford, PhD, one of the study's researchers. "But for men who are already consuming alcohol, I think the results of this study suggest that modest consumption of red wine—four to eight 4-ounce drinks per week—is the level at which you might receive benefit. More than that may have adverse effects on health."

Caution: The healthiest pattern of drinking is one or two drinks a day—*not* eight glasses once per week.

• **For kidney cancer—protection** (with a long footnote). Researchers at Harvard Medical School analyzed data from 12 studies on alcohol and kidney cancer and found that one drink a day was associated with a 30% lower risk.

"However," says Jung Eun Lee, ScD, one of the researchers, "alcohol drinking is associated with increased risks of cancers of the oral cavity, larynx, pharynx, esophagus, liver and breast and probably the colon and rectum. Therefore, maintaining a healthy weight and avoiding smoking are the principal means to reduce the risk of kidney cancer, and may reduce the risk of many other cancers as well."

• **For liver cancer—the next step after cirrhosis.** Ninety percent of cases of liver cancer develop in scarred, cirrhotic livers—and alcoholism is the leading cause of cirrhosis.

Sobering thought: One to 2% of alcoholics develop liver cancer every year.

• **For non-Hodgkin's lymphoma—less risk.** Researchers at Yale analyzed health data from more than 15,000 people and found that drinkers had a 27% lower risk.

• **For colon cancer—rotgut.** Analysis of 10 years of health data for more than 10,000 Americans showed that one or more drinks per day was linked to a 70% increase in the risk of colon cancer—if the drink was liquor. Wine or beer had no effect.

Who shouldn't drink: If you're pregnant...if your father or mother suffered from alcoholism...if you're on a blood-thinning medication like warfarin...if you have breast cancer or a family history of the disease...if you're about to drive, operate heavy machinery or do anything that requires normal reaction time—*don't drink.*

the same to colon, breast, ovarian and stomach cancer cells.

A key component of olive oil (oleic acid) even tamped down the activity of Her-2/neu, the gene that drives many aggressive cases of breast cancer. "This is a novel mechanism linking the Mediterranean diet and cancer," say researchers from the Comprehensive Cancer Center of Northwestern University, in the *European Journal of Cancer.*

What to do: Buy a bottle of olive oil! Choose the richest in anticancer factors—extra-virgin, the first pressing of oil from olive. (Refined virgin or virgin is the second pressing.)

Researchers estimate the cancer-preventing amount is 1 ounce per day—two tablespoons or six teaspoons.

Try this: "In the Mediterranean diet, olive oil is consumed cold as a dressing for salads and pastas and used for sautéing and deep frying," says Brian Lockwood, PhD, in *Alternative Medicine Review.*

"Or you can drizzle it over slices of crusty bread or onto open-face sandwiches, or use it on a baked potato or add it to mashed potatoes instead of butter," says Linda Stradley, author of *What's Cooking, America* (Chehalem) and culinary master of the Web site by the same name (*www.whatscookingamerica.net*).

She says to use extra virgin for salads, dressings and vinaigrettes. "It also tastes great on cooked vegetables or brushed onto fish or meat before serving." For sautéing or frying, she recommends a blend of extra virgin and virgin.

Store your olive oil in a kitchen cabinet located away from the direct sunlight and the stove, adds Stradley.

BLACK COHOSH CUTS BREAST CANCER RISK

The herb black cohosh is typically taken to control hot flashes and other symptoms of menopause. But women with breast cancer or breast cancer survivors have been told *not* to take this herb—because it was thought to be a weak estrogen that might stimulate the growth of estrogen-sensitive breast cancer cells.

New thinking: Recent research shows that black cohosh doesn't stimulate the growth of estrogen-sensitive breast cells—in fact, it inhibits them, says Francis J. Brinker, ND, a naturopathic doctor, clinical assistant professor at the Program of Integrative Medicine at the University of Arizona College of Medicine and author of *Complex Herbs—Complete Medicines* (Eclectic Medical Publications). Scientists are also discovering the herb might inhibit breast cancer.

➤ Breakthrough Study

Doctors at the University of Pennsylvania School of Medicine studied more than 2,500 women and found that those who took black

BREASTFEEDING IS GOOD FOR BREASTS, TOO

A woman who has her first baby after the age of 25 doubles her risk for breast cancer. But a study conducted by researchers at the University of Southern California shows that breastfeeding can erase the risk.

"Breastfeeding may have a protective effect that negates the increased risk of breast cancer associated with late pregnancies," says Giske Ursin, MD, PhD, associate professor of preventive medicine, and one of the researchers who conducted the study.

Her motherly advice is, if you're having a baby after 25—breastfeed.

cohosh had a 61% lower risk of developing breast cancer. Those who took Remifemin—a popular black cohosh formulation—had a 53% lower risk. There was no reduction linked to the use of other herbs, including ginseng and red clover.

Recommended: Consider liquid Remi-Femin, a 60% ethanol extract of black cohosh root, with a dose of 2 mg, taken twice daily, says Dr. Brinker.

NATURAL SUPPORT

Seven out of 10 cancer patients don't settle for conventional medicine alone. They also use *complementary and alternative medicine* (CAM), such as nutritional or herbal supplements, says Keith I. Block, MD, medical director of the Block Center for Integrative Care in Evanston, IL, editor of the *Journal for Integrative Cancer Therapies* and author of the upcoming *Life Over Cancer* (Bantam).

Cancer patients choose CAM, says Dr. Block, to boost the therapeutic power of conventional treatment…for a greater sense of control and hope…because they believe CAM works…and as a last resort when conventional treatment has failed.

As CAM has become more popular among cancer patients, cancer researchers have intensified their investigation of natural treatments. And the newest research (and decades of successful clinical use by complementary cancer specialists) shows that CAM can work. But it's important to remember that these treatments are not *alternatives* to conventional care, says Dr. Block. *They are integrated with it, to…*

• **Boost the curative,** life-extending power of chemotherapy;

• **Reduce toxic side effects from chemotherapy and radiation** (approximately 30% of cancer patients stop potentially life-saving and life-extending treatment because of side effects);

• **Help prevent cancer recurrence;** and

• **Increase overall health and well-being,** improving the quality of life and perhaps extending it.

Here are the best science-based breakthroughs in complementary and alternative treatments for cancer.

GINSENG—LIFT THE FOG OF FATIGUE

"Cancer-related fatigue is one of the most profound and distressing issues cancer patients face," says Debra L. Barton, PhD, from the Mayo Clinic. "This unique type of fatigue can have many causes, and for patients who have completed cancer therapy, fatigue is among their foremost concerns, second only to fear of disease recurrence." Well, there may be a new solution for cancer-related fatigue—ginseng, the Asian and American herb traditionally used to chase away everyday fatigue.

▶ *Breakthrough Study*

Dr. Barton and her colleagues at the Mayo Clinic gave either a placebo or a daily supplement of American ginseng (in varying doses) to 282 cancer patients. Patients taking high doses of ginseng reported more energy. They also said that fatigue was interfering less with their daily activities. And they noted greater well-being—physical, mental, emotional and spiritual. The study was presented at the annual meeting of the American Society of Clinical Oncology.

What to do: Talk to your oncologist about whether ginseng is right for you.

TO MAXIMIZE COMPLEMENTARY TREATMENTS—START ASAP, BUT TALK TO YOUR ONCOLOGIST FIRST

"Decades of clinical experience with natural treatments for cancer shows that starting them *as soon as possible* after diagnosis is the best way to maximize their power to improve health and increase the likelihood of survival," says Dr. Block.

But not all natural medicines work for everyone, adds Dr. Block. "Treatment should be individualized. As soon as possible after diagnosis, talk to your oncologist about natural medicines that might benefit *you*."

Red flag: Talk to your oncologist *before* using natural treatments. Without medical supervision, nutritional supplements and herbs might negatively impact cancer.

Example: Nutrients and herbs that thin the blood, such as vitamin E and ginkgo, are contraindicated in cancer patients with low levels of platelets (cells that assist in blood clotting) from chemotherapy.

Suggested intake: The study tested daily doses of 750, 1,000 or 2,000 mg of American ginseng. Only those taking 1,000 or 2,000 mg got positive results.

Warning: Many ginseng products don't contain the amount or type of herb advertised on the label, says the supplement watchdog group, ConsumerLab.com. *They tested many types of American ginseng and approved two products as reliable...*

- **Hsu's Root to Health American ginseng** (500 mg per capsule)
- **Puritan's Pride American Ginseng** (500 mg per capsule)

ANTIOXIDANTS AND CHEMOTHERAPY

Oncologists often advise their patients *not* to take antioxidant supplements such as vitamin C or vitamin E during chemotherapy and radiation treatments. These medical therapies destroy cancer cells by causing oxidative damage, and antioxidants are thought to be counterproductive. But new scientific research shows the *opposite* is true. Antioxidant supplements aren't powerful enough to counter chemotherapeutic medicines or radiation...but they can reduce the side effects of those treatments...and may also battle tumors and extend life, says Dr. Block.

▌▌▌➡ *Breakthrough Study*

Researchers from the University of Illinois at Chicago and the Institute for Integrative Cancer Research and Education in Evanston, IL, analyzed 19 studies involving 1,554 cancer patients who took antioxidants during chemotherapy. *They found...*

- **Protection from nerve damage.** Only 31% of cancer patients (lung, head, neck, ovarian, testicular) taking vitamin E supplements during chemotherapy experienced peripheral neurotoxicity (tingling, numbness and/or burning pain in the hands and feet), compared to 86% of those who didn't take the antioxidant.

- **59% higher survival rates.** In postmenopausal women with breast cancer, the 43-month survival rate was 78% among women taking vitamin A—and 19% among women not taking the antioxidant.

New thinking: Antioxidants can diminish toxicity, and improve treatment tolerance, tumor response and survival rates. Most cancer patients are better off using antioxidants in conjunction with chemotherapy and radiation than not, conclude the researchers, in *Cancer Treatment Reviews.*

What to do: Share this research with your oncologist and discuss whether antioxidants are right for you.

☀ See Block K.I., et al. *Cancer Treatment Reviews* 33, no. 5: 407–18. Or contact Keith Block, MD, at the Institute for Integrative Cancer Research and Education, 1800 Sherman Avenue, Suite 350, Evanston, IL 60201 (847-492-3040 or fax 847-492-30450); e-mail *kblock@block medical.com*.

ASTRAGALUS—STOPPING LUNG CANCER DEATHS

The herb *astragalus* has been used as a tonic in Traditional Chinese Medicine for thousands of years. Scientific studies show it strengthens the immune system, increasing the activity of cancer-fighting immune cells (macrophages and natural killer cells) and blocking the activity of immune compounds that increase cancer-worsening inflammation (T-helper cell type 2 cytokines). Now, research shows the herb can also boost the power of chemotherapy to treat advanced lung cancer.

▌▌▶ *Breakthrough Study*

Researchers from the School of Public Health at the University of California, Berkeley, analyzed 34 studies involving 2,815 patients with advanced non-small cell lung cancer who were treated with either chemotherapy alone, or with

---

HEAD AND NECK CANCER— FOR A FOUL PROBLEM, AN ESSENTIAL SOLUTION

Patients with incurable head and neck cancer can develop infected skin ulcers near their tumors, with smells so foul that even family and friends stay away. Doctors in Germany, Australia and England have begun supplementing standard antibiotics with a natural remedy of twice-daily rinses with 5 milliliters (about 0.2 ounces) of antiseptic essential oils. *For more than 60 patients, the results have been miraculous...*

"All patients experienced a complete resolution of the foul smell by only the third or fourth day of therapy," say the doctors, in the journal *Phytomedicine*.

But not only did the smell go away—in some cases, after a few weeks of treatment, so did the ulcers! (The tumors continued to grow, however.)

Needless to say, patients were very happy. "The patients experienced great personal relief upon resolution of their malodorous conditions," say the doctors. "Quality of life improved significantly with the resulting reintroduction of social contact with relatives and friends."

Essential oil therapy "should have a significant place in modern palliative care and oncology," the authors conclude.

The treatment used was Klonemax, a product in development in Australia. It consists of 70 mg eucalyptus oil, 50 mg tea tree oil, 45 mg lemongrass oil (*Cymbopogon citratus*), 45 mg lemon oil (*Citrus limon*), 7 mg clove leaf oil (*Syzgium aromaticum*) and 3 mg thyme oil (*Thymus vulgaris*), in a 40% ethanol base.

Share this research with the oncologist and oncology nurse, and discuss whether a treatment with essential oils is right for you or your loved one.

Helpful: A licensed nurse practitioner with the certification CCAP (certificate in clinical aromatherapy) is fully qualified to administer this treatment.

☀ *Phytomedicine* 13, no. 7 (July 10, 2006): 463–67. Or contact the study's corresponding author, Patrick H. Warnke, at the Department of Oral and Maxillofacial Surgery, University of Kiel, Germany; e-mail *warnke@ mkg.uni-kiel.de*.

chemotherapy *and* astragalus-based Chinese herbs.

Results: Those taking astragalus had a 33% lower risk of death after 12 months. (In two studies, people who took astragalus for two years had a remarkable 42% reduced risk of death.) Patients taking astragalus also had a 24 to 46% better tumor response (reduction in size).

Astragalus-based Chinese herbal medicine may increase the effectiveness of chemotherapy, write the researchers, in the *Journal of Clinical Oncology.*

What to do: Share this research with your oncologist and discuss whether astragalus is right for you.

☀ *Journal of Clinical Oncology* 24, no. 3: 419–30. Or contact the study's author, John Colford, MD, PhD, at the University of California, Berkeley, 140 Warren Hall, MC 7360, Berkeley, CA 94720; e-mail *jcolford@berkeley.edu.*

STOP MOUTH ULCERS WITH GLUTAMINE

Chemotherapy can damage the mucous lining of the digestive tract, which stretches from the inside of the mouth to the rectum.

A common result is *oral mucositis* (OM)—the mucous lining of the mouth and throat become inflamed, ulcerated, easy prey for infection and just plain old painful.

Enter *glutamine.* This amino acid is the primary fuel for the daily maintenance and rebuilding of the mucous lining of the digestive tract—and glutamine supplements can help limit or stop its destruction by chemotherapy.

⫸ *Breakthrough Studies*

Researchers at the University of Connecticut Health Center gave either glutamine powder or a placebo to 326 cancer patients who were undergoing chemotherapy and developing OM.

Results: Those taking glutamine experienced a significant reduction in the severity of the OM compared to those taking the placebo. In fact, many of those who developed OM during their first cycle of chemotherapy and then took glutamine *didn't* develop OM during their second cycle of chemotherapy treatment. "Glutamine powder is safe and effective for preventing and treating OM in patients receiving cancer chemotherapy," says Douglas E. Peterson, DMD, PhD, the study's lead researcher.

What to do: The researchers used the glutamine product Saforis. A typical therapeutic dose is 5 to 10 grams, twice daily, says Dr. Keith I. Block.

Share this research with your oncologist and discuss whether glutamine is right for you.

☀ See *Cancer* 109, no. 2 (Jan. 15, 2007): 322–31. Or contact the study's corresponding author, Douglas E. Peterson, at the Dept. of Oral Health and Diagnostic Sciences, School of Dental Medicine, and the Carole and Ray Neag Comprehensive Cancer Center, University of Connecticut Health Center, 263 Farmington Ave., Farmington, CT 06030-2875; e-mail *peterson@nso.uchc.edu.*

RESIST RECURRENCE— WITH A HEALTHY DIET

When you think about how to survive cancer —about how *not* to have a deadly recurrence of your disease—you probably think about chemotherapy, radiation and surgery, and not about the foods in the produce department at your supermarket. But scientists have found that the same healthy diet that can prevent cancer can also prevent its recurrence.

IIII➤ *Breakthrough Studies*

• **Colon cancer.** Researchers at the Dana-Farber Cancer Institute in Boston analyzed the diets of more than 1,000 patients with Stage III colon cancer (cancer in the colon and nearby lymph nodes) who had been treated with surgery and chemotherapy.

Results: Those who ate a standard "Western" diet (emphasizing red and processed meats, sweets and desserts, French fries and refined grains) were three-and-half times more likely to have their cancer recur than those eating a "prudent" diet (emphasizing fruits and vegetables, poultry and fish).

Recommended: "We know from previous research that diet and lifestyle influence people's risk of developing colon cancer," says Jeffrey Meyerhardt, MD, MPH, who led the study. "Our results suggest that people treated for Stage III colon cancer can actively improve their odds of survival by their dietary choices."

He theorizes that the Western diet increases levels of the hormone insulin, which in turn triggers the release of growth factors that trigger and fuel tumors.

• **Prostate cancer.** Researchers analyzed data from 25 studies that looked at the progression of prostate cancer and diet.

Results: Diets high in saturated fat—found mainly in meat—were linked to triple the risk of dying from the disease.

Recommended: "For men diagnosed with prostate cancer, the key to improving the odds of survival is avoiding high-fat fare and instead choosing fruits, vegetables, beans and other cancer-fighting vegetarian foods," says Susan

Berkow, PhD, CNS, one of the study's researchers and a nutrition scientist with the Physicians Committee for Responsible Medicine. "Many of the nutrients found in those foods appear to inhibit the growth of malignant cells."

• **Breast cancer.** For more than a decade, researchers at the Moore Cancer Center at the University of California, San Diego, studied 1,490 women with early stage breast cancer.

Results: Women who ate a healthy diet and exercised regularly had half the risk of dying from the disease—even if they were overweight.

Recommended: "Even if a breast cancer survivor is overweight, if she eats at least five servings of vegetables and fruits a day, and walks briskly for thirty minutes, six days a week, her risk of death from the disease goes down," says John Pierce, PhD, who led the study.

RELIEVE NAUSEA WITH ACUPUNCTURE

The nausea and vomiting that typically follow sessions of chemotherapy can strand you on the roller coaster from Hell. Time to get off that awful ride. Acupuncture, the healing technique from Traditional Chinese Medicine, in which thin, tiny needles are painlessly inserted into specific points to stimulate and balance *chi*, or life-energy, is a natural treatment that improves the performance of nausea-beating drugs.

"There is so much scientific evidence about the efficacy and safety of acupuncture for nausea and vomiting," says Amit Sood, MD, codirector of research in the Complementary and Integrative Medicine Program at the Mayo Clinic. Evidence that shows acupuncture can also help relieve other side effects of conventional cancer therapy.

ⵊⵊⵊ➡ *Breakthrough Studies*

• **Nausea and vomiting.** Researchers analyzed 11 studies that tested whether acupuncture, electro-acupuncture (applying mild electric stimulation to inserted needles) or acupressure (applying manual pressure to points rather than needles) could help relieve nausea and vomiting in cancer patients receiving standard medical treatment for the problem.

Overall, acupuncture decreased vomiting after chemotherapy an additional 26%, with electro-acupuncture being particularly effective. Acupressure was effective at reducing the severity of acute nausea.

• **Postchemotherapy hot flashes.** Chemotherapy often triggers menopause—and hot flashes. In a study in Sweden, 12 weeks of treatment with electro-acupuncture reduced daily hot flashes from an average of eight to four.

• **Joint pain from aromatase inhibitors.** For postmenopausal women with hormone-positive breast cancer, the estrogen-suppressing class of drugs called *aromatase inhibitors* (AI) are standard treatment. Problem is, they can cause joint pain, leading some women to stop taking the drug. Researchers at Columbia University treated 21 women with AI-triggered joint pain with acupuncture. After six weeks, they had 33% less pain; their worst pain was 38% less severe; and they had a 46% reduction in the interference of pain with daily activity.

• **And more.** Doctors at the University of Colorado Cancer Center say that acupuncture can also help relieve depression in cancer patients, sometimes more effectively than an antidepressant...improve breathlessness in end-stage cancer...improve dry mouth in people with oral cancer who have received salivary gland radiation...and help with chronic fatigue after chemotherapy.

What to do: For information on nausea-relieving acupressure devices, please turn to page 187 of Chapter 7, "Digestive Disorders."

To find an acupuncturist near you, see the information on page 33.

FLAXSEED—SLOW PROSTATE TUMORS BY 40%

Chronic inflammation is known to fuel the growth of tumors. Omega-3 fatty acid, a nutrient abundant in fish and flaxseeds, is a potent *anti-inflammatory,* slowing tumor growth and shrinking tumors in animal studies. Research shows it may do the same for men with prostate cancer.

ⵊⵊⵊ➡ *Breakthrough Study*

Researchers at Duke University Medical Center, the University of Michigan and the University of North Carolina studied 140 men with prostate cancer who were scheduled to undergo prostate surgery in 30 days. They divided them into four presurgical groups—men taking 30 grams (about one ounce) of flaxseed daily; men eating a low-fat diet and taking flaxseed; men eating a low-fat diet; and a control group using none of the regimens.

Results: After the surgery, they found the tumors of the men taking flaxseed had grown at a 30 to 40% slower rate than those of the other men.

"We are excited that this study showed that flaxseed is safe and associated with a protective effect on prostate cancer," says Wendy Demark-Wahnefried, PhD, RD, a researcher in Duke's School of Nursing and the lead researcher of the study, which was reported at the annual meeting of the American Society of Clinical Oncology in 2007.

WALK AWAY FROM FATIGUE

Doctors often tell cancer patients to "rest and take it easy" if they become fatigued during chemotherapy and radiation. After all, life has become tough enough without the burden of having to get out and exercise. But new studies show that "taking it easy" may be hard on you.

||||➤ *Breakthrough Study*

Researchers in England studied 66 men undergoing radiation therapy for prostate cancer, dividing them into two groups—one started to walk regularly and the other didn't.

Results: Four weeks later, the men who didn't exercise were much more fatigued. Those who started a program of regular walking had no increase in fatigue.

Important: Other studies show that regular exercise during cancer treatment can decrease pain and improve appetite.

What to do: Talk to your oncologist about starting a walking program of 30 minutes, at a moderate pace, five or more days a week.

How it works: Dr. Demark-Wahnefried theorizes that the omega-3 fatty acids in flaxseeds might stop cancer cells from lumping together, curbing tumor growth. Other researchers speculate that *lignans*, a natural estrogen (phytoestrogen) in flaxseed, might reduce blood supply to tumors.

What to do: The men used ground flaxseed, mixing it in drinks or sprinkling it on yogurt and other foods.

"Flaxseed is easily ground using an inexpensive coffee grinder or blender," says Kaye Effertz, executive director of AmeriFlax, a group that promotes the healthfulness of flaxseed and flaxseed oil. "Unground flaxseed can have a shelf life of several years if stored in a cool, dry location away from bright light."

SOOTHING SUPPORT WHEN YOU NEED IT MOST

There's a full-time massage therapist at the Mayo Clinic Cancer Center, but she's not giving backrubs to stressed doctors during lunch breaks. She's treating *cancer patients*—relieving their anxiety and pain.

"Our cancer patients asked us for these services," says Dr. Amit Sood. "They don't dislike the conventional medicine we offer—in fact, they love it and they trust it—but they wanted something more."

It's not hard to see why.

When you're diagnosed with cancer—when you suddenly have to deal with a life-threatening illness and the often serious side effects of conventional treatment—you need care that is not only medical but also tender and loving. Care that can ease your disease-burdened body and mind. Here are the types of alternative TLC that doctors say can work.

||||➤ *Breakthrough Studies*

● **Art Therapy—drawing away distress.** "Art therapy is the therapeutic use of art making, within a professional relationship," says Donna J. Betts, PhD, an art therapist. "Through creating art, and reflecting on the process and results, those with illness can better cope with symptoms, stress and traumatic experiences." At the Northwestern Memorial Hospital in Chicago, cancer patients who participated in a one-hour art therapy session had significant reductions in anxiety and distress, and "overwhelmingly expressed the desire to continue with the therapy," say the researchers.

☀ American Art Therapy Association, Inc., 11160-C1 South Lakes Dr., Suite 813, Reston, VA 20191 (888-290-0878, 703-212-2238); e-mail *info@arttherapy.org* or visit *www.arttherapy.org*.

• **Faith—comfort you can believe in.** "For patients confronting a life-threatening illness such as advanced cancer, religious coping can be an important factor influencing their quality of life," say doctors at the Yale University School of Medicine. In a study of 170 cancer patients, they found those who dealt with their disease using "religious coping"—prayer, attendance at services, counseling from clerics, reading spiritual or religious books, et cetera —had fewer physical symptoms, and were less depressed and anxious than those who didn't. In fact, those who had "negative religious coping," such as anger at God, had more symptoms, and were more depressed and anxious.

• **Foot Reflexology—relief from the bottom up.** Foot reflexology teaches that each organ and system in the body has a corresponding point on the foot, and that massaging those points can provide healing and stress relief. Studies in the United States, Italy and Korea have found that foot reflexology can reduce anxiety in cancer patients…decrease nausea, vomiting and fatigue in breast cancer patients undergoing chemotherapy…and reduce pain in patients with advanced cancer.

☀ Reflexology Association of America, Administrative Office, PO Box 714, Chepachet, RI 02814 (401-578-6661, fax 401-568-6649). You can find a reflexologist in your area at its Web site, *www.reflexology-usa.org*.

• **Hypnosis—before surgery for better recovery.** In a study at New York's Mt. Sinai Medical Center, 200 women scheduled to receive either a breast biopsy (an operation to remove a suspected tumor for testing) or a lumpectomy (an operation to remove a tumor) were divided into two groups. Before surgery, one group was hypnotized for 15 minutes by a psychologist and one group wasn't. The hypnosis group reported less intense pain, and less nausea, fatigue, discomfort and emotional upset after surgery. They also spent less time in surgery (11 minutes) and required less anesthesia, lowering costs by an average of $773. "The combination of potential improvements in symptom burden for the hundreds of thousands of women facing breast cancer surgery each year, and the economic benefit for institutions, argues persuasively for more widespread application of brief presurgical hypnosis," says Guy Montgomery, PhD, who led the study.

☀ You can request a referral to a qualified medical hypnotherapist by contacting the American Psychotherapy and Medical Hypnosis Association (APMHA), Wenatchee, WA 98801 (509-662-5131); e-mail *admin@apmha.com* or visit *www.apmha.com*.

• **Massage—less depression, less anger …and a stronger immune system.** In a study conducted at the Touch Research Institutes at the University of Miami, women with breast cancer who received massage therapy for 30 minutes, three times a week were less depressed and angry than women who didn't get massages. The massaged women also had higher blood levels of two types of cancer-battling immune cells.

☀ American Massage Therapy Association (AMTA), 500 Davis Street, Suite 900, Evanston, IL 60201-4695 (877-905-2700 or 847-864-0123, fax 847-864-1178); e-mail *info@amtamassage.org* or visit *www.amtamassage.org*. To find a licensed massage therapist near you, AMTA recommends *www.findamassagetherapist.org*.

• **Mindfulness Meditation—ease stress.** Researchers at the Dana-Farber Cancer Institute in Boston analyzed nine studies on mindfulness meditation for cancer patients—and found that those who practiced the focusing, calming technique had less stress, better coping and better overall well-being.

☀ To locate a class in mindfulness-based meditation in your area, visit the Web site of The Center for Mindfulness in Medicine, Health Care, and Society, of the University of Massachusetts Medical School, at *www.umassmed.edu/cfm,* which includes a state-by-state directory of instructors and classes throughout the United States.

• **Tai Chi—for survivors, more strength.** Cancer patients who practiced tai chi for 12 weeks—the gentle, flowing exercise from China—had greater fitness, strength and ability to function. "Tai chi may be an effective intervention for cancer survivors," say the researchers, from the University of Rochester School of Medicine and Dentistry, in New York.

☀ There is no national licensing for teachers of tai chi, says the National Center for Alternative and Complementary Medicine. When selecting a tai chi teacher, they recommend you ask the teacher about his/her training and experience.

• **Yoga—protect your peace of mind.** Nearly 40 studies have been conducted on yoga and cancer. In one of the most recent, researchers at the University of Texas M. D. Anderson Cancer Center, in cooperation with a yoga research institution, divided 61 women with breast cancer into two groups—one practiced yoga three times a week and the other didn't. After one week, those doing yoga reported lower levels of daytime fatigue and better general health. "Yoga could help reduce the treatment-related side effects that accumulate in cancer patients over time," says Lorenzo Cohen, PhD, director of the Integrative Medicine Program at M. D. Anderson.

☀ You can find a member of the International Association of Yoga Therapists—a group of yoga teachers trained in helping people with illness—at *www.iayt.org.*

5

DEPRESSION & OTHER EMOTIONAL DOWNERS
DRUG-FREE WAYS TO EASE SADNESS AND ANXIETY

Unhappy=unhealthy. That's the surprising emotional equation discovered by scientists at Carnegie Mellon University in Pittsburgh. Reviewing a decade of research on emotions and health, they found that people with more positive emotions had fewer symptoms, less pain and less chronic illness. They also discovered that happier people are less likely to catch colds!

"We need to take seriously the possibility that positive emotions are a major player in disease risk," says Sheldon Cohen, PhD, a professor in the Department of Psychology at Carnegie Mellon.

This chapter takes that possibility *very* seriously by offering you effective, drug-free ways to tame the three most dangerous emotional beasts—depression, anxiety and hostility.

medication. And no wonder. Rates of depression have nearly tripled since World War II! But for many people who opt for an antidepressant, there's a better way, says Charles Barber, a lecturer in psychiatry at Yale University School of Medicine and author of *Comfortably Numb: How Psychiatry Is Medicating a Nation* (Pantheon).

"Through direct-to-consumer advertising and the promise of a quick fix, the pharmaceutical industry convinces people that drugs are the only answer to feeling down," he says. "But without an industry to promote them, non-drug approaches that could help millions of depressed people are often overlooked."

Time to remedy that situation—with drug-free remedies that can help chase away a temporary or chronic case of the blues.

NATURAL REMEDIES TO RELIEVE DEPRESSION

Doctors write about 230 million prescriptions for antidepressants every year—more than any other type of

TAKE ACTION AGAINST DEPRESSION—EXERCISE

Take an antidepressant. Take a walk. If you want to beat depression, there's no difference. They work equally well.

WHAT IS DEPRESSION?

It depends who you ask. Some say it's a biologically caused disease, like diabetes. Some say it's not a disease at all, but a pattern of behaviors. But all the experts agree that when you're depressed, you're *suffering,* and you need help—either self-help, professional help or both.

What are the symptoms? Depression can be *mild, moderate* or *severe*—labels along a continuum, from a temporary case of the blues, to relentless emotional agony that can lead a person to consider (and even commit) suicide, explains Michael Terman, PhD, a professor in the Department of Psychiatry at Columbia University Medical Center. *When you're depressed...*

• You feel down in the dumps—sad or "empty inside."

• You've lost interest in your daily activities. Pleasure is rare.

• You've lost your appetite and have lost weight, or you binge (typically on carbohydrates) and have gained weight.

• You can't sleep or you oversleep (maybe 10 hours or longer) and have to drag yourself out of bed.

• You move at a super-slow or super-fast (manic) pace.

• Your sex drive is stalled.

• You have trouble concentrating—you find yourself rereading the same paragraph three times, or unable to follow the storyline in a TV show.

• You're agitated and restless, or you're tired and lethargic.

• You feel like a failure—that you're worthless and have let down your family and friends.

• You think a lot about death and that maybe you'd be better off dead.

• You see suicide as a solution.

If you've had five or more of those symptoms for longer than two weeks, you're considered "severely depressed" or "clinically depressed"—and you definitely need to see a clinician—your family physician, or a psychologist or psychiatrist. (Keep in mind, however, that medication is only one medical option for clinical depression. You can also consider drug-free treatments such as cognitive-behavioral therapy, behavioral therapy or psychotherapy, all discussed in this chapter.)

If you have fewer than five of the above symptoms, your depression is more on the mild or moderate side, and self-treatment is a reasonable option, says Dr. Terman.

Surprising: Many people—middle-aged men in particular—are depressed but don't know it, say experts. They just think life after forty is like that. It isn't! If a few of the above symptoms match your daily experience—*you're depressed.* Consider using the drug-free approaches in this chapter, or talk to your family doctor or a mental health professional.

▶ *Breakthrough Study*

Researchers in the Department of Psychiatry and Behavioral Sciences at Duke University Medical School studied 202 people with depression (71% mild; 39% moderate or severe), dividing them into four groups.

One group exercised three times a week at a gym, with supervision. One group exercised three times a week at home, without supervision. One group didn't exercise but took the antidepressant medication *sertraline* (Zoloft). One group didn't exercise and took placebo pills.

Result: After four months of treatment—*exercise worked just as well as the antidepressant in relieving depression!*

Forty-seven percent of the people who took medication were no longer depressed, compared to 45% in the gym-based exercise group and 40% in the home-based exercise group. The placebo group had a far lower rate of recovery.

"Exercise is comparable to antidepressant medications in the treatment of depression," says James A. Blumenthal, PhD, a professor at Duke University Medical Center who led the study.

Why exercise works: "The mechanisms aren't known," says Dr. Blumenthal. But he has some theories. Regular exercise might give you more confidence, the belief that you *can* change your life—a depression-defeating attitude psychologists call "self-efficacy." Exercise might distract you from negative thoughts. It might improve your self-image.

And, of course, exercise also affects you *physically,* says Dr. Blumenthal—and might relieve depression by boosting happiness-stimulating hormones and feel-good brain chemicals such as serotonin.

But if the "why" of exercise isn't known, the "what" is a proven fact. "Patients who would like to engage in exercise therapy can achieve significant relief from the symptoms of their depression," says Dr. Blumenthal.

What to do: Ten minutes of slow, warm-up walking...followed by 30 minutes of brisk walking or jogging...with 5 minutes of slow, cool-down walking...three times a week—that was the "exercise prescription" for depression used in the study at Duke University Medical School.

Weight lifting works too: Researchers at Harvard Medical School found that weight lifting significantly reduced clinical depression in 32 depressed people. (For weight-lifting routines, see page 15 in Chapter 1, "Aging and Longevity" and pages 58–59 in Chapter 3, "Back Pain, Headaches and Other Pain Problems."

Important: Studies show that if you're inactive, you're at greater risk for *developing* depression.

HEART DISEASE, DEPRESSION AND EXERCISE

Consider these three facts...

1. Forty percent of people become depressed after having a heart attack or a *stent,* an artery-expanding procedure for heart disease.

2. Depression increases the risk for a second heart attack or worsening arterial blockage.

3. Studies show that antidepressant medications increase the risk of death and hospitalization in those with heart disease!

It's reasonable to conclude that antidepressants aren't a smart option for depressed people with heart disease—and that's just what scientists have concluded...

"There is a need to identify alternative approaches for treating depression in heart patients," says Dr. James Blumenthal. "Exercise may be one such approach. It improves cardiovascular functioning and mood, is relatively inexpensive and avoids the side effects sometimes associated with medication use."

Standout scientific evidence: Dr. Blumenthal and his colleagues studied people who suffered a heart attack and developed depression—and then either exercised or stayed sedentary. Compared to their sedentary counterparts, exercisers reduced their symptoms of depression—*and* cut their risk of death by 50%.

If you have heart disease, talk to your cardiologist about whether regular exercise is right for you.

LIGHT THERAPY—A BRIGHT IDEA FOR S.A.D.

It's early October, the days are shortening—and you're dreading the return of winter. But not because of the bad weather.

You're dreading the carbohydrate binges and weight gain...the heavy-limbed fatigue... the brain fog and irritability. You're dreading the return of your *depression,* which often lifts during the sunny days of summer but falls like a suffocating blanket of black snow when winter rolls around.

If that sounds like you, you probably have *Seasonal Affective Disorder* (SAD)—depression that tends to settle in during late fall and lift in late spring. (This particular misery loves company—mild to severe SAD afflicts one out of every four Americans.)

What's the best remedy for your dark mood?

Light. Lots of light.

"A person with a deep winter depression can snap completely out of it in less than a week's time with light therapy," says Dr. Michael Terman, one of the world's leading experts in Light Therapy for depression.

⫸ *Breakthrough Study*

Researchers commissioned by the American Psychiatric Association analyzed eight studies on light therapy and found that it relieved SAD (*and* nonseasonal depression)—in many cases, just as effectively as antidepressant drugs!

What happens: The "light box" used in light therapy is a bank of bright lights on a stand, positioned above eye level and shining down at your eyes.

You don't look at the lights, however. You look downward—at (for example) your laptop, a book or your breakfast. A session is 30 minutes.

Why it works: There are three mechanisms at work, explains Dr. Terman.

Light therapy stimulates energizing adrenal hormones.

It also boosts serotonin levels, the feel-better neurotransmitter increased by some antidepressant drugs. And it resets your "circadian rhythm"—the internal clock that controls

sleep-wake patterns, which can trigger depression when it's out of whack.

What to do: A study conducted at Columbia University Medical Center showed that the best treatment for SAD is a 10,000-lux fluorescent light box, used for 30 minutes a day, immediately after waking up. (*Lux* is a measurement of perceived light—10,000 lux is the light you would perceive walking on the beach about 40 minutes after sunrise. The lighting in a normal room is about 750 lux.)

Helpful: Light therapy for SAD is not a one-size-fits-all treatment. The effective timing of your therapy depends on your circadian rhythm and whether you're a "morning person" or an "evening person." In fact, a study shows that light therapy is *twice* as effective for SAD if it's timed to an individual's circadian rhythm—80% of people get better, compared to 40%.

The Web site of the Center for Environmental Therapeutics (*www.cet.org*) offers an automated Morningness-Eveningness Questionnaire (MEQ) that will help you determine the best time for you to use light therapy.

Examples: If you score 16 to 18 on the MEQ—in other words, you're an extreme evening person—light therapy should be started at 8:45 a.m. If you score 85 to 86—you're an extreme morning person—light therapy should be started at 4:15 a.m. If you score 42 to 45—you're what's called an "intermediate"—light therapy should be started at 7:00 a.m.

Smart idea: If light therapy works for you, should you start it every fall to prevent the problem? Not necessarily, says Dr. Terman—SAD might not strike every year. Instead, be on the lookout for the signs of impending SAD—trouble getting up in the morning, tiredness during the day, carbohydrate cravings—and start treatment *after* they show up.

Precaution: If you're starting therapy, have an eye checkup—you shouldn't use the therapy if you have diabetic retinopathy, which might be worsened by the bright lights. Also, if you take drugs that can sensitize eyes to light—for example, psychiatric drugs such as *imipramine* (Tofranil)—you should wear special filtering wraparound sunglasses that eliminate the transmission of the shorter wavelengths that can damage "photosensitized" eyes. The sunglasses are available from *www.noir-medical. com,* or by calling 800-521-9746. The model to use is the UV Shield Orange 49%, L60.

Symptoms such as headaches and eye irritation occur in about one-third of people in the first week or so; the problems usually go away after about five days.

Treating Nonseasonal Depression

Light therapy can be just as effective treating recurrent or chronic (nonseasonal) depression, says Dr. Terman. In fact, it can boost the power of antidepressant drugs, speeding improvement.

What most people don't know: SAD can be mild, moderate or severe. If it's severe, it's usually restricted to winter. If it's mild or moderate—the majority of cases—you're likely to be recurrently or chronically depressed, with winter worsening the condition. That's why people with so-called "nonseasonal depression" may find relief with light therapy—because nonseasonal depression isn't all that different from SAD! In fact, says Dr. Terman, depressed people who stay in bed with the shades drawn to "escape the world" may miss the early morning light that synchronizes the body's internal clock to local time, upsetting circadian rhythms and worsening depression.

New study: Dr. Terman and a team of researchers from the Department of Psychology at Wesleyan University treated 32 depressed patients for five weeks with either bright light (10,000 lux, for one hour after waking up) or another nondrug treatment. Depression ratings improved an average of 54%, with half the people in the study getting completely better.

Dr. Terman has found that light therapy can treat other kinds of depression besides SAD and nonseasonal depression—bipolar depression (manic-depression); depression during and after pregnancy; and "refractory depression" that resists treatment by drugs, electroconvulsive therapy or both.

Research also shows the therapy holds promise for many nondepressive conditions, including insomnia, eating disorders, adult attention deficit hyperactivity disorder, premenstrual syndrome, Parkinson's and Alzheimer's.

How to Choose a Light Box

It can be confusing, says Dr. Terman, because there are so many different varieties—big and small sizes, white and colored lights, fluorescent and LED lamps, cheap and expensive price tags. *He offers these six criteria to guide you in your selection...*

1. The light box was used in a rigorous scientific study that showed light therapy works. You're buying a proven device.

2. The light box provides 10,000 lux of illumination at a comfortable sitting distance—the illumination used in many studies. If the box doesn't have specifications that allow you to figure this out, don't buy it.

3. The fluorescent lamps of the light box have a smooth diffusing screen that filters out UV rays, which are harmful to your eyes and skin.

4. The light box provides white light, not colored light. "Full spectrum" lamps and blue lamps provide no added benefit, in spite of what the accompanying hype might say.

5. The lights in the box project downward from above, to minimize glare.

101

6. The light box is large enough. If you're using a small light box, even seemingly insignificant head movements can take your eyes out of therapeutic range.

ℹ️ The Web site of the organization supervised by Dr. Terman—the Center for Environmental Therapeutics (*www.cet.org*)—has a store that sells a light box that meets all the above criteria, the Day-Light from Uplift Technologies. You can order at the CET site, or call the company directly at 800-387-0896. (Products purchased at the site fund scientific research into light therapy.)

Caution: Self-treatment with light therapy is fine if you have mild or moderate SAD or nonseasonal depression, says Dr. Terman. However, if you have true clinical depression (described in the box, "What Is Depression?" on page 98), you should only use light therapy under the supervision of a doctor or mental health professional.

FISH OIL FOR DEPRESSION

The American Psychiatric Association recommends eating fish three times a week.

That's right—the *American Psychiatric Association.* Not the American Heart Association …not the American Diabetes Association…not even the American Fisheries Association.

The reason psychiatrists are fans of finned food—it contains two unique *fatty acids,* the building blocks of biologically important fats. They are EPA (*eicosapentaenoic acid*) and DHA (*docosahexaenoic acid*), otherwise known as "omega-3" fatty acids (a designation based on the arrangement of their molecules).

Without omega-3s, the outer covering of brain cells (neurons) would fall apart. With not enough omega-3s, neurons fall short.

They generate less serotonin, the neurotransmitter that sends feel-good messages from cell to cell. *Dopamine,* another neurotransmitter linked to depression, does a shoddy job. *Dendrites,* the branching extensions that channel messages into and out of the cell, have fewer branches. And there are fewer synapses, the bridge between cells.

In other words, a deficiency of omega-3s—very common among Americans, who eat a lot more hamburgers than salmon steaks—is a sad story for your mind and mood. Very sad.

⏩ *Breakthrough Studies*

People living in countries where seafood is rarely eaten have a 65-fold greater risk of developing depression, says Joseph Hibbeln, MD, one of the world's top experts in omega-3 fatty acids and mental health. *Fortunately, taking omega-3 supplements can help solve the problem…*

• **Depression.** Researchers in Taiwan analyzed the results of 10 studies in which omega-3 was used to treat depression—and found a "significant antidepressant effect," with EPA and DHA supplements improving the condition by 69%.

• **Bipolar disorder.** The same analysis found EPA and DHA improved the symptoms of bipolar disorder (manic-depression) by 69%.

• **Postpartum depression.** The risk of depression after childbirth is 50-fold greater in countries with a low dietary intake of seafood, says Dr. Hibbeln. He also found that new mothers with low levels of DHA in their breast milk were more likely to become depressed. But, he says, studies show that supplementing with EPA and DHA decreases depression after (and during) pregnancy by 50%.

"It would be a shame if inadequate dietary intakes of omega-3 fatty acids change the emotional experience of pregnancy and childbirth from happiness to depression and despair," he says.

• **Suicide attempts.** Among patients hospitalized with emotional problems, those with the lowest blood levels of DHA had the most suicide attempts over the next three years, say Irish researchers. But, in another study, suicidal thinking was dramatically reduced among people taking 2 grams a day of EPA and DHA.

What to do: Follow the recommendation of the American Psychiatric Association, says Dr. Hibbeln. Eat fish three times a week, or supplement your diet with a minimum of 1 gram of EPA and DHA daily.

ℹ️ Fish oil supplements are widely available. The Nordic Naturals brand used in many scientific studies has proven the value of fish oil; their Ultimate Omega product contains 650 milligrams (mg) of EPA and 450 mg of DHA, or 1.1 grams.

Trap: Larger doses don't produce better results. In a study that tried to determine the right dose of omega-3s for depression, larger doses than 1 gram per day were less effective.

SAFFRON, THE HAPPINESS SPICE

Think *saffron*, and you probably think of the world's most expensive spice, and the golden-yellow color of saffron-containing dishes, such as Spanish paella or Indian biryani. What you probably don't think of is depression. But some psychiatrists do.

Ⅲ➡ *Breakthrough Studies*

Doctors at the Psychiatric Research Center at the Tehran University of Medical Sciences in Iran (the country that produces 80% of the world's saffron) studied 40 people with depression, dividing them into two groups. One group received the antidepressant *fluoxetine* (Prozac). The other group received saffron capsules.

ANTI-ANTIDEPRESSANTS

When the first type of antidepressant fails, the doctor usually tries a second. When the second type fails, he usually prescribes a third. And that usually doesn't work either.

New finding: The largest depression study ever conducted showed that when depressed patients don't get better on a second round of antidepressants, they're unlikely to improve with a third.

This study "underscores the persistence of depression and its resistance to current [drug] treatments," says Robert Freedman, MD, editor-in-chief of the *American Journal of Psychiatry,* the medical journal where the study appeared.

Problem: "There has been enormous investment in the development of new antidepressants, yet there has not been an enormous improvement in the effectiveness of treatment for depression," says Dr. Michael Terman. "The standard antidepressant has not fulfilled its promise. Yes, it works very well with certain people—when it works. But the conventional medication strategy with antidepressants has several problems. It often doesn't work. When it does work, it takes five to six weeks to see improvement. Additionally, antidepressants can have a range of side effects, from dry mouth to sexual dysfunction. And when the drug is stopped, depression commonly returns."

Solution: However, says Dr. Terman, many nondrug alternatives reliably produce lasting results in less than a week, such as light therapy. You'll find them in this chapter.

Result: After six weeks, *both* groups had the same level of relief from depression.

"The results of this study indicate the effectiveness of *Crocus sativus* [saffron] in the treatment of mild to moderate depression," say the researchers, in the *Journal of Ethnopharmacology*.

In another study by the same team of researchers, saffron matched the depression-ending power of *imipramine* (Tofranil), a drug in the tricyclic class of antidepressants.

Suggested intake: The researchers used 30 mg a day.

🛈 EXIR Saffron Dietary Supplements are available at *www.amazon.com*.

PSYCHOTHERAPY—STICK WITH IT, STAY WELL

Psychotherapy is the verbal give-and-take with a psychologist or psychiatrist to help you understand and resolve the problems that underlie your depression—in the past and the present, in yourself and in your relationships. And studies show it can relieve those problems and lift depression—in fact, as effectively as antidepressant medications. But a new study shows it works best *if you stick with it.*

▐▐▐➡ *Breakthrough Study*

Researchers in the Department of Psychiatry at the University of Pittsburgh studied more than 200 women with recurrent depression. They found that of those who underwent psychotherapy and got better, 74% stayed depression free for more than two years *if* they continued with once-a-month psychotherapy sessions.

"These women remained *really* well—basically symptom free," says Ellen Frank, PhD, who led the study. (And she says the same would probably hold true for men, since other studies show little difference in how men and women respond to psychotherapy.) If you can't arrange or afford once-a-month treatment, check in with your therapist at least once every couple of months, she advises. "It's hard for people with depression to spot when depression is returning. Seeing the therapist every now and then can help you identify and prevent a recurrence."

What to do: To find a therapist, Dr. Frank suggests getting a recommendation from a friend or colleague you trust, or calling the Department of Psychiatry at a local university medical center. You can also use the "Psychologist Locator" at the Web site of the American Psychological Association (APA) at *www.apa.org* or call the APA's referral service at 800-964-2000.

NEGATIVE IONS ARE VERY POSITIVE

Why do most of us feel better when we stand by a waterfall? Is it the natural beauty, the sound of

---

ECO-THERAPY—GET OUTSIDE YOURSELF

Researchers at the Centre for Environment and Society at the University of Essex in England asked people to go for two very different types of walks—outside in a country park, surrounded by woods, meadows and lakes; or inside, in a mall, surrounded by stores. After each walk, they measured the exercisers' mood—and found the outdoors walk decreased mild, everyday depression five times more than the indoor walk!

"Exercising outdoors in a green environment is a lot more effective in enhancing your mood than an equivalent amount of indoor exercise," say the researchers. "It offers an ideal way of getting rid of the blues."

rushing water—or the *negative ions*? Scientists are thinking negative.

To understand negative ions, let's take a quick trip to the atomic level. (Don't pack your toothbrush—you'll be right back.) In this electromagnetic environment, atoms are orbited by particles with either a positive (proton) or a negative (electron) charge. An atom with an unequal number of protons and electrons is called an *ion;* if there are more electrons, it's a *negative ion.*

Back to the everyday world. When atoms in the air are thoroughly jostled—by the surge and retreat of surf, by the constant pour of a waterfall, by the turbulence of a spring thunderstorm—the air becomes loaded with negative ions. And for some reason unknown to scientists, negative ions boost mood. Even when they're generated by a machine.

DR. DOLPHIN WILL SEE YOU NOW

Pets might be the world's best psychologists.

Researchers at the University of Leicester Medical School in England recruited 25 depressed Americans, dividing them into two groups. One group was assigned to swim with, play with and take care of bottlenose dolphins at the Roatan Institute for Marine Sciences in Honduras, for one hour a day. The other group swam and snorkeled in a beautiful coral reef for one hour a day.

Result: Both groups had a significant improvement in their depression symptoms —but interacting with dolphins had *twice* the antidepressive effect as swimming at the coral reef.

What to do: There probably aren't too many dolphins at your local pet store. But scientific studies on "pet therapy" have shown the antidepressant benefit of owning a dog or a cat, caring for a canary, watching a fish tank, riding a horse and even raising a cow.

▶ *Breakthrough Studies*

Researchers at Columbia University Medical Center studied people with SAD (seasonal affective disorder) and bipolar depression (manic-depression), asking them to use negative ion generators in their bedrooms. (The devices used in the study generated many negative ions —"high-density negative ions," in scientific parlance.)

After three weeks, their depression ratings improved by 48%. Another group was treated with low-density negative ions. Their depression ratings improved by only 23%.

In a second study, 30 people with chronic depression improved their depression ratings by 52% after five weeks of one-hour treatments with a negative ion generator, right after waking up.

"High-density ionization is an active antidepressant and can be considered as an alternative to medication," says Dr. Terman.

What to do: The people in the study placed the ionizer two feet away from the bed, with the flow of ions directed toward the pillow. A timer turned the ionizer on about 90 minutes before their typical wakeup time.

Other tips from Dr. Terman on using a negative ion machine to beat depression…

● **Place the unit away from other electrical appliances,** such as a phone, clock radio or TV and grounded objects such as walls or a radiator. Both appliances and grounded objects attract ion flow, diminishing the impact of negative ions.

● **Use a timer to turn on the ionizer about 90 minutes before you typically wake up** (the method used in the study at Columbia), or simply turn the unit on at bedtime and turn it off when you wake up. Keeping it on 24/7 is not a problem.

● **To maximize negative ions, humidify the room too.**

● **Place the ionizer above mattress level,** on a bedstand or chair.

There are many negative ion machines out there. Which work to beat depression?

"Most machines don't specify their output of negative ions, so there's no way to determine an adequate antidepressant dose," says Dr. Terman. And specified output or not, most machines manufactured for air purification can't produce the level of negative ions needed to combat depression.

🛈 Dr. Terman recommends using the same type of unit that worked to beat depression in his studies, the Sphere FreshAIR Negative Ionizer, which is available at the Web site of the Center for Environmental Therapeutics (*www.cet.org*) or by calling the manufacturer at 866-569-3236. (Profit from units bought at the CET site support research into environmental therapy for depression.)

ST. JOHN'S WORT—BETTER THAN PROZAC

Possessed by a spirit? Daunted by a demon? Stunned by a witch's spell? Try St. John's wort.

That was typical self-help advice in the Middle Ages, when this saintly herb was used to counter non-saintly forces of a supernatural kind. Well, today's demon is depression—and St. John's wort is still on the job.

⫸ *Breakthrough Studies*

Researchers from the University of Essen in Germany asked nearly 400 people with

---

SICK AND DEPRESSED? PRAY FOR RELIEF

When you're feeling low, consider getting help from on high.

New study: Harold G. Koenig, MD, a professor of psychiatry and behavioral sciences at Duke University Medical Center in North Carolina, evaluated the depression levels and the "religious characteristics" of 1,424 hospital patients, all of them over 50.

Four hundred eleven patients had major depression, 585 had mild or moderate depression and 428 weren't depressed. *The depressed patients were...*

• Less likely to have a religious affiliation,

• Less likely to pray, and

• Less likely to read scripture.

And in a study of nearly 870 people over 50 with heart failure and chronic lung disease who were also depressed, Dr. Koenig found a 53% faster recovery rate from depression among those who were reliably religious—the people who attended a place of worship *and* prayed regularly *and* studied religious texts *and* believed in God.

How does religion protect against depression, particularly among people with ill health?

"Religious beliefs can be a source of hope, meaning and purpose for those facing difficult life problems, especially medical illness," says Dr. Koenig. "It gives people a sense that they are cared for and helped. It's not surprising that religious belief and activity generates optimism and helps protect against depression." He also notes that the social side of religion—belonging to a community, attending services—buffers against depression.

What to do: "People who are religious should be encouraged that science is showing their beliefs make a difference," says Dr. Koenig. "Those who are ill and depressed should make use of those beliefs that may be a central source of comfort and hope."

However: What if you're ill and *angry* with God? "It is important to see a trained pastoral counselor or chaplain who can help you work through these issues," he says.

moderate depression to take either an extract of St. John's wort, the antidepressant drug *citalopram* (Celexa), or a placebo.

Result: The herb worked just as well as the drug to reduce the symptoms of depression—but half the people taking the drug had side effects, compared to 17% of those on the herb (and 30% of those on the placebo).

"St. John's wort extract is a good alternative to antidepressants in the treatment of people with moderate depression," say the researchers.

In a similar study of 135 depressed people, researchers in the Depression Clinical and Research Program at Massachusetts General Hospital in Boston found that 900 mg a day of an extract of St. John's wort outperformed *fluoxetine* (Prozac) in relieving depression.

How it works: St. John's wort may help boost levels of feel-good brain chemicals such as serotonin, dopamine and GABA, says Hyla Cass, MD, an assistant clinical professor of psychiatry at UCLA School of Medicine and author of *St. John's Wort: Nature's Blues Buster* (Avery).

What to do: "It makes a lot of sense to try the natural way of healing before plunging into the risky world of pharmaceutical drugs," says Christopher Hobbs, an herbalist and author of *St. John's Wort: The Mood Enhancing Herb* (Interweave Press). "St. John's wort is a logical first step toward effectively and safely relieving symptoms of depression."

ℹ The company ConsumerLab.com tested many brands of St. John's wort to see if they contained the amount of the herb stated on their labels—and many didn't! The brands that did were Gaia Herbs, Kira, Nature's Resource, New Chapter, Puritan's Pride, Sundown and 21st Century.

MARRIAGE—VOWING NOT TO BE DEPRESSED

Single and depressed? Tie the knot.

Depressed people get a bigger psychological boost from marriage than the nondepressed, say researchers from Ohio State University, who analyzed psychological data from more than 3,000 people who were unmarried in 1987 and married in 1994.

"We thought depressed people would be *less* likely to benefit from marriage, because the depression of one spouse can put a strain on the marriage and undermine marital quality," says Adrienne Frech, one of two researchers who conducted the study.

Why the added boost for the formerly unmarried morose? "Marriage may give depressed people a greater sense that they matter to someone, while people who weren't depressed prior to marriage may have always thought that way," says Kristi Williams, PhD, assistant professor of sociology at Ohio State University, and the study's other researcher.

Suggested intake: 300 mg, three times a day, of an extract standardized to provide 24 mg of hyperforin, the active ingredient.

Warning: Studies show that St. John's wort interacts with many different medications, in some cases undercutting efficacy and in others increasing the risk of side effects.

"If you are on a prescription medication, do not take St. John's wort," says Francis Brinker, ND, a naturopathic doctor, clinical assistant professor at the Program of Integrative Medicine at the University of Arizona College of Medicine and author of *Herb Contraindications and Drug Interactions* (Eclectic Medical Publications).

He also advises you not to take the herb if you are photosensitive (allergic to the sun), and to discontinue taking it two weeks before elective surgery, because it might interact with anesthesia.

COGNITIVE THERAPY— THINKING YOURSELF WELL

"I'm a total failure. I never do anything right!"

"This proves the world is no damn good."

"I never get a break."

"I just can't control myself."

Those kinds of negative thoughts can lead to depression, say psychologists who practice cognitive therapy. But by learning how to recognize and change these and other *cognitive distortions,* you can banish the blues.

IIIII➤ *Breakthrough Studies*

Doctors at the University of Pittsburgh studied more than 400 people with clinical depression who didn't get better with *citalopram* (Celexa) and then switched to either another medication or to cognitive therapy.

Result: Both groups did equally well, with about 25% of patients depression free after three months. On the downside, cognitive therapy took a little longer to work; on the upside, it didn't have any side effects.

And in a study published in the *Journal of the American Medical Association,* researchers from the Department of Psychology at the University of Pennsylvania found that ten sessions of cognitive therapy were more effective than other types of treatments in preventing repeat suicide attempts in people who had recently tried to commit suicide.

How it works: Cognitive therapy is based on the principle that your feelings result from your *cognitions*—the messages you give yourself via your thoughts, says David D. Burns, MD, a clinical professor at the Stanford University School of Medicine and author of *Feeling Good* (Avon). "In fact," he says, "your thoughts often have much more to do with how you feel than what is actually happening in your life." By learning to change the way you think about things, he explains, you can change your basic values and beliefs. "And when you do, you will often experience profound, lasting and positive changes in your mood, outlook and productivity."

Counterproductive Thoughts

Dr. Burns describes 10 cognitive distortions…

1. **All-or-nothing thinking.** Seeing things in black-and-white categories.

2. **Overgeneralization.** You see a single negative event as a never-ending pattern of defeat.

3. **Mental filter.** You pick out a single negative detail and dwell on it.

4. **Disqualifying the positive.** You reject positive experiences by insisting they "don't count."

5. **Jumping to conclusions.** You make a negative interpretation even though the facts don't support it.

6. **Magnification or minimization.** You exaggerate the importance of things (such as a goof-up) or inappropriately shrink things (such as a personal strength).

7. **Emotional reasoning.** You assume your negative emotions reflect the way things really are.

8. **Should statements.** You try to motivate yourself with shoulds and shouldn'ts.

9. **Labeling and mislabeling.** You describe an event with language that is emotionally loaded.

10. **Personalization.** You see yourself as the cause of a negative event that you weren't responsible for.

Try this: Dr Burns says to write down your negative thoughts, identify the cognitive distortions you're using and substitute a "rational response."

For example, you think, "I never do anything right." That's an *overgeneralization,* he says. The rational response is "Nonsense! I do a lot of things right."

Or you think "I'll make a fool of myself." That's *labeling*. The rational response is "I may appear foolish, but that doesn't make me a fool."

ⓘ The books *Feeling Good: The New Mood Therapy* (Avon) and *The Feeling Good Handbook* (Plume), both by Dr. Burns, are a complete guide to using cognitive therapy to overcome depression. Or you can find a cognitive therapist through the "Find A Therapist" feature of the Association for Behavioral and Cognitive Therapy, *www.abct.org*, or by calling 212-647-1890.

SAMᴇ—A NUTRIENT FOR A NEW YOU

You may have heard of Sammy Davis, Jr.…Same old, same old…and S.A.M.E. (Okay, you probably haven't heard of the Society of American Military Engineers.) But *SAMe*…what in the Sam Hill is that? Well, if you're depressed, this oddly named natural compound might be one of the best things that ever happened to you.

▶ *Breakthrough Study*

Researchers at Yale Prevention Research Center analyzed the results of 11 studies on SAMe (*S-adenosyl-methionine*) and depression, and found the natural compound had a "favorable and significant" effect on relieving the problem.

Who should take SAMe? "A patient with mild depression who has a strong interest in natural remedies," says David Mischoulon, MD, PhD, a psychiatrist at Harvard Medical School. Or, he says, if antidepressants haven't worked for you, or you've been daunted by their side effects, you might want to try taking SAMe

DEFEATING DEPRESSION ONE ACTION AT A TIME

Studies show that *Behavioral Activation Therapy* is as effective as cognitive therapy or antidepressants in clearing up depression, says Christopher Martell, PhD, a psychologist in private practice in Seattle, clinical associate professor at the University of Washington and coauthor of *Overcoming Depression One Step at a Time: The New Behavioral Activation Approach to Getting Your Life Back* (New Harbinger).

New thinking: What is behavioral activation? Committing to a depression-defeating action—even if you don't feel motivated to do it. Example: You may not feel like going for a walk, but if you take a walk in spite of how you feel, you may improve your mood.

Trap: You commit to something that's not likely to occur, such as getting up at 6:00 a.m. when you've been getting out of bed at 10:00 a.m.

Solution: Break the action down into small steps. Try to get up at 9:45 a.m. a couple of days during the week. Once you're doing that, get up at 9:30 a.m. In other words, take small, doable steps with a high likelihood of success.

"Set a limit on what you're going to accomplish so that it's actually doable, instead of having the continual experience of failing because you're trying to do too much," says Dr. Martell.

supplements, with your doctor's approval and supervision.

He also points out that SAMe works *faster* than antidepressants…and may help boost the power of tricyclic antidepressant drugs such as *amitriptyline* (Elavil).

How it works: No one knows for sure. Scientists do know that SAMe helps produce neurotransmitters, the brain chemicals that regulate mood and phospholipids, a crucial factor in strong, well-functioning brain cells.

Suggested intake: "Start with a dosage of 1,600 mg a day—either 800 mg twice a day, or 400 mg four time a day—for about two or three weeks, or until you start to feel the antidepressant effects," says Sol J. Grazi, MD, an assistant professor at the University of Colorado School of Medicine, and author of *SAMe: The Safe and Natural Way to Combat Depression and Relieve the Pain of Osteoarthritis* (Prima). Once you're feeling better, he recommends gradually reducing the dosage to 800 mg or even 400 mg a day, as long as your symptoms don't return.

 SAMe supplements are widely available.

MAGNETS—BEYOND THE REFRIGERATOR DOOR

How could holding a big magnet to your head help cure depression? Scientists don't know. They just know that it does—particularly in people who don't seem to get any better taking antidepressants.

▶ *Breakthrough Study*

Doctors at the University of Pennsylvania and 23 other hospitals and clinics in the United States, Canada and Australia studied 310 people with clinical depression who hadn't been helped by antidepressants. Half received four to six weeks of 35-minute, five-days-a-week treatments with *transcranial magnetic stimulation* (TMS)—holding an electromagnetic coil to the head and turning on an electric current, sending magnetic waves into the brain. Half received a fake TMS treatment.

Approximately 17% of the patients receiving TMS got better, compared to 8% of the patients receiving the fake treatment. There were few side effects.

"TMS provides a well-tolerated treatment option to patients whose depression is

YOGA—BENT ON FEELING BETTER

Neurotransmitters are brain chemicals that control mood. GABA—*gamma-aminobutyric acid*—is one of the most important. When GABA levels are high, you're likely to be happy and relaxed. When GABA levels are low, you're likely to be depressed and anxious. Yoga increases GABA.

The study: Researchers at Boston University measured before-and-after GABA levels in two groups. One group practiced yoga for an hour, and the other group read for an hour. Yoga boosted GABA by 27%; reading didn't budge the neurochemical.

"Yoga should be explored as a treatment for disorders with low GABA levels, such as depression," says Chris Streeter, MD, an assistant professor of psychiatry and neurology.

Other recent scientific developments: Yoga reduced depression levels in alcoholics in rehab...an analysis of five studies on yoga and depression showed "beneficial effects"... yoga worked better than antidepressants in 30 people with depression...yoga eased depression (and anxiety, anger and confusion) in 13 psychiatric patients...yoga eased depression in 28 college students.

☀ The Web site of the magazine *Yoga Journal*—*www.yogajournal.com*—has a directory of yoga teachers, with a search function to find teachers and classes in your zip code. Search the "Teachers and Studios" category. Or check the Yellow Pages under "Yoga." To find a yoga therapist—a yoga teacher trained to work with people with various health problems—check out the Web site of the International Association of Yoga Therapists at *www.iayt.org.*

otherwise treatment-resistant," says John P. O'Reardon, MD, associate professor of psychiatry at the University of Pennsylvania, and lead author of the study. "Since TMS is administered via the scalp and therefore goes directly to the brain, it avoids the side effects common to anti-depressant drugs, such as weight gain, drowsi-ness and sexual dysfunction." (Common sexual problems from antidepressants include erectile dysfunction, delayed ejaculation and lowered sexual desire.)

"TMS offers new hope to patients," he says.

Other studies have found TMS can help depression in patients with Parkinson's disease (a common problem)...help patients with recur-rent depression who have had a relapse...and improve memory in depressed patients.

Talk to your doctor about whether TMS is right for you.

ANXIETY—FROM PANIC TO PEACE

There's a difference between normal fear and anxiety, explains Robert L. Dupont, MD, clinical professor of psychiatry at Georgetown University School of Medicine, founding president of the Anxiety Disorders Association of America and coauthor of *The Anxiety Cure* (Wiley).

"*Fear* is the experience of an immediate, real danger," he says. "*Anxiety* is the body's signal of possible, future danger, a sort of emo-tional early warning system."

And when you're *chronically* anxious—"if your heart sinks whenever you hear a siren or whenever your phone rings, because it *might* be the police telling you that one of your loved ones has been killed"—then you may have an anxiety disorder, says Dr. Dupont. If so, you're one of about 25 million chronically anxious Americans.

Other signs of anxiety disorder, says Dr. Dupont, include...

● **You experience panicky feelings—** even a full-scale panic attack—when you leave home, drive on a highway, go to a shopping mall or get on an elevator.

● **Your intense feelings of worry,** which most other people do not experience, wake you up at night or come unexpectedly at any time of day.

● **You spend hours every day think-ing about,** fearing and expecting these anx-ious, panicky feelings.

● **You give up important activities in your life** because of anxiety and the fear of panic attacks.

There are many theories about the cause of chronic anxiety, says Edward H. Drummond, MD, a psychiatrist in private practice in New Hampshire. Genes...past experiences...daily stress. But, whatever the cause, he says, "there are many other treatments for anxiety besides medications, such as relaxation techniques." And scientists are finding that one of the best relaxation techniques for chronic anxiety is autogenic training...

AUTOGENIC TRAINING— "I AM SUPREMELY CALM"

"I am supremely calm"...Easier said than done, right? No, easily done *because* it's said—when you practice the anxiety-reducing mind-body relaxation exercise called *autogenic training.*

▶ *Breakthrough Studies*

Researchers in England divided 93 nursing students into three groups. One group learned autogenic training (AT), one group received "laughter therapy" (told jokes and watched funny videos) and the third group didn't receive

111

any training. After two months, those who learned AT had far lower anxiety levels than either of the other two groups, along with lower blood pressure and lower pulse rates.

● **Post-traumatic stress disorder.** In another study, Japanese researchers tested out AT on firefighters with post-traumatic stress disorder (PTSD). After two months, their PTSD had significantly lessened.

● **Anxiety and heart disease.** Researchers in England found that AT reduced anxiety in patients who had had a coronary angioplasty (an invasive medical procedure that widens a disease-narrowed artery with an inflatable balloon).

Why it works: "Autogenic training teaches you to create a feeling of warmth and heaviness throughout your body, thereby experiencing a profound state of physical relaxation and mental peace," explains Raymond Lloyd Richmond, PhD, a psychologist in private practice in San Francisco.

What to do: Here are Dr. Richmond's instructions for one session of AT…

Practice in a quiet place. Remove your shoes and wear loose clothing. Lie flat on your back in bed or on a carpeted floor, or sit in a comfortable chair. Warm up with deep breathing, exhaling to a mental count that is twice as long as you inhale. *Then mentally repeat the following phrases…*

● **My arms and legs are getting limp, heavy and warm (1–2 times)**

● **My arms and legs are getting heavier and warmer (1–2 times)**

● **My arms and legs are completely heavy and warm (1–2 times)**

● **I feel supremely calm (1–2 times)**

● **My chest feels warm and pleasant (6–8 times)**

WHAT IS ANXIETY DISORDER?

There are seven distinct types of anxiety disorders and they are among the most common emotional problems in the United States, affecting more than 25 million people, says Reneau Z. Peurifoy, a psychologist in private practice in Citrus Heights, CA, and author of *Overcoming Anxiety* (Owl Books). *He describes the seven disorders…*

1. **Generalized anxiety disorder** (GAD). You experience unrealistic or excessive anxiety and worry about two or more life circumstances for more than six months. You also have six or more of 18 symptoms of anxiety, such as feeling shaky, dry mouth and trouble falling or staying asleep.

2. **Panic disorder.** You have unexpected panic attacks—with symptoms such as shortness of breath, dizziness and racing heartbeat—for no apparent reason.

3. **Panic disorder with agoraphobia.** You tend to avoid places or situations where escape might be difficult or embarrassing, or where help might be unavailable in the event of a panic attack.

4. **Social phobia.** You're afraid of embarrassing or humiliating yourself in social situations.

5. **Obsessive-compulsive disorder.** An obsession is a persistent idea, thought, image or impulse that is senseless or repulsive and intrudes on your awareness; a compulsion is an action repeated in a ritualistic fashion. Compulsions are usually done in response to an obsession—for example, if you fear contamination (the obsession) you might engage in excessive hand washing (the compulsion).

6. **Simple phobia.** Also called a specific phobia, these can involve fear of flying, heights, insects, et cetera.

7. **Post-traumatic stress disorder.** Severe stress and anxiety resulting from a traumatic event, such as major surgery, a natural disaster, assault, rape or wartime combat duty.

● **My heartbeat is calm and steady** (6–8 times)

   ● **I feel supremely calm (6–8 times)**

End the session by counting backward from 5 to 1 and then repeating...

   ● **Eyes open.** Supremely calm. Fully alert.

He recommends practicing this two or three times a day. "If you don't feel the results of what you are saying," he advises, "take the time to repeat" the phrase.

☀ Dr. Richmond provides a free, three-month course in autogenic training at his Web site, *www.guidetopsychology.com*. Other resources include the book *Autogenic Training* by Kai Kermani (Souvenir Press), and the CD *Progressive Relaxation and Autogenic Training* by Carolyn McManus.

AMINO ACIDS—HIGH PROTEIN FOR ANXIETY

Protein is composed of 22 building blocks called *amino acids*. Scientists divide them into *essential* (you can only get them from food) and *nonessential* (the body manufactures them). Two of those 22 amino acids may be particularly "essential" for people with chronic anxiety.

||▶ *Breakthrough Studies*

Researchers in Japan asked 108 healthy people with high levels of chronic anxiety to take either a placebo or a supplement of the amino acids L-lysine and L-arginine for one week. At the end of the week, they gave all the participants a mentally stressful written test and measured blood levels of their stress hormones.

Result: The people taking the amino acids had much lower anxiety levels during and after taking the stressful test, and had lower levels of anxiety-generated stress hormones.

In another study, the researchers gave either L-arginine and L-lysine or a placebo to 29 anxious people for 10 days before they gave a public speech. Right after the speech, those taking the amino acids had lower levels of stress hormones and less sweaty skin (galvanic skin response)—in fact, they had the same level of hormones and skin response as people with typically low levels of anxiety.

"These results point to a combination of L-lysine and L-arginine as a potentially useful dietary intervention in healthy people with high levels of mental stress and anxiety," say the researchers.

Why it works: The researchers theorize that the two amino acids affect serotonin

---

TEST ANXIETY—OMEGA-3 FATTY ACIDS EARN AN "A"

You feel so nervous about that upcoming test you can hardly study—a self-fulfilling prophecy for failure.

"Test anxiety is an incapacitating academic syndrome," say researchers from the Gonda Brain Research Center in Israel. Could brain-balancing omega-3 fatty acids help? To find out, the researchers gave students with test anxiety a nutritional supplement that included omega-3s. They had improved concentration, less fatigue, better ability to organize their notes and other study materials and got a good night's sleep before the next day's test. (The researchers don't say whether they got better grades.)

Suggested intake: Research shows a fish oil supplement containing 1 gram of EPA (eicosapentaenoic acid) and DHA (docosahexaenoic acid) helps improve mood and calm the mind. Fish oil supplements are widely available. The Nordic Naturals brand has been used in many scientific studies that have proven the value of fish oil; their Ultimate Omega product contains 650 mg of EPA and 450 mg of DHA, or 1.1 grams.

"receptors" in the digestive tract and brain, increasing levels of the good-feeling chemical.

Suggested intake: The researchers used a daily dose of 2.5 to 3 grams of lysine and 2.5 to 3 grams of arginine.

ℹ️ L-lysine and L-arginine supplements are widely available.

Caution: Arginine can stimulate genital or oral herpes (cold sores) in those infected with the virus.

DENTAL ANXIETY? SNIFF AN ORANGE

Sugar causes cavities. So does dental anxiety…

A survey shows that people who are afraid of the dentist—about 15% of the population—have fewer dental checkups (no surprise) and more cavities. Your nose can help your teeth.

⫸ *Breakthrough Study*

Researchers at the Medical University of Vienna in Austria asked 200 people who were waiting for a dental procedure to sniff the essential oil of either lavender or orange. The odors reduced anxiety and improved mood, say the researchers, and could help fearful dental patients.

What to do: Take a small bottle of either lavender or orange essential oil (or a combination of both) to the dentist's office, and sniff it in the waiting room.

ℹ️ Serenity Synergy, which contains lavender and sweet orange essential oils, is available from Arlys Naturals. The company also sells Anti-Stress Synergy, which contains several citrus essential oils (pink grapefruit, lemon) and lavender; Calm Synergy, which contains lavender and Harmony Synergy, which contains lavender and pink grapefruit essential oils. Visit the Web site of Arlys Naturals, *www.arlysnaturals.com,* or call 877-502-7597 or 954-523-9513; e-mail *susan@arlysnaturals.com.*

EASE MEDICAL ANXIETY WITH HYPNOSIS

A long device with a light and a camera on the end is snaked into your colon…

A narrow tube is inserted into your breast and a wire clips off possible cancerous tissue…

The anesthesiologist asks you to count backward from one hundred, while the surgeon looks over his scalpels…

Medical tests and surgery are guaranteed to produce *anxiety*—anxiety about possible pain and discomfort, anxiety about possible postprocedure announcements of a dreadful disease. Self-hypnosis can help.

⫸ *Breakthrough Studies*

● **For colonoscopy.** Doctors at Baylor University in Texas taught six people about to have colonoscopy a self-hypnosis technique for relaxation. Compared to people who didn't have hypnosis, they had less anxiety, less pain, less need for sedating medication during the procedure and quicker recovery after the procedure, with fewer incidents of dizziness and nausea.

● **For breast biopsy.** Doctors at Harvard Medical School taught self-hypnosis to 82 of 236 women undergoing breast biopsy. The women who didn't learn the technique had more than double the level of anxiety before the procedure. "Hypnosis provides powerful anxiety relief without undue cost," say the researchers.

● **For invasive circulatory and kidney procedures.** A group of patients undergoing invasive testing for circulatory and kidney conditions received self-hypnosis. They had less anxiety and used fewer pain-relieving drugs than other patients undergoing the procedures, and the procedures were shorter, say doctors from Harvard Medical School. The benefits were greatest for those with the highest levels of anxiety before the procedures.

• **For surgery.** Doctors at Yale University School of Medicine taught a group of presurgical patients self-hypnosis techniques, while others received standard care. Those learning self-hypnosis had a 56% decrease in anxiety when they entered the operating room—while the standard-care group had a 47% increase! "Hypnosis significantly alleviates preoperative anxiety," say the researchers.

What to do: "Prior to a medical procedure or surgery, hypnosis can reduce anticipatory fear, anxiety and tension, and increase confidence by developing a calmer, positive state of mind," says Josie Hadley, founder and director of the California Institute for Medical Hypnosis and coauthor of *Hypnosis for Change* (New Harbinger).

Self-hypnosis starts with an "induction" that relaxes the body, explains Hadley. Then it continues with a "suggestion." *Here is the process she recommends...*

1. **Beginning the induction.** Take a nice deep breath, close the eyes and begin to relax.

2. **Systematic relaxation of the body.** Just think about relaxing every muscle in your body—relax your face and jaw...your temples, eyes and eyelids...the back of your neck and your shoulders...your lower back...your arms...your chest...your stomach...your legs...your toes.

HEY, PUTTERS—ACUPUNCTURE CURES THE YIPS!

About 30 to 50% of golfers experience *the yips*—an involuntary muscular jerk, spasm or cramp during putting, usually of putts shorter than five feet, and usually during competitive or tournament play. The problem, which tends to strike older, experienced golfers, adds about five strokes a round. Golfers are often told to change their grip or their putter—or even to take a tranquilizer! Maybe the clubhouse needs an acupuncturist.

New approach: A 65-year-old man with more than 30 years of golfing experience asked for an acupuncture treatment for the yips, reports Palle Rosted, MD, an acupuncturist in England, in the journal *Acupuncture in Medicine*. (Acupuncture is a technique of Traditional Chinese Medicine, in which tiny, painless needles are inserted into specific points to balance and increase chi, the fundamental life force that energizes the body.)

"On average, he was playing golf three times a week and had a handicap of fourteen," says Rosted. "The yips started two years earlier, for no apparent reason. During the attacks, he feels that his upper extremities are frozen when he is making a short putt. Initially, he tried to solve the problem by changing to the left hand—he is right-handed—without success."

After one treatment, the symptoms disappeared!

Rosted continued to treat his patient every other week, for five treatments. When he checked up on him two years later, the golfer "was still enjoying his golf using his right hand, without symptoms of the yips."

What happens: No one knows what causes the yips, but a report from the Mayo Clinic speculates that it's caused by anxiety, overuse of muscles, or both. In this case, the acupuncture points used were intended to decrease anxiety and muscular tension.

What to do: Consider seeing an acupuncturist—and tell the practitioner that the yips were successfully eliminated in one case by treatment at the points GV20, EX-HN-1 (*Si Shen Cong*) and TE5. To locate an acupuncturist near you, (see page 333 in Chapter 12, "Men's Health").

3. **Creating imagery of deeper relaxation.** Drift and float into a deeper and deeper level of total relaxation. Feel a heavy, heavy weight being lifted off your shoulders.

4. **Deepening the trance.** You are in an elevator taking you to a special, peaceful and beautiful place. Feel yourself begin to descend. As you watch the number of floors passing, relax more and more. You see the number ten…and now the number nine…and now the number eight…

5. **Induction.** A pleasant calm flows over you, and as you relax more and more, you know you are being taken care of. You can just flow with the deep relaxation. By the time you enter (the surgery) (the procedure), you are completely relaxed. The (surgeon) (the medical personnel) are experts and are extremely capable. You are just fine, you are just fine. Now imagine you are (in recovery) (finished with the procedure). You feel relaxed, you are just fine. You feel comfortable and relaxed. All is well.

☀ If you would like to learn self-hypnosis from a qualified medical hypnotherapist, you can request a referral by contacting the American Psychotherapy and Medical Hypnosis Association (APMHA), 1100 Kittitas Street, Wenatchee, WA 98801 (509-662-5131); e-mail *admin@apmha.com* or visit *www.apmha.com*.

WHAT CAN I DO ABOUT WORRYING?

Worrying itself is not a problem, says Steve Shearer, PhD, of the Anxiety and Stress Disorders Institute of Maryland. "Worry is a normal response when you are unsure about things. It may help you feel more prepared in the short run. It may even help you feel some control over what could happen. Worry may 'work' at that time—but it can become a bad habit."

Worry is a bad habit when you can't control it, he explains—when it gets in the way of daily activities, makes your life miserable and disturbs your sleep. Worry, he says, becomes a problem when it becomes a way of life.

Fortunately, there are ways to escape the worrying.

▸ *Breakthrough Study*

There are many ways to worry less, says Dr. Shearer. His recommendations, from the journal *American Family Physician*…

● **Remember that nearly all worries are only thoughts.**

● **Remember that bad things that you worry about hardly ever happen.** Worry won't protect you from the rare bad things that do happen.

● **Stop trying to get rid of worries.** It doesn't work, and it may make things worse. Instead, accept worry, but don't give it your full attention whenever you think of it.

● **Use "worry periods" for 10 to 20 minutes at set times during the day.** Give your worries your full attention only at these times. At other times, remind yourself to save thinking about a worry until your next worry period.

● **Find out what things calm you.** Try to do things such as exercise, relaxation, massage, prayer, yoga, music, journal writing or taking a hot bath. Do it to calm yourself—not to get rid of your worries.

● **Being sure about things is only a feeling—it is rarely real.** Practice noticing and accepting the many things each day that you can't feel certain about and can't control.

● **Ask yourself, Am I making too much of the risk?** Will this even matter next week? What would I be feeling if I were not worrying? Am I giving in to my worries instead of managing them? What can I do instead of worrying more?

EXERCISE AND PANIC ATTACKS

Panic attacks don't happen when you're faced with a truly panicky situation—a tiger that's escaped from its cage, a tidal wave at a beach resort, an avalanche on a ski slope. No, they're *self-generated*...based on the fear of having another panic attack!

Reneau Z. Peurifoy, a psychologist in private practice in Citrus Heights, CA, and author of *Overcoming Anxiety* (Henry Holt), describes the typical development of a "panic disorder"...

You're a high-anxiety person and one day (for no apparent reason) you suddenly develop a "panic attack"—a rapid heartbeat, deep and rapid breathing (hyperventilation), muscle tension, dry mouth and many other symptoms of the classic fight-or-flight response. You're *frightened*. You see a doctor who tells you that your problem is "just nerves." But as an anxious person you start *worrying*—that the symptoms will recur, and that you'll lose control. You start paying close and near-constant attention to your internal sensations, such as your heartbeat and breathing. And you become *so* worried about having another panic attack—so overwrought and so concerned—that you trigger another one! You are now in the vicious, self-generated "anxiety/panic" cycle of panic disorder, explains Dr. Peurifoy.

Your way out might be a workout.

▐▶ *Breakthrough Studies*

Researchers at Southern Methodist University in Texas studied 39 people with panic disorder—and found the more physically inactive the person, the greater their level of "anxiety

---

THE CURE FOR "HEALTH ANXIETY"

Hypochondria are the persistent and distressing preoccupations with fears and thoughts that you have a serious illness, says Dr. Shearer. You talk to your doctor to reassure yourself that you're not sick. You read medical textbooks. You look at Web sites. You look in the mirror, checking your "symptoms"—again and again and again. And you tend to pay attention to "evidence" that confirms your suspicions and ignore evidence that doesn't. About 6% of Americans suffer from a mild or severe form of this type of "health anxiety," says Dr. Shearer. *But there is a cure...*

• Stop seeking reassurance. "If you repeatedly seek reassurance from your physician or spouse, encourage them to gradually withhold the reassurance that only perpetuates the problem," he says. "Stop 'investigating' on the Internet. The relief you feel will not last, and you will just feel the need to check more. Sometimes your checking can scare you more."

• Try cognitive therapy. A study in the *Journal of the American Medical Association* showed that six sessions of cognitive therapy significantly lower hypochondriacal symptoms, beliefs and attitudes. The therapy helps you spot and correct "cognitive distortions," such as exaggerating the importance of benign symptoms or identifying a normal bodily function as a symptom. You can find a cognitive therapist near you through the "Find a Therapist" feature of the Association for Behavioral and Cognitive Therapy, *www.abct.org,* or by calling 212-647-1890.

• Read a book. *Worried Sick? The Exaggerated Fear of Physical Illness: How to Put Physical Symptoms Into Perspective, How to Avoid Unnecessary Worry* by Fredric Neuman (Hadrian).

sensitivity" to the physical symptoms of a possible panic attack, and the greater the overall severity of their panic disorder.

In another study, the researchers found that 10 weeks of regular exercise (running) was as effective as medication in relieving the symptoms of panic disorder.

How it works: "Desensitization to the physical sensations of panic is achieved by creating sensations similar to those in panic," explains Elke Zuercher-White, PhD, a psychologist in private practice in California and author of *An End to Panic* (New Harbinger). "Your aim is to achieve the new experience of feeling panic-like sensations without fearing them."

GINGKO—FOR ANXIETY ABOUT ALZHEIMER'S

The herb *gingko biloba* is often recommended to slow, stop or reverse memory loss. But a lot of older people also *worry* about memory loss and a dismal descent into dementia. Gingko can help with that, too.

The study: Doctors at the Clinic for Psychiatry and Psychotherapy in Giessen, Germany, gave 107 people with "generalized anxiety disorder" either ginkgo or a placebo. After one month, those taking the herb had nearly twice the reduction in anxiety as those taking the placebo.

"Ginkgo may be of particular value in older people with anxiety about mental decline," say the doctors, in the *Journal of Psychiatric Research.*

Suggested intake: The dose used in the study was 480 mg a day.

Caution: Ginkgo biloba can boost the power of blood-thinning medications for heart disease, such as aspirin or *warfarin* (Coumadin), and of glucose-lowering oral medications for diabetes, such as *metformin* (Glucophage). Take ginkgo biloba only after a conversation with your doctor or pharmacist.

"Exercise can create physical sensations such as rapid heartbeat and sweating that produce fear in people with panic disorder," agrees Jasper A. J. Smits, PhD, in the Department of Psychology at Southern Methodist University. "The activity may provide necessary exposure to these sensations so that patients with panic disorder can begin to recover."

What to do: Talk to your doctor, psychologist or psychiatrist about whether exercise is right for you.

TUNE OUT WORRY WITH MUSIC

There's a reason those angels are playing harps—music can be heavenly. Soothing, peaceful, soul satisfying. The exact opposite of anxiety.

▶ *Breakthrough Studies*

Doctors studying music and anxiety usually test the peace-creating power of tunes in the most anxiety-producing situations—medical tests, procedures and advanced illness…

● **Heart surgery.** Sixty adults over 65 scheduled for heart surgery were divided into two groups. One group listened to music during and after surgery and the other group did not. Those listening to music had much less anxiety—and after the surgery, they were removed from their respirators sooner.

● **Advanced illness.** Researchers at the Cleveland Clinic Cancer Center tested music therapy on 200 cancer patients. Not only did it reduce their anxiety, but it also lessened pain and helped relieve shortness of breath. It even cheered up visiting family members. "Music therapy is invaluable," say the researchers.

● **Kidney disease.** Thirty-six patients with kidney disease on *hemodialysis* (the mechanical cleansing of blood) were divided into two groups. One group listened to music during hemodialysis and the other group did not. The music group had much less anxiety.

- **Burns.** Doctors in Korea divided burn patients into two groups. One group listened to self-selected music through headphones while their dressings were being changed, and the other group did not. The music group had much lower levels of anxiety and pain.

- **Colonoscopy.** People who listened to self-selected music during a colonoscopy requested much less sedation than those who didn't listen to music, and reported much less discomfort, say doctors in India.

- **Cesarean delivery.** Women listening to music during a cesarean delivery had much lower levels of anxiety than women who didn't, say doctors in Taiwan.

- **Outpatient surgery.** Doctors in Australia divided people undergoing outpatient surgery into two groups. One group listened to self-selected music and the other group did not. The music group had significantly reduced anxiety compared to the nonmusic group.

What to do: Notice that most of these studies used *self-selected* music. Those angels dig harps—but country music might be your idea of cloud nine. "There is no one style of music that is more therapeutic than all the rest," says a spokesperson for the American Music Therapy Association. "Individual preferences are what is important."

YOGA FOR STAGE FRIGHT

Your heart is racing, your breathing is fast and shallow, you're trembling and dizzy and you just broke out in a sweat. Are you standing on the edge of a cliff? No, you're standing behind a podium near the edge of a stage…about to give a speech…and you've got a curtain-lowering case of *stage fright*—reportedly the number one fear among Americans.

"The deep fear associated with public speaking or performance as a musician, singer or actor is the fear of embarrassment and negative evaluation by others—the fear of making a fool of yourself," says Janet E. Esposito, a licensed clinical social worker and author of *In The SpotLight: Overcome Your Fear of Public Speaking and Performing* (Strong Books). Stage fright, she says, takes a toll on self-confidence and self-esteem, and can lead to missed career opportunities. What to do?

Practice yoga!

▶ *Breakthrough Study*

Sat Bir S. Khalsa, PhD, an assistant professor of medicine at Harvard Medical School, conducted a study on yoga and stage fright—formally known as "performance anxiety"—with musicians attending the summer fellowship program of the Tanglewood Music Center, the Boston Symphony Orchestra's academy for advanced musical study.

Performance anxiety afflicts nearly 70% of musicians, says Dr. Khalsa. "It can lead to serious professional consequences for the performer, including leaving the profession." He also notes that medications typically used to control anxiety, such as *paroxetine* (Paxil), could impair performance.

To see if yoga could decrease performance anxiety, Dr. Khalsa enrolled 10 musicians in a two-month course at the Kripalu Center for Yoga and Health in Lenox, MA, during which they practiced yoga postures, meditation and deep breathing and also attended a weekly class to discuss yoga- and meditation-inspired strategies to overcome performance anxiety.

Results: By the end of the two months, their scores for performance anxiety during solo performances had decreased by an average of nearly 20%. A second study on musicians and yoga produced similar reductions in performance anxiety.

Why it works: "Yoga improves the physical and psychological capacity to cope with stress, and induces a state of peace and harmony," says Dr. Khalsa. "For someone with performance anxiety, it's very useful."

Try this: If you want instant relief from stage fright, try *slow breathing,* says Dr. Khalsa. *His instructions...*

"Keep your mental focus on the breath—whether it's the sound of the breath, or the flow in and out of your nostrils or the feeling in the abdomen and chest. When your mind wanders, simply bring it back to the breath in a nonjudgmental, nonstressful way. Breathe as slowly as you can comfortably breathe—absolutely normally, without any sense of 'air hunger' or the need to breathe more. Just intend to *slow* your breath. This process is the opposite of anxiety, and will help overcome performance anxiety whenever you're experiencing it."

KAVA WORKS, BUT IS IT SAFE?

"Kava has been shown beyond reasonable doubt to have an anti-anxiety effect," say researchers from England who analyzed all the current scientific research on herbs for anxiety. But is this calming herb from the South Pacific safe? Maybe not.

The study: Researchers at the University of Sydney investigated the effect of kava on the liver, after previous studies had shown liver damage among kava-takers. The researchers found that *kavain*—one of the active ingredients in the herb—narrowed blood vessels in the liver and damaged liver cells.

What to do: Kava has been banned in several European countries because of concerns about liver damage, and the FDA has issued a consumer advisory about the herb. For now, consider less worrisome ways to lower anxiety...

To find a yoga class near you, use the Yoga Directory at the Web site of *Yoga Journal* magazine, *www.yogajournal.com.* Or check your local Yellow Pages for yoga teachers and yoga schools in your area.

Also helpful: Janet E. Esposito offers a few additional tips for reducing stage fright...

● **Accept your fearful feelings—they'll pass more easily.**

● **Think about past successes.**

● **Prepare ahead of time and be well practiced and rehearsed.**

● **Stand in a self-assured, confident posture**—even if you don't feel that way.

● **Focus on your purpose for speaking or performing.**

● **Give up trying to be perfect**—know it's okay to be human and make mistakes.

You'll find more information and tools for overcoming stage fright at Janet E. Esposito's Web site, *www.performanceanxiety.com.* In The Spotlight, LLC, PO Box 494, Bridgewater, CT 06752 (877-814-7705 or 860-210-1499, fax 203-743-1110); e-mail *jesposito@performance anxiety.com.*

HOSTILITY CAN HURT YOUR HEART

"High hostility may predict heart disease more than other risk factors, such as cholesterol..."

"Harboring hostility may be linked to unhealthy lungs..."

"Hostility increases hypertension risk..."

Those are just a few of the many headlines about hostility and health from recent years. Hostility has also been linked to slower wound healing...adult asthma...more inflammation (a contributor to diseases diverse as heart disease, arthritis, Alzheimer's and diabetes)…and even gum disease.

Hostility is the strong and constant tendency to feel impatient…annoyed…irritable…cynical…and blaming. You feel like the world is against you and you need to do something about it—now! That mind-set, say scientists, generates stress hormones that raise blood pressure, damage arteries, weaken immunity, batter your brain and gut—and shorten your life.

"Anger is a toxin to your body," says Redford Williams, PhD, a professor in the Department of Psychiatry and Behavioral Science at Duke University Medical Center and author of *Anger Kills: Seventeen Strategies for Controlling the Hostility That Can Harm Your Health* (Harper). "Hostile persons must develop skills to counter their natural tendencies."

A good place to start is to practice the skill of forgiveness.

FORGIVE FOR GOOD HEALTH

"Forgiveness may serve as an antidote to the health-eroding process of hostility," says Everett L. Worthington, Jr., PhD, a professor in the Department of Psychology at Virginia Commonwealth University in Richmond and author of *The Power of Forgiving* (Templeton Foundation) and many other books about forgiving.

⮞ *Breakthrough Studies*

Researchers in the Veterans Affair New York Harbor Healthcare System studied 99 people. First, the participants described their own level of forgiveness—whether or not they typically forgave people who hurt them.

Those with the highest level of forgiveness had the lowest blood pressure.

Next, the high-forgivers and low-forgivers were asked to recall an event that made them angry. Both groups had a spike in blood pressure—but the blood pressure of the high-forgivers returned to normal more quickly.

"Forgiveness may be related to overall reductions in blood pressure levels and may aid in cardiovascular recovery from stress," say the researchers.

Other studies show similar health benefits from forgiveness…

• **People who are more forgiving have fewer symptoms of ill health,** use fewer medications, sleep better and have less fatigue, report researchers from the Department of Psychology at the University of Tennessee.

• **Angry people who took a forgiveness training course had significant reductions in blood pressure,** report researchers from the Florida Hospital in Orlando.

• **Of 61 people with chronic low back pain,** those with higher scores in forgiveness had lower levels of anger *and* pain, say doctors at the Duke University Medical Center.

What to do: "The decision to forgive someone can take place instantly," says Dr. Worthington.

"It's like flipping on a light switch. You can decide, 'I'm going to change my behavior toward this person who harmed me. I won't get even with them. I won't hold this against them. I'll try to treat them fairly.' " You can make that decision not because you feel loving toward the person, but because you care about your own health, says Dr. Worthington. That *decisional forgiveness* will help you feel more positive, he says.

But if you want truly profound results—permanently replacing feelings of anger with feelings of forgiveness—you need to take the next step to *emotional forgiveness*.

"Even though you've made the decision to forgive, you may still be really angry," he says. You may think about the hurt, talk to your spouse, rehearse it moment by moment. It takes time to replace all those negative, unforgiving, health-eroding emotions—hostility, resentment, bitterness, hatred—with the positive emotions of empathy, sympathy, compassion and love.

Dr. Worthington says there are five steps to reach emotional forgiveness. The initial step is the one you've already taken—deciding to forgive. *The other five steps, says Dr. Worthington, are the way to R.E.A.C.H. forgiveness…*

R: **Recall the hurts.** Select the event that hurt you and write about what happened. Don't inhibit any negative emotions. But don't excessively blame the transgressor, either. Try to describe the event as objectively as possible.

E: **Empathize** (sympathize, show compassion, experience love). To empathize, talk to a friend or counselor as if you were the offending person talking. Write yourself a letter from the offending person's viewpoint. To sympathize, reflect on the person's background—possible reasons why he/she may have hurt you, such as addiction or a troubled childhood. To show compassion, think about how you could help the person. To experience love, talk about how you have loved this person in the past, and how you might act lovingly again.

A: **Altruistic gift of forgiveness.** You may want to forgive because it's good for your health. This is a "self-enhancement motive," says Dr. Worthington, and it's a good one. But you may also want to forgive out of an "altruistic motive"—to bless an offender, or out of humility, he says. Think about a time you transgressed and received forgiveness. Think about your emotions when you were forgiven—usually feelings of freedom, lightness and joy.

Consider whether you wish to give that gift to your offender.

C: **Commit to the forgiveness you experience.** Once you experience emotional forgiveness, make a public statement, which will help you hold on to your forgiveness at a later time. This might be in the form of a written letter, or simply telling someone else that you have experienced emotional forgiveness.

H: **Hold on to forgiveness in the face of doubts.** "You've worked through a lot of deep-seated unforgiveness and, after much effort, you win freedom from unforgiveness and blame," says Dr. Worthington. "Then you come face-to-face with the transgressor—a meeting that may generate anger, as a result of the past. You may doubt that you have truly forgiven. This is because you have bought into the idea that if you forgive, you must necessarily forget. Realistically, a wound is rarely forgotten. You usually still have a reaction to the painful or angering experience. This understanding will help you deal with your doubts that your experience of emotional forgiveness is genuine."

☀ Dr. Worthington's books on learning how to forgive include *Forgiveness and Reconciliation* (Brunner-Routledge), *The Power of Forgiving* (Templeton Foundation), *Handbook of Forgiveness* (Brunner-Routledge), *Five Steps to Forgiveness* (Crown) and *To Forgive Is Human* (InterVarsity).

OMEGA-3s—BETTER THAN COUNTING TO 10

Detectives take note…the culprit in the next murder you investigate might be a nutritional deficiency.

"Nutritional deficiencies of the omega-3 fatty acids EPA (eicosapentaenoic acid) and DHA (docosahexaenoic acid) found in fish oil may increase the risk of impulsivity and rage, resulting in homicidal behavior," says Joseph R. Hibbeln, MD, a scientist at the government's National Institute of Alcohol and Abuse and Alcoholism, and one of the top experts in the world on the role of omega-3 fatty acids in emotional and mental well-being.

That's because EPA and DHA are a must for the health of *neurons*, or brain cells. Without them, brains go bad. And so, apparently, do people.

||||➤ *Breakthrough Studies*

Researchers at the Kaiser Permanente Center in Oakland, CA, compared hostility levels and omega-3 intake in 3,581 people. Those who ate fish rich in omega-3 fatty acids, such as wild salmon, were 18% less likely to be hostile.

Other researchers have found similar results...

• **Less anger.** When healthy Japanese students took omega-3 supplements they felt less anger. The same was true of older people in Thailand.

• **Fewer verbal outbursts.** A person with "borderline personality disorder" is quick to perceive insults and pick a fight, and angry a lot of the time. When women with the disorder took 1 gram of EPA a day, they had 75% fewer angry verbal outbursts, says a study in the *American Journal of Psychiatry*.

• **More agreeable.** In a study of 105 normal people, researchers at the University of Pittsburgh found that the higher the blood level of DHA and EPA, the more agreeable the person.

"Ensuring optimal intakes of omega-3 fatty acids shows considerable promise in preventing aggression and hostility," says Dr. Hibbeln.

What to do: His advice is to eat fish three times a week, or take a daily fish oil supplement with 1 gram of EPA and DHA.

ℹ️ Fish oil supplements are widely available. The Nordic Naturals brand used in many scientific studies has proven the value of fish oil; their Ultimate Omega product contains 650 mg of EPA and 450 mg of DHA, or 1.1 grams.

WALKING—TAKE IT OUT ON THE ROAD

Feel like kicking the dog? Use your feet in a slightly different way.

||||➤ *Breakthrough Study*

Japanese researchers studied 119 people, dividing them into two groups. One group participated in a four-week walking program and one group didn't. The people who walked had significant decreases in anger and hostility compared to the nonwalkers.

What happens: The researchers conducted tests that showed four weeks of regular walking shifted the nervous system toward greater *parasympathetic functioning*—the part of the nervous system responsible for calming down rather than revving up emotions.

What to do: Use the walking routine in the study—1 hour a day, six days a week, at a reasonably brisk pace of about four miles an hour (one mile in 15 minutes).

6

DIABETES & INSULIN RESISTANCE
NATURAL CONTROL FOR THE SUGAR DISEASE

The numbers tell the bitter story of the sugar disease. The rate of type 2 diabetes has *doubled* in the past two decades, from 5 to 10% of American adults, with 1.3 million new cases every year, totaling nearly 20 million people. How are most folks with type 2 being treated? With drugs.

The average person with type 2 diabetes takes between nine and 13 drugs. Two or three drugs to lower chronically high blood sugar. Two or three drugs to lower blood pressure, a risk factor for heart attack and stroke, the diseases that kill four out of five people with diabetes. A drug to lower high cholesterol, another risk factor for heart disease. Maybe drugs to help control or slow the possible complications of diabetes—nerve damage, lost eyesight, slow kidney function. It's not that those drugs are bad.

"Diabetes medications can be lifesaving," says Neal Barnard, MD, an adjunct professor of medicine at George Washington University School of Medicine and author of *Dr. Neal Barnard's Program for Reversing Diabetes* (Rodale). "They can reduce your blood sugar and, over the long run, cut your risk of complications."

But, he says, drugs should be used only if diet and lifestyle changes don't do the job.

You may want to start with a slice of whole-wheat toast.

DIABETES-FIGHTING DIETS

HIGH-FIBER DIET— GO WITH THE GRAINS

Foods rich in fiber slow down digestion so that a steady supply of glucose is released into the bloodstream. That's the ideal dietary scenario for the prevention and control of diabetes: *balanced* blood sugar, rather than a roller coaster of big spikes (hyperglycemia) and sudden crashes (hypoglycemia).

But fiber is found in many foods—fruits, vegetables, grains, beans. Do some balance blood sugar better than others? Yes, say German scientists, in the *Archives of Internal Medicine*.

▶ *Breakthrough Study*

Researchers at the German Institute of Human Nutrition studied the eating habits of more than 25,000 men and women, aged 35 to 65, analyzing dietary data from 1994 to 2005. Those who ate the most amount of daily fiber had a 27% lower risk of developing diabetes, compared to those who ate the least. But only one kind of fiber worked—*cereal fiber*, from whole grains such as wheat, oats, barley and rye. A high intake of fiber from fruits and vegetables didn't reduce diabetes risk.

Why cereal fiber works best: Scientists don't know for sure. But another team of German researchers, reporting in *Diabetes Care*, found that when 13 people ate bread enriched with 31 grams of cereal fiber every day for three days, their insulin sensitivity improved by approximately 10%.

Suggested intake: Those with the lowest risk of diabetes got an average daily intake of 16.6 grams of cereal fiber, the equivalent of ¾ cup of Kellogg's All-Bran. Other excellent sources of cereal fiber include whole-wheat bread and whole-grain rye bread, at 3 grams per slice, and buckwheat groats (kasha) and brown rice, at about 10 grams per cup.

Also helpful: A study conducted at the Creighton Diabetes Center in Nebraska showed that when people ate a breakfast cereal made with fiber-rich barley, their postmeal rise in blood sugar was *six times lower* than when they ate oatmeal.

That's because barley is particularly rich in *beta-glucan*, a type of fiber that's uniquely effective at slowing digestion, says C. Walt Newman, PhD, professor emeritus at Montana State University and author of *Barley for Food and Health* (Wiley).

ℹ️ He recommends a special type of barley flakes, with two to three times more beta-glucan, available from NuWorld Nutrition, 816 6th Avenue NE, Perham, MN 56573 (800-950-3188), or e-mail *nuworld@eot.com*.

PGX—A SUPER-SUPPLEMENT FOR THE FIBER-CHALLENGED

The American Diabetes Association recommends a daily fiber intake of 35 grams for men and 25 grams for women. But if you're like most people, you only get *half* the recommended amount. How can you make up the difference?

"I would suggest a fiber supplement for people who aren't meeting the recommended daily intake of fiber," says Joanne L. Slavin, PhD, RD, a professor in the Department of Food Science and Nutrition at the University of Minnesota and an expert on fiber.

But there are a lot of fiber supplements on the market—chitosan, psyllium, glucomannan, pectin, guar gum, mixed fibers. Is there one type that's best for a person with diabetes?

Yes, says Vladimir Vuksan, PhD, professor in the Department of Nutritional Sciences at the University of Toronto and chair of the Nutrition Committee of the Canadian Diabetes Association.

It's a supplement featuring *viscous*, or soluble fiber, the kind found in many fruits, vegetables, grains and beans. Viscous fiber forms a thick, slowly absorbed gel in the digestive tract, lowering and steadying blood sugar levels. And the viscous fiber supplement that studies show is *most* effective in balancing blood sugar, says Dr. Vuksan, is PolyGlycoplex (PGX).

PGX is a unique fiber supplement, made from the root of the Japanese konjac plant and a blend of two other viscous fibers. Studies show PGX has six times the viscosity of psyllium (the fiber in Metamucil) and a uniquely powerful ability to stop the diabetes-worsening spikes in blood sugar levels that can occur after eating.

In studies on people with severe diabetes led by Dr. Vuksan and published in *Diabetes Care*, PGX reduced insulin resistance by 40%—double the effect previously seen with other types of fiber.

🏛 A DIABETES GLOSSARY

Quick definitions of scientific terms used throughout this chapter.

Glucose. Blood sugar, your body's primary fuel.

Glucose tolerance. How your body responds to a big dose of sugar—the better your glucose tolerance, the less chance diabetes will develop or worsen. Healthy levels of blood sugar are balanced, steady and stable—not fluctuating wildly, with huge ups and downs.

Fasting glucose. A measurement of blood sugar levels taken after you haven't eaten for eight hours—70 to 100 mg/dl (milligrams per deciliter) is normal; 126 or higher means you have diabetes.

Postprandial glucose. Your blood sugar level after a meal. High, postprandial spikes of glucose contribute to and worsen diabetes.

A1C (glycated hemoglobin). The percentage of hemoglobin (red blood cells) that have been frosted (glycated) by blood sugar. It is the best measure of *long-term* blood sugar control—over the past two to three months. For someone with diabetes, 7% or less means the disease is "well controlled." Ten percent or higher, it's "poorly controlled." Decreases of 0.5 to 1% (or more) are considered significant.

Insulin. A hormone manufactured by the pancreas, insulin controls blood sugar levels, moving glucose out of the bloodstream and into muscle, fat and liver cells. Insulin is the key that opens cellular locks—so glucose can enter the cell and blood sugar levels stay steady.

Insulin receptors. The locks on muscle and fat cells.

Insulin sensitivity. The more sensitive your receptors—the more easily the key fits into the lock—the better. Insulin sensitivity is *good*.

Insulin resistance. Either the key, the lock or both aren't working well. Insulin resistance is also called *prediabetes* and is the primary feature of the metabolic syndrome, which also includes overweight and circulatory problems. Insulin resistance is *bad*.

Type 2 diabetes. Nine out of ten people with diabetes have type 2—a condition of insulin resistance and high glucose levels. (In type 1 diabetes, the body can't produce insulin.) Because it's the focus of this chapter, every time we say diabetes, we mean type 2.

In another study in *Diabetes Care*, people with prediabetes who sprinkled PGX on their food had a reduction in "bad" LDL of 22%—the same amount as seen with low-dose statin drugs!

"There is nothing more powerful than PGX," says Dr. Vuksan. "It has a dramatic effect on blood sugar levels and heart disease risk factors such as LDL cholesterol, and it's easy to take."

How it works: There are several mechanisms, he says. PGX slows the absorption of carbohydrates in the intestine. It reduces appetite, by creating a long-lasting feeling of fullness and perhaps by affecting hormones in the gut. It helps produce more "friendly" bacteria in the colon, and they generate substances that reduce the production of cholesterol. It lowers the production of cholesterol in the liver.

What to do: PGX is readily available and easy to take, in a powdered form that you can sprinkle on food, mix into a drink or use as a supplement.

☀ A variety of PGX-containing products are available at *www.naturalfactors.com*, in their Slim Styles and WellBetX line of products. They are also available in most health-food stores in the US. Follow the dosage recommendation on the label, says Dr. Vuksan. To order, go on-line.

Or in the United States, contact Natural Factors Nutritional Products Inc., 1111 80th Street SW, Suite 100, Everett, Washington, 98203 (425-513-8800 or 800-322-8704); e-mail *us_custservice@naturalfactors.com*.

In Canada, contact Natural Factors Nutritional Products Ltd., 1550 United Boulevard, Coquitlam, BC, Canada V3K 6Y7 (604-777-1757 or 800-663-8900); e-mail *custservice@natural factors.com*.

LOW GLYCEMIC INDEX DIET— DIGEST SLOWLY, HEAL FAST

The glycemic index (GI) is a 100-to-0 measurement of how quickly or slowly dietary carbohydrates—starches, sugars and fibers—turn into blood sugar in the bloodstream. The slower the better for preventing and controlling diabetes.

- **High-GI foods** score 100 to 70. *Examples:* instant mashed potatoes (97), cornflakes (92), pretzels (83).
- **Moderate-GI foods** score 69 to 56. *Examples:* pancakes from mix (67), cantaloupe (65), cheese pizza (60).
- **Low-GI foods** score 55 to 0. *Examples:* carrots (47), rolled oats (42), skim milk (32), cherries (22).

||||▶ *Breakthrough Study*

Johanna Burani, MS, RD, is a nutritionist, certified diabetes educator and author of *Good Carbs, Bad Carbs* (Marlowe). She studied 21 people with diabetes who had followed a low-GI diet for two years or more, lowering the average GI of their meals from 59 to 44. Low was the way to go.

They had an average 1.5% drop in A1C, from 7.5 to 6.0. They lost an average of 17 pounds. And many reduced their need for diabetes medications, with two people eliminating medications completely (with their doctor's supervision and approval).

Why the Low-GI Diet Works

When carbohydrates turn into glucose quickly, blood sugar levels shoot up—and then crash down. When carbohydrates turn into glucose slowly, blood sugar levels stay steady. Studies show that *small* fluctuations in blood sugar levels benefit your health in a number of ways:

- **Diabetes** is better controlled.
- **Prediabetes** is less likely to develop into diabetes.
- **Weight loss** is easier, because you feel fuller at meals and less hungry an hour or two later.

How to Switch to a Low-GI Diet

Simply substitute low-GI foods for high-GI foods, says Jennie Brand-Miller, PhD, a professor in Human Nutrition at the University of Sydney in Australia and author of many books on the glycemic index, including her latest, *The New Glucose Revolution for Diabetes* (Marlowe). Her six rules of thumb:

- **Use breakfast cereals** based on oats, barley and bran.
- **Use breads with whole grains.** Sourdough is also good.
- **Eat fewer potatoes.**
- **Enjoy all other types of fruits and vegetables.**
- **Use basmati, long-grain or brown rice.**
- **Enjoy pasta and noodles.** (Firm, briefly cooked, "al dente" style is best, says Burani.)

☀ *www.glycemicindex.com*, a search engine with the GI rating of nearly 2,000 foods.

LOW-FAT VEGAN DIET TOPS THE ADA DIET

It was the dietary equivalent of a prizefight—with the prize being better control of diabetes.

Ninety-nine people with diabetes went on either the American Diabetes Association (ADA) diet or a low-fat vegan diet for 22 weeks.

In the ADA corner, a diet with...

• **Carbohydrate levels kept steady** through the day, and day by day;

• **Low levels of saturated fat from meat and dairy foods,** but plenty of mono-unsaturated fat from foods such as avocados, walnuts and olive oil and

• **A 500-a-day calorie deficit** to help the typically overweight person with diabetes shed pounds.

In the low-fat vegan corner, a diet with...

• **No animal products** (meat, poultry, fish, dairy, eggs);

LOW-GI ON THE GO—USE YOUR PDA

Researchers at the University of Massachusetts Medical School counseled 31 people with "poorly controlled" diabetes about the low-GI diet and then left them on their own—except for a handy PDA (personal digital assistant) with a database of the glycemic index. After six months of using the hand-held device, they were successfully eating lower GI foods—and had lower A1C, weight and blood pressure.

☀ You can find downloadable glycemic index software for a PDA at *www.glycemic dietsw.com.* For GI software for your home computer, go to *www.nutrigenie.biz.*

• **A bare minimum of fat** from high-fat veggie foods such as avocados, olive oil, nuts and seeds;

• **No carbohydrates high on the "glycemic index"** (a measurement of how fast carbs digest)—no foods with white sugar or white flour, no cold cereals (except for bran cereals), no pineapples or watermelon, no big baking potatoes and

• **Calorie-wise, the diet allowed unlimited portions**—those on the low-fat vegan diet could eat as much as they liked of the foods allowed.

▶ *Breakthrough Study*

After 22 weeks, the winner was...the low-fat vegan diet. *Here are the victor's stats...*

• **Fewer drugs.** By the end of the study, 43% of the vegan group had reduced their diabetes medications, compared to 26% of the ADA group.

• **Lower A1C.** It fell 1.23% in the vegan group but only 0.38% in the ADA group.

• **More weight loss.** The vegan group lost more than twice as much weight—an average of 14.3 pounds, compared to 6.8 for the ADA group.

• **Lower LDL cholesterol.** Seventy-five percent of people with diabetes die of heart disease or stroke, so any drop in artery-clogging "bad" LDL cholesterol is potentially life-saving. The vegans' LDL dropped 21%, while the ADA-eaters saw a drop of 11%.

Why the Vegan Diet Won

The hormone insulin signals insulin receptors to allow blood sugar into the cell, keeping blood sugar levels steady, explains Dr. Barnard, lead author of the study. With a low-fat vegan diet, there's less fat to clog up the muscle cells, allowing the hormone to reach receptors more easily and do its job.

How to Go on a Low-Fat Vegan Diet

Do it in two steps, advises Dr. Barnard, a low-fat vegan himself.

1. Check out your options. Eat bacon and eggs for breakfast? Think about oatmeal instead. Go to the store, buy some oatmeal (along with flavor-boosting cinnamon and raisins), cook it, and see if you like it. Or try low-fat meat substitutes you might enjoy, such as vegetarian sausages. Go through the same process for lunch and dinner. Also visit your favorite restaurants and sample vegan entrees, such as pasta marinara or vegetarian sushi.

2. Test-drive the diet for three weeks to see if you like it. After a week, you'll probably notice glucose levels are down, you have more energy and you're losing weight.

You might also find your food preferences changing, as when someone switches from full fat to skim milk. At first skim milk tastes strange, then it tastes fine, then you can't go back to whole milk because it tastes like cream. You'll probably have the same type of experience switching to a low-fat vegan diet, says Dr. Barnard.

"People often think going on a low-fat vegan diet sounds hard," says Dr. Barnard. "But going blind and ending up on dialysis—possible consequences of uncontrolled diabetes—is what is hard. This diet is every bit as easy as any other diet. I eat this way and I love it."

ℹ️ Dr. Barnard has written a book about his diet—*Dr. Neal Barnard's Program for Reversing Diabetes: The Scientifically Proven System for Reversing Diabetes Without Drugs* (Rodale).

DON'T PIG OUT...ON PORK

Hogs are happy with Harvard.

Scientists at Harvard Medical School and Simmons College in Boston analyzed 10 years of dietary data from nearly 70,000 women, aged 38 to 63. They divided the women into two groups: Those who ate a "prudent" diet with plenty of fruits, vegetables, beans, fish, poultry and whole grains; and those who ate a "Western" diet with lots of red meat, sweets, desserts and refined grains. Among the Western group, those eating the most red meat (beef, pork, lamb) had a 26% increased risk of diabetes *per serving*. In other words, a woman eating three servings of red meat a day had a 52% higher risk of developing diabetes than a woman eating one serving. But *processed* red meats were the worst, with hot dogs increasing diabetes risk by 43% per serving and bacon by 49%, says Teresa Fung, ScD, RD, lead author of the study and associate professor of nutrition at Simmons College.

And hold the fries. A similar study by Harvard researchers in the *American Journal of Clinical Nutrition* showed that women eating a lot of French fries had a 21% higher risk of diabetes compared to women who almost never ate them.

One possible reason why foods like hamburgers and hot dogs increase the risk of diabetes is *advanced glycation end products,* chemicals that are formed from intense heat like grilling and that can decrease insulin sensitivity. Dr. Fung urges you to take those foods off your personal menu. "Red and processed meats have also been linked to heart disease and colon cancer," she says. "First reduce your intake to one serving a week. After three or four weeks, cut back to one serving a month."

LOSE THE WEIGHT WITH MEAL REPLACEMENTS

"Weight loss is the *only* cure for type 2 diabetes," says Zhaoping Li, MD, PhD, an associate professor of clinical medicine at the Center for

Human Nutrition, in the David Geffen School of Medicine at UCLA.

Fat isn't an inert lump on the body, she explains. Just like the thyroid, adrenal and other glands of the endocrine system, fat cells pump out *hormones*, chemicals that tell cells what to do. Unfortunately, the hormones generated by fat cells "contradict" another hormone, *insulin*, which instructs muscle cells to absorb glucose. The result is *insulin resistance*, a condition that causes or worsens diabetes. Losing weight is the only way to control or reverse insulin resistance, she says. And one of the most effective ways for a person with diabetes to lose weight is with meal replacements—eating packaged entrees, soups, shakes, puddings or bars instead of a regular meal.

▶ *Breakthrough Study*

For one year, Dr. Li studied 77 people with diabetes, dividing them into two groups. One group used meal replacements (MR)—two a day for three months, and one a day for the next nine months. The other group followed dietary recommendations from the American Diabetes Association (ADA). *The results...*

Weight loss: After a year, the MR group had lost an average of 10 pounds, compared to five pounds for the ADA group. A loss of 10 pounds is often enough to reverse or control insulin resistance.

Blood sugar: A1C dropped twice as much in the MR group—0.30% compared to 0.15% in the ADA group.

Medication use: The MR group reduced their use of diabetes medications by 15% more than the ADA group.

C-reactive protein: This risk factor for heart disease fell 26% in the MR group, compared to 7% in the ADA group.

Why Meal Replacements Work

Weight-loss diets are hard to follow, with most people underestimating their daily caloric intake by 20 to 30%, says Dr. Li. When you lose weight with meal replacements, you don't have to figure out calories. Plus, you're far less tempted to overeat. You just eat the entree, shake or bar—and that's that.

☀ Dr. Li's patients used Slim-Fast during the study, which is available in most supermarkets and drugstores. Another scientifically tested and widely used meal-replacement system is Health Management Resources, with products available on the Web at *www.hmrprogram.com*, or by calling 800-418-1367.

Talk with your doctor to see if meal replacements are a good way for you to lose weight.

HEALING FOODS

DARK CHOCOLATE—KIND TO BLOOD SUGAR

If you're healthy and want to prevent diabetes, a little bit of chocolate might help. As long as you eat the dark variety.

▶ *Breakthrough Study*

Every day for two weeks, researchers in Spain gave 15 healthy people either dark or white chocolate. Then they gave them a glucose tolerance test. Compared to those eating white chocolate, those eating dark chocolate had 10% greater insulin sensitivity and 45% less insulin resistance. Why is dark better than white? Because unlike white, it's rich in *polyphenols*, powerful antioxidants that help insulin do its job efficiently.

Suggested intake: To get a hefty dose of polyphenols, look for dark chocolate containing 70 to 85% cocoa solids, which supplies 150 calories and a minimum amount of fat and sugar, says Roger Corder, MD, an expert in polyphenols and health. Eat about 1 ounce a day.

One-ounce bars from Scharffen Berger chocolates—look for 70% Cacao Bittersweet Chocolate or 82% Cacao Extra Dark. They're available in Whole Foods and other stores, by calling 800-930-4528, or on the Web at *www.scharffenberger.com* or *www.artisanconfection.com.*

ALCOHOL OKAY AT 1–2 DRINKS A DAY

Historically, people with diabetes have been told *not* to drink because alcohol can play havoc with blood sugar, particularly on an empty stomach. Now, however, the American Diabetes Association says that moderate drinking with a snack or meal—no more than 1 drink a day for women and 2 a day for men—is A-okay (as long as your doctor agrees). Here's why.

▶ *Breakthrough Study*

Swedish researchers conducted a "meta-analysis" of 13 studies on diabetes and alcohol, finding that *moderate* intake reduced the risk by 30%.

In the United States, researchers at the Boston Medical Center analyzed dietary and health data from more than 8,000 people. They found those imbibing more than 20 drinks a month had a 66% lower risk of developing the metabolic syndrome—a potentially deadly combination of insulin resistance, high blood pressure, high triglycerides, extra abdominal fat and low HDL (good) cholesterol.

Note: Immoderate drinking—more than 1 drink a day for women and 2 drinks a day for men—*increases* the risk of diabetes.

THE POWER OF RED WINE

Some scientists studying alcohol and diabetes think red wine might be particularly good for you because it's uniquely high in antioxidants. To test that theory, researchers at the Nutrition Program of North Carolina University and Duke University Medical Center asked people with diabetes to drink 5 ounces a day of antioxidant-rich muscadine red wine, for 28 days. (Muscadine grapes are grown in the southeast US and are typically used in dessert wine and port.) At the end of the four weeks, they had lower levels of blood glucose, insulin and A1C—all signs of improved blood sugar control.

"I've changed my habits because of conducting this study," says Leon Boyd, PhD, a professor of food science at North Carolina University. "I drink more muscadine wine and other red wines, and more red grape juice."

Dr. Boyd prefers wines from Duplin Winery, one of the south's largest, which specializes in muscadine wines, including their two most popular red dessert wines, Hatteras Red and Carolina Red. Duplin Winery, PO Box 756, Rose Hill, NC 28458 (800-774-9634); e-mail *info@duplinwinery.com,* or go on-line at *http://catalog.duplinwinery.com.*

How alcohol protects: It lowers A1C, a biomarker for long-term blood sugar control.

It also increases good HDL cholesterol and lowers *fibrinogen,* a protein that puts you at greater risk for artery-clogging clots. Those two benefits are *crucial,* because people with diabetes have four times greater risk of dying from heart disease than people without.

New finding: In healthy people, drinking either wine, beer or gin (liquor used in study) with a meal reduces postmeal levels of blood sugar by up to 37%, yet another way moderate drinking may protect against diabetes, say Australian researchers in the *American Journal of Clinical Nutrition.*

Definition of a drink: One drink is 5 ounces of wine, 12 ounces of beer, or 1½ ounces of 80% distilled spirits or liquor, such as whiskey or vodka.

Who shouldn't drink: If you're pregnant...if your father or mother suffered from alcoholism ...if you're on a blood-thinning medication like *warfarin*...if you have breast cancer or a family history of the disease...if you're about to drive, operate heavy machinery or do anything that requires normal reaction time—*don't drink.*

WHEY PROTEIN TAMES HIGH-GI MEALS

Can you have your high-carbohydrate cake and eat it too? Maybe—if you follow it with whey protein powder.

▐▌▶ *Breakthrough Study*

For two days, researchers from Lund University in Sweden and the University of Copenhagen in Denmark asked 14 people with diabetes to eat what they shouldn't—fast-digesting, sugar-imbalancing, high-glycemic carbohydrates. White bread for breakfast. Instant mashed potatoes for lunch.

On one of the two days, the researchers supplemented the high-glycemic meals with a powder made from *whey protein*, a liquid by-product produced during cheese-making. Those eating the meal produced 37% more sugar-controlling insulin after the whey-supplemented breakfast and 57% more after the lunch.

Research shows that milk boosts the production of insulin. This study, say the scientists, shows it's the whey protein in milk that does the trick. Whey protein, they conclude, might help balance blood sugar in people with diabetes, and reduce or even eliminate the need for medications and their possible adverse affects.

DON'T GOT DIABETES? MAYBE YOU GOT MILK

Those milky white moustaches might be a sign of good health.

Researchers at Harvard Medical School analyzed dietary data from more than 41,000 men and found that every serving of a low-fat dairy product decreased the risk of diabetes by 9%.

Why it works: Researchers at Tufts-New England Medical Center theorize that the calcium, magnesium and vitamin D in the milk do the trick, by improving the body's ability to produce and use insulin.

A serving of dairy: 8 ounces of milk, 1.5 ounces of cheese or 6 to 8 ounces of yogurt. Choose low fat.

Suggested intake: A 28-gram dose of whey protein powder, approximately a 1-ounce serving, dissolved in 8 ounces of water, with breakfast and lunch.

ℹ Designer Whey has been used in many of the scientific studies showing whey powder boosts health, says Michael Zemel, PhD, director of the Nutrition Institute at the University of Tennessee. Designer Whey is widely available in supermarkets, drugstores and health-food stores throughout the United States, or on the Web at *www.designerwhey.com.* NEXT Proteins, PO Box 2469, Carlsbad, CA 92018 (760-431-8152).

POMEGRANATE JUICE STOPS OXIDATION

People with diabetes are often told *not* to drink fruit juices because they're loaded with sugar. Pomegranate juice should be the exception.

▐▌▶ *Breakthrough Study*

Israeli researchers in the Lipid Research Laboratory at the Rambam Medical Center in

Haifa asked 10 people with diabetes to drink about two ounces a day of pomegranate juice for three months. Before and after the three months, they took several measurements of *oxidation*.

What is oxidation? Oxygen *supports* life but it can also *spoil* it—through oxidation. Oxygen rusts metal and rots fruit. *High levels of blood sugar spawn the oxidants that can rust and rot you from the inside out…*

• **They oxidize LDL cholesterol**, clogging arteries—one reason most people with diabetes die of heart disease or stroke.

• **They damage small blood vessels** in your kidneys, eyes and feet—the cause of severe diabetic complications such as kidney disease, blindness and foot ulcers.

• **They fracture DNA.**

Reducing oxidation can help slow those body-damaging processes. And that's just what pomegranate juice does.

The results: The Israeli scientists found pomegranate juice caused these changes in oxidation…

• **39%** *decrease* in the oxidation of LDL

• **56%** *decrease* in **TBARS,** a group of vicious oxidants that attack arteries and veins

• *141% increase* in **glutathione,** a powerful antioxidant

Drinking pomegranate juice can power antioxidation, helping slow the development of circulatory disease in diabetes, say the researchers in the medical journal *Atherosclerosis.*

Suggested intake: Toast to your health every day with a nonalcoholic spritzer of two to four ounces of pomegranate juice and four to eight ounces of sparkling water.

ⓘ POM Wonderful is a widely available brand with 100% pomegranate juice from concentrate and with no added sugar, colors or flavorings. Lakewood Pomegranate Juice, available at Whole Foods supermarkets and health-food stores, is 100% juice, not from concentrate.

SAY "NUTS" TO DIABETES

In the glycemic index—the rating system for how quickly foods digest and turn into blood sugar (glucose), with 100 being the fastest and 1 the slowest—white bread is among the speediest with a rating of 70. So it's no surprise that when Canadian researchers wanted to see how almonds affected blood sugar, they fed 15 healthy volunteers two meals—white bread, and white bread with almonds. Before and after each meal, the researchers took three measurements—glucose, insulin and *protein thiols*, a measurement of protection against oxidation, a type of heart-harming cellular damage triggered by high levels of glucose in the blood.

▶ *Breakthrough Study*

The concentration of protein thiols was *five times* higher after the meal with almonds. And this measurement correlated exactly with lower post-almond levels of glucose and insulin. In other words, almonds slowed the digestion of carbohydrates *and* protected the body against oxidation.

"Incorporating almonds in the diet may help in the management of blood glucose levels and the onset of diabetes, while promoting a healthy heart," says Cyril Kendall, PhD, a professor at the University of Toronto and a coauthor of the study.

Suggested intake: Eat a handful of almonds (about twenty) with a meal, advises Dr. Kendall. That's one ounce, or about 150 to 200 calories. To compensate for the extra calories, cut a less-than-healthy snack out of your diet, he says. Some equivalents: 1 ounce of pretzel nuggets, 1 Drake's Yodel, 1½ ounces of full-fat cheese or 2 handfuls of jelly beans.

Walnuts Are Good, Too

In an Australian study of 58 people with diabetes, adding a handful of walnuts a day to the diet lowered "bad" LDL cholesterol and increased "good" HDL cholesterol.

Ditto for peanut butter: Scientists at the Harvard School of Public Health found that people who ate peanut butter five or more times a week had a 21% lower risk of diabetes than people who almost never ate it.

Or any type of nut: The same study found that people who ate a one-ounce serving (a handful) of *any* type of nut five or more times a week cut their risk of diabetes by 27%, compared to people who almost never ate nuts.

COFFEE FOR 60% LESS RISK

You may want to buy stock in Starbucks. Or at least pay a visit. In the past few years, study after study has shown that coffee can protect against diabetes. One of the most recent.

▶ Breakthrough Study

Researchers in Finland analyzed 13 years of dietary and health data from more than 22,000 men and women. Those who drink three to six 8-ounce cups of coffee a day had a 29% lower risk of developing diabetes than those drinking two or fewer cups. Among people who drank seven or more cups a day, the risk dropped by 34%. And among those who were overweight or didn't exercise, drinking seven or more cups of coffee a day reduced the risk by 50%. "If you drink coffee daily, you may prevent diabetes," says Dr. Gang Hu, MD, PhD, a senior researcher at the University of Helsinki and one of the scientists who conducted the study.

People with prediabetes also benefit: In a study conducted at the University of California-San Diego, researchers analyzed coffee intake in 317 people with prediabetes —levels of blood sugar above normal, but not high enough to be defined as diabetes. Those drinking coffee regularly had a 60% lower risk of developing diabetes, compared to those who never drank coffee. Coffee, say the researchers, has a "striking protective effect."

Coffee protects those with diabetes against heart disease: The Finnish researchers found people with diabetes who drank five to six cups of coffee a day had a 30% lower risk of dying from heart disease and a 36% lower risk of dying from stroke, compared to people with diabetes who didn't drink coffee.

Why it works: Researchers surmise that several factors in coffee—the caffeine, minerals in coffee like magnesium, or an antioxidant called *chlorogenic acid*—may help regulate blood sugar.

Regular or decaf? Both caffeinated and decaffeinated work, says Rob M. van Dam, PhD, an assistant professor in the Department of Nutrition at the Harvard School of Public Health and an expert on coffee and diabetes. He advises you drink it black, or use sugar substitutes and/or low-fat milk.

SOY SLOWS KIDNEY DAMAGE

Ten to 20% of people with diabetes suffer from kidney disease, or *diabetic nephropathy*, says Francine Kaufman, MD, past president of the American Diabetes Association and author of *Diabesity* (Bantam). In fact, diabetes is the leading cause of kidney failure, or *end-stage renal disease*, accounting for nearly half of all cases. Why?

The high sugar levels of diabetes gradually weaken and destroy small blood vessels in the

DRINKING COFFEE FOR TWO?

Four percent of pregnant women develop *gestational diabetes*—high blood sugar levels that not only increase a mother's risk of developing type 2 diabetes in the future, but also increase her baby's risk of breathing problems at birth and obesity and diabetes as a child or adult. If you're a woman planning to get pregnant...consider a coffee break.

Researchers at the University of Washington School of Public Health and Community Medicine in Seattle talked to 1,744 healthy pregnant women in the early months of their pregnancy, asking them how much coffee they drank *before* they got pregnant. Women who drank two to four 8-ounce cups of caffeinated coffee a day had a 50% lower risk of developing gestational diabetes than women who didn't drink coffee.

Caution: Coffee drinking *during* pregnancy was not protective. Most experts recommend drinking no more than two 8-ounce cups of caffeinated coffee a day during pregnancy, or a limit of 300 milligrams of caffeine.

kidneys, explains Dr. Kaufman. These twin organs cleanse the blood of toxins and excess water. With advancing kidney failure, a person with diabetes can suffer from water retention, with puffiness in the legs and face; difficulty breathing, as lungs fill with excess fluid; high blood pressure; headaches; unrelenting fatigue; and heart failure.

Accumulating toxins can also trigger dry skin and intense itching, insomnia, nausea and vomiting, confusion, urinary tract infections and hearing problems. At the end of the road is complete kidney failure, requiring dialysis (blood cleansing with a surgical shunt or a machine) or a kidney transplant.

Soy may help slow this debilitating process.

▐▐▶ *Breakthrough Study*

Scientists in the Division of Nutritional Sciences at the University of Illinois studied 14 men aged 53 to 73 with diabetes and nephropathy. They asked the men to take soy protein—in the form of vanilla-flavored *isolated soy protein powder* (ISP), mixed with water, juice or food.

The men had a 9.5% drop in urinary levels of the protein *albumin*. Higher levels are a sign of kidney damage.

"This was a very significant and unexpected clinical result," says John W. Erdman, Jr., PhD, a professor of nutrition at the University of Illinois and the researcher who led the study. Dr. Erdman and his colleagues had hypothesized that ISP might *stop* the rise in albumin but not *reverse* it.

Why soy works: The scientists have two theories. Soy contains high levels of *isoflavones*, an estrogen-like compound that may help restore kidney function. Soy also delivers high levels of the amino acid arginine, which increases nitric oxide, a biochemical that improves blood flow to the kidneys and other organs.

The ISP given to the men in this study was Supro from Solae. Two widely available Supro-containing products are NOW Foods Soy Protein Isolate and Scifit Soy Protein Isolate. They are available in a variety of flavors, including vanilla, chocolate and strawberry.

Suggested intake: Use 2 grams of powder per 9 pounds of body weight—if you weigh 180 pounds, for example, use 40 grams a day. (Divide body weight by 9 and multiply by 2.)

Divide the dose between two meals, says Dr. Erdman. For example, 20 grams at breakfast and 20 grams at lunch. Try mixing ISP with a glass of juice in the morning and a cup of yogurt at lunch.

AN APPLE A DAY MIGHT KEEP DIABETES AWAY

The theory sounded good. Flavonoids—antioxidants in foods with red, yellow, blue and other deep colors—might protect the insulin-producing cells of the pancreas from oxidative damage, preventing diabetes. But when scientists at Harvard analyzed nine years of dietary and health data from more than 38,000 women, they found that eating a diet with plenty of flavonoid-rich foods such as citrus fruits, leafy greens, broccoli, tomatoes, grapes and berries *didn't* protect against diabetes. Except for one fruit. The apple.

Women who ate one or more apples a day had a 28% lower risk of developing diabetes, compared to women who didn't eat apples. The researchers didn't speculate as to why. But that shouldn't stop you from snacking once a day on a Golden Delicious, or a McIntosh, or a Fuji, or...

Caution: Some people may have trouble digesting the carbohydrates in soy, says Dr. Erdman. To avoid digestive upset, introduce ISP gradually—10 grams the first week, 20 grams the second, 30 the third and so on, until you're using the dose right for you.

NUTRITIONAL SUPPLEMENTS FROM A TO ZINC

ALPHA-LIPOIC ACID FOR DIABETIC NEUROPATHY

Twenty-five percent of people with diabetes develop *diabetic neuropathy* —glucose-caused damage to nerves throughout the body, particularly in the hands, arms, feet and legs (peripheral neuropathy).

You experience tingling and prickling. Numbness. And pain—from annoying, to burning, to stabbing, to excruciating. Drugs hardly help.

"Many studies have been conducted on drugs for diabetic neuropathy, and no drug is really effective," says Anne L. Peters, MD, professor of medicine and director of the USC Clinical Diabetes Programs, and author of *Conquering Diabetes* (Hudson Street Press). But, she adds, there is a nutritional supplement that may help, alpha-lipoic acid (ALA), a vitamin-like antioxidant manufactured by the body.

▶ *Breakthrough Study*

Scientists at the German Diabetes Center at Heinrich Heine University in Dusseldorf studied 181 people with diabetic neuropathy, dividing them into two groups. For five weeks, one group received a daily dose of 600 milligrams (mg) of ALA; the other got a placebo. Throughout the study, the researchers asked patients about tingling and prickling, numbness and pain.

Within two weeks, those taking ALA had a 51% reduction in pain and numbness—nearly twice that of the placebo group.

This degree of relief is as powerful as painkillers used to treat diabetic neuropathy, says the researchers in *Diabetes Care*.

But painkillers don't relieve numbness, which can cause someone with diabetes not to notice a sore on his/her foot...leading to an infected ulcer...and to gangrene...and to the amputation of one or more toes, a foot or a leg, a fate that befalls 82,000 people with diabetes every year.

How it works: The researchers theorize that ALA improves blood flow to the nerves, citing another study on ALA and diabetes that showed the nutrient increased arterial blood flow by 44%.

Suggested intake: 600 mg a day, say the researchers, as do scientists in the Department of Neurology at the Mayo Clinic, who reviewed the study. Higher doses aren't more effective, and may cause nausea, vomiting and vertigo.

ℹ️ Widely available brands of ALA supplements containing 600 mg per pill/capsule include Natrol, NOW Foods, Doctor's Best and Pure Encapsulations.

CALCIUM/VITAMIN D—FOR STRONG BONES *AND* BLOOD

If you're a middle-aged woman who turns on the TV, reads a newspaper or pages through a magazine, you're probably tired of hearing that getting plenty of calcium and vitamin D helps prevent osteoporosis. Enough already. You *know*.

TEAM UP WITH BENFOTIAMINE

If you take alpha-lipoic acid (ALA) for diabetic neuropathy, you may also want to take *benfotiamine*, a highly absorbable form of thiamine (vitamin B-1), says Dr. Peters. "Taking ALA together with benfotiamine, a super B vitamin, may help benefit people with neuropathy," she says.

Like ALA, benfotiamine has been studied in Germany, where researchers looked at 40 people with diabetic neuropathy, dividing them into two groups. For three weeks, one group received 200 milligrams a day of benfotiamine, while the other group got a placebo. After three weeks, the benfotiamine group was doing much better—less tingling and prickling, less numbness and far less pain. No side effects were noted.

☀️ To order benfotiamine, go to *www.benfotiamine.net*, or call 888-493-8014.

What you may not know: This nutritional duo might also prevent diabetes.

⫸ *Breakthrough Study*

Researchers at Tufts-New England Medical Center in Boston analyzed 20 years of dietary data from more than 83,000 women. They found that those getting 1,200 milligrams of calcium and 800 IU of vitamin D from diet and supplements were 33% less likely to develop diabetes than women getting half or less of that amount.

"There is a potential beneficial role for both calcium and vitamin D intake in reducing the risk of type 2 diabetes," say the researchers in *Diabetes Care*.

They theorize the nutrients work by improving the body's glucose control. They also point out that the combo may do its best work stopping prediabetes from turning into type 2.

ℹ️ Try Os-Cal, a widely available daily supplement that provides both calcium and vitamin D, says Dr. Peters. Os-Cal offers four products, with varying levels of calcium and vitamin D, in caplet and chewable forms. Choose a product that fits your budget and preferences. For more information, see *www.oscal.com*.

CHROMIUM PICOLINATE— CONTROL DIABETES

First, let's talk about what taking a dietary supplement of the trace mineral chromium probably *won't* do. It won't prevent diabetes. The FDA is adamant about that, calling chromium's power to block diabetes "highly uncertain."

But one type of chromium supplement, taken at a high enough dosage, can help you *control* diabetes if you've already got it.

TYPE 1 DIABETES—SHIELD YOUR CHILD WITH VITAMIN D

Five percent of those with diabetes have *type 1* —a disease in which the body's immune system attacks and destroys the insulin-producing beta cells of the pancreas. The assault usually starts in infancy and continues for months or years. By the time type 1 is diagnosed—often in puberty—80% of beta cells have been destroyed. After that, survival depends on daily insulin injections.

Unlike type 2, most scientists don't think of type 1 diabetes as preventable. They might be wrong.

A study by English researchers published in *Lancet*, one of the world's most prestigious medical journals, found that Finnish children given daily doses of vitamin D-rich cod liver oil during their first year of life were 78% less likely to develop type 1 diabetes than children not given cod liver oil.

How did vitamin D prevent type 1? No one knows for sure, says Michael F. Holick, MD, PhD, director of the Vitamin D, Skin and Bone Research Laboratory at Boston University Medical Center. But there's a theory—a slow-acting viral infection triggers type 1 diabetes, and vitamin D prevents the virus by powering up immune cells.

Should your infant and child get supplemental vitamin D?

Yes, says Susan Harris, DSc, author of "Vitamin D in Type 1 Diabetes Prevention," in the *Journal of Nutrition*. "All infants and children should receive between two hundred and one thousand IU of supplemental vitamin D, particularly if they have limited sun exposure, live in northern areas, are dark skinned or are exclusively breastfed." (Most of these factors cut down vitamin D production, which is triggered by sunlight on the skin. Breast milk is low in vitamin D.)

And, she adds, parents of children with the highest risk for type 1 diabetes—children with a mother, father, brother or sister with type 1—should consider giving their child a supplement of 1,000 to 2,000 IU.

Is there a risk of overdose from that much vitamin D? "To suffer from an overdose of vitamin D, a person needs to get more than ten thousand IU a day, every day, for six months," says Dr. Holick. "Not getting *enough* vitamin D is the real risk."

⫸ *Breakthrough Study*

In a study published in *Diabetes Technology and Therapeutics* in 2007, two research scientists reviewed 15 clinical studies on chromium involving nearly 1,700 people with different types of diabetes—type 1, type 2, gestational and steroid-induced. All the studies used *chromium picolinate*, at daily doses between 200 and 1,000 micrograms (mcg). And all the studies showed chromium picolinate *worked*—balancing blood levels of glucose and improving the body's production and use of insulin, the hormone that moves glucose out of the bloodstream and into cells. Why is this particular form of chromium effective? (Chromium is available in many forms, such as chromium polynicotinate, chromium aspartate, chromium acetate and chromium oxide.) Because your body can absorb it.

"All of the studies using the more bioavailable chromium picolinate have reported positive effects, with greater effects at one thousand mcg per day compared with two hundred mcg per day," says Richard Anderson, PhD, a researcher at the Beltsville Human Nutrition Center in Maryland and author of 70 studies on chromium. Other, less absorbable forms of chromium don't have the same track record.

Why it works: Chromium helps control blood sugar three ways, explains Dr. Anderson. It helps your cells make more insulin receptors; boosts an enzyme that helps those receptors work and blocks an enzyme that turns those receptors off. "If chromium were a drug for diabetes, everybody would have touted it as a 'wonder drug,'" says Dr. Anderson. "But effective nutritional treatments almost never get that kind of positive attention."

Suggested intake: For people with diabetes, Dr. Anderson recommends a minimum of 600 mcg of chromium picolinate a day, taken in three doses of 200 mcg. "Three times a day is better than once a day for maximum absorption," he explains. And, he says, you should take chromium separately from meals or multivitamin/mineral supplements. "There are many factors—including starch, calcium and iron—that can interfere with the absorption of chromium." (However, if you don't think you'll remember to take the supplement three times a day, take 600 mcg once a day, away from meals and other supplements.)

ⓘ Look for Chromax, a brand of chromium picolinate used in many studies. You can find it in most drugstores.

L-ARGININE BOOSTS DIET AND EXERCISE

In the body, the amino acid L-arginine turns into nitric oxide, which relaxes arteries. Studies show L-arginine improves the circulation of those with diabetes, whose glucose-battered

DIACHROME—THE 42 BILLION DOLLAR NUTRITIONAL SUPPLEMENT

Forty-two billion dollars. That's the amount of money four economists at Widener University in Pennsylvania estimate could be saved if all of the million-plus people newly diagnosed each year with diabetes took Diachrome, a nutritional supplement containing chromium and biotin. Each person would save an average of $36,000 over a lifetime—on drugs not taken and medical costs not incurred. Why are these economists forecasting Diachrome? They've been reading studies like the one reported in 2007 in *Diabetes/Metabolism Research and Reviews*...

Four hundred forty-seven people with diabetes took either Diachrome or a placebo for 90 days. Before and after supplementation, researchers measured their A1C.

To control diabetes, the American Diabetes Association recommends an A1C below 7%. But studies show that a drop of even 1% among those with an A1C of 10% or higher can reduce the complications of diabetes, such as heart disease, kidney failure and blindness, reduce diabetes-related deaths—and reduce healthcare costs.

In this study, those taking Diachrome had an A1C drop of 1.76%, compared to 0.68% for the placebo group. And that drop was among people who were *already* taking medications to control diabetes.

"Patients with uncontrolled type 2 diabetes present an ongoing clinical challenge to health professionals," says Cesar Albarracin, MD, a Texas-based physician who led the study. "Prescribing another antidiabetic medication can increase the risk of unwanted side effects, including weight gain and could place an added financial burden on the patient." This study, he continues, "shows that adding Diachrome to antidiabetic medications can help patients reach their blood sugar goal simply, effectively and safely." And maybe save a lot of money too!

Why does Diachrome work? Both chromium and biotin help control how carbohydrates turn into blood sugar—and the two nutrients together regulate the process better than either one by itself.

ⓘ Diachrome is widely available in supermarkets and drugstores. If you have type 2 diabetes, talk to your doctor to see if it's right for you. Follow the dosage recommendation on the label.

arteries are often stiff and clogged. It also relaxes muscle cells so they're more sensitive to insulin, the hormone that regulates blood sugar.

But L-arginine isn't a L-oner. It can team up with diet and exercise—the key components of diabetes control—to improve your health.

⦀⮕ *Breakthrough Study*

Italian doctors put 33 overweight people with diabetes on a low-calorie diet and exercise regimen for 21 days, dividing them into two groups—one got 8.3 grams of L-arginine a day and the other got a placebo. By the end of the three weeks, the L-arginine group was in much better shape, inside and out. *Tests showed those taking L-arginine had…*

• **More weight loss and fat loss,** including belly fat.

• **Retained more muscle,** or lean body mass. (Losing calorie-burning muscle during dieting makes it harder to *maintain* weight loss.)

• **Lower daily blood sugar levels.**

• **Lower levels of** *fructosamine* (a combination of protein and glucose), a measurement of long-term blood sugar control.

• **Increased levels of nitric oxide.**

• **More relaxed arteries.**

• **Lower levels of** *adipokines,* artery-damaging chemicals released by fat cells.

"L-arginine treatment resulted in an additive effect compared with a diet and exercise training program alone on glucose [blood sugar] metabolism and insulin sensitivity," write the researchers in the *American Journal of Physiology—Endocrinology and Metabolism.*

Suggested intake: The dose used in the study—8.6 grams per day—is similar to doses used safely in studies on other conditions, including heart disease, infertility and pressure ulcers. However, for long-term use, only take L-arginine with your doctor's approval and supervision.

ℹ️ L-arginine supplements are widely available in retail stores, on-line and in catalogs. Brands offering supplements with 1-gram pills include Jarrow Formulas, Source Naturals and KAL. Carlson and NOW offer L-arginine in powder form, to mix with water or juice.

Also try: Nutrisoda Immune, a sugar-free beverage available at supermarkets nationwide, supplies 2 grams of L-arginine in every 8-ounce serving, says Jennifer Ashley, RD, LD, a dietitian in Minneapolis, MN.

MAGNESIUM—FIX THE DEFICIENCY

The Diabetes Detectives (aka scientists) have been collecting clues and they've nailed one of the culprits—low levels of the mineral magnesium.

⦀⮕ *Breakthrough Studies*

• **Preventing diabetes.** Scientists at the German Institute of Human Nutrition analyzed 11 years of dietary data from more than 25,000 adults and found those with the highest intake of magnesium had a 23% lower risk of developing diabetes (*Archives of Internal Medicine*).

• **Improving insulin sensitivity.** Scientists at the University of South Carolina analyzed eight years of dietary data from more than 1,000 adults. Those with an intake of 325 mg or more of magnesium a day had greater insulin sensitivity than those getting less than 325 mg (*American Journal of Epidemiology*).

• **Preventing the metabolic syndrome.** Doctors at Northwestern University studied nearly 5,000 Americans, aged 18 to 30. Over 15 years, more than 600 developed the *metabolic syndrome,* a prediabetic condition. Those with the highest intakes of magnesium were 31% less likely to develop the syndrome (*Circulation*).

• **Treating diabetes.** Scientists from Harvard Medical School analyzed nine studies in which doctors gave an average of 360 mg of supplemental magnesium per day to 370 people with diabetes, for one to four months. Blood sugar levels among those taking the mineral were "significantly lower" than those not taking it (*Diabetic Medicine*).

• **Preventing complications.** Italian doctors examined 290 patients with diabetes. Forty-nine percent had low blood levels of magnesium. And the lower the level, the higher the risk for the complications of diabetes—low levels of "good" HDL cholesterol; high levels of artery-clogging triglycerides; high blood pressure; reduced kidney function (*Journal of the American College of Nutrition*).

• **Preventing kidney disease.** Doctors at UCLA tracked the development of kidney disease over five years in 550 patients with diabetes. Those with the lowest intake of magnesium had the highest rate of kidney disease (*Clinical Nephrology*).

Why it works: Magnesium is a key player in the production and function of insulin, the hormone that regulates blood sugar, ushering glucose out of the bloodstream and into the cells.

What to do: Get more magnesium in your diet, say researchers from the Harvard School of Public Health.

Best food sources…

• **Nuts** (almonds, cashews and Brazil nuts)

• **Wheat** (whole wheat, wheat germ, wheat bran)

• **Whole grains** (millet, rye, brown rice, barley)

• **Soy products** (soybeans, tofu)

• **Vegetables** (avocados, beets, broccoli, cauliflower, carrots, celery, asparagus, green peppers, winter squash)

• **Greens and seaweed** (collard greens, dandelion greens, dulse, kelp)

• **Meat** (beef, chicken)

• **Miscellaneous** (banana, brewer's yeast, cheddar cheese, garlic)

Take a supplement. A supplement can ensure a person with diabetes gets enough magnesium.

Suggested intake: For maximum absorption, she recommends magnesium citrate, with a daily dose of 300 to 400 milligrams.

ℹ Widely available brands offering magnesium citrate supplements with this dosage include NutriCology, NOW Foods, Swanson Health Products and Allergy Research.

OMEGA-3 HELPS DEFEAT DEPRESSION

It's a sad fact about sadness—people with diabetes have a 40% higher risk of developing depression than people who don't have the disease. Doctors don't know why, though some think it's the stress from having a chronic disease. What docs do know, however, is that antidepressant medications aren't all that helpful. Fifty to 60% of depressed people with diabetes treated with the drugs don't get any better.

• **Omega-3 fatty acids**—a type of fat found in fatty fish such as salmon and tuna—might provide an extra helping of happiness.

▶ *Breakthrough Study*

Writing in the journal *Diabetes Medicine*, Dutch scientists point to three important scientific findings…

• **People with a low intake of omega-3** are more likely to develop diabetes.

• **People with diabetes** are likely to be depressed.

141

- **A high intake of omega-3** can prevent and/or treat depression.

They conclude that "supplementation with omega-3 may be a safe and helpful tool to reduce the incidence of depression and to treat depression in type 2 diabetes."

Other benefits: Even if omega-3 doesn't dissolve depression, it's still good for you, reducing the risk of artery-clogging clots and cooling down artery-damaging inflammation. Studies on diabetes and omega-3 show the nutrient might: prevent blindness from diabetic retinopathy, by reducing damage to blood vessels in the retina; lower blood pressure, a risk factor for stroke; and lower the risk of heart attacks, the primary killer of people with diabetes. Not a bad day's work for one nutrient!

Recommendation: "I frequently recommend an omega-3 supplement for my patients with type 2 diabetes, especially if they suffer from depression," says Jennifer Warren, MD, director of the Physicians Healthy Weight Center in Hampton, NH.

Suggested intake and product: "My favorite supplement is Nordic Naturals, for several reasons," says Dr. Warren. "It doesn't cause 'fishy' burps. It's concentrated, which means patients take fewer capsules. And it's not contaminated with mercury or other heavy metals. I generally recommend Pro-Omega, at a dosage of one to two capsules per day."

ZINC GUARDS YOUR HEART

Studies show that low blood levels of the trace mineral zinc put you at higher risk for heart disease. Well, people with diabetes *already* have a fourfold higher risk of heart disease. Could low zinc levels make the problem worse? Yes, say scientists, in *Diabetes Care*.

||||➤ *Breakthrough Studies*

Finnish scientists analyzed more than a decade of dietary and health data on zinc and heart disease from more than 1,000 people with diabetes. The results weren't heartening. Those with the lowest blood levels of zinc had a 37% higher risk of a heart attack and a 70% higher risk of dying from heart disease.

Why it works: Zinc might protect the heart of a person with diabetes in several ways, say the scientists. It triggers enzymes that help the heart function. It's an antioxidant, protecting blood vessels from free radicals and other cell-damaging bad guys. It boosts the manufacture and function of insulin, helping normalize blood sugar. (All that extra blood sugar damages the arteries of a person with diabetes.)

Best food sources of zinc: Want to get more zinc in your diet? Head for the seashore. The best source is oysters, with four times more zinc than any other food. (Shrimp also scores well.) Meats are rich, with beef and turkey leading the pack. Among nuts, favor pumpkin seeds, pecans, peanuts, almonds and walnuts. Among grains, choose whole wheat, rye and oats. (Wheat germ is another good source.) Legumes deliver too, with chickpeas, lima beans and split peas the richest.

Supplement common sense: "Zinc supplementation might be useful in preventing heart disease in people with type 2 diabetes," say the Finnish scientists. But take a zinc supplement only with your doctor's okay and supervision. Long-term use of high-dose zinc supplements (more than 150 mg a day) can *harm* your heart, by lowering levels of "good" HDL cholesterol. They can also damage the gut and immune system. And because zinc and copper are on either side of a metabolic seesaw, high levels of zinc (50 mg a day) can block copper, another essential mineral.

Suggested intake and product: Take 30 milligrams a day of L-Opti-Zinc or Opti-Zinc, two highly absorbable forms of the mineral, says Dina Khader, MS, RD, a nutritionist in private practice in Mt. Kisco, NY. L-Opti-Zinc or Opti-Zinc are found in many widely available brands, including Jarrow Formulas, Life Extension, NOW Foods, Nutraceutical Sciences Institute (NSI), Solaray, Solgar and Source Naturals.

EXERCISE AND ACTIVITY

STEP OUT WITH A PEDOMETER

Regular exercise can lower your risk of developing type 2 diabetes by 30 to 50%, says JoAnn E. Manson, MD, DrPH, a professor of medicine and women's health at Harvard Medical School. *Just 30 minutes of "moderate-intensity" activity a day (such as brisk walking) can help you…*

- **Lower blood sugar**
- **Increase insulin sensitivity**
- **Decrease insulin resistance**
- **Lower high blood pressure**
- **Lower cholesterol and triglycerides**
- **Lower the risk of blood clots,** the trigger of most heart attacks and strokes
- **Strengthen arteries**
- **Shed pounds**
- **Douse disease-causing inflammation**

Other studies show that exercise is equally effective at *controlling* diabetes, with regular exercisers having an average drop of 0.6% in A1C—the same reduction achieved by many diabetes medications.

But maybe your garage is the Shrine of Good Intentions, with once-coveted exercise machines gathering dust in the corners. How do you start—and stick with—a regular exercise program? Use a pedometer.

▶ *Breakthrough Studies*

Researchers at the University of New Mexico Health Sciences Center in Albuquerque studied 30 people with diabetes, dividing them into two groups. One group got a pedometer (a small device that clips to your belt or waistband and displays the number of steps you take each day) and were instructed to walk 10,000 steps a day. The other group was told to keep doing whatever they were already doing.

After six weeks, the pedometer group had…

- **Increased their daily physical activity by 70%,**
- **Increased their levels of "good" HDL cholesterol,**
- **Increased the number of calories they burned per minute** even when *not* exercising (a sign of adding muscles and decreasing fat), and
- **Decreased plasma *activator inhibitor 1,*** a biochemical sign they were less likely to generate blood clots, the trigger of most heart attacks and strokes.

A pedometer, say the researchers, may be an "effective tool for promoting healthy lifestyle changes" in "previously inactive people" with type 2 diabetes.

In another study, published in the journal *Preventive Medicine,* researchers at the University of Tennessee found that 18 overweight women with a family history of type 2 diabetes who were given a pedometer and instructed to walk 10,000 steps a day significantly lowered daily blood sugar levels and blood pressure.

- **Why a pedometer works.** "Because it gives you instant, accurate feedback," says

James Hill, PhD, a professor at the University of Colorado and coauthor of *The Step Diet* (Workman), which features the pedometer-measured walking program as the best way to achieve long-term weight-control. "If your goal is eight thousand steps a day, you can look at your pedometer and right away know how you're doing."

What to do: Dr. Hill says to buy a pedometer in the $5 to $20 range. (Cheaper pedometers aren't as accurate.) Wear it for three to four days, writing down your step count at the end of each day. Then calculate your average daily steps. Next, increase your daily step count by 2,000—an increase of about 15 to 20 minutes of walking a day, or 1 mile, or about 100 calories. How to do that?

"Take a walk before work, after work or at lunch," says Dr Hill. "Walk the dog. Walk on the weekend. Walk rather than drive to a destination, such as a local store. If you drive, park farther away. Use the stairs rather than an elevator."

And, says Dr. Hill, if you're motivated to continue increasing your daily steps by *another* 2,000, and perhaps *another* 2,000 after that, until you hit 10,000 (a number often cited by authorities as ideal for disease prevention and fitness)—go for it! Your pedometer will be "coaching" you every step of the way.

Precautions: People with diabetes need to take a few precautions before they start an exercise program, says Dr. Peters.

• **Check with your doctor first.** "If you are over thirty-five, you need to check with your primary physician to be sure it is okay for you to start exercising," she says. "If you have a

WHY WASHING DISHES IS GOOD FOR YOU

Aerobic exercises such as brisk walking or biking are only one type of physical activity—a level of activity exercise scientists label as "moderate to vigorous intensity." But there's also "light-intensity" physical activity, such as washing the dishes, ironing and weeding. The amazing news is those activities can also help keep blood sugar under control!

Scientists at the University of Queensland in Australia and the International Diabetes Institute studied 173 middle-aged men and women who didn't have diabetes. For one week, they measured all their physical activity with an accelerometer, a device that records any degree of action. They also measured their blood sugar levels every day.

Those who engaged regularly in light-intensity activity had average blood sugar levels that were nearly twice as low as those who were mostly sedentary.

"Substituting light-intensity activity for television viewing or other sedentary time may be a practical and achievable strategy to reduce the risk of type 2 diabetes," says Genevieve Healy, PhD, the study's lead researcher.

Light-intensity activity includes...

• *Cleaning.* Straightening, dusting, sweeping, mopping, vacuuming, ironing, scrubbing the floor, washing dishes, cleaning the garage, washing and waxing the car, washing windows, hanging the laundry, making the bed.

• *Food and kitchen activities.* Food shopping with a grocery cart, putting away groceries, cooking, baking.

• *Other household and domestic activities.* Feeding the pets, bathing the dog, watering plants, playing with children, carrying small children, pushing a stroller, trimming shrubs or trees, weeding, loading or unloading a car.

• *Recreation.* Fishing, slow ballroom dancing such as the waltz or foxtrot, playing a musical instrument, bowling, billiards, croquet, horseshoes, shuffleboard.

Important: Even if you get more light-intensity activity, 30 minutes a day of moderate-to-vigorous activity is still important for good health, says Dr. Healy.

heart problem, increasing exercise could cause a heart attack."

● **Make sure your eye exams are up to date.** "Exercise can complicate untreated diabetic eye damage," she says.

STRENGTH-TRAINING— MUSCLE ASIDE DIABETES

If you had to choose a bodyguard, would you pick Arnold Schwarzenegger or Lance Armstrong? You'd probably pick Arnie, the weightlifter, over Lance, the bicycler. Well, the same might go for a "bodyguard" to protect you from diabetes.

⫸ *Breakthrough Studies*

Researchers in the Department of Diabetes and Rheumatology at a hospital in Austria asked 39 men and women with diabetes to participate in a strength-training (lifting weights) program. *After four months, they had positive changes in several important measurements of diabetes…*

● **Decrease in A1C from 8.3% to 7.1%,**

● **Decrease in daily blood glucose levels from 204 to 147,**

● **Decrease in insulin resistance of 22%,**

● **Decrease in total cholesterol, from 207 to 184,**

● **Decrease in "bad" LDL cholesterol, from 120 to 106,**

● **Decrease in triglycerides, from 229 to 150 and**

● **Increase in "good" HDL cholesterol, from 43 to 48.**

"Strength-training may play an important role in the treatment of type 2 diabetes," say the researchers in the *Archives of Physical Medicine and Rehabilitation*.

Prevention, Too

In another study, researchers at Purdue University asked 36 healthy people in their mid-60s to participate for 12 weeks in a resistance-training program in a gym. After the 12 weeks, their glucose tolerance improved by 25 to 30%. "This is a profound improvement, helping to decrease the risk of type 2 diabetes in a group of people who, because they are older, are at higher risk for the disease," says Wayne W. Campbell, PhD, a professor in the Department of Foods and Nutrition at Purdue and the study's lead researcher.

Why it works: Moving muscles activates *glucose transporters* within the cell, moving them from below to within the membrane, where they help the cell absorb more glucose, lowering blood sugar, explains Stephen Headley, PhD, a professor of exercise science and sports studies at Springfield College in Massachusetts and an expert in using exercise to help control and reverse disease.

What to do: "A person with diabetes should use lighter weights and more repetitions," says Dr. Headley. "Working with a knowledgeable trainer at a gym or a personal coach, determine a weight that you can lift about ten times. When you can lift that weight fifteen times, switch to a higher weight." (The typical recommendation is to determine a weight you can lift six to eight times, and switch to a higher weight when you can do 12 repetitions.) Consider strength training two or three times a week.

Routine: The strength-training routine used in the Purdue study.

At every session…

Upper back seated row…Leg extension… Chest press…Leg curl…Latissimus dorsi pull down…Double leg press…Shoulder raise and seated calf press *or* Hip adductor and hip abductor exercises.

RELAX AND HEAL WITH YOGA

It almost seems like you can't drive down a city street without passing a yoga center—where instructors teach the unique stretches, breathing exercises and meditation techniques of this 4,000-year-old system of personal and spiritual development from India.

What you may not know: Yoga is also used as a *therapy* for healing—including control of diabetes.

▷ Breakthrough Study

Researchers at the Center for the Study of Complementary and Alternative Therapies at the University of Virginia Health Systems reviewed more than two dozen scientific studies on yoga for type 2 diabetes. *The studies found the practice of yoga could...*

- **Cut fasting glucose by up to 34%,**
- **Decrease postprandial glucose by up to 33%,**
- **Decrease A1C by up to 27%,**
- **Reduce total cholesterol by up to 20%,**
- **Decrease "bad" LDL cholesterol by up to 8%,**
- **Decrease VLDL cholesterol (a particularly nasty variety) by up to 15%,**
- **Increase "good" HDL cholesterol by up to 4%,**
- **Decrease triglycerides by up to 12%, and**
- **Decrease body weight by up to 8%.**

Yoga practice, the studies showed, could also reduce the need for glucose-controlling medications and reduce episodes of angina.

"The published research offers evidence that yoga may improve risk profiles and clinical outcomes in adults with type 2 diabetes," says Kim E. Innes, PhD, who led the study.

LIFT WITH CAUTION

As with all types of exercise, people with diabetes who strength-train need to take several precautious, says Dr. Headley.

- Before you begin, talk with your doctor to see if strength-training is right for you. If you have diabetic eye disease, such as retinopathy, strength-training might further damage the weakened blood vessels of your eyes.
- Check glucose levels before working out—they should be above 100 to start. If they're not, drink some fruit juice or eat a piece of hard candy.
- Always carry hard candy or fruit juice with you to use if you become hypoglycemic while exercising.
- Strength-train with a partner, who can make sure you don't drop a weight if you suddenly become hypoglycemic.
- Check with your doctor every three months to see if you need an adjustment in your diabetes medication—strength-training can improve long-term blood sugar control.

How yoga works: By reducing stress, says Dr. Innes, yoga might reduce the level of adrenal hormones such as cortisol that can worsen diabetes.

The practice of yoga also stimulates the *vagus nerve*, which extends from the brainstem to the abdomen, and helps control heart rate, breathing and digestion. Stimulating the nerve can tone the heart, improve mood, boost energy and balance hormones and blood chemistry.

And, she points out, yoga philosophy encourages a healthy lifestyle that can lead to weight loss, which can help control diabetes and its circulatory complications.

- **Find a yoga therapist.** To find a yoga therapist near you—a person who teaches yoga for better health and healing—go to the Web site of the International Association of Yoga Therapists at *www.iayt.org*, click on "Find a

Yoga Therapist," and enter your town and state in the form provided. Or contact IAYT, 115 S. McCormick Street, Suite 3, Prescott, AZ 86303 (928-541-0004); e-mail *mail@iayt.org.*

☀ *Yoga as Medicine: The Yogic Prescription for Health and Healing* by Timothy McCall, MD (Bantam). It provides yoga breathing exercises and a 14-exercise yoga routine specifically designed for people with type 2 diabetes.

HERBS AND SPICES

FENUGREEK—POWERFUL FOE OF DIABETES

Fenugreek is an herb with a planetary pedigree. The ancient Egyptians used it to embalm mummies. The ancient Romans, on the other hand, used it to calm mommies, giving it to women in labor to ease birth. In traditional Chinese medicine, fenugreek is touted as a tonic. Ditto for Ayurveda, the ancient system of natural medicine from India, where they also put fenugreek to culinary use in chutneys and curries. And, in the United Kingdom, they say fenugreek seeds "exert antidiabetic effects" by cutting down the amount of carbohydrates absorbed from a meal.

That's the word from scientists at the University of Ulster in Northern Ireland, writing in the *British Journal of Nutrition.* They're one of several scientific teams from around the world that have conducted more than 70 studies on fenugreek and diabetes. *These studies show fenugreek can...*

- **Balance daily blood sugar levels;**
- **Lower A1C**, a measure of long-term blood sugar control;
- **Increase enzymes** that help regulate blood sugar;

PRECAUTIONS FOR YOGIS WITH DIABETES

"Yoga is generally very safe," says Dr. McCall. But, he adds, there are important precautions for people with diabetes...

Consult an eye doctor first. "Anyone with diabetes and retinal disease should avoid inverted postures—such as shoulder stands, headstands and even standing forward bends—and other practices which raise pressure in the eyes, unless given clearance by an ophthalmologist," says Dr. McCall.

Monitor your medications. Yoga works. What once was an appropriate dose of glucose-controlling oral medications or insulin may be too much. "If you're taking medication to lower blood sugar levels, carefully monitor your readings after you begin yoga practice, because glucose levels may drop dangerously low, causing a hypoglycemic reaction," says Dr. McCall. If you think you need to change your medication, consult your doctor.

Don't follow the recommendation not to eat before yoga. "The general recommendation for doing a yoga practice is to avoid eating for several hours before—but this may not be a good idea for people on diabetes medication, whose blood sugar may plummet," says Dr. McCall.

If you have peripheral neuropathy, take extra care. "Since you may not be able to feel your feet, take care with balancing poses such as the Tree Pose," says Dr. McCall. Do those poses near a wall, so you can catch yourself if necessary. And practice with shoes on, to avoid injury to your feet, he adds. Consider using a pair of comfortable, thick-soled shoes reserved for yoga, so you won't track dirt into the yoga studio or onto your mat.

Avoid strenuous classes. Some types of yoga—such as Hot, Vinyasa and Power—may be too strenuous for people with diabetes, especially those with complications, says Dr. McCall. When in doubt, check with the teacher first. Your best bet is to start with a private session.

- **Activate insulin signaling in fat cells and liver cells,** a key to blood sugar regulation;

- **Lower triglycerides,** a blood fat that can increase the risk of heart disease;

- **Lower total cholesterol;**

- **Increase HDL "good" cholesterol;**

- **Thin blood,** reducing the risk of blood clots;

- **Slow diabetic retinopathy,** eye damage that can lead to blindness and

- **Fight cell-damaging oxidants.**

Most of the studies mentioned above were conducted using laboratory animals with diabetes. (Not many pharmaceutical companies foot the hefty bill for human studies on herbs.) But there have been five studies conducted on fenugreek, diabetes and people. Here's the latest.

▐▐▐➤ *Breakthrough Study*

Doctors at the Jaipur Diabetes Center in India divided 25 people newly diagnosed with diabetes into two groups. One group received a daily, 1-gram dose of fenugreek seed extract. The other group started a diet and exercise program.

Two months later, both the diet/exercise and fenugreek groups had similar and substantial decreases in daily glucose levels. But the fenugreek group had *greater* decreases in insulin levels and in insulin resistance.

"Fenugreek seeds and diet/exercise may be equally effective strategies for attaining glycemic control in type 2 diabetes," says Ethan Basch, MD, a member of the editorial board of the *Journal of Herbal Pharmacotherapy.*

And, he and his colleagues add, in a report on the "Therapeutic Applications of Fenugreek" in the *Alternative Medicine Review,* "fenugreek may hold promise" for people with prediabetes, lessening the chance that it will progress to type 2 diabetes.

Product and suggested intake: "For people with diabetes, I recommend Fen-Gre from Standard Process," says Thomas Von Ohlen, MS, CN, director of the Advanced Center for Nutrition in Fairfield, CT. "The typical response is a drop in fasting blood sugar levels from 60 to 80 mg/dl within four months." He suggests a 270 mg capsule, taken twice a day, with the approval and supervision of a physician. "Whenever a diabetes patient is on a medication, we keep an open line of communication with the physician, to make sure they are aware of the possible need to change medication dosages as the patient's condition improves, based on consistent changes in blood sugar readings."

ℹ Fen-Gre is available on-line from *www.standardprocess.com.* Standard Process Inc., 1200 W. Royal Lee Drive, Palmyra, WI 53156 (800-558-8740).

PYCNOGENOL FOR FOOT ULCERS

If you're a person with diabetes, odds are 1 in 5 that sooner or later you'll find yourself hospitalized with a foot problem—and that doctors will have to amputate a toe or foot. Nine times out of ten, the foot problem started with a foot ulcer.

Foot ulcers plague people with diabetes for a couple of reasons. Foot deformities (common in diabetes) cause pressure in unusual areas, such as the tops of the toes. A sore forms but goes unnoticed—because nerve damage (diabetic neuropathy) has numbed the foot. Poor circulation slows healing. The ulcer doesn't close, gets larger, gets infected...and the foot or one or more toes has to go.

Obviously, *healing* the ulcer can prevent amputation. "The primary goal of treatment of diabetic foot ulcers is wound closure," says

Robert Frykberg, DPM, a podiatrist at Des Moines University in Iowa. But if wound closure were easy, amputation wouldn't be common. *Now for the good news…*

A person with a diabetic foot ulcer has a new, powerful (and natural) option for wound healing: Pycnogenol, the water extract of the bark of the maritime pine tree, which grows along the coast of southwest France.

▐▐▐▶ *Breakthrough Studies*

A team of doctors from universities in Italy and Germany treated 30 patients with diabetic foot ulcers with one of four treatments…

1. Pycnogenol, taken as a supplement and topically applied to the ulcer

2. Supplement only

3. Topical only or

4. Standard medications for foot ulcers, such as antibiotics.

Of those receiving the combined Pycnogenol treatment, 89%—nine out of ten—had *complete healing* of foot ulcers after six weeks. The rate was 85% on the supplement alone and 84% with topical application alone. Meanwhile, only 61% of those receiving standard medications had total healing.

"Combined systemic and local application of Pycnogenol may offer a new treatment for diabetic ulcers," say the researchers.

Why it works: In another study by the same team of doctors, 60 people with diabetes but without foot ulcers were given either 150 mg of Pycnogenol a day or a placebo. Those who received the supplement had a greater increase in the microcirculation of the foot, while those on the placebo didn't. This finding, say the researchers, shows not only *why* Pycnogenol heals foot ulcers—by improving circulation to the foot—but that it can also help *prevent* them.

In another study, the same researchers used 200 mg of Pycnogenol a day to reduce cramps and muscle pain in people with diabetes—a big help if you're trying to start or maintain a sugar-controlling exercise program.

Talk to your doctor about Pycnogenol. Your physician can find the complete citations to the articles discussed in this section at *www.pycnogenol.com* and work with you to decide if Pycnogenol is the right treatment (or preventive remedy) for you.

Product and suggested intake: Many companies sell Pycnogenol-containing supplements and topical products in supermarkets, drugstores, health-food stores and on the Internet. Working with your doctor, follow the supplement parameters used in the studies—150 to 200 mg a day, in 50 mg doses taken three to four times a day.

CINNAMON—NATURE'S INSULIN-LIKE SPICE

In 2003, scientists published a remarkable finding in the journal *Diabetes Care*…

Thirty people with diabetes who took 1 to 3 grams of cinnamon for 40 days had significant decreases in health measurements every doctor who treats diabetes likes to see fall. *Decreases of up to…*

- **29% in fasting blood sugar;**
- **27% in LDL "bad" cholesterol;**
- **26% in total cholesterol; and**
- **30% in triglycerides, a blood fat linked to heart disease.**

In 2006, Dutch researchers reported a study in which 40 people with diabetes took 3 grams of cinnamon a day for four months. They had a *three times* greater drop in fasting blood sugar levels than people with diabetes who didn't take the herb.

The good news about cinnamon and blood sugar keeps on coming—for those with diabetes *and* those who want to prevent it...

IIII▶ *Breakthrough Study*

Swedish researchers studied 14 healthy people, feeding them the same meal twice—rice pudding, with or without a hefty sprinkling of cinnamon. The cinnamon-spiced meal significantly lowered postmeal levels of blood sugar.

How cinnamon works: The herb mimics the action of insulin, explains Richard Anderson, PhD, a researcher at the Beltsville Human Nutrition Research Center in Maryland, and the coauthor of 10 scientific studies on cinnamon, including the 2003 breakthrough study. "Cinnamon stimulates insulin receptors on fat and muscle cells the same way insulin does, allowing excess sugar to move out of the blood and into the cells."

Suggested intake: Try to get ¼ to 1 teaspoon daily, says Dr. Anderson. Sprinkle it on hot cereals, yogurt or applesauce. Use it to accent sweet potatoes, winter squash or yams. Try it with lamb, beef stew or chilies. It even goes great with grains such as couscous and barley, and legumes such as lentils and split peas.

Supplementing, with the right dose: "I like cinnamon supplements, because they're an easy way to deal with high blood sugar and high blood fats," says Dr. Peters. "You can take a cinnamon supplement with every meal."

Consider taking 1 to 3 grams per day, says Dr. Anderson, which was the dosage range in the 2003 study; 3 grams were used in the 2006 study.

ℹ️ One gram cinnamon capsules are widely available, including from Nature's Bounty, Mason Natural, and Good 'N Natural brands.

SALACIA OBLONGA CAN BLOCK CARBS

A class of drugs for type 2 diabetes—*alpha-glucosidase inhibitors* such as Precose (arbacose) and Glyset (miglitol)—work by blocking the absorption of carbohydrates from your digestive tract, lowering glucose and insulin. A study in the *Journal of Clinical Nutrition* shows an herb can do the same thing.

IIII▶ *Breakthrough Study*

The herb is *Salacia oblonga*. It's native to India, where for thousands of years Ayurvedic physicians—practitioners of an ancient system of natural medicine—have used the root to treat diabetes.

To test the herb, American researchers concocted a high-carbohydrate drink, adding either 480 or 240 mg of *S. oblonga* extract. Then they asked 66 people with diabetes who hadn't eaten for a while to chug one of three versions of the drink...

1. Just the drink

2. The drink with 480 mg of extract or

3. The drink with 240 mg.

For the next three hours, the scientists measured their blood levels of glucose and insulin. Those getting the herb-enhanced drink had *much* lower glucose levels compared to those who got the carb-only drink: 27% lower for 480 mg, and 19% lower for 240 mg. Insulin was also, 19% lower for 480 mg and 12% lower for 240 mg.

"S. oblonga works similarly to alpha-glucosidase inhibitors, and could be an ideal nutritional therapy for type 2 diabetes," says Jennifer Williams, MPH, the clinical scientist who led the study. "People often find it tough to stick with dietary restrictions, and S. oblonga might allow a person with diabetes to eat a carbohydrate-rich meal without a big spike in blood sugar."

How to use: The Japanese use S. oblonga as a food ingredient and supplement to control diabetes and obesity. But, as with all nutritional and herbal therapies, those with diabetes should only use S. oblonga with the approval and supervision of their physician.

Where to find: You can order S. oblonga on-line from India-based companies, at the following English-language Web sites...

🛈 *www.salaciaoblongacapsules.com.* Botanika, 34 Old Cannought Place, Dehra Dun-248001, Uttaranchal, India (00-91-135-271-5222); e-mail *info@salaciaoblongacapsules.com.*

www.herbscancure.com/salacia.htm. IvyComm Systems, 1405, Sector 14, Faridabad HR 121007 India (00-91-981-818-1405).

BANABA—ANCIENT HERB, MODERN SUCCESS

It's called *banaba* in the Philippines, *bang-lang* in Cambodia, *bungor* in Malaya and *jalal* in India. For thousands of years, folk healers in these southeast Asian countries have used the many-named plant to lower blood sugar. Scientists are catching on.

⫸ *Breakthrough Studies*

Japanese researchers in the Department of Diabetes and Clinical Nutrition at Kyoto University gave 31 people with diabetes and other blood sugar problems either corosolic acid (the active ingredient of banaba) or a placebo. Then they gave them a big dose of dietary sugar, in what's called a *glucose tolerance test.* An hour later...90 minutes later...and 2 hours later...those taking the banaba had much lower blood sugar levels.

In a similar study conducted in the United States, 10 people with diabetes were given banaba for 2 weeks—and their high blood sugar dropped by 30%.

Why it works: Corosolic acid stimulates cells to absorb glucose, say the researchers.

Suggested intake: 32 to 48 mg a day of a banaba extract standardized to 1% corosolic acid (CRA), the active ingredient.

🛈 The US study used Glucosol, a soft-gel formulation found in many products, including Glucotrim from NSI, Gluco Trim from NOW Foods and Glucosol/Rx-Blood Sugar from Nature's Plus.

GINSENG FOR BETTER BLOOD SUGAR CONTROL

Ginseng root is one of the most popular herbs on the market, with nearly 5% of American adults taking it to boost energy and alertness. If you have diabetes, ginseng may also boost your efforts to control blood sugar—even if you're already taking diabetes medications!

⫸ *Breakthrough Study*

Researchers in the Department of Nutritional Sciences at the University of Toronto studied the effect of ginseng on 19 people with well-controlled diabetes. They divided them into two groups. For three months, one group took 6 grams of ginseng a day and the other took a placebo. For the next three months, the groups reversed, with ginseng-takers taking the placebo and placebo-takers taking ginseng. Throughout the study, researchers measured A1C, glucose tolerance, blood levels of insulin and insulin sensitivity.

They also evaluated the safety of the herb, testing liver and kidney function, blood chemistry and blood pressure levels. *After six months, those taking the ginseng had up to...*

- **11% better glucose tolerance**
- **38% lower insulin levels**
- **33% greater insulin sensitivity**

"It is very important to note that these effects were achieved in people with well-controlled diabetes who were *already* taking diabetes medications," says Vladimir Vuksan, PhD, professor in the Department of Nutritional Sciences at the University of Toronto and a researcher who has conducted more than a dozen studies on ginseng and diabetes. "In other words, even if a person's diet and medication regimen is working, ginseng may *still* improve blood sugar control."

Suggested ginseng variety and dose: This is where it gets tricky, says Dr. Vuksan…

There are many different kinds of ginseng, he explains. There's Asian, or *panax ginseng*… sometimes called Chinese or Korean, sometimes derived from wild plants and sometimes from cultivated varieties…sometimes red (dried and steamed) and sometimes white…sometimes powdered and sometimes in the form of a water- or alcohol-based extract. And then there's American, or *panax quinquefolius*…with the same type of variability.

In a study published in *Diabetes Care*, Dr. Vuksan and his colleagues reviewed studies that analyzed 317 batches of various kinds of ginseng—and found huge differences in the level of ginsenosides (perhaps the main active ingredient in the herb). Other research conducted by Dr. Vuksan shows some ginsengs lower blood sugar…some have no effect…and some actually raise it. "The use of herbs such as ginseng in diabetes must be approached cautiously," he says.

So be cautious…talk to your doctor about whether supplementing your regimen with ginseng is a good idea, and do so only with your physician's approval and supervision.

If you and your doctor decide ginseng is right for you, look for a brand that combines both Asian (Korean) and American ginseng. Dr. Vuksan says future research may show this combination might be "the ultimate herbal treatment of diabetes."

🛈 Two widely available products with both Asian and American ginseng approved by ConsumerLab.com (a company that tests nutritional and herbal supplements to verify their potency and purity) are Action Labs Guaranteed Potency Ginseng Powermax, from Nutraceutical Corporation, and TruNature (Costco) Triple Energy Extract, from Inverness Medical Nutritionals Group. Follow the dosage recommendations on the label, says Dr. Vuksan.

Latest Development

Preliminary studies conducted by Dr. Vuksan show that combining ginseng *with* the fiber supplement PGX (discussed on page 125) provides even greater benefits in controlling blood sugar than ginseng alone.

HAWTHORN MAY LOWER HIGH BLOOD PRESSURE

People with diabetes often have high blood pressure, a risk factor for heart attack and stroke. High blood pressure can also increase the risk of eye and kidney disease, common complications of diabetes. The herb hawthorn may help lower blood pressure—even if you're already taking pressure-lowering medication.

⫸ *Breakthrough Study*

Researchers at the University of Reading in England studied 79 people with diabetes, 56 of whom were taking medications for high blood pressure. For 16 weeks, 40 people took a daily dose of 1,200 mg of hawthorn extract, while 39 took a placebo. Researchers measured blood pressure levels at the beginning and end of the study.

Among those taking the herb, diastolic blood pressure (the lower reading) dropped three points. There was no change in those taking the placebo.

Why it works: The active ingredient in hawthorn are *flavonoids*, which relax blood vessels, says Ann F. Walker, PhD, a member of the National Institute of Medical Herbalists in the UK, senior lecturer in human nutrition at the University of Reading and the lead scientist on the study.

Suggested intake: Look for a hawthorn extract standardized to a minimum of 1.8% vitexin (the active ingredient). With your doctor's approval and supervision, consider taking 1,200 mg a day, the amount used in the study. Although this is higher than the typical dose of hawthorn recommended by herbalists, it's the level necessary to lower high blood pressure, says Dr. Walker. This is a safe level of intake, she adds.

ℹ️ Widely available brands of standardized hawthorn extract include Pure Encapsulations Hawthorn Extract (500 mg), Nature's Way Standardized Hawthorn Extract (300 mg), NOW Foods Hawthorn Extract (300 mg) and Nature's Plus Extended Release Hawthorn (300 mg).

MIND–BODY HEALING

LAUGHTER—MORE ABOUT THE BEST MEDICINE

Joan: *Hey, June, did you hear about the artists who held a competition?*

Joan: *No? How did it turn out?*
June: *It was a draw.*

If you laughed at that joke, you may have lowered your blood sugar.

▶ *Breakthrough Study*

Researchers in Japan studied 19 people in their 50s and 60s with diabetes. On the first day of the study, they ate lunch—and then listened to a boring lecture. Over the following two hours, their average postmeal glucose level rose 123 mg. On the second day, they had the same meal —then watched a comedy routine. This time, their glucose rose 77 mg—about 37% less!

Laughter lessens the typical postmeal rise in glucose, say the researchers in *Diabetes Care*.

Why it works: More muscular activity, less stress (negative emotions are known to increase glucose levels), or both, say the researchers.

In two subsequent studies on laughter and diabetes, the Japanese researchers found...

International Journal of Molecular Medicine. Three months of laughter therapy in people with diabetes lowered blood levels of renin, a biochemical that can raise blood pressure, damaging arteries and veins. "Laughter therapy can be used as a nonpharmacological treatment for the prevention of diabetic complications," they say.

Journal of Psychosomatic Research. Twenty-three people with diabetic kidney disease (nephropathy) who watched a comedy show lowered their levels of a receptor gene and a biochemical (*prorenin*) that worsens the condition. The study, say the researchers, strongly indicates "the beneficial effects of laughter on preventing the worsening of diabetic nephropathy."

What to do: Page through joke books. Watch DVDs of standup, sitcoms and comedic movies. Humor is very subjective, but there's plenty of funny material out there. Some recommendations from "jollytologist" Allen

Klein, author of *The Healing Power of Humor* (J.P. Tarcher) and many other books and joke collections...

● **Stand-Up Videos.** *Robin Williams Live on Broadway; Bill Cosby, Himself; Johnny Carson: The Johnny Carson Collection; Milton Berle: Mad World of Comedy.*

● **Comedic Videos.** *Some Like It Hot; Tootsie; Dr. Strangelove; Annie Hall; Duck Soup* (the top five comedies selected by the American Film Institute).

● **Joke books.** *The Penguin Dictionary of Jokes, Wisecracks, Quips and Quotes* by Fred Metcalf (Penguin); *Oxford Dictionary of Humorous Quotations* by Ned Sherrin (Oxford University Press); *An Encyclopedia of Humor*, by Lowell Streiker (Hendrickson).

☀ You can order many of these and other laughter-inducing products at *www.allenklein.com*.

THREE EASY WAYS TO TEE-HEE

Find it hard to laugh? Try these tips from Annette Goodheart, PhD, psychotherapist, "laughter counselor" and author of *Laughter Therapy.*

Fake it till you make it. "Your diaphragm is stupid," says Dr. Goodheart, with a smile. "If you fake the laughter—just say 'ha-ha' or 'tee-hee' over and over—your diaphragm will kick in like a car engine and you'll start laughing."

Smile more. "The more you smile, the more the muscles of your face are prepared to laugh," she says.

Laugh with strangers. If you walk past people who are laughing, don't hold back—laugh along with them.

For more information about Dr. Goodheart and laughter counseling, see her Web site, *www.laughtercoach.com*, or e-mail her at *teehee@teehee.com*.

BIOFEEDBACK—LESS STRESS, LOWER SUGAR

When you think of illnesses caused or complicated by stress, you probably think of headaches, ulcers or heart disease. But *diabetes*? What does stress have to do with uncontrolled blood sugar? A lot, say scientists.

Stress is a *stimulant*—it pumps sugar into the bloodstream and releases hormones that destabilize sugar levels. And when you're stressed, you're less likely to exercise and eat right, factors that help keep sugar balanced.

A literally groundbreaking study highlights the stress/sugar connection. Japanese researchers compared blood sugar levels in people with diabetes in two cities hit by earthquakes: Kobe, where there was a lot of death and destruction; and Osaka, where there wasn't. On average, people in Kobe with diabetes had higher levels of blood sugar—and those who lost relatives or property had the highest levels.

Any stress that shakes you up is bad news for blood sugar. The good news is stress-reduction techniques can solve the problem.

➤ *Breakthrough Study*

Doctors from the Department of Psychiatry at the Medical University of Ohio in Toledo divided 39 people with diabetes into two groups. One group received biofeedback and relaxation training; the other, educational information about the disease. Biofeedback and relaxation training *reduced* blood sugar by 11%; in the education group, levels *increased* slightly. "Patients with type 2 diabetes could significantly improve blood sugar control through the use of biofeedback and relaxation training," say the researchers in *Diabetes Care.*

How biofeedback works: You're hooked up to a machine that monitors stress-sensitive body activity such as skin temperature or muscle tension, and gives you feedback—a beep or flashing light—when you're stressed. You learn to recognize signs of tension, with or without the machine. And when you *know* you're tense, you can do something about it—with relaxation techniques such as deep breathing.

☀ To find a nearby biofeedback practitioner…

Visit the Web site of the Association for Applied Psychophysiology and Biofeedback, at *www.aapb.org*. Click "Find a Provider" on the home page, and the "Provider Directory" near the bottom of the next page. *To contact:* Association for Applied Psychophysiology and Biofeedback, 10200 W. 44th Avenue, Suite 304, Wheat Ridge, CO 80033 (800-477-8892 or 303-422-8436); e-mail *AAPB@resourcenter.com*.

Visit the Biofeedback Certification Institute of America, at *www.bcia.org*. Click, "How Can I Find a BCIA Certified Provider Near Me?" Contact: BCIA, 10200 W. 44th Ave., Suite 310, Wheat Ridge, CO 80033-2840 (303-420-2902 or 866-908-8713); e-mail *bcia@resourcenter.com*.

SOCIAL SUPPORT—FRIENDS ARE THE BEST MEDICINE

"Diabetes is an immense challenge," says Francine Kaufman, MD, past-president of the American Diabetes Association and author of *Diabesity*. "After the diagnosis, nothing will be as it was before. You will have to develop the skills to manage your disease yourself—to check blood sugar four or five times a day, take medication and eat to balance blood sugar. You will need to see your doctor every three months—with the specter of fearsome diabetes complications. And on top of everything else, there are the costs in money and time."

But you don't have to go it alone. "Friends, family, coworkers and other people with diabetes can be a real source of support," says Dr.

DIAGNOSED WITH DIABETES? BLAME YOUR BOSS

Your job can get to you. And to your pancreas.

Israeli researchers at Tel Aviv University studied nearly 700 employed, healthy men and women for three to five years—managers, professionals, nonprofessionals, self-employed. At the end of the study period, the researchers gave everyone a questionnaire assessing their level of chronic burnout—emotional exhaustion, physical fatigue and mental weariness. Those with the highest level of burnout were 84% more likely to have been diagnosed with diabetes during the study. What's the connection between burnout and blood sugar?

Burnout can cause high cholesterol and inflammation, two conditions that interfere with the cell's ability to use blood sugar, explains Samuel Melamed, PhD, the scientist who led the study.

What to do: First, figure out if you're a victim of burnout, says Dr. Melamed. Do the following statements describe you?

I feel fed up. I feel like my batteries are dead. I feel tired. I feel physically drained. I have difficulty concentrating. I feel I'm not thinking clearly.

If that sounds like you, you're probably burned out. Dr. Melamed's advice is to identify what and who is bothering you at work, and—if you can—avoid or reduce your contact with those situations and people.

Also important: Eat a healthy diet. Get enough sleep. And be assertive—don't say yes to stressful tasks or commitments you can't handle.

For more ways to handle burnout, see the section on burnout in Chapter 16, "Stress, Insomnia and Fatigue," page 415.

Peters. Support...and much better diabetes control.

⫸ *Breakthrough Studies*

Researchers in England analyzed 11 scientific studies that look at "group-based diabetes education programs"—meeting with other people with diabetes to learn self-management strategies for the disease. More than a year after attending such a program, people who participated had A1C levels an average 1% lower than people who didn't. They also had lower fasting blood sugar levels, weighed less, had lower blood pressure and less need for diabetes medications.

And, in Holland, researchers at Maastricht University found similar results in people who participated in ongoing "peer support" groups—even over the Internet or on the phone.

What to do: Get in touch—and get better!

☀ The American Diabetes Association maintains a state-by-state listing of education programs at *www.diabetes.org/education/edustate2. asp.* American Diabetes Association, National Call Center, 1701 North Beauregard Street, Alexandria, VA 22311 (800-342-2383); e-mail *AskADA@diabetes.org.*

The Defeat Diabetes Foundation maintains a state-by-state listing of Diabetes Education Programs and Peer Support Groups at *www. defeatdiabetes.org/support_groups.htm.*

For more information, you can also contact government organizations:

National Diabetes Information Clearinghouse (NDIC), One Information Way, Bethesda, MD 20892-3560 (800-860-8747); e-mail *ndic@ info.niddk.nih.gov* or visit on-line at *www.diabetes. niddk.nih.gov.*

National Diabetes Education Program (NDEP), One Diabetes Way, Bethesda, MD 20814-9692 (888-693-6337); e-mail *ndep@ mail.nih.gov* or visit on-line at *www.ndep.nih.gov.*

7

DIGESTIVE DISORDERS
GREAT NEWS FOR YOUR GUT

Digestion—the body's processing of food into energy—is like breathing: You hardly think about it until something goes wrong. Unfortunately for us Americans, something is going wrong a lot of the time.

One third to one half of American adults have a digestive problem—more than 62 million people. And those problems are the number two reason Americans seek medical attention, right behind the common cold. "There is an *epidemic* of digestive illness in the US," says Elizabeth Lipski, PhD, CCN, a nutritionist in Asheville, NC, and author of *Digestive Wellness* (McGraw-Hill). Why is our collective gut so upset?

Not because of an Alka-Seltzer shortage. It's our modern lifestyle, explains Dr. Lipski. "We eat unnatural, processed foods. We don't exercise regularly. We don't get enough sleep. All those habits undermine healthy digestion. And nonstop stress also targets the digestive system, which has more nerve endings than the spine."

In many cases, she says, a seemingly unsolvable digestive problem, such as chronic heartburn, will vanish after a person takes a closer look at his or her lifestyle and makes healthful modifications—eating more whole foods…going for regular walks…relaxing now and then with a hobby or other enjoyable activity…getting enough sleep.

"*Self-care* is the key to digestive wellness," she emphasizes. And, says Dr. Lipski, self-care includes nutritional, herbal and other drug-free remedies.

DRUG-FREE WAYS TO DOUSE HEARTBURN

Heartburn happens when stomach acid doesn't stay put. Instead, it refluxes back into the esophagus, the tube between the mouth and stomach. Your chest or throat (or both) *burn*—maybe for a few minutes, maybe for a couple of hours. You might even taste the regurgitated acidic stomach contents. Yuck!

Occasional heartburn is a fact of life for 60 million Americans. For another 25 million Americans, it can occur twice a week, even at night, and may not back off when treated with over-the-counter medication. Those folks have what doctors call *gastroesophageal reflux disease* (GERD).

GERD is no fun. People with the problem commonly report they enjoy life (and food) a whole lot less. But GERD can do more than ruin your day. It can end your life—with long-term damage that literally erodes the lining of the esophagus, a problem that can advance from esophageal irritation (*esophagitis*) to *esophageal adenocarcinoma*, a once rare but now common cancer that has quadrupled in incidence over the last 20 years…along with a similar rise in the incidence of GERD.

If you have GERD, a doctor may prescribe an acid-suppressing proton pump inhibitor (PPI), such as Nexium (the second biggest-selling drug in the world), or Prevacid. And you'll probably be told to take that drug every day for the rest of your life. Fine and dandy for your esophagus. But as far as your bones are concerned, that once-a-day drug regimen might be a big mistake.

New danger: Doctors at the University of Pennsylvania School of Medicine analyzed data from more than 145,000 people and found that those taking a PPI daily for one year had a 21% higher risk of hip fracture than people not taking the drug. And the longer they took PPIs, the higher the risk—41% higher after two years, 54% higher after three years and 59% after four years. For those on the highest doses of the drug, the risk was 265% higher!

PPIs cut down your body's ability to absorb bone-protecting calcium, explains Yu-Xiao Yang, MD, the lead author of the study published in the *Journal of the American Medical Association.* "The general perception among physicians and the public is that PPIs are relatively harmless, but that may not be the case," he says.

In fact, other studies show PPIs more than double your risk of colds and flu, and increase your risk of pneumonia by 63%—because there's too little stomach acid to kill viruses and bacteria, and they migrate into your respiratory tract.

Fortunately, there are many safe, effective drug-free remedies for heartburn and GERD.

FIBER HELPS, FAT HURTS

Seven out of 10 people with heartburn say fatty foods trigger their symptoms. But scientists have never provided conclusive evidence that fat (or any other food component) is the culprit. Until now.

IIII➤ *Breakthrough Study*

Gastroenterologists at the Houston Veterans Affairs Center analyzed a year's worth of dietary data from nearly 400 people. Those *most likely* to have heartburn got 40% of their calories from fat, while those *least likely* got 30%. Those with the most heartburn also ate 14% more saturated fat and 13% more cholesterol. (High fat intake and heartburn were particularly linked in people who were overweight.)

The researchers also found that people eating the most fiber—about 20 grams a day—were the *least likely* to have heartburn (no matter what their weight).

What happens: There are two possible mechanisms for the fat/heartburn connection, say experts.

Fatty foods—particularly foods rich in saturated fat and cholesterol, such as red meat—relax the *lower esophageal sphincter* (LES), the muscular valve that stops acid from seeping out of the stomach.

Or dietary fat may lower your pain threshold, making you more sensitive to acid in the esophagus, says Ronnie Fass, MD, a gastroenterologist and professor of medicine at the University of Arizona.

(While the heartburn-causing effect of fat is well understood, scientists don't know how fiber works to prevent heartburn, says Hashem

El-Serag, MD, the lead author of the study published in the medical journal *Gut*.)

What to do: You can limit fat to 30% of calories *and* increase the fiber in your diet by maximizing your intake of vegetables, fruits and whole grains, says Chris Meletis, ND, a naturopathic physician in Beaverton, OR, and executive director, Institute of Healthy Aging.

Recommended: Five to nine daily servings of vegetables (½ cup) and fruits (1 small or medium-size piece); four to five daily servings of whole grains (1 slice of bread, 1 cup of ready-to-eat cereal, ½ cup of cooked rice, cooked pasta or cooked cereal).

And since saturated fat and cholesterol are linked to heartburn, Dr. Meletis says to cut your intake of red meat to one or two 4-ounce servings a week, a portion about the size of a deck of cards.

THE CHEWING GUM CURE

Regurgitated stomach acid can destroy teeth. A team of British dentists theorized that chewing gum might help prevent the problem—by increasing the rate of swallowing, which can wash acid out of the esophagus.

To test their idea, the dentists fed 31 people with reflux two fatty meals designed to produce heartburn. After one of the meals, the people chewed sugar-free gum for half an hour; after the other meal, they didn't.

Those who chewed gum had 37% less reflux.

"Chewing sugar-free gum for half an hour after a meal can reduce acid esophageal reflux," says Dr. Rebecca Moazzez, the lead author of the study, in the *Journal of Dental Research*.

Now there's a remedy with teeth in it.

ACUPUNCTURE—A BOOST TO MEDICATION

When a proton pump inhibitor (PPI) such as Nexium doesn't stop GERD, a doctor often doubles the dose from once to twice a day. But this strategy usually doesn't improve GERD symptoms, says Dr. Fass, director of the GI Motility Laboratory at the University of Arizona Health Sciences Center. So, Dr. Fass and his colleagues teamed up with experts in natural medicine and acupuncture to try a different approach.

⫸ *Breakthrough Study*

Thirty patients with GERD who weren't getting better on a standard dose of PPI were divided into two groups. In one group, the PPI dose was doubled; in the other, acupuncture was added to the standard dose. After four weeks, the acupuncture/PPI group had less daytime heartburn, nighttime heartburn and acid regurgitation. (They also felt healthier in general.) The group with the doubled dose didn't see any improvement. (And they didn't notice any change in general health, either.)

"Adding acupuncture is more effective than doubling the proton pump inhibitor dose in controlling GERD-related symptoms in patients who failed standard-dose proton pump inhibitors," says Dr. Fass.

Why it works: People who don't respond to PPI often have a hypersensitive digestive tract that can be calmed by acupuncture, explains Dr. Fass.

What to do: "Patients who do not achieve symptom relief with once-a-day PPI should consider adding acupuncture instead of switching to a twice-a-day dose of PPI," he says. Talk to your doctor about this option.

☀ See page 33 for how to find an acupuncturist near you.

LIFESTYLE FIXES—WHAT SCIENCE SAYS WORKS

There are lots of lifestyle recommendations out there for preventing heartburn—eat smaller meals...don't consume acidic foods and beverages such as tomatoes, coffee or tea...don't drink alcohol...loosen your belt...and many more. They're all worth trying. But which of those recommendations have been *scientifically* shown to work? Here's the scoop from some of the world's top medical schools and clinics.

⫸ *Breakthrough Studies*

Tilt the head of your bed. An analysis of 16 studies on lifestyle and heartburn by gastroenterologists at Stanford University School of Medicine in California shows that elevating the head of the bed a few inches reliably reduces nighttime heartburn. The reason is that a little extra gravity stops acid from flowing back into the esophagus.

"Use a 4x4 or 4x6 piece of wood under the legs at the head of the bed," says Dr. Lipski. "It's such a small change you won't even notice it, but it's enough extra gravity so that it works."

● **Sleep on your left side.** It reduces nighttime heartburn, say the Stanford doctors, because acid drains out of the esophagus faster.

● **Lose weight.** Doctors at the Baylor College of Medicine found that overweight people (body mass index higher than 25) have a 54% higher risk of heartburn and obese people (body mass index higher than 30) have a 278% higher risk. The extra fat increases pressure on the stomach, forcing acidic stomach contents into the esophagus.

● **Don't smoke.** Longtime smokers (cigarettes, pipes or cigars) have a 70% greater risk of heartburn symptoms, say Swedish researchers from the Karolinska Institute in Stockholm, because smoking weakens the lower esophageal sphincter.

● **Cut back on the salt.** Ditto for people who always use lots of table salt, say the Swedes, though the reason is not known.

● **Exercise regularly.** Thirty minutes of physical exercise such as jogging or swimming at least once a week decreased the incidence of heartburn by 50%, in the Swedish study. Strengthening the diaphragm, which works with the lower esophageal sphincter, helps to keep acid in place.

● **Cut back on sugary sweets and white bread.** They increase symptoms, say doctors at

BUBBLE TROUBLE

Should people with heartburn avoid carbonated beverages?

"It makes sense to do so," says Peter Crookes, MD, an associate professor in the Department of Surgery at the University of Southern California (USC).

Dr. Crookes is so confident because of a study he and his colleagues conducted. Nine healthy volunteers (including himself) drank carbonated beverages such as cola and carbonated bottled water. Next, they underwent a unique test developed at USC to measure the strength of the lower esophageal sphincter (LES), the muscular passageway between the esophagus and stomach that relaxes to let food through and squeezes shut to keep acidic stomach contents where they belong.

After drinking the carbonated beverages, LES strength levels decreased by 30 to 50%, a diseaselike drop. Tap water, on the other hand, had *no* effect.

"We've always suspected that there were dietary components that were increasing the prevalence of heartburn and GERD in America," says Dr. Crookes. "The increasing consumption of carbonated beverages parallels the increasing incidence of reflux disease, so they may be an important factor driving the increase.

the Charite University Medical Center in Berlin, Germany, though the reason is unknown.

- **Don't ban these beverages.** The Stanford and Swedish doctors found that several beverages, such as alcohol, tea and coffee, frequently blamed for heartburn had *no* effect.

INDIGESTION

You *don't* have heartburn. You *don't* have an ulcer. You *don't* have stomach cancer. You're *not* taking a nonsteroidal anti-inflammatory drug (NSAID), such as aspirin or ibuprofen, a common cause of stomach injury and pain. So what *is* your problem?

When doctors rule out all the testable causes for frequent tummy troubles, they call the condition *functional dyspepsia*. (You call it indigestion or a stomachache.) The mix of symptoms can include gnawing or burning pain in the upper abdomen, above the navel; feeling uncomfortably full after eating only a little food; bloating and belching and nausea or vomiting.

GI experts don't know for sure what causes indigestion. Some theorize that nerves in the digestive tract are misfiring. Others speculate that intestinal muscles are either too active or not active enough. But whatever the cause, drugs aren't much help.

Over-the-counter and prescription drugs used for dyspepsia (and there are dozens, from Alka-Seltzer to Zantac) are not "substantially effective," says Jay W. Marks, MD, former associate director of the Division of Gastroenterology at Cedars-Sinai Medical Center in Los Angeles. In fact, a study shows that three out of five people with dyspepsia still have symptoms after a year of taking supposedly dyspepsia-defeating drugs.

Which is why it might be a good idea to try drug-free ways to soothe your stomachache.

THE WONDER OF IBEROGAST

There's no standard therapy for functional dyspepsia because no therapy has been proven to work, say German doctors in the *American Journal of Gastroenterology*. That's why they tested the herbal remedy Iberogast, which is an extract of clown's mustard plant (*Iberis amara*, an herb found in Spain and Western Europe) combined with eight other digestion-regulating herbs—lemon balm leaf, chamomile flower, caraway fruit, peppermint leaf, licorice root, angelica root, milk thistle fruit and greater celandine herb.

⫸ *Breakthrough Studies*

The German doctors asked 315 patients with dyspepsia to take either Iberogast or a placebo for eight weeks. Compared to the placebo group, those taking Iberogast had a much greater reduction in symptoms such as abdominal pain, nausea and fullness.

Complete relief: In another German study, published in the journal *Digestion*, 43% of people with dyspepsia taking Iberogast had "complete relief" after eight weeks—compared to 3% of people taking the placebo.

Effective and safe: Swiss doctors from University Hospital Zurich and German researchers from the University of Heidelberg analyzed the results of several studies on Iberogast, in which 273 people with dyspepsia took either the herbal preparation or a placebo. Iberogast was far more effective—significantly reducing stomach pain, abdominal cramps, nausea and heartburn—and produced no significant side effects. "From the point of view of efficacy and safety," says Jorg Melzer, MD, one of the doctors who conducted the study, Iberogast is a "valid therapeutic option" for the treatment of dyspepsia.

"Iberogast is the best-studied and safest preparation available for indigestion, and should be the first choice for treating this problem," says Olaf Kelber, MD, a German doctor who has studied the remedy. "You should always have a bottle in your luggage when traveling!"

Why it works: Researchers at the Royal Adelaide Hospital in Australia gave either Iberogast or a placebo to 29 healthy men and then repeatedly measured their stomach function for 2 hours after a meal. The herbal formula relaxed the muscles of the stomach, increasing its size by 41% compared to the placebo group. (More stomach room means less uncomfortable feelings of fullness.) It also improved *antral motility*—the strength of muscular "pressure waves" in the part of the stomach that connects to the small intestine. (Faster digestion means less chance indigestion can take hold.) These two effects might underlie the "therapeutic efficacy" of Iberogast in dyspepsia, say the researchers, in the *American Journal of Gastroenterology*.

New thinking: Writing in the journal *Phytomedicine*, an international team of doctors from Germany, Poland and Australia say dyspepsia is caused by a "large number of mechanisms." But drugs for dyspepsia typically target only *one* of those mechanisms, increased acid secretion, they add—and are "unlikely to be effective in all patients." Iberogast, on the other hand, has nine plant extracts, which together address the range of mechanisms that can trigger dyspepsia. The herbal treatment—not the drug—is the treatment more likely to be "advantageous" in treating dyspepsia, say the doctors.

Suggested dosage: Twenty drops a day, three times a day, says Dr. Kelber. You can take the drops directly, or mix them with one to two ounces of warm water and drink before, with or after a meal.

☀ Iberogast is manufactured in the US by Medical Futures, and can be ordered from eVitamins, at *www.evitamins.com* (888-222-6056); and Emerson Ecologics, *www.emersonecologics. com* (800-654-4432), *cs@emersonecologics.com*.

ARTICHOKE LEAF EXTRACT PROVIDES RELIEF

The French adore the *artichaut*—they've been using it for indigestion for centuries, post-foie gras. The German Commission E—recognized by experts worldwide as the last word on the therapeutic use of herbs—also recommends the *artischocke* for digestive complaints. Now researchers are finding that supplements of *artichoke leaf extract* (ALE) can provide digestive relief.

⫸ *Breakthrough Studies*

Doctors at the University of Reading in England gave ALE to 454 people with dyspepsia. After two months, they had a 40% reduction in symptoms and their overall quality of life improved.

In a similar study conducted by German gastroenterologists at the University of Essen, 244 patients with dyspepsia took either ALE or a placebo for six weeks. Those taking ALE had a 20% greater improvement in symptoms and a 40% greater improvement in quality of life.

Why it works: By stimulating the secretion of bile, a digestive fluid that helps breakdown fat, easing and speeding digestion.

Suggested dosage: 640 milligrams (mg) of standardized extract, three times a day, is the dosage that has been used in most clinical studies on dyspepsia and ALE, says Jamie Joy,

PharmD, director of experiential education at the University of Arizona College of Pharmacy.

ℹ️ ALE supplements are widely available, in many brands.

Precautions: Don't use ALE if you're allergic to artichokes or to related plants such as daisies, ragweed, marigold, echinacea and chrysanthemums, says Dr. Joy. Also, stay away from the herb if you have gallstones or bile-duct obstructions, as bile-stimulating ALE could worsen those conditions.

POTATO JUICE THERAPY

In the late 1800s, patients with indigestion at the famous sanatorium in Zurich founded by Dr. Maximilian Bircher-Benner were treated with potato juice, an unusual remedy. But the natural-minded Bircher-Benner (if you munch on muesli for breakfast, you're eating his invention) was only following European folk tradition, which had long favored the lowly spud as a remedy for stomach complaints.

Fast-forward to the twenty-first century, when Professor Dr. Sigrun Chrubasik at the University of Freiburg in Germany suffered from heartburn, tried potato juice, got relief… and decided to conduct a scientific study on the remedy.

⦀➡ *Breakthrough Study*

Dr. Chrubasik and her colleagues asked 42 patients with dyspepsia to drink a glass of potato juice twice a day—after getting up in the morning and before going to bed at night. If their stomach problems persisted, the amount was doubled. Overall, symptoms of indigestion decreased by 45%, with the researchers considering the treatment of 29 of the 42 patients a success. "I recommend that patients with dyspepsia consider trying this self-treatment

before they try over-the-counter or prescription drugs," says Dr. Chrubasik.

Suggested intake: The patients in the study drank 100 milliliters (3½ ounces) of potato juice, twice a day. If symptoms persisted for two or three days, the amount was doubled to 7 ounces twice a day.

ℹ️ Dr. Chrubasik recommends Biotta Organic Potato Juice Plus (with fennel), the Swiss-manufactured bottled juice used in the study. Biotta juices are available at many natural-food supermarkets and health-food stores, but their potato juice is not currently available in the United States.

Try this: Drink 6 ounces of freshly juiced potato juice, once a day, says Steven Bailey, ND, a naturopathic doctor in Portland, OR, and author of *Juice Alive* (Square One). For a tasty combination, blend it with 10 ounces of carrot juice and juice from ¼ inch of ginger root.

However: Don't juice potatoes that have been poorly stored and sprouted, and wash potatoes thoroughly before juicing.

THE HOTTEST CURE AROUND

Capsaicin—the active ingredient in cayenne—is a red-hot painkiller. It can short-circuit C-type nerve fibers that send pain messages to the brain. Italian doctors at the University of Bologna decided to try it out on stomach pain. They gave either 800 mg of capsaicin or a placebo before meals to 30 people with dyspepsia. After three weeks, those taking capsaicin had a 60% decrease in stomach pain, uncomfortable feelings of fullness and nausea—compared to a 30% decrease for the placebo group. Capsaicin, say the researchers, is a "potential therapy for functional dyspepsia." Cayenne supplements are widely available.

GALLSTONES

The gallbladder is a storage tank for *bile*, a liver-manufactured, acidic soup of cholesterol, salts, proteins and other ingredients that help the body break up fat. After a meal, bile squirts out through tubes into the small intestine. And all is right with your digestive world. *Unless you trip over a stone…*

Twenty million Americans have gallstones, from microscopic shards to golfball–size chunks. And every year, 500,000 of them require surgery to remove the gallbladder, when stones block a tube or inflame the organ and its surroundings. The resulting pain can range from discomfort to agony.

While there are unavoidable risk factors for forming gallstones, such as gender (hormones double a woman's risk), age (over 60) and genes (stones run in your family)—nutritional experts say you can probably *prevent* stones from forming *if* you follow a few key dietary guidelines. So choose your weapon for battling gallstones—a scalpel…or a set of silverware.

PREVENTION IS POSSIBLE WITH NUTRITION

Researchers from the University of Kentucky Medical Center and Harvard Medical School analyzed decades of dietary and health data from two massive, ongoing research projects. The Nurse's Health study involved nearly 70,000 women, and the Health Professional's Follow-up study involved more than 42,000 men. The results, published in many scientific studies, show that gallstones are preventable…with smart nutrition.

"The same diet that is good for preventing diseases such as heart disease and type 2 diabetes is good for preventing gallstones," says Edward L. Giovannucci, MD, ScD, an associate professor at Harvard Medical School and coauthor of many of the studies.

And while the researchers may not always know the biochemical mechanism behind the dietary protection, they've proven the protection is real.

⫸ *Breakthrough Studies*

● **Refined carbohydrates.** *Consume with caution.* Women who ate the most quick-digesting, refined carbohydrates such as white flour and sugar had a 35% higher risk of having gallbladder surgery than women who ate the least. Men eating the most refined carbohydrates had a 59% higher risk of gallstone disease than men eating the least.

● **Fiber.** *Bulk up for protection.* Women who ate the most fiber had a 13% lower risk of gallstone surgery than women who ate the least. The most protective fiber was insoluble, the type found in whole grains; high consumption lowered risk by 17%.

Theory: Recirculating bile acids contribute to stone formation; fiber binds with those acids, ushering them out of the body.

● **Fruits and vegetables.** *Mom was right, of course.* Women who ate the most fruits and vegetables had a 21% lower risk of gallstone surgery than women who ate the least.

● **Fat.** *Un- is number one.* Men who ate the most polyunsaturated and monounsaturated fats—found in vegetable oils, nuts and fish—had an 18% lower risk of gallstone disease than men who ate the least.

Important: The healthy fats were part of an "energy-balanced" diet, say the researchers. The men ate more healthy fats but didn't overdo it on calories.

● **Trans fats.** *A fat with gall.* No wonder laws are being passed to make sure trans fats (found in processed foods such as baked goods and margarine, and in shortening used for deep-frying in fast-food restaurants) don't trespass your lips. Men who ate the most trans fats had a 23% higher risk of gallstone disease than men who ate the least.

• **Protein.** *Vegetable is better than animal.* Women who ate the most vegetable protein, from foods such as beans and nuts, had a 21% lower risk of gallbladder surgery than women who ate the least. Women who ate the most animal protein had a 7% higher risk for the surgery than women who ate the least.

• **Nuts.** *All they're cracked up to be.* Men who ate five or more servings of nuts per week had a 30% lower risk of gallstone disease than men who almost never ate nuts. (A serving is a handful.) For women eating the most nuts, the risk of gallbladder surgery was 25% lower.

Theory: Phytosterols, a component of nuts, block cholesterol absorption, reducing the risk of stone formation. (Hardened cholesterol is the main component of most stones.)

• **Iron.** *For men, a mineral to minimize.* Men eating the most *heme* iron (found in meat, fish and poultry) had a 21% higher risk of gallstone disease than men eating the least.

Theory: Too much heme iron in a man's diet triggers the formation of cholesterol crystals in bile.

• **Magnesium.** *Maximize.* Men who got the most dietary magnesium—abundant in whole grains, beans, dark leafy greens, broccoli and bananas—had a 23% lower risk of gallstone disease than men who got the least.

Theory: Low levels of magnesium create blood sugar imbalances that can form stones.

• **Coffee.** *Consume without concern.* Women who drank four or more cups of caffeinated coffee a day had a 28% lower risk of gallstone disease than women who didn't drink any coffee. For two to three cups, the risk was 22% lower; for one cup, 9% lower. For men drinking

YO-YO IS A NO-NO

Scientists at the University of Kentucky Medical Center in Lexington found that men who did the most yo-yo dieting—repeatedly losing and regaining weight—had a 42% higher risk of developing gallstones than men who maintained their weight. The highest risk was found among those with the biggest fluctuations in weight and the most lose/gain cycles. (See Chapter 14, page 350, for ways to shed weight and keep it off.)

four or more cups of caffeinated coffee, the risk of gallstone disease was 45% lower; for two to three cups, 40%.

Theory: Coffee stimulates the release of *cholecystokinin*, a hormone that triggers gallbladder contractions, making the organ a less hospitable environment for stone formation.

And don't forget to exercise: Researchers at the University of Pittsburgh found that postmenopausal women who got the least physical activity had a 57% higher risk of gallstone disease than women who got the most.

IRRITABLE BOWEL SYNDROME

Your abdomen bloats and cramps. You pass so much gas you think you might be contributing to global warming. You barely cope with the overdrive of diarrhea or the stall of constipation, or an alternating assault of both.

Your problem (and that of 36 million other Americans) is irritable bowel syndrome (IBS), the most common gastrointestinal disorder, accounting for 10% of doctor's visits and 50% of referrals to gastroenterologists. But the fact that doctors see a lot of IBS doesn't mean they understand the condition or treat it effectively.

Like any *syndrome*, IBS is a well recognized but unexplained set of symptoms—medical science knows *what* is happening but not *why*. A diagnosis of irritable bowel syndrome isn't made by detecting telltale biochemical or structural changes unique to IBS—it's made after other digestive disorders have been ruled out, such as colon cancer or inflammatory bowel disease.

At that point, the typical doctor—generalist or gastroenterologist—offers a predictable prescription of seemingly sensible, bowel-calming advice to eat more fiber, drink more water, get more exercise and reduce stress.

While that regimen may work for some, it fails many, says Dr. Lipski. Because it overlooks a common but often ignored trigger of IBS—*food sensitivity*.

SOLVING FOOD SENSITIVITY

To understand food sensitivity, you first need to understand what it is *not*—food allergy.

• **Food allergies** are relatively rare, affecting 1 to 2% of the population. Like inhaled pollen or mold, the ingested food attracts the immune system's IgE antibodies, which identify it as "foreign" and attack it, sparking the release of *histamine* and *cytokines*, inflammatory chemicals that cause tissue to swell, eyes to tear, skin to itch and other allergic symptoms. Eggs, milk, nuts, shellfish, soy and gluten-containing foods such as wheat are common allergy-causing foods.

• **Food sensitivity** involves other antibodies, such as IgA, IgG and IgM. Their attack isn't launched immediately—it can occur hours or even days after eating. The resulting symptoms tend to be chronic rather than acute, and they can show up in any organ or system of the body. For example, they can affect the brain, with migraines...the joints, with rheumatoid arthritis...the skin, with eczema...or the digestive tract, with IBS.

Which means that *eliminating* foods to which you're sensitive might eliminate IBS.

▶ *Breakthrough Study*

Researchers at the University of Kansas Medical Center put 20 people with IBS on elimination-rotation diets to treat food sensitivity. After one year, most had less digestive pain, more normal stool frequency and an improved quality of life—the satisfying experience of minimized symptoms and control over the condition.

IBS is always challenging to treat, says Jeanne Drisko, MD, the lead author of the study, in the *Journal of the American College of Nutrition*. But, she continues, "identifying and appropriately addressing food sensitivity in IBS patients" results in a sustained improvement in both symptoms and quality of life.

What to do: Here's the elimination regimen Dr. Lipski uses successfully with her IBS patients...

For one week, eat an elimination diet consisting solely of foods that rarely cause reactions, such as all fruits (except citrus), all vegetables (except tomatoes, eggplant, potatoes and peppers), white rice, fish and chicken. To add extra taste, use olive and safflower oils, and herbs and spices.

If after seven days you are symptom free, food sensitivity is likely triggering your IBS.

Next, reintroduce one category of food, every two to three days. Start with one of the foods that account for 80% of food sensitivity, such as beef, citrus, dairy products, egg, pork or wheat.

For two days, eat the elimination diet *and* as much of the reintroduced food as you like. If IBS symptoms return, you have detected a sensitivity.

If you develop symptoms, discontinue the food; wait until the symptoms disappear to reintroduce another food. If you don't get symptoms, go on to the next food after the two days of eating the previous one.

Repeat this process, reintroducing foods one by one, until you no longer experience or trigger symptoms.

For the next six months, avoid all foods that caused IBS during the elimination diet, which will help your bowel heal. After six months, try a "rotation diet"—reintroduce the offending foods (as long as they don't cause symptoms), but eat any offending food (such as wheat) no more than once every five days.

An elimination-rotation diet requires patience and commitment. But the results can change your life.

Also helpful: If you have food sensitivity, digestive enzyme supplements can help reduce gas and bloating, says Dr. Lipski. Companies that make effective digestive enzyme products include Tyler Encapsulations, Transformation Enzymes, Enzymetica and Enzymatic Therapy. These products are widely available in stores, on-line and in catalogs. Find a product that works for you, and take one capsule with every meal.

PEPPERMINT OIL FOR IBS

Have a mint. That's the classic advice for digestive upset. Now doctors are finding that taking a mint—specifically, a pill of peppermint oil—can soothe the digestive symptoms of IBS.

⫸ *Breakthrough Studies*

Italian doctors asked 57 patients with IBS to take either peppermint oil or a placebo for four weeks. Seventy-five percent of the patients taking peppermint oil showed a 50% reduction in symptoms—abdominal bloating, abdominal pain or discomfort, diarrhea, constipation, feeling of incomplete evacuation, pain at defecation,

DRUGS DON'T WORK WELL

Doctors have tried a range of drugs for IBS—*bulking agents* for constipation, *antidepressants* to affect brain chemicals that play a role in digestion, *spasmolytics* to decrease cramping. But a review by Dutch doctors of 40 studies on medications for IBS concluded, "The evidence of efficacy of drug therapies for IBS is weak." And in some cases, the side effects of the drug are a lot worse than the syndrome. *In fact, they could be fatal...*

Latest development: In 2007, the FDA pulled the IBS drug *tegaserod maleate* (Zelnorm) from the market when studies showed it increased the risk of heart attack and stroke tenfold.

Good news: Find and eliminate food sensitivity, use natural remedies to help control symptoms, work with your doctor to detect and treat infections—and you can resolve the symptoms of IBS *without* drugs, says Dr. Lipski.

urgency at defecation and passage of gas or mucus. The placebo had little or no effect.

"Peppermint oil improves abdominal symptoms in patients with IBS," the doctors conclude, in the journal *Digestive and Liver Disease.*

"Taking into account the currently available drug treatments for IBS," say another team of researchers, in *Phytomedicine,* "peppermint oil may be the drug of first choice in IBS patients...to alleviate general symptoms and to improve quality of life."

How it works: By relaxing the muscles of the digestive tract.

Suggested intake: One or two capsules daily, between meals.

ⓘ The researchers used enteric-coated peppermint oil, which prevents the oil from dissolving in the stomach. One widely available enteric-coated product is Pepogest. (The Italian researchers used Mintoil, which is not available in the United States.)

Caution: Don't use the remedy if you have heartburn because it relaxes the lower esophageal sphincter, the muscular valve that keeps acidic contents in the stomach.

PROBIOTICS—THE "FRIENDLY" BACTERIA

Antibiotics *kill* bacteria. Probiotics *are* bacteria —friendly bacteria that live in a neighborly way in your colon, where they help regulate digestion, keep inflammation in check and reduce the secretion of substances that trigger diarrhea.

Grown in a controlled environment and packaged in a pill or added to a food, probiotics are now used to treat IBS, with dozens of scientific studies testing their effectiveness. Unfortunately, sometimes the studies show probiotics work and sometimes the studies show they don't.

The problem is that many studies use different varieties of friendly bacteria. Are any of those varieties *uniquely* effective in taming the symptoms of IBS? Yes, say scientists.

▐▐▶ *Breakthrough Study*

Researchers at the University of Michigan, led by Darren Brenner, MD, evaluated all of the many studies using probiotics to treat IBS, reporting their results at the annual meeting of the American College of Gastroenterology. They found that only one type of probiotic, *bifidobacterium infantis 35624*, consistently improved the symptoms of IBS—abdominal pain and discomfort, bloating and distension, and bowel movement difficulty.

"*B. infantis 35624* is a probiotic that specifically relieves many of the symptoms of IBS," agrees Peter Whorwell, MD, a professor of gastroenterology at the University of South

Manchester in England, who has conducted research on many different strains.

How it works: By decreasing inflammation in the digestive tract.

ℹ️ B. infantis 35624 can be found in the product Align, which is widely available.

Suggested intake: One capsule per day, the dosage recommendation on the label.

ULCERS

D octors used to think that peptic ulcers (located in the stomach or its intestinal neighbor, the *duodenum*) were caused by factors such as heavy drinking and harrying deadlines—a kind of badge of courage for hard-driving male executives. (Men get three times more ulcers than women, with men over 45 at highest risk.) Now, scientists know that two-thirds of ulcers are caused by

ARE YOU INFECTED?

Food sensitivity triggers approximately 50 to 75% of IBS. Another 25% is caused by infections.

Recent findings: Israeli doctors studied 564 travelers. Those who developed traveler's diarrhea had a *five times higher* risk for later developing IBS (*Clinical Infectious Diseases*).

Reviewing eight studies, American scientists found a *seven times higher* risk of IBS among those who'd had infectious gastroenteritis, an infection of the stomach (*American Journal of Gastroenterology*).

What to do: If you suspect an infection has triggered IBS, see your doctor, says Dr. Lipski. Ask for a CDSA—a comprehensive digestive stool analysis, which can detect abnormal bacteria, fungi and parasites. If the test is positive, your doctor can prescribe the appropriate antibiotic.

Helicobacter pylori (*H. pylori*), bacteria that can infest the stomach and small intestine. (The other third are caused by long-term use of nonsteroidal anti-inflammatory drugs such as aspirin or ibuprofen, which increase the risk of ulcers *fortyfold*.)

Rod-shaped *H. pylori* burrow into and weaken the mucous coating, setting the stage for acid to carve out the ulcers that gnaw at the guts of 10% of Americans at some time in their lives. And while the dull ache of an ulcer is mostly bothersome, the condition can turn brutal (and fatal) if the ulcer breaks through the stomach wall, bursts a blood vessel or if swelling and scarring block the passage of food.

Accurate detection of *H. pylori* and triple therapy to eradicate it (with two drugs to kill the bacteria and one to reduce stomach acid) is the best way to banish an ulcer, with a 90% cure rate. But natural remedies can lend a significantly helping hand.

LACTOFERRIN AND PROBIOTICS

Lactoferrin is a peptide, or protein subfraction, of milk; studies show that it strengthens immunity and kills harmful bacteria, including *H. pylori*. Probiotics are "friendly" bacteria that help protect and restore the health of the digestive tract. Together, they can turn triple therapy into a home run.

⏭ *Breakthrough Study*

Italian researchers from the University of Pisa gave 206 ulcer patients either standard triple therapy (Group A) or triple therapy *with* lactoferrin and probiotics (Group B).

The therapy was a success in 72% of the patients in Group A—and 89% of patients in Group B! But Group A not only had *less* success, they also had *more* side effects.

"The addition of lactoferrin and probiotics could improve the standard eradication therapy for *H. pylori* infection—lactoferrin serving to increase the eradication rate and probiotics to reduce the side effects of antibiotic therapy," say the researchers, in the *American Journal of Gastroenterology.*

What to do: Lactoferrin and probiotic supplements are widely available. Talk to your doctor about adding them to your triple-therapy treatment regimen. (For more information on how to pick the best probiotic supplement, see the box on page 171.)

EASE "TRIPLE THERAPY" SIDE EFFECTS

Triple therapy is effective—but potentially unpleasant. The combo of medicines can cause nausea, dizziness, headaches and/or diarrhea. Some patients decide the treatment isn't worth it and stop taking the drugs. Supplementing triple therapy with *Saccharomyces boulardii*—a strain of yeast that normalizes the functioning of the digestive tract—might help.

⏭ *Breakthrough Study*

Turkish doctors in the Department of Gastroenterology at Gazi University in Ankara studied 124 patients with *H. pylori* infection who were receiving two weeks of triple therapy, dividing them into two groups. One group took daily supplements of *S. boulardii*, while the other took placebos.

During the therapy, twice as many people in the placebo group experienced diarrhea, and three times as many had stomach pain. After the therapy, the placebo group had 38% more gastrointestinal discomfort. Overall, say the researchers, *S. boulardii* improved "treatment tolerability."

ⓘ Try Florastor, a widely available *S. boulardii* supplement that has been proven effective in more than a dozen clinical studies. Follow the dosage recommendation on the label.

SALT—INSULTING YOUR INJURY

Twenty percent of people under 40 and 50% of people over 60 are infected with *H. pylori*. Why do only some of them get ulcers? (And stomach cancer, another disease triggered by *H. pylori*?) Diet might be one reason. Particularly a diet high in salt.

⏩ *Breakthrough Study*

Epidemiological research—data on health and disease in thousands of individuals—has linked a high intake of salt with a higher risk of an *H. pylori* infection causing an ulcer.

To see if that data has a biological basis, scientists in the Department of Microbiology and Immunology at the Uniformed Services University of the Health Sciences in Bethesda, MD, studied the effect of salt on *H. pylori* bacteria. They found that high concentrations of salt warped *H. pylori* cells—they stopped dividing normally and became elongated. They also found that extra salt activated a gene that makes it more likely *H. pylori* bacteria will turn nasty and trigger an ulcer.

"These changes may help explain why a high-salt diet is associated with increased risk of ulcers in people infected with *H. pylori,*" says D. Scott Merrell, PhD, one of the researchers who conducted the study.

What to do: If you're over 60, you have an increased risk of an *H. pylori* infection *and* an increased risk of high blood pressure—two reasons to reduce salt intake. And reducing salt

intake is particularly important if tests show you're infected with *H. pylori*, says Dr. Merrell.

Recommended: "It's important to remember that most of our daily salt intake doesn't come from the saltshaker but from the salt *added* to many foods," says Dr. Merrell. He advises to choose low- or no-salt versions of foods. Stay away from foods that are cured, pickled or smoked. Avoid high-salt condiments, such as soy sauce, mustard and ketchup. Just say no to olives. If possible, don't cook with salt. For extra flavor, use spices, herbs, lemon and/or vinegar. Keep the saltshaker off the table.

KIDNEY STONES— PREVENTABLE PAIN

The intense pain of passing a kidney stone—typically, a hard mass of congealed calcium crystals—has been compared to childbirth. In other words, the *most* intense pain there is. Ouch!

Unfortunately, if you've passed one stone, chances are 50-50 that you'll make and pass another stone within five years…and another …and another. That's especially true for men between the ages of 40 and 60, who for some unknown reason have the highest risk of kidney stones.

Is there any way to resign from the yearly ranks of the half-million people who rush to emergency rooms, seeking relief from the excruciating pain of passing a stone? (Not to mention the other 2.5 million who visit the doctor, looking for a reliable way to forestall the next agonizing event.)

Is there any way to *prevent* new stones from forming? Quite a few ways, actually.

HOW TO CHOOSE (AND USE) THE BEST PROBIOTIC

"Probiotics are 'friendly' bacteria in your digestive tract that mount a variety of defenses against disease," says Lynne McFarland, PhD, a research scientist in the Veterans Administration Puget Sound Health Care System in Seattle, and coauthor of *The Power of Probiotics* (Hayworth). "They help regulate the immune system. They prevent disease-causing agents from becoming attached to the intestinal wall. They generate *bacteriocins*, a kind of internal antibiotic. They produce enzymes that attack toxins."

But not all probiotic supplements provide the same benefits, says Dr. McFarland. *When choosing a probiotic supplement for healing, here's what to look for...*

Buy from a reputable manufacturer. Dr. McFarland sent a variety of probiotic supplements to independent laboratories—and found that more than a third of the supplements didn't contain the type or amount of probiotics advertised on the label! "To get a quality product, buy from an established manufacturer that sells a wide variety of supplements," she advises.

Match the strain to the disease. A particular strain of probiotic bacteria may not solve your particular health problem, says Dr. McFarland. Choose the strain that research shows can help the condition you're trying to treat. (Use this chapter as a guide.)

Take a sufficient dose. For a probiotic to work, you need to take a lot of it—typically, about 10 billion organisms, says Dr. McFarland. That number appears on a label as 1x10(10)—shorthand for 1 times 10 to the 10th power.

Choose freeze-dried. In freeze-drying a probiotic—a process also known as *lypholization*—manufacturers reduce the temperature and suck the air out of the bacteria, stabilizing them.

"Freeze-dried probiotics are the best quality," says Dr. McFarland. "Unlike a probiotic that requires refrigeration, you don't need to worry if it was kept cold during the long distribution process, from manufacturer to store."

LEMONADE THERAPY REDUCES KIDNEY STONES

Eighty percent of kidney stones are formed from calcium oxalate crystals. Most others are formed from uric acid. Doctors try to prevent the recurrence of both types of stones by prescribing *potassium citrate*. The citrate helps stop calcium crystals from sticking together. The drug also reduces the acidity of urine, making a uric acid stone less likely. But potassium citrate isn't without side effects; some patients experience nausea and/or diarrhea. And the drug can interfere with diuretics or ACE inhibitors for high blood pressure. Perhaps you'd prefer a simpler, natural therapy.

||||➡ *Breakthrough Study*

Researchers from the Comprehensive Kidney Stone Center at Duke University studied 22 patients with kidney stones—11 who had been on long-term "lemonade therapy" for an average of 44 months, and 11 who had been taking potassium citrate for an average of 42 months. They analyzed how many stones those drinking lemonade had formed before they started their therapy and afterward—stones passed, stones surgically removed and new stones seen in imaging tests. And they looked at levels of urinary citrate in both groups.

Both the potassium citrate group and the lemonade group showed an increase in urinary citrate—482 mg per day for those taking potassium citrate, and 383 mg a day for those drinking lemonade. *And all that extra citrate wasn't wasted...*

While on lemonade therapy, stone formation decreased from an average of one stone per year to 0.13 per year—a reduction of 87%.

None of the patients needed any medical intervention during their 3½ years on lemonade therapy—no drugs, no surgery, no conventional treatments of any kind.

"Lemonade therapy appears to be a reasonable alternative for kidney stones patients who cannot tolerate potassium citrate," says Glen Preminger, MD, professor of urologic surgery and director of the Comprehensive Kidney Stone Center.

What to do: Mix ½ cup of concentrated lemon juice with 7 cups water. Add a sugar substitute to taste. Drink throughout the day.

Also helpful: Scientists at the University of Texas Southwestern Medical Center asked 13 people (nine healthy, four recurrent stone-formers) to drink 13 ounces of orange juice with every meal for one week. (The study used Minute Maid orange juice, from frozen concentrate.) Urine samples showed the orange juice increased the amount of citrate in the urine and reduced acidity. It also reduced the tendency of calcium oxalate and uric acid to form crystals.

"Orange juice could play an important role in the management of recurrent kidney stones, and may be considered an option in patients who can't tolerate potassium citrate," says Clarita Odvina, MD, the scientist who conducted the study and assistant professor of internal medicine at the University of Texas Southwestern Medical Center.

An excellent choice to help you do that is lemonade, discussed above. But perhaps the easiest (and healthiest) fluid to drink in large quantities is water. And the best water to drink to prevent kidney stones may be mineral water rich in bicarbonate.

⫸ *Breakthrough Study*

Researchers at the Medical School of Hanover in Germany asked 34 recurrent stone-formers to drink either 48 ounces of mineral water with a high level of bicarbonate or the same amount of water with a low mineral content, for three days. At the start and the end of the study, they measured various urinary parameters that contribute to stone formation—acidity, citrate, the tendency of calcium oxalate to form stones (supersaturation) and the tendency of uric acid to form stones (precipitation).

After three days, those drinking the mineral water had significantly better measurements in *all* those categories.

"Bicarbonate water can be recommended for the prevention of calcium oxalate and uric acid urinary stones," say the researchers, in the *World Journal of Urology*.

ⓘ Popular mineral waters with high levels of bicarbonate include San Pellegrino, Perrier and Vittel.

DRINK MINERAL WATER

Drinking fluid—*lots* of fluid—is the most important action for preventing new kidney stones.

Reason: A high volume of urine stops calcium oxalate from crystallizing.

Recommendation: Pass 48 to 64 ounces of water a day. (Not drink: Pass.)

INDIVIDUALIZE YOUR DIET

Over the decades, many different types of diets have been recommended for preventing kidney stones, with a low-calcium diet leading the list. But, as one researcher recently noted, "There is not ample evidence to confidently recommend dietary changes." Now there is.

⫸ *Breakthrough Studies*

When researchers at Harvard Medical School analyzed 14 years of diet and health data from more than 45,000 men, they found that the best dietary factors for preventing kidney stones *varied*—depending on the men's age and weight. For example, high levels of calcium were protective in men *under* 60, but didn't cut the risk in men *over* 60.

"Our results confirm the importance of individual dietary factors in the development of symptomatic kidney stones," says Eric N. Taylor, MD, in the *New England Journal of Medicine.* "Dietary recommendation for stone prevention should be tailored to the individual patient."

For men under 60…

● **Calcium.** High intake decreased risk by 21%. Best foods: Low-fat dairy products.

Important: Kidney stones are made of calcium oxalate—but dietary calcium binds to oxalate in the intestine, *reducing* the amount of oxalate in the urine and *decreasing* the risk of stones.

For all men…

● **Potassium.** High intake decreased risk by 46%.

Best foods: Avocado, lima beans, potato, tomato, banana, flounder, cantaloupe.

● **Magnesium.** High intake decreased risk by 29%.

Best foods: Kelp, cashews, molasses, brewer's yeast, buckwheat, millet, rye.

● **Fluids.** High intake cut risk by 29%.

For men who aren't overweight…

● **Animal protein.** High intake increased risk by 38%.

For women…

In a study similar to the one conducted with men, researchers at Harvard Medical School analyzed diet and health data from more than 96,000 women aged 27 to 44. *They found…*

STAY AWAY FROM OXALATES

Oxalates are a component of food that contributes to calcium oxalate, the main material of most kidney stones. If you're trying to prevent a stone, stay away from these high-oxalate foods, say researchers, in the *New England Journal of Medicine…*

Walnuts, hazelnuts, peanuts, almonds, beets, spinach, rhubarb, parsley, chives, chocolate, cocoa, wheat germ, brown rice and tea.

● **Calcium.** High intake cut risk by 27%.

Important: There was no increased risk from calcium supplements.

● **Fluid.** High intake cut risk by 32%.

● **Animal protein.** High intake increased risk by 16%.

● **Sugar.** High intake upped risk by 31%.

What to do: Emphasize the factors that decrease risk and cut back on the factors that increase risk.

Also important: For five years, Italian researchers studied 120 men prone to forming kidney stones. They found that a diet low in salt and animal protein, with normal amounts of calcium, reduced the risk of stone formation by 51%, compared to the traditionally recommended low-calcium diet. The men ate no more than 3 ounces of red meat a day, with fish the preferred alternative. Salt was not used in cooking or added to food, but there was an unlimited use of spices.

CONSTIPATION

What's a normal bowel movement? Let's start this section by settling that number one issue, once and for all.

MORE POUNDS, MORE STONES

Researchers at Harvard Medical School analyzed data on weight and kidney stone formation in nearly 46,000 men, 94,000 older women (34 to 59), and 102,000 younger women (27 to 44). They found…

Men weighing more than 220 pounds had a 44% higher risk of kidney stones than men weighing less than 150 pounds. For overweight women, the increased risk was 89% (older women) to 92% (younger women) higher.

Men who gained more than 35 pounds since age 21 had a 39% higher risk of kidney stones than men who didn't gain weight. For women, gaining weight increased risk by 70% (older) to 82% (younger).

"Obesity and weight gain increase the risk of kidney stone formation," say the researchers, in the *Journal of the American Medical Association*.

For ways to lose weight, please turn to Chapter 14 on page 350.

"It is normal to have one to three soft bowel movements each day," says Dr. Lipski.

Normal, she explains, because such movements are a sign of efficient, fairly rapid "transit time"—the hours between eating and evacuation. Transit times of 24 hours or less have been linked to lower rates of type 2 diabetes, heart disease, colon cancer, gallstones, hemorrhoids and other diseases. What's *not* normal is…

Infrequent bowel movements (less than one each day). Painful bowel movements. Hard stool. Straining at stool. A sudden slowdown in bowel movements, from normal to not. If any of those problems persists for three months or more, you're officially constipated—along with approximately 15% of your fellow Americans.

There are many serious medical conditions that can cause constipation, such as colon cancer and Parkinson's disease, so a doctor should check out any substantial and sustained change

in your bowel habits. But once disease has been ruled out as the cause, it's time for relief.

FIBER SUPPLEMENTS— THE NATURAL LAXATIVE

Eating high-fiber foods, drinking more water and getting regular exercise can all help clear up constipation, says Dr. Lipski. But many Americans rely on laxatives, and it costs them $750 million per year. There's a better (and cheaper) way.

Breakthrough Study

Doctors at the New York Methodist Hospital in Brooklyn added a fiber supplement to the diet of 92 people (all older than 65) who were taking one or more laxatives—docusate, milk of magnesia with Cascara, or senna. Over the next 36 months, 63 of the people were able to stop taking laxatives without slipping back into constipation. And the cost of treating constipation was decreased by more than $40 a year per person.

"The fiber supplement was a safe and convenient alternative to laxatives and decreased the cost of medical care," say the doctors.

The doctors used the product Regularity Plus, a fiber supplement. You can order at *www.ndlabs.com*, or by calling 888-263-5227, Nutritional Designs Direct, 51 Watermill Lane, Great Neck, NY 11021; *nddirect@ndlabs.com*.

Suggested dosage: Seven grams of fiber (one tablespoon, in a glass of water or juice), twice a day, with meals.

Also helpful: Konjac glucomannan—a high-fiber supplement made from the root of a Japanese plant—has been found to relieve constipation, with a study in the journal *Nutrition* showing it improved defecation frequency by 27%, and stool weight by 26%. (Without *any* of the side effects sometimes caused by fiber supplements, such as cramping, bloating and gas.) Brands include Nature's Way and Swanson.

Suggested intake: 1.5 grams per meal.

FOOD TO GO

What foods are best at beating constipation? Here's what scientists from around the world are saying.

▐▐▐▶ *Breakthrough Studies*

Rye bread and yogurt. Doctors in Finland asked 59 otherwise healthy women with constipation to eat two pieces of fiber-rich rye bread *and* a cup of yogurt every day for three weeks—fiber to speed up and soften bowel movements; lactobacillus-rich yogurt to provide the "friendly" intestinal bacteria that would help decrease possible GI discomfort from an increase in dietary fiber. The two foods did the trick. The addition of fiber increased the number of bowel movements per day, decreased transit time and softened stools, and the yogurt reduced bloating, cramping and gas. The doctors recommend fiber-rich rye bread and lactobacillus-containing yogurt for the treatment of

---

FOUR POPULAR LAXATIVES THAT DON'T WORK

Scientists in the Division of Gastroenterology at the University of Iowa Carver College of Medicine in Iowa City analyzed more than 30 years of studies on laxatives and found four that are commonly used—but don't work! *They are...*

• Milk of magnesia

• Senna (Ex-Lax)

• Bisacodyl (Carter's Little Pills)

• Stool softeners (docusate)

---

constipation, in the *European Journal of Clinical Nutrition*.

Kiwifruit. Doctors at the Queen Mary Hospital in Hong Kong gave 33 constipated patients a ripe kiwifruit in the morning after breakfast and in the evening after dinner, for four weeks. More than half of the patients improved, with average bowel movements per week doubled from two to four, and laxative use reduced by 50%. "Kiwifruit is reported to have a laxative effect, and is a good source of dietary fiber," says Annie On-on Chang, MD, a gastroenterologist in Taiwan and the lead researcher for the study published in the *World Journal of Gastroenterology*. "Based on this study, I recommend it to my patients with chronic constipation."

Useful: The variety was Hayward, the lime-green, tart kiwifruit typically found in supermarkets. A ripe fruit has a slightly soft texture.

Magnesium. Researchers in Japan analyzed data on diet and constipation in nearly 4,000 Japanese women aged 18 to 20. The lower the intake of magnesium, the higher the incidence of constipation.

Recommended: Magnesium-rich foods include kelp, wheat bran, wheat germ, almonds, cashews, blackstrap molasses, brewer's yeast, buckwheat, Brazil nuts, filberts, peanuts, millet, pecans, walnuts, rye, tofu, coconut and brown rice.

LOSE WEIGHT, STAY REGULAR

Low-calorie diets are great for losing weight. But they're not so great for staying regular. Taking a dietary supplement of probiotics (friendly, gut-regulating bacteria) and *prebiotics* (which feed probiotics in the bowel) can help.

TO MOVE YOUR BOWELS, MOVE THE REST OF YOU...

Dutch researchers studied 43 men and women with chronic constipation, dividing them into two groups. Both groups received advice about increasing fiber and fluid intake, but only one group added 30 minutes of brisk walking to their daily regimen. After three months, the walking group had fewer incomplete defecations, less straining at stool and a smaller percentage of hard stools. They also had speedier transit times, down from an average of 80 hours to 58. The nonwalking group didn't see any benefits. (Neither group followed the advice to increase fiber and water intake.) People with chronic constipation should get regular physical activity, say the researchers.

What to do: Walk 30 minutes at a brisk pace, five or more days a week.

⏮️ *Breakthrough Study*

Italian doctors from Palermo studied 297 obese people who were on a diet of 1,400 or 1,200 calories a day and who were constipated. For two months, the dieters were supplied with supplements containing the probiotic *bifidobacterium* and the prebiotic FOS (*fructooligosaccharides*). Those who took the supplement "showed a greater improvement of constipation" than those who didn't, say the researchers.

Why it works: Weight loss can disrupt the internal ecosystem—the balance of good and bad bacteria in your colon—resulting in a condition called *dysbiosis* that causes or worsens constipation, explain the researchers. Probiotics and prebiotics deliver a dose of good bacteria—and solve the problem.

❶ Products containing bifidobacterium and FOS prebiotics include Jarrow Bifidus Balance + FOS; Pro Dophilus w/ FOS, from ProHealth;

SymBiotics with FOS Powder, from Allergy Research Group/Nutricology

Follow the dosage recommendation on the label.

CONSTIPATION AND COLON CANCER—IS THERE A LINK?

Yes, say Japanese scientists, writing in the *European Journal of Cancer*. They studied more than 40,000 men and women for seven years. Those with constipation (less than one bowel movement per day) had a 35% higher risk of colon cancer than those with a daily bowel movement. Among laxative users, the risk for colon cancer was 31% higher than nonusers. And for those who used laxatives twice a week or more, the risk of colon cancer was nearly three times higher than nonusers.

MECHANICAL MASSAGE FOR CONSTIPATION

Clearing up a case of constipation has just gotten a helping hand. *From a machine...*

⏮️ *Breakthrough Study*

Doctors at the University of Thrace in Greece studied a newly developed, abdomen-massaging, anticonstipation machine—Free-Lax—on 30 older, severely constipated people from Greece and Israel, who used it for 20 minutes a day for four months. Bowel movements per week increased from an average of 1.4 to 3.9... stools were larger in 21 patients...and stool consistency changed from hard to soft in 23 of 25 patients. There were no side effects. "External mechanical vibration of the abdomen helped to relieve severe constipation," say the researchers, in the *World Journal of Gastroenterology*.

How it works: You use the device while sitting down. It rests on your lap while attached to your abdomen by an adjustable belt. Two disks face the abdomen and vibrate when the machine is turned on. The vibration, say the researchers, may work by duplicating the natural "peristaltic" motions of the bowel that propel stool.

☀ *www.free-lax.com.* You can contact the manufacturer via an e-mail inquiry at this Israeli-based, English-language Web site. The five-pound piece of equipment device is currently sold in Israel and Europe, where it is approved as a medical device. It includes a user's manual, which specifies that it should not be used if you're pregnant, under 15, have had surgery in the past six months, have damaged vertebrae or an untreated hernia. It costs about $400, which sounds steep, but…"long-term use of this device will be less expensive than most other therapies commonly used today," say the doctors who conducted the study.

www.cure-constipation.com. This US-based site offers the same product as Free-Lax under the name U-G-O.

HEMORRHOIDS

Veins around or inside the anus can be, well, a pain in the backside.

We're talking hemorrhoids, of course. Aging is the main cause of these swollen anal veins—half of Americans over 50 have them. Chronic constipation or diarrhea can also trigger them. So can pregnancy.

Hemorrhoids are mostly harmless. But they can bleed, itch, burn and just plain old hurt. Persistent symptoms (for example, an internal hemorrhoid that protrudes out of the rectum, doesn't go away and becomes irritated and painful) may require medical care to shrink or even surgically remove the hemorrhoid. But

CURING EXTREME CONSTIPATION

You're trying to go to the bathroom—but you just can't seem to relax the muscles of your pelvic floor (the anal muscles used to stop the flow of urine or inhibit the passing of gas). Doctors call this "pelvic floor dyssynergic-type constipation"—and it afflicts about one third of constipated people who are referred by gastroenterologists to subspecialists in constipation. *Laxatives don't help all that much. Biofeedback does…*

Gastroenterologists at the Center for Functional GI and Motility Disorders at the University of North Carolina at Chapel Hill treated 84 patients with dyssynergic-type constipation. All of them were given training to learn to relax the muscles of the pelvic floor. But 30 were also given biofeedback (using an electromyography machine that electronically indicated when pelvic muscles were relaxed)…30 took a tranquilizer one to two hours before attempting defecation…and 24 took a placebo.

After three months, biofeedback had relieved constipation in 70% of the patients, compared to 38% taking placebos and 23% taking tranquilizers.

Biofeedback can work to treat pelvic floor dyssynergia, say the researchers—*if* the biofeedback therapist uses electromyography.

Important: Biofeedback *doesn't* work for "slow transit" constipation, the most common type. A study shows only 8% of people with slow transit constipation found biofeedback effective, compared to 71% of people with pelvic floor dyssynergia.

What to do: If you have been diagnosed with pelvic floor dyssynergia, talk to your gastroenterologist about instrument-based biofeedback training to relax the muscles of your pelvic floor. To find a biofeedback therapist near you, please see the information on page 155.

the best treatment of all to keep hemorrhoids and their symptoms at bay is all natural.

FIBER SUPPLEMENTS SOOTHE SYMPTOMS

If you've got recurring bouts of bothersome hemorrhoids, your doctor will probably tell you to increase dietary fiber and drink more water. The purpose is to help soften stool, stop straining and spare your anal veins. Trouble is, most people don't follow that commonsense advice.

Good alternative: Get in the habit of taking fiber supplements.

⏸▶ *Breakthrough Study*

A team of doctors from the United States, Canada and Spain analyzed studies on hemorrhoids and fiber supplements, involving 378 patients. *Compared to placebo, fiber supplements...*

- **Decreased the risk of persistent symptoms by 47%,**
- **Decreased the risk of bleeding by 50%, and**
- **Decreased the risk of recurrence.**

The use of fiber supplements shows a "consistent beneficial effect for symptoms and bleeding in the treatment of symptomatic hemorrhoids," say the doctors, in the *American Journal of Gastroenterology*.

What to do: There are many different fiber supplements on the market. Popular brands include psyllium-based Metamucil and Benefiber. Follow the dosage recommendation on the label. Be sure to drink at least 8 ounces of water with any fiber supplement—or you could wind up with even worse constipation!

GO AHEAD AND EAT THOSE RED HOT CHILI PEPPERS!

Spicy foods supposedly cause and worsen hemorrhoids. Doctors in Italy decided to put that belief to the test. They asked 50 people with hemorrhoids to take either a capsule containing red-hot chili powder or a placebo after lunch. Over the next 48 hours, neither group had more hemorrhoid symptoms—no additional bleeding, swelling, burning, itching or pain.

"There is no scientific evidence that a spicy meal based on red-hot chili pepper worsens hemorrhoidal symptoms," says Donato F. Altomare, MD, associate professor of surgery at the University of Bari.

FLAVONOIDS TO STRENGTHEN VEINS

Flavonoids are the palette of the plant world, the pigments that (along with carotenes) color vegetables, fruits and herbs in reds, yellows and blues.

There are more than 6,000 flavonoids, a handful of which are frequently touted for their health benefits, such as the catechins in green tea and the isoflavones in soy. One type of flavonoid—the *hesperidin* in citrus fruits—is particularly helpful in restoring the health of veins. And that includes the swollen veins of hemorrhoids.

⏸▶ *Breakthrough Studies*

Researchers from the United States, Canada and Spain analyzed 14 studies on flavonoids and hemorrhoids, involving more than 1,500 patients. *They found the nutrient...*

- **Decreases the risk of bleeding by 67%,**
- **Cuts the risk of persistent pain by 65%,**
- **Cuts the risk of itching by 35%, and**

• **Decreases the risk of recurrence of hemorrhoids by 47%.**

Other studies have found that flavonoids can...

• **Treat an acute episode of hemorrhoids.** For seven days, Chinese doctors gave either flavonoids or a placebo to 90 patients suffering from an acute episode of hemorrhoids. Those receiving the flavonoids had less pain, swelling and bleeding. Flavonoids, say the doctors, "can be considered an effective and well-tolerated agent in the treatment of acute episodes of hemorrhoids," in the journal *Current Medical Research and Opinion*.

• **Improve symptom control after hemorrhoid surgery.** Surgeons in Italy divided patients who had just received a hemorrhoidectomy (surgical removal of hemorrhoids, a procedure with significant postoperative pain and other complications) into two groups. One group received standard antibiotic and anti-inflammatory drugs to prevent infection and relieve pain; the other group received those drugs *and* flavonoids. *The flavonoid group had...*

• **44% less pain,**

• **76% less difficulty in completely emptying bowels,**

• **55% less bleeding and**

• **55% less itching.**

Used with antibiotics and anti-inflammatory drugs, flavonoids can "reduce both the duration and the extent of postoperative symptoms and wound bleeding following hemorrhoidectomy," say the researchers, in the medical journal *Diseases of the Colon and Rectum*.

• **Improve the effectiveness of coagulation therapy.** A common treatment for hemorrhoids is *infrared photocoagulation*, or coagulation therapy. The doctor focuses an intense beam of infrared light on the swollen vein, creating scar tissue that cuts off blood supply to the hemorrhoid, which falls off after seven to 10 days.

Doctors at the Saint Savvas Hospital in Athens, Greece, divided patients with bleeding hemorrhoids into three groups. The first group received coagulation therapy; the second received flavonoids; the third received *both* treatments. Five days after treatment, those receiving coagulation therapy and flavonoids had far less bleeding than people receiving either therapy alone.

The flavonoid used in these studies was *micronized purified flavonoid fraction*, or MPFF, a specially processed flavonoid derived from the hesperidin in citrus rinds. It is very similar to an over-the-counter flavonoid product called *diosmin*.

How it works: Nearly 40 years of scientific research shows that diosmin safely strengthens veins, improves microcirculation and reduces inflammation.

Suggested intake: 500 mg, twice a day, according to the *Alternative Medicine Review*. For an acute episode of hemorrhoids, the recommended dose is 1,000 mg three times daily for four days, followed by 1,000 mg twice daily for three days, and then a maintenance dose of 500 mg daily for two months or the length of time determined by you and a health-care professional.

Diosmin is an ingredient in the following products, which are available in retail stores, on the Internet, or in supplement catalogs: DiosMin Flavonoid Complex, from LifeTime (this product contains several other herbs traditionally used to strengthen veins, such as butcher's broom and horse chestnut); Diosmin, from Baywood; Diosmin-HMC, from Thorne Research and Ultra DiosVein Diosmin/Hesperidin, from Swanson.

ANAL FISSURES—A SITZ BATH IS WHERE IT'S AT

A hemorrhoid isn't the only medical problem that bothers your behind. An anal fissure—a little tear in the lining of the anal canal, often from straining at stool—can also bleed and hurt. Ninety percent of anal fissures go away on their own. But that doesn't mean you don't want relief while it's healing. A special kind of hip-first soak called a *sitz bath*—along with some extra bran—might be your best bet.

▶ *Breakthrough Study*

A gastroenterologist at the University of Copenhagen in Denmark studied 96 patients with a first, acute (painful) episode of anal fissure. He divided them into three treatment groups. One group used hydrocortisone ointment; one used lidocaine ointment and one group took twice-daily sitz baths and added bran to their diets.

During the first and second week of treatment, the bath/bran patients had a much greater decrease in their average "symptom score" than the ointment groups—less pain, less bleeding and less itching. After three weeks, they also had the highest percentage of healed fissures—87%, compared to 82% for the hydrocortisone group and 60% for the lidocaine group.

"Warm sitz baths plus an intake of bran came out as the treatment of choice for an acute first episode of anal fissure," says Steen Jensen, MD, the doctor who conducted the study. "This treatment is cheap, has no potential serious side effects and brings the best and quickest relief of symptoms."

What to do: Soak your hips and buttocks in a bathtub or big bowl of hot water (104°F) for 15 minutes, twice a day, after defecation in the morning and at bedtime. (If possible, soak after each stool.) Continue for two weeks.

Dr. Jensen asked his patients to add unprocessed bran to their diets, but he says that bran tablets may be more convenient and work just as well. There are many varieties of bran tablets available. Follow the dosage recommendation on the label.

DIARRHEA

You can get it on a trip to a foreign country. Or after a trip to the pharmacist, if your doctor has prescribed antibiotics.

The problem is the frequent watery stools of diarrhea.

Chronic diarrhea requires careful medical attention to figure out the cause, which can range from contaminated water to cancer. But *preventing* a couple of dismal days of diarrhea is a lot easier.

PROBIOTICS PREVENT DIARRHEA

Twenty percent of people taking antibiotics—a lot of them over 65—develop what doctors call "antibiotic-associated diarrhea" (AAD).

What happens: The antibiotic kills off "good" intestine-protecting bacteria, allowing "bad" antibiotic-resistant bacteria (*Clostridium difficile*) to multiply and wreak havoc.

Result: Sometimes AAD is mild, clearing up soon after you stop the drug. Sometimes, however, AAD turns serious—even fatal—as *C. difficile* takes over, causing not only diarrhea but also high fever, bloody stools, nausea, abdominal pain and dehydration. (*C. difficile* can even poke a deadly hole in your colon!) Doctors call this condition *Clostridium difficile disease*, or CDD.

WHAT TRAVELERS SHOULD KNOW ABOUT DIARRHEA—AND OFTEN DON'T

"Don't drink the water."

You know not to do *that* when you visit a developing country, where traveler's diarrhea is just about as common as, well, water. (The risk is 15 to 20% in the Caribbean and Eastern and Southern Europe; 20 to 50% in Africa, Southeast Asia and Latin America.)

But a study by researchers at the University of Alberta in Edmonton found that many vacationers who were heading off to Mexico weren't aware that traveler's diarrhea can also be caused by...

- *Viruses.* Wash your hands as often as possible, or use a hand-sterilizing product before eating, says Julie Johnson, PhD, the lead researcher on the study. (Only 56% of the vacationers knew that hand washing was an effective way to help prevent traveler's diarrhea.)

- *Ice cubes.* Don't add them to bottled drinks.

- *Brushing your teeth.* Use bottled water (not tap) to rinse.

- *Salads.* Raw fruits and vegetables are a no-no. Get your fiber elsewhere, for now.

- *Partially cooked beef or chicken.* Ask for well done. And only eat recently cooked foods, advises Dr. Johnson.

- *Other high-risk foods.* Unpasteurized milk, soft cheese (in Mexico) and luncheon meat.

- *Chlorine tablets.* Yes, it's not a bad idea to add them to water, but they're not foolproof—diarrhea-causing microorganisms such as Cryptosporidium can shrug off the chlorine.

Recommended: You can counter bad bacteria with probiotics—nutritional supplements that replenish your intestines with billions of good bacteria.

▶ Breakthrough Study

Dr. Lynne McFarland analyzed 31 studies on probiotics and AAD and CDD. Reporting in the *American Journal of Gastroenterology,* she found that probiotics...

- **Significantly reduced the risk of developing AAD by 57%.**

- **Effectively cleared up CDD, outperforming placebos by 41%.**

What to do about AAD: If you've been prescribed antibiotics, talk to your doctor about also taking probiotics to help *prevent* AAD, says Dr. McFarland.

Recommended: Take probiotics along with the antibiotics, and for two weeks to a month afterward, to reestablish beneficial bacteria.

Dr. McFarland says that three types of probiotics have been proven to prevent AAD...

- ***Lactobacillus rhamnosus GG.*** This probiotic is available in Allergy Research Group Russian Choice Immune or Nutricology Russian Choice Immune. Many other brands of probiotics also include *L. rhamnosus.*

- ***Saccharomyces boulardii.*** This probiotic is available in Florastor. For more information on *S. boulardii,* see page 169 in this chapter.

- ***Probiotic mixtures.*** Mixed probiotics—combining *L. acidophilus* and *L. bulgaricus;* or *L. acidophilus* and *Bifidobacterium lactis;* or *L. acidophilus* and *Bifidobacterium infantis*—are available in many products.

What to do about CDD: CDD usually develops after taking antibiotics in a hospital setting—and antibiotics are used to treat it. In many cases, however, the antibiotics don't kill the bacterial spores, which germinate, and CDD recurs—even over a period of years. If you're taking a 10-day course of antibiotics for

CDD, take probiotics during that time and for one month afterward, advises Dr. McFarland.

The only probiotic scientifically proven to work for CDD is *S. boulardi*. The dosage that works: 2x 10/10TH, or 20,000,000 billion. In milligrams it's 250 mg, four times a day.

INFLAMMATORY BOWEL DISEASE

Six hundred thousand Americans suffer from inflammatory bowel disease (IBD)—chronic and sometimes severe inflammation and ulceration of the digestive tract. Some have ulcerative colitis, which hits the colon and rectum. Others have Crohn's disease, which can strike anywhere along the tract. Both types are episodic, sometimes active, sometimes in remission. When the disease is active, the symptoms—commonly, abdominal pain, bloody stool and diarrhea—can range from mild to monstrous, with dozens of loose, bloody bowel movements a day, and severe abdominal cramping. Long-term consequences can be severe too, including arthritis and colon cancer.

Scientists don't know the cause of (or cure for) IBD. Powerful anti-inflammatory drugs, steroids and immunosuppressant drugs are typically used to reduce inflammation. Side effects from these medications are common, from the temporary (heartburn and headache), to the chronic (type 2 diabetes and osteoporosis). Yet even with drug treatment, surgery is often required, to remove a disastrously diseased section of the bowel.

It's no wonder, then, that nearly 60% of people with IBD use natural remedies to calm symptoms, reduce their need for drugs and slow the disease. Here are the most effective.

PROBIOTICS CAN STOP ACTIVE DISEASE

The intestinal tract is populated by bacteria. Some are good, helping food digest. But some are bad. Usually the good guys keep the bad guys in check. Doctors theorize that inflammatory bowel disease is caused or complicated when bad bacteria take over, inflaming the mucous lining of the intestine. Taking a probiotic supplement can give the good guys the upper hand.

▶ *Breakthrough Studies*

• **Achieving remission during active disease.** Doctors at the University of Alberta in Canada gave probiotics or a placebo to 32 people with active "mild to moderate" ulcerative colitis that wasn't responding to conventional medical treatment. After six weeks, 53% of the patients on probiotics had gone into complete remission, and another 24% had a positive response.

• **Preventing relapse during inactive disease.** Doctors at the Catholic University of Rome gave 187 patients with inactive ulcerative colitis either probiotics or the anti-inflammatory drug mesalazine, a standard treatment. Probiotics were *more effective* than the drug at preventing relapse. Probiotics could be "a good therapeutic option for preventing relapse" in ulcerative colitis, say the doctors.

• **Treating arthritis.** Arthritis is a common complication of IBD. Dutch doctors gave probiotics to 16 IBD patients with arthritis, and 10 had an improvement in symptoms. (The doctors also note that none of the patients had a relapse while on the supplement.) Probiotics, say the doctors, "may be an alternative treatment for arthritis in patients with IBD."

• **Treating pouchitis.** In 80% of cases, severe ulcerative colitis is treated with surgery in which the colon is removed and a "j-pouch" is created between the small intestine and the rectum. Sadly, many patients *continue* to experience symptoms—because of bouts of inflammation (and infection) in the pouch, with frequent, urgent bowel movements, cramping, bleeding and bloody stools. This condition is called *pouchitis*. Doctors in Italy gave probiotics for four weeks to 23 patients with pouchitis. Sixteen patients went into remission and stayed in remission for the next six months of probiotics treatment.

ⓘ In many studies on ulcerative colitis and probiotics, doctors have used VSL#3, a supplement with eight different strains of friendly bacteria. (Four strains of *lactobacillus,* three strains of *Bifidobacterium* and one strain of *Streptococcus*). It is available at *www.vsl3.com,* or by calling 866-438-8753. Use it with your doctor's approval and supervision.

FISH OIL CUTS RELAPSE RATE IN CROHN'S

To stop new bouts of Crohn's, patients with the disease are typically prescribed the "immuno-modulator" infliximab (Remicade). This medication can have serious and even fatal side effects, from pneumonia, pancreatitis (inflammation of the pancreas) and liver damage, to an increased risk for lymphoma (blood cancer). Doctors are searching for an effective yet safe drug to stop relapses. They may have found one.

⬛⬛⮕ *Breakthrough Study*

Researchers in Israel and Canada analyzed the data from four studies using fish oil to prevent new episodes of active Crohn's disease. They found the "remarkably safe" supplement cut the one-year relapse rate by 50%. Fish oil supplements may turn out to be an effective alternative treatment for the disease, says Dan Turner,

MD, a gastroenterologist in the inflammatory bowel disease unit at the Shaare Zedek Medical Center at the Hebrew University in Jerusalem. If a patient (or a parent of a child with Crohn's) asks him about using fish oil, he usually gives the okay to go ahead and try the supplement.

Important: The studies that worked used enteric-coated fish oil capsules that dissolve in the small intestine rather than the stomach, such as Epanova, a prescription-only fish oil.

ⓘ Over-the-counter enteric-coated fish oil products are widely available, and include Nature's Way Fisol Fish Oil and NOW Omega-3 Odor Controlled, Enteric.

What to do: If you have Crohn's, talk to your doctor about whether you should add a fish oil supplement to your therapeutic regimen. In the studies, a typical dose was a supplement containing 1.8 grams a day of EPA (*eicosapentaenoic acid*) and 900 mg a day of DHA (*docosahexaenoic acid*).

CURCUMIN—THE CALMING SPICE

If you like Indian food, you like turmeric, the yellow spice used to flavor curries.

The active ingredient in turmeric—*curcumin*—is also spicing up the pages of medical journals, with laboratory, animal and human studies showing the herb can counter an amazing range of conditions, from Alzheimer's disease and arthritis to...well, to ulcerative colitis.

⬛⬛⮕ *Breakthrough Studies*

Doctors in Japan studied 82 patients with inactive ulcerative colitis, dividing them into two groups. Both groups took standard anti-inflammatory medications for the disease. But 43 patients also took curcumin, while 39 took placebos.

After six months, only two people receiving curcumin had relapsed—compared to eight in the placebo group.

"Curcumin seems to be a promising and safe medication for maintaining remission in patients with quiescent ulcerative colitis," say the researchers.

And in a study conducted at Columbia University in New York, curcumin improved symptoms in five patients with Crohn's disease and five with pouchitis. The doctors called the results "encouraging."

How it works: Curcumin decreases the production of many types of chemicals that power inflammation, such as tumor necrosis factor, interleukin, thromboxane and leukotriene.

Suggested intake: One gram after breakfast and one gram after dinner.

ℹ Curcumin supplements are widely available. Use with the approval and supervision of your doctor.

CELIAC DISEASE

From sea to shining sea there are a lot of amber waves of grain out there—and two to three million Americans who practically get sick just thinking about them…

Those are the folks with *celiac disease*, a genetic disorder in which the body can't deal with *gluten*, the protein found in wheat, rye and barley. And if you have celiac disease, you have an autoimmune disease—eating gluten causes your immune system to attack and ruin the lining of the intestinal tract. The resulting symptoms run the gamut from digestive insults such as abdominal pain, bloating, diarrhea and constipation, to celiac-caused chronic conditions such as anemia, osteoporosis and even cancer.

As of now, there's only *one* way to treat the disease.

THE GLUTEN-FREE DIET

"A strict gluten-free diet for life is the only treatment for celiac disease," says Shelley Case, RD, a consulting dietitian in Saskatchewan, Canada, a member of the Medical Advisory Boards of the Celiac Disease Foundation and the Gluten Intolerance Group, and author of *Gluten-Free Diet* (Case Nutrition Consulting). But, she adds, staying on such a diet can be a huge challenge.

"Wheat and wheat-based products are major staples of the North American diet," she says. "Hectic lifestyles result in more meals eaten away from home and reliance on packaged, convenience foods, which often contain wheat. Another major challenge is that gluten is a hidden ingredient in many foods."

How to stay gluten-free? You need the right information and a smart strategy to implement it, she says, in the medical journal *Gastroenterology*. Here are her tips for success.

Get your information from top sources.

A lot of the information on celiac disease (CD) and a gluten-free diet (GFD) is outdated, inaccurate and conflicting, says Case. The best sources of information are celiac organizations; local celiac support groups and up-to-date books, magazines and Web sites that specialize in information about CD and GFD.

● **Top organizations.** Celiac Disease Foundation, 13251 Ventura Blvd. #1, Studio City, CA 91604 (818-990-2354, fax 818-990-2379); e-mail *cdf@celiac.org* or on-line at *www.celiac.org*.

American Celiac Disease Alliance, 2504 Duxbury Place, Alexandria, VA 22308 (703-622-3331); e-mail *info@americanceliac.org* or on-line at *www.americanceliac.org*.

Gluten Intolerance Group of North America, 31214 124th Ave. SE, Auburn, WA

98092-3667 (253-833-6655, fax 253-833-6675); e-mail *info@gluten.net* or on-line at *www.gluten.net*.

Canadian Celiac Association, 5170 Dixie Road, Suite 204, Mississauga ON L4W 1E3 (905-507-6208 or 800-363-7296, fax 905-507-4673); e-mail *info@celiac.ca* or on-line at *www.celiac.ca*.

• **Top resource book.** *Gluten-Free Diet: A Comprehensive Resource Guide* by Shelley Case, RD, *www.glutenfreediet.ca*. (In its fourth edition, this book is recommended by the National Institutes of Health and the American Celiac Alliance.)

• **Top cookbooks.** *The Gluten-Free Gourmet* cookbook series (Holt) by Bette Hagman. (Titles include *The Gluten-Free Gourmet, The Gluten-Free Gourmet Cooks Comfort Foods, The Gluten-Free Gourmet Bakes Bread* and many others.)

Gluten-Free Quick & Easy and *Gluten-Free 101* by Carol Fenster, *www.carolfenster.com*.

• **Top magazine.** *Gluten-Free Living* magazine; 560 Warburton Avenue, 2nd Floor, Hastings-on-Hudson, NY 10706 (800-324-8781); Subscription inquiries at *info@gluten freeliving.com* or *www.glutenfreeliving.com*.

• **Top restaurant and travel information.** *Let's Eat Out! Your Passport to Living Gluten and Allergy Free* and other *GlutenFree Passport* guides by Kim Koeller and Robert La France, and the Web sites *www.glutenfreepassport.com*.

Bob and Ruth's Gluten-free Dining & Traveler Club, 205 Donerail Court, Havre de Grace, MD 21078 (410-939-3218); e-mail *info@boband ruths.com* or on-line at *www.bobandruths.com*.

• **Put together a team.** Managing CD is too tough to do on your own. You need a team, says Case. You're the *team* leader, and members should include your family, doctor, dietitian and your celiac support group.

WATCH OUT FOR THESE SNEAKY FOODS

Licorice. Corn flakes. Beer. You don't think of those foods as containing wheat, rye or other grains with gluten—but they do! Here is a list of other frequently overlooked foods that may contain gluten, from Shelley Case, RD.

Warning: Baked beans; chocolate bars; communion wafers; dry roasted nuts; gravy; icings and frostings; imitation bacon bits; marinades; meat loaf; processed meats and poultry; salad dressings; sauces; sausage products; seasonings; flavored herbal teas and coffees; self-basting poultry; soups, soup bases, broth, bouillon cubes; soy sauce; stuffings; thickeners.

Caution: Doctors are often misinformed about CD, says Case. They might recommend a GFD diet *before* medical tests to confirm the disease, which can interfere with the diagnosis. They might not emphasize the importance of a GFD. They might rely on outdated information. Find a physician you're comfortable with who *knows* about CD.

Important: The physician should refer you to a dietitian with expertise in CD, for a nutritional assessment, diet education and meal planning. The nutritionist should also help you adapt to the emotional and social challenges of a GF lifestyle.

Bottom line: If you follow the GFD, you'll reduce the risk of further complications from CD and improve your quality of life, says Case.

NAUSEA

"You make me want to throw up." Well, if you were saying that to your *body*, you might have to say it to your stomach, or brain, or liver, or appendix, or pancreas, or

DO YOU HAVE CELIAC DISEASE?

An estimated 1% of the population has celiac disease (CD)—with many people now developing it later in life, between the ages of 40 and 70. But 95% of those with CD don't know they have it!

CD is the single most *underdiagnosed* disease, says Shelley Case, RD. In fact, a study of more than 2,600 adults with CD (conducted by Case and a team of Canadian researchers, and published in the journal *Digestive Diseases and Sciences*) revealed that it typically takes nearly *12 years* for a person with CD to receive an accurate diagnosis. And since CD can attack multiple systems in the body, producing multiple symptoms, those might be 12 (or more) years of skin rashes, anemia, digestive upset, constipation and diarrhea, extreme fatigue, migraines, depression, infertility and miscarriages, canker sores...and the list goes on.

With symptoms like that, you doctor may have misdiagnosed you with irritable bowel syndrome, lactose intolerance, fibromyalgia or diverticulosis. (Many doctors don't think to test for CD because they were taught in medical school that it is a rare condition, found mostly in children.) How can you find out if have CD? *Case advises you to talk to your doctor about these medical tests...*

1. The EMA (IgA endomysial) and TTG (IgA tissue transglutaminase) blood tests, which are 90 to 95% accurate in screening for CD.

2. A small intestine (duodenum) biopsy, which is the definitive test to confirm the diagnosis.

Better: Celiac disease can appear in patches, so a single biopsy sample may show you're CD-free, even though you're not. Make sure the doctor takes not one but at least four to six samples.

Trap: Do not start a gluten-free diet before the blood test and biopsy. For these tests to detect CD, your body needs to be reacting to gluten *at the time* of the test.

Good news: If you've been suffering from lots of unresolved health problems, receiving a diagnosis of celiac is good news—because now you can solve your problems! "A strict gluten-free diet—a healthy diet that emphasizes fruits, vegetables, lean meats, dairy foods, nuts, seeds, legumes and non-gluten grains such as corn and rice—can clear up most if not all of the symptoms of CD," says Case.

gallbladder, or immune system, or heart or kidneys. In other words, there are a *lot* of physical problems that can trigger nausea, and not all of them have to do with a tortured tummy. (And don't forget pregnancy, surgery, chemotherapy, boating...)

If your nausea won't go away, you need to see the doctor, of course. But no matter what the cause, there are drug-free ways to feel a lot less queasy.

ACUSTIMULATION FOR POSTOPERATIVE RELIEF

Acupuncturists call it P6—the point about two inches down from the palm side of your wrist, in the middle of your forearm, right between two tendons. Stimulation of that point with acupuncture (tiny, painless needles) or acupressure (using fingers or a device that applies steady, gentle pressure) is strong medicine for the common problem of postoperative nausea. In fact, it's *stronger* than medicine.

⁕ *Breakthrough Studies*

Researchers at the University of Texas Health Sciences Center in Houston analyzed 33 studies on "acustimulations" (acupuncture, acupressure and electrical stimulation of acupoints) for postoperative nausea and vomiting. *They found acustimulation...*

● **Reduced nausea by 40%,**

• **Reduced vomiting by 49% and**

• **Reduced use of "rescue antiemetics"** (a second round of medications given after routine, post-op antinausea medications don't work) by 47%.

"Acustimulation is just as effective as medications in reducing nausea and vomiting symptoms for postoperative adult populations," say the researchers.

Important: Acupressure was just as effective as acupuncture or *electrical stimulation* of acupoints. A study illustrating that finding...

• **Half as much postoperative nausea.** Doctors in Turkey asked postoperative surgical patients to wear either an acupressure band with a plastic bead at the P6 point or a similar band with the bead at another point...

• 63% of those with the "fake" acupressure band developed nausea, compared to 33% with the real band.

• 61% of those with the fake band vomited during the first 24 hours after surgery, compared to 25% of those with the real band.

"Acupressure at the P6 meridian point is an effective alternative for the prevention of nausea and vomiting" after surgery, say the researchers, in the *European Journal of Anesthesiology.*

ⓘ Doctors in the Department of Anesthesiology and Pain Management at the University of Texas Southwestern Medical Center used the ReliefBand, which stimulates the P6 acupoint with mild electrical waves, on patients after plastic surgery—with excellent results (less nausea, less use of rescue antiemetics, more patient satisfaction with quality of recovery and a quicker time to home readiness). The product is available from on-line vendors, or direct from the manufacturer Neurowave Medical Technologies, at 312-334-2505, or by e-mailing *info@neurowavemedical.com.*

There are many other brands of P6-stimulating acupressure products, including Sea-Bands, Medicmates Anti-Nausea Acupressure Bands and the Acu-Strap.

Important: Acupressure wrist bands have also been used successfully to reduce nausea from morning sickness, motion sickness and chemotherapy.

GINGER—THE ANTINAUSEA HERB

If you lived in Asia anytime before drugs were invented (say, in the last 2,000 to 3,000 years) and gone to a local herbalist for a nausea remedy, it's likely you would have been given the herb ginger. Modern physicians are discovering ginger was—and is—a smart solution.

||||➡ *Breakthrough Studies*

• **For postoperative nausea.** Doctors in Thailand analyzed five studies using ginger to reduce postoperative nausea and vomiting, involving 363 patients.

Result: Ginger reduced postoperative nausea and vomiting by 31%. In a separate analysis of just vomiting, ginger reduced the incidence by 39%.

"Ginger is an effective option in the prevention of postoperative nausea and vomiting," says Nathorn Chaiyakunapruk, PhD, the lead researcher for the study, in the *American Journal of Obstetrics and Gynecology.*

• **For morning sickness.** Most pregnant women don't want to take drugs during pregnancy, including antinausea drugs that may increase the risk of birth defects. But morning sickness can drive any woman to her gynecologist, pediatrician or family doctor, looking for relief.

187

"A safe and effective medication [for nausea] would be a welcome addition to the therapeutic repertoire," say Italian researchers at the University of Naples. And they found one...

Analyzing data from six studies on ginger and morning sickness, involving 675 pregnant women, they found ginger was as effective as antinausea drugs in relieving nausea, and that there were no significant side effects for the mother or (on follow up) her baby. "Ginger may be an effective treatment for nausea and vomiting," say the researchers, in the journal *Obstetrics and Gynecology*.

"Ginger offers the clinician and the pregnant woman a safe alternative to prescription medications for nausea," agrees Eva Bryer, CNM, a midwife in California.

● **For chemotherapy-induced nausea.** Forty-one people with leukemia who were undergoing chemotherapy were given an antinausea drug and either ginger or a placebo. Those who received the drug and the ginger reported far less nausea.

● **For seasickness.** During their first sea voyage, naval cadets were given 1 gram of ginger or a placebo. Those taking the herb had less nausea, dizziness, cold sweats and vomiting.

How it works: Possibly by binding to receptor sites on neurochemicals in the brain that trigger nausea, so that those chemicals can't be activated, say German researchers.

Suggested intake:

● **For surgery.** 1 gram, 1 hour before surgery.

● **For morning sickness.** "I recommend 1 gram, two to four times per day," says Bryer. "Use it continuously until your symptoms abate."

● **For seasickness.** 1 gram, 1 hour before boarding.

● **For chemotherapy.** 1 gram, 1 hour before chemotherapy.

ⓘ Ginger supplements are widely available.

Red flag: A few people experience a mild stomachache after taking ginger—not the result you want when you're trying to relieve nausea!

Solution: Take ginger in pill or capsule form rather than as a loose powder or tea.

EYES, EARS & TEETH
SHARP SENSES, PROBLEM-FREE TEETH AND GUMS

GOOD CARBS AND FATS FIGHT CATARACTS

Like a camera, your eye has a small light-focusing lens, tucked behind the cornea and pupil. Unlike a camera, your lens is made of protein and water. And, as the years pass, its precise array of protein fibers is *oxidized*, like rusting metal. The frizzled fibers collapse into light-blocking clumps—your vision clouds, blurs, dims, even yellows. You have a cataract.

Stronger glasses and better lighting can help. But, eventually, many of the more than 20 million Americans with cataracts (including 50% of Americans over 65 and 70% over 75) choose cataract surgery, the most frequent operation among the over-65 set. The cornea is cut, the lens is sucked out and an artificial lens is inserted.

Cataract surgery has a 90% success rate in improving eyesight. But surgery is surgery—scalpels, anesthesia, discomfort, risk, bills...the works. You want to avoid it, if possible. You want to stay cataract free for as long as possible.

"Prevention is the most effective way to address cataracts," says Allen Taylor, PhD, director of the Laboratory for Nutrition and Vision Research at the Jean Mayer USDA Human Nutrition Research Center on Aging at Tufts University. He estimates that if all of us Americans could delay cataract formation by an average of 10 years, our total number of "visually disabling" cataracts would drop by 45%. And you *can* delay or prevent cataracts. Just take a closer look at what you're eating.

⫸ *Breakthrough Studies*

• **Vegetable oils increase risk.** Dr. Taylor and a team of researchers at Harvard Medical School examined 15 years of dietary data from 440 women aged 53 to 73. Those who ate the most linoleic acid—the omega-6 polyunsaturated fatty acid found in vegetable oils such as safflower, sunflower, corn, soybean and cottonseed—were twice as likely to develop cataracts.

Theory: Easily oxidized linoleic acid becomes concentrated in the lens of the eye—and is oxidized.

• **Fish oil reduces risk.** Dr. Taylor's team also examined 16 years of dietary data from more than 71,000 women. Those who ate omega-3 fatty acids from fatty fish, such as wild salmon and mackerel an average of once a week, had a 12% lower rate of cataract surgery than women who didn't eat fatty fish regularly.

Theory: Omega-3 fatty acids prevent oxidation and strengthen the lens.

● **Slow-digesting carbs reduce risk.** After looking at fats, Dr. Taylor and his colleagues at Tufts turned their attention to carbohydrates, analyzing dietary data from more than 3,300 people aged 60 to 80. They figured out who ate a high glycemic index (GI) diet loaded with refined carbohydrates such as white bread that *quickly* turn into glucose (blood sugar), and who ate a low glycemic index diet, emphasizing unrefined carbs such as whole-wheat bread that *slowly* turn into glucose.

Those who ate the high-GI diet had a 30 to 40% increased risk of developing cataracts.

Theory: Consistently high levels of glucose in the bloodstream damage the protein in the lens.

Food Strategies for Cataract Prevention

Good Fats: For cooking, avoid omega-6 oils (sunflower, safflower, corn, soybean and cottonseed), choosing omega-3 oils such as olive, canola and flaxseed. Eat at least one four-ounce serving of fatty fish per week, such as salmon, mackerel, herring, sardines, lake trout or albacore tuna.

Good Carbohydrates: To maximize your intake of low-GI foods, follow these six guidelines from Jennie Brand-Miller, PhD, a professor in Human Nutrition at the University of Sydney in Australia and coauthor of *The New Glucose Revolution* (Marlowe & Company) and many other books on the glycemic index...

● **Use breakfast cereals based on oats, barley and bran.**

● **Use whole-grain breads.** Sourdough is also low-GI.

● **Reduce the amount of potatoes you eat.**

● **Enjoy all other types of vegetables and fruits.**

● **For rice, use basmati, long-grain or brown.**

● **Enjoy pasta and noodles.** (Firm, briefly cooked "al dente" style is low-GI.)

AGE-RELATED MACULAR DEGENERATION

The number one cause of severe vision loss and virtual blindness in older Americans is *age-related macular degeneration* (AMD), a disease that erodes the eyesight of 20% of those aged 65 to 74 and 35% of those 75 or older.

In AMD, the sweet spot of your inner eye—the retina's *macula*, a collection of specialized cells that deliver sharp, fine-print vision to the brain—deteriorates over time. The result is an advancing blight of blurry vision, with wavy lines in the middle of your visual field eventually widening to a blotch and then to a barrier. Books, faces, the TV screen, stairs, road signs, the road—all are eventually enveloped in AMD's independence-ending fog.

There is no cure for AMD, and medical treatments are minimally effective. But there are drug-free ways to prevent or slow the disease. Don't turn a blind eye toward them.

⫸ Breakthrough Studies

● **Lutein and zeaxanthin.** Scientists from the Age-Related Eye Disease Study analyzed six years of health data from 4,500 people aged 60 to 80 and found that those who had the highest dietary intake of *lutein* and *zeaxanthin*—pigments found in dark green and yellow vegetables—were the least likely to develop sight-robbing AMD.

Why it works: "These yellow pigments work as a filter to protect the central retina from damage," say Drs. Marc and Michael Rose, ophthalmologists (and identical twins!) in private practice in California, and authors of *Save Your Sight!: Natural Ways to Prevent and Reverse Macular Degeneration* (Grand Central).

Recommended: Take an eye-protecting supplement with 6 to 10 milligrams (mg) of lutein and 0.3 to 1 mg of zeaxanthin, they suggest. And maximize your intake of foods rich in the two nutrients, such as kale, spinach, collard greens, broccoli, zucchini, Brussels sprouts, corn, peas and eggs.

Red flag: "Whether you're eating lutein- and zeaxanthin-rich foods or taking the supplements, try not to do so at the same meal during which you're taking a beta-carotene supplement or eating beta-carotene–rich foods, such as carrots, sweet potatoes or cantaloupe," say Drs. Rose and Rose. "They compete for absorption in the digestive tract and for transport to the eye."

• **Good carbohydrates.** Scientists at the Laboratory for Nutrition and Vision Research at Tufts University in Boston analyzed dietary and health data from more than 4,000 men and women. They found that those eating a diet with foods high on the glycemic index—fast-digesting, refined carbohydrates such as white bread and white rice that quickly turn into blood sugar (glucose)—were more likely to develop advanced, vision-robbing AMD. In fact, the more refined carbs they ate, the higher the risk.

"Many cases of AMD could be prevented if individuals ate a low-GI diet rich in unrefined carbohydrates," says Allen Taylor, PhD, director of the Laboratory.

Recommended: To follow a low-GI diet, see the six simple guidelines for low-GI eating in the item on cataracts, on the opposite page.

• **Fish.** The dictionary says that *fisheye* is an unfriendly or suspicious look—but fish is *very* friendly to your eyes. Researchers at Harvard Medical School analyzed the diets of 681 older men, including 222 with AMD. The men who had eaten two or more servings a week of fatty fish, such as salmon or mackerel, had reduced their risk of AMD by 22%. A similar study conducted by the Centre of Vision Research at the University of Sydney found a 40% reduction for those eating fatty fish once a week.

What happens: The omega-3 fatty acids in fatty fish may protect the cells of the retina in several different ways, say researchers from the government's National Eye Institute—by boosting circulation, reducing the cell-harming effects of sunlight, cutting inflammation and improving the efficient communication within cells (cell signaling) that helps keep them healthy and young.

Recommended: Consider a salmon steak for lunch or dinner, once or twice a week. Or try other fatty fish, such as mackerel, herring, sardines, lake trout and albacore tuna.

• **Overweight.** Being obese—20 to 30 pounds overweight, or more—increases the risk of AMD by 93%, says a study in the journal *Ophthalmology*.

Recommended: For easy, effective ways to lose weight, turn to Chapter 14, "Overweight."

• **Smoking.** No surprise here—smokers have twice the risk of developing AMD and four times the risk of the disease advancing to a vision-destroying stage, say researchers.

Recommended: Quitting cuts risk by about 20%. Better yet, don't start.

• **Heavy drinking.** Five drinks or more a day drown the retina in a sixfold higher risk for AMD, say researchers from the Department of Preventive Medicine at the University of Southern California. Heavy beer drinking is at the bottom of this particular barrel, tripling the risk of advanced AMD.

Recommended: If you drink, do so moderately—no more than one or two drinks a day for men, and no more than one for women. (For more information on alcohol and health, see page 131 in Chapter 6, "Diabetes and Insulin Resistance.")

Caution: This item discusses the gradual type of age-related macular degeneration known as "dry." The rarer "wet" type advances rapidly. The first symptom—straight lines look wavy. See an eye-care professional immediately.

GLAUCOMA—PROTECTION FOR THE OPTIC NERVE

Sitting at the back of the eyeball like a wizard in a cave, the retina transforms light into electrical signals that flash to the brain along the retina's *optic nerve*, a cablelike bundle of more than a million nerve fibers.

In glaucoma, the optic nerve is damaged.

At first, the outer edge of sight—peripheral vision—is stolen. As glaucoma progresses, vision narrows to a tunnel. The final stage is blindness, with glaucoma causing 10% of all cases in the United States.

The most common cause of glaucoma is faulty plumbing. The flow of tissue-nourishing fluid inside the eyeball doesn't drain properly, nerve-damaging pressure builds and the fragile fibers of the optic nerve die off.

Nearly three million Americans have glaucoma. Those at higher risk include African-Americans over 40, everyone over 60 (with older Hispanics particularly prone) and people with a family history of the disease.

If you're at high risk, the best prevention is an eye exam every two years to detect pressure buildup before it can damage the optic nerve. Pressure-lowering drugs and/or surgery can slow or correct the problem. But, says one of the world's top glaucoma specialists, drug-free remedies can also help.

▶ *Breakthrough Study*

While drugs and surgery can lower pressure, one thing they *can't* do is directly protect nerve cells, says Robert Ritch, MD, an ophthalmologist at Glaucoma Associates of New York and a professor at New York Medical College. But, he says, many natural compounds *can* shield the cells of the optic nerve from damage and death, slowing glaucoma. *He presents the best of those drug-free remedies in the* Canadian Journal of Ophthalmology…

• **Fish oil.** If it works for an aging rat, it might work for you, says Dr. Ritch—an animal study shows that upping the intake of omega-3 fatty acids from fish oil lowers pressure inside the eyeball (intraocular pressure). He also points to an Italian study in which a supplement combining DHA (an omega-3 fatty acid), vitamin E and B vitamins improved the vision and retinal health of 30 people with glaucoma.

• **Ginkgo biloba extract.** Dr. Ritch is particularly enthusiastic about the eye-healing potential of ginkgo biloba extract (GBE). "Gingko biloba has several biological actions that combine to make it a potentially important agent in the treatment of glaucoma," he says. GBE may help glaucoma by thinning blood and improving circulation to the eye, stopping spasms in blood vessels that can reduce blood flow, fighting cellular damage from oxidation (a kind of internal rust), extending the life of cells and slowing or stopping a process that kills nerve cells called *excitotoxicity*. *He cites several studies that show the eye-protecting power of GBE…*

Doctors at the Glaucoma Research and Diagnostic Center at Indiana University gave 11 people with glaucoma either 40 mg of GBE or a placebo, three times a day, for two days. Those taking GBE had a 23% increase in blood flow to the eye—without an increase in blood pressure, heart rate or pressure inside the eye.

In a study from Italy, 27 people with glaucoma took either 40 mg of GBE three times a day for one month or a placebo. While taking GBE, their visual field (the total range of peripheral and central vision) improved by 23%—compared to no change for the placebo group.

● **Methylcobalamin.** This form of B-12 can protect nerve fibers and even help regenerate damaged nerve cells, says Dr. Ritch. In a study from Japan, 14 people with glaucoma received methylcobalamin supplements for four years, while another group of 22 glaucoma patients didn't receive the nutrient. After the four years, only two people (14%) in the B-12 group had a reduction in their visual field—compared to 13 people (59%) among those not taking B-12.

What to do: Share this research with your ophthalmologist and discuss whether any of these nutritional or herbal supplements are right for you.

The scientific citation for Dr. Ritch's paper on drug-free approaches to glaucoma is Ritch, R. *Canadian Journal of Ophthalmology* 42 (2007): 425–38.

WHEN GLAUCOMA IS AN EMERGENCY

There are many different types of glaucoma. The type discussed in this chapter, *primary open angle glaucoma*, is the most common form. It develops slowly, is painless and usually doesn't produce symptoms until it's advanced. Another, rare form of the disease is *angle closure glaucoma*—a medical emergency in which pressure inside the eyeball rises quickly, with possible symptoms including severe eye pain, blurred vision, halos around lights, reddening of the eye, nausea and vomiting. If you have those symptoms, seek medical care immediately. Surgery can correct the problem.

☀ Your doctor can contact Dr. Ritch at Robert Ritch, MD, Glaucoma Associates of New York, The New York Eye and Ear Infirmary, 310 East 14th Street, Suite 304, New York, NY 10003 (212-477-7540); e-mail *ritchmd@earthlink.net.*

DRY EYES? THINK BLINK

Forty million Americans suffer from dry, reddened eyes—eyes that sometimes sting, burn, itch or otherwise hurt, with a feeling that something gritty or sandy is *in* your eye…eyes that may feel tired and strained, and are sensitive to light, with blurred vision.

What happens: The "tear film" that should uniformly cover and moisten your cornea is parched, breaking up between blinks into streaks and dot-size puddles—and plenty of irritating dry spots in between.

The causes of dry eye are many. Age can dehydrate the eye; menopause, for example, is particularly tough on the tear film. Medications that dry up mucous, such as antihistamines and decongestants, can dry up the tear film too. So can some diseases, such as diabetes and rheumatoid arthritis. A common side effect of LASIK—laser-assisted surgery for vision correction—is a lifetime of dry eyes.

And one of the biggest culprits is staring at a computer screen for hours at a time, a habit for many of us, at work and at home. Seventy-five percent of people who spend long hours in front of a monitor complain of dry eyes. Two simple strategies can help.

▶ *Breakthrough Studies*

● **Less blinking.** Blinking is the main way eyes stay wet. But when attention is riveted to the computer, you tend to blink less, say specialists in dry eyes at the National Institute of

Occupational Health in Denmark, who have intensively studied the problem. A typical blink rate is 15 per minute; steady computer work cuts it to 10, or even 5. And complex, difficult mental tasks also decrease blinking, says Peder Wolkoff, PhD, one of the Danish researchers.

What to do: Take breaks to maintain moist eyes and normal blink frequency, advises Dr. Wolkoff. If you use a computer for lengthy periods, your eye breaks should add up to about five minutes per hour, agree experts from the Mayo Clinic. During each break, rest your eyes by closing your lids for several seconds and then consciously increase your blink rate after you open your eyes, they advise.

● **Low humidity.** Dry, hot rooms are hard on eyes, says Dr. Wolkoff. In fact, a study at the University of Texas showed that for every 10% drop in humidity, there is a 30 to 60% increase in evaporation of moisture from the surface of the eye.

What to do: Ideal humidity to prevent dry eyes is between 35 and 45%, say the UT researchers. At home, use a *hygrometer* (available at most hardware stores) to check humidity. If it's low, turn on the humidifier, setting the humidity level at about 40%, using the appliance's humidity meter.

What most people don't realize: The first line of treatment for dry eyes is (not surprising) eye drops and artificial tears. However, many leave a sticky plasticlike film at the edge of the eyelid...cut the "oxygen permeability" of soft contact lenses, further fatiguing eyes...and may contain preservatives that irritate the eye. The best, study-proven lubricants without those drawbacks are Refresh Endura, Soothe and Tears Again, says Dr. Wolkoff.

FOLATE SLOWS HEARING LOSS

You're out to eat with your wife, and from across the intimate, candlelit table for two, she says, "I love you"—but you can't hear her.

You walk into a room where your grandson is watching TV and he calls out "Grandpa"—but you can't hear him.

Yes, being hard of hearing *is* hard...on happiness!

Doctors call the problem "age-related hearing loss," or *presbycusis* (pre-bih-KU-sis), and it muffles the lives of about 30 million Americans—49% of 60-year-old men and 26% of women. (They say women are better listeners; now you know one reason why.)

Age-related hearing loss is caused by the gradual death of thousands of tiny hair-shaped, sound-sensitive cells in the *cochlea*, or inner ear.

The first type of hearing to go is the higher frequencies, such as the voices of women and children. As hearing worsens, background noise—other conversations, the TV—can turn sound into slosh. As time passes, your hearing gets worse.

There is no cure for age-related hearing loss. But you might be able to slow it down. With a vitamin.

||||▶ *Breakthrough Study*

Researchers in Holland studied 712 men and women aged 50 to 70. For three years, half took a daily supplement of the B-vitamin folate, while the other half took a placebo.

Result: Those who took folate had 70% less hearing loss in a range of tones and sounds that hearing experts call "speech frequencies."

"A benefit of this size could reduce the proportion of men who are hearing-aid candidates at age seventy-five from thirty-three percent to twenty-two percent," says Robert A. Dobie, MD, a professor in the Department of Otolaryngology at the University of California, Davis.

Why it works: Folate may protect the genetic material (DNA) in hair cells, helping them stay alive longer, say the Dutch researchers.

Suggested intake: 800 micrograms (mcg) daily, about twice as much as in a typical multivitamin.

ℹ️ Folate and B-vitamin supplements are widely available.

Caution: Always take folate with B-12 (400 to 1,000 mcg) because folate supplementation can mask a B-12 deficiency, a dangerous condition, says Michael Murray, ND, a naturopathic doctor and author of *Encyclopedia of Nutritional Supplements* (Three Rivers Press).

CELL PHONES—MORE CALLS ARE COSTLY...TO HEARING

Researchers in India found that people who used mobile phones for more than an hour a day for four years had 23% more high-frequency hearing loss in their right ears (the ear most typically used for conversations) than people who used mobile phones more than an hour a day for a year or two.

Red flags: "A warm feeling in your ear, or ringing in the ear or a feeling it is clogged up, are warning signs of hearing loss, and cell phone users with those symptoms should consider reducing or stopping use," says Naresh K. Panda, the scientist who led the study, which was reported at the annual meeting of the American Academy of Otolaryngology—Head and Neck Surgery. If you don't have those symptoms, "use cell phones only when necessary," he cautions.

Better: Using headsets or ear buds is a safer choice than a mobile phone held up to the ear, says Dr. Panda.

AFTER THE ROCK CONCERT, TAKE MAGNESIUM

Past the outer ear...past the ear canal...past the eardrum...past the chain of three tiny bones called the *malleus, incus* and *stapes*...is the *cochlea*, the inner ear. A snail-shaped coil, it houses a chamber filled with four rows of thousands of "hair cells," specialized fibers that translate sound waves into electrical signals for the auditory nerve to speed to the brain.

Loud sounds—a jet taking off, high-volume music, the roar of a vacuum cleaner—turn the cochlea into a torture chamber for hair cells. The buffeted cells tear and break, like branches in a hurricane. Tiny veins contract, cutting off blood supply and withering cells. The hair cells die in droves.

While a loud noise such as an explosion can cause hearing loss, if the noise exposure is loud *and* sustained *and* recurrent, noise-induced hearing loss is nearly guaranteed. Nine out of 10 professional musicians, for example, develop some degree of hearing loss.

Common sense can help you keep your sense of hearing. Limit your exposure to noxious noise, such as loud concerts or hours of too-loud headset use. When exposure is inevitable—such as airplane travel, mowing the lawn with a power mower or vacuuming—use ear protection, such as earplugs or noise-reducing earmuffs.

You can also take a supplement of the mineral magnesium.

▐▐▶ *Breakthrough Study*

Researchers in the Department of Communications Disorders at the University of Haifa in Israel studied 20 men, giving them either 170 mg of magnesium or a placebo and then exposing them to loud noise. On the days the men took magnesium, they had less temporary hearing loss.

"Magnesium provides significant protection against temporary hearing loss," say the researchers.

In earlier research, published in the *American Journal of Otolaryngology*, the same team of Israeli scientists gave either 170 mg a day of magnesium or a placebo for two months to 300 recruits in basic training—training that included "repeated exposure to high levels of noise while using earplugs." The men taking the magnesium had significantly less *permanent* hearing loss than the men taking the placebo.

"These two studies on hearing loss introduce a new, natural agent for the prevention and possible treatment of noise-induced cochlear damage," says Joseph Attias, MD, who led both studies.

What to do: If you've been exposed to loud noise, follow it with a dose of magnesium. If loud noise is a part of your life, help prevent hearing loss with daily intake.

Suggested intake: Both studies used 170 mg of magnesium *aspartate*, a form of the mineral that is widely available in nutritional supplements.

HIGH-TECH HEARING AIDS—SMALLER, BETTER

Only 20% of people with hearing loss that leads to communication problems decide to use hearing aids. And 25% of people *with* hearing aids don't wear them, because of problems with background noise.

ⅢⅢ▶ *Breakthrough Study*

That's too bad, says Harold Kim, MD, an otolaryngologist at the Wilson Ear Clinic in Portland, OR. In the last 10 years, hearing aids have gone high-tech. No more large, conspicuous devices. No more squealing feedback. No more second-rate sound. "Today's hearing aids offer higher fidelity, greater overall amplification and amplification of specific frequencies and more accurate detection of the direction of the sound."

Dr. Kim highlights the newest features in a report in the journal *Otolaryngology–Head and Neck Surgery*...

- **Digital signal processing.** Yes, like TV, movies and just about every other technology, hearing aids have gone from analog to digital, improving clarity and reducing distortions of all kinds. Digital hearing aids can also include programs for different types of hearing, such as quiet listening or noisy backgrounds.

- **Directional microphones.** The hearing aid of yore had an "omnidirectional microphone" that picked up and amplified *every* sound. The newer microphones "preferentially" amplify sounds in front of you and suppress sounds behind you. Conversations are clearer. (Unless somebody is talking behind your back.)

- **Open-fitting hearing aids.** These new "vented" aids don't block the ear canal or give you the sense you have an earplug. They also eliminate the echo or hollow sound that often annoys hearing aid users when they talk. "Open-fitting aids are best for people with normal or near-normal hearing in the low frequencies, with hearing loss in the higher frequencies," says Dr. Kim. (Your audiologist can let you know if you're in that category.)

- **Wireless CROS aids.** CROS aids are for people with single-sided deafness—they use two hearing aids, routing signals from the "bad" ear to the "good" ear. They require a wire to connect the two aids, and they produce poor sound. The new, wireless varieties use FM or BlueTooth technology to help eliminate those problems.

A NATURAL TREATMENT FOR SUDDEN DEAFNESS

Yesterday you could hear. Today you're deaf. That's the shocking reality of sudden deafness, or what experts call *sudden sensorineural hearing loss* (SSHL)—suddenly and rapidly losing hearing in one or both ears, over one to three days. It strikes an estimated 4,000 Americans a year, most of them over 40.

You may notice it when you wake up in the morning or when you make the day's first phone call. Maybe you're dizzy or there is a ringing in your ears (tinnitus), or you heard a sudden "pop" right before your hearing vanished.

Two-thirds of those with SSHL recover within a week or two. For the rest, hearing loss may be permanent.

Experts say there are more than 100 possible causes for sudden deafness, from the immune system mistakenly attacking the inner ear, to a drug reaction, to a head injury. In most cases, however, no cause is found.

Sudden hearing loss should mean a trip to the emergency room. You'll probably receive steroids—powerful, multipurpose drugs that calm inflammation and swelling and suppress the immune system. (Emergency treatment should be followed by a medical workup to discover possible underlying causes of the problem.) But steroids only tend to work when hearing loss isn't severe, and in people under 40.

A drug-free approach that can help is hyperbaric oxygen treatment (HBOT)—breathing 100% oxygen in a pressurized chamber.

⬛➡ *Breakthrough Study*

Researchers in Belgium studied 216 patients with sudden hearing loss who weren't helped by steroids, giving them HBOT two to three days after deafness struck. Another group of patients didn't get any HBOT. Those who got HBOT the quickest after the hearing loss had a *sevenfold* improvement in hearing, compared to those who didn't get HBOT.

In another study on HBOT, by researchers at Weill Medical College of Cornell University, in New York City, nine people with sudden hearing loss who didn't improve after two weeks of treatment with either steroids or antiviral drugs received 90 minutes of HBOT every day, for 10 days. Two patients had "dramatic improvement," says Samuel H. Selesnick, MD, one of the doctors who conducted the study.

Theory: A lack of oxygen flow to the inner ear may trigger sudden deafness. The oxygen may also help kill viruses that cause the problem.

What to do: Talk to you doctor—as soon as possible after the onset of sudden hearing loss—about whether hyperbaric oxygen is available in your area and an option for you.

☀ You can find a state-by-state guide to hyperbaric oxygen chambers at the Web site of the Undersea and Hyperbaric Medical Society, *www.uhms.org*. On the home page, go to the "Resource Library", where you will find the "Chamber Directory" for the US. *Information:* Undersea and Hyperbaric Medical Society, 21 West Colony Place, Suite 280, Durham, NC 27705; Phone: (877) 533-UHMS, (919) 490-5140; fax: (919) 490-5149; e-mail: *uhms@uhms.org*.

Red flag: Counseling to help you pick the right hearing aid is crucial, says Dr. Kim. "Poorly done, it is a significant reason why many people don't accept and use their hearing aids." *Good counseling includes…*

1. A history of problem areas with hearing.

2. An audiogram—a hearing test.

3. Advice as to the best hearing aid for you—one or both ears; behind-the-ear, in-the-ear, in-the-canal, or completely-in-the-canal; and the specific type, along with options.

4. Instructions to use the hearing aid.

New approach: "There have been tremendous strides in hearing aids, with newer models providing high-fidelity amplification more accurately tailored to the needs of the hearing aid user," says Dr. Kim. "With these advances, the elimination or reduction of hearing impairment with the use of hearing aids is a *reality*. This fact needs to be relayed to the four out of five people who stand to benefit from amplification with a hearing aid but choose not to acquire one."

Hear, hear, Dr. Kim!

FOR TINNITUS, TRY LOW-PITCHED SOUNDS

Sixty million bells, buzzers and beeps, with some humming, roaring and hissing, for good measure.

If that sounds like a lot of noise, it is.

It's the noise of *tinnitus*—the relentless, often high-pitched racket *inside* the head of each one of the 60 million men and women with this hearing disorder, many of them over 55 years old.

Commonly called "ringing in the ears" (though it can also sound like crickets chirping, bacon frying, horns blaring or...well, you get the pinging, puttering point), tinnitus can range from the mild to the maddening.

You might be able to disregard the sound. Or it might be so loud and intrusive that you have trouble getting to sleep, hearing conversations or concentrating. The constant aural annoyance can leave you frustrated and even depressed.

What causes tinnitus? Scientists can't say for sure. It's often entwined with age-related hearing loss...can follow a lifetime of exposure to loud noise...can be the symptom of a disease, such as Meniere's (an inner ear disorder)...or can be caused or worsened by medications, such as the regular use of aspirin or antibiotics.

Treatments are nothing to cheer about. Doctors have tried drugs such as antidepressants and migraine medications, but without much success. Usually, you're told to reduce stress and cut back on dietary factors that might notch up the volume, such as coffee and alcohol. And that's it! But the best (and newest) treatment of all may be—believe it or not—another sound.

‖‖➡ *Breakthrough Study*

Many tinnitus researchers have attempted to treat tinnitus with "masking"—using a high-pitched sound to counter the one in your head, says Fan-Gang Zeng, PhD, director of the Hearing and Speech Lab at the University of California, Irvine, School of Medicine. "For a masker to work, it has to be close to the pitch of the tinnitus, and louder than the tinnitus. But if the tinnitus is loud and unpleasant, the masker is likely to be louder and even more unpleasant. As a patient, which poison do you pick?"

But in the process of treating a patient with tinnitus so severe a louder sound was out of the question, Dr. Zeng discovered that a low-pitched sound could work just as well. The sound was what he describes as a "calming, pleasant tone" of 40 to 100 hertz of frequency, applied with headphones through a regular MP3 player. (An MP3 player is a digital music-playing device, such as an iPod, that you use to download music from the Internet.)

In just 90 seconds, the low-pitched sound suppressed the high-pitched ringing and provided what the patient described as a high level of continued relief.

"We are very surprised and pleased by the success of this therapy," says Dr. Zeng. "Hopefully, with further testing it will provide needed relief to the millions who suffer from tinnitus.

HOMEOPATHY FOR SEVERE, DISABLING TINNITUS

The theory behind the healing technique of *homeopathy* is the substances that can give you the symptoms of a disease can actually cure you of the disease when taken in minuscule amounts. For tinnitus, that theory may be a reality.

New study: Doctors in the Martha Entenmann Tinnitus Research Center at the State University of New York gave 11 people with severe, disabling tinnitus a homeopathic/herbal remedy for the condition. After three months, seven of the 11 had positive results—they reported their tinnitus was far less intense and less annoying. They also had less middle ear pressure, an objective sign of disease improvement, say the doctors, in the *International Tinnitus Journal.*

ℹ️ Clear Tinnitus, from Clear Products, a combination of homeopathic remedies and herbs. Follow the dosage recommendation on the label.

☀️ Clear Tinnitus is available in pharmacies and health-food stores, and on the Internet at *www.cleartinnitus.com.*

"This treatment does not represent a cure," he emphasizes. "It is only effective when applied to the ear, after which the ringing can return."

What to do: While Dr. Zeng and his colleagues are refining their treatment, you can put a version to work for yourself, with an MP3 player, a pair of headphones and some downloads of recordings of low-pitched sounds. The treatment can also work with earphones or speakers, using any type of playing device, he says.

Karen Ramirez—a composer, "conceptual sound designer" and tinnitus-sufferer in Toronto, Canada—has created a Web site stocked with hour-long MP3 downloads with low-pitched and pleasing sounds for tinnitus. The site refers to Dr. Zeng's research...allows you to listen to 15-second samples of all the recordings for sale

at the site...provides an exchange or money-back guarantee for the dissatisfied...and walks the uninitiated through the download process. The best four MP3 files for sound masking are Rain on the River, Windy Mountain Valley, Cave by the Waterfall and Turbine Hall.

☀️ The friendly, witty and somewhat irreverent Web site (featuring the slogan, "Because tinnitus sucks") is at *www.whitenoisemp3s.com;* e-mail *whitenoisemp3s@gmail.com.*

THE BEST TOOTHBRUSH FOR GUM DISEASE

We're gumming up our body's works—with gum disease.

Forty-eight percent of Americans have *gingivitis*—infected, swollen, bleeding gums. Among those over 65, the rate is 85%. About one-third of those with gum disease end up with *periodontal disease,* when gums (and surrounding bone) erode and recede.

The result, of course, is tooth loss. *And maybe even loss of life...*

What most people don't realize: Gum disease can increase your risk for high blood pressure, heart disease, stroke, type 2 diabetes and even certain types of cancer, says Thomas Van Dyke, DDS, a professor in the Goldman School of Dental Medicine at Boston University. The worse the gum disease, the greater the risk.

Maybe your jaw just dropped, and your gums with it. How can a seemingly minor condition like gingivitis lead to a severe, life-threatening chronic illness? *Dr. Van Dyke explains...*

Gum disease is fueled by *biofilm,* or plaque—a multilayered, mineral-encrusted, bacterial base camp on your teeth. White blood cells—the infantry of your immune system—rush to the area to fight the bacteria. In the process, they release chemicals that create an *inflammatory response*, the telltale redness and swelling that signals an immune system in defense mode. But inflammation has a downside—it damages tissue, causing or complicating many diseases.

The inflammation from gum disease can cause chronic disease in two ways, says Dr. Van Dyke. Mouth bacteria travels to other parts of the body, sparking inflammation, and local inflammation in the gums sets off alarms that trigger body-wide inflammation.

What to do?

Just what your dentist, hygienist, kindergarten teacher, mother and the surgeon general have been telling you to do since your first visit from the tooth fairy—to bust up biofilm, brush your teeth twice a day. But one brush may do a better job than all the others.

▶ *Breakthrough Study*

The scientific literature on toothbrushes (consisting of hundreds of studies) is a bit like a debate among nerds at a Star Wars convention, arguing over who has the most powerful Lightsaber. There's the dual-action power toothbrush…the ionic toothbrush with the lithium battery…the multi-tufted, flat-trimmed, end-rounded nylon filament brush…the twin-motor sonic toothbrush, not to mention the Deep Clean, the Curvex and the Spinbrush Pro.

Well, the scientists from the Cochrane Collaboration, an organization that recruits specialists to analyze and interpret scientific evidence in particular areas of health, letting docs know which treatments really work and which don't—took a hard and soft-bristled look at 42 rigorous studies on toothbrushes, plaque removal and gingivitis, involving nearly 4,000 people.

Result: One type of powered toothbrush works better than all the rest, either powered or manual—a brush with "rotation oscillation action" (the brush head rotates first in one direction and than the other).

This type of brush removes more plaque than manual brushes (up to 17%), and is better at reducing inflammation and bleeding, the signs of gum disease.

Other powered brushes didn't outperform the manual variety. They included brushes with a circular motion (Teledyne), counter oscillation (Interplak), side-to-side motion (Sonicare) and ultrasonic vibration (Ultrasonex).

ℹ The power toothbrushes that rotate and oscillate are from Oral-B, and there are many different types, including Oral-B Triumph and Oral-B Professional Care. You can find out more about these products at *www.oralb.com*. (For an excellent step-by-step refresher course on brushing and flossing, visit the "Daily Care" section of the "Learning Center" at the Web site.)

Important: Any toothbrush works if you use it twice a day, and use it correctly, says Dr. Van Dyke. Hold the bristles at a 90-degree angle to the gums, wiggling rather than scrubbing.

And may the floss be with you. "It helps you clean between teeth in areas that a toothbrush can't reach," he says. "Use the same twice-a-day timing."

AFTER GUM SURGERY, TAKE B VITAMINS

You have *periodontitis*—colonies of entrenched bacteria called tartar have weakened your gums, which have pulled apart from your teeth, forming deep, infected "pockets." The dental hygienist did a "deep cleaning," scraping off the tartar, smoothing out rough spots on the root of the tooth where bacteria like to gather and inserting into the pockets tiny, round particles of slow-releasing antibiotics called microspheres. Whew!

But, at your last checkup, the dentist said the situation still wasn't under control. Your gum disease continues to progress and you need "flap surgery"—lifting the gums, removing the tartar beneath and sewing them up tighter to the teeth. Whew again.

Ready for some good news? If you take B vitamins after the surgery, you may have better results.

IIII▶ *Breakthrough Study*

Dental researchers in the Department of Periodontics at the School of Dentistry at the University of Michigan studied 30 people after flap surgery, dividing them into two groups. One group took a daily B-complex supplement, while the other took a placebo. After 30 days, the dentists measured "clinical attachment levels"—the degree to which gums were successfully adhering to teeth.

Result: Those taking the B vitamins had attachment levels nearly twice that of the placebo group.

What to do: Consider taking a B-vitamin supplement every day for one month after flap surgery, says Rodrigo Neiva, DDS, MS, who led the study.

Suggested intake: The B-complex vitamin used in the study consisted of 50 mg each of thiamine, riboflavin, niacinamide, pantothenate and pyridoxine (B-6). B-complex supplements are widely available.

ANTIOXIDANTS AGAINST GUM DISEASE

If you want to nurture healthy gums and keep your teeth, consider what you put in your mouth—diets rich in antioxidants may help prevent advanced gum disease.

IIII▶ *Breakthrough Study*

An international team of researchers from the Goldman School of Dental Medicine at Boston University and the School of Dentistry at the University of Birmingham in England analyzed data on blood levels of antioxidants and severe gum disease (*periodontitis*) in more than 11,000 people.

Result: Those with the highest blood levels of antioxidants—beta-carotene, selenium, vitamin C, vitamin E and others—were 47% less likely to develop periodontitis.

Theory: The researchers explain how antioxidants might save your teeth...

Bacteria infect the gums. The immune system fights back, generating the classic immune

---

BRUSH, FLOSS—AND SLEEP

Your gums need rest too.

Scientists from the Department of Preventive Dentistry at Osaka University in Japan studied 219 people with periodontal disease for four years, matching lifestyle factors with the progression of the disease.

Result: The disease progressed more slowly in those who got seven to eight hours of sleep, compared to those who got six hours or less.

"This study points out that there are lifestyle factors other than brushing and flossing that may affect oral health," says Preston D. Miller, Jr., DDS, former president of the American Academy of Periodontology. "Simple lifestyle changes, such as getting more sleep, may help people improve or protect their oral health."

Warning: Although sleep had a significant impact, smoking was the number one lifestyle cause of worsening gum disease. (Sleep was number two.) High stress levels and heavy drinking also played a role.

201

response—the swelling and redness known as *inflammation*. Inflammation creates what scientists call *reactive oxygen species* (ROS)—oxygen-containing molecules that destroy tissue (in this case, gums and bone) just like oxygen browns the flesh of a sliced apple. Antioxidants protect the gums against ROS.

What to do: Eat more antioxidant-rich foods, of course.

Surprising: Researchers at the US Department of Agriculture measured the antioxidant content of 100 foods and found some unexpected standouts among those richest in the nutrients. *The antioxidant superstars…*

- **Beans** (small red bean, red kidney bean, pinto bean, black bean)

- **Berries** (blueberry, cranberry, blackberry, raspberry, strawberry)

- **Apples** (Red Delicious, Granny Smith, Gala)

- **Artichokes**

- **Plums and prunes**

- **Pecans**

- **Sweet cherries**

FOR BAD BREATH, TRY GOOD BACTERIA

Breath mints. Chewing gum. Mouthwash. Toothpaste. Those are some of the products used by the 40 million Americans with bad breath to try to sweeten the problem.

They can add *streptococcus salivarius K12* to the list.

▶ *Breakthrough Study*

Streptococcus salivarius K12 is a *probiotic*—a "good" bacteria that can shove aside "bad" bacteria in your body that are up to no good. In this case, the bad bacteria hang out on your tongue and in your mouth and throat, generating smelly sulfur-containing molecules that are the "bad" in bad breath.

Scientists in the Department of Microbiology and Immunology at the University of Otago in New Zealand have created an approach to bad breath that first gets rid of bad bacteria and then replaces it with good—Streptococcus salivarius K12, a cousin of Streptococcus thermophilus, a good bacteria used to make yogurt.

In recent research, the scientists studied 23 people with bad breath, also known as *halitosis*. For three days, they gargled with a mouthwash containing the antiseptic *chlorhexidine*. A few times a day during those three days they also sucked on lozenges that either contained S. salivarius K12 or were look-alike, taste-alike placebos.

Result: A week later, 85% of those using the bacteria-containing lozenges had substantial reductions in the sulfur-generating bacteria that cause bad breath—while only 30% of the placebo group had similar reductions.

The researchers then examined the study participants' saliva in test tubes. They found that S. salivarius K12 stymied the growth of halitosis-causing bacteria.

"The replacement of bacteria implicated in halitosis by colonization with competitive bacteria such as S. salivarius K12 may provide an effective strategy to reduce the severity of halitosis," says Jeremy Burton, PhD, at the University of Otago, the researcher who led the study.

What to do: If you'd like to try S. salivarius K12 for the control of bad breath, there are a full range of "K"-containing products formulated by the New Zealand researchers—a mouthwash (used twice a week), probiotic lozenges (used twice a day), a gel to help clean the tongue of bad bacteria and colonize it with good (used once or twice a day), and a bacteria-removing tongue scraper designed to help remove the bad bacteria while not damaging the surface of your tongue (used with the gel, once or twice a day).

☀ You can buy the products separately or in a kit at *www.breezecare.com/usa*. E-mail for questions *dentist@breezecare.com*; e-mail for orders *sharon@breezecare.com*.

CITRUS OIL—FOR HEALING CANKER SORES

It's a cheeky disease.

First, there's the tingling and burning, the early warning system that's telling you it's already too late. Then a tiny, round ulcer carves a crater in the lining of your cheek or lips, or on your gums. But while it might be little in size, it's big in discomfort. The red-ringed, gray-floored ulcer feels as bad as it looks, stinging today, tomorrow and for the rest of the week.

You have a canker sore, or what doctors call an *aphthous ulcer*.

You might get one every now and then. Or you might get them constantly and in bunches, a common condition called *recurrent aphthous stomatitis*.

The cause? For the genetically prone, it could be a jab or a jolt to the tissue, from toothbrushing, say, or the corner of a taco chip. As for the rest of us, doctors don't know, though they're reasonably sure it's not stress or an infection. They do know, however, that the immune system is riled up, sending cells to the area that haul inflammation and irritation in their wake.

Whatever ushers in the ulcer, the oft-recommended treatments are standard. Use over-the-counter gels, creams and pastes, perhaps

TONGUE SCRAPER BEATS TOOTHBRUSH

Want fast relief from bad breath? Tidy your tongue.

In a scientific article in the journal of *General Dentistry*, researchers with the US Navy Dental Corp looked at two studies on tongue scraping to reduce bad breath—and found the devices worked 20 to 30% better than brushing the tongue with a toothbrush to get rid of the sulfur-generating bacteria that cause bad breath, or halitosis. Scraping also helped breath stay sweeter longer.

Surprising: Tongue scrapers are particularly effective for bad breath caused by chronic sinus infections. "A common reason for bad breath is postnasal drip, which coats the back area of the tongue with bacteria-rich mucous," says June Lee, DDS, from the Academy of General Dentistry. "A tongue scraper is often effective in relieving bad breath caused by sinus drainage."

What to do: Scrape the middle and back of the tongue using any one of the many tongue scrapers that are commercially available, she says. "Cleaning the tongue is quickly and easily accomplished, and tongue scrapers are easy to transport and inexpensively priced. Everyone from children to older people should be able to incorporate this technique into their oral care regimen."

Also helpful: A study by researchers at the University of Illinois found that Big Red—a cinnamon-flavored chewing gum made by Wrigley's—reduced halitosis-causing bacteria in the mouth by more than 50%. "The product, which contains plant essential oils, doesn't just mask foul mouth odor," says Christine Wu, DDS, professor of periodontics and one of the authors of the study. "It temporarily eliminates the bacteria that cause bad breath."

with a corticosteroid to reduce inflammation and/or a numbing anesthetic to relieve pain.

Compared to a natural remedy with citrus oil and magnesium salts, those canker sore remedies are second-rate.

⫸ *Breakthrough Study*

Israeli researchers from the Department of Medicinal Chemistry and Natural Products at the Hebrew University of Jerusalem studied 48 patients with canker sores, dividing them into two groups.

One group was treated with Kank-A, from Blistex—a tincture that (like many products on the market) contains an anesthetic (*benzocaine*) to numb the area and dries to form a protective barrier that (hopefully) spares the ulcer from more irritation and speeds healing.

The other group was treated with a tiny, tabletlike patch that immediately forms a soft, elastic covering over the ulcer—and delivers citrus oil and magnesium salts to the area. *They were sore winners...*

• **Faster healing.** On average, the citrus/magnesium patch healed the canker sores in 24 hours—compared to 120 hours for the benzocaine-barrier. That's one day versus five days! (A study on the popular barrier product Orabase shows that it produces healing in about eight days.)

• **Pain relief.** The study participants used a numerical scale to describe their pain level. The pain level of those using the citrus/magnesium patch was 3.7 after 12 hours—compared to 6.3 for the benzocaine-barrier. After 24 hours, the pain level among the citrus/magnesium group was 2.3, compared to 5.7 for the benzocaine-barrier.

• **Side effects.** Everyone who used the benzocaine-barrier product reported side effects, such as numbing, tingling, local pain from applying the product and a bad taste—one hour after using it, and in the days following. Only 44% of the citrus/magnesium group reported those side effects (except that nobody experienced a bad taste)—and *only* one hour after applying the patch. After that, it was clear sailing.

"The benefit to canker sore sufferers is quite clear," says Avner Shem, MD, the doctor who led the study. "The oral patch heals canker sores in a day, stops pain and protects the sore from food and drink irritants for eight to twelve hours."

Why it works: In combination, citrus oil and magnesium salts dramatically lower the level of inflammatory immune cells and factors, while the patch adheres for eight hours and speeds healing, says Dr. Shem.

ℹ The patch containing citrus oil and magnesium salts is Canker Cover, from Quantum Healing.

What to do: Follow the recommendations for use on the label, applying a patch every eight to 12 hours until healing is complete.

☀ Canker Cover is widely available, at most drugstores and other national retail chains, or call 800-448-1448 to find a store near you that sells the product. You can also purchase the product on-line at *www.cankercover.com.* Quantum, Inc., PO Box 2791, Eugene, OR, 97402 (800-448-1448, 541-345-5556 or fax 541-345-4825); e-mail *orders@quantumhealth. com.*

A SURPRISING REMEDY FOR DRY MOUTH

Your salivary glands are like springs in your mouth and throat, supplying you with a constant flow of refreshing fluid. But age, disease or medications can dry up those springs. The condition is called dry mouth, or *xerostomia* (zeer-o-STO-me-uh). And it can dehydrate your health.

Too little saliva is tough on your gums and teeth, which require steady cleansing to resist disease and decay. Your lips can crack and the corners of your mouth split. Dessert might taste like the desert; saliva is a crucial ingredient in any "mouth-watering" recipe. Swallowing, once as natural as blinking, can turn into a choked chore. And your breath might smell like a drained wetland. Water, water!

Yes, experts sensibly suggest those with dry mouth sip water throughout the day. They also recommend you chew sugar-free gum or suck on sugar-free lozenges, and use moisturizing gels/sprays and saliva substitutes. But dentists in Finland—who say that there is no "satisfactory treatment" for dry mouth—have discovered another and very effective way to moisten the problem.

⫸ *Breakthrough Study*

The Finnish dentists, from the Institute of Dentistry at the University of Tulku, studied 28 people who had suffered from dry mouth for at least a decade (with some afflicted for 30 to 40 years), dividing them into two groups. One group received "individually prescribed homeopathic medicine" and the other group a placebo for six weeks. Before and after the six weeks, the researchers measured their saliva flow and asked them to describe their condition.

Result: "The group taking the homeopathic medicine experienced a significant relief of xerostomia, whereas no effect was found in the placebo group," say the researchers. In fact, all but two of the 15 people taking a homeopathic remedy had a notable improvement. After the six weeks, the researchers gave homeopathic remedies to the people who had been taking the placebo—and over the next three months, most of them got better too!

"Homeopathic treatment, specifically designed for oral dryness, in most cases gives a useful and long-lasting improvement of symptoms," say the researchers. "These patients experienced improved quality of life, with less nighttime awakening and fewer other mucosal symptoms. Thus, homeopathy could be a valuable addition to patients whose systemic diseases and/or medications have led to severe oral discomfort."

Why it happens: "Homeopathic medicine is a natural pharmaceutical science," says Dana Ullman, MPH, a homeopath in Berkeley, CA, and author of *The Homeopathic Revolution* (North Atlantic) and other books on homeopathy, and founder and director of the Homeopathic Educational Services (*www. homeopathic.com*). "The homeopathic practitioner seeks to find a substance that in large doses would cause similar symptoms to those the sick person is experiencing. When the match is made, the substance is then given in very small, safe doses, often with dramatic effects." He compares the process—known to homeopaths as the "law of similars"—to immunization and to the use of small doses of an allergen, such as ragweed, to treat a ragweed allergy.

What to do: In the Finnish study, the homeopathic treatments were individualized—the remedies (with strange-sounding names, such as *Arsenicum album* or *Thuja occidentalis*) were matched to the individual's physical, mental and emotional symptoms. An over-the-counter homeopathic treatment may not work as well. It's better to find a homeopath to recommend one.

☀ To find a homeopathic practitioner near you, visit the Web site of the North American Society of Homeopaths (NASH), *www.homeopathy.org*, which includes an extensive state-by-state registry of members certified by NASH. NASH, PO Box 450039, Sunrise, FL 33345-0039 (206-720-7000 or fax 208-248-1942). In Canada, NASH, 9 Bantry Avenue, Richmond

Hill, ONT L4B 4J4, Canada (905-886-1060); e-mail *NashInfo@homeopathy.org*.

ALA—A COOL NUTRIENT FOR A BURNING MOUTH

About a million women over 50 are on fire. Or at least their mouths are.

"Burning mouth syndrome is a poorly defined disorder that primarily affects post-menopausal women," says Audrey Kunin, MD, a dermatologist and author of *The DERMAdoctor Skinstruction Manual* (Simon & Schuster). "Areas most commonly affected include the tip of the tongue, the hard palate at the top of the mouth and the inside of the lower lip."

The symptoms of burning mouth syndrome (BMS) include a scalding sensation, dry or sore mouth, tingling and numbness on the tip of the tongue and a bitter or metallic taste.

What's the cause? Doctors are mostly flummoxed. *But they've come up with a long list of possible culprits, including...*

• **Anemia and B-vitamin deficiencies** ("Supplementation with vitamin B complex, B-12 and iron has helped many patients," says Dr. Kunin.)

• **Blood sugar problems,** including the metabolic syndrome and type 2 diabetes

• **Salivary gland problems**

• **Infection with candida fungus**

• **Thyroid problems**

• **The hormonal changes of menopause**

• **Allergies, to foods or food additives**

• **Denture problems** (with fit, or an allergy to the materials in the denture)

• **Nerve damage**

• **Heartburn**

DRUG-CAUSED DRY MOUTH

There are more than 400 prescription and over-the-counter medications that can cause dry mouth—and taking more than one of them can further increase your risk. The most common dehydrating meds are for depression, anxiety, high blood pressure, back pain (muscle relaxants), allergies, urinary incontinence and Parkinson's disease.

If you develop dry mouth after starting a prescription drug, talk to your physician about an effective alternative.

Other known causes: Sjogren's syndrome (an autoimmune disease), head and neck radiation for cancer, poorly controlled diabetes, menopause, depression and stress.

• **Psychological problems, such as depression and anxiety**

In most cases, however, a cause is *never* found. But that doesn't mean there isn't a way to reduce the pain.

▶ *Breakthrough Study*

Italian researchers studied 192 otherwise healthy women with BMS, dividing them into four groups.

One group was treated with two months of psychotherapy—two, one-hour sessions per week. A second group received two months of a daily supplement of 600 mg of the antioxidant alpha-lipoic acid (ALA). A third group received both treatments. And a fourth group didn't receive any treatment.

Result: The group receiving both the ALA supplement and psychotherapy had the greatest pain relief, more than those with either ALA or psychotherapy alone, says Felice Femiano, MD, a professor at the University of Medicine and Surgery in Naples.

In an earlier study, Dr. Femiano gave 44 patients with BMS either ALA or a placebo, and found a "significant symptomatic improvement" among those who took ALA—an improvement that continued for one year in more than 70% of the patients.

Dr. Femiano also compared ALA to a mouthwash and a drug used to treat dry mouth—and found ALA was of "remarkable benefit."

How it works: ALA can help soothe nerve pain—and Dr. Femiano thinks BMS may be a "neuropathy," or nerve problem, triggered by psychological stress. (For more information on ALA and neuropathy, see page 136 in Chapter 6, "Diabetes and Insulin Resistance.")

What to do: Talk to your doctor about daily treatment with 600 mg of ALA, psychotherapy or both.

To find a therapist, get a recommendation from a friend or colleague you trust, or call the department of psychiatry at a local university medical center, says Ellen Frank, PhD, a professor in the Department of Psychiatry at the University of Pittsburgh. Or you can also use the "Psychologist Locator" at the Web site of the American Psychological Association (APA) at *www.apa.org* or call the APA's referral service at 800-964-2000.

Widely available brands of ALA supplements containing 600 mg per pill/capsule include Natrol, NOW Foods, Doctor's Best and Pure Encapsulations.

STOP COLD SORES IN THREE DAYS

Talk about overstaying your welcome!

After your first infection with the *herpes simplex 1* virus—from a kiss, a facial towel in the guest bathroom, sharing a spoon over a bowl of ice cream—the virus takes up residence in nerve cells deep in your body and doesn't budge. Until a sunburn, flu, deadline or some other stress weakens your immune system enough for the virus to travel to the skin and burst out as a *cold sore*—a coin-size collection of tiny, painful, fluid-filled blisters, typically around your lips, and embarrassingly blatant and uncomfortable on a patch of raised and reddened skin.

The virus usually rages for about seven to 10 days, with the blisters eventually drying, crusting and disappearing in about 21 days.

Sadly, there is no permanent cure for cold sores. But there is a drug-free way to shorten an episode, and maybe keep them from dropping in quite so often.

▶ *Breakthrough Study*

Researchers from the UCLA Geffen School of Medicine and Southern California University of Health Sciences studied 120 people with cold sores, asking them to apply an ointment with the amino acid L-lysine as its principal ingredient.

During the outbreak, they evaluated them for several symptoms, including tingling, itching, burning, tenderness, prickling, soreness, bumps and swelling, number of blisters, oozing of blisters and crusting of blisters. They also took photographs of the episode, and asked the participants to keep a cold sore diary. A participant was considered "cured" if the sore crusted and disappeared.

Result: Remarkably, 40% of the participants were free of cold sores by the third day, 87% by the sixth day. By day 11, nobody had cold sores. In many cases, the blisters didn't even crust—they just disappeared!

How it works: The amino acid L-lysine stops the herpes virus from replicating, short-circuiting the sore.

ℹ️ The product used in the study was SuperLysine+, from Quantum Health, a combination of L-lysine and other antiherpes nutrients and herbs, such as zinc and echinacea, an immune-strengthening herb. It is available as a stick applicator, a salve or a tincture.

What to do: In the study, the participants applied a cream of SuperLysine+ every two hours while awake.

☀️ You can find SuperLysine+ in most Whole Foods and health-food stores, or order it on-line at *www.quantumhealth.com*. Quantum, Inc., PO Box 2791, Eugene, OR 97402 (800-448-1448, 541-345-5556 or fax 541-345-4825); e-mail *orders@quantumhealth.com*.

Also helpful: Supplements of L-lysine and/or zinc may block cold sores. In a study of 45 people, daily doses of 300 to 1,200 mg of L-lysine cut down the number and severity of episodes. And when Italian researchers gave a daily dose of 22.5 mg of zinc sulfate to 20 people with more than six episodes of cold sores a year, the episodes decreased to an average of three a year, and each episode lasted an average of only 5.7 days.

1

HEART DISEASE & STROKE
EASY WAYS TO CLEAN YOUR ARTERIES

As you read this sentence, somebody in America will have a heart attack. By the end of this paragraph, somebody will have died from one. And by the end of the third or fourth paragraph, somebody will have had a stroke, too. *Multiply those tragic events by the half-million or so minutes in a year, and they look like this...*

- **Heart disease,** the number one killer of Americans—with more than 1.4 million of us suffering a heart attack every year, and 560,000 dying.

- **Stroke,** the number three killer—striking 780,000 Americans yearly, killing 150,000.

All told, more than 80 million Americans (nearly 40 million over the age of 60) have some form of *cardiovascular disease* (CVD)—heart disease, stroke, high blood pressure, high cholesterol, angina, heart failure, peripheral arterial disease and all the other misfortunes that can foul up our primary pump and its network of arteries and veins.

Modern medicine offers many ways to keep that network working. "Without question, there have been enormous advances in the tools available to the modern physician

for treating patients with heart disease," says Julian Whitaker, MD, director of the Whitaker Wellness Institute in Newport Beach, CA, and author of *Reversing Heart Disease* (Grand Central Publishing). "However," he says, "most of the advancements now available to modern physicians are tools for managing the problem once it has become manifest." But CVD can be *prevented*—even *reversed*—with non-drug, nonsurgical approaches, such as diet, nutritional supplements and exercise, says Dr. Whitaker.

"Recent research has shown that a number of effective natural medicines, along with diet, exercise and stress reduction, can reduce your risk of heart disease and stroke," agrees David Heber, MD, PhD, director of the UCLA Center for Human Nutrition and author of *Natural Remedies for a Healthy Heart* (Avery). ("Please be sure to check with your doctor before making *any* changes in diet, medication or exercise," he adds.)

Here are the best of those recent drug-free breakthroughs for the healing and lifelong health of your precious cardiovascular system.

HEALTH BY THE NUMBERS

Cholesterol problems (high total cholesterol, high "bad" LDL cholesterol and low "good" HDL cholesterol), high levels of triglycerides (another type of blood fat) and high blood pressure are three risk factors for heart disease and stroke. Government agencies and medical experts have established numerical categories and goals to help you and your doctor effectively control cholesterol, triglyceride and blood pressure levels.

LEVEL	CATEGORY
Total Cholesterol	
Less than 200 mg/dL*	Desirable
200 to 239	Borderline high
240 and above	High
LDL Cholesterol	
Less than 100	Optimal
100 to 129	Near optimal/above optimal
130 to 159	Borderline high
160 to 189	High
190 and above	Very high
HDL Cholesterol	
60 mg/dL and above	The higher, the better
40 to 59 mg/dL	Protective against heart disease
Less than 40 mg/dL	A major risk factor for heart disease
Triglyceride	
Less than 150	Normal
150 to 199	Borderline high
200 to 499	High
500 or higher	Very high
Blood Pressure	
Lower than 120/80 mm Hg**	Normal
120/80 to 139/89	Caution (Prehypertension)
140/90 to 159/99	High (Stage 1 Hypertension)
160/100 or higher	Very High (Stage 2 Hypertension)

*Cholesterol and triglyceride levels are measured in milligrams (mg) of cholesterol per deciliter (dL) of blood.

**A blood pressure reading includes two numbers—the upper "systolic" number and the lower "diastolic" number. Systolic measures the pressure of blood against artery walls as the heart beats; diastolic, as the heart rests. The measurement is in millimeters of mercury—"mm Hg" (original blood pressure devices used a column of mercury to measure the pressure). In describing your blood pressure reading, your doctor might say, "Your blood pressure is one hundred thirty over eighty-five," meaning 130 systolic over 85 diastolic. To be diagnosed with high or very high blood pressure, your readings must consistently be at those levels, not just once or twice.

THE FOOD "PORTFOLIO"— INVEST IN YOUR HEART

You got the results back from your most recent cholesterol test, and the level of "bad" artery-clogging LDL cholesterol was 150, or "borderline high." Your doctor says that failing to lower LDL will increase your risk for a heart attack. He recommends an LDL-cutting statin, the most common type of drugs used to lower cholesterol.

Do you have any other choice?

Yes, says an international team of 17 researchers, led by scientists from the Clinical Nutrition and Risk Modification Center at the University of Toronto.

Their studies show that you can use *diet* to lower LDL cholesterol by up to 30%—the same level of decrease you'd expect from one of the so-called "first-generation" statins, such as lovastatin (Mevacor).

Their secret is *combining* the four most powerful cholesterol-lowering foods into one dietary portfolio.

▐▌▐▌▶ *Breakthrough Study*

The researchers call their cholesterol-lowering diet the "portfolio" because, like a financial portfolio, it includes a variety of "investments" for best results.

In earlier studies on the portfolio, published in the *Journal of the American Medical Association* and the *American Journal of Clinical Nutrition*, people who followed the diet for one month in a controlled environment (a laboratory set up for food studies) reduced LDL cholesterol by 30%—the same amount as another group who didn't eat the diet and took a statin.

But does the portfolio produce dividends in a "real world" setting, outside the lab? *That's what the researchers looked at next...*

For one year, 66 people (average age, 59) who had participated in the lab-based portfolio research continued to eat the diet, which emphasized...

● **Plant sterols,** such as found in certain types of margarine. (Plant sterols have a similar chemical structure to cholesterol, and block its absorption.)

● **Soy protein,** such as in soy milk, soy burgers and tofu.

● **Viscous** (soluble) fiber, such as in oatmeal.

● **Almonds.**

Result: As in the laboratory, LDL cholesterol was no match for the portfolio...

LDL fell by an average of 13%. And nearly one-third of the participants had a drop of more than 20%.

"Such reductions approach the levels seen with first-generation statins, which have been associated with a twenty-five to thirty-five percent reduction in deaths from heart disease," says David Jenkins, MD, who led the study.

The diet also raised good HDL cholesterol, the type that carries fat away from arteries, he says.

Why it works: "The different modes of action of the four components of the dietary portfolio contribute to their additive effect," says Dr. Jenkins. Plant sterols reduce cholesterol absorption...viscous fibers affect bile acid, a key component in the body's manufacture of cholesterol...soy proteins cut the liver's production of cholesterol...and the monounsaturated fat in almonds directly lowers LDL.

Newer approach: "The benefit of statins to individuals at high risk for cardiovascular disease is not in question here," emphasizes Dr. Jenkins. "However, we don't know the *long-term* effects of these drugs on the millions of people with moderately increased LDL who take them for prevention of heart disease. And taking a statin may give people the false impression that they have nothing further to do to protect their health—thereby stopping them from making serious lifestyle changes. Emphasizing dietary changes—eating the LDL-lowering portfolio foods—can boost the success rate of statins, while providing additional health benefits. And the portfolio is a possible alternative for those who don't want to take drugs."

What to do: The real-world portfolio diet has real-world challenges, says Dr. Jenkins. "The participants found it easiest to incorporate single items such as almonds and margarine into their daily lives. The viscous fiber and soy protein were more challenging, since they require more meal planning and preparation. We considered it ideal if the participants were able to follow the diet three-quarters of the time."

Eating The Portfolio Way

Try to include foods from one or more portfolio categories with each meal…

● **Plant sterols.** Plant sterol-enriched margarines, such as Benecol and Take Control. Plant sterols in supplement form.

Examples: Replace butter and margarine with sterol-enriched margarine. Take a phytosterol supplement, such as Mega Strength Beta Sitosterol from Source Naturals, or Heart Choice Phytosterols from Vitamin Shoppe. (Follow the dosage recommendation on the label.)

● **Soy protein.** Soy-based foods such as soy milk, soy burgers, soy hot dogs and soy cold cuts. Tofu.

Examples: Drink a glass of soy milk. Eat a soy burger for lunch instead of a hamburger. Enjoy a vegetable stir-fry with tofu—use extra firm, low-fat. (For more information on enjoying soy foods, turn to page 349 in Chapter 13, "Osteoporosis.")

● **Viscous fibers.** They are found in grains such as oats and barley, psyllium products such as Metamucil and vegetables such as eggplant and okra.

Examples: Stir Metamucil into soy milk for a snack (a common strategy among those in the study). Eat oat bran cereal.

● **Almonds.** Eat a handful of almonds (about 20) every day.

● **Other advice.** For maximum cholesterol-lowering power, consider following this additional dietary advice, says Dr. Jenkins…

Maximize your intake of other whole grains such as brown rice and whole wheat, and beans, such as lentils and chickpeas. Eat five to nine servings of fruits and vegetables a day.

Limit meat to three or fewer servings a week, and each serving to three or fewer ounces (a bit smaller than a pack of cards). Have three or fewer eggs a week, emphasizing egg whites, or use egg substitutes.

Limit dairy foods to two or fewer servings a week, and choose fat-free or low-fat versions.

For cooking, use olive or canola oil.

Smart idea: "Save the experimenting for the evening, when you have more time to prepare more complicated meals," says Dr. Jenkins.

DON'T FORGET THE MACADAMIAS

The cholesterol-lowering almonds in the portfolio diet featured on page 211 are what scientists call a "tree nut"—and the Food and Drug Administration has okayed heart-healthy claims for *all* tree nuts (almonds, walnuts, pistachios, hazelnuts, pecans, pine nuts), *except* for three that have a lot of fat. On the nut-not list are macadamias, Brazil nuts, and cashews. *Well, a team of researchers at Penn State University decided to see if macadamias deserved dietary disrespect from the Feds…*

New study: For five weeks, they asked people with slightly elevated cholesterol to eat a standard American diet or that same diet with 1.5 ounces (about ½ handful) of macadamias added per day. (The two diets were adjusted to contain the same amount of total fat.) The folks eating the macadamias had a drop in total cholesterol of 9.4% and a drop in LDL of 8.9%.

How did macadamias cut cholesterol?

Theory: Macadamias have the same amount of monounsaturated fat as olive oil, the star of the heart-healthy Mediterranean diet.

"I think the bottom line is that macadamia nuts should be included in the list of nuts to have a health claim," says Penny Kris-Etherton, PhD, RD, a distinguished professor of nutritional sciences at Penn State and coauthor of the study.

What to do: Eat macadamia nuts as a snack, mix them into meals, use them as a salad topping, include them in baked goods such as cookies and muffins.

SHOULD OATMEAL STILL BOWL US OVER?

More than a decade ago, the government's Food and Drug Administration gave their stamp of approval to a health claim on the label of oatmeal and oat bran products: "Diets low in saturated fat and cholesterol that include soluble fiber from oatmeal may reduce the risk of heart disease."

But we know what can happen to dietary guidelines, right? Once-timely food pyramids start to look as if the pharaohs built them; the goodness of once-hallowed carbohydrates are hotly debated; recommended dietary allowances for individual nutrients bounce up and down like a basketball. Is it time to rethink oatmeal and oat bran?

⫸ *Breakthrough Study*

Not if you still want to prevent heart disease, says James W. Anderson, MD, professor of medicine and clinical nutrition at the University of Kentucky College of Medicine. Dr. Anderson is the coauthor of a scientific paper in the *American Journal of Lifestyle Medicine*, which reviewed the last 15 years of research on oatmeal and health.

"Since the 1980s, oatmeal has been scientifically recognized for its heart health benefits, and the latest research shows this evidence endures the test of time," says Dr. Anderson. "Eating oatmeal should be embraced as a lifestyle option for the millions of Americans at risk for heart disease."

What are those "heart health benefits" exactly? *Well, eating oatmeal regularly can…*

- **Lower total cholesterol**

- **Lower bad LDL-cholesterol,** without affecting good HDL-cholesterol

- **Change the physical characteristics of LDL particles,** making them larger and less dense—and therefore less likely to form arterial plaque

- **Reduce the risk for high blood pressure.**

In fact, says Dr. Anderson, for most people with moderately high cholesterol, regularly eating oatmeal and oat bran is probably a better choice than taking a cholesterol-lowering drug. "Lifestyle choices should be the first line of therapy for most patients with moderate cholesterol risk, given the expense, safety concerns and intolerance related to cholesterol-lowering drugs."

Why it works: Oats contain a type of soluble fiber called *beta-glucan*. It binds with liver-produced bile acids, ushering them out of the body; this triggers the liver to manufacture more bile acids—and in doing so it burns up cholesterol. And when it reaches the colon, beta-glucan generates compounds called short-chain fatty acids that interfere with cholesterol production.

What to do: "In individuals with total cholesterol levels above two hundred twenty, eating the equivalent of three grams of soluble oat fiber typically lowers total cholesterol by eight to twenty-three percent," says Michael T. Murray, ND, a naturopathic doctor and author of *Heart Disease and High Blood Pressure* (Prima). "This is highly significant, because with each one percent drop in total cholesterol, there is a two percent decrease in the risk of heart disease. Three grams of soluble fiber are provided by approximately one bowl of ready-to-eat oat bran cereal or oatmeal." (All oatmeal—whether it's standard, quick or instant—comes from cholesterol-lowering whole grains.)

"My advice," says Dr. Murray. "Eat oatmeal or oat bran often."

WHAT? EGGS CAN *HELP* MY CHOLESTEROL?!?

Yes, that is in fact the remarkable finding of a team of eggheads—sorry, *scientists*—in the Department of Nutritional Sciences at the University of Connecticut. Read on, and you'll never look at an egg the same way again. (Particularly if you're over 50, trying to prevent heart disease and think of eggs as little cholesterol time bombs.)

▐▐▶ *Breakthrough Study*

The researchers studied 42 people—29 post-menopausal women aged 50 to 68, and 13 men aged 60 to 80. For one month, they ate three eggs a day (yes, *three*), delivering 640 mg of dietary cholesterol. Then, after three weeks of not eating eggs, they ate an "equal volume" of cholesterol-free egg substitute every day, again for one month.

Result: The researchers, led by Christine M. Greene, PhD, note that about one-third of people are "hyper-responders" to dietary cholesterol—when they eat it, their blood cholesterol climbs. And sure enough, about one-third of the people in this study had significant increases in total cholesterol after eating eggs for one month, while the others didn't.

New thinking: But the researchers had cholesterol measurements taken by Liposcience, a high-tech lab in Raleigh, NC. That lab didn't just measure total cholesterol, and "bad" LDL and "good" HDL. They also measured the size of the LDL and HDL particles. And that's crucial, because the newest, best understanding of the link between cholesterol and heart disease says that it's not LDL per se, but *smaller, denser* particles of LDL—what researchers called sdLDL—that really mess up your arteries and cause heart disease. And that same new understanding says that larger HDL particles are also more protective than smaller ones. "Traditional lipoprotein cholesterol measurements fail to consider this variability in size distribution," says Dr. Greene.

Well, Dr. Greene and her colleagues found that the cholesterol hyper-responders had an increase in larger, less "artherogenic" (artery-clogging) LDL particles after they ate eggs.

They also had higher levels of HDL, and larger HDL particles.

In other words, eggs only raised cholesterol in about one-third of people who ate eggs every day—and the type of cholesterol was unlikely to increase the risk for heart disease!

Dr. Greene also notes that eating more eggs increased blood levels of lutein and zeaxanthin, two *carotenoids* (similar to the beta-carotene in carrots) that are crucial in preventing age-related macular degeneration, the leading cause of blindness in people over 60. (For more on those two nutrients and their role in protecting eyesight, see page 190 in Chapter 8, "Eyes, Ears and Teeth.")

"This study indicates that egg consumption may be permitted—even encouraged—among healthy older people, with minimal concerns about increasing the risk of heart disease," says Dr. Greene.

What to do: Stop worrying about eating eggs! *In fact, Dr. Greene urges you to include them in your diet...*

"Eating eggs regularly has been shown to provide many nutritional benefits, such as higher daily intakes of vitamins C, E and B-12, in addition to folate," she says. "Deficiencies in these vitamins have been linked to an increased risk of cardiovascular disease, as well as cancer and Alzheimer's. The addition of eggs to the diet could actually *prevent* heart disease, particularly among older people who are at increased risk."

☀ To discover more ways to enjoy eggs, visit the Web site of the American Egg Board at *www. incredibleegg.org.* American Egg Board Office, 1460 Renaissance Drive, Park Ridge, IL 60068 (847-296-7043 or fax 847-296-7007); e-mail: *aeb@aeb.org.*

Books: *Eggs* by Michel Roux (Wiley). *The Good Egg: More Than 200 Fresh Approaches from Breakfast to Dessert* by Marie Simmons (Houghton Mifflin).

SOLVE HIGH PRESSURE WITH POTASSIUM

The natural, plant- and meat-based diet of our Stone Age ancestors had *16 times* more potassium than sodium (salt).

As a result, our prehistoric kidneys were built to *excrete* potassium and *conserve* sodium.

"This mechanism, however, is unfit for the sodium-rich and potassium-poor modern diet," explains Nicolaos Madias, MD, from Tufts University School of Medicine, in the *New England Journal of Medicine.*

That diet has *four times* more sodium than potassium.

"The end result of the failure of the kidneys to adapt to the modern diet," he says, "is an excess of sodium and a deficit of potassium—in hypertensive patients."

Hypertension. High blood pressure. The relentless, heartbeat-by-heartbeat, defectively forceful push of blood against the walls of the arteries. Seventy-three million Americans have it. Another 69 million have prehypertension, a systolic blood pressure reading of 120 to 139, or a diastolic reading of 80 to 89. And years of elevated blood pressure is the leading risk factor behind 75% of strokes and 50% of heart disease.

To help lower high blood pressure, you can cut sodium. But there's a better, easier way to do the job...

Increase potassium.

⫸ *Breakthrough Study*

Potassium has usually been viewed as a minor factor in high blood pressure and stroke, but it actually has a critical role, says Dr. Madias. *He cites studies that show...*

• **Lower intake of dietary potassium** increases blood pressure levels by 7 systolic and 6 diastolic.

• **Low intake of potassium increases the risk of stroke by 28%.**

• **On average, African-Americans have the same sodium intake as whites** but much lower potassium intakes—and higher rates of hypertension.

• **Potassium supplements can reduce or even eliminate** the need for medication to control hypertension.

"A modified diet that approaches the high potassium-to-sodium ratio of the diets of human ancestors is a critical strategy for the primary prevention and treatment of hypertension," says Dr. Madias.

What to do: "In people with high blood pressure, too little potassium in the diet is as bad as too much sodium," agrees Richard D. Moore, MD, PhD, author of *The High Blood Pressure Solution: Natural Prevention and Cure with the K Factor* (Inner Traditions). ("K" is the chemical symbol for potassium.)

He recommends taking three dietary steps to correct the potassium/sodium imbalance.

1. Eat more high-potassium foods. Fresh fruits, fresh vegetables, skim or low-fat milk and yogurt, grains, chicken, fish and lean meat.

Best: Potassium superstars include bananas, potatoes, prunes and apricots, cantaloupe and spinach. Dr. Moore is particularly passionate about the potato: "Potatoes have a potassium-to-sodium ratio of approximately one hundred thirty to one."

2. Avoid salty foods. There's very little natural salt in the modern diet; it's almost all *added* to processed foods. Dr. Moore's no-no list includes most canned foods, salted nuts, potato chips and most crackers (unless labeled "unsalted" or "no added salt"), processed meats, commercially baked breads (unless they are marked "low salt"), commercially prepared desserts, olives, anchovies, canned sardines, commercially prepared dill pickles, soy sauce, bacon, most cheeses, most peanut butters, canned or bottled tomato juice, creamed cottage cheese, instant pudding and most instant hot cereals.

3. Use a salt substitute for table salt. There are many available, such as Nu-Salt, AlsoSalt, NoSalt and Morton Salt Substitute.

Example: Here's a menu from Dr. Moore for a day with four times more potassium than sodium…

LOSE THE WEIGHT, LOWER THE PRESSURE

Thirty-three percent of Americans have high blood pressure. Sixty-six percent of Americans are overweight. Do the two problems have anything to do with each other? *Yes…*

New study: Fifty percent of overweight people with high blood pressure have high blood pressure *because* they're overweight, estimate Italian researchers…

When they put 210 men and women with hypertension on a low-calorie diet for six months, 49% of the women and 53% of the men lost at least 5% of their weight—and they also lowered their blood pressure by 5%.

They reported their findings at the American Heart Association's annual Conference of the Council for High Blood Pressure Research.

What happens: "We are now beginning to understand the underlying mechanisms of the adverse effects of obesity on cardiovascular health," say researchers from Belgium, in the journal *Nature*. They explain that fat tissue releases compounds that raise blood pressure…*and* cholesterol…*and* thicken blood, raising the risk of clots…*and* increase inflammation, which speeds the buildup of arterial plaque.

See Chapter 14, "Overweight," for dozens of easy ways to shed extra pounds.

- **Breakfast.** Eight ounces orange juice, banana or melon, 8 ounces skim milk
- **Lunch.** Chef's salad (raw vegetables, greens, sprouts, strips of Swiss cheese totaling 1 ounce and slices of hard-boiled egg, oil and vinegar dressing), 8 ounces skim milk, 1 cup grapes
- **Snack.** Mixed dried fruit
- **Dinner.** Spaghetti with meatless tomato sauce, baked acorn squash (brown sugar, no butter), ⅔ cup asparagus with lemon, 8 ounces skim milk

---

FOR A HAPPY HEARTBEAT, TRY BEET JUICE

Scientific studies show that diets rich in fruits and vegetables—such as the DASH diet (Dietary Approaches to Stop Hypertension) and the vegetarian diet—lower blood pressure and protect you against heart disease and stroke. But *why*?

Researchers theorized that the pressure-lowering star players were antioxidant vitamins such as beta-carotene that stop oxidation, the internal rust that turns your arteries into junkyards of plaque. But when scientists gave thousands of people nutritional supplements of beta-carotene and tracked their health, they found rates of heart disease went *up*.

New thinking: Among fruits and vegetables, the *green, leafy vegetables* such as spinach have the strongest protective effect against heart disease, with every additional daily serving reducing risk by 23%. These vegetables contain high levels of *nitrates*—a chemical that transforms in the body into nitrite, which in turn becomes *nitric oxide*, which…relaxes blood vessels…reduces artery-damaging inflammation… and thins the blood, preventing artery-plugging clots. The less nitric oxide on the arterial scene, the higher the risk of high blood pressure, heart

disease and stroke. Could the nitrates in vegetable-rich diets lower blood pressure?

Scientists at the famed William Harvey Research Institute in London decided to answer that question in an unusual way. They asked a bunch of people to drink beet juice.

▶ *Breakthrough Study*

Led by Amrita Ahluwalia, PhD, the researchers studied 14 healthy people, dividing them into two groups. One group drank 16 ounces of beet juice (which is rich in nitrates) and one group drank water. For three hours before and 24 hours afterward, the researchers regularly measured blood pressure, blood levels of nitrites and the rate of blood clotting.

Result: The water drinkers had no increase in nitrites and no drop in blood pressure or blood clotting.

The beet juice drinkers, on the other hand, had a 16-fold rise in blood nitrites starting 30 minutes after drinking the juice. Those levels peaked at 90 minutes, stayed that way for six hours and remained elevated for 24 hours.

And as their nitrite rose, their systolic blood pressure fell—starting to drop an hour after drinking the juice and plummeting by more than 10 points. There was also a reduction in blood clotting.

"These findings suggest that dietary nitrate underlies the beneficial effects of a vegetable-rich diet, and highlights the potential of a natural, low-cost approach for the treatment of heart disease," says Dr. Ahluwalia. "Our research suggests that drinking beet juice, or consuming other nitrate-rich vegetables, such as leafy greens, might be a simple way to maintain a healthy cardiovascular system and might be an additional approach that one could take in the modern-day battle against rising blood pressure."

What to do: Go green. Leafy, green vegetables include spinach, kale, collards, Swiss chard, mustard greens, turnips greens, bok choy and romaine lettuce.

Try to get one cup of steamed or two cups of raw leafy green most days, says Steven Pratt, MD, coauthor of *SuperFoods Rx* (Harper).

His tips for quick ways to get more spinach and other leafy greens into your diet are to layer cooked spinach or other greens in a lasagna...steam spinach and serve sprinkled with fresh lemon and grated Parmesan cheese...add a handful of spinach to soup...dress leftover leafy greens with balsamic vinegar dressing and sprinkle with some sesame seeds...add chopped greens to an omelet along with chives, tomato, bell peppers and onion...shred various greens along with romaine lettuce in a shell...shred greens onto tacos and burritos. (And don't forget the borscht!)

ⓘ Biotta Beet Juice, with pressed organic beetroots. It is available in natural-food supermarkets and health-food stores.

BLACK AND BLUE IS GOOD FOR YOU

Raspberries, strawberries, blueberries, lingonberries, chokeberries, blackberries...

Those were just some of the types of berries consumed (whole, pureed or juiced) by 72 middle-aged men and women. The results were berry, berry good for their hearts.

▶ Breakthrough Study

Researchers at the National Public Health Institute in Finland recruited those 72 folks (each with at least one risk factor for heart disease, such as mild high blood pressure, high LDL cholesterol or low HDL cholesterol) and divided them into two groups. One group ate four-and-half ounces of berries every day for two months. The other didn't.

● **Less risk of blood clots.** Those who ate the berries had an 11% drop in the clumping activity of red blood cells, a risk factor for blood clots and heart attacks. The nonberry group didn't have any change.

● **Higher HDL.** HDL jumped 5.2% in the berry group, with no change in the nonberry.

● **Lower blood pressure.** In those with the highest blood pressure, systolic readings dropped by 7.3. Again, there was no change in the berryless.

The researchers also saw big boosts in blood levels of *polyphenols*, the powerful antioxidants in berries—not surprising, since the researchers estimate the berry eaters were ingesting three times as many polyphenols as the berry bereft.

"The regular consumption of berries may play a role in the prevention of cardiovascular disease," say the researchers, in the *American Journal of Clinical Nutrition*.

What to do: Try to eat one to two cups of berries a day, says Dr. Pratt, MD. "Each polyphenol in each berry has something to contribute. Don't limit your berry consumption to any particular kind. Eat them all!" But shamelessly enamored of his favorite, the blueberry, he suggests you might...sprinkle them on yogurt...mix them into hot oatmeal...toss them onto cold cereal...whip them into a smoothie...drop them into pancake batter...or simply snack from a big bowl.

THIRTY LIFE-SAVING CALORIES OF CHOCOLATE

Thirty calories a day of dark chocolate—a piece about the size of a Hershey's Kiss—could help prevent a fatal stroke or heart attack.

TUBBY TUMMY? DRINK CRANBERRY JUICE

The more fat you have around your middle, the higher your risk of heart disease. *Cranberries could help you out...*

New study: Researchers at Laval University in Canada studied 30 men, with an average age of 51 and very sizable guts ("abdominally obese" was the term the scientists used). When the men drank a daily eight-ounce glass of cranberry juice for four weeks, their level of heart-protecting HDL cholesterol rose anywhere from 9 to 14%, a very significant boost. (That's profound protection—every 1% drop in HDL increases the risk of heart disease by 3%.)

"We theorize that polyphenols [natural antioxidants in berries] may be causing this effect—supporting the idea that consumption of foods such as cranberry juice can be cardioprotective," say the researchers, in the *British Journal of Nutrition*.

IIII➤ *Breakthrough Study*

Researchers at the University Hospital of Cologne in Germany studied 44 people, aged 56 to 73. All of them had either prehypertension or Stage 1 hypertension. They divided them into two groups. For the next 18 weeks, one group ate 30 calories a day of dark chocolate—chocolate loaded with a natural compound called flavanols—while the other received the same amount of no-flavanol white chocolate.

At the beginning and end of the study, the researchers measured blood pressure levels and blood levels of nitric oxide, a biochemical that relaxes arteries. *The results will please chocoholics everywhere...*

• **Systolic blood pressure fell** by an average 2.9 points and diastolic by 1.9 points. (And lest you think this small drop in blood pressure is no big deal—experts estimate that for every three-point drop in systolic blood

pressure, there is an 8% decrease in the risk of death from stroke, a 5% decrease in the risk of death from heart disease and a 4% decrease in the risk of death from any cause.)

• **86% of the study participants had hypertension** at the beginning of the study; only 68% did at the end.

• **Those who ate dark chocolate also had a tenfold increase in nitric oxide levels.**

• **White chocolate was a whitewash**— no change in blood pressure, no rise in nitric oxide.

"The inclusion of small amounts of flavanol-rich dark chocolate as part of a usual diet efficiently reduced blood pressure and improved the formation of vasodilative [artery-expanding] nitric oxide," says Dirk Taubert, MD, PhD, who led the study, published in the *Journal of the American Medical Association*.

Why it works: Dr. Taubert theorizes that the flavanols in dark chocolate trigger the production of nitric oxide, which relaxes the arteries, lowering blood pressure.

New thinking: "The most intriguing finding," he says, "is that small amounts of commercially available dark chocolate have the potential to lower blood pressure comparable to comprehensive dietary modifications that are proven to reduce the incidence of heart disease." (He's referring to the much-studied DASH diet—high in fruits, vegetables and low-fat dairy products and generally low in saturated fat—and the PREMIER intervention—which adds to the DASH diet recommendations for weight loss, sodium reduction, increased physical activity and limited alcohol intake.)

"Long-term adherence to complex behavioral changes is often low, and requires continuous counseling," he says. "Adding small amounts of flavanol-rich cocoa into the habitual diet is a modification that is easy to adhere to, and therefore may be a promising behavioral approach to lower blood pressure in individuals with above-optimal blood pressure."

In other words, it's easy (even delightful) to eat a little tidbit of dark chocolate every day to lower your blood pressure—but it's hard to consistently eat more fruits…more vegetables… more low-fat dairy products…lose weight…cut salt…exercise more…and drink less…

What to do: To get a hefty dose of flavanols, look for dark chocolate containing 70 to 85% cocoa solids. Thirty calories of dark chocolate is about one-fifth of an ounce, or a piece of chocolate the size of a Special Dark Chocolate Hershey's Kiss.

More good news for your heart: Reducing high blood pressure isn't the only heart-healthy benefit from eating dark chocolate. *Other recent studies have found…*

• **Dark chocolate + sterols = hearty results.** Every day for one month, 49 people with high cholesterol ate two CocoaVia dark chocolate bars (with plant sterols, a cholesterol-like compound that blocks the absorption of dietary cholesterol). Their LDL dropped by 5.3% and their total cholesterol by 2%. Systolic blood pressure fell 6 points.

• **Death rate 1,280% higher—without chocolate.** Researchers at Harvard Medical School studied the Kuna Indians who live on islands near Panama and drink five cups of flavanol-rich cocoa a day. They found that when the Indians moved to the mainland and stopped imbibing their favorite drink, their average death rate from heart disease was nearly *13 times* higher.

THE ORGANIC ADVANTAGE

Organic produce is free of pesticides, herbicides and other synthetic chemicals. That has to be good for you, one way or another. But are organic foods better for your *heart*?

New study: Researchers at the University of California, Davis, conducted a 10-year study comparing the level of two *flavonoids* in tomatoes grown in organic and nonorganic fields. (They studied the tomato because it's the number two most-eaten vegetable in the American diet, with potatoes number one.) The researchers found that *quercetin* was 79% higher and *kaempferol* was 97% higher in the organic tomatoes.

"These flavonoids are antioxidants and their dietary intake has been linked to a lower risk of heart disease and stroke," says Alyson E. Mitchell, PhD, who led the study. "We went into the study expecting to find higher levels, but didn't expect to find levels *this* much higher."

Nonorganic farmers will just have to ketchup.

Good news: Speaking of tomatoes and your heart, Israeli researchers found that a diet loaded with tomatoes increases HDL cholesterol by 15%…a study in the *American Journal of Clinical Nutrition* found that tomato extract supplements thin the blood, reducing the risk of artery-clogging blood clots…a study in the *American Heart Journal* found that tomato extracts reduce high blood pressure…and researchers from the Division of Nutritional Sciences at the University of Illinois, in an article on the tomato in the *Journal of Nutrition*, say that "increased intakes" of the vegetable decrease the risk of heart disease and stroke, and that the tomato "is of undeniable importance as part of a healthy diet."

Also try: The tomato extract studied by the Israeli researchers was Lyc-O-Mato. They used a daily dosage of 250 mg for two months to decrease systolic blood pressure from 144 to 134 and diastolic blood pressure from 87.4 to 83.4, in 31 people who weren't taking drugs for high blood pressure.

Resource: Lyc-O-Mato is an ingredient in many brands of lycopene supplements, another flavonoid in tomatoes.

• **Lower risk of artery-plugging blood clots.** Researchers at Johns Hopkins University found that the blood of people who eat chocolate regularly takes slightly longer to clot than the blood of people who don't—and they theorize the flavanols in chocolate may have a biochemical effect similar to blood-thinning aspirin. They recommend one ounce a day of dark chocolate.

• **Less risk of stroke?** Researchers from Harvard Medical School found that older people who drank a flavanol-rich beverage had improved blood flow to the gray matter of their brains for the next 2 to 3 hours. Dark chocolate may be an "extremely promising" way to decrease the risk of stroke, they say, in the *Journal of Cardiovascular Pharmacology.*

• **You're not getting older; you're getting more responsive to chocolate.** Harvard researchers found that the circulatory systems of people over 50 are particularly responsive to the effect of chocolate, producing more artery-relaxing nitric oxide than people under 50.

Bottom line: Eighteen percent lower risk of death from heart disease.

And a team of researchers from the Harvard School of Public Health analyzed data from more than 136 studies on chocolate and health. They found chocolate can lower blood pressure, beat back artery-damaging inflammation, reduce risky blood clotting, increase HDL and decrease LDL…leading to an overall 18% reduction in death from heart disease among people eating the most chocolate, compared to those eating the least. Semi-Sweet!

FISH OIL—WAVE GOODBYE TO HEART DISEASE

There are about as many scientific studies on fish oil and heart disease as there are, well, *fish.*

Cardiologists recently dove into all those studies to make practical sense of their findings, publishing their conclusions and recommendations in the *Mayo Clinic Proceedings.*

⫸ *Breakthrough Study*

"The most compelling evidence for the cardiovascular benefit provided by omega-3 fatty acids in fish oil comes from three large studies of thirty-two thousand people who either received omega-3 fatty acid supplements or a placebo," says James O'Keefe Jr., MD, a cardiologist from the Mid America Heart Institute in Kansas City, MO.

Result: These studies found that the two omega-3 fatty acids in fish oil—EPA (eicosapentaenoic acid) and DHA (docosahexaenoic acid)—reduced heart attacks and death from heart disease by anywhere from 19 to 45%.

"These findings suggest that intake of omega-3 fatty acids, whether from fatty fish or fish oil supplements, should be increased, especially in those with or at risk for coronary artery disease."

You're at risk for heart disease if you have one or more of the following factors (and the more the scarier)—you're over 65; you're a man; one or both of your parents had heart disease; you're African- or Mexican-American, an American Indian or a native Hawaiian; you smoke; you have high total cholesterol; you have high LDL cholesterol; you have low HDL cholesterol; you have high blood pressure; you're overweight (particularly with a waist size of more than 40" for men and 35" for women); you have type 2 diabetes.

What to do: Dr. O'Keefe recommends a daily intake of 1 gram of omega-3s (a total of 1,000 mg of EPA and DHA) for those with or at risk for heart disease, and 500 mg for healthy, prevention-minded people. Eating herring, mackerel, salmon or tuna at least two times a week supplies a daily average of 400 to 500 mg of EPA and DHA.

"People who need to consume higher levels of omega-3 may choose to use fish oil supplements to reach those targets," says Dr. O'Keefe.

What you may not know: People with high levels of triglycerides—a blood fat similar to cholesterol that can also threaten the heart —should take 3 to 4 grams of fish oil a day (3,000 to 4,000 mg of DHA and EPA). "Research shows that this dosage lowers triglyceride levels by twenty to thirty percent," says Dr. O'Keefe.

If you're taking statins to lower cholesterol —don't think you're covered. "Combination therapy with omega-3 fatty acids and a statin is a safe and effective way to improve cardiovascular health beyond the benefits provided by statin therapy alone," says Dr. O'Keefe.

Trap: Don't depend on your family doctor to recommend statins and fish oil—a study in the *Journal of the American Board of Family Medicine* found that only 17% of family doctors regularly prescribe fish oil to those with heart disease, even with all the evidence showing the supplement may help prevent heart attacks and death from heart attacks.

There are few side effects from fish oil, except for occasional nausea, upset stomach, or a fishy burp, says Dr. Keefe. "Taking the supplement at bedtime or with meals may help reduce burping and upset stomach symptoms."

🛈 When choosing a fish oil supplement, it's best to use the same supplement that scientific studies used, says Harry Preuss, MD, CNS, professor of medicine at Georgetown University Medical Center, a certified nutrition specialist and coauthor of *The Natural Fat-Loss Pharmacy* (Broadway). The most studied supplement, he says, is the brand Nordic Naturals.

The Nordic Naturals product that supplies (and slightly exceeds) the level of EPA and DHA

recommended by Dr. O'Keefe—1,000 mg of EPA and DHA a day—is Ultimate Omega. It delivers 650 mg of EPA and 450 mg of DHA. For those with high triglycerides who need

WHAT ABOUT MERCURY?

You're told to eat tuna to help your heart. You're told tuna contains mercury, a nerve-damaging toxin. To tuna or not to tuna, that is the question. What is the answer?

New finding: Researchers in the Department of Medicine at Harvard Medical School wanted to find out. They analyzed hundreds of scientific studies on fish (and fish oil) and heart health, and on the health risks from mercury and other pollutants found in fish, such as PCBs (polychlorinated biphenyls) and dioxins. Their results, published in the *Journal of the American Medical Association*...

Eating more fish or taking fish oil reduced deaths from heart disease by 36%—and premature deaths from any cause by 17%. (Thank you, Dr. Poseidon!)

There are *no* substantive health risks from eating fish—such as "subclinical neurodevelopmental deficits" in children caused by mercury, or cancer in adults caused by PCBs and dioxin.

Recommended: "The benefits of modest fish consumption (one to two servings a week) outweigh the risks among adults and, excepting a few selected fish species, among women of childbearing age," says Dariush Mozaffarian, MD, DrPH, who led the study.

Red flags: Those high-mercury species include swordfish, shark and golden bass (also known as tilefish) from the Gulf of Mexico.

In fact, says Dr. Mozaffarian, *not* eating fish because of fear of pollutants is a whale-sized mistake. "Avoidance of modest fish consumption due to confusion regarding risks and benefits could result in thousands of excess deaths from heart disease annually."

It turns out that the question about toxins in fatty fish was a red herring, so to speak. It's no mystery after all—salmon, tuna, mackerel, anchovy (and herring) are good for you.

to take higher doses of fish oil, consider the Ultimate Omega Liquid, which supplies 813 mg of EPA and 563 mg of DHA per tablespoon. (A recent survey of more than 6,000 supplement users by the highly respected ConsumerLab.com, which independently evaluates supplement quality, found that Nordic Naturals was the number one rated fish oil brand, with 95% satisfaction.)

☀ You can find the Nordic Naturals product line at its Web site, *www.nordicnaturals.com*. Call 800-662-2544. Nordic Naturals products are widely available in retail stores, in catalogs and on the Internet.

DON'T LIKE FISH? EAT WALNUTS

Maybe all that vile cod liver oil your mother insisted you take scarred your taste buds for life.

Maybe your high school teacher forced you to read *The Old Man and the Sea*. Twice.

Maybe to you a mackerel in the oven smells something like the inside of an old tennis shoe.

Maybe you just don't like fish, fish oil, fishing or even playing Go Fish.

Well, that doesn't mean you have to pass on the heart-protecting benefits from the type of omega-3 fatty acids found in fatty fish and fish oil supplements. Mother Nature spread those omega-3s around.

▐▐▶ *Breakthrough Studies*

There's *another* omega-3 fatty acid besides the EPA (eicosapentaenoic acid) and DHA (docosahexaenoic acid) found in fish oil. It's ALA, or alpha-linolenic acid. *And it does a great job protecting your heart...*

● **Less risk of heart disease and heart attacks.** Researchers at Harvard Medical School analyzed diet and health data from more than 45,000 men. They found that those with a *low* intake of fish-based omega-3s but a *high* intake of ALA had a 47% lower risk of heart disease and a 58% lower risk of heart attacks than men with a low intake of EPA and DHA and a low intake of ALA.

"Plant-based omega-3s may particularly reduce heart disease risk when seafood-based omega-3 intake is low," say the researchers, in the journal *Circulation*.

● **Lower total cholesterol and LDL.** In a study of 23 men and women with risk factors for heart disease, researchers at the University of Pennsylvania found that adding ALA-rich walnuts, walnut oil and flaxseed to their diet lowered total cholesterol by 11%, LDL cholesterol by 12% and triglycerides by 18%.

"This research shows that walnuts can play a role in reducing cardiovascular disease risk factors," says Penny M. Kris-Etherton, PhD, RD, who led the study.

● **Lower blood pressure.** Greek researchers studied 59 men with an average age of 53, supplementing their diet with flaxseed oil for three months. The men had an average decrease in blood pressure from 3 to 6%.

"This level of reduction would be expected to considerably reduce the overall risk for heart disease," says George K. Paschos, BSc, in the *European Journal of Clinical Nutrition*.

Why it works: Simple. ALA converts to EPA in the body. In a study by researchers at Emory University in Atlanta, 56 people who took flaxseed oil capsules for three months had a 60% increase in blood levels of EPA.

What to do: Easy strategies work best, say researchers and doctors.

● **Canoodle with canola oil.** Substitute ALA-rich canola oil and canola-based margarine for vegetable oils and spreads, say researchers from the University of Illinois and Pennsylvania

State University. They analyzed the diets of more than 9,000 people, and estimated that switching to canola-based products from vegetable-oil based products would increase the intake of ALA by 73%.

● **Favor flaxseed oil and flaxseeds.** "Flaxseed oil is the richest source of ALA," says Artemis P. Simopoulos, MD, president of the Center for Genetics, Nutrition and Health in Washington, DC, and coauthor of *The Omega Diet* (Collins).

"Add flaxseed oil to salad dressings or soups and sauces just before serving," she recommends. "If you like, you can mix it with juice and glug it down like medicine. Or stir it into flavored yogurt or cottage cheese. If you can't tolerate the taste, consider taking flaxseed oil capsules."

Dr. Simopoulos is also a big fan of flaxseeds. "They have a subtle, nutty flavor, so you can grind them into a fine meal and add them to breads, muffins, pancakes, waffles, cereals and cakes, with little change in texture or flavor. Plan to use about one to two tablespoons of flaxseed meal or 'flax meal' per cup of flour. You can grind your own flax meal in a food grinder or coffee grinder, or you can buy it ground."

● **While away with walnuts.** "Add walnuts to salads and baked goods, or eat a small handful each day as a snack," says Dr. Simopoulos.

Surprising: Researchers in Spain added eight shelled walnuts to a fatty meal of salami-and-cheese sandwich on white bread. They found the walnuts helped preserve the elasticity and flexibility of arteries, which typically become rigid as soon as they're barraged by postmeal fat. "This demonstrates that the protective fat from walnuts actually undoes some of the detrimental effects of a diet high in saturated fat," comments Robert A. Vogel, MD, a professor of medicine at the University of Maryland.

THE WORST MEAL FOR YOUR HEART

Actually, it's the worst *two* meals...

New finding: As part of the US government's Atherosclerosis Risk in Communities study, researchers at the University of Minnesota analyzed nine years of diet and health data from more than 9,500 people.

They found that those who ate two or more servings of meat a day (imagine two burger patties, and you get the picture) had a 25% higher risk of developing the *metabolic syndrome,* which includes several risk factors for heart disease, such as high blood pressure, low levels of HDL cholesterol and a hefty waist size.

Another food the study found hurts your heart—diet soda.

And now for the side dish. "It's not just meat that adds inches to the waist, increases blood pressure and lowers HDL—it's fried foods as well," says Lyn Steffen, PhD, MPH, RD, who led the study.

In other words, the worst meal for your heart is a burger, fries and diet soda. Sound familiar? It did to Dr. Steffen.

"Fried foods are typically synonymous with commonly eaten fast foods, so I think it's safe to say that these findings support a link between fast-food consumption and an increase in metabolic risk factors for heart disease," she says.

Those ads are right. You *do* deserve a break today—from fast food!

Better: A tip on eating in a fast-food restaurant without eating the burger, fries and soda, from cardiologist Stephen Sinatra, MD, coauthor of *The Fast Food Diet* (Wiley)...

"Have grilled chicken instead of the beef patty, eliminating or reducing the condiments...order a club soda with lemon...and substitute a baked potato, without butter or sour cream topping, for the fries. You'll easily cut the calorie load by half while feeling just as full. You'll also be getting a lot less fat—good for your heart as well as your hips."

THE HEALTHIEST DIET AFTER A HEART ATTACK

Is it the low-fat, low-cholesterol diet touted by the American Heart Association? Is it the olive-oily Mediterranean diet, which studies show protects entire populations from heart disease?

It's both.

⫸ *Breakthrough Study*

Scientists at the Providence Medical Research Center in Spokane, WA, asked 202 people who had suffered a heart attack within the past six weeks to eat the American Heart Association's "Step II" low-cholesterol, low-fat diet, or a Mediterranean-style diet with more fat, particularly monounsaturated fat from foods such as olive oil. Each participant had a one-on-one counseling session with a dietician in the first month of following the diet, and one session every three months for the next two years.

Four years later, the researchers tallied the number of "cardiovascular complications"—chest pain that medication couldn't control, heart attacks, strokes, hospitalizations for heart failure and deaths.

Result: "We did not find even a suggestion of a difference between the two groups," says Katherine R. Tuttle, MD, who led the study.

But when the two groups were combined, and compared to a *third* group of heart attack victims that didn't receive any dietary counseling, those who followed the low-fat or the Mediterranean diet had nearly 70% fewer cardiac complications.

"The good news is that *either* diet is a good choice," says Dr. Tuttle.

What to do: If you're recovering from a heart attack and want to eat healthier, *don't* try to do it without help.

"It's difficult to maintain a new diet on your own, without support and encouragement," says Dr. Tuttle. "To meet your dietary goals, you need to see a dietician regularly and repeatedly."

And the diet you end up following should mirror one of the two used by the participants in this study...

The participants in both groups limited their cholesterol intake to no more than 200 mg a day, and saturated fat (from foods such as meat and dairy products) to no more than 7% of their calories. (The average American consumes *twice* that much saturated fat, says Dr. Tuttle.)

Those assigned to the AHA diet kept their fat intake to less than 30% of their total calories.

The ADA diet emphasized fruits and vegetables and lean meats, and restricted cholesterol-rich and saturated fats such as fatty red meats, butter and cream.

For those on the Mediterranean diet, the calories from fat was 40%. But the fat was good omega-3 and monounsaturated fat—from eating fish three to five times a week, as well as liberal amounts of olive oil, avocados and nuts.

☀ To find a nutritionist to help you with your diet, see the "Find a Nutritional Professional" feature on the home page of the American Dietetic Association, *www.eatright. org*. The search function allows you to locate a professional within your zip code, specializing in heart disease, for individual counseling. American Dietetic Association, 120 South Riverside Plaza, Suite 2000, Chicago, IL 60606-6995; 800-877-1600.

Books: The Mediterranean Prescription: Meal Plans and Recipes to Help You Stay Slim and Healthy for the Rest of Your Life by Angelo Acquista, MD (Ballantine); *The Miami Mediterranean Diet: Lose Weight and Lower Your Risk of Heart Disease with 300 Delicious Recipes* by Michael Ozner, MD (Benbella Books); *The*

LOW-FAT VS. LOW-CARB— AND THE LOSER IS...

You're trying to lose weight to cut your risk of heart disease. Is a low-carbohydrate diet a good choice? *Maybe not...*

New study: Researchers at the Medical College of Wisconsin asked 20 overweight people to participate in a six-week, head-to-head competition (head of lettuce vs. headcheese) between low-fat and low-carbohydrate diets. They found that the low-carb diet caused "reduced flow-mediated dilation"—a narrowing of the arteries that is an early sign of high blood pressure and heart disease. The low-fat diet *improved* flow-mediated dilation.

"Low-carbohydrate diets are significantly higher in total grams of fat, protein, dietary cholesterol and saturated fats than are low-fat diets," says Shane Phillips, MD, a study researcher. "While a low-carbohydrate diet may result in weight loss and improvement in blood pressure, similar to a low-fat diet, the higher fat content is ultimately more detrimental to heart health."

Recommended: If you're trying to cut calories to lose weight and help your heart, go low-fat, not low-carb, says David D. Gutterman, MD, who led the study. "The composition of the diet may be as important as the degree of weight loss in determining the effect of dietary intervention on circulatory health."

New American Heart Association Cookbook (Clarkson Potter).

NEWS FOR MIDDLE-AGED TEETOTALERS

It's almost a cardiac commandment, enshrined by the American Heart Association and other Arterial Authorities—if you're not currently a drinker: Thou Shalt Not Drink.

And there are plenty of reasons not to.

So-called "immoderate drinking" (more than two drinks a day for men and more than one a day for women) can be a scourge—from alcoholism to car accidents, from stroke-inducing binges to health-battering beer bellies.

However: Scientific studies show that "moderate drinking" (one to two drinks a day for men, or one drink a day for women) dramatically lowers the risk of heart disease, stroke and other circulatory problems. (A drink is 5 ounces of wine, 12 ounces of beer or 1½ ounces of 80% distilled spirits or liquor, such as whiskey or vodka.) *For example, if you drink moderately, you're...*

- **42% less likely to have a heart attack** or die of heart disease—even *with* an otherwise healthy lifestyle that includes not being overweight, not smoking, exercising every day and eating a healthy diet;

- **32% less likely to have a heart attack** if you have high blood pressure;

- **34% less likely to suffer congestive heart failure** and

- **23% less likely to have a stroke.**

Now a new study shows that middle-aged nondrinkers who decide to start drinking moderately might be making a heart-smart decision.

▐▐▐▶ *Breakthrough Study*

Researchers at the Medical University of South Carolina analyzed 10 years of health data in nearly 8,000 people between the ages of 45 and 64 who were nondrinkers. During that time, 6% began drinking moderately.

Result: After four years, the new drinkers had decreased their risk of developing heart disease by 38% compared to the nondrinkers —independent of whether they exercised, were overweight or had other risk factors for heart disease, such as high cholesterol.

"This study shows a substantial cardiovascular benefit from adopting alcohol drinking in middle age," says Dana E. King, MD, who led the study.

"Any such benefit must be weighed with caution against the known ill consequences of alcohol consumption," she says. "But while caution is clearly warranted, the study demonstrates that new moderate drinking lowers the risk of cardiovascular disease."

What to do: "For carefully selected individuals, a heart-healthy diet may include limited alcohol consumption, even among individuals who have not included alcohol previously," says Dr. King.

"Alcohol consumption can be part of a healthy lifestyle," agrees Eric Rimm, ScD, an associate professor at the Harvard School of Public Health, who has conducted many scientific studies on the link between moderate alcohol consumption and health.

What happens: Dr. Rimm explains that moderate intake of alcohol protects against

THE GREAT GRAPE

A drink or two a day can lower your risk of heart disease by more than 40%. But that drink doesn't *have* to be alcoholic.

What you may not know: "Recent studies have documented that grapes and grape juices are equally cardioprotective as red wine," say researchers at the University of Milan, in Italy. (Hey, if wine-loving Italians are admitting that Concord is as good as Chianti, it must be true!) *The evidence...*

- **Lower LDL, higher HDL.** Researchers in Spain studied 41 people, asking them to drink 3½ ounces (100 milliliters) of red grape juice every day for 14 days. After two weeks, they had lower LDL cholesterol and higher HDL cholesterol. "Red grape juice may favor a reduction in cardiovascular disease risk," say the researchers, in the *American Journal of Clinical Nutrition.*

- **Better blood flow.** Researchers from Brazil studied 16 people with high cholesterol, asking them to drink an 8-ounce glass of purple grape juice every day for two weeks—at which point an ultrasound showed the arteries in their forearms had relaxed, widening by 60%. "Grape juice may protect against coronary artery disease," say the researchers.

- **Lower blood pressure.** Korean researchers asked 40 people with high blood pressure to drink Concord grape juice every day for two

months. Diastolic blood pressure fell by an average of 6.2 and systolic by 7.2. "Consuming Concord grape juice may favorably affect blood pressure in hypertensive individuals," say the researchers.

- **Less inflammation.** Researchers at the Whitaker Cardiovascular Institute at the Boston University School of Medicine asked 20 people with heart disease to drink purple grape juice for two weeks. After the two weeks, they had lower levels of biomarkers showing their blood was less likely to form an artery-blocking blood clot, and their HDL cholesterol rose from 45 to 50. "Purple grape juice may attenuate [lessen] cardiovascular disease and, specifically, inhibit thrombosis [blood clots]," say the researchers, in *Arteriosclerosis, Thrombosis, and Vascular Biology,* the journal of the American Heart Association.

What happens: Purple and red grape juice are loaded with *polyphenols*, plant compounds such as resveratrol and anthocyanins that cut the manufacture of cholesterol and reduce artery-damaging inflammation.

ⓘ Welch's Concord grape juice was used in the study by the researchers from the Boston University School of Medicine. Drink an 8-ounce glass daily.

heart disease and stroke by increasing good HDL cholesterol and by lowering fibrinogen, a factor that increases the risk of artery-clogging blood clots. And he says that *any* type of alcohol—wine, beer or spirits—provides the benefit, because the *ethanol* in the alcohol conveys the heart-protecting power. But he also offers these cautions...

Warning: If you're pregnant...if your mother or father suffered from alcoholism...if you're on a blood-thinning medication such as aspirin or *warfarin* (Coumadin)...if you have breast cancer or a family history of the disease...if you're about to operate heavy machinery or do anything that requires normal reaction time...don't drink.

(For more information on alcohol and health, see page 3 in Chapter 1, "Aging and Longevity," and page 131 in Chapter 6, "Diabetes and Insulin Resistance.")

POMEGRANATE JUICE— FORTIFYING HEARTS

Forty-five people with heart disease. Nearly half had suffered heart attacks. Most had high blood pressure. Nearly all had high cholesterol. Everyone was taking cholesterol-lowering statins. Most were on several other drugs, including blood thinners, blood pressure drugs and beta-blockers to ease circulatory stress on the heart.

Could a daily glass of healthful fruit juice help regenerate those damaged hearts? Yes, say researchers.

⫸ *Breakthrough Study*

Doctors from the Preventive Medicine Research Institute in Sausalito, CA, and the University of California, San Francisco, studied those 45 people (average age, 69) with heart disease, dividing them into two groups. For three months, one group drank 8 ounces of pomegranate juice a day; the other group drank a look-alike, taste-alike drink.

At the beginning and end of the three months, the doctors gave both groups a *myocardial perfusion test*—a sophisticated "stress test" that uses a CAT scan to measure blood flow to the heart during exercise.

Result: After three months, the group drinking pomegranate juice had a 17% *increase* in blood flow to the heart, while the faux-fruit group had a *decrease* of 18%.

And those are very important test results. A recent study from researchers at the Cedars-Sinai Medical Center in Los Angeles shows that the *best predictor* of whether a person with heart disease will have a heart attack is the amount of blood flow to the heart as measured by a myocardial perfusion test.

The researchers also found that episodes of angina—intense chest pain caused by a heart gasping for more oxygen—decreased by 50% in the pomegranate group and increased by 38% in the non-pom group. And while they point out these numbers aren't "statistically significant," they probably pleased the pomegranate-drinking heart patients!

Why it works: "Pomegranate juice contains powerful antioxidants such as polyphenols, tannins and anthocyanins," says Dean Ornish, MD, the founder, president and director of the Preventive Medicine Research Institute in Sausalito, one of the study's researchers and author of *Dr. Dean Ornish's Program for Reversing Heart Disease* (Ballantine). These antioxidants, he explains, can stop the artery-clogging oxidation of LDL...cut the formation of the notorious "foam cells" that brew arterial plaque...reduce "platelet formation," the clumping of red blood cells that can lead to an artery-blocking clot...trigger the release of artery-relaxing nitric oxide (NO)…and decrease the production of NO-dissolving "superoxide."

More good news: There have been several other studies showing the heart-helping benefits of pomegranate juice…

• **Tops in pacifying LDL.** Researchers at the Center for Human Nutrition at the University of California in Los Angeles found that pomegranate juice had 20% more antioxidant activity—more power to stop the artery-clogging oxidation of LDL cholesterol—than red wine, Concord grape juice or orange juice.

• **Reverses clogged arteries.** Israeli researchers asked 10 people with heart disease to drink pomegranate juice for one year. Those who drank the juice had up to a 30% decrease in the thickness of their arterial plaque—while another group of heart patients not drinking pomegranate juice had a 9% increase.

• **Doesn't do drugs.** Earlier research had indicated that pomegranate juice might interfere with the action of medications, as grapefruit juice does. Researchers at Tufts University found that wasn't the case. "Pomegranate juice does not produce drug interactions," says David J. Greenblatt, MD, a professor in the Department of Pharmacology and Experimental Therapeutics, who led the study.

What to do: "Daily consumption of pomegranate juice may have important clinical benefits" in people with heart disease, says Dr. Ornish. If you've got high blood pressure, high cholesterol or diagnosed heart disease—consider quaffing eight ounces a day.

ℹ The study used POM Wonderful, a widely available brand, with 100% pomegranate juice from concentrate, and with no added sugar, colors or flavorings.

"COMPETENT EATING" SATISFIES YOUR HEART

It's not just *what* you eat but *how* you eat that keeps your heart healthy.

▌▌▌➡ *Breakthrough Study*

Scientists in the Department of Nutritional Sciences at Pennsylvania State University, led by Barbara Lohse, PhD, RD, studied 48 people with LDL levels over 110 (99 or below is considered optimal).

They found that those who were less "competent eaters" were five times more likely to have LDL over 130 *and* had lower levels of HDL cholesterol…*and* had higher blood pressure…*and* were seven times more likely to have triglycerides over the normal level of 150. In other words, competent eaters were a lot healthier, even among folks with a risk factor for heart disease.

New thinking: "Competent eaters have positive attitudes about eating and therefore are relaxed about it," says Ellyn Satter, MS, RD, LCSW, a family therapist, author of *Secrets of Feeding a Healthy Family* (Kelcy Press) and many other books and the dietician who, based on decades of clinical experience, developed the "competent eating" model studied by the scientists at Penn State.

She says most people today *aren't* competent eaters. "They feel more or less ambivalent and anxious about eating and doubt their ability to do a good job with food management. They carry around standards of what and how much they *should* eat, often ill defined. And they feel ashamed of themselves when they like—and eat—food that falls short of their standards."

The two keys to competent eating, she says, are 1) *permission* to choose enjoyable food and eat it in satisfying amounts, and 2) the *discipline* to have regular, reliable, rewarding meals and snacks and to pay attention when eating them.

She describes some ways to become a more competent eater...

• **Planning.** "You don't just grab food when you're hungry," says Satter. "You plan your snacks and meals—whether you cook from scratch, microwave, eat takeout or eat in a restaurant."

• **Enjoyment.** "You go to some trouble to make food taste good, and take the time to tune in and enjoy your food," she says. "Eat foods you like, and let yourself be comfortable with and relaxed about what you eat. Enjoying eating

supports the natural inclination to seek variety, the keystone of healthful food selection."

• **Internal regulation, not outer rules.** "Pay attention to your sensations of hunger and fullness to determine how much to eat," says Satter. "Go to the table hungry, eat until you feel satisfied and then stop, knowing another meal or snack is coming soon when you can do it again."

• **Positive discipline, not negative restrictions.** "There is positive discipline in feeding yourself well," says Satter. "It takes discipline to set up regular and predictable mealtimes, to plan the shopping list, to get the food in the house, to do the cooking and cleanup,

TRANS FATS— THEY'RE STILL OUT THERE

In 2007, the Girl Scouts decided to take the fatal fat out of their cookies. (Good deed!) In the same year, trans fats were exiled from entire cities, with the mayor of the Big Apple declaring them banned from deep-fried apple fritters and apple piecrusts found within the boundaries of New York City. (Trans fats are created when vegetable fats are "partially hydrogenated" to improve their texture and taste for use in cookies, pastries and crackers, and their durability for use in deep-fat fryers in restaurants.)

But is your *supermarket* safe?

New finding: Researchers at the University of Minnesota spent some serious scientific time inside a Wal-Mart, tallying the trans fats in foods found in the snack aisle and the cookie aisle. And many of those foods *had* been transformed since the FDA issued its edict requiring food companies reveal the amount of trans fats in their products on the "Nutrition Facts" portion of the label. Now it's macho for nachos to say they contain "0 grams" of trans fat. *But...*

Red flags: Movie buffs, beware the microwave popcorn! It's very likely to contain more than three grams of trans fats per serving.

Two other categories that still call for extra caution are cookies and snack cakes (think Twinkies), with nearly half those products containing substantial amounts of trans fats. Only about 25% of snack chips and crackers continue to contain trans fats.

Surprising: The lower the price of the pack of cookies, cakes, chips or crackers, the more likely it is to contain trans fats.

"Consumers need to read product labels because trans fat content of individual products can vary considerably," says Matthew Alpers, MPH, who led the study.

Better: Consumer products with *no* trans fats. A recent study from researchers at the Harvard School of Public Health found that people who eat the most trans fats have *three times* the likelihood of developing heart disease, compared to those who eat the least. "Food additives should be allowed to be used only if there is reasonable certainty of no harm," says Walter Willett, MD, PhD, from the Department of Nutrition at the Harvard School of Public Health. "The present FDA position of allowing trans fats in the food supply is indefensible, and large numbers of Americans are dying prematurely."

to set aside time to eat, to tune in when you are eating. On the other hand, the discipline becomes negative when you get caught in the *shoulds* and *oughts*—what to eat, what to avoid, how much to eat. 'I must eat it because it is good for me.' 'That is way too fattening.' 'I mustn't let it go to waste.' "

• **The bottom line is pleasure.** "To keep up the day-in, day-out effort of structured meals, those meals must be richly rewarding to plan, prepare, provide and eat," she says. "Being able to eat the foods you like, in satisfying amounts, gives your eating order and stability. Foods that are no longer forbidden become ordinary foods that you can eat in ordinary ways."

What most people don't realize: "Contrary to the fears of the food cops—both internal and external—we don't have a slothful inclination toward overindulgence," says Satter. "Rather, we overeat because we are *restrained* eaters—we chronically restrict ourselves. We restrict ourselves until we can't stand it anymore, then we overeat. Setting aside food restriction is like nutritional judo—going *with* the natural drive to eat as much as you want rather than fighting *against* it. After people learn to trust and honor their true and legitimate needs, they find that rather than periodically cutting loose and eating a great deal of high-calorie food, they eat moderately and consistently of all food, all the time and find it genuinely satisfying."

☀ You can find out more about Ellyn Satter and Eating Competence at *www.ellynsatter.com.* Ellyn Satter Associates, 4226 Mandan Crescent, Madison, WI 53711 (800-808-7976, 608-271-7976 or fax 866-724-1631); e-mail *info@ellyn satter.com.*

SIP THE TEA, SKIP THE MILK

Teatime is a good time for your heart.

Black tea is loaded with powerful plant compounds called *polyphenols*—specifically, *catechins* and *theaflavins. In test tube, animal and human studies, these polyphenols…*

• **Protect heart cells from** *oxidation,* the rustlike metabolic mayhem that is the harbinger of heart disease.

• **Prevent oxidation of LDL cholesterol,** which can damage arteries.

• **Tamp down the activity of** *nuclear factor kappa B,* a cellular component that activates the genes of a mob of molecules that can wreck arteries.

• **Slow the unchecked growth of vascular smooth muscle cells,** which narrows arteries.

• **Cut down on platelet aggregation,** the clumping of blood cells that can lead to an artery-plugging blood clot.

• **Relax and expand narrowed arteries.**

• **Reduce total cholesterol by 4%** and LDL cholesterol by 8%, prompting researchers at the government's Beltsville Human Nutrition Research Center to declare that tea "may reduce the risk of coronary heart disease."

New thinking: Inflammation plays a key role in arterial disease, leading to heart attacks and strokes. LDL cholesterol accumulates on the endothelium—the inner lining of the artery—irritating endothelial cells. Inflamed by this "foreign" invasion, *monocytes*—a type of white blood cell in the immune system—rush to the scene. They become *macrophages*, big immune cells that literally gobble up LDL. But in the microscopic cauldron of heart disease, those well-intended, cholesterol-stuffed macrophages turn into the frothy, fatty "foam" cells that accumulate as arterial plaque.

Tea polyphenols confront inflammation. *They can help...*

- **Stop white blood cells** from sticking to and burrowing into LDL-laden arterial walls.

- **Cut the production of** *chemokines*, a kind of bait for white blood cells.

- **Restrain monocytes**, the early form of a macrophage.

"The development of heart disease is multifactorial and involves processes that appear to be affected by tea ingredients," says Verena Stangl, MD, an expert on tea and health, in the *European Heart Journal.*

In fact, studies show that drinking one or more cups of black tea a day reduces the risk of developing stroke-causing high blood pressure by 46%...of heart disease by 36%...of heart attacks by 44%...and of death after heart attack by 31%.

Tea, it seems, is a cup of cardio-cure. But maybe not if you add milk.

▶ *Breakthrough Study*

"Experimental and clinical studies indicate that tea exerts protection against cardiovascular diseases," says Dr. Stangl. "However, a question of much debate is whether the addition of milk modifies the biological activities of tea."

To answer that question, she and her colleagues studied 16 people (average age, 59). Over three days, they drank . . . Day 1) 17 ounces of freshly brewed black Darjeeling tea; Day 2) the same tea with 10% skimmed milk added; Day 3) 17 ounces of boiled water. Two hours after drinking the beverage, Dr. Stangl used ultrasound to measure the width of the brachial artery in the forearm. Wider is healthier.

COFFEE—GOOD FOR THE 65+ HEART

Is coffee good or bad for your heart?

The more coffee you drink, the more likely you are to have a heart attack, say Finnish researchers, in the *Journal of Nutrition*...

Coffee cuts the risk of death from heart disease by up to 24%, say Norwegian researchers, in the *American Journal of Clinical Nutrition.*

Coffee drinking doesn't increase or decrease the risk of heart disease, say Harvard researchers, in the journal *Circulation*...

Give me a break, says you, in annoyance.

Well, if you're over 65, you may want to make that a coffee break...

New finding: The confusion about coffee and heart disease may just be confusion about the age of the person drinking the coffee, says James A. Greenberg, MD, of the Brooklyn College of the City University of New York.

He and his colleagues analyzed nine years of diet and health data from more than 6,500 people.

They found that only in people *over 65* was there a link between drinking caffeinated coffee and a healthy heart—with those drinking 4 or more cups a day having a 53% lower risk of dying from heart disease; those drinking 2 to 3 cups having a 32% lower risk; and those drinking 1 to 2 cups having a 23% lower risk.

There was *no* "protective effect" for those under 65.

And the protection *didn't* extend to seniors with very high blood pressure, or so-called "stage 2 hypertension" of 160/100 or above.

Theory: Coffee boosts blood pressure slightly after a meal. And low blood pressure (hypotension) after a meal—common among those over 65—has been linked to deadly heart attacks!

Bottom line: Unless you have very high blood pressure, if you're one of the 80% of Americans who enjoy one or more cups of coffee a day, there's no reason to cut your intake. And if you're over 65 and don't have stage 2 hypertension, you may want to drink a little more.

Result: On the day they drank black tea, the artery relaxed and widened by 4%, compared to the water. But drinking tea *and* milk "completely blunted" that affect—with *no* extra widening.

To verify her results, Dr. Stangl experimented with the arteries and arterial cells of laboratory animals. Black tea relaxed the arteries and triggered the production of artery-relaxing nitric oxide in arterial cells. Adding milk "completely inhibited" that Effect.

Later, she measured the heart-helping polyphenols in tea after milk was added. "Addition of ten percent milk to tea selectively and markedly decreased the concentrations of various catechins," she says.

"The addition of milk to black tea completely prevents the favorable health effects of tea on vascular function," says Dr. Strangl. And in the restrained language of science, she adds that her finding "may have broad implications on the mode of tea preparation and consumption."

What to do: Well, you may want to narrow that implication to your kitchen, your teapot and your teacup. For the sake of your heart, sip the tea but skip the milk—at least every now and then!

BRUSH YOUR TEETH, PROTECT YOUR HEART

Yes, eating healthy foods is necessary for protecting and healing your heart. *But they may not do your heart much good if you don't brush and floss afterward...*

New finding: Scientists know that people with periodontal disease—advanced gum disease—have a higher risk of heart disease. Researchers at Howard University in Washington, DC, analyzed data from 11 studies on gum and heart disease, and found that people with the *highest* levels of bacteria in their gums also had the *highest* level of systemic, whole-body bacterial exposure, and the *highest* degree of arterial blockage.

Theories: Bacteria from the mouth travel to the arteries, sparking the inflammation that weakens arterial walls, allowing the accumulation of artery-clogging plaque.

"Extended bacterial exposure from chronic, advanced gum disease may be what ultimately leads to cardiovascular disease," says Kenneth S. Kornman, DDS, PhD, the editor of the *Journal of Periodontology*, where the study appeared.

"This study shows how taking care of your teeth and gums can help you take care of your heart," adds Susan Karabin, DDS, president of the American Association of Periodontology.

ONE DAY A MONTH, *DON'T* EAT

Mormons have lower rates of heart disease than other Americans. One possible reason is that they fast—they *don't* eat one day out of every month. But you don't have to convert to get the benefits.

▐▐▶ *Breakthrough Study*

"People who fast seem to receive a heart-protective benefit, and this appears to hold true in non-Mormons who fast as part of a health-conscious lifestyle," says Benjamin D. Horne, PhD, MPH, an assistant professor at the University of Utah, who studied the effect of various lifestyle factors on the heart in more than 7,000 people in Utah.

He found that those who fasted once a month were 39% less likely to be diagnosed with heart disease. "Fasting was the strongest predictor of lower heart disease risk in the nearly seven thousand people we surveyed, including non-Mormons," says Dr. Horne.

Why is fasting good for your heart?

"When you abstain from food for twenty-four hours or so, it reduces the constant exposure of the body to foods and blood sugar," says Dr. Horne. "One of the major problems in the development of the metabolic syndrome—the constellation of risk factors such as high blood pressure, overweight and low HDL cholesterol, which leads to heart disease and diabetes—is that the insulin-producing beta-cells of the pancreas become desensitized to blood sugar. Routine fasting may allow them to resensitize—to reset to a baseline level so they work better."

What to do: With your doctor's permission, abstain from eating solid foods for one day a month. "Drink only water," says Allan Cott, MD, author of *Fasting: The Ultimate Diet* (Hastings House). "I advise you to drink at least two quarts of water on the day of the fast. Drink mineral water, if possible."

☀ *Fasting: The Ultimate Diet* by Allan Cott, MD (Hastings House); *Fasting and Eating for Health: A Medical Doctor's Program for Conquering Disease* by Joel Fuhrman, MD (St. Martin's).

VITAMINS AND HERBS

TOP THREE SUPPLEMENTS TO PROTECT AGING HEARTS

What's the biggest risk factor for cardiovascular diseases—for clogged arteries, congestive heart failure and stroke?

"Age itself," says Tory M. Hagen, PhD, of the Linus Pauling Institute at Oregon State University. Aging can be a biochemical train wreck, he explains.

Antioxidant levels fall, leaving cells vulnerable to oxidation (think rust and rotting apples but happening *inside* your body)…there's a decline in levels of specialized "stress response" enzymes that help your cells cope with change and challenge…and the DNA in mitochondria—the metabolic batteries inside every cell—erodes and decays.

But you can help maintain the cellular status quo—you can slow aging *and* the risk of heart disease and stroke—with "diets enriched in micronutrients," says Dr. Hagen. Food alone might not do it, however, because "inadequate nutritional intake is rampant" among those over 65, affecting nearly half of otherwise healthy people. You may need supplements.

⮕ *Breakthrough Studies*

Here are the nutrients and supplements that may help prevent heart disease or reduce its impact, says Dr. Hagen, in the journal *Pharmacological Research*…

• **Vitamin C to prevent heart disease.** Studies show that people with the highest intake of vitamin C (400 mg a day) have the lowest rates of death from heart disease.

Why it works: Vitamin C helps maintain flexible arteries by triggering the release of nitric oxide, a biochemical that relaxes and expands arterial walls.

Recommendation: "Most every adult should take one thousand milligrams of vitamin C a day as part of a daily supplement regimen," advises Stephen Sinatra, MD, cardiologist and coauthor of *Reverse Heart Disease Now* (Wiley).

• **Folate to prevent stroke.** A team of US and Chinese researchers analyzed eight studies on folic acid and stroke and found that people who took supplemental folic acid for more than three years lowered their risk of stroke by 29%. "Folic acid supplementation can effectively reduce the risk of stroke," say the researchers, in the *Lancet*.

Why it works: Folic acid lowers levels of *homocysteine*, an amino acid often linked to weakened, disease-prone arteries.

Recommendation: "Take the whole range of B-complex vitamins, not just one or two," says Dr. Sinatra. "If you concentrate on just one, you may cause a relative deficiency in the other B factors. For general prevention, a good multi-vitamin contains enough of the B vitamins."

PINE BARK—LESS SWELLING FROM BP MEDS

Thirty-five percent of people who take medications for high blood pressure get some degree of *edema*—swelling of the feet and ankles. (It's one reason why 25% of people prescribed antihypertensives stop them within the year.)

New approach: Italian researchers studied 53 patients with high blood pressure who were taking either a beta-blocker or an ACE inhibitor (two commonly prescribed antihypertensives) and developed edema.

Eight weeks after taking Pycnogenol—an extract of the bark of the maritime pine tree—their edema was reduced by 37%.

Why it works: Pycnogenol is packed with *polyphenols*, the same type of heart-helping plant compounds found in blueberries, purple grapes, green tea and dark chocolate. And those compounds improve *microcirculation*, the flow of blood through tiny blood vessels called capillaries, says Gianni Belcaro, MD, PhD, who led the study. As microcirculation improves, swelling goes down.

What to do: If you have edema from blood pressure meds, talk to your doctor about Pycnogenol.

Suggested intake: The dosage used in the study was 50 mg, three times a day.

🛈 Pycnogenol-containing supplements are widely available from many different brands.

● **Fish oil supplements to prevent a second heart attack.** Omega-3 fatty acids found in fish oil supplements can not only protect you from heart disease and death from heart attack—if you've had a heart attack and take a fish oil supplement, you're less likely to suffer a second attack.

Why it works: Omega-3s thin the blood, helping to prevent artery-plugging clots...help stop the abnormal heart rhythms that can trigger a heart attack...and stabilize arterial plaque, so chunks don't break off and block an artery.

Suggested intake: "For prevention, take one gram a day," says Dr. Sinatra—a combined total of 1,000 mg of EPA (eicosapentaenoic acid) and DHA (docosahexaenoic acid).

(For more information on fish oil supplements, see page 221 of this chapter.)

NIACIN—THE BEST WAY TO INCREASE HDL

You've read about this good/bad duo so many times, they might seem as familiar to you as Luke Skywalker and Darth Vader or Cain and Abel.

There's bad LDL cholesterol, the low-density lipoprotein that slings fat onto the walls of your arteries like a demonic short-order cook. And then there's good HDL cholesterol, which dutifully hauls fat away from the arteries and back to the liver, where it can be disposed of properly. You hear a lot about lowering LDL, but not quite so much about increasing HDL. But both are important.

New finding: Researchers at the University of Washington analyzed data from more than 83,000 heart patients and found that decreasing LDL by 40% *and* increasing HDL by 30% lowers the risk of heart attack or stroke by

70%— a much greater reduction than just lowering LDL.

Problem: Torcetrapib, a new drug that increased HDL by 60%, was shelved when clinical studies showed that it had side effects that *increased* heart problems and death rates.

Solution: "One of the few reliable ways to increase HDL is with therapeutic doses of niacin, a B-vitamin," says Allan Magaziner, DO, the medical director of the Magaziner Center for Wellness and Anti-Aging Medicine in Cherry Hill, NJ, and coauthor of *The All-Natural Cardio Cure* (Avery).

If you're one of 15 million Americans taking an LDL-lowering statin, you may want to talk to your doctor about adding niacin, a new approach called "combination therapy."

▶ *Breakthrough Study*

In a study reported in the journal *Atherosclerosis,* doctors divided 292 patients with high LDL (average, 197) into four groups. Two groups received a statin *and* niacin; one group received two statins simultaneously; and one group received one statin. All four groups had similar decreases in LDL of 50%. But only those receiving the statin *and* niacin had substantial increases in HDL.

What to do: Adding niacin to your cholesterol-lowering regimen might work something like this, says Dr. Magaziner…

Start with 500 mg a day. Every week, increase by 500 mg until you reach 2,000 mg a day, in three divided doses, with meals. Be certain to use *nicotinic acid*, not *niacinamide*, a form of the B-vitamin that does not lower cholesterol.

Red flag: In rare cases, high-dose niacin therapy can elevate levels of enzymes that cause liver damage. If you take more than 2,000 mg a day, your treatment must include regular blood tests for these enzymes.

• **Preventing the "niacin flush."** The most common (but harmless) side effect of niacin is *flushing*—a warm, itchy, rashlike reddening of the face, neck and chest, lasting about 10 minutes. It's caused by *vasodilation*, the artery-widening power of niacin. Choose flush-free niacin, or *inositol hexanicotinate*, says Dr. Magaziner. Combined with inositol, another B-vitamin, this form of niacin prevents the flush without reducing niacin's effectiveness.

ℹ No-Flush Niacin, from Solgar. Visit *www.solgar.com* to find a store near you.

STOP STATIN SIDE EFFECTS WITH COENZYME Q10

More than 15 million Americans take a *statin,* a class of medications that inhibits the action of *HMG-CoA reductase,* an enzyme involved in producing cholesterol. In fact, since their introduction in 1987, statins such as Lipitor, Mevacor and Zocor have become the most-prescribed medications in the United States, with many doctors touting them as a wonder drug, with few side effects. But what your doctor doesn't know about statins can hurt you, says Beatrice Golomb, MD, PhD, who heads the Statin Effects Study (collecting reports of statin side effects) at the University of California, San Diego School of Medicine.

▶ *Breakthrough Study*

Dr. Golomb and her colleagues asked 650 people who took a statin and reported a side effect to complete a survey that included questions about how the doctor responded when told about the problem.

Surprising: About 50% of doctors dismissed the possibility that the statin caused the problem—even though statin-triggered side effects such as muscle problems, memory loss and nerve pain are widely reported in the medical literature. About 25% endorsed the possibility that a statin was the cause. Another 25% were noncommittal, neither dismissing nor endorsing the possibility. The results were published in the journal *Drug Safety*.

Dr. Golumb says some possible side effects from statins are...

• **Muscle pain, fatigue and exercise intolerance.** The most commonly reported side effects in the Statin Effects Study, bothering 60%.

• **Memory loss and other cognitive problems.** The second most commonly reported type of side effect in the Statin Effects Study. One statin-taker with an apparent case of dementia saw her problem *reversed* when she discontinued statins.

• **Peripheral neuropathy.** Tingling, numbness or burning pain in the hands, arms, feet or legs, caused by nerve damage. The third most common side effect in the Statin Effects Study. In a study by researchers in Denmark, statin-takers had a 16-fold higher risk of developing peripheral neuropathy, compared to people not taking the drug.

• **Irritability, sleep problems, sexual problems.** These side effects are also frequently reported in the Statin Effects Study.

What to do: You need to protect yourself from the possible side effects of statins, says Dr. Magaziner. A cause of many of these side effects—statin-triggered damage to the *mitochondria*, microscopic structures in cells that generate energy. The remedy, says Dr. Magaziner—take Coenzyme Q10 (CoQ10), a nutrient that nourishes mitochondria.

Suggested intake: 150 to 300 mg daily.

ℹ️ Dr. Sinatra recommends *hydrosoluble* CoQ10, which he says is the most absorbable. Look for the word "Q-Gel" on the label. CoQ10 brands with Q-Gel include Swanson, Country Life and Life Extension. "For maximum absorption, take CoQ10 with meals," he advises.

Also helpful: Dr. Sinatra gives CoQ10 to *all* his heart patients. "CoQ10 offers impressive benefits for cardiovascular disease by reenergizing heart cells," he says. *In the Q-Gel form, he recommends these daily intakes...*

• **60 to 120 mg for prevention of heart disease;**

• **180 to 360 for angina pectoris, cardiac arrhythmia and high blood pressure;**

• **300 to 360 for moderate heart failure** or

• **360 to 600 for severe heart failure.**

HIGH-DOSE MULTIPLE FOR HEART FAILURE

Five million Americans have *chronic heart failure* (also called *congestive heart failure*)—your primary pump is weak and can't supply the body with the blood and oxygen it needs, leading to swelling (edema), breathlessness and fatigue. A high-nutrient supplement might help.

▐▐▶ *Breakthrough Study*

Cardiologists in England and Germany studied 28 people with heart failure (average age, 75) for nine months, dividing them into two groups. One group received a high-dose multivitamin-mineral supplement, while the other group took a placebo.

• **Enlarged heart shrinks.** In one type of heart failure, the chamber of the lower left side of the heart (left ventricle) abnormally enlarges to try to compensate for the heart's weakness. After nine months, those taking the supplement had a *decrease* of "left ventricular volume" of 13%—in other words, the ventricle got smaller. Those in the placebo group had an increase of 4%.

● **More powerful pumping.** At the same time, the pumping power of the left ventricle (left ventricle ejection fraction) increased by 5.3%. The placebo group didn't have any increase.

● **Better life.** The supplement group also had a 10% improvement in their overall "quality of life"—less fatigue, breathlessness, ankle swelling, and depression; better appetite, sleep, mobility and social activities. Those taking the placebo had a slight decrease of 1%.

"Long-term multiple micronutrient supplementation can improve" heart failure, say the researchers, in the *European Heart Journal*.

Why it works: "Using single supplements to correct only one deficiency when multiple deficiencies exist may be useless," says Klaus Witte, MD, who led the study. "On the other hand, micronutrients may have synergistic [positively interacting] effects." Specifically, he says...severe thiamine deficiency can cause heart failure, and thiamine can improve heart function...multiple nutrients decrease *oxidative stress*, the oxygen-caused cellular destruction that is increased in people with heart failure...people with heart failure have lower levels of coenzyme Q10, a powerful antioxidant, in the wall of the heart...selenium, vitamin C and vitamin E can relax and expand arteries...B vitamins such as folate, B-6 and B-12 can reduce *homocysteine*, an amino acid linked to heart disease.

What to do: Talk to your primary-care physician or cardiologist about taking a megadose vitamin-mineral supplement comparable to the one used in the study. *If your doctor wants to read the study, the citation is...*

Witte, K., et al., *European Heart Journal* 26 (2005): 2238–44.

If your doctor wants to e-mail the study leader, he is Klaus K. A. Witte, MD, at *klaus witte@hotmail.com*.

Suggested intake: The supplement contained calcium, 250 mg; magnesium, 150 mg; zinc, 15 mg; copper, 1.2 mg; selenium, 50 micrograms (mcg); vitamin A, 32,000 IU; thiamine, 200 mg; riboflavin, 2 mg; vitamin B-6, 200 mg; folate, 5 mg; vitamin B-12, 200 mcg; vitamin C, 500 mg; vitamin E, 400 IU; vitamin D, 400 IU; coenzyme Q10, 150 mg.

ⓘ Cardi-Rite, from Carlson Laboratories, contains all the nutrients listed above, in generally similar amounts.

☀ *www.carlsonlabs.com*. J.R. Carlson Laboratories, Inc., 15 College Drive, Arlington Heights, IL 60004-1985 (888-234-5656, 847-255-1600 or fax 847-255-1605); e-mail *carlson@carlson labs.com*.

HAWTHORN FOR A STRONGER HEART

"If I had chronic heart failure, I would certainly consider using hawthorn extract," says Max H. Pittler, MD, PhD, deputy director of complementary medicine at Peninsula Medical School in Exeter, England. Here's the reason why.

▶ *Breakthrough Study*

Dr. Pittler and his colleagues reviewed 14 scientific studies on herbal extracts of hawthorn (a flowering shrub related to the rose), involving 855 people. *Compared to a placebo, they found hawthorn extract...*

● **Increased maximal workload** (the maximum intensity of activity a person can do in an exercise stress test) by 46%,

- **Increased exercise tolerance** (a measurement of endurance in an exercise stress test) by 43%,

- **Decreased pressure heart-rate** (a measurement of oxygen used by the heart) by 58%, and

- **Decreased shortness of breath** and fatigue by 59%.

"There is good evidence that, when used alongside conventional therapy, hawthorn extract can bring additional benefits," says Ruoling Guo, BSc, MSc, PhD, a researcher on the study.

How it works: The extract boosts the strength of the heart's contractions as it pumps, says Dr. Pittler—increasing blood flow through the arteries and reducing irregular heartbeats.

What to do: Talk to your doctor about whether hawthorn extract is right for you.

ℹ In many of the successful scientific studies using hawthorn, an extract of the hawthorn's flower and leaf (not the widely available hawthorn berry) worked. And the extract was "standardized" to the active ingredient in the flower and leaf—18.75% *oligomeric procyanidins.* The only product available in the United States that uses standardized flower and leaf extract is HeartCare, from Nature's Way.

Suggested intake: The studies used 150 to 300 mg daily, in two or three divided doses.

Precaution: Hawthorn extract is a powerful herbal medicine. It can improve the performance of several heart-helping medications for blood pressure and heart disease, such as statins and digitalis—and stronger isn't always better. (Think overdose.) If you have heart failure, or are taking medications for cholesterol or heart disease, use hawthorn extract only with the approval and supervision of your cardiologist.

OH WELL, IT STILL ANNOYS VAMPIRES

"Garlic doesn't work to lower cholesterol."

That's the conclusion of Christopher Gardner, PhD, at the Stanford Prevention Research Center, after he and his colleagues asked 192 people with high LDL cholesterol to either take garlic supplements (aged or powdered) or eat raw garlic every day for six months.

Unfortunately for garlic aficionados, the participants' LDL cholesterol readings were nearly identical at the beginning and the end of the study.

"If garlic was going to work, in one form or another, then it would have worked in our study," says Dr. Gardner. "The lack of effect was compelling and clear. We took cholesterol measurements every month for six months and the numbers just didn't move. There was no effect with any of the three garlic interventions—powdered garlic, aged garlic or raw garlic—even though fairly high doses were used."

Dr. Gardner says garlic can still be a valuable part of the diet if used to increase the consumption of healthy dishes, such as a stir fry or a Mediterranean salad. "But if you choose garlic fries as a cholesterol-lowering food, then you blew it," says Dr. Gardner. "The garlic doesn't counteract the fries."

REHABILITATE BETTER WITH MAGNESIUM

Exercise therapy is a big part of "cardiac rehabilitation"—a closely monitored and regular program of aerobics, such as walking on a treadmill or pedaling on a stationary bicycle, that slowly but surely (and safely) strengthens your ailing ticker so that it can start keeping time with your life.

Well, just as a race-car can have mag (magnesium) wheels for better performance, consider adding some mag as you take those laps on the way to better health.

⫸ *Breakthrough Study*

Researchers at the Human Performance Laboratory at Texas A&M University reviewed recent scientific literature on magnesium and the heart—and concluded the mineral was magnificent for…

• **Strengthening the *left ventricle*,** the part of the heart that pumps blood to the rest of the body;

• **Relaxing and therefore widening arteries,** allowing for more blood flow—and doing so as effectively as cholesterol-lowering medications and

• **Decreasing chest pain** in people with angina.

To see if magnesium could help cardiac patients rehabilitate a little bit better, they studied 53 men with heart disease—men who had suffered a heart attack…or undergone coronary bypass surgery…or had an angioplasty, with a wire-mesh stent inserted to reverse a blockage in an artery…or had an abnormal angiography, a test that detects severe arterial blockage.

For six months, the men (average age, 61) took pills twice a day: either 270 mg of magnesium or a placebo. At the beginning and end of the six months, the researchers measured: the pumping strength of the left ventricle; VO2max, the lung capacity's for oxygen (a sign of fitness); and an electrical measurement of the health of the heartbeat during exercise, called "factor K."

Result: Those taking the magnesium had…

• **An improvement in the strength of the left ventricle** of 14%, compared to a slight decrease in the placebo group;

• **An increase in lung capacity** of 8%, compared to no change for the placebo group; and

• **An improvement in factor K** of 31%, compared to no change in the placebo group.

Why it works: When the men started the study, they were magnesium *deficient*, say the researchers. ("More than half of all Americans may be deficient in magnesium," says cardiologist Dr. Sinatra. "Most patients with cardiovascular disease—especially acute disease—are depleted.") By replacing the missing magnesium, the men's hearts were strengthened both at rest and during exercise—probably because the extra magnesium improved blood flow to the heart.

What to do: "In patients with magnesium deficiency, magnesium supplementation should be given," says Serge P. von Duvillard, PhD, the director of the Human Performance Laboratory at Texas A&M University and one of the researchers who conducted the study.

"To check for a deficiency, ask your doctor for a red cell magnesium or ionized magnesium test," says Dr. Sinatra. "These tests yield more accurate measurements of functional magnesium. Standard blood-level tests often turn up falsely normal results."

But whatever the results, Dr. Sinatra's advice is straightforward—"Cardiovascular patients should take supplemental magnesium."

Suggested intake: "I recommend four hundred to eight hundred milligrams a day, regardless of food intake," says Dr. Sinatra.

ⓘ Magnesium citrate, the type of magnesium used in the study. Magnesium citrate supplements in larger doses (200 mg and up) are available from Solgar, NSI (Nutritional Sciences Institute), NOW Foods and many other manufacturers.

Helpful: If your doctor wants to read the study, the citation is *British Journal of Sports Medicine* 40 (2006): 773–78.

Your doctor can contact Dr. von Duvillard via e-mail at *serge_vonduvillard@tamu-commerce.edu.*

VITAMIN D PREVENTS PAD

You couldn't find a parking spot close to the mall entrance and had to walk a hundred yards or so—but halfway there your calves were seized by a cramp as vicious and painful as the bite of a pit bull…

You have *peripheral artery disease*, or PAD. Eight to 12 million Americans are in the same listing boat.

In PAD, the arteries of the legs are clogged and narrowed with plaque. Whenever you ask your legs to do a little extra work—walk up stairs, stroll to the mailbox—your leg muscles can't get enough oxygen, and your calves, thighs or hips start to cramp, a symptom doctors call *intermittent claudication*.

Treatments include exercise (a start-and-stop walking regimen that considers your pain, providing plenty of rest), lowering cholesterol with diet and medications or even surgery to clear clogged arteries. But you may not have needed any of those therapies—if you'd gotten enough vitamin D.

⫸ *Breakthrough Study*

Researchers at Albert Einstein College of Medicine analyzed diet and health data from nearly 5,000 people. Those with the lowest blood levels of vitamin D (less than 17.8 nanograms per milliliter, or ng/mL) were 64% more likely to have PAD than those with the highest levels (more than 29.2 ng/mL). In fact, for every 10 ng/mL drop in vitamin D from the highest level of intake, the risk of ending up with PAD increased by 29%.

But this startling finding about PAD—reported at the American Heart Association's annual Arteriosclerosis, Thrombosis and Vascular Biology conference—is only the latest in a series of breakthroughs about the role of vitamin D in heart disease…

● **Low vitamin D, high blood pressure —a deadly combination.** Researchers at Harvard Medical School analyzed five years of diet and health data from nearly 1,800 people and found that people with the lowest blood levels of vitamin D had a 62% greater risk of a "cardiovascular event" (heart attack, heart failure or stroke) than those with the highest levels. Those with low vitamin D levels *and* high blood pressure had *twice* the risk (200%) of a cardiovascular event.

"EPHEDRA-FREE" CAN STILL HURT YOUR HEART

You probably remember ephedra, the now-banned metabolism-boosting herbal supplement that helped millions of people lose weight…and a couple of dozen people lose their lives, from ephedra-caused heart attacks. Well, many supplement manufacturers are now making "ephedra-free" products featuring bitter orange (*citrus aurantium*), a supposedly safer herb that also boosts metabolism. *But bitter orange might leave an aftertaste—of the afterlife…*

New findings: Cardiologists at Tufts-New England Medical Center report a case of angina caused by bitter orange, in the *Mayo Clinic Proceedings*…researchers at the University of California, San Francisco, studied 15 healthy adults, giving them a single dose of bitter orange—and it sent blood pressure skyrocketing…researchers at Mercer University in Atlanta report the case of a 55-year-old woman without high blood pressure or high cholesterol who had a heart attack after taking bitter orange for a year. They conclude, "The use of *C. aurantium* containing supplements may present a risk for cardiovascular toxicity."

What to do: "Don't use bitter orange for weight loss," says Dr. Harry Preuss. "Its safety is not proven. For now, if you see 'bitter orange' or 'citrus aurantium' on the label of a weight-loss product, consider it an orange alert."

"A growing body of evidence suggests that low levels of vitamin D may adversely affect the cardiovascular system," says Thomas J. Wang, MD, who led the study. "Cellular receptors for vitamin D are found in many different types of tissue, including the muscle cells of the circulatory system and the endothelium, the inner lining of the body's blood vessels. Our data raise the possibility that treating vitamin D deficiency could reduce cardiovascular risk."

And there are many people with vitamin D deficiency. "Low levels of vitamin D are highly prevalent in the United States, especially in northern latitudes with less sunshine," says Dr. Wang. "Twenty to thirty percent of the population in many areas has moderate to severe vitamin D deficiency."

What to do: For a complete discussion about vitamin D deficiency and expert advice to correct it effectively and efficiently with vitamin D supplements (diet and sun exposure aren't reliable), see page 9 in Chapter 1, "Aging and Longevity."

WHAT SCIENTISTS DON'T KNOW ABOUT VITAMIN E

In 2004, a meta-analysis of 19 studies on vitamin E and heart disease involving 136,000 people showed an *increased* death rate among people taking a daily dose of more than 400 IU of the nutrient. Eek!

In 2008, a meta-analysis of 15 studies on vitamin E involving hundreds of thousands of people showed that for every additional 30 IU of the nutrient in the diet (from food or supplements) the risk of heart disease fell by 4%. Yippee!

What the E is going on?

▶ *Breakthrough Study*

Every study ever conducted on vitamin E and heart disease is "fatally flawed," say Balz Frei, PhD, director of the Linus Pauling Institute at Oregon State University, and Jeffrey Blumberg, PhD, director of the Antioxidants Research Laboratory at the Jean Mayer USDA Human Nutrition Research Center on Aging at Tufts University, in the journal *Free Radical Biology and Medicine*. Why?

• **They used too little of the vitamin.** The newest research shows that it takes anywhere from 1,600 to 3,200 IU of vitamin E a day to reverse the oxidation of cholesterol, the artery-clogging process that vitamin E—a powerful antioxidant—is intended to stop. That amount has rarely been tested, says Dr. Frei.

• **They didn't measure oxidation.** Imagine conducting a study to test a statin drug, which lowers cholesterol, without measuring cholesterol at the beginning and end of the study. Ridiculous, right? Well, says Dr. Frei, that's just what has been done with studies on vitamin E. "Oxidative stress was never measured in these trials, and therefore we don't know whether it was actually reduced or not."

• **They used the wrong form of the vitamin.** It's now known that natural forms of vitamin E (the d- types) are better absorbed than synthetic forms (the dl- types). Studies need to be done with the right type of the vitamin, says Dr. Frei.

• **They didn't make sure to take it with a meal.** Vitamin E supplements taken without a fat-containing meal are largely useless, because vitamin E needs dietary fat to be absorbed.

"Only when we do these studies right will we answer questions about the value of vitamin E in preventing and treating cardiovascular disease," says Dr. Frei.

Try this: Should you take vitamin E in the meantime? "Some studies on vitamin E have been flawed in terms of design and the type of vitamin used," agrees Dr. Sinatra. However, he says, "I am a strong believer in vitamin E." *He recommends…*

- **Take the right amount…**Take no more than 400 IU daily, as *part* of a comprehensive supplement program. "You may even find enough E as part of a multivitamin supplement," says Dr. Sinatra.

- **Take the right type…** "Vitamin E is usually sold as a single compound called alpha-tocopherol," says Dr. Sinatra. "Optimally, it should be accompanied by the family of other vitamin E compounds, including gamma-tocopherol and tocotrienols."

- **Take in a natural form…** "Avoid vitamin E with the designation of dl-alpha-tocopherol, which is synthetic vitamin E," he says. Look for the d- designation.

- **Take with meals.** "Vitamin E is fat soluble, so take it with food."

EXERCISE AND ACTIVITY

FITNESS—YOUR SHIELD AGAINST STROKE

Your dad died of a stroke…you have high blood pressure…and type 2 diabetes… you're more than a couple of pounds overweight…and your cholesterol is quite high. Are you doomed to suffer stroke, jr.?

Not if you're fit.

▐▐▐▶ *Breakthrough Study*

That's the startling news from Steven P. Hooker, PhD, who, with his colleagues at the Prevention Research Center of the University of South Carolina Arnold School of Public Health, analyzed 18 years of health data on more than 60,000 people, aged 18 to 100, who participated in a study at the Cooper Aerobics Center in Dallas.

When they started, each participant took a treadmill test to measure their CRF—*cardiorespiratory fitness,* or the fitness of the heart and lungs.

Results: Men who were the most fit had a 40% lower risk of stroke compared to men who were the least fit; the fittest women had a 43% lower risk. And that lower risk was the case whether the men smoke, drank, had a family history of cardiovascular disease, were overweight, had high blood pressure, diabetes or high cholesterol. Fitness ruled! But how "fit" is fit? Well, those folks weren't fitness fanatics— their fitness level was achieved by 30 minutes of brisk walking, five days a week. (Or a similar activity, such as riding a stationary bike.)

"We found that a low-to-moderate amount of aerobic fitness for men and women across the whole adult age spectrum would be enough to substantially reduce stroke risk," says Dr. Hooker. (And in a similar analysis of 26,000 men and women, the University of South Carolina researchers found that the fittest had a 31% lower risk of heart disease.)

- **Good news—even 10 minutes works!** In another recent study, researchers in Ireland found that even *three days* a week of 30 minutes of brisk walking lowered systolic blood pressure by five points. (And those daily 30 minutes could be split up into three, 10-minute walks.) "Moderate intensity physical exercise *below* the recommended level of five days a week still makes a difference to health," says Mark Tully, MD, who led the study.

What to do: "Brisk walking each day will change your life," says John A. McDougall, MD, author of *The McDougall Program for a Healthy*

Heart (Plume). "Walking provides all the benefits of a good aerobic workout, without the dangers that competitive sports present. And walking is safe if you have had a heart attack because there's little chance of overexerting yourself. If you feel angina pain come on, stop walking and rest until it passes. Then resume your walk at a more leisurely pace." *His tips for a successful walking program...*

● **See your doctor first.** "Your doctor may want to give you a complete physical and basic blood tests," says Dr. McDougall. "Once your doctor gives you the green light, start the walking program."

● **Then visit the shoe store.** "Be sure your walking shoe has a firm heel, a thick resilient sole, provides plenty of arch support and has a wide toe," says Dr. McDougall.

Smart idea: "Some experts recommend that a walking shoe should be a half-size larger than the size you're used to, in order to accommodate a thicker sock and give your foot plenty of breathing room," says Dr. McDougall.

● **Go slow.** "Don't launch yourself into your walk at top speed," he says. "Start out slow and work your way up to a more brisk pace as you feel your circulation improving and your energy rising."

● **Start with three walks a week.** "I recommend that you start walking three times per week and that each session last fifteen to twenty minutes," he says. "Avoid hills. Maintain this schedule for two to four weeks, until you feel your strength improving. Then increase your time to twenty-five to thirty minutes. After a few

RxERCISE

Regular exercise is powerful medicine for your heart. *Consider the evidence...*

● **Surviving after an angioplasty.** Italian researchers studied 168 people aged 70 and older who had undergone an angioplasty after a heart attack—the surgical insertion of a small inflatable balloon into a blocked artery to widen it. In the month after the procedure, among those who walked, gardened or biked every day for 30 minutes or more, only 4% died. Among those who exercised daily for 15 to 30 minutes, 18% died. Among those who didn't exercise, 23% died. The study was reported in the *American Heart Journal.*

● **More walking, fewer heart attacks.** Researchers in Finland found that men with the most leisure activity—daily walking or cycling—had 34% lower risk of heart attack or stroke, compared to men with the least activity; for active women, the risk was lowered by 46%.

● **Increasing good HDL, lowering triglycerides.** Researchers in the West Virginia University School of Medicine analyzed 10 studies on exercise and blood fats, involving more than 1,200 people with heart disease. Regular exercise increased HDL and lowered heart-threatening triglycerides.

● **Even 10 minutes reduces risk.** Spikes in blood fats after eating are a risk factor for heart attacks. Researchers in the UK found that even 10 minutes of brisk exercise, three times a day, could cut postmeal blood fat levels.

● **Lean is mean—but lean and fit is better.** Researchers in England studied 113 normal weight men—and found that those who were fit had lower total cholesterol and lower LDL cholesterol than those who weren't fit.

Bottom line: Less than half of US adults meet the government's recommendations for heart-healthy exercise, says William L. Haskell, PhD, of Stanford University, who was part of an expert panel convened by the American Heart Association and the American College of Sports Medicine. *The panel's advice for cutting your risk of heart disease, stroke and high blood pressure...*

At a minimum, walk briskly for 30 minutes, five days a week.

weeks, gradually increase your speed and the distance you walk during your thirty minutes."

• **Take the talk test.** "Can you talk effortlessly while you're walking?" asks Dr. McDougall. "If you have trouble talking, you're walking too briskly. Slow down or rest."

• **Pick an inspiring path.** "Walk in places that inspire you," he says. "The ideal place for walking lifts your mood, gets your mind off your problems and makes you lighter of spirit."

Bottom line: "Getting out there and taking a walk is what it's all about," agrees James A. Levine, MD, PhD, of the Mayo Clinic. "You don't have to join a gym; you don't have to check your pulse. It doesn't cost you anything. You just have to switch off the TV, get off the sofa and go for a walk. You can do it now, this minute. Walking is for everyone."

FOR BEST RESULTS, *BELIEVE* IN EXERCISE

If you believe everyday physical activity such as cleaning and gardening can make you healthier —it probably will!

⫸ *Breakthrough Study*

Researchers in the Department of Psychology at Harvard University studied 84 women housekeepers from seven different hotels. At the beginning of the study, the researchers asked the women how much exercise they got—two-thirds said they didn't work out regularly and one-third said they never exercised. The researchers also took basic health measurements—weight, blood pressure, body fat—which confirmed the women were indeed sedentary.

Then, in four of the hotels, 44 women were told—via a presentation, posters and brochures—that cleaning hotel rooms is good, calorie-burning exercise, and satisfies the surgeon general's requirement for an active lifestyle. The women in the other three hotels weren't given any new information.

Four weeks later, all the women were asked again about their exercise habits. Eighty percent of the 44 women who had been told their work was healthy said they were exercising regularly—even though their actual level of physical activity hadn't changed! *They also had...*

• **Lost an average of two pounds,**

• **Lowered their systolic blood pressure by 10%,**

• **A lower percentage of body fat and**

• **A more healthful waist-to-hip ratio.**

Meanwhile, there was very little change in those parameters in the other group.

"Exercise affects health in part—or in whole—via the placebo effect," says Ellen J. Langer, PhD, one of the researchers who conducted the study. "Whether the change in physiological health was brought about directly or indirectly, it is clear that health is significantly affected by mind-set."

PUT ON A SWEATER, PREVENT A HEART ATTACK

Cardiologists in Pakistan reviewed how many people showed up week by week at the emergency room of the Punjab Institute of Cardiology with heart attacks or angina. Between January 1 and 15, the number was 3,029; the yearly two-week average was 1,250. What was happening in January?

It was *cold.* Cold weather constricts blood vessels, causing the heart to work harder, which triggers more episodes of angina and more heart attacks.

The solution is in cold weather, make sure the chest is covered with warm clothing, such as a wool sweater, say the cardiologists at the Institute. Also, keep your head, hands and feet warm.

Bottom line: In other words, *believe* your daily physical activity is helping your heart stay healthy—and your heart will probably agree with you!

WEAK HEART? START WALTZING

People with chronic heart failure may not feel like they have much to kick up their heels about. All the more reason to start dancing.

ⅢⅢ➡ *Breakthrough Study*

"Our research suggests that dancing is a new choice of exercise training for patients with heart failure," says Romualdo Belardinelli, MD, director of cardiac rehabilitation and prevention at Lancisi Heart Institute in Ancona, Italy.

In an earlier study, Dr. Belardinelli and his colleagues had found that dancing a few times a week—specifically, slow and fast waltzes—improved the functioning of the heart and the quality of life in people who had suffered heart attacks.

This time, Dr. Belardinelli studied 110 people (average age, 59) with chronic heart failure—on average, the pumping power of their heart was less than 40% from normal.

One group of 44 participated in supervised exercise training on a stationary bicycle or treadmill, three times a week for eight weeks. Another group of 44 people was on the same three-day-a-week schedule, but they danced, alternating between slow (5 minutes) and fast (3 minute) waltzes, lasting 21 minutes. A third group of 22 patients didn't exercise.

At the start of the study and eight weeks later, the participants underwent exercise stress tests to evaluate heart functioning and also filled out a quality-of-life questionnaire, rating how heart failure affected their sleep, sex life, level of worry and depression and participation in everyday activities such as hobbies and housework.

"The results indicate that dancing improves the functional capacity of the heart," says Dr. Belardinelli. *In fact, the dancers had slightly stronger hearts and higher fitness levels than the conventional exercisers…*

• **18% improvement in oxygen capacity** of the lungs, compared with 16%;

• **21% improvement in time to muscle fatigue,** compared with 20% and

• **19% improvement in "cardiocirculatory fitness,"** compared with 18%.

There was no improvement among those who didn't exercise.

The new dancers were also the happiest of the three groups. "Surprisingly, quality of life was more significantly improved in the dancing group, compared to the exercise group," says Dr. Belardinelli—with scores decreasing (lower scores reflect fewer problems) from 56 to 41 in the dance group, compared with 58 to 48 in the exercise group.

What to do: Check with your doctor to see if you're good to go…out on the town. If so, let your fingers do the dancing, and check the Yellow Pages under "Dancing Instruction" for classes near you. Or dance at home.

☀ The DVD, Learn to Dance Waltz, Volumes I and II, from *www.dancecrazy.com*. Call 877-507-3403 or e-mail *info@dancecrazy.com*.

WEED OUT HEART DISEASE (IN YOUR GARDEN)

When you think of cardiac rehabilitation, you probably think of walking on a treadmill, electrodes attached to your chest, and a nurse with a clipboard dutifully recording your pulse and your progress.

Well, start thinking earthworms, spades and zinnia seeds.

▐▌▶ *Breakthrough Study*

Researchers at the Rusk Institute of Rehabilitation Medicine at the New York University School of Medicine studied 107 people in cardiac rehab, dividing them into two groups. One group received a standard, classroom-based educational session about heart disease. The other group received a session of "horticultural therapy," which the American Horticultural Therapy Association defines as "a process that uses plants and plant-related activities through which participants strive to improve their well-being." (In other words, you get your hands a little dirty for the sake of your heart.)

Before and after the sessions, the researchers asked the participants to fill out a questionnaire about mood, and checked their heart rates.

Result: Before the sessions, there was no difference in mood or heart rate between the two groups. Afterward, however, the people who hung out with plants had a decrease in "total mood disturbance" of up to 18%, while the mood of the classroom group didn't change. And the heart rates of the horticulturally helped fell by an average of four beats per minute, while there was no change in the classroom group.

"These findings indicate that horticultural therapy improves mood, suggesting that it may be a useful tool in reducing stress and an effective component of cardiac rehabilitation," says Matthew Wichrowski, MSW, HTR, who led the study.

But not only does horticultural therapy enhance mood and reduce stress, says Wichrowski—it also "provides mild to moderate exercise to maintain physical ability, while at the same time providing something tangible to be satisfied and proud of."

SECONDHAND HEART DISEASE

One activity you definitely *don't* want to do: hang out with people who are smoking, *ever. Even a little bit of secondhand smoke can damage your heart...*

Newest research: Led by Andrea Venn, PhD, researchers at the University of Nottingham in England analyzed data on the blood levels of *cotinine*—a breakdown product of nicotine—in more than 7,500 people who had never smoked. (Cotinine is a biochemical giveaway—if you've got it in your blood, you've either smoked or been around smokers.) The researchers also looked at blood levels of C-reactive protein, homocysteine and fibrinogen, three compounds that link to higher rates of heart disease.

Surprising: People with both low *and* high levels of cotinine had high levels of the three cardio-hurting compounds.

"Our study shows very low levels of exposure to secondhand smoke may be associated with appreciable increases in cardiovascular risk," says Dr. Venn.

Shockingly, the researchers found that fibrinogen and homocysteine levels of people exposed to secondhand smoke were about 35 to 45% of the levels seen in *smokers.* In other words, in terms of damage to your health—for every two to three cigarettes they smoke, you smoke one.

What most people don't realize: "Even when participants in the study weren't exposed to smoke at the workplace or at home, many had low or high levels of cotinine in their blood," says Dr. Venn. "These people may be exposed in bars or restaurants or perhaps in other people's homes, such as those of relatives or friends. This suggests that even people exposed to low levels of second-hand smoke may be at increased risk for heart disease."

Fortunately, she adds, "secondhand smoke is an *avoidable* cause of heart disease."

Horticultural therapy doesn't mean that you have to buy bonsai or apprentice yourself to a neighbor with a green thumb. It includes decorating rooms with plants and caring for them, helping at a community garden or even just going on a nature walk, says Wichrowski. Even tending one African violet on a windowsill qualifies!

☀ *www.ahta.org.* The American Horticultural Therapy Association, 201 East Main Street, Suite 1405, Lexington, KY 40507-2004 (800-634-1603, 859-514-9177 or fax 859-514-9166); e-mail the Association director, Gaye Horton, at *ghorton@amrms.com.*

www.med.nyu.edu/rusk/glassgardens. Glass Garden, Rusk Institute, New York University Medical Center, 400 East 34th Street, New York, NY 10016 (212-263-6058); e-mail *glass gardenrusk@nyumc.org* or *matthew.wichrowski @nyumc.org.*

LOWER THE PRESSURE WITH YOGA

Could the gentle poses and stretches of yoga be as powerful as prescription medication in lowering high blood pressure? Scientists at Yale think so.

‖‖➡ *Breakthrough Study*

Researchers at the Prevention Research Center at Yale University School of Medicine analyzed 12 studies that used mind-body therapies—yoga, meditation and guided imagery—to treat high blood pressure.

Result: Yoga was number one—reducing blood pressure by an average of 19 points diastolic and 13 points systolic, compared with an average of 12 and 7 for the other therapies. The studies also showed that yoga reduced the risk of dying from heart disease or stroke.

Why it works: "There are a number of ways in which the practice of yoga can benefit people with hypertension," says Timothy McCall, MD, medical editor of *Yoga Journal* magazine and author of *Yoga as Medicine* (Bantam). He explains that regular yoga practice lowers stress—which may directly lower high blood pressure, or help people forgo lifestyle choices such as unhealthy eating and smoking that can increase blood pressure.

Find a yoga therapist: To find a yoga therapist near you—a person who teaches yoga for better health and healing—go to the Web site of the International Association of Yoga Therapists, *http://iayt.org*, click on "Find A Yoga Therapist" and enter your town and state in the form provided. Or contact IAYT, 115 South McCormick Street, Suite 3, Prescott, AZ 86303 (928-541-0004); e-mail: *prescott@ iayt.org.*

Warning: "In any posture, avoid what's known as the Valsalva maneuver—holding your breath and bearing down as you would to pass a bowel movement," says Dr. McCall. "Doing so can cause a major spike in blood pressure." For those whose pressure is not well-controlled with medication or other measures, other precautions include avoiding postures that involve backbends, inversions (such as a headstand) and balancing your body on your arms. "If your breath is smooth and even, and you feel at ease, your blood pressure is likely to be stable during yoga practice," he says.

☀ *Yoga as Medicine: The Yogic Prescription for Health and Healing* by Timothy McCall, MD, (Bantam). It provides a complete yoga routine designed for a person with high blood pressure, as well as helpful practices for dealing with stress.

For more information on yoga and heart disease, see page 146 in Chapter 6, "Diabetes and Insulin Resistance."

HEALING WITH FEELING

SHORT FUSE, SHORTER LIFE

There's "state" anger and "trait" anger, say psychologists. One is more deadly than the other.

"State" anger is when you're angry at something in particular—the driver who cuts you off in traffic, the mistaken charge on your credit card bill. In state anger, you get angry and you get over it.

"Trait" anger is when you're angry at everything in general, and you're angry a lot—angry at the alarm clock for waking you up, *again*... angry at your wife for spending so *long* in the bathroom...angry at all those *other* drivers on the road slowing you down on your way to work. In trait anger, you get angry, you stay angry and your anger is more intense.

Trait anger can be a one-way ticket to heart disease.

⫸ *Breakthrough Study*

Researchers at the Medical University of South Carolina analyzed eight years of health data from more than 2,000 men, aged 48 to 67, with prehypertension.

Result: They found that those who scored the highest on a questionnaire measuring trait anger were nearly 1.7 times as likely to develop high blood pressure as those scoring the lowest...and 90% more likely to go on to develop heart disease.

More evidence: Needless to say, this isn't the first study that shows the link between anger and heart disease...

● **Hot under the collar, hot in the bloodstream.** Researchers at Duke University Medical Center studied 313 men (average age, 50) and found that those with the highest levels of anger and hostility also had the highest levels of two biomarkers for inflammation, a risk factor for heart disease.

● **Don't freak out your defibrillator.** Researchers at the Center for Arrhythmia Prevention at Harvard Medical School studied more than 1,000 people with heart disease who had "implantable cardioverter defibrillators" (devices that regulate the rhythm of the heart, preventing infarction-causing arrhythmias). They found that those who became moderately angry *tripled* the risk of having a life-threatening heart rhythm disturbance, while those who became very angry, furious or enraged increased the risk 17-fold.

● **Women aren't exempt.** Researchers at the University of Pittsburgh found that women who scored highest on measurements of hostility were 35% more likely to have heart disease than women who scored lowest.

What happens: "Anger causes perturbations of the heart," explains Paul Pearsall, PhD, a psychoneuroimmunologist and author of *The Heart's Code* (Broadway). "It makes it beat more rapidly, increasing the risk of damage to the inner lining of our arteries. Blood sent spurting by the agitated heart 'shoots' the tiny blood cells called platelets like bullets, so that they scrape and nick artery walls, creating pockets for the deposit of vessel-blocking plaque. Anger increases stress hormones, which cause fat cells in our body to release fat into the blood, causing even more clogging of our arteries. The excess stress hormones from anger also cause the platelets to become more sticky, increasing the risk of a blood clot."

What to do: Exercise may be a good option, says Marty S. Player, MD, who led the study at the Medical University of South Carolina. (For more information on exercise and other ways to overcome hostility and anger, see the "Hostility" section on pages 120 to 123 of Chapter 5, "Depression.")

Here are more tips on anger control from Redford Williams, MD, and Virginia Williams, PhD, authors of *Anger Kills: 17 Strategies for Controlling the Hostility That Can Harm Your Health* (Harper).

• **First, figure out if your anger** is justified. "Consider the objective facts of the situation that stimulated your hostile thought, feeling or action," they say. Is it worth your continued attention? *If not...*

• **Shout—at yourself.** "When you become aware of having a hostile attitude or thought, shout 'at' it to 'Stop!' If you're in the company of others—for example, listening to your surly teenager—you will want to make your 'shout' a silent one, of course. On the other hand, if you're alone, go ahead and shout 'Stop!'—at the top of your lungs, if you wish."

• **Distract yourself.** "Simply getting your mind off the anger can often be effective," they say. "Quickly look around to find something else to capture your attention. When you become annoyed by the wait in the supermarket line, for example, you can leaf through a magazine on sale adjacent to the checkout. Alternatively, just watch the people around you."

• **Listen!** Rather than trying to hear and understand, do you find yourself instead busily concentrating on your own thoughts? "Most hostile people are very self-involved," they say. "You must simply learn to listen. While the other person is talking, look him or her straight in the eyes, lean toward him or her with an intent expression of interest as well as a positive facial expression, and *never* interrupt—*always* wait until the other person is finished speaking before you say a word."

A SAD DAY FOR YOUR HEART

Researchers in Holland analyzed data from 28 different studies and found that depression increased the risk of heart attack by 60%. In fact, they found depression was *the most important risk factor* for developing cardiovascular disease!

What to do: See the extensive section on "depression" on pages 97 to 111 in Chapter 5, "Depression and Other Emotional Downers." You'll find dozens of practical, drug-free ideas for overcoming depression, including the best way to counter depression *after* a heart attack—thereby possibly avoiding a second! (Depression can triple your risk of another attack.)

• **Laugh—at yourself!** "When hostile people engage in humor, it is often negative and attacking—ridicule," say Drs. Williams and Williams. "The hostile person will laugh at the expense of someone else's failure. Try instead to make *your own* foibles or the circumstances that are temporarily overwhelming you the object of your humor. If you find yourself in a compromised position, for example, try making fun of your own sense of self-importance and your own ridiculousness."

RELAX AND RECOVER

Prepare yourself for some stressful news. About stress.

Unrelenting, high levels of stress—a bad marriage, financial worries, chronic illness—can increase the risk of cardiovascular disease by 68%.

Now relax and take a deep breath. Relaxation techniques and deep breathing can deflate heart-harming stress.

IIII➤ *Breakthrough Studies*

Dutch researchers analyzed data from 27 studies on relaxation techniques and heart disease. *They found that people who had suffered a heart attack and then regularly practiced relaxation techniques had...*

• **Fewer episodes of angina;**

• **Fewer arrhythmias, abnormal heartbeats** that can cause a heart attack and

• **Fewer deaths from a second heart attack.**

"Relaxation is an important ingredient of cardiac rehabilitation, in addition to exercise," they say.

And in a recent study from Massachusetts General Hospital Hypertension Program, 100 people with hypertension, aged 55 and older, were taught the "relaxation response" or attended weekly counseling sessions on controlling high blood pressure. After 20 weeks, 32% of those in the relaxation response group had lowered their pressure sufficiently to reduce the dose of one of their medications, compared to 14% in the counseling group.

"The counseling group received an intensive amount of good-health information and reported making fairly dramatic lifestyle changes, but only the relaxation response group was able to significantly reduce their use of antihypertensive medications," says Jeffrey Dusek, PhD, who led the study.

To practice the relaxation response, follow these instructions from Herbert Benson, MD, one of the study researchers and coauthor of *The Relaxation Response* (Harper)...

1. Pick a focus word, short phrase or prayer that is firmly rooted in your belief system.

2. Sit quietly in a comfortable position.

3. Close your eyes.

4. Relax your muscles, progressing from your feet to your calves, thighs, abdomen, shoulders, head and neck.

5. Breathe slowly and naturally, and as you do, say your focus word, sound, phrase or prayer silently to yourself as you exhale.

6. Assume a passive attitude. Don't worry about how well you're doing. When other thoughts come to mind, simply say to yourself, "Oh well," and gently return to your repetition.

7. Continue for 10 to 20 minutes.

8. Do not stand immediately. Continue sitting quietly for a minute or so, allowing other thoughts to return. Then open your eyes and sit for another minute before rising.

9. Practice the technique once or twice daily. Good times to do so are before breakfast and before dinner.

Best: The best relaxation technique for lowering blood pressure may be the one that Dr. Benson first studied in the 1970s: transcendental meditation (TM), and on which he based the Relaxation Response technique. That's the conclusion of a recent study from James W. Anderson, MD, of the University of Kentucky, in *Current Hypertension Review*. Dr. Anderson and his colleagues reviewed 107 studies on stress reduction and high blood pressure and found that TM reduced systolic pressure by an average of 5 points and diastolic by 2.8—more than any other relaxation technique.

"The magnitude of the changes in blood pressure with the transcendental meditation technique are at least as great as the changes found with major changes in diet or exercise that doctors often recommend," says Dr. Anderson. "Yet the transcendental meditation technique does not require a change in lifestyle. Thus, many patients with mild hypertension or prehypertension may be able to avoid the need to take blood pressure medications—all of which have adverse side effects. Individuals

TAKE A DEEP BREATH

"Deep breathing is one of the simplest yet most effective stress management techniques," says Dr. Dean Ornish. "If you practice deep breathing for a few minutes each day, you'll find that events don't upset you as much as before. Also, whenever you do feel upset, anxious or worried, taking a few, slow deep breaths can break the stress cycle." *His instructions...*

1. Exhale completely through your nose.

2. Place your right hand on your chest and your left hand on your abdomen.

3. Then begin by filling your lower lungs with air, which causes the abdominal area to expand. As you do this, your left hand should begin to rise but your right hand will not.

4. After filling your lower lung area, keep inhaling as you allow more air to rise, filling your lower chest, this should cause your right hand to rise. Feel your rib cage expand as you inhale.

5. Keep inhaling and feel the air rising even higher in your chest. As the air reaches the top of your lungs, you will feel your collarbones begin to rise. (At this point, be careful not to draw your abdomen inward.)

6. To exhale, repeat the same process in reverse—that is, from the top to the bottom.

7. First, exhale and allow some air to escape from the top of your chest, and feel your collarbones lowering as you do so.

8. Next, continue exhaling as you feel the upper and then the lower parts of your chest contracting.

9. Finally, allow the remaining air to be expelled from your abdominal area, and your abdominal muscles to contract, thereby pushing out whatever air remains.

10. Since exhaling is the most relaxing phase of breathing, take longer to exhale than inhale. Many teachers advise that a 2:1 ratio is ideal. For many people, this takes some practice. Start slowly and don't force it. If you feel any shortness of breath or gasping, you are pushing too hard.

with more severe forms of hypertension may be able to reduce the number or dosages of their blood pressure medications under the guidance of their doctor."

☀ You can find the nearest certified teacher of TM by visiting the Web site *www.tm.org*, and clicking on "Where to Learn," or calling 888-532-7686; e-mail: *tminfo@tm.org*.

Helpful: You can find complete instructions for several other relaxation and stress-reduction techniques in the book. *For...*

● **Autogenic Training,** see page 111 in Chapter 5, "Depression."

● **Guided Imagery,** see page 393 in Chapter 16, "Stress, Insomnia and Fatigue."

● **Mindfulness-Based Stress Reduction,** see page 38 in Chapter 2, "Arthritis," and page 397 in Chapter 16, "Stress, Insomnia and Fatigue."

● **Body-Scan Technique,** see page 401 in Chapter 16, "Stress, Insomnia and Fatigue."

● **Mantram (or mantra),** see page 402 in Chapter 16, "Stress, Insomnia and Fatigue." Both TM and the Relaxation Response are examples of mantram meditation.

SIESTA THERAPY

Einstein and Edison were apparently enamored of the mid-afternoon nap. Twenty-first-century scientists say those geniuses had the right idea.

IIII➤ *Breakthrough Study*

Researchers in Greece analyzed six years of health data from more than 23,000 people. They found that those who regularly took siestas—napping in the afternoon at least three times a week, for 30 minutes each time—had 37% fewer deaths from heart disease than non-nappers.

What happens: There is considerable evidence that stress increases the risk of heart disease and death from heart disease, and an afternoon siesta may act as a stress-releasing process, says Dimitrios Trichopoulos, MD, PhD, at the Harvard School of Public Health.

What to do: "If you can take a midday nap, do so," says Dr. Trichopoulos.

SOCIALIZE AND SURVIVE

Are you married? Do you live with another person? Have you seen or had telephone contact with a family member today? Are you at home alone for less than two hours every day?

The answers to those questions could indicate whether you're going to live or die.

IIII➤ *Breakthrough Studies*

Researchers in Spain studied 371 people, aged 65 or older with heart failure. Those who had a high rating on their social network—who answered yes to all four of the above questions—had 87% fewer hospital readmissions.

And in a three-year study of 102 women, Swedish researchers found that those who were socially isolated and depressed had *five times* the thickness of new artery-clogging plaque, compared with women who weren't socially isolated or depressed. The results, they say, "suggest a direct psychosocial effect on the atherosclerotic process."

What to do: "Create an inventory to find where your support is, or could be," says cardiologist Bruno Cortis, MD, author of *Heart & Soul: A Psychological and Spiritual Guide to Preventing and Healing Heart Disease* (Villard). *Grab a pencil and quickly jot down the answers to the following questions…*

- **Who would listen to me, no matter what?**
- **Who would lend me money?**
- **Who would come in the middle of the night?**
- **Who notices how my health is?**
- **Who notices how my projects are going?**
- **Whom do I think of calling when I want to have fun?**
- **If I received some wonderful, unexpected news** that had to be kept a secret for a time, whom would I tell?

"If you aren't happy with all your answers, you need to make an effort to expand your social support base," he says. "Start by finding people who like what you like. If you find

GOT A CAT?
YOUR HEART IS PURRING

Okay, cat lovers, you were right all along…

Surprising: Researchers at the University of Minnesota analyzed 10 years of cata…no, *data*…from more than 4,000 people, ages 30 to 75. They found that people who never owned a cat were 40% more likely to die of a heart attack.

But don't despair dog owners. It may not be your dog. *It may be you…*

High stress levels are known to increase the risk of cardiovascular disease, and "maybe cat owners tend not to have high-stress personalities, or they are just that type of people that are not highly affected by anxiety or high-stress situations," says Adnan Qureshi, MD, who led the study.

people through activities you enjoy, these things make them happy, too, so you already have a bond even though you may not have met yet."

But, says Dr. Cortis, don't worry if you don't ever have a long list of friends. "Many people find a few really dependable friends are enough support. To add others, take the initiative. Make the first move to get to know people. You'll find the best way to find a friend is to be one."

SOCIAL SUPPORT THAT BACKFIRES

Sometimes family members and friends think they're providing social support—when they're doing just the opposite!

New finding: Fifty-nine patients in the hospital for heart disease at Weill Medical College of Cornell University told researchers there were five types of social support they found extremely unwelcome...

TIME TO CALL 911

These are the warning signs of a heart attack and a stroke, from the American Heart Association and the American Stroke Association.

HEART ATTACK

• **Chest discomfort.** Most heart attacks involve discomfort in the center of the chest that lasts more than a few minutes, or that goes away and comes back. It can feel like uncomfortable pressure, squeezing, fullness or pain.

• **Discomfort in other areas of the upper body.** Symptoms can include pain or discomfort in one or both arms, the back, neck, jaw or stomach.

• **Shortness of breath** with or without chest discomfort.

• **Other signs** may include breaking out in a cold sweat, nausea or lightheadedness.

For women: "Fatigue, nausea, upper body aches, perspiring and shortness of breath are the *only* symptoms in about 20% of women who have a heart attack," says Marianne J. Legato, MD, of Columbia University. Other warning signs of a heart attack in women can include irregular heartbeat, jaw pain or pain in the upper abdomen or back during physical activity or intense emotion.

Warning: "A person with chest pain typically waits *six hours* before going to the emergency room—often too late to receive treatments that can stop or reverse damage to the heart, brain and other vital organs," says

Maurice A. Ramirez, DO, an emergency room doctor at the Pasco Regional Medical Center in central Florida. Don't make that mistake.

STROKE

• **Sudden numbness or weakness of the face, arm or leg,** especially on one side of the body.

• **Sudden confusion,** trouble speaking or understanding.

• **Sudden trouble seeing** in one or both eyes.

• **Sudden trouble walking,** dizziness, loss of balance or coordination.

• **Sudden, severe headache** with no known cause.

Warning: "Do you want to take a risk that you're *not* having a stroke, and not go to the emergency room—and end up disabled for the rest of your life?" asks Dr. Ramirez. "Absolutely not. If numbness develops suddenly during the day, call 911. If you woke up with numbness—a likely scenario for localized nerve damage—you can drive to the emergency room. And if the weakness or trouble speaking go away, you should still call 911. Even a temporary disconnection between your brain and the rest of your body is cause for concern."

Bottom line: If you don't receive treatment for a stroke within six hours, your odds of future disability are 50%. If you receive treatment within two hours, there is a 70% chance of full recovery.

- **Too many telephone calls.** *"I don't like it when there are too many phone calls. I hate the phone ringing all the time." "They were becoming too demanding. If she called, she expected me to drop what I was doing and talk to her."*

- **Too much expression of emotion.** *"I know she worries because she cares, but she worries too much." "They argue and fight about who is going to take care of me." "They drive me crazy with concern." "I don't want anyone to pity me, cry over me or try to search for encouraging words to say. Just be quiet and support me."*

- **Unsolicited advice or information about health.** *"People talk and give advice when all I want them to do is listen to me." "Don't tell me things that are going to worry me."*

- **Information without means of implementation.** *"I really don't like it if someone tells me all the things I should be doing, but doesn't teach me how to do those things." "They always tell me that I should do this or that, but it's easy for them to say. It's not their body."*

- **Taking over.** *"They treat me like an invalid. I'm an independent person, respect that." "I like to drive, but my son tells me I can't drive because of my condition. He drives me everywhere."*

"Patients described actions of their social network that were *intended* to be supportive but instead were perceived as problematic—because they were in excess of what was needed, they didn't match what was desired or they contributed to negative feelings," says Carla Boutin, MD, who conducted the study.

What to do: "If you're trying to give support, understand that in spite of your best intentions to help, you might be perceived as unhelpful," says Dr. Boutin. "Set realistic goals that balance your need to give and be supportive with the needs of your recipient. Encourage the person receiving the support to let you know if it's not helpful—let the person describe the type, amount and timing of support she or he needs."

10

Immune System & Respiratory Disorders
Beat the Bugs, Breathe Better

Think of them as your own personal army... your biological bodyguards...your cellular cops. It's your *immune system*—and it's *very* intent on protecting you.

There are the B cells, the brains of the bunch, keeping a database of every invader, so the rest of the crew can recognize and respond to bad guys. There are the antibodies, specialized warriors, each trained to take on and defeat a specific enemy—say, this year's flu virus. There are the *macrophages*—Greek for "big eater"—that literally gobble up trespassers. There are the natural killer cells, taking infected cells out of commission. There are the multitalented T cells, which do everything from attacking invaders to restoring order.

And if you took a walk today, or complimented your spouse or drank a glass of tomato juice—those heroes of your immune system probably paused for a microsecond, gave you a round of applause and then vigilantly went back to 24/7 protection.

Yes, simple lifestyle changes can liven up your immune system...

"Taking control of your immune system means being proactive about your health," says Mark Liponis, MD, medical director of Canyon Ranch Health Resorts and coauthor of *UltraPrevention* (Atria). He explains that good food, regular exercise and positive emotions inspire your immune system.

"You can rejuvenate your immune system by taking the right nutritional supplements and herbs and maintaining a healthy lifestyle," adds Robert Rountree, MD, coauthor of *Immunotics* (Perigree Trade)—the name he has given to immune-boosting nutritional and herbal remedies.

For example, just by going for a walk, you rev up your natural killer cells, get T cells working harder and even generate more antibodies if you've just had a flu shot!

Let's start by discovering drug-free ways to help your immune system repel the most common of all attackers—cold and flu viruses.

Colds and Flu

Your head aches...your nose is running... your eyes are watery...your throat is sore...and your constant coughing and sneezing is like the Greek chorus for a 10-day tragedy.

256

Yes, you have another cold. (Most adults get two to four colds a year.) Throw in a high fever, nausea, chills, sweats and overall muscle achiness, and you probably have the flu.

In both cases, a virus has got your number, infecting your respiratory system. And in both cases, the standard advice is to rest, get plenty of fluids and do your best to endure the week or two of mucus-filled misery. For a cold, doctors often recommend you take symptom-easing over-the-counter medicines, such as pain relievers or decongestants. For flu, a physician might prescribe an antiviral, which shortens the suffering by about a day, as long as you start taking them in the first day or two of your symptoms.

That standard advice is sensible. But when it comes to drug-free remedies, the standard is skepticism. For example, a major health organization that helps people with respiratory ills says *none* of the claims for nondrug cold remedies is solidly supported by scientific studies. Is *that* sensible?

No, says Dr. Rountree, "Immunotics can reduce the severity of symptoms and speed recovery from a cold," he says. As for the flu, immunotics "can help your body kick out the virus faster, so you'll have less discomfort."

His number one immunotic for colds is the herb echinacea. Many other scientists agree with him.

58% FEWER COLDS WITH ECHINACEA

"The significance of this finding becomes clear when you consider Americans suffer from one billion colds annually and spend about $1.5 billion annually for doctor's visits and another $2 billion annually on nonprescription cough and cold treatments," says Craig Coleman, PhD, an assistant professor at the School of Pharmacy of the University of Connecticut.

What finding is he talking about? The fact that the herb echinacea *works*.

⫸ *Breakthrough Studies*

Often touted for preventing and treating colds, echinacea is the most popular medicinal herb in the United States—40% of people who use natural products use echinacea. But some research (including a much-publicized study in the prestigious *New England Journal of Medicine*) shows the remedy *doesn't* work to stop, shorten or ease a cold.

To help settle the issue, researchers at the School of Pharmacy of the University of Connecticut analyzed results from 14 rigorous studies on echinacea and colds, involving nearly 3,000 people. *They found...*

• *Fewer colds.* Taking echinacea reduces the risk of catching a cold by 58%.

• *Shorter colds.* Treating a cold with echinacea shortens the length of a cold by an average of 1.4 days.

"The take-home message from our study is that echinacea does indeed have powerful cold prevention and cold treatment benefits," says Dr. Coleman, who led the study.

But why did the *New England Journal of Medicine* study show that echinacea *didn't* work? The study had two problems, says Dr. Coleman. It used the least common form of echinacea (*angustifolia*), not the one most people take (*purpurea*). And the dose was three times lower than recommended.

What to do: There are more than 800 echinacea-containing products on the market, from different species of the plant (*purpurea*, *angustifolia* and *pallida*), containing different plant parts (roots, leaves, flowers, seeds), in different forms (extracts in pills and capsules, liquid tinctures and teas) and in different doses. Is there a way to navigate that herbal maze and find a product likely to work?

Recommended: Use a tincture, says Peter Holyk, MD, director of the Contemporary Health Innovations clinic, in Sebastian, FL.

"The tincture works through local action in the mouth and throat against viruses and bacteria, *and* by stimulating the immune system, increasing the production of immune factors such as white blood cells, lymphocytes and macrophages, which are immune system factors that fight cold and flu viruses," he says.

A brand of tincture that is widely available in health-food supermarkets and health-food stores—and widely endorsed by herbalists for potency and purity—is Herb Pharm. Their echinacea products include Super Echinacea, Echinacea Root and Golden Echinacea.

www.herb-pharm.com. Herb Pharm, PO Box 116, Williams, OR 97544 (800-348-4372); e-mail *info@herb-pharm.com.*

Suggested intake: "Take echinacea preventively when you're more likely to get a cold, such as when you're under stress, or traveling and exposed to more microbes," says Amanda McQuade Crawford, a medical herbalist in private practice in California.

If you're using a tincture preventively, take 1 teaspoon (5 milliliters), twice a day, for 1 to 14 days, she says. (Taking echinacea for long periods of time can actually *weaken* your immune system, say experts.)

If you're using echinacea to shorten a cold and ease symptoms, Crawford says to take ½ teaspoon (2 milliliters) of a tincture every hour, up to 6 teaspoons (30 milliliters) a day, for no more than two days.

Caution: If you have a ragweed allergy, you may also be allergic to echinacea.

C ISN'T FOR COLDS

Do you run marathons? If so, it's likely that supplementing your diet with vitamin C can help you outrun a cold. For the rest of us, vitamin C's cold-preventing powers might be quite pedestrian.

Newest finding: Researchers at the University of Helsinki in Finland and Australian National University analyzed results from 30 studies on vitamin C and colds, involving more than 11,000 people taking at least 200 milligrams (mg) of C a day.

The underwhelming results were 4% less risk of catching a cold and 8% shorter colds.

However: Marathon runners and soldiers on subarctic missions—people under extreme physical stress—had 50% fewer colds if they used daily vitamin C supplements.

Recommendation: "It doesn't make sense to take vitamin C three hundred and sixty-five days a year to lessen the chance of catching a cold," says Harri Hemilä, MD, PhD, who has studied the vitamin for 25 years.

Dr. Hemilä still thinks studies could show vitamin C might help prevent colds in children, and treat pneumonia. "Linus Pauling—the Nobel Prize–winner and author of *Vitamin C and the Common Cold* [Buccaneer Books]—was overly optimistic," says Dr. Hemilä. "But he wasn't completely wrong."

ELDERBERRY EXTRACT FOR FAST FLU RECOVERY

Don't fool with the flu.

Influenza virus is a *killer,* hospitalizing more than 200,000 Americans a year and killing 36,000, many of them over 65.

If you're over 50…if you're an adult with a chronic illness such as heart disease, type 2 diabetes or COPD…if you're living in an assisted-care facility…if you're a health care worker—get a flu shot.

But flu shots aren't perfect.

In 2007 to 2008, for example, the shot was only 44% effective—because two out of the three components of the vaccine didn't match the season's flu viruses. So what do you do when you got the shot but you still get the flu—and its dismal delivery of fever, nausea, chills, sweats, coughing, sore throat and head-to-toe muscle aches? Try the berries of black elder (*Sambucus nigra*).

⫸ *Breakthrough Study*

"Elderberry has been used in folk medicine for centuries to treat influenza, colds and sinusitis," says Zichria Zakay-Rones, MD, in the Department of Virology at the Hebrew University-Hadassah Medical School, in Israel.

To put it to the test, he and his colleagues studied 54 people who had symptoms of influenza for at least 48 hours, dividing them into two groups. One group received a syrup of black elderberry extract; the other got a look-alike, taste-alike placebo.

Result: Ninety percent of the people taking the elderberry extract had nearly total symptom relief after three days, compared with seven days for the placebo group.

For example, on Day 4, on a scale of 1 to 10, with 10 being "no problems," and 1 being "pronounced problems," the people in the two groups had…

Aches/pains: 9.8 elderberry; 0.5 placebo

Frequency of coughing: 8.7 elderberry; 0.6 placebo

Mucous discharge: 9.2 elderberry; 1.0 placebo

Nasal congestion: 9.2 elderberry; 0.6 placebo

Overall: 9.7 elderberry; 0.9 placebo.

"Duration of the flu can be reduced by three to four days with elderberry syrup," says Dr. Zakay-Rones. "It offers an efficient, safe and cost-effective supplement to the present medications for preventing and treating influenza."

How it works: "A flu virus enters a cell by puncturing the cell membrane with tiny spikes of an enzyme designed to destroy the membrane," says Dr. Rountree. "Once inside, the virus uses the cell's own machinery to reproduce itself. Elderberry knocks out the flu virus in two ways. First, it binds to the viral spikes, preventing them from piercing the cell membrane. Second, it inhibits the chemical action of the enzyme designed to weaken the membrane. The end result is that elderberry makes it difficult, if not impossible, for the flu virus to reproduce."

ℹ️ The researchers used the product Sambucol. "Sambucol is the only black elderberry preparation shown effective in clinical studies," says Russell Greenfield, MD, at the University of North Carolina–Chapel Hill School of Medicine. "It has no known side effects or negative interactions." Sambucol is widely available in retail stores and on the Internet.

Suggested intake: One tablespoon, four times a day, with meals, as soon as you have flu symptoms and for the next five days.

☀️ *www.sambucolusa.com.* Call 866-613-5057 or e-mail *feedback@sambucolusa.com.*

THE RHINOVIRUS—NO MATCH FOR HAPPINESS

You have a sunny disposition. Your gloomy friend lives under a dark cloud. But that doesn't have anything to do with who catches a cold and who doesn't. After all, a cold-causing rhinovirus surfing on a sneeze toward your respiratory tract doesn't care whether you're smiling or frowning. Or does it?

⫸ *Breakthrough Study*

Researchers in the Department of Psychology at Carnegie Mellon University studied 193 healthy people (ages 21 to 55). *Using psychological tests, they divided them into two groups…*

- **Those with a "positive emotional style" (PES)**, represented by vigor (lively, full of pep), well-being (happy, cheerful) and calm (at ease), or

- **Those with a "negative emotional style" (NES)**, represented by depression (sad, unhappy), anxiety (on edge, tense) and hostility (angry).

Next, they inoculated both the happy and the unhappy with nasty nasal drops containing a cold virus.

Result: The people with a positive emotional style were *three times less likely* to have the signs and symptoms of a cold than those with a negative style!

"These results indicate that positive emotional style may play a more important role in health than previously thought," says Sheldon Cohen, PhD, who led the study.

More evidence: Older people with PES have better health and fewer symptoms, and fewer strokes…positive people with rheumatoid arthritis or fibromyalgia have less pain…after a heart attack, positive people are less likely to be rehospitalized for heart problems…and positive women undergoing assisted fertilization are more likely to get pregnant.

What happens: In another study, Dr. Cohen and his colleagues infected 234 healthy adults with rhinovirus and then measured various immune components. Those with PES had fewer cold symptoms *and* lower levels of an immune factor (interleukin-6, or IL-6) linked to more severe symptoms. "This analysis supports the hypothesis that PES influences illness expression through its impact on IL-6 production," says Dr. Cohen.

Recommended: "About fifty percent of our happiness comes from our genes," says Kathleen Hall, director of the Stress Institute, in Atlanta, and author of *A Life in Balance: Nourishing the Four Roots of True Happiness* (AMACOM). "But there is still around fifty percent of happiness that is determined by our attitude, behaviors and values. We can learn techniques to be happy." *Her recommendations…*

- **Be grateful.** "Daily gratitude exercises result in higher levels of happiness," says Dr. Hall. Keep a gratitude journal. Take 5 to 10 minutes every evening to write down gifts you received that day, such as moments of natural beauty or gestures of kindness from others. Write, "I am grateful to _____ for _____."

- **Smile.** "Begin the practice of intentionally smiling," says Dr. Hall. "When you put a smile on your face, you release more 'happiness hormones' such as serotonin and endorphins."

- **Play.** "We were meant to play," she says. "Children do it. Animals do it all their lives. From playing golf to playing cards—play is fun and fun is happiness."

- **Laugh.** "Laugh as often as possible, which also releases happiness hormones," she says. "Rent a funny movie, go on-line to a humorous site, or read a joke book."

- **Forgive.** "Happy people know forgiveness sets the soul free," says Dr. Hall. "Decide to let go of judgment and resentment."

In other words, warm up your cold shoulder and don't get a cold.

GINSENG EXTRACT—LESS COLDS FOR SENIORS

If you're over 65, your immune system ain't what it used to be.

Your white blood cells—the germ-killing warriors of the immune system—don't multiply as quickly or get on the march quite as fast. Once on the move, they don't transform as rapidly into the mature cells (macrophages) that literally gobble up the type of viruses that cause colds and flu. And even when those cells do mature, they don't produce the same level of virus-killing compounds. Your immune system isn't retired, but it's not working overtime and maybe not even full time.

Well, you definitely don't want your immune system taking time off when cold and flu season rolls around. Ginseng extract can help immune cells stay on the job.

▐▐▶ Breakthrough Study

Researchers at the University of Alberta in Canada studied 43 people over 65 years old, dividing them into two groups. Every day for four months, starting in September, one group took a supplement containing a patented extract of the root of American ginseng; the other group took a placebo.

Results: In November and December, those taking ginseng extract had 33% fewer colds than the placebo group. And the colds they got were shorter, only 5.6 days, compared to 12.6 days.

Why it works: The researchers tested the supplement COLD-fX, which is processed to contain a high level of polysaccharides, a compound in ginseng root, says Janet E. McElhaney, MD, who led the study. Laboratory tests have shown COLD-fX boosts the production of white blood cells and increases the level of virus-slaying compounds generated by macrophages, such as interleukin and tumor necrosis factor. And when human cells were infected with the flu virus, adding COLD-fX to the mix sparked the production of more virus-killing interferon.

ℹ COLD-fX.

Suggested intake: The study used two capsules a day, containing 200 mg per capsule.

More good news: In other studies testing COLD-fX…279 people aged 18 to 65 took either the supplement or a placebo for four months—those taking the ginseng had 25% fewer colds, symptoms were 31% less severe and colds were 35% shorter…198 flu-vaccinated people living in assisted-care and nursing homes took either COLD-fX or a placebo—nine of those on the placebo got the flu, compared to one on COLD-fX.

☀ COLD-fX is widely available in retail stores. For information call 877-490-3300 or fax 416-226-2224. Visit on-line at *www.coldfxusa.com* or e-mail *info@coldfx.com*.

BOOST YOUR FLU SHOT— WITH EXERCISE

It's one of the unkind paradoxes of the passing years…

As you age, your immune system weakens, and you become easier prey for flu viruses. But the annual flu shot—which works by activating the immune system to produce specific antibodies that fight off the year's crop of viruses—doesn't offer as much protection to an aging immune system.

"A significant number of older adults do not develop a protective antibody level following immunization with influenza vaccine, leaving these individuals potentially vulnerable to infection," says Marian L. Kohut, PhD, an associate professor at Iowa State University.

Is there *anything* you can do to encourage those antibodies?

"In terms of therapies we can employ to boost immunity, there aren't a lot options," says Dr. Kohut. "Most have side effects or aren't practical. But we found that older people who *exercise* have a better response to the influenza vaccine."

IIII➤ Breakthrough Study

Dr. Kohut and her colleagues studied 27 people aged 64 or older, dividing them into two groups. One group exercised regularly at a moderate pace for 25 to 30 minutes, 3 days a week, for 10 months. The other didn't. At the beginning and end of the study, both groups received the flu vaccine.

Result: After the second vaccination, the exercisers produced many more antibodies to the virus than the nonexercisers.

In earlier research, Dr. Kohut and her colleagues studied people 62 or older, categorizing them into three groups. One group exercised

vigorously 3 or more times every week; one group was "moderately active" (exercising fewer than 3 times a week, with less intensity, for shorter periods of time); and one group didn't exercise at all. All three groups were inoculated with the flu vaccine.

Two weeks later, the vigorous exercisers had the most antibodies—and the moderate exercisers had more than the nonexercisers. (Dr. Kohut also found stronger immune responses in people who were more optimistic, had the most social activity, took a daily vitamin and had less perceived stress.)

"The practice of regular, vigorous exercise was associated with enhanced immune response following influenza vaccine," she says, adding that "lifestyle factors" may also influence immune response.

ONE-A-DAY FOR FEWER SICK DAYS

Want to keep working when everybody around you is down with a cold or the flu? Look for a multitasking nutritional supplement.

The study: Researchers from the University of North Carolina School of Medicine and Wake Forest School of Medicine studied 130 people, dividing them into two groups. For one year, one group took a standard daily multivitamin and mineral supplement and the other group took a placebo. During that time, the researchers kept track of their infections and sick days.

• **Thirty percent fewer infections.** Seventy-three percent of the placebo group experienced an infection during the year, mostly colds and flu. Only 43% of the supplement group had an infection.

• **Fewer sick days.** Fifty-seven percent of the placebo group took sick days because of infections, mostly colds. Only 21% of the supplement group took sick days.

What happened: "Correction of micronutrient deficiencies would be the most bio-

logically plausible explanation for our results," say the researchers. "Even mild nutrient deficiencies can impair immune response.

"Multivitamin and mineral supplements are convenient and relatively inexpensive," they add. "The widespread implementation of this preventive measure could ease the burden of suffering in our society."

What to do: Look for a supplement similar to that used in the study, which, say the researchers, "contained amounts of vitamins and minerals very similar to those found in most commercially available multivitamin and mineral supplements." *The dosages...*

Vitamin A, 4,000 IU; beta-carotene, 1,000 IU; B-1 (thiamine), 4.5 mg; B-2 (riboflavin), 3.4 mg; B-3 (niacin), 20 mg; B-6 (pyridoxine), 6 mg; B-12 (cyanocobalamin), 30 mcg; vitamin C (ascorbic acid), 120 mg; vitamin D, 400 IU; vitamin E, 60 IU; vitamin K, 20 mcg; biotin, 0.03 mg; pantothenic acid, 15 mg; folic acid, 400 mcg; calcium, 120 mg; magnesium, 100 mg; manganese, 4 mg; copper, 2 mg; iron, 16 mg; zinc, 22.5 mg; iodine, 150 mcg; selenium, 105 mcg; chromium, 180 mcg.

Dr. Kohut sums up her research on exercise and immunity for those over 60: "Exercise is a very attractive way to partially restore the function of the aging immune system. It is noninvasive. It can be conducted in many different environments, indoors and out. And it has important health benefits for many other chronic diseases, including arthritis, heart disease, stroke, peripheral vascular disease, diabetes, osteoporosis and chronic obstructive pulmonary disease."

What to do: Dr. Kohut recommends a minimum of three exercise sessions per week, 30 minutes each time. How intensely should you exercise? "Intensely enough to work up a sweat," she says. The people in her study did that using a treadmill, an exercise bike (a recumbent bike is often more comfortable for those over 60, she says), a rowing machine, a stair climber, a cross-country skiing machine or NuStep (an exercise machine that works out arms and legs).

SCIENCE SAYS IT'S SO— STAY WARM AND DRY

"There is a widespread and longstanding belief that connects the common cold with exposure to a cold environment, including wet clothes, feet and hair—that the onset of a cold is a direct result of a chill," says Ronald Eccles, BSc, PhD, DSc, director of the Common Cold Centre of Cardiff University in Wales. But is that a cold, hard fact?

▌▌▶ *Breakthrough Study*

To find out, Dr. Eccles and his colleagues studied 180 healthy students—and chilled half of them. The chilled group sat in a 77°F room, took off their shoes and socks and kept their feet in a bowl of 50°F water for 20 minutes.

(If the water temperature started to rise, helpful sadists—no, *assistants*—dumped in some ice.) The other half kept their shoes and socks on, and put their feet in an empty bowl for 20 minutes. (The personal sacrifices made for the sake of science!) Right after the faux and freezing footbaths, and over the next four to five days, both groups recorded any cold symptoms—runny nose, stuffed nose, sore throat, sneezing or cough.

Chilling the feet *didn't* trigger any immediate symptoms. But in the next couple of days, the chilled group had nearly twice as many cold symptoms. And after four days, 29% of the chilled had a cold, compared to only 8% of the nonchilled.

Bottom line: "The results support the belief that exposure to chilling may cause the onset of common cold symptoms," says Dr. Eccles.

Theory: Perhaps chilling triggers constriction of the circulatory system in the upper airways, lowering defenses against an already-present cold virus, he says.

What to do: What your mother told you to do! Put on your sweater! Don't forget your scarf! Don't get your hair wet! Keep your feet dry—or you'll catch your death of cold!

FOR ACUTE SINUSITIS, AVOID ANTIBIOTICS

Every year, 40 million Americans get *acute sinusitis*—a mucus-packed viral, fungal or bacterial inflammation of the sinus cavities around the nose that is the caboose on the train of one out of every 50 colds.

Twenty million people go to the doctor with the problem, and 90% are prescribed antibiotics. In fact, 15 to 20% of *all* outpatient antibiotic prescriptions are for acute sinusitis.

Red flag: Antibiotics don't work for sinusitis, and they can contribute to the increasingly common problem of *antibiotic resistance*—untreatable bacterial infections. (The more antibiotics prescribed—individually and collectively—the more bacteria mutate to resist them.)

||||➤ *Breakthrough Studies*

Two hundred forty people with an acute sinus infection were given one of four treatments for the problem—an antibiotic, a nasal corticosteroid, both or neither. None of the treatments was any better than the other treatments. "Among patients with the typical features of acute bacterial sinusitis, neither an antibiotic nor a topical steroid alone or in combination are effective in altering the symptom severity, the duration or the natural history of the condition," say the researchers in the *Journal of the American Medical Association.*

Researchers in Switzerland analyzed nine studies on acute sinusitis and antibiotics, involving more than 2,500 people. "Antibiotics offer little benefit for patients with acute sinusitis," they conclude in *The Lancet.* "Given the cost, adverse events and bacterial resistance associated with antibiotic use, they are not justified, even if a patient reports symptoms for longer than ten days."

More anti-antibiotic evidence...Finnish researchers reviewed 57 studies involving more than 15,000 people with acute sinusitis. The studies showed that people typically get better after two weeks—whether they take antibiotics or not. "Clinicians need to weigh the small benefits of antibiotic treatment against the potential for adverse effects for both individuals and the general population," say the researchers.

Drug-free relief for chronic sinusitis: If sinusitis becomes chronic—if it lasts longer than four weeks—there *is* something effective you can do, and it doesn't have to involve medications...

New finding: Researchers in England analyzed eight studies that looked at *nasal saline irrigation*—gently and slowly washing out your nasal passages with a saline solution—as a treatment for chronic sinusitis.

"Saline is beneficial in the treatment of the symptoms of chronic sinusitis when used as the sole treatment," they say.

In another study, a team of researchers in the University of Michigan Health System found nasal saline irrigation was far more effective than nasal saline spray in reducing symptoms from chronic sinusitis.

ⓘ Sinus Rinse, from NeilMed. The product is available at most drugstores and many national retail chains.

☀ *www.neilmed.com, www.sinusrinse.com, www.nasalrinse.com.* NeilMed Pharmaceuticals, Inc., 601 Aviation Blvd., Santa Rosa, CA 95403 (877-477-8633, 707-525-3784 or fax 707-525-3785); e-mail *questions@neilmed.com.*

THE AFRICAN HERB FOR ACUTE BRONCHITIS

In the language of the Zulu tribe of Africa, *umckaloabo* means "heavy cough"—and it's also the name for a local species of geranium whose roots are used by tribal healers as a remedy for coughs and upper respiratory tract infections.

It wasn't too long before the rest of the world discovered the herb. A liquid extract of the roots of the plant (*Pelargonium sidoides*) has been available in Germany since the early 1980s as an over-the-counter remedy for acute bronchitis—the viral infection of the bronchial tract, and its symptoms of coughing, chest pain, phlegm, wheezing and breathlessness. And German doctors have tested it to see if it works.

▐▌▌▶ *Breakthrough Study*

German researchers from the University of Freiburg studied 217 people with acute bronchitis, dividing them into two groups. One group got the African herbal remedy and the other group a placebo. After one week, the symptoms of the herbal group had improved 30% more than the placebo group.

In an earlier study, the researchers gave the herb to 205 people with acute bronchitis (or a sudden worsening of chronic bronchitis). After one week, their symptoms had decreased by 55%.

Pelargonium sidoides is an "effective treatment for acute bronchitis in adults," say the researchers, in the journal *Current Medical Research and Opinion.*

Why it works: The herb contains a range of immune-supporting natural compounds that activate virus-eating white blood cells and kill bacteria.

ⓘ Umcka ColdCare, from Nature's Way. This brand includes many products; look for Original Drops.

Suggested intake: Follow the dosage recommendations on the label.

CAN THIS SUPPLEMENT BEAT THE BIRD FLU?

"The avian flu situation in Indonesia is grave, and the risk of mutation into a human pandemic form will worsen if more is not done, the U.N. warned last week..."

"The government in the West Bengal state of India claimed to have wiped out its outbreak, then found new cases. Since the disease was found in crows, it presumably crosses borders easily..."

"In Egypt, newly emerging strains found even in vaccinated flocks suggest that bad vaccine matches are speeding mutations..."

That bad news is, of course, about the bird flu—or, as an expert might say, the H5N1 avian influenza virus. Those same experts are imagining scenarios similar to the 1918–19 flu pandemic but worse—a flu lasting one to three years, killing 180 million people worldwide, and infecting one-third of the US population.

The virus itself is nastier than a vulture. It replicates fast, pumping out uniquely toxic components that quickly cripple the lungs and lead to death in about 50% of cases.

And it's resistant to just about everything modern medicine uses to fight a virus—interferon, corticosteroids, antiviral inhibitors. But even if an antiviral such as *oseltamivir* (Tamiflu) worked on the bird flu—and there's no certainty it will—the predicted stockpile of the drug will only cover 20% of the population. Meanwhile, a vaccine is being...researched.

Is there *anything* you can do to shoo away this threat?

Yes, is the (theoretical) answer of Harvey Lederman, MD, medical director of the Pioneer Valley Family Practice in Northampton, MA, and former associate clinical professor at Yale and Tufts University School of Medicine, and Howard Friel, an expert on emerging viruses and climate change, writing in the journal *Medical Hypotheses.*

There, they present a "carefully designed nutritional supplement formulation that may antagonize the major pathogenic processes of H5N1 in humans. In the absence of vaccine, drug and surgical remedies, this nutritional supplement formula provides a rational and cost-effective approach to H5N1 influence at the individual and organizational level."

Based on scientific research (they cite more than 100 studies in their paper), *they say the*

WHEN TO CALL THE DOCTOR

A cold or flu can turn nasty fast, morphing into pneumonia, says Dr. Rountree. He says to call your doctor if you experience any of these symptoms—shortness of breath, especially at rest; rapid breathing; fever of higher than 102°F; coughing up thick, yellow or green mucus or blood. If you have flulike symptoms with a severe headache and a stiff neck, you may *not* have the flu—you may have viral meningitis, an infection of the brain and spinal cord that is a medical emergency.

or fax 412-494-0155). *www.houseofnutrition.com.* House of Nutrition. Call 800-277-9861 or e-mail *info@houseofnutrition.com.*

www.myvitanet.com. Valuc Nutrition Center/Kowalski Chiropractic, 6540 Riverside Drive, Dublin, OH 43017 (800-807-8080); e-mail *customerservice@myvitanet.com.*

www.betterlife.com. betterlife.com, 2380 North Tustin Avenue, Santa Ana, CA 92705 (800-317-7150, 714-547-1620 or fax 714-464-4153); e-mail *info@betterlife.com.*

vitamins, minerals, herbs and phytochemicals in the supplement (29, all told) could…

● **Stop the virus from replicating**—by affecting the genetic structure (RNA) of the virus, and by boosting the viral-repelling power of human cells

● **Destroy the virus itself**

● **Cool the inflammatory process in the respiratory system**

● **Protect the lungs from virus-related damage**

"Taken preventively and throughout the duration and recovery of an H5N1 infection, the nutritional supplement formula may aid humans infected with HFN1 influenza to survive with a reduced likelihood of major complications," says Dr. Lederman.

This is all *theory*—hypothesis, speculation, conjecture. Nobody with bird flu has taken this supplement. It has never been tested or proven. On the other hand, there aren't many reliable remedies out there.

ⓘ Hi-Vidomin Nutritional Immune Multi, from Douglas Labs.

☀ *www.douglaslabs.com.* Douglas Laboratories, 600 Boyce Road, Pittsburgh, PA 15205 (800-245-4440, 888-368-4522, 412-494-0122

HAY FEVER AND OTHER AIRBORNE ALLERGIES

You have a cold—the stuffed and runny nose, the watery, itchy eyes, the sneezing, the sinus pressure, the fatigue. Only you have it in May. And June. Then July. August too. Come September, your "cold" still hasn't gone away—because what you have isn't a cold. It's *hay fever,* or *allergic rhinitis.*

Forty million Americans—perhaps due to allergy-prone genes, a birthday during pollen season or infancy around secondhand smoke—are snuffling right along with you. Like you, their immune systems are on semipermanent red alert, with snarling immune cells programmed to respond to "allergens" such as particles of pollen, flakes of pet dander, microscopic dust mites and floating mold spores—the everyday stuff of life that other people's immune systems just shrug off. An immune system in overdrive releases inflammatory biochemicals such as histamine that trigger the red, itchy, watery, wearying symptoms of hay fever. (Though it's not caused by hay and you don't have a fever. Talk to Noah Webster about that one.)

Your physician and/or an allergy specialist can help you keep hay fever under control. And drug-free remedies are nothing to sneeze at.

THE SEVEN-HERB SOLUTION FOR HAY FEVER

You thought black pepper made sneezing *worse*, right? Not when it's mixed with herbal extracts of Indian gooseberry, Harda, Bedda Nut tree, Indian walnut, ginger root and Indian long pepper. Then it makes sneezing—and watery eyes and a runny, stuffy nose—better. Much better.

▐▐▌▶ *Breakthrough Study*

Those herbal extracts (all from the medicine chest of *ayurveda*, India's ancient system of natural healing) are the ingredients of an anti-allergy formula developed over a decade and then tested by scientists at the Natural Research Center in Bangalore, India.

The scientists asked 503 people with hay fever to take the formula for 12 weeks. One hundred fifty-one participated in a classic double-blind, randomized, placebo-controlled study (half got the formula and half didn't, and nobody knew who was getting what). The other 374 were in an "open" study, in which everybody knew they were getting the formula.

Result: Nine out of 10 people taking the herbal formula said they had a reduction in their hay fever symptoms—sneezing, runny nose, nasal congestion and itchy, watery eyes. The level of relief ranged from 40% to *complete relief* in about one-third of the participants.

Compared with the placebo group, those taking the herbal formula also had improvements in two measurements of nasal congestion—"mucociliary clearance" (whether mucus is loitering or moving along) and "nasal expiratory flow rate" (how fast you can breathe out of your nose). And in blood tests, those taking the formula had lower levels of *eosinophils*, immune cells that signal an allergic reaction.

The herbal formula is "effective in patients with allergic rhinitis," say the scientists, in the *International Journal of Clinical Pharmacology Research*.

Why it works: Studies show that the formula has several modes of action, explains Debasis Bagchi, PhD, a professor of Pharmacy Sciences at Creighton University Medical Center, in Omaha, NE.

In an allergic reaction, mast cells break-down (degranulate) and release histamine, which triggers symptoms. The formula helps keep mast cells stable. The formula also lowers the production of several other "inflammatory mediators" that contribute to allergic reactions, such as trypsin, hyaluronidase and 5-hydroxytryptamine. And this potent antioxidant neutralizes destructive molecules called free radicals, which can damage the body's respiratory and immune systems.

Important: Another advantage of the formula—the study in India showed it had no significant side effects. "For many people, the side effects of allergy medications, such as nervousness, headache, fatigue and drowsiness, are worse than the symptoms themselves," says Dr. Bagchi. "The formula can be taken before allergy seasons starts—or even all year round, if breathing difficulties are a problem—without debilitating side effects."

ℹ The name of the formula is Aller-7, and it is an ingredient in supplements from various manufacturers, including Aller-7 Plus from Abundance; Aller-7 from GNC; Liquid Aller-7 from HerbaSway Laboratories; Aller-7 and Aller-7 Support from Natural Factors; Aller-7 from Nature's Plus; AllerSense from Preferred Nutrition; Aller-7 and Aller-7 Support from

Reliance and Aller-7 from Swanson Health Products.

Suggested intake: "The recommended adult dosage used in the studies was 660 mg twice daily with meals, for 6 to 12 weeks, and then 330 mg twice daily, thereafter," says Dr. Bagchi.

A NEW AIR FILTER FOR FEWER SYMPTOMS

The very best treatment for allergies? Avoid the allergen!

But how do you avoid *pollen*—when during hay fever season there are 400 particles per square meter of air?

How do you avoid *dust mites* (those creepy microscopic creatures that feast on dead skin) with as many as 1,000 per gram of dust?

How do you avoid *animal dander*—when it's frequently found in places animals have

ARE YOU ALLERGIC TO CHRISTMAS?

Ho-ho-achoo...

New study: Canadian allergist Michael Alexander, MD, at the University of Western Ontario, asked four of his patients to keep close track of their allergy symptoms during Christmas season, comparing them to four Jehovah's Witnesses (who don't celebrate Christmas). He found the Yuletide group had far more symptoms—and that those symptoms started around the time Christmas trees were put up and ended shortly after the trees were tossed. He then investigated a couple of Christmas trees, and found they were naturally garlanded with mold spores—a common allergen.

What to do: Be a bit of a humbug and bring home the *artificial* tree next Christmas.

never been (carried there on the clothes of us cat- and dog-loving humans).

How do you avoid *mold,* with billions of often-odorless spores spread on the wind?

The answer? You *can't.*

But a new study shows that a particular new air filter may work especially well in helping reduce the number of particles penetrating your respiratory tract.

➤ *Breakthrough Study*

Sleep is a tough time for the allergic—the nocturnal nose often clogs, and symptoms tend to be worse at night and early in the morning. You may find yourself feeling drowsy during the day, a problem often made worse by drowsiness-causing allergy medications. If you could only turn your bedroom into an allergen-free oasis, you could improve your ability to cope with allergies.

"Bedrooms are the primary focus of avoidance strategies because of the amount of time spent there," says Richard Morris, MD, of the Allergy and Asthma Care clinic, in Minneapolis. "Air filtration is a logical avoidance approach, but its effectiveness has been limited. The air breathed while sleeping in the bed is locally contaminated with allergens from the bedding before they can reach a filter on the floor. And carpet-bound allergens aren't filtered."

Because of those and other problems with air filters, Dr. Morris and his colleagues at the University of Minnesota created a new type of air filter—one that delivers filtered air to the *head of the bed,* creating "an envelope of air that is 99% free of allergenic particles around the head of the sleeping person."

They tested it out, asking 13 people with seasonal ragweed allergies to put the air filter in their bedrooms—during ragweed season.

Dr. Morris measured allergy symptoms, quality of life and daytime sleepiness in the three weeks before they used the filter, during one week of use, and one week after.

- **Better sleep.** All participants said they slept better.

- **Fewer symptoms.** Seventy-seven percent of the people said they had fewer allergic symptoms, with an average 26% reduction of symptoms in the morning and a 24% reduction in the evening.

- **Less daytime sleepiness.** Daytime drowsiness fell by 29%.

- **Feeling better.** Seventy-five percent said their quality of life improved—they felt better and functioned better during the day.

The results were reported in the journal *Allergy and Asthma Proceedings.*

"This is one of the very few studies analyzing the *clinical* effectiveness of air filtration on allergic disease," says Dr. Morris. "Most studies on air filters document airborne allergen levels, but not clinical improvement. This study showed positive effects, and they persisted at least a week after removal of the filtration unit. And people's sleep was not disturbed by the unit."

Trap: "Many—and perhaps most—allergic patients don't follow their allergist's advice to get rid of their house pets and carpets," says Dr. Morris. "Dust mite avoidance, though routinely recommended, is difficult and moderately expensive. Closing one's windows to avoid pollen means limiting fresh air. For these and other reasons, environmental control is seldom attained."

Solution: "Air filtration for the allergic person's bedroom could be a desirable and unique remedy," he says.

The allergists tested the PureNight air filtration system.

Why it works: The system combines two devices—a supereffective HEPA filtration

unit *under* the bed, and a fan that delivers a *laminar* or streamlined flow of filtered air to a zone around the sleeper's head. Most air-filtration units eliminate about 60% of particulates; PureNight eliminates 99% of particles.

And Dr. Morris says that because hay fever season is a "more intense, acute allergic stimulus" than any other, PureNight "should provide protection regardless of the specific allergy or environment."

www.purenight.com. To order by phone call 800-248-9500; HALO Innovations Inc., 111 Cheshire Lane, Suite 700, Minnetonka, MN 55305 (952-259-1500 or fax 952-278-1000); e-mail *sales@haloinnovations.com.*

HOW TO KILL DUST MITES IN THE WASH

Change the temperature setting on your washing machine from warm to hot and you may do a lot less sneezing.

New finding: Researchers from Yonsei University in Seoul, South Korea, washed cotton sheets using hot or warm settings, measuring the before-and-after level of three allergens—dust mites, dog dander and pollen. *They found...*

- **Hot water (140°F) killed 100% of dust mites,** while warm water (86°F to 104°F) killed only 6%.

- **Hot water removed 90% of dog dander,** warm water 60%.

- **Hot water removed 97% of pollen,** compared to 95% at 104°F and 69% at 86°F.

Also try: If your delicate clothes can't take the heat, the researchers suggest washing clothes on the warm setting, and then rinse *twice* with cold water, at least 3 minutes each time to get rid of allergens.

FOUR DRUG-FREE WAYS TO GET ALLERGY RELIEF

Using antihistamines or steroids to treat allergic symptoms can be hazardous to your health, says Jacqueline A. Krohn, MD, director of the Los Alamos Medical Center, in New Mexico, and coauthor of *The Whole Way to Allergy Relief and Prevention* (Hartley & Marks). "Many antihistamines cause drowsiness, so someone who is already fatigued from allergic reactions becomes more tired. And even though newer antihistamines cause drowsiness in only ten percent of people taking them, they can cause heart arrhythmias if they're taken with the antibiotic erythromycin, or with antifungal drugs such as *ketoconazole* (Nizoral), *fluconazole* (Diflucan) or *itraconazole* (Sporanox). Oral steroids can lead to cataracts, high blood pressure, ulcers, diabetes, edema and suppression of adrenal gland function. Repeated use of inhaled steroids can cause perforation of the nasal septum."

Fortunately, there are safer, natural, drug-free ways to get symptomatic relief.

▶ *Breakthrough Studies*

• **Butterbur—as effective as Allegra.** Researchers in Switzerland asked 330 patients with hay fever to take either an extract of the leaf of the herb butterbur; *fexofenadine* (Telfast, Allegra); or a placebo. Both butterbur and fexofenadine were equally effective in relieving symptoms—less sneezing, nasal congestion, itchy eyes and nose, red eyes and skin irritation. "Butterbur extract should be considered an alternative treatment for intermittent allergic rhinitis," say the researchers. (And they note that butterbur *didn't* cause drowsiness.)

However: The Swiss researchers used an extract of butterbur *leaf* (Tesalin), which is not available in the United States. But a similar study from the Asthma and Allergy Research Group in Scotland compared butterbur *root* (Petadolex) and fexofenadine—and found them both equally effective. The dosage in the study was 50 mg, twice daily.

Warning: Only use Petadolex—other butterbur extracts may contain substances toxic to the liver.

• **MSM—less fatigue.** Researchers at the Center of Integrative Medicine in Graham, WA, asked 50 people with hay fever to take a daily dose of MSM (methylsulfonylmethane), a supplement known to decrease inflammation. They checked on them once a week for the next four weeks. "Respiratory symptoms were reduced significantly" after the first week... "energy levels increased significantly" by the end of the second week and participants felt less and less fatigue through the next two weeks. "MSM supplementation of 2,600 mg a day...may be effective for the reduction of symptoms associated with seasonal allergic rhinitis," say the researchers.

"MSM offers prompt and powerful relief of pollen allergies," agrees Stanley W. Jacob, MD, author of *The Miracle of MSM* (Putnam). "It may be as effective as any antihistamine on the market."

• **Spirulina—reduces cellular inflammation.** Researchers in the Division of Allergy and Clinical Immunology in the School of Medicine at the University of California, Davis, asked people with hay fever to take either a spirulina-based dietary supplement or a placebo for three months. (Spirulina are blue-green algae harvested from commercial ponds and dried into powdered or tablet form. Advocates often promote it as a superfood because of its range and level of nutrients and antioxidants.) Those taking the supplement had lower levels of interleukin-4, an immune factor called a "cytokine," which plays a major role in allergic reactions. This study, say the researchers in the *Journal of Medicinal Food*, "demonstrates the protective effects of spirulina towards allergic rhinitis."

ℹ️ The study used 2,000 mg a day of Earthrise spirulina, which is widely available.

☀️ *www.earthrise.com.* Earthrise Nutritionals, 2151 Michelson Drive, Suite 258, Irvine, CA 92612 (800-949-7473, 949-623-0980 or fax 949-623-0990); e-mail *lina@earthrise.com.*

• **Fish oil—prevents hay fever.** An allergic response is an inflammatory reaction of the immune system—you're suffering those symptoms because your immune cells are spraying friendly fire as they fight off what they perceive to be an invader (pollen, dust, mold). The fatty acids in fish oil (EPA, or eicosapentaenoic acid; DHA, or docosahexaenoic acid) are *anti-inflammatory*. Researchers in Japan found that those with the highest intake of EPA and DHA had a 44% lower risk of having allergic rhinitis. Similarly, German researchers found that those with a high intake of EPA had a 55% lower risk. "Dietary factors might affect the clinical manifestation of hay fever," they say, in the journal *Allergy*.

What to do: For information on how to increase your intake of EPA and DHA, see page 221 in Chapter 9, "Heart Disease and Stroke."

BEATING ALLERGIES BY A NOSE

If you have allergies, many of your problems are with your *nose*, right? So doesn't it make sense to treat your nose?

⫸ *Breakthrough Study*

Researchers at the Nasal Dysfunction Clinic in the School of Medicine at the University of California in San Diego studied 211 people—people with hay fever, aging rhinitis (age-related changes in nasal secretions that cause clogging and postnasal drip), atrophic rhinitis (chronic inflammation of the nose) and postnasal drip.

Twice a day, for three to six weeks, they rinsed out the inside of their noses with a Waterpik and a saline solution, using a nasal adapter. At the beginning and end of the study, the participants filled out a questionnaire rating the intensity of 30 different nasal symptoms.

Result: An average of 23 of those 30 symptoms improved.

PREVENT HAY FEVER—EAT MORE PLANTS (WITH SOY SAUCE)

German researchers analyzed diet and health data for 547 people and found that those with the highest blood levels of carotenoids—compounds like beta-carotene and lycopene that color carrots orange and tomatoes red—were 56% less likely to have hay fever.

"A diet high in fruits and vegetables might have a protective effect on hay fever in adulthood," say the researchers.

Surprising: If you're planning to eat those carrots and tomatoes in a stir-fry, you may want to add some tofu—and a dash of soy sauce.

Japanese researchers at the Fukuoka University School of Medicine analyzed health data from more than 1,000 people and found that those who ate the most soy products—soybeans, tofu, soy sauce and the like—had the lowest risk of allergic rhinitis. Other Japanese scientists studied a nutritional supplement made from soy sauce carbohydrates (*shoyu polysaccharides*, or SPS), and found it reduced sneezing and nasal stuffiness, compared to a placebo.

"Soy sauce would be useful in an anti-allergic therapy utilizing daily foods," they say, in the *International Journal of Molecular Medicine*.

"Nasal irrigation is effective in improving symptoms" in people with sinonasal disease, says Terence M. Davidson, MD, one of the researchers.

More good news: In a study of 10 kids with seasonal allergies, three-times-a-day nasal irrigation improved symptoms and cut the use of antihistamines. "This treatment was tolerable, inexpensive and effective," say the researchers.

What to do: Here are Dr. Davidson's step-by-step instructions for using the Waterpik for nasal irrigation…

1. Purchase or otherwise obtain an *adjustable* Waterpik, the kind that is traditionally used for oral hygiene. Nasal attachments to the Waterpik for nasal irrigation are available. *The three commercially available nasal adapters are…*

    • The Ethicare Nasal Adapter made by Ethicare Products, PO Box 5027, Fort Lauderdale, FL 33310 (800-253-3599); e-mail *mail@ethicareinc.com* or visit on-line at *www. ethicare.com.*

    • The Grossan Nasal Adapter made by Hydro Med Inc., 10200 Sepulveda Blvd., Suite 150, Mission Hills, CA 91345 (800-560-9007) e-mail *customerservice@hydromedonline.com* or visit on-line at *www.hydromedonline.com.*

    • The Anthony Products nasal irrigator from Anthony Products (API), 7740 Records Street, Indianapolis, IN 46226 (800-428-1610); e-mail *api@anthonyproducts.com* or visit on-line at *www.anthonyproducts.com.*

2. Fill the Waterpik bowl to a volume of 500 cc (17 ounces) with warm tap water. Many prefer body temperature water at 97°F; others prefer slightly cooler temperature. Plain water burns, as does hypertonic saline. Normally, one, two or at the most three teaspoons of salt are added to the 500 cc of tap water. Most people do well with a single teaspoon. The pressure adjustor should be turned to the lowest pressure. Lean over the sink holding the Waterpik nasal adapter first to one nostril, then the other. Irrigate each nasal cavity. Sometimes the water runs through the pharynx and out the mouth and sometimes it will run out the opposite nostril. Each nasal chamber is irrigated until clean. Some patients irrigate with 250 cc (8 ounces) on one side and then 250 cc (8 ounces) on the other. Others alternate back and forth using 50–100 cc (1.7 to 3.4 ounces) at a time on each side.

3. Most people benefit from twice-daily irrigations. Many irrigate once a day and a few will irrigate three, four or even more times a day. Dr. Davidson's recommendation is to begin with twice-daily irrigations, then adjust and modify to comfort and benefit.

SHINGLES

You thought you already had chicken pox…well, your chicken pox cleared up, but the virus—*varicella*—never went away. It just moseyed down some nerve fibers beneath the skin and hibernated in nerve cells for a couple of decades. But as you age, the immune cells that vigilantly guard against varicella's return can weaken, losing the spry strength needed to keep the virus in check. And you can become one of the 500,000 Americans a year—most of them over 60—who gets herpes zoster, or *shingles*. In fact, one-third of *all* adults over 60 will get shingles eventually.

Shingles usually announces itself with pain or itching, then shows up a couple of days later as a rash of blisters on one side of your body, wrapping itself in a wide, mid-torso band from spine to breastbone.

Those blisters might itch a little. Or they might hurt like the dickens, with a slight breeze across your skin feeling like a flogging.

In about 20% of cases, after the rash fades (usually in a few weeks) the pain remains—for months or even years, a difficult-to-treat condition called *postherpetic neuralgia*. "It can be quite painful and can result in impairment to a person's quality of life that is comparable to people with congestive heart failure, type 2 diabetes or major depression," says Michael Irwin, MD, a professor at UCLA, who has studied the disease.

A herpes zoster vaccine can help prevent shingles; an antiviral drug can reduce the severity and length of an attack, and lower the risk of postherpetic neuralgia. And there are drug-free approaches that can help prevent the disease and boost the power of the vaccine.

TAI CHI PLUS VACCINE STOPS SHINGLES

Tai chi—a meditative, relaxing, slow-moving martial art from China—may help an older immune system defend itself against shingles.

▌▌▌➡ *Breakthrough Study*

Led by Dr. Irwin, researchers at the University of California in Los Angeles and UC-San Diego studied 112 people (aged 59 to 86; average age, 70), dividing them into two groups.

One group took 40-minute tai chi classes, three times a week. The other group spent those 40 minutes attending educational classes about health.

After four months, both groups received an injection of Varivax, a vaccine to prevent an infection of the varicella-zoster virus (VZV), which causes shingles.

Result: A sign of the effectiveness of the vaccine is "cell-mediated immunity" (CMI)—a measurement of the immune system's specific activation against VZV. At the start of the study, the two groups' CMI were the same. But within 10 weeks of receiving the vaccine, the tai chi group had developed twice the CMI to VZV as the education group—and the same level typically seen in 30- to 40-year-olds who receive the vaccine!

Perhaps even more remarkable, the tai chi group had a level of CMI about 40% higher than typically produced by the vaccine alone. (They also had less pain, more vitality, more mental clarity and better physical functioning than the education group.)

"Dr. Irwin's research team has demonstrated that a centuries-old behavioral intervention, tai chi, resulted in a level of immune response similar to that of a modern biological intervention, the varicella vaccine, and that tai chi boosted the positive effects of the vaccine," says Andrew A. Monjan, PhD, of the government's National Institute of Aging, which funded the study.

Why it works: "There are several ways tai chi may affect immunity and health, including relaxation and exercise, both of which have been shown to strengthen the immune system," says Dr. Irwin.

Good news: "These are also exciting findings because the positive results of the study have implications for other infectious diseases," says Dr. Irwin. "Since older adults often show blunted protective responses to vaccines, this study suggests that tai chi is an approach that might complement and augment the efficacy of other vaccines, such as influenza."

☀ If you want to learn tai chi, look in the Yellow Pages under "Tai Chi" to find a course near you. The best instructor is an experienced one, with many years of teaching the martial art. Tai chi courses are often taught at the local YMCA.

For an instructional DVD, consider the best-selling Tai Chi for Seniors, available on-line at *www.taichiforseniorsvideo.com*. Tai Chi for Seniors, 801 Tupper St. Suite 1111, Santa Rosa, CA 95404 (800-497-4244); e-mail *chigung@mindspring.com*.

FRUITS AND VEGETABLES DO IT AGAIN

If your diet is low in vitamins and minerals, the virus-fighting cells of your immune system are likely to be sluggish—and you may put yourself at greater risk for getting shingles, says Sara L. Thomas, PhD, at the London School of Hygiene and Tropical Medicine. That's especially true for people over 60, who have *immunosenescence*—immune systems that, after a lifetime of fighting viruses, bacteria and other relentless invaders, are showing signs of wear and tear.

IIII➤ *Breakthrough Study*

Dr. Thomas and her colleagues analyzed the diets of 243 people with shingles and 483 people without the disease.

Result: They found that those over 60 who ate one to two servings of fresh and/or frozen vegetables a day had nearly *six times* the risk of getting shingles, compared to those who ate five or more daily servings. People who ate less than one serving of vegetables a day had more than nine times the risk.

People who ate less than one serving of fresh fruit a week were three times more likely to get shingles compared to those who ate three or more servings a week.

And when the researchers analyzed the combined intake of fruits and vegetables, they found that those who ate less than one serving of fresh and/or frozen fruits and vegetables a day had a 3.4 higher risk of shingles than those who ate eight or more servings a day.

NATURAL TREATMENTS FOR POSTHERPETIC NEURALGIA

"Postherpetic neuralgia can cause pain, paralysis and depression, but conventional treatments for this condition are not satisfactory, and there is room for natural treatments," say Eric Yarnell, ND, RH, a naturopathic doctor, and Kathy Abascal, JD, RH, an herbalist, in the journal *Alternative and Complementary Therapies*. Here are their two recommendations. Discuss them with your doctor.

• **Topical capsaicin (cayenne).** "This is the best and most widely studied herbal remedy for the problem," say Drs. Yarnell and Abascal. It may work by overactivating the nerve fibers (C fibers) that cause pain, thereby depleting "substance P," the brain chemical that creates the sensation of pain.

"The cream may itch and burn the first few times you apply it," they say. "Make sure

to wear gloves, or wash your hands thoroughly afterward with soap and water, so you don't transfer the capsaicin to sensitive body parts."

ℹ Capsaicin creams are widely available; for dosage and application, follow the directions on the label.

• **Rose-scented geranium.** This oil was as effective as capsaicin in one study, they say. For application, dilute the oil in mineral oil or another type of oil for skin care (almond oil, soy oil, and so on). Use a 1-to-10 (10%) dilution.

ℹ Rose-scented geranium for topical use is available at *www.100pureessentialoils.com*. 100% Pure Essential Oils and Aromatherapy Products Online, 20 Pine Court, Cromwell, CT 06416 (877-203-9904); e-mail *info@100puressentialoils.com*.

However: The researchers also investigated the relationship between seven individual nutrients and the risk of shingles—vitamin A, B-6, C, E, folic acid, zinc and iron. Low intake of any one of those nutrients *didn't* increase the risk for shingles. In other words, an individual nutrient such as vitamin C did not protect against shingles—it was fruits and vegetables.

"A 'cocktail' of nutrients such as those found in fruits and vegetables may act together, particularly in older individuals, to maintain immune health and prevent zoster," says Dr. Thomas, in the *International Journal of Epidemiology.* "Our findings provide a further reason to eat at least five servings of fruits or vegetables per day."

What to do: Same old adage: Get at least five servings a day. (And eight is even better, as the study shows.) A vegetable serving is ½ cup. A fruit serving is one small or medium-size piece.

CHRONIC OBSTRUCTIVE PULMONARY DISEASE

Which diseases kill the most Americans? You can probably name the top three—heart disease, cancer and stroke. *But can you name number four...?*

It's *chronic obstructive pulmonary disease* (COPD).

COPD kills 120,000 Americans every year —more than accidents, diabetes, Alzheimer's or the flu.

What happens: The airways of the lungs are like an upside-down tree—the trunk is the *windpipe;* the large branches are tubes called *bronchi;* the twigs are *bronchioles.* At the tip of the bronchioles are tiny air sacs called *alveoli,* where cellwide blood vessels shunt oxygen into

the bloodstream and carbon dioxide out. In COPD, airways and air sacs lose their elasticity, like old hoses and balloons...inflamed airway walls thicken, while their cells pump out scads of airway-clogging mucus (sputum)...and the walls of air sacs collapse. (Chronic bronchitis involves the bronchi, while emphysema involves the bronchioles and alveoli; most people with COPD have both.)

The earliest symptoms of COPD might be a chronic cough and sputum. Later, you may find yourself unexpectedly short of breath while carrying groceries, climbing stairs or going for a brisk walk. As the disease advances, respiratory difficulties can turn into disasters. You wheeze, can't take a deep breath and sometimes feel like you can't breathe at all. Walking across the room is a chore. Eventually, your best friend could be an oxygen tank.

"COPD can't be cured," says Robert G. Crystal, MD, chief of the Division of Pulmonary and Critical Care Medicine at the New York-Presbyterian Hospital/Weill Cornell Medical Center. But, he says, there are ways to control symptoms, slow the progress of the disease and enjoy an active, healthier life. Drug-free treatments can help. Starting with exercise.

COPD—MORE EXERCISE IS BETTER

Two top medical organizations—the American College of Chest Physicians, and the American Association of Cardiovascular and Pulmonary Rehabilitation—have issued new exercise and lung rehabilitation guidelines for patients with COPD.

Better: They recommend a training program including aerobics (such as walking) and strength training, conducted under the supervision and guidance of a pulmonary therapist. Engaging in *both* these types of exercises, they say, can reduce and control breathing difficulties, improve quality of life and decrease the use of medical care and the length of hospital stays.

"As COPD advances and people begin to have more lung dysfunction, they tend to exercise *less*," says Dr. Crystal. And that's a big reason why people with COPD also have a higher risk of heart disease and depression, he says. "Exercise can help those problems. It conditions the heart muscle, lowering the risk of heart disease. It helps you feel better about yourself, and therefore less depressed. And it strengthens skeletal muscle—the muscles of your arms and legs and back and torso—allowing you to do more rather than less. Under appropriate guidance, exercise is very good for a person with COPD."

⫸ *Breakthrough Study*

The new exercise recommendations were published in *Chest*, the journal of the American College of Chest Physicians. *They include…*

• **Lower body training.** Walking or riding a stationary bicycle. Both low- and high-intensity training produces benefits. But the higher the intensity, the greater the benefit.

Benefit: Strengthens leg muscles, to help you move about more easily for longer periods.

• **Upper body training.** Strength training exercises for the arm and shoulder muscles.

Benefit: Stronger muscles provide more support to the ribcage and improve breathing. Upper body training also decreases the amount of oxygen required for everyday activities, such as carrying groceries, cooking dinner, making the bed, vacuuming, taking a bath or shower and combing hair.

• **Length of program.** Twelve weeks or more.

Benefit: Programs of six to 12 weeks produce benefits—but only for 12 to 18 months after the program ends. If you want sustained benefits, train longer.

☀ To find an expert in pulmonary rehabilitation near you, contact the American Association of Cardiovascular and Pulmonary Rehabilitation at 608-831-6989, or your local chapter of the American Lung Association. To find your local chapter, call 800-LUNGUSA, or use the "Find Your Local Chapter" function at the association's Web site, *www.lungusa.org.*

TWELVE MILLION HAVE COPD— BUT DON'T KNOW IT

Twenty-four million Americans have COPD— *but half of them don't know it.* Why not?

Trap: Because lungs have so much capacity and strength, or "reserve," the early stages of COPD are symptom-free.

Solution: Spirometry can detect the disease—a medical test using a spirometer, a breathing device that measures lung capacity (the amount of air lungs can hold) and lung strength (exhalation speed after taking a deep breath).

However: A study by researchers at UCLA and the University of Toronto found that only 22% of primary-care physicians used the test—even in patients with symptoms of COPD! Spirometry is underused and primary-care physicians underdiagnose COPD, say the researchers, in the journal *Chest.*

Better: Here's what to do, says Dr. Crystal…

If you are a current or former smoker (the cause of 90% of all cases of COPD)…if you were exposed for years to secondhand smoke or occupational dust and fumes (other common causes of COPD)…if you have the early symptoms of COPD, such as chronic cough or increased sputum production…tell your doctor that you want to know if there is any damage to your lungs, and ask for a spirometry.

COLD CUTS AND COPD

What do French fries, bologna and pie à la mode have in common? They all can increase your risk of COPD.

||||➡ *Breakthrough Studies*

Researchers in the Department of Nutrition at Harvard Medical School analyzed 16 years of diet and health data from more than 70,000 women. Women who ate a "prudent pattern" (with plenty of fish, fruits and vegetables and whole grains) had a 25% lower risk of developing COPD, compared with women eating a "Western" pattern (with plenty of cured and red meats, French fries, refined grains and desserts).

The researchers found similar results when analyzing 12 years of diet and health data from more than 40,000 men. Those eating the prudent pattern had a 50% lower risk of being diagnosed with COPD than those eating the Western pattern.

"It makes sense that people who eat diets with lots of fruits and vegetables—diets high in antioxidant nutrients such as vitamin C—have better lung health," says Dr. Crystal.

What happens: Oxidation, he explains, is what spoils meat and rusts bridges. And since 90% of people with COPD are current or former smokers, it's also what has happened to their lungs—because one puff of a cigarette delivers one hundred trillion oxidants. Antioxidants provide (partial) protection.

Recommendation: "People with COPD should eat a high-antioxidant diet," says Dr. Crystal. You may also want to take a supplement containing vitamins E and C, and the mineral selenium, which Dr. Crystal says are "the most important antioxidant nutrients."

PURSED LIPS HELP COPD

In chronic obstructive pulmonary disease, the key word is obstructive.

"Think of yourself breathing out through a large straw," says Dr. Crystal. "You could

STAY OUT OF THE HOSPITAL— GET MORE MAGNESIUM!

Doctors do their best to keep people with COPD from having "acute exacerbations" of the problem that put them in the hospital. They give vaccinations, hoping that the flu or pneumonia won't latch onto weakened lungs. They give drugs such as anti-inflammatory steroids and fluid-reducing diuretics to stop a case of acute bronchitis. But when doctors at St. Luke's Hospital in Pennsylvania studied 100 people with COPD who were admitted to the hospital for an acute exacerbation, they discovered that over a two-year period only *one factor* predicted whether those folks ended up back in the hospital.

Surprising new risk factor: "The sole predictor of frequent hospital readmission were blood levels of magnesium," says Surya Prakash Bhatt, MD, who led the study. "This is an easily modifiable risk factor," he adds.

What to do: Emphasize high-magnesium foods in your diet. They include nuts (almonds, cashews, Brazil nuts), wheat (whole wheat, wheat germ, wheat bran), other whole grains (millet, rye, brown rice, barley), soy products (soy substitutes such as soy milk or soy hamburgers, tofu), vegetables (avocado, beets, broccoli, cauliflower, carrot, celery, asparagus, green pepper, winter squash), leafy greens and seaweed (collard greens, dandelion greens, dulse, kelp), meat (beef, chicken), bananas, brewer's yeast, cheddar cheese and garlic.

For insurance, however, take a supplement. For maximum absorption, try magnesium citrate, with a daily dose of 300 to 400 mg. Widely available brands offering magnesium citrate supplements with this dosage include NutriCology, NOW Foods, Swanson and Allergy Research.

do it, but it would be harder, because of the obstruction. A person with COPD has to work much *harder* to breathe out, particularly in the latter stages of the disease. Stronger respiratory muscles can help."

And scientists have discovered the best way to strengthen those muscles.

⫸ *Breakthrough Study*

Researchers in the Veterans Administration Greater Los Angeles Health Care System studied 40 people with COPD, asking them to practice one of two techniques to improve breathing—either pursed-lip breathing or "expiratory muscle training" (using a device to increase the strength of exhalation).

The researchers monitored lung strength several ways, including measuring how long it took to become breathless during a six-minute walk, and having the participants fill out a questionnaire about the ease or difficulty of daily functioning (such as washing the dishes, climbing stairs and taking out the garbage).

Result: Only those learning pursed-lip breathing had "sustained improvement" in the time it took them to become breathless during the six-minute walk and in daily functioning.

What to do: Here are instructions on pursed-lip breathing from the American College of Chest Physicians...

Step 1: Relax your neck and shoulder muscles. Inhale slowly through your nose, and count to two in your mind.

Step 2: Pucker your lips as if you are whistling. Exhale slowly and gently through your lips while you count to four or more in your head. Always exhale for longer than you inhale. This allows your lungs to empty more effectively.

Practice this breathing technique until it works well for you, and use it often throughout the day.

ADULT ASTHMA

Have your bronchial tubes attacked you today—the muscles around the airway tightening in spasm, the tubes clogged with phlegm, you wheezing, coughing and short of breath, your chest tight as a knot?

If so, you're one of an estimated 30 million Americans (70% of them adults) who suffer from asthma, a disease in which airways become inflamed, constricted and clogged with mucus, says Richard Firshein, DO, medical director of the Firshein Center for Comprehensive Medicine in New York City, and author of *Reversing Asthma* (Warner).

You can have asthma attacks occasionally or every day...they can be mild, moderate or severe (or even fatal)...and they can be triggered by factors as diverse as the soot from a cloud of diesel engine, the pollen from an oak tree or the protein from a peanut.

Conventional doctors typically treat asthma with one or more prescription medications, says Dr. Firshein. Steroid-containing bronchodilators (also called inhalers) open airways and reduce inflammation. But drugs do not *solve* the problem of asthma, he says.

Danger: Long-term use of steroid inhalers may contribute to serious side effects, including osteoporosis and cataracts.

Better: Yes, work with your doctor to find the asthma drugs that work best to control your symptoms and help you recover and repair after an asthma attack. But also work with your doctor to find drug-free approaches to control the disease, thereby reducing (or even eliminating) the need for asthma medications.

New scientific research points to some of the best drug-free treatments that can help you and your doctor manage the disease.

BREATHE SMARTER, STOP AN ASTHMA ATTACK

"This is a significant endorsement in a major medical journal of a nondrug technique for the management of mild asthma—an endorsement that, if it were being given to a medication, would produce a billion-dollar drug."

Those are the words of Dr. Firshein, an expert in asthma—and the nondrug technique he's talking about is a breathing exercise.

⏸▶ *Breakthrough Study*

Researchers at the University of Sydney in Australia taught 57 asthmatics breathing techniques, which they practiced twice daily for 30 weeks.

Result: The number of times they used inhalers declined by 86%, and the amount of medication inhaled each time decreased by 50%.

"Breathing techniques may be useful in the management of patients with mild asthma symptoms," say the researchers, in the journal *Thorax.*

What to do: "A person with asthma can use breathing exercises to build up the strength of the lungs, and prevent asthma attacks or help stop an attack in progress," says Dr. Firshein.

"There are a number of different breathing techniques, and I have created one—the Firshein Technique—that is an effective combination of the others. It is the one I use myself and teach to my patients."

Dr. Firshein says the most effective technique for strengthening the lungs…

• **Establishes a rhythm of breathing,** coordinating breath with heartbeat;

• **Exhales slightly longer than loose inhales;**

• **Builds "back pressure" in the lungs;** and

• **Uses abdominal breathing,** activating the diaphragm, a muscle necessary for good respiratory control.

How to do the Firshein Technique…

Sit down. Put one hand on your stomach, with the palm open and flat against your stomach; use this hand to monitor that your abdomen is rising and falling as you breathe. Use the thumb of the other hand to feel for the pulse point of the hand on your stomach. Let yourself relax. Next, synchronize your breathing with your heart rate. Breathe in through the nose, with the pulse—inhale 2-3-4-5. Breathe out through the mouth, with the pulse—exhale 2-3-4-5-6-7. Blow out through pursed lips, which builds back pressure. Continue for 10 to 15 minutes, practicing twice a day, or any time you're having an asthma attack.

Caution: If you are in the midst of an overwhelming and serious asthma attack or allergic response, breathing exercises may not be effective, says Dr. Firshein. In almost all other cases, this exercise can help regulate breathing.

TAKE CoQ10—AND TAKE FEWER STEROIDS

The anti-inflammatory corticosteroids in asthma inhalers, such as Aerobid and Pulmicort, are the most commonly used drugs for asthma, with medical sources calling them the cornerstone of treatment for the disease. They may be —but good health is crumbling.

"The side effects of long-term use of steroids keep mounting," says Dr. Firshein. They include high blood pressure, heart disease, osteoporosis, weight gain, weakened immunity, poor wound healing, thinning skin, severe acne, joint pain, cataracts…to name a few.

Is there any way to contain the damage?

279

Yes, say a team of scientists in Slovakia. Take steroids *and* the nutritional supplement coenzyme Q10 (CoQ10).

IIII▶ *Breakthrough Study*

In a study reported in the journal *Allergy*, the researchers found that 56 adult asthmatics (average age, 56) on steroids had blood levels of CoQ10 that were 45% lower than a group of healthy people.

Next, the researchers gave 41 steroid-using asthmatics either a daily dose of CoQ10 or a placebo.

Result: After 16 weeks on the nutrient—with blood levels of CoQ10 rising fourfold—the asthma patients were able to use 74% fewer steroids to control their asthma. In other words,

---

WHY ASHTMA IS SPREADING (IT'S THE MARGARINE)

The rates of asthma are increasing. "There are a number of possible explanations," says Dr. Firshein. The increase in pollution, particularly the lung-penetrating particles from diesel fuel...the increase in allergens, as pollens and grasses of all kinds spread into new areas...and the increase in the dietary intake of inflammation-causing fats, such as the polyunsaturated fats and trans fats in margarine.

New study: Researchers in Germany studied the diets of 105 people newly diagnosed with adult asthma, comparing them to a similar nonasthma group. The surprising finding is that "a high margarine intake increased the risk of onset of asthma in adulthood" by 73%.

What to do: You may want to avoid margarine, of course. Or use a margarine that has no trans fats, is low in inflammatory saturated fats and contains anti-inflammatory omega 3 fatty acids.

🛈 Canola Harvest, with flaxseed oil.

---

for every four puffs of an inhaler they needed previously, they now needed only one.

Needless to say, the researchers recommend supplementation with CoQ10 in patients with asthma.

Why it works: "CoQ10 is a biochemical sparkplug," says Dr. Firshein. "Every second, energy factories called mitochondria are at work inside each of our thirty trillion cells, turning oxygen into pure energy. CoQ10 is instrumental in this process. But not only does CoQ10 assist in fueling the body, it is also a uniquely powerful antioxidant."

Knowing about these unique features of CoQ10, *the Slovakian researchers theorize that an asthma-steroid-CoQ10 connection might work like this...*

1. Asthma is an *inflammatory* disease—a trigger such as soot from diesel fuel enters the asthmatic's hypersensitive bronchi and lungs...the immune system perceives it as an "invader" and rushes to the area...and inflammation is the result.

2. Inflammation begets oxidation—the creation of destructive molecules called "reactive oxygen species," or free radicals, that oxidize cells, an internal process similar to what happens to an apple when it is cut open and browns.

3. Oxidation worsens inflammation, and inflammation produces more oxidation, in a vicious cycle.

4. Steroids are taken to calm the inflammation and break that cycle. And they do, temporarily. But they also damage mitochondria and drain the body of antioxidant CoQ10—increasing oxidation...and inflammation... and the need for more steroids!

5. Supplementing an asthmatic's diet with CoQ10 can interrupt this process—regenerating damaged mitochondria, reducing

oxidation, reducing inflammation and allowing asthmatics to take fewer steroids.

What to do: Talk to your doctor about whether CoQ10 should be included in your regimen. "There is no treatment that works for everyone," cautions Dr. Firshein.

Suggested intake: The study used a daily dosage of 120 mg of coenzyme Q10.

ℹ The researchers used the highly absorbable Q-Gel form of coenzyme Q10, which is available in brands such as Swanson, Country Life and Life Extension.

FISH OIL STOPS EXERCISE-INDUCED ASTHMA

"About twenty percent of all asthma episodes are *exercise-induced,*" says Dr. Firshein. "We don't know precisely why exercise-induced asthma occurs. Our best guess is that during intense exercise, fluid from the lining of the lungs is lost faster than it can be replaced."

But whatever the cause, fish oil might be able to prevent it.

⮕ *Breakthrough Study*

Researchers at Indiana University studied 16 asthmatics with "exercise-induced bronchoconstriction"—asthma attacks triggered by exercise. For three weeks, they gave the asthmatics a daily dose of either fish oil capsules with two types of omega-3 fatty acids—EPA (eicosapentaenoic acid) and DHA (docoheanoic acid). Before, during and after the three weeks, the researchers measured lung function and levels of inflammation.

Result: While on the fish oil, the asthmatics had normal lung function, lower levels of inflammation—and reduced use of steroid-containing brochodilators.

Fish oil supplements could be a "nonpharmacological intervention" for asthmatics, say the researchers, in the journal *Chest.*

Why it works: "Omega-3 fatty acids—found in fatty fish such as salmon, tuna and mackerel, and in fish oil supplements—are a natural anti-inflammatory," says Dr. Firshein.

Important: Omega-3 fatty acids quiet two types of inflammatory reactions in asthma, explains Dr. Firshein, the immediate, or acute reaction of an asthma attack; and a secondary, or late-phase reaction, which occurs hours after the attack and can last for weeks. The late-phase reaction causes the most damage to airways and is responsible for chronic asthma.

What to do: Take a daily omega-3 nutritional supplement, he recommends.

Suggested intake: One to 2 grams of a mixture of DHA and EPA.

ℹ Dr. Firshein recommends Arctic Omega, a pharmaceutical-grade fish oil that is free of contaminants. The product is widely available. Order on-line at *www.arcticomega.com,* call 831-332-5296 or e-mail *sales@arcticomega.com.*

Warning: "Studies have shown that fish oil may actually intensify asthma in the ten percent of asthmatics who are sensitive to aspirin," says Dr. Firshein.

SPRAY CLEANERS—KEEP THEM AWAY FROM *ADULTS*

They're spritzing the windows, spraying the furniture and squirting a misty blast or two of air freshener in the kitchen and bedroom. They're doing it in Spain, England, Holland, Canada, Italy, Sweden, Germany and Greece. And wherever they're doing it—wherever homeowners are using cleaning and freshening sprays—they're getting asthma.

▶ *Breakthrough Study*

The international team of researchers who conducted the European Community Respiratory Survey—one of the largest-ever studies of airway diseases—focused on 3,503 people who said they did the cleaning in their homes and who didn't have asthma at the start of the study.

The reason—it's been proven that maids, janitors and other cleaning workers have a much higher rate of asthma than the rest of the population. And many products used in professional cleaning are the same as those used in

---

TWO MORE DRUG-FREE WAYS TO EASE ASTHMA

Coenzyme Q10 and fish oil are the two anti-asthma supplements featured in this section. But there are two other remedies that recent scientific studies show can help ease symptoms and reduce the need for drugs.

▶ *Breakthrough Study*

• **Butterbur.** "The main concern with inhaled corticosteroid treatment for asthma is the potential for dose-related systemic effects, including adrenal suppression, osteoporosis, growth inhibition, skin bruising, cataracts and ocular hypertension (increased pressure in the eye)," says Ulrich Danesch, PhD, at the University of Heidelberg, in Germany.

Could a natural product help reduce the intake of corticosteroids?

To find out, Dr. Danesch asked 80 people with asthma (64 adults) to take an extract of the herb butterbur for two months—an herb that previous studies have shown is anti-inflammatory, and can loosen and relax the chest-tightening bronchial spasm of asthma.

Result: The number of asthma attacks decreased by 48%. The length of an average attack shortened by a remarkable 91%. And the severity of symptoms—cough, difficulty breathing, chest tightness, difficulty exhaling, wheezing, mucus—lessened by 69%. About half of the people in the study were able to reduce their medication. In all, 95% of the asthmatics said butterbur was either very good or good at treating their asthma—and 90% of their doctors agreed.

"This study suggests that butterbur extract is an effective and well-tolerated therapy for the treatment of asthma," says Dr. Danesch.

ℹ️ The study used the product Petadolex, which has been used in Germany as a medication since 1972, and became available in the US as a dietary supplement in 1997. It is available from many brands, including Swanson, Enzymatic Therapy and Rainbow Light.

Suggested intake: Adults took 50 mg, three times daily.

• **Genistein (soy isoflavone).** Scientists at the Feinberg School of Medicine at Northwestern University in Evanston, IL, analyzed the diets of more than 1,000 people with asthma. They found only *one* nutrient—genistein, an *isoflavone* in soy—matched "airflow obstruction" in asthma—the more genistein a person consumed, the less severe their asthma.

In another study—to explore *why* genistein helps asthma—the same team of researchers gave 13 asthmatics isoflavone supplements for four weeks, and measured the production of inflammation-causing white blood cells called *eosinophils* that are a sign of an asthma attack.

Result: Eosinophil levels dropped by 33%, and asthma symptoms decreased by 16%.

Dietary supplementation with soy isoflavones may influence airway inflammation, says Ravi Kalhan, MD, who led the study, and there is a "potential role for soy isoflavones in the treatment of asthma."

Suggested intake: 100 mg of soy isoflavones, including 29 mg of genistein.

ℹ️ The researchers used NovaSoy, a soy isoflavone ingredient found in more than 125 brands of supplements; look for NovaSoy in the ingredient list on the label.

---

homes. Could cleaning at *home* increase the risk of asthma?

Result: Nine years later, 6% of the home cleaners *did* have asthma. And those who used household cleaning sprays at least once a week were 50% more likely to have developed asthma, compared with people with less use!

The more spraying, the more asthma. Those who used cleaning sprays four to seven days a week more than doubled (211%) their risk of developing the disease; and those who used three or more types of sprays more than one day a week nearly tripled (296%) their risk.

Red flags: Of the 15 types of sprays surveyed, the three that did the dirtiest work on lungs were air-freshening sprays, furniture sprays and glass-cleaning sprays. (Others on the list included stain removers; oven sprays; ironing sprays; sprays for carpets, rugs and curtains and so on.)

The use of nonaerosol cleaning products was *not* associated with asthma. "The application through spraying is likely to facilitate respiratory exposure to these components, explaining why we have observed associations with the use of sprays but not liquid cleaners," says Spanish researcher Jan-Paul Zock, PhD, of the Centre for Research in Environmental Epidemiology.

"Frequent use of household cleaning sprays may be an important risk factor for adult asthma," he adds. How important? "Cleaning products could account for as much as fifteen percent, or one in seven cases of adult asthma."

What to do: "Vapors from common cleaning products can cause throat and lung irritation along with burning of the eyes, nose and throat in healthy adults," says Dr. Firshein. "Most of these cleaners, disinfectants and air fresheners contain chemicals such as ammonia, ethanol or acetone. These toxic chemicals can sensitize lungs, because they are often delivered through aerosolized mists that can be drawn deeply into the lungs, causing serious irritation and damage. There are mild cleaners that are much less toxic."

He recommends the brands Simple Green and Envirocide, which are widely available. "Using these will benefit everyone," he says.

www.simplegreen.com. Simple Green, 15922 Pacific Coast Highway, Huntington Harbor, CA 92649 (800-228-0709 or fax 562-592-3034).

For Envirocide products, visit on-line at *www.labsafety.com.* Lab Safety Supply, Inc., PO Box 1368, Janesville, WI 53547-1368 (800-356-0783 or fax 800-543-9910).

SLEEP APNEA

Twelve million Americans stopped breathing last night—hundreds of times.

They're all alive this morning. But barely. Take Joe, for example. He woke up with a sore throat and a headache—as usual. He feels so tired, he can hardly read the morning paper without drifting off. And the rest of Joe's day isn't much livelier.

Joe has *sleep apnea.*

What happens: In this sleep disorder—which can strike anyone but specializes in men over 65—the muscles at the back of the throat and the top of the airway relax during sleep. (Docs rarely find a cause, though being overweight is often blamed.) As the muscles sag, your airway narrows or shuts. You breathe less or stop breathing altogether for 10 seconds or longer. Your brain jars you awake. You snort, grunt, gasp, cough, *breathe.* And fall back asleep, never remembering your little exile from the Land of Nod. But that brief, breathless interlude happens over and over and over again—for some people, more than once a minute, all night long.

But even though you don't know you're waking up repeatedly, your spouse probably does. Because it's likely that as a significant other, you're also a significant snorer—when people with apnea saw wood, they bring the chainsaw.

But sleep apnea is more tragedy than comedy. Daytime sleepiness can and does cause car accidents, not to mention a general state of listless misery. And those mini-suffocations are a constant nightmare for you heart, doubling or tripling your risk for high blood pressure. Fifty percent of people with apnea end up with

hypertension, itself a prelude to heart disease and stroke; the disorder increases the risk of dying from heart disease by 30%. Memory problems, depression and erectile dysfunction are three other common apnea-caused complaints. Talk about a bad night's sleep!

If your spouse is grousing about your roaring snoring…if you frequently wake up with a headache…if daytime fatigue is your default setting…see your doctor—and decide with your physician if you need to see a sleep specialist, who can conduct overnight tests to determine if you have apnea or not, and recommend an effective treatment. (All too often, apnea remains *un*diagnosed and *un*treated—increasing the risk for all the apnea-related problems mentioned

THE SALT ASSAULT

Scientists have shaken loose many facts about asthma and sodium (salt)—and "the studies to date…have provided support for the hypothesis that increased dietary intake of sodium may increase the severity of the disease in those with asthma," says Timothy Mickleborough, PhD, an assistant professor at Indiana University.

In other words, if you eat a salty diet, your asthma may get worse!

To test that theory, Dr. Mickleborough conducted a study.

The study: He asked 15 asthmatics to go on a low-salt or high-salt diet for two weeks. Lung function after a "challenge" of exercise was measured before and after the two-week period.

Result: While on the low-salt diet, the asthmatics had better lung function—while the lung function of those on the high-salt diet got worse. In a similar one-week study, a low-salt diet improved postexercise lung function by about 20%.

What happens: Animal studies show that high-salt diets boost the production of inflammation-causing white blood cells, causing

abnormally rapid breathing, such as seen in exercise-induced asthma.

Recommendation: "Eating a low-sodium diet may improve lung function in adults with asthma, while eating a lot of sodium seems to have a detrimental effect," says Dr. Mickleborough. "A low-sodium diet should be considered a therapeutic option for adults with asthma."

What to do: Since there's very little salt in natural foods, the key to reducing salt is reducing processed foods, says Richard D. Moore, MD, PhD, author of *The High Blood Pressure Solution* (Healing Arts). His no-no list includes most canned foods, salted nuts, potato chips and most crackers (unless labeled "unsalted" or "no added salt"), processed meats, commercially baked breads (unless they are marked "low salt"), commercially prepared desserts, olives, anchovies, canned sardines, commercially prepared dill pickles, soy sauce, bacon, most cheeses, most peanut butters, canned or bottled tomato juice, creamed cottage cheese, instant pudding and most instant hot cereals.

You should also use a salt substitute for table salt, says Dr. Moore. There are many available, such as Nu-Salt, AlsoSalt, NoSalt and Morton Salt Substitute.

above.) Surgery is one way out, trimming excess tissue from your throat. But drug-free devices offer the best treatments. Surprisingly, one of them is a musical instrument.

DIDGERIDOO— BLOW APNEA AWAY

It's the world's oldest wind instrument and probably the easiest to learn—the didgeridoo, a cross between a log and a tuba, first made from termite-hollowed eucalyptus branches and saplings by the aboriginal peoples of northern Australia, who played the wide-mouth instrument's deep and distinctive drone during ceremonial dances, while clapping boomerangs kept the beat.

But what does a didgeridoo have to do with sleep apnea? Read on, mate.

▐▐▶ *Breakthrough Study*

Sleep apnea ranges from mild to severe, defined by how many times an hour you're bothered by reduced breathing (hypopnea) or suspended breathing (apnea). Five to 14 is mild; 15 to 30 is moderate; more than 30 is severe.

For people with severe sleep apnea, the gold standard of treatment is *continuous positive airway pressure* therapy, or CPAP. (You can read about CPAP on page 286.) But using this device involves sleeping in a cumbersome mask. Hence, CPAP is not for everybody.

"For moderately affected persons who complain about snoring and daytime sleepiness, CPAP may not be suitable, and other effective interventions are needed," say a team of respiratory specialists at the University of Zurich, in the *British Medical Journal.*

Well, one of those researchers is a didgeridoo instructor—and he found that many of his students said they snored less and had less daytime fatigue after taking up the instrument.

(In one person, apnea incidents fell from 17 to two an hour!) Maybe learning and playing the didgeridoo—which involves an unusual technique called "circular breathing"—trains the upper airway muscles in the back of the throat, so that the muscles are less likely to relax at night and block breathing. (Playing the didgeridoo doesn't involve learning any fingering or reading music.)

To test that theory, the researchers, led by Milo Puhan, MD, PhD, recruited 25 people with moderate sleep apnea (most of them men over 50), dividing them into two groups—one group received four once-a-week didgeridoo lessons, and the other was put on a "waiting list" for instruction.

The doo-ers were also asked to practice at home for 20 minutes, five days a week, on a 4½-foot-long, 1½-inch-wide plastic instrument, with a mouthpiece about an inch wide. ("Acrylic didgeridoos are easier for beginners to learn on than conventional wooden didgeridoos," note the researchers. And that must have been the case—they practiced an average of six days a week, for 25 minutes a session, more than they were asked to do.)

Before and after the lessons began, the researchers took measurements that included daytime sleepiness, on a scale of 1 to 24, with 11 and up being excessive; the severity of sleep apnea; and the sleep partner's rating of sleep disturbance, on a scale of 1 to 10 (10 being tantamount to "I'm filing for divorce").

Results: The didgeridoo definitely did it. *After four months, those playing the instrument had...*

• **Fewer hourly episodes.** On average, hourly episodes of breathing cessation and reduction dropped from 22.3 to 11.6. For the nonplaying group, episodes started at 20.3 and fell to 15.4.

• **Less daytime sleepiness.** The rating of didge players went from 11.8 to 7.4, while the non-didge went from 11 to 9.6.

• **Happier partners.** The partners played along—their sleep dissatisfaction fell from an average of 6 to 2. The partners of the non-didge group started at 6 and ended up at 5.

The researchers summed up their results: "Four months of training of the upper airways by didgeridoo playing reduces daytime sleepiness in people with snoring and obstructive sleep apnea syndrome. The reduction of the apnea-hypopnea incidents per night indicated that the collapsibility of the upper airways decreased. In addition, the partners of participants in the didgeridoo group were much less disturbed in their sleep."

And they note that the improvement in daytime sleepiness was in line with what is typically accomplished by the CPAP device.

"Our results may give hope to the many people with moderate obstructive sleep apnea syndrome and snoring, as well as to their partners."

What to do: Visit *www.didgeridoostore. com,* run by the informative, friendly and encouraging folks at the Didgeridoo Store, in Oakhurst, CA. The site includes a wide selection of didgeridoos (including plastic instruments for as little as $28)…advice on how to pick one that's right for you…a range of instructional DVDs, CDs and CD-ROMs to learn the instrument…*and* free instructions on the Web site itself, including sound clips. There, you can learn about how to create the "drone" that characterizes the didgeridoo ("You blow down the tube with loose lips, creating a vibration that echoes down the tube, coming out amplified as a drone"), and the "circular breathing technique" (described by the researchers as "inhaling through the nose while maintaining airflow through the instrument, using the cheeks as bellows").

The concept of "dreamtime" figures prominently in the aboriginal culture. Play the didgeridoo, and you should get a lot more of it!

☀ *www.didgeridoostore.com.* The Didgeridoo Store, 49522 Road 426, Oakhurst, CA 93644 (866-468-3434, 559-642-6434 or fax 559-683-3216); e-mail *didgeridoostore@aol.com.*

HOW TO STAY WITH CPAP— DESPITE THE DISCOMFORT

The gold standard for treating moderate to severe sleep apnea is "continuous positive airway pressure" therapy (CPAP)—a machine the size of a shoebox that generates a constant gentle flow of pressurized air into a flexible tube connected to a strapped-on breathing mask.

If just *reading* that description made you feel uncomfortable, you're hardly alone—many people who start using these devices don't like them and stop using them. Reasons include (among many others) skin irritation, claustrophobia, dry mouth, the noise, the smell, having to maintain and clean the equipment—and the fact that it's not exactly sexy to wear an oxygen mask to bed every night.

The problem is that CPAP *works.* A review of 36 studies involving more than 1,700 people showed the devices decreased daytime sleepiness, lowered blood pressure, cut apnea episodes by eight an hour and improved memory problems. In fact, for people with moderate or severe sleep apnea (15 or more episodes per hour) they work far better than so-called "oral appliances" (mouthpieces that help keep the airway open)—cutting apnea episodes by nearly 20% more. (Oral appliances are a good option for people with mild sleep apnea, with less than 15 episodes per hour. Researchers also emphasize that they're a positive option for people with moderate sleep apnea who decide not to use CPAP.)

Is there a way to make the CPAP experience more pleasant? Well, sleep specialists from the American Academy of Sleep Studies recently completed a five-year evaluation of what works and doesn't work with CPAP, including what helps people with apnea stick with the treatment (what doctors call "adherence"). Led by Peter Gay, MD, of the Mayo Clinic, here's what they're saying, in the journal *Sleep*.

IIII▶ *Breakthrough Studies*

• **Humidify.** Many studies have found that using a room temperature or heated humidifier helps eliminate dry mouth, nose and throat—a major reason why people stop using CPAP.

• **Wear a nasal mask.** You have options for the mask—nose and mouth, or just mouth, or just nose, or nasal prongs rather than a mask. In one standout study, 19 out of 20 people thought a nasal mask was more comfortable than a full-face mask.

Better: In another study, doctors found that a *nasal pillow mask*—providing more comfort for the tube-to-nose connection—was a favorite of many patients. You can find these types of masks, such as the Breeze, at *www.cpapplus.com,* a site for CPAP equipment.

ℹ️ CPAP Supplies Plus/Direct, 10481 164th Place, Orland Park, IL 60467 (877-791-3195 or fax 708-364-0166); e-mail *info@cpapplus.com.*

• **Consider an APAP.** That's short for automatic positive airway pressure—the device only pumps out air when it senses you're having an apnea episode. A study in the journal *Respiration* found CPAP and APAP were equally effective—but 65% of people with sleep apnea preferred the APAP. One possible reason is less flowing air, less mouth dryness.

A DRINK AT LUNCH, SLEEP APNEA AT NIGHT?

Sleep experts know that having a drink around bedtime worsens sleep apnea. Alcohol weakens throat muscles, so that they slouch more easily during sleep, and it blunts your respiratory response to an oxygen shortage. But what about a glass of wine at lunch or a beer after work? Does drinking *earlier* in the day make apnea worse?

New finding: Researchers at the University of Wisconsin studied more than 1,400 people with sleep apnea. They found that any drinking—not just at night—worsened the condition, with every additional drink increasing the risk of more nighttime breath stoppages by 25%.

Recommended: "Persons with sleep apnea might benefit from generally reduced alcohol consumption, and not just avoidance near bedtime," says Paul E. Peppard, PhD, in the *Journal of Clinical Sleep Medicine.*

• **Get good follow-up.** Two of the biggest complaints of people using CPAP are that they can't get the pressure right, and they have trouble using the mask. The solution is to stay in touch with your sleep specialist! That's particularly important in the first few weeks of the therapy, when you'll experience the most difficulties and side effects. Once you're settled in, the doctors from the American Academy of Sleep Medicine recommend once-a-year follow-up.

• **Join a support group.** Researchers at the Buffalo School of Nursing of the State University of New York found that people using a CPAP who joined a support group were better able to accommodate to the device…gained more practical knowledge about how to use it…were more motivated to persist with the device…and felt part of a caring community.

AUTOIMMUNE DISEASES

Sometimes, as they say, you are your own worst enemy. Having an autoimmune disease is one of those times.

What happens: Your immune system works by developing "antibodies" to invaders such as viruses and bacteria—specialized molecules that recognize and destroy the intruders.

TENNIS BALL, 40; APNEA, LOVE

When you're lying on your back (*supine,* in the lingo of sleep science), you're more likely to have apnea—the tongue can flop back… it's easier for throat muscles to sag into the airway…and tonsils are set up for a breath-blocking tumble. That's why some experts recommend *positional therapy* for apnea—techniques to keep you off your back.

There are alarms that sound when you turn onto your back, and cushions specially designed to stop supine sleeping. But, say Israeli researchers, there's nothing wrong with putting a couple of tennis balls into play.

New study: Doctors in the Sleep Disorders Unit at Lowenstein Hospital in Ramana, Israel, asked 50 people with sleep apnea to use the "tennis ball technique," which the American Sleep Apnea Association describes as "putting tennis balls in a tube sock and pinning the sock to the back of a nightshirt." (They don't specify Wilson, Penn or Dunlop.)

Six months later, 38% of the patients were still sleeping with tennis balls…and said their daytime alertness had improved, their quality of sleep was better and their snoring was softer.

"Positional therapy appears to be a valuable form of therapy," say the researchers.

However: Sleep experts say the tennis ball technique works best for younger, thinner people, is unlikely to work if you're overweight and is contraindicated in those with chronic shoulder pain.

In an autoimmune disease, your immune system develops antibodies to…you!

To your pancreas (type 1 diabetes)…your thyroid gland (Grave's disease, Hashimoto's thyroiditis)…your joints (rheumatoid arthritis)…to the myelin sheath around nerves (multiple sclerosis)… to many different parts of the body, including the skin, joints, heart, lungs, blood, kidneys and brain (systemic lupus erythematosus).

What causes this self-destructive process?

Doctors don't know, though factors can include a family history of the illness or having another autoimmune disease. And there's often a triggering incident, such as an infection.

There are more than 80 autoimmune diseases, afflicting 10 million Americans, 75% of them women. Some common autoimmune diseases are covered in other chapters, such as rheumatoid arthritis (Chapter 2); celiac disease, Crohn's disease and ulcerative colitis (Chapter 7); and psoriasis (Chapter 15).

Here you'll find natural approaches that might help ease the course of two other common autoimmune diseases—systemic lupus erythematosus (lupus) and multiple sclerosis (MS).

RELIEVE FATIGUE— WITH EXERCISE

"Fatigue is a major symptom in multiple sclerosis, lupus and rheumatoid arthritis, and can cause a range of physical, psychological and social problems," says Jane Neill, RN, PhD, of Flinders University in Australia.

Studies show that 81% of people with lupus, 70% of people with MS and 57% of people with rheumatoid arthritis suffer from fatigue. "Any measures that can reduce people's fatigue are to be welcomed," says Dr. Neill. Welcome, exercise.

288

IIII▶ *Breakthrough Studies*

Dr. Neill and her colleagues analyzed data from 38 studies on exercise and three autoimmune diseases—lupus, multiple sclerosis and rheumatoid arthritis.

"Our review showed that aerobic exercise can significantly reduce fatigue" in all three conditions, she says.

What to do: The level of aerobic exercise that helped is a minimum of 30 to 60 minutes, three times a week.

And many different types worked—walking, home exercise bikes, swimming, jogging and supervised classes.

Important: Other research has shown that resistance-training (lifting weights) is particularly helpful for people with MS, improving walking speed, strength and overall "functional ability."

Any exercise program has to be suitable for *you,* emphasizes Dr. Neill, taking into account your pain, your day-to-day stress and your general mobility.

She recommends you talk to your healthcare professional, who should determine your level of fatigue, assess your symptoms and help you design an exercise routine.

DHEA FOR LUPUS

Imagine a disease that develops slowly or quickly…strikes any or every part of the body…is mild or severe…flares and goes out again or burns permanently.

That's the inflammatory autoimmune disease *lupus* (systemic lupus erythematosus, or SLE, the most common form of the disease). Approximately 1.5 million Americans have it, most of them women between the ages of 15 and 45.

When the disease is severe, the list of possible symptoms reads like Job's—no, Joan's—diary—mouth sores and skin lesions, fatigue and fever, fingers that turn blue during stress, a butterfly-shaped rash across the cheeks and nose, joint pain and swelling, memory problems and brain fog.

Remarkably, an over-the-counter supplement—DHEA—might help.

IIII▶ *Breakthrough Studies*

DHEA is short for *dehydroepiandrosterone*—a hormone secreted by the adrenal gland that helps regulate the immune system. Although no one knows the cause of lupus, doctors have observed that people with the problem often have low levels of DHEA. Could increasing levels of the hormone help reduce symptoms?

In a study published in the journal *Autoimmunity,* Swedish researchers gave 41 women with SLE either DHEA or a placebo for six months. The study focused on "health-related quality of life"—how good or bad you feel day to day, in terms of your energy, mood, sleep, work, recreation, sex life and physical health.

Those taking the DHEA had improved "mental well-being and sexuality" compared with those taking the placebo, say the researchers.

In another study of 120 women with lupus, doctors in Taiwan focused on *flares*—the sudden worsening of symptoms that is the hallmark of the disease. Those taking DHEA for six months had 16% fewer flares.

And in a study of 20 women with lupus conducted by a psychologist, those taking DHEA had improved memory and learning abilities, compared with those taking a placebo.

Why it works: In another study by Taiwanese researchers, 30 women with lupus who took DHEA had lower levels of *interleukin-10*—an inflammation-causing immune factor

—than women who took a placebo. "This finding may suggest why DHEA could significantly reduce lupus flares," say the researchers, in the *Annals of Rheumatic Diseases.*

Suggested intake: In the two Taiwanese studies, women took 200 mg a day of DHA; in the Swedish study, the dose was 35 to 45 mg a day.

Recommended: An independent review of DHEA products by ConsumerLab.com gave an "Approved" rating to many brands of DHEA, including Doctor's Trust, Natrol, Nature's Bounty, Puritan's Pride, Solaray and Vitamin World.

Warning: DHEA is a powerful hormone with many potential side effects, such as acne and hair loss in women and lowering heart-protecting "good" HDL cholesterol. Take it only with the approval and supervision of your doctor.

DIET AND SUPPLEMENTS FOR MULTIPLE SCLEROSIS

Each nerve cell in the central nervous system of the brain and spine has a branching extension called an *axon* that is insulated by a fatty wrapper called the *myelin sheath.* In multiple sclerosis, the immune system attacks the myelin sheath.

The central nervous system is the switchboard between mind and body. When messages are mangled, symptoms are severe.

You can have mental and emotional problems, such as poor memory and depression. Problems with balance and walking. Double vision and slurred speech. Eventually, as the system shorts out, you can lose total function, including blindness and paralysis.

The condition, which afflicts 300,000 Americans, can be treated with medications, but "benefits are only partial," says Bianca Weinstock-Guttman, MD, at the Baird Multiple Sclerosis Center for MS Treatment and Research, at State University of New York, in Buffalo.

But remember, the myelin sheath is made out of *fat.* And omega-3 fatty acids in fish oil are known anti-inflammatory nutrients. Perhaps supplying people with MS with the healthiest possible combination of fats could improve the disease.

⫸ *Breakthrough Study*

Dr. Weinstock-Guttman and 13 colleagues at SUNY-Buffalo, and another MS center at the Cleveland Clinic, studied the effect of a low-fat diet and two forms of fat supplements on 31 people with the "relapsing-remitting" form of MS—the most common form of the disease in its earliest stages, with symptoms flaring (relapsing) and disappearing (remitting).

For one year, they were divided into two dietary groups...

One group went on the American Heart Association Step 1 diet, with 30% of calories from fat and olive oil supplements (with monounsaturated fatty acids), dubbed the Olive Oil group (OO).

The other group partook of a low-fat diet, with 15% of calories from fat and fish oil supplements (with polyunsaturated omega-3 fatty acids), dubbed the Fish Oil group (FO).

At the beginning, the middle and the end of the study, the scientists measured levels of physical health, mental and emotional health, the impact of fatigue on daily activity, and occurrences of flare-ups.

Result: The FO group had better physical, mental and emotional health.

The OO group had less fatigue.

The FO group had lower levels of *cytokines* and *chemokines*—immune compounds that cause inflammation.

Both groups had a reduction in flare-ups.

Bottom line: "Both fish oil and olive oil might have potential to improve the immune dysfunction in MS patients, although the fish oil effects are more efficient and prompt," says Dr. Weinstock-Guttman. However, she says, the most obvious benefits—in overall health and in immunological parameters—were in people who took fish oil.

Recommended: Eat a diet with no more than 30% of calories from fat and take 3 grams a day of omega-3 fish oil supplements, the level used in the study.

☀ The AHA diet with 30% of calories from fat can be found in *The New American Heart Association Cookbook* (Clarkson Potter).

A diet with 15% of calories from fat is featured in *Everyday Cooking with Dr. Dean Ornish: 150 Easy, Low-Fat, High-Flavor Recipes* (Collins).

To find out more about omega-3 fatty acids and fish oil products, see pages 221–223 in Chapter 9, "Heart Disease and Stroke," which recommends the Nordic Naturals brand of omega-3 fatty acids.

ⓘ Consider the Ultimate Omega-D3 product from Nordic Naturals; taking 3 grams per day (six capsules). See also the effect of vitamin D on multiple sclerosis (below).

PREVENT AND TREAT MS— WITH VITAMIN D

"If you live below the longitude of Atlanta, Georgia, for the first ten years of your life—in other words, in a sunny climate—you have a fifty percent reduced risk of developing multiple sclerosis for the rest of your life," says Michael F. Holick, PhD, MD, director of the Vitamin D, Skin and Bone Research Laboratory at Boston University Medical Center. "But if you live in New York, Boston or Chicago for the first ten years of your life—in other words, in a not-so-sunny climate—you have a hundred percent increased risk of developing MS."

Why is sunshine connected with multiple sclerosis? Because vitamin D (the nutrient created in the skin by the sun) protects you against the disease, perhaps by strengthening your immune system, says Dr. Holick.

But don't give up if you're an adult. A study from researchers at the Harvard School of Public Health shows that getting 400 IU daily of vitamin D from a supplement reduces the risk of MS by 41%, compared with those not getting a supplement.

The newest finding is that vitamin D might even protect you *after* you have multiple sclerosis.

⫸ *Breakthrough Study*

For one year, researchers in Finland studied 23 patients with MS and 23 healthy people, tracking their blood levels of vitamin D and the relapses of disease in those with MS.

Result: *All* of the 21 relapses during the study occurred when the blood levels of vitamin D were at their lowest.

What to do: For a complete discussion of vitamin D, and how to boost blood levels (supplements of 1,000 IU a day are a must, says Dr. Holick), see page 9 in Chapter 1, "Aging and Longevity."

11

MEMORY LOSS & ALZHEIMER'S DISEASE
RETAIN YOUR BRAIN

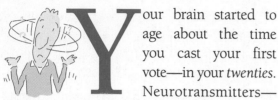

Your brain started to age about the time you cast your first vote—in your *twenties*. Neurotransmitters— chemicals that relay messages between brain cells, so you can think, concentrate and remember—are less efficient. Brain cells start to die off; in fact, your entire brain starts to *shrink*. And for someone on the sad path to Alzheimer's, the weedy tangles and dense plaques of abnormal proteins that eventually choke off brain function begin to grow—in some cases, before the age of 30.

Those brain changes weaken memory, eventually eroding your ability to learn a new language, recall names or remember where you put your keys. Nearly half of people 50 or older complain of mild, age-related memory problems...one in three over 70 suffers from impaired memory...and one in seven over 70—nearly 4 million people—has dementia. That's the bad news.

Good news: Studies show that approximately 65% of aging—including memory-erasing aging of the brain—is not caused by genes but by *lifestyle*, says Gary Small, MD, director of the UCLA Center on Aging and the Semel Institute Memory Research Center and

coauthor of *The Memory Prescription* (Hyperion). "That means it's never too late—or too early— to take action to prevent or restore memory loss," he says.

Dr. Small's breakthrough research shows that the best ways to keep your brain healthy and your memory sharp are nourishing foods, regular exercise, brain-sharpening mental activity and stress reduction.

THE FOUR BEST WAYS TO IMPROVE MEMORY

"There are four key ways to slow, stop or possibly reverse the brain aging that can cause memory loss," says Dr. Small. "They are mental activity, a healthy diet, stress reduction and physical conditioning." And he has the scientific evidence to prove it.

▷ *Breakthrough Study*

Led by Dr. Small, scientists at the UCLA Center on Aging studied 17 people (average age, 53) with age-related memory impairment. Eight went on a 14-day program consisting of memory training, a brain-healthy diet, regular aerobic exercise and stress reduction techniques. The other nine were to maintain their current habits. Before and after the program, all 17 people were tested for memory and mental ability, and had brain scans.

Result: After 14 days, those on the program had an average 20% improvement in mental abilities, including memory. Their brain scans showed a 5% greater efficiency in an area that controls memory.

"Using this protocol, we literally rewired one of the memory centers in the brain in just two weeks," says Dr. Small. They published the results in the *American Journal of Geriatric Psychiatry.*

What to do: Dr. Small offers these suggestions for putting into practice the essence of his 14-day program…

• **Memory training.** Memory involves two basic functions, he says—*learning* (getting information into your memory stores) and *recall* (pulling it out).

"My favorite strategy to improve memory involves three skills that are the foundation of any effective memory-training program." He calls those skills, *"LOOK, SNAP, CONNECT"*…

• **LOOK—Actively observe what you want to remember.** "The single biggest reason people don't remember is that they don't pay attention," he says. "By making a conscious decision to absorb information—by looking or listening carefully, and even by feeling, tasting and smelling carefully—you can fix information in your memory stores."

THE THREE STAGES OF MEMORY LOSS

Memory loss is a gradual process that memory experts have partitioned into three stages…

• **Age-related memory impairment.** You feel like your memory isn't what it used to be, and standard memory tests show you're right—compared to the average 20-year-old, your memory is impaired. But compared to the average 65-year-old (if you're 65), your memory is normal. "About forty percent of people aged sixty-five or older—sixteen million Americans—have age-related memory impairment. Only about one percent of them will progress to dementia each year," says Dr. Small.

• **Mild cognitive impairment.** You begin to forget things you usually remember, like a dentist's appointment. Your nearest and dearest also notice your memory worsening. A memory test shows that, compared to people your age, your memory is below par. "About ten percent of people sixty-five years or older have mild cognitive impairment, and nearly fifteen percent of them develop Alzheimer's each year," says Dr. Small.

• **Dementia.** Your memory loss is severe and debilitating. From finding the right word to finding your way home, you can't remember. Eventually, you can't remember your own name. Alzheimer's is the most common cause of dementia, disorienting 1 in 10 Americans over 65, 1 in 7 over 70 and 1 in 2 over 85. Reduced blood flow to the brain—usually after a stroke—is another cause; called *vascular dementia*, it affects nearly 20% of those with dementia.

New thinking: Dr. Small and his colleagues at UCLA conducted sophisticated brain scans of people with mild cognitive impairment—and found the same plaques and tangles of abnormal protein found in people with Alzheimer's; their results were published in the *New England Journal of Medicine.* "It looks like these abnormal proteins build up over a lifetime," says Dr. Small. "Alzheimer's disease may be the end result of the aging of the brain—which means that lifestyle choices that slow aging can help prevent or slow memory loss, too."

Important: If you think you're developing memory problems, see your physician, says Dr. Small. He can conduct standard memory tests… diagnose your level of memory loss, if any…determine if there is an underlying cause for memory problems, such as a deficiency of vitamin B-12… and recommend possible treatments.

For example, if you drive to a new location by following directions—a process requiring your full attention—you'll probably remember how to get there on your own, days or even weeks later. But if you were a passenger on that trip—and not paying close attention to every turn and landmark—you're likely to get lost the first time you try to find the location on your own.

LOOK exercise: Look around the room and notice a piece of furniture or any other object. Stare at it and observe as many details as possible. Then close your eyes and think about those details. Now do this exercise for a second item. Afterward, jot down the names of the two objects you studied. Tomorrow, look at your notes, close your eyes and try to recall as many details as possible.

● **SNAP—Create mental snapshots of memories.** Can you remember the details of the objects you observed in the LOOK exercise? "As you try to recall the information, you're probably attempting to re-create the image in your mind's eye," says Dr. Small. This is SNAP—creating a mental snapshot of information you want to remember.

"Transforming information into mental images is one of the most effective ways to fix them into your long-term memory storage," he says.

"Bright, colorfully enhanced SNAPS stick best in the memory, as do those with three dimensions, movement and detail. Distorting or exaggerating one or more aspects of your SNAP can also make it easier to learn and recall later," says Dr. Small. "If I park my car on level 3B of a parking garage, and want to remember where I parked, I might visualize three giant bumblebees hovering over my car."

SNAP exercise: Visualize each of the following words, but alter them slightly so they become unusual in some way. (For example, for

the word "fork," imagine a fork dancing on its tines.) Football. Rock star. Orange.

● **CONNECT—Link the mental snapshots together.** "Developing ways to connect mental SNAPs together is a basic element of nearly all memory techniques," says Dr. Small.

In CONNECT, you associate two or more SNAPS so you can remember the connection—a skill, he says, that "will help you remember birthdates and names, and allow you to never again forget the name connected to a face."

There are several ways to CONNECT, says Dr. Small. Place one image on top of the other...make one image rotate or dance around the other...have one image crash into or penetrate the other...merge or melt the images together...wrap one image around the other.

For example, in remembering the name *Weinberger*, you might connect SNAPs of a bottle of wine falling on a burger, he says.

"To connect the name to the face, LOOK at the person's face and search for a distinguishing feature, whether it is a pug nose, prominent chin, puffy hair or large ears—and link it to the name," says Dr. Small.

"For example, if Mrs. Beatty has full lips, focus on her mouth to create a memorable face SNAP. Her name SNAP is easy—if you are a movie buff, you'll see the actor/director Warren Beatty. Connect the two snaps in your mind's eye with the image of Warren Beatty kissing her lips."

CONNECT exercise: Create a single visual image to link the following groups of three words—shack, slinky, flower.

"Learn these techniques and see how you can apply them to everyday memory tasks, such as remembering names and faces, and remembering your to-do list," says Dr. Small. "You'll quickly see benefits in your life."

● **Brain-healthy diet.** Fast-digesting carbohydrates such as sugar and white flour cause spikes in blood sugar levels, which can lead to type 2 diabetes—a disease that cuts down on circulation to the brain. *The key to a brain-healthy diet is to control blood sugar levels throughout the day, by...*

• Emphasizing healthy, slow-digesting carbohydrates. That includes most whole grains, beans and legumes and fresh fruits and vegetables.

• Eating smaller portions. "Don't eat one or two big meals," he says. "Eat five or six times a day—three meals and in-between-meal snacks. And don't overdo it on calories."

• Snacking on carbohydrate-protein combos. "Eat fresh fruit and cottage cheese, or almonds and raisins," he says.

There are two categories of nutrients that are particularly nourishing for the brain, says Dr. Small...

• **Omega-3 fatty acids.** The membranes of brain cells are made out of fat. Getting enough omega-3 fatty acids—eating two servings a week of fatty fish such as salmon, mackerel, herring, albacore tuna; and including walnuts, flaxseeds, canola and their oils in your diet—helps keep brain cell membranes soft and flexible. On the other hand, minimize omega-6 fatty acids, found in vegetable oils, margarine, mayonnaise, most processed foods and fried foods. They can contribute to chronic brain inflammation.

• **Antioxidants.** Oxidative stress—internal rust from everyday cellular wear and tear—can accelerate brain aging, says Dr. Small. Antioxidants can stop the process.

"Fruits and vegetables are high in antioxidants," he says. Among the fruits richest in antioxidants include berries, cherries, kiwi, oranges, plums, prunes, raisins and red grapes. Among the vegetables are avocados, beets, Brussels sprouts, broccoli, corn, eggplant, onions, red bell peppers and spinach.

"Include them in your diet as often as possible," he advises.

• **Aerobic exercise.** "Exercise increases blood flow to the brain and helps control overweight, a risk factor for Alzheimer's," says Dr. Small.

• Walk. "I recommend taking a daily, brisk walk with a friend, which will also reduce stress, as you talk about the day, and improve social relationships, which studies show is also good for the brain."

• **Stress reduction techniques.** "Chronic mental stress triggers the release of stress hormones that cause wear and tear on the brain," says Dr. Small.

He recommends practicing a relaxation technique daily to reduce stress. "The other way to decrease stress is to become more realistic about what you can and can't take on," he says. "Many people commit to too much. Delegate some responsibilities."

• **Tighten and Release Muscle Unwinder.** *Here are Dr. Small's how-to instructions for an easy, effective, stress-relieving relaxation technique...*

"Lie down or sit in a comfortable chair. While the rest of your body remains comfortable and relaxed, slowly clench your right fist as tightly as you can. Focus on the tension in your fist, hand and forearm. After five seconds, relax your hand and let your fingers and wrist go limp. Notice the contrast between the sensation of tension and relaxation in those muscles, and hold that tension for five seconds. Then let your arm straighten and drop gently to your side. Feel the sensation of your muscles relaxing. Repeat the exercise for your left side. Continue this sequence of tensing and releasing different muscles groups throughout your body, including shoulders, abdomen, buttocks, thighs and legs."

Books by Dr. Small include *The Memory Prescription* (Hyperion), *The Memory Bible* (Hyperion) and *The Longevity Bible* (Hyperion).

He has helped develop a handheld brain-exerciser for better memory, called *Brain Games,* from Mattel.

Based on his 14-day study, Dr. Small developed a one-day program for memory improvement, called the One-Day Brain Boot Camp. To find out more about it, contact the UCLA Memory & Aging Center, at 310-825-0545 or visit on-line at *www.npi.ucla.edu/memory/.*

A NEUROPEPTIDE FOR A PEPPIER MEMORY

First, a peptide primer...

A *peptide* is a chain of amino acids, the building blocks of protein.

A *neuropeptide* is a peptide in your brain.

There are hundreds of different neuropeptides, and some launch a biochemical cascade that produces specific emotions and behaviors—such as *oxytocin*, a peptide of nine amino acids that is released in large quantities during labor and breastfeeding, prompting maternal-infant bonding.

Another neuropeptide is *cerebrolysin*, approved in more than 30 countries for use as an intravenous medication to treat Alzheimer's disease. The theory is it activates a gene that allows more neuron-nourishing glucose into the brain and/or triggers brain cells to sprout more signal-sending dendrites.

N-PEP-12 is a compound derived from cerebrolysin.

It is far less potent, but you can take it in pill form.

And it can improve memory.

In fact, says Thomas Crook, PhD, former head of geriatric psychopharmacology at the National Institutes for Mental Health and author of *The Memory Advantage* (Select Books)—the improvement is equivalent to reversing 11 to 12 years of mental aging!

▶ *Breakthrough Study*

Dr. Crook and his colleagues studied 54 people (average age, 68), with age-related memory impairment. They were asked to take N-PEP-12 or a placebo for 30 days. At the beginning and end of the study, the participants took several tests measuring mental function, including a standard memory test.

Result: The memory of those taking N-PEP-12 improved by 15%, and was 27% better than the placebo group.

Now, that might not sound like a big difference. But, says Dr. Crook, that level of memory boosting was as if the folks taking N-PEP-12 had gone back in time by more than a decade—the 68-year-olds were remembering as if they were 56 again.

And he points out that those taking N-PEP-12 not only improved on memory tests—they *said* their memory had improved.

"That kind of 'subjective' improvement is almost unheard of in one-month memory studies," says Dr. Crook. Usually, the participants don't notice an actual improvement in memory—even when their scores on memory tests have improved.

Dr. Crook also notes that the level of memory improvement seen after one month (1.6 on the standard "ADAS-cog" memory test) is similar to that required by the FDA for approval of drugs to treat Alzheimer's (a minimum of 2.0)—even though Alzheimer's studies last a minimum of six months. "An effect size of one point six on the ADAS-cog memory Score alone, after one month of treatment, compares very favorably with the effect size of drugs currently approved to treat Alzheimer's disease," he says.

In another study on N-PEP-12, Dr. Crook and his colleagues gave a single dose of the neuropeptide to six people (average age, 63) and measured their memory skills right before they took the supplement and six hours later. There was a significant improvement in memory—and an increase in electrical activity in brain areas associated with memory.

ℹ️ N-PEP-12 is available in the supplement MemoProve.

Suggested intake: "Follow the dosage recommendation on the label," says Dr. Crook. More is not better, he cautions.

☀️ *www.memoprove.com.* MemoMind Pharma, 225 Main Street, Suite 305, Westport, CT 06883; e-mail *joe@memomind.net.*

MEDITERRANEAN DIET PREVENTS ALZHEIMER'S

It might help protect you against heart disease, cancer, diabetes, Parkinson's disease and even (if you're pregnant) premature delivery.

It's the Mediterranean diet—a culinary combination featuring fruits and vegetables, fish (rather than red meat), whole grains and beans, more fat from monounsaturated olive oil and less from polyunsaturated safflower, corn and sunflower oils and moderate alcohol intake, with a nod toward red wine.

And a recent study shows it's also good for your brain.

▐▐▐▶ *Breakthrough Study*

Scientists at the Taub Institute for Research on Alzheimer's Disease and the Aging Brain studied the health and diet of more than 2,000 people over the age of 65, for 4 to 12 years, asking each study participant to rate their "adherence" to the Mediterranean diet. During the study, 262 participants developed Alzheimer's disease.

Result: Those who ate a Mediterranean-type diet were 40% less likely to develop

SLOW MEMORY LOSS BY 85%— HAVE A GLASS OF WINE!

Every year, 15% of people with the advanced type of memory loss known as "mild cognitive impairment" fade into Alzheimer's. Now, wine-loving Italian scientists may have found a way to slow down that process—just remember to drink a glass of vino every day!

New finding: Researchers at the Center for Aging Brain at the University of Bari in Italy studied 121 people with mild cognitive impairment (aged 65 to 84) for three-and-a-half years. Those who had one drink a day (mostly wine) developed Alzheimer's at an 85% slower rate than those who didn't drink. (More than one drink a day didn't slow the rate further.)

What happens: "Alcohol consumption may protect against dementia by improving the health of the blood vessels in the brain," says Vincenzo Solfrizzi, MD, PhD, one of the researchers who conducted the study.

What to do: "The most beneficial way to drink wine for health is in the classic French style—one 4- to 5-ounce glass of wine per meal," says Roger Corder, PhD, MRPharmS, professor of experimental therapeutics at the William Harvey Research Institute and author of *The Red Wine Diet* (Avery).

Dr. Corder thinks that red wine is your best bet for lifelong health. Other scientists agree. Experts at the Litwin-Zucker Research Center for the Study of Alzheimer's Disease and Memory Disorders, in New York, say that studies show moderate consumption of red wine lowers the risk of Alzheimer's disease. And in a recent study, they found that *resveratrol*—an antioxidant found mainly in red wine and grapes—destroys amyloid-beta, the toxic protein found in the brains of people with Alzheimer's.

Alzheimer's compared with those who didn't. Those in the middle range of adherence were 15% less likely to develop the disease.

How it works: "The Mediterranean diet might help prevent Alzheimer's by improving the health of blood vessels in the brain, reducing inflammation or providing a high level of brain-protecting antioxidants," says Nikolaos Scarmeas, MD, who led the study.

And, yes, Dr. Scarmeas eats the Mediterranean diet himself. "It's very easy for me, because I'm Greek and have eaten this way since I was born," he says.

"But it's easy for anyone to follow this diet, because it's very tasty and it's not low-fat."

☀ *The Mediterranean Diet* by Marissa Cloutier, MS, RD (Harper); *The Mediterranean Prescription: Meal Plans and Recipes to Help You Stay Slim and Healthy for the Rest of Your Life* by Angelo Acquista, MD (Ballantine); *My New Mediterranean Diet Cookbook* by Jeannette Seaver, (Arcade Publishing).

WANT TO REMEMBER NEW INFO? TAKE A NAP

There are two types of long-term memory (the memories that never disappear or only vanish after many years)—memories of "what" (what you read yesterday, what happened yesterday) and memories of "how" (how to drive, how to play the piano).

A nap can help "how" memories take up permanent residence in your brain. (Good news if you're taking golf lessons, learning an instrument, memorizing the steps of a new dance, learning tai chi.)

||►*Breakthrough Studies*

Researchers at the University of Haifa in Israel and the University of Montreal in Canada taught a group of people a new hand movement—a specific sequence of repeatedly touching the thumb to other fingers. After learning the movement in the morning, some people napped in the afternoon and some stayed awake. That evening, the researchers tested to see whether the nappers or the non-nappers remembered the movement better.

The nappers performed the movement faster and more accurately.

"A daytime nap speeds up the consolidation of 'how' memory in the brain, improving performance," says Avi Karni, MD, a professor at the Center for Brain and Behavior Research at the University of Haifa.

In a second experiment, the researchers wanted to see if a nap might help solve a common memory problem. You learn a how-to task, then you learn another one soon afterward—and completely forget how to do the first!

The researchers taught several groups of people a sequence of thumb-to-finger moves—and then taught them a second sequence two hours later. Of the four groups, only those that napped shortly after learning the first sequence remembered it. "This part of the study demonstrated, for the first time, that a nap can help how-to memory become immune to interference and forgetting," says Dr. Karni, who led the study.

Researchers at the Laboratory of Cognitive Neuroscience and Sleep at the City University of New York conducted a similar experiment with "what" memory.

At 11:30 a.m., they had 33 people memorize unrelated pairs of words; at 1:00 p.m., some napped and some stayed awake; at 4:00 p.m., they conducted a test to see who remembered the most words. Those who did the best job memorizing the words during the initial training session *and* took a nap remembered the most word pairs. A daytime nap benefits memory performance, say the researchers.

What to do: When you've just learned something and want to recall it later, head for the couch, the recliner or the bed—and take a memory-enhancing nap!

GOOD FATS, GOOD THINKING

It's smart to be a fathead—as long as it's the right kind of fat.

⫸ *Breakthrough Studies*

Study after scientific study shows that omega-3 fatty acids—the DHA (*docosahexaenoic acid*) and EPA (*eicosapentaenoic acid*) found in fatty fish such as salmon, albacore tuna, mackerel and herring and the ALA (*alpha-linolenic acid*) found in plant foods such as walnuts, flaxseed and canola—nourish the brain.

On the other hand (or lobe), many studies show that a diet rich in omega-6 fatty acids—found in corn, peanut and sunflower oils, in most margarines and in fried foods—is bad for the brain.

What you may not know: "The brain requires more omega-3 fatty acids than any other system in the body," says Andrew L. Stoll, MD, of Harvard Medical School, author of *The Omega-3 Connection* (Simon & Schuster). "With sufficient quantities of omega-3 fatty acids in the diet, the membranes surrounding our brain cells perform their crucial functions normally. Without sufficient quantities of omega-3 in the diet, the brain cells use substitute fats such as omega-6, which have vastly different properties than omega-3s."

What are those "crucial functions"? The fatty membrane of the brain cell is like a skilled executive assistant, organizing the movement of information into and out of the cell, explains Dr. Stoll. When omega-3 isn't on the job, your brain is literally disorganized. *With omega-3 on the job, your brain can be much more efficient...*

● **Slowing cognitive decline in older men.** Dutch researchers studied 210 healthy men aged 70 to 89, for five years. Compared with those who didn't eat fish, those who ate fish (with an average daily intake of about 400 mg of EPA and DHA) developed cognitive decline (poor memory) at a slower rate. "A moderate intake of EPA and DHA may postpone cognitive decline," say the researchers, in the *American Journal of Clinical Nutrition.*

● **Better memory in people with mild cognitive impairment.** Twelve people with mild cognitive impairment took supplements that included DHA. They showed a "significant improvement of immediate memory," say Japanese researchers, in *Neuroscience Research.*

● **Preventing Alzheimer's.** Scientists from the French National Institute of Health and Medical Research studied 8,000 men and women over aged 65 for four years. None of the participants had dementia at the start of the study. Four years later, 183 had Alzheimer's and 98 had other types of dementia. *Fats may have determined their fate...*

● Eating a diet rich in ALA from canola, flaxseed and walnut oil may have reduced dementia risk by 60%.

● Eating fish at least once a week may have lowered the risk of dementia by 40% and Alzheimer's by 35%. (This was true only of the 90 to 95% of the study participants—those not carrying the APOE e4 gene for Alzheimer's.)

● Eating a diet loaded with omega-6 oils, but containing little or no omega-3 or fish, may have doubled the risk of developing dementia.

"We have identified dietary patterns associated with lowering a person's risk of dementia or Alzheimer's," says Pascale Barberger-Gateau, PhD, a study researcher.

And in a nine-year study of nearly 900 men and women aged 55 to 88, people with the highest dietary intake of DHA (from eating fish three times a week) were 47% less likely to get dementia from any cause, and 39% less likely to get Alzheimer's disease, say scientists from the Human Nutrition Research Center at Tufts University.

● **More omega-3, less cognitive decline in mild Alzheimer's.** People with very mild Alzheimer's disease who took omega-3 supplements with 1.7 grams of EPA and 600 milligrams (mg) of DHA had a slower rate of cognitive decline than people not taking the supplements, say Swedish researchers, in the *Archives of Neurology.*

● **More omega-3, less agitation and depression in Alzheimer's.** Scientists in Sweden studied 200 people with mild Alzheimer's, dividing them into two groups—one got fish oil supplements and one got a placebo. Those getting omega-3 who also had the gene for Alzheimer's (APOE e4) showed less agitation, a symptom typical of the disease. Those who didn't have the gene showed less depression, another common symptom.

● **More DHA, less brain-toxic protein.** Researchers often study Alzheimer's by breeding mice to produce the two characteristic signs of the disease—*tau*, a protein that ties many-branched brain cells into knots (tangles); and *beta amyloid*, a protein that forms clumps (plaques) that block communication between brain cells.

Scientists at the University of California-Irvine fed Alzheimer's mice various diets, rich in either omega-3 or omega-6 fatty acids. Only those mice receiving extra DHA had lower levels of both tau and beta.

DON'T BE SWEET TO YOUR BRAIN

If you can't remember what beverage you ordered at lunch, it may have been a can of soda, with its dozen teaspoons of sugar...

● **Diabetes and mild cognitive impairment.** Researchers at Columbia University studied nearly 1,000 people, aged 65 or older, for an average of six years. Those with diabetes had a significantly higher risk of mild cognitive impairment. "Our results provide further support to the potentially important role of diabetes in the development of Alzheimer's disease," say the researchers, in the journal *Archives of Neurology.*

● **Prediabetes and Alzheimer's.** Researchers at the Uppsala University in Sweden studied more than 2,000 middle-aged men for 30 years, and found that those who developed prediabetes were one-and-a-half times more likely to develop Alzheimer's.

What happens: Writing in the journal *Neurobiology of Aging*, researchers at the Salk Institute for Biological Studies in La Jolla, CA, say their experiments show that increased levels of blood glucose in the brain damages brain blood vessels, speeding the development of Alzheimer's disease and vascular dementia.

Bottom line: Diabetes may increase the risk of Alzheimer's by 30 to 65%.

What to do: In an eight-year study of more than 22,000 people over age 50 with diabetes, scientists at Kaiser Permanente Research Division in Oakland, CA, found that those with the poorest blood sugar control were 78% more likely to develop dementia.

"Effective blood sugar control may lower the risk of another diabetes-related complication—dementia," says Rachel A. Whitmer, PhD, who led the study.

For ideas about how to control blood sugar, please see Chapter 6, "Diabetes and Insulin Resistance," on page 124.

DHA works by cutting levels of *presenilin*, an enzyme required for the manufacture of beta amyloid, say the scientists, in the *Journal of Neuroscience.*

"We are greatly excited by these results, which show us that simple changes in diet can positively alter the way the brain works and lead to protection from Alzheimer's disease pathology," says Frank M. LaFerla, PhD, codirector of the Institute for Brain Aging and Dementia at Irvine.

Recommended: For complete information on maximizing the intake of omega-3 fatty acids in your diet, from foods and/or supplements, see page 221, in Chapter 9, "Heart Disease and Stroke."

REVERSE AGE-RELATED MEMORY LOSS BY 10 YEARS

You go out for a walk to get your heart beating faster. To make it stronger, fitter. *Younger.*

Now, a scientific study shows that you can exercise your brain to make your *memory* stronger and fitter. And much, much younger.

⯈ *Breakthrough Study*

Researchers at the University of Southern California Andrus Gerontology Center and the Mayo Clinic studied 524 healthy people aged 65 and older, dividing them into two groups.

One group spent one hour a day exercising on a computer-based brain fitness program. They did the mental exercises five days a week, for eight to 10 weeks.

On the same schedule, the other group took computer-based educational programs. (Learning is an excellent way to build brain-power.)

Result: The group that used the brain fitness program took 10 years off the age of their memories—that is, they performed on memory tests like people *10 years* younger! And they didn't just do better on the memory test. Seventy-five percent of those using the brain fitness program said they could remember phone numbers and names better—and where they left their keys! (Or their wallet or reading glasses or the car in the mall parking lot...)

"The changes we saw in the brain-building group were remarkable," says Elizabeth Zelinski, PhD, who led the study. "From a researcher's point of view, the results were very impressive. People got better at the mental tasks they trained for. Those improvements generalized to four standardized memory tests. And people also perceived improvements in memory in their day-to-day lives.

"Cognitive decline is not an inevitable part of aging," she adds. "Doing the properly designed cognitive activities can actually enhance abilities as you age." She reported the study results at the annual meeting of the Gerontological Society of America.

ℹ️ The study used the Brain Fitness Program Classic, from Posit Science.

How it works: The program features six computer-based exercises that the company says are "designed to be very easy to use, even for computer novices."

The exercises improve "working memory," explains Dr. Zelinski—the type of memory that retains information (new names, a shopping list, directions from the airport to your niece's wedding) long enough to either act on it or transfer it to long-term memory.

It also improves "narrative memory"—the details of the stories told to you every day by a spouse, coworkers, friends and teachers. Better narrative memory allows you to engage confidently in new and enjoyable activities, such as taking a class or traveling.

And the brain exercises are designed to increase the levels of "neuromodulators"—neurotransmitters and hormones that keep the mind sharp but typically decline with age.

☀ *www.positscience.com*. Posit Science Corporation, 225 Bush Street, 7th Floor, San Francisco, CA 94104 (800-514-3961, 415-394-3100 or fax 415-986-2829).

FOR BETTER MEMORY, GINKGO IS A GO

At 200 million years and counting, ginkgo is the oldest living species of tree, and an extract of *ginkgo biloba* from its lovely fan-shaped leaves is *the* remedy for memory—used by practitioners of Traditional Chinese Medicine for thousands of years to treat memory loss...recommended by the world-renowned herbal experts of Germany's Commission E for "memory deficits"...and taken by scores of Alzheimer's-anxious Americans, who spend more than $140 million a year on the memory-enhancing herb.

Well, if you've just blown out 85 candles on your birthday cake, you may want to join them. (Even if memory loss is not a problem.)

⏣➡ *Breakthrough Study*

For three years, researchers at the Layton Aging and Alzheimer's Disease Center at Oregon Health & Sciences University studied 118 people aged 85 or older—oldsters with *no* memory problems. Half the group was asked to take a daily ginkgo supplement and half weren't.

Result: At the end of the three years, those who had reliably taken the supplement had a 68% lower risk of developing mild memory problems.

There have been more than 50 other studies on ginkgo biloba and memory, showing it can enhance memory, help prevent Alzheimer's and soften dementia's memory-robbing blows.

How it works: Ginkgo biloba improves circulation to the brain by thinning blood and relaxing arteries...decreases oxidative damage, the cellular rust that ages neurons...and boosts levels of neurotransmitters, brain chemicals that speed messages from one neuron to another. "Ginkgo is a premier example of an herb that can keep your brain sharp by stimulating blood flow and brain function," says James A. Duke, PhD, author of *The Green Pharmacy* (Rodale).

Suggested intake: Most studies on ginkgo and memory have used between 150 and 250 mg of ginkgo biloba extract (GBE) a day.

ℹ GBE is widely available. Look for an extract standardized to its active ingredients—24% ginkgo flavone glycoside and 6% terpene lactones (ginkgolides and bilobalide).

Caution: A few people taking GBE suffered severe internal bleeding, such as that found with an intracerebral hemorrhage (stroke), says Francis Brinker, ND, a naturopathic doctor, clinical assistant professor at the Program of Integrative Medicine at the University of Arizona College of Medicine and author of *Herb Contraindications and Drug Interactions* (Eclectic Medical Publications). Some were also taking GBE with blood-thinning drugs such as aspirin, ibuprofen and *warfarin* (Coumadin) that decrease platelet aggregation, the clumping of blood cells that can lead to an artery-clogging blood clot. Did GBE boost the potency of the blood-thinners, causing the bleeding?

Subsequent studies showed that GBE does *not* decrease platelet aggregation, says Dr. Brinker. People who suffered a bleeding episode while taking GBE probably experienced what doctors call an "idiosyncratic reaction"—a genetic peculiarity in the metabolizing of a particular drug or herb.

Even though GBE does not pose a general risk of bleeding, it is unknown who will or won't bleed when they take the herb. *Caution is best, so Dr. Brinker advises…*

If you're taking Coumadin or any other drug prescribed for blood thinning, or are regularly using nonsteroidal anti-inflammatory drugs (aspirin, ibuprofen, naproxen, the Cox-2 inhibitors)—don't take GBE.

FORGETFUL? CALL A FRIEND

Which activity is better at improving brain-power and memory—spending 10 minutes doing a crossword puzzle or spending 10 minutes talking with a friend?

They work equally well.

▶ *Breakthrough Study*

Scientists at the University of Michigan Institute for Social Research conducted two experiments.

First, they studied 3,610 people, aged 24 to 96. For each person, they matched data on the level of mental functioning (measured by a mental exam that included a memory test) and data on the level of social interaction (how often each week the person talked on the phone or got together with friends, neighbors and relatives).

Result: Overall, those with the higher levels of social interaction had the best performances on the mental exam!

Next, they studied 76 people, dividing them into three groups. One group socialized for 10 minutes (discussing current events); one group did a crossword puzzle and took a reading comprehension test for 10 minutes; and one group watched a 10-minute clip of *Seinfeld*, a TV comedy. After those 10-minute activities, all the participants took a test measuring memory and speed of mental functioning.

Result: "We found that the short-term social interaction, lasting for just ten minutes, boosted participants' memory and intellectual performance as much as engaging in the so-called intellectual activities, says Oscar Ybarra, PhD, who led the study. "This experiment shows that social interaction directly affects memory and mental performance in a positive way."

Visiting with a friend or neighbor may be just as helpful in staying sharp as doing a daily crossword puzzle, he says.

Dr. Ybarra notes that while social *interaction* may improve memory, social *isolation* may have a negative effect.

New findings: Researchers at the Rush University Medical Center in Chicago conducted a study showing that people who are socially isolated—with a small social network, unmarried and participating in few activities with others—have an increased risk for dementia.

In a subsequent four-year study of 823 people, with an average age of 81, the Rush researchers found that those who scored highest on a yearly measurement of loneliness were twice as likely to develop Alzheimer's.

What to do: Here are three tips for increasing social interaction, from Dr. Gary Small…

● **Increase empathy.** "Develop and maintain your empathy skills," says Dr. Small. "Listen to others, try to identify with their feelings and let them know that you understand."

● **Nurture intimacy.** "If you are in an intimate relationship, make efforts to nurture it," he says. "Schedule time together, share feelings without criticizing and stay in touch with friends and other couples."

● **Enjoy a pet.** "Pets can also be enjoyable, stress-reducing companions," he says.

COFFEE STIMULATES MEMORY

Coffee beans are good for the ole bean...

New study: For four years, French researchers studied the caffeine intake and mental abilities of more than 4,000 women over 65 years old. They found that those who ingested caffeine equivalent to three or more cups of coffee and/or tea a day were 30% less likely to have had a decline in memory. At age 80 and older, the three-a-day coffee/tea drinkers were 70% less likely to have worsening memory.

"Caffeine is a psychostimulant that appears to reduce cognitive decline in women," says Karen Ritchie, PHD, of the French National Institute for Health and Medical Research.

The researchers also studied nearly 3,000 men but found no memory boost. Why not? "Women may be more sensitive to the effects of caffeine," says Dr. Ritchie. "Their bodies may react differently to the stimulant, or they may metabolize caffeine differently."

Drinking coffee or tea didn't *prevent* dementia, however. "It might be that caffeine slows the dementia process rather than preventing it," she says.

What to do: Play Sudoku at Starbucks.

IT'S NOT TOO LATE FOR FOLATE

A brain cell—a neuron—is, well, brainy.

Smart enough to grab information with fingerlike *dendrites*, pitch the info into its nucleus for processing and then transmit fresh facts to its brainy neighbors via the cablelike *axon*, which propels the new know-how across synapses between neurons via clever chemical packets called neurotransmitters. What a whiz!

But brain cells are stupefied by too much homocysteine. An excess of this amino acid (a working part of protein) is a neuron's worst nightmare.

Homocysteine can damage a neuron's DNA, the genetic gears of cellular machinery

...oxidize the cell, crusting its shine with biochemical rust...trigger *excitotoxicity*, a flash flood of neuron-damaging chemicals...and even cause *apoptosis*, the sudden death of a cell. If that weren't bad enough, homocysteine also batters and clogs blood vessels in the brain.

No wonder high levels of the amino acid have been linked to brain atrophy—the loss of so many neurons that the brain literally shrinks. And linked to the final results of all that neuronal erosion—the everyday trauma of mild cognitive impairment, and the terminal tragedy of Alzheimer's disease.

But the how-to of protecting your brain from homocysteine is simple as a supplement—just take folate, a B vitamin.

▶ Breakthrough Studies

Korean researchers conducted a 30-month study of 518 people, aged 65 and older. At the study's start and finish, they measured blood levels of folate.

After 30 months, 45 people had dementia. But those with low folate levels at the beginning of the study were *3.5 times more likely* to have developed the brain disease.

And in a recently completed six-year study, scientists at the Taub Institute for Research on Alzheimer's Disease and the Aging Brain, at Columbia University in New York, focused on 965 people aged 65 or older. They found that those who got the most folate—through diet *and* supplements—had a 50% lower risk of dementia. (Food alone or supplements alone didn't do the trick.) And vitamins B-6 and B-12 —nutrients often pegged to the risk of dementia—didn't put a dent in dementia rates.

"Our results suggest that a higher intake of folate is related to a lower risk of Alzheimer's disease," says Jose A. Luchsinger, MD, MPH, who led the study. "We found this association for total folate intake—dietary and supplement—but not for dietary or supplement sources alone. That suggests that what is important is total intake of folate, from both sources."

And in a three-year study from Dutch researchers of hundreds of people aged 50 to 70 with high homocysteine levels, those who took a daily supplement of 800 mcg of folate a day for three years had better memory (and information processing speed), compared with a group that didn't take the vitamin.

What to do: "First, see your doctor and ask for a blood test that measures homocysteine," says Kilmer S. McCully, MD, a proponent of the link between high homocysteine levels and disease and author of *The Homocysteine Revolution* (McGraw-Hill).

The optimal level is eight or less micromoles per liter of blood.

Borderline levels are between eight and 12. If higher than 12, it's wise to take action to increase folate and lower homocysteine. *Dr. McCully's advice...*

• **Take a multivitamin supplement.** A multivitamin provides folate insurance—and compensates for the decreased ability to absorb vitamins as you age. Look for a supplement with 400 to 1,000 mcg of folate.

Dr. McCully thinks B-6 and B-12 also play an important role in lowering homocysteine, and says a multivitamin should include at least 5 to 10 mg of B-6 and 100 to 200 mcg of B-12.

ⓘ Good, nationally available brands include Twin Labs, Solgar, Centrum, Carlson, Sundown and Theragram, he says.

• **Eat folate-rich foods.** They include leafy green vegetables, broccoli, Brussels sprouts, asparagus, beans, citrus fruits, fortified breakfast cereals, brown rice and liver.

To get more B vitamins in your diet, says Dr. McCully, avoid processed foods, eat more fresh fruits and vegetables, eat more whole grains and legumes, and have one to two servings a day of either fresh fish, poultry, meat, eggs or dairy products.

MUSIC FOR BETTER POSTSTROKE MEMORY

The days and weeks right after a stroke can be agonizing for the victim and for his family and friends—particularly the struggle to speak again, to remember and say words that once flowed so easily and effortlessly.

Is there anything you can add to standard rehabilitation to help a stroke victim recover memory faster?

Yes, start playing his favorite music.

||||▶ *Breakthrough Study*

Scientists in the Cognitive Brain Research Unit at the University of Helsinki in Finland studied 54 people who had suffered a stroke, working with them after admittance to the hospital. Most had problems with memory and other mental processes and with movement. The researchers divided them into three groups. One group listened to music for one to two hours a day; one group listened to audio books and one group didn't receive either type of "listening" therapy. Otherwise, all three groups received standard stroke rehabilitation. Right after the stroke, and three and six months later, the researchers asked the stroke victims to take a wide range of tests to evaluate memory, mental power and mood.

Result: "We found that three months after the stroke, verbal memory improved by sixty percent in music listeners, eighteen percent in audio book listeners and twenty-nine percent in nonlisteners," says Teppo Särkämö, PhD, who led the study.

"Similarly, focused attention—the ability to control and perform mental operations—

MAINTAIN YOUR BRAIN— WITH MEDITATION

Inside your skull—in your cerebral cortex at the surface of the brain; in the cerebellum, in back at the bottom; in the hypothalamus, deep within—your brain is, well, *shrinking. Aging is the reason. But time might be no match for meditation...*

New study: Scientists at Emory University studied 13 people who meditated regularly and 13 similarly aged and educated non-meditators, using brain scans to measure how much "cerebral gray matter" they had left. The nonmeditating group had the normal age-related decline in gray matter. The meditators didn't!

"Regular practice of meditation may have neuroprotective effects and reduce the cognitive decline associated with normal aging," says Giuseppe Pagnoni, PhD, in the Department of Psychology and Behavioral Sciences.

Another study, by scientists at the University of Pennsylvania, also found that meditation changes the brain—their tests showed that when people meditated 30 minutes a day for two months, they increased their ability to quickly and accurately move and focus attention, a process psychologists call "orienting."

What to do: The participants in the study at the University of Pennsylvania practiced a meditation technique called "Mindfulness Meditation." Instructions for practicing this technique are on page 397 in Chapter 16, "Stress, Insomnia and Fatigue," where you'll also find resource information for classes on mindfulness meditation, mindfulness-based CDs and tapes and books about mindfulness.

improved by seventeen percent in music listeners. But no improvement was seen in audio book listeners and nonlisteners." Those results were essentially the same six months after the stroke, he says.

The researchers also found that those listening to music were less depressed and confused.

"As a result of our findings, we suggest that everyday music listening during early stroke recovery offers a valuable addition to a patient's care—especially if other active forms of rehabilitation, such as speech therapy, are not yet feasible at this stage," says Dr. Särkämö. "Music provides an individually targeted, easy-to-conduct, and inexpensive means to facilitate cognitive and emotional recovery."

And there's plenty of opportunity to implement the therapy, he says. "Other research has shown that during the first weeks and months after stroke, the patients typically spend about three-quarters of their time each day in non-therapeutic activities, mostly in their rooms, inactive and without interaction. However, this time window is ideal for rehabilitative training, from the point of view of brain plasticity. Our research shows that listening to music during this crucial period can enhance cognitive recovery and prevent negative mood."

Why it works: "Music listening activates a widespread network of brain regions related to attention, word processing, memory, motor functions and emotional processing," says Dr. Särkämö. The music might increase the ability of the brain to repair and renew its neural networks after the damage, he explains. Or it might directly stimulate damaged areas of the brain.

What to do: If you have had a stroke or are caring for someone who has—strike up the band!

"We thought it was important for stroke victims to start listening to music as soon as possible during the acute poststroke stage, as the brain can undergo dramatic changes during the first weeks and months of recovery," says Dr. Särkämö.

The stroke victims listened, one to two hours a day, to their selected, favorite music. Sixty percent selected popular music—pop, rock or rhythm and blues; 20% selected classical or spiritual; 10% selected jazz and 8% selected folk music.

PREVENT ALZHEIMER'S— WALK 10 MINUTES A DAY

Ten minutes. About the time it takes to read the morning paper. Or microwave and eat a TV dinner. Or prevent Alzheimer's disease.

⫸ *Breakthrough Studies*

Led by Eric Larson, MD, MPH, researchers at the University of Washington in Seattle studied 1,740 people, aged 65 or older, without serious memory loss. At the beginning of the study, they were asked how often they exercised. Six years later, 158 had developed dementia, with 107 of those having Alzheimer's disease.

Result: Those who exercised three or more times a week, for at least 15 minutes each time, were 38% less likely to have gotten dementia. Even walking for as little as 10 minutes reduced the risk of developing Alzheimer's by 32%.

And a recent study by Italian researchers shows that people aged 65 and older who regularly walk and engage in other types of physical activity (such as gardening and housework) reduce their risk of *vascular dementia* (the second most common cause of dementia, after Alzheimer's disease) by 27%. "It's important to note that an easy-to-perform activity like

YOUR BELLY AND YOUR BRAIN

People with the most belly fat in their 40s are more likely to develop dementia in their 70s.

That's the finding of a team of researchers led by Rachel A. Whitmer, PhD, of the Kaiser Permanente Division of Research, in Oakland, CA. "And considering that fifty percent of adults in this country have an unhealthy amount of abdominal fat, it's a disturbing finding," she says.

The researchers analyzed 30 years of health data from more than 6,500 people, and found that, compared with people with a normal weight and a normal-size belly, people with the biggest bellies were nearly *three times* more likely to develop dementia.

Overall, the researchers divided belly size into five levels of bigness, from normal (1) to biggest (5)—and found that risk and waist size were (unfortunately) a perfect fit. Those in level 2 had a 20% increased risk for dementia...those in level 3, 49%...those in level 4, 67%...and those in level 5, a 270% increased risk. (When the researchers combined obesity *and* extra abdominal fat, the risk nearly quadrupled, to 360%.)

What's the link between belly and brain? "Research needs to be done to determine what the mechanisms are that link abdominal obesity and dementia," says Dr. Whitmer. However, she points out that researchers have *already* linked a bigger belly at midlife to an increased risk for heart disease and stroke—with the understanding that extra abdominal fat acts like a gland, releasing inflammatory hormones and immune compounds that damage arterial cells. "The brain may also be a target organ for the harmful effects of central obesity," she says.

"Another study showed that higher abdominal fat in elderly adults was tied to greater brain atrophy," adds Dr. Whitmer. "And autopsies have shown that changes in the brain associated with Alzheimer's disease may start in young to middle adulthood. These findings imply that the dangerous effects of abdominal obesity on the brain may start long before the signs of dementia appear."

What to do: See Chapter 14 on page 350 for ways to help you lose abdominal fat quickly and safely.

walking provides the same cognitive benefits as other, more demanding types of exercise," says Giovanni Ravaglia, MD, who led the study.

Even people who already have Alzheimer's benefit from exercise. French researchers conducted a yearlong study of 134 people with Alzheimer's in nursing homes. Those who participated in a one-hour, twice-a-week exercise program had a slower decline in their ability to perform activities of daily living—bathing, dressing, eating and using the toilet. They report their results in the *Journal of the American Geriatric Society*.

Theory: Exercise boosts the delivery of blood and oxygen to the brain…triggers the release of compounds that strengthen brain cells…and eases cell-damaging stress.

What to do: "Just like you brush your teeth every day, try to exercise every day," says Dr. Larson. He recommends a minimum of 15 minutes, while shooting for 30.

"Most people find that walking is the easiest way to exercise regularly," he says. "If you can't walk, finding something else to do, such as swimming, biking, weight training or stretching—whatever you like to do, and *will* do on a regular basis."

CAN CURRY STOP ALZHEIMER'S?

Why are rates of Alzheimer's among 70- to 79-year-olds in India four times lower than those in America—in fact, among the "lowest ever reported," according to an article in the journal *Neurology*?

Maybe it's all the yellow spice (known as turmeric) that Indians eat.

Because many scientists think that one of turmeric's main components—*curcumin*—can help prevent Alzheimer's disease.

⫸ *Breakthrough Studies*

Writing in the journal *Current Alzheimer's Research*, scientists from the Alzheimer's Research Center in the UCLA Department of Neurology present the promising power of curcumin to battle Alzheimer's…

● **Antioxidant.** In laboratory animals, curcumin stops the artery-harming oxidation of fats and cell-killing oxidation of DNA—two possible causes of Alzheimer's. Studies even show that curcumin is a far more potent antioxidant than vitamin E.

● **Anti-inflammatory.** When the immune system battles an invader, it leaves behind a wake of inflammation (for example, the redness and swelling around a healing cut). But *chronic* inflammation (from stress, sugary foods, extra pounds and other immune-stimulating bugaboos of modern life) can backfire, causing or worsening disease—including Alzheimer's.

"Curcumin has been shown to have anti-inflammatory effects and may have a role in slowing Alzheimer's disease through this mechanism," says John M. Ringman, MD, who coauthored the paper on curcumin with four of his colleagues. Curcumin can stop the production of enzymes that produce pro-inflammatory immune factors, and limit the inflammatory damage of immune cells already on the warpath.

● **Lowers cholesterol.** High levels of cholesterol may spur the spread of *beta-amyloid*, the toxic brain plaque that is to Alzheimer's what arterial plaque is to heart disease. In one study, a supplement of 500 mg a day of curcumin lowered total cholesterol by 12%.

● **Thins blood.** Too thick, clot-prone blood may play a role in Alzheimer's disease, or in vascular dementia—and studies show that curcumin can thin blood.

• **Anti-amyloid.** Curcumin can curb beta-amyloid—stop it from forming and destroy it once it starts to form.

• **Eases Alzheimer's in animals.** In laboratory animals bred to form beta-amyloid plaques, feeding them curcumin decreases oxidation…decreases inflammatory immune factors…decreases levels of beta-amyloid by up to 50%…and improves memory.

"Animal studies are highly suggestive of efficacy for curcumin against Alzheimer's disease via multiple possible mechanisms," say the researchers. "Curcumin is a promising agent in the treatment and/or prevention of Alzheimer's disease, and further study is warranted." And those doctors at UCLA are conducting the research—curcumin is being tested in clinical trials, with people with mild to moderate Alzheimer's taking high-dose supplements of a special formulation of the herb.

New finding: But while you're waiting for the results of that research, scientists in Singapore have conducted a study pointing to curcumin's power to block the memory loss that often *precedes* Alzheimer's…

"Curcumin shows promise for the prevention of Alzheimer's disease," say researchers at the National University of Singapore, led by Tze-Pin Ng, MD, in the Department of Psychological Medicine. To find out whether it might keep that promise, Dr. Ng and his colleagues studied more than 1,000 people, aged 60 to 93.

They asked them about their consumption of yellow curry—whether they ate it never or rarely (less than once every six months), occasionally (more than once every six months but less than once a month), often (more than once a month but less than once a week) or very often (once a week or more).

They also gave the study participants a standard memory test called the "minimental state examination" (MMSE).

Curcumin, it turns out, might be renamed curc*umind*…

Those who ate curcumin-rich yellow curry occasionally, often or very often had higher scores on the MMSE—and a 35 to 38% lower risk of "cognitive impairment" (the stage before Alzheimer's disease). In fact, the researchers point out that curry eaters were mentally 10 years younger than the never-curry group. "These findings provide the first epidemiological evidence supporting a link between curry consumption and cognitive performance," say the researchers, in the *American Journal of Epidemiology*.

What to do: "If you enjoy Indian cuisine, by all means enjoy these delicious foods," says Holly Lucille, ND, RN, a naturopathic doctor in private practice in Los Angeles. But, she points out, American meals rarely contain curry. "That's why turmeric/curcumin supplements are suddenly quite popular," she says. Her advice is to look for a high-potency turmeric extract from turmeric root (*Curcuma longa*), standardized to contain 90% curcuminoids, the active ingredient.

Suggested intake: Dr. Ng points out that a 200 mg supplement of curcuminoids helps to reduce the oxidation of LDL cholesterol and normalize blood levels of fibrinogen, a clotting factor.

ℹ The independent consumer research organization ConsumerLab.com tested curcumin and turmeric supplements and found that many didn't contain the dosages listed on the label—and some contained lead! Curcumin/turmeric products that met their approval included Douglas Laboratories, New Chapter, NOW, Nutraceutical Sciences Institute, PhysioLogics,

HELP THE HEART, HELP THE BRAIN

There are numerous blood vessels in your brain. And by keeping them healthy—by lowering high blood pressure and high cholesterol, by doing *exactly* what you do to keep your heart healthy—you can keep dementia in check...

New thinking: Scientists at the University of Washington in Seattle autopsied more than 3,400 men and women participating in a long-range study on brain health, and found that about one-third of all cases of dementia were caused by damage to the small blood vessels in the brain. (Forty-five percent were caused by Alzheimer's, and 10% by other degenerative brain changes.)

The key to preventing this type of vascular damage is to prevent high blood pressure and/or type 2 diabetes, says Thomas Montine, MD, PhD, who led the study.

Researchers from the University of Pittsburgh agree with him. They conducted brain scans of healthy people, people with mild cognitive impairment and people with Alzheimer's. In all three groups, those with high blood pressure had lower blood flow to the brain.

"These results suggest that hypertension changes blood flow to the brain and may contribute to the development of Alzheimer's disease," says Cyrus Raji, MD, a study researcher.

"This study demonstrates that good vascular health is also good for the brain," adds Oscar L. Lopez, MD, professor of neurology and psychiatry, and another study researcher.

And a new study of nearly 10,000 people shows that men in their early 40s with total cholesterol levels above 240 are 150% more likely to develop dementia, and those with levels between 221 and 248 are 125% more likely to develop the disease. "Our findings show it would be best for patients to reduce high cholesterol levels in their forties to reduce the risk of dementia," says Alina Solomon, MD, who led the study.

Hypertension and high levels of cholesterol are both important risk factors for Alzheimer's disease, say scientists from the Taub Institute for Research on Alzheimer's Disease and the Aging Brain.

"By changing these modifiable risk factors for vascular disease, it may be possible to prevent or delay dementia," adds Kannayiram Alagiakrishnan, MD, in the Division of Geriatric Medicine at the University of Alberta.

For information on controlling hypertension and high cholesterol, see Chapter 9, "Heart Disease and Stroke," on page 209.

Pure Encapsulation, Puritan's Pride, Vitamin Shoppe and Vitamin World.

As with all herbal and nutritional supplements, it's prudent to consult with your doctor or pharmacist before taking curcumin.

CHECKMATE DEMENTIA

You're 75. You figure that at this point in your life, you're either going to get Alzheimer's or not—there's nothing you can do. Well, your brain has another idea.

||||➤ *Breakthrough Studies*

For five years, researchers at the Rush Alzheimer's Disease Center in Chicago studied more than 700 people with an average age of 80. Every year, they gave them cognitive tests and asked them about their daily activities.

Result: After five years, those who had participated regularly in mentally stimulating activities—who regularly played chess, or read a newspaper, or attended plays, or visited the library or did crossword puzzles—were 2.6 times less likely to develop Alzheimer's disease or dementia, compared with people who weren't as mentally active.

And that result held up even when the researchers figured in other factors theorized to influence the risk of Alzheimer's, such as earlier levels of mental activity, current social relationships, intensity of daily physical activity and socioeconomic status.

Better: The study also found that mentally stimulating activities lowered the risk of developing mild cognitive impairment—the interim stage between age-related memory loss and dementia.

What to do: "Almost any mental activity will fulfill the brain's needs," says Dharma Singh Khalsa, MD, president and medical director of the Alzheimer's Prevention Foundation, in Tucson, AZ, and coauthor of *Brain Longevity* (Grand Central Publishing). "Among the most productive are reading, writing, drawing, playing word games, playing board games, building, conversing and engaging in stimulating hobbies. The important thing about mental activity is not what you do, but merely that you do it."

GIVE YOUR BRAIN SOME JUICE

An apple a day keeps the doctor away. You've heard that, of course. But how about this—A glass of apple juice every other day keeps Alzheimer's away.

||||▶ *Breakthrough Study*

Researchers at the Vanderbilt School of Medicine analyzed about a decade of diet and health data from nearly 2,000 men. They found that those who drank fruit or vegetable juices at least three times a week had a 76% lower risk of developing Alzheimer's disease than those who drank

juice less than once per week. And the risk was 16% lower among those who drank juice one to two times a week.

"Fruit and vegetable juices may play an important role in delaying the onset of Alzheimer's disease," say the researchers, in the *American Journal of Medicine.*

Reason: "The theory is that the brain accumulates damage due to oxidation as we age, and if you can protect the brain from that damage you can protect the person from Alzheimer's disease and other causes of dementia," says Dr. Larson, one of the researchers who conducted the study. Juice is made using the parts of the fruit with the highest concentration of antioxidants, he says.

Recommendation: Dr. Larson says grape, apple and orange juices are very rich in antioxidants and could be the most effective at preventing Alzheimer's disease. *However, he offers a couple of cautions…*

Red flags: Look for 100% juice, not 10% juice…check the list of ingredients to make sure there isn't added sugar…and more isn't necessarily better—the study participants with the most protection drank an eight-ounce glass of fruit or vegetable juice three times per week, or every other day.

HUPERZINE-A, BRAIN HERB FROM CHINA

The class of drugs typically used to treat Alzheimer's disease is *cholinesterase inhibitors.*

The enzyme AChE (*acetylcholinesterase*) lowers levels of an important brain chemical called *choline acetyltransferase* that sends messages between neurons; cholinesterase inhibitors cut levels of AChE.

The drugs include *donepezil* (Aricept), *rivastigmine* (Exelon), *galantamine* (Reminyl) and *tetrahydroaminoacridine* (Tacrine).

They're used mostly for people with mild to moderate Alzheimer's—but they don't work for everybody, the improvement they provide is usually very minimal, they don't slow the disease and many patients stop using them because of side effects.

Fortunately, there's a natural (and perhaps more effective) alternative—the herb, huperzine A, an extract of Chinese club moss (*Huperzia serrata*).

IIII➡ *Breakthrough Study*

Chinese researchers in the Department of Geriatrics at Sichuan University recently evaluated six studies of huperzine A, involving 454 patients.

They found the herb improved mind and memory, strengthening general cognitive function, helped with agitation, depression and other behavioral disturbances and improved day-to-day functioning.

Plus, there were hardly any side effects—and those that occurred weren't any different from the everyday health problems of people in the placebo groups, which mean they probably weren't caused by huperzine A.

Huperzine A, conclude the researchers, can have beneficial effects in Alzheimer's.

How it works: Scientists in the Department of Psychiatry at Georgetown University Hospital took a close look at all the research on huperzine A. They concluded the herb penetrates the brain better than tacrine or donepezil...does a better job than tacrine or galantamine in shutting down AChE...may protect brain cells against oxidation...may help rescue injured neurons...and may help cut down the creation and toxicity of beta-amyloid, the pernicious protein that chokes off brain cells in Alzheimer's.

WHY IT'S SMART TO BE CONSCIENTIOUS

A new scientific study shows that not only are Boy Scouts cheerful, thrifty, brave and clean—they're also less likely to get Alzheimer's.

At least that might be the case if they spent a lifetime following the Scout Oath to "do my best to do my duty," and obeying the Scout Law to be "trustworthy, loyal and helpful." Those are some of the characteristics (along with self-discipline, purposefulness and dependability) of a trait that psychologists call *conscientiousness*. A trait that might benefit the brain. (Who said virtue has to be its own reward?)

New finding: Scientists at the Rush University Medical Center in Chicago studied nearly 1,000 older Catholic clergy for 12 years. At the beginning of the study, the participants were given a questionnaire that measured "conscientiousness," with statements to agree or disagree with, such as, "I am a productive person who always gets the job done."

None of the participants had Alzheimer's when the study began in 1994; 12 years later, 176 had the disease.

And compared with those who were the least conscientious, those who were the most conscientious were 89% less likely to have Alzheimer's. They were also less likely to have "mild cognitive impairment" (the interim stage between age-related memory loss and dementia).

Reason: Conscientious people might be more *resilient*—more able to cope with negative life events and chronic psychological distress, which have been linked to dementia, says Robert S. Wilson, PhD, who led the study.

What to do: Dr. Wilson's finding expands scientific knowledge about Alzheimer's, but he isn't recommending practical action to take based on his breakthrough. So for now perhaps the best advice is to be as conscientious as you can—and Be Prepared.

In other words, huperzine A may do a lot *more* than cholinesterase inhibitors in helping fight the disease.

Plus, the brain doesn't seem to build a tolerance to huperzine A, as it does to the synthetic drugs, which tend to stop working after a few years of use.

They cite numerous studies in which huperzine A improved the memory and mental state of Alzheimer's patients—including a study that added it to an already-existing drug regimen of cholinesterase inhibitors, boosting their power.

The researchers also describe the most recent US study of the huperzine A—people with Alzheimer's were either taking the herb or a placebo for four months, and then were invited to continue with the herb for the next six months. "So far," they say, "only thirty-six of the two hundred ten people enrolled have discontinued treatment, even though many subjects enrolled in the huperzine A trial after failing to tolerate standard cholinesterase inhibitors… suggesting good tolerability" of huperzine A.

Put another way, cholinesterase inhibitors tend to have numerous unpleasant side effects; huperzine A doesn't.

However, the researchers don't endorse huperzine A over cholinesterase inhibitors, saying that more research is necessary before recommending the herb for Alzheimer's.

Suggested intake: Studies typically use a dose of 200 to 400 mcg a day. (In one US study, the intake was 50 mcg the first week, 100 mcg the second, 150 mcg the third and 200 mcg the fourth.)

 Huperzine A is widely available.

Caution: Although huperzine A has shown itself to be a safe and effective herb, with little downside, it is a potent, brain-changing compound, with possible side effects (mostly mild and usually temporary) that include drowsiness, dizziness, nausea and diarrhea. Only use the herb with the approval and supervision of a physician.

12

MEN'S HEALTH
BE POTENT ALL OVER

Big boys don't cry. And they don't get sick, either. And if by any chance they do get sick, they don't complain about it.

Those are the cultural stereotypes most guys grow up with, says Jed Diamond, PhD, a California-based psychologist, author of *The Irritable Male Syndrome* (Rodale) and founder and director of the MenAlive health program.

"In our culture, a woman is taught to think positively about her health—to get regular checkups, to care about her health and that of her family," he says. "Male conditioning is just the opposite. A man is taught that being sickly isn't manly. And to 'tough it out' when he's in pain." All of which, he adds, is a big part of why men typically die so much earlier than women.

Maybe you're ready to live a healthier, longer life—in spite of being male! The key is to change your *attitude,* says Dr. Diamond. *And the best three ways for a man to do that are…*

● **Talk to your wife.** Ask your wife or girlfriend to stop nagging you about seeing a doctor and instead *reward* you for taking care of yourself—for instance, by greeting you at the door in sexy lingerie after you return from a doctor's appointment or a workout at the gym.

● **Talk to your friends.** Don't be afraid to talk to your buddies about your health. After all, you can hardly turn on the TV without seeing a commercial about erectile dysfunction or prostate problems. These days, it's acceptable for a man to talk openly about health problems.

● **Talk to yourself.** Be a decisive and determined man. Tell yourself that vibrant health is your birthright and that it's A-okay to take care of yourself—starting today!

But better health doesn't necessarily mean popping a pill, says Dr. Diamond. "Men are savvy—one reason they stay away from doctors is they know drugs and surgery can *wreck* health. Most men want a self-reliant, nonmedical form of care." To prevent illness, he recommends regular exercise and a diet rich in natural foods. And if you develop a health problem, try out the natural remedies discussed in this chapter.

ERECTILE DYSFUNCTION

Eighteen percent of American men— nearly 20 million very unhappy guys— suffer from *erectile dysfunction* (ED): The inability to get and keep an erection, most or all of the time. ED becomes more common with age, afflicting 5% of 20-year-olds but 70% of 70-year-olds. Yet no matter what your age, it's possible to get and stay hard during sex—*without* popping a prescription potency pill and risking side effects ranging from heart failure and blindness to headaches and nausea. (The latest warning from the FDA says taking prescription pills, such as Viagra, Cialis and Levitra, may cause sudden hearing loss in one ear, within hours or days after starting the medication. There have been 29 reports of this side effect, and the loss was permanent in about 20 cases.)

EXERCISE FOR BETTER BLOOD FLOW

Why do 90% of men with ED have at least one risk factor for heart disease, such as high blood pressure or high cholesterol?

Why does ED afflict 50% of men with diabetes—a circulation-damaging condition that cuts lives short with heart attacks and strokes?

Why? Like heart disease, ED is often caused by *poor circulation*—there isn't enough blood flow to the penis to start and sustain an erection.

"Heart health is tantamount to erectile health," says Mark A. Moyad, MD, MPH, director of complementary and preventive medicine in the Department of Urology at the University of Michigan Medical Center in Ann Arbor.

And, just as with heart disease, you can prevent or treat ED…with heart-pumping, circulation-boosting exercise.

||||➡ *Breakthrough Study*

Researchers at the Johns Hopkins Bloomberg School of Public Health in Baltimore looked at health data from more than 2,100 men. The men who hardly exercised—who hadn't walked, cycled, jogged or otherwise broken an aerobic sweat in the past month—were much more likely to have ED than men who exercised regularly.

In a similar study, researchers at the Harvard School of Public Health surveyed nearly 32,000 men aged 53 to 90—and found that those who exercised regularly had a 30% to 40% lower risk of developing ED than men who hardly exercised.

"Increasing exercise levels may be an effective, drug-free way to prevent and treat erectile dysfunction," says Elizabeth Selvin, PhD, MPH, an assistant professor in the Department of Epidemiology at Johns Hopkins.

What to do: According to Harvard researchers, you can lower your risk of developing ED by 30% to 40% if you exercise regularly, engaging in one or a combination of the following weekly activities…

- **Running, 3 hours per week,** at 6 mph (10 min/mile)
- **Running, 4 hours per week,** at 5 mph (12 min/mile)
- **Ski machine,** 3 to 4 hours per week
- **Stationary bicycle,** 3 to 4 hours per week (moderate pace)
- **Tennis (singles),** 4 hours per week
- **Calisthenics,** 4 hours per week (push-ups, pull-ups, jumping jacks, sit-ups, etc., performed vigorously)
- **Rowing machine,** 4 to 5 hours per week (moderate pace)
- **Weight-lifting,** 5 to 6 hours per week
- **Heavy outdoor work,** 5 to 6 hours per week (carpentry, installing rain gutters, building a fence, gardening with heavy power tools such as a tiller, walking with a power mower, etc.)
- **Walking, 6 hours per week** (on a level, firm surface at 4 mph, a very brisk pace)
- **Walking, 8 hours per week** (on a level, firm surface at 3.5 mph, a brisk pace)

To cut the risk of ED by 20 to 30%, exercise at least ½ the weekly amount of one or a combination of the above activities.

WHY ITALIANS ARE BETTER LOVERS?

Oysters. Champagne. Truffles. Those are the foods that supposedly get you (and your partner) in the mood. But there are plenty of less exotic (and probably more effective) aphrodisiacs in your kitchen—an apple, a slice of whole wheat bread, an avocado.

⫸ *Breakthrough Study*

Researchers at the University of Naples in Italy studied 65 men with ED and the metabolic syndrome (a circulation-choking combination of high blood sugar, high blood pressure, overweight, elevated triglycerides, high "bad" LDL cholesterol and low "good" HDL). They asked 35 of those men to go on a Mediterranean diet.

Two years later, nearly half the men on the Mediterranean diet scored 22 or higher out of 30 on the International Index of Erectile Function. *Which meant they had...*

• **Better erections**, with more penetration and better ability to maintain an erection after penetration.

• **More intense orgasms.**

• **More sexual desire.**

• **More sexual satisfaction.**

• **More overall satisfaction with life.** (Not hard to figure out why.)

"A Mediterranean-style diet might be effective in reducing the prevalence of ED in men with the metabolic syndrome," say the scientists in the *International Journal of Impotence Research.*

How to tell if you have the metabolic syndrome: If you're a guy with a waistline of 40 inches or more you probably do, says

WANT TO GET TURNED ON? TURN OFF THE TV

Guys who watch TV more than 20 hours a week have a 30% higher risk of developing ED, say researchers from Harvard School of Public Health. (And that's particularly true for men *under* 60.)

And Italian researchers found that couples with no TV in the bedroom have twice as much sex as those with broadcasts in the boudoir—eight times a month, compared to four. For those over 50, the statistics were even more dismaying. A TV in the bedroom cut sex from seven times a month to once or twice. The researchers also found that violent shows were more likely to deaden sex than reality shows.

So if sex seems like a remote possibility...put down the remote and go for a walk instead! Or change the channel from *24* to *Dancing With the Stars.*

Richard Anderson, PhD, a nutrition researcher at the government's Beltsville Human Nutrition Research Center in Maryland. (If your waistline is less than 40 inches, ask your doctor for tests to detect the problem—blood pressure, cholesterol and triglycerides, plus glucose level.)

What to do: Eat more fish, whole grains, fruits, vegetables, beans, walnuts, avocados and olive oil. (The last three foods are rich in heart-healthy monounsaturated fats, a key component of the Mediterranean diet.)

Eat less red meat, full-fat dairy products, refined carbohydrates (such as white bread) and sugar-rich, salt-rich processed foods such as doughnuts and potato chips.

☀ *The Sonoma Diet* by Connie Gutterson, RD, PhD (Meredith); *The Mediterranean Diet* by Marissa Cloutier, RD, MS (Avon); and *The Miami Mediterranean Diet* by Michael Ozner, MD (Cambridge).

PELVIC FLOOR EXERCISES FOR STRONGER ORGASMS

Your pelvic floor muscles—the muscles that help you stop the flow of urine and prevent gas from passing—can also help you reverse ED.

⫸ *Breakthrough Study*

Fifty-five men with ED were divided into two groups. One group learned pelvic floor exercises. The other received advice about positive lifestyle changes, such as how to quit smoking and lose weight.

After three months, the men who learned the pelvic floor exercises had much higher scores on the International Index of Erectile Function—more sexual desire; harder, more dependable erections and stronger orgasms. Overall, they were more satisfied with sex. (And so were their partners, who were also surveyed.)

At that point in the study, the men who weren't in the pelvic floor group learned the techniques. After another three months, 22 of the 55 men—40%—had achieved completely

normal erections. Another 19 men had better erections.

"Pelvic floor muscle exercises are effective in treating men with erectile dysfunction and should be the first-line approach to treat the problem for men who prefer a more natural approach—who don't want to take medication for ED," says Grace Dorey, PhD, a physical therapist at Somerset Nuffield Hospital in Taunton, England, and the lead researcher for the study, published in the *British Journal of General Practice*. Or, she says, men can use the exercise along with medical treatments, to boost their effectiveness.

What to do: Here are instructions for exercises to strengthen your pelvic floor, from the researchers who conducted the study.

Stand with your feet slightly apart and tighten your pelvic floor muscles—the same tensing action as if you were stopping the flow of urine or stopping yourself from passing gas.

Look in a mirror—if you're doing the exercise correctly, you'll see the base of the penis move a bit nearer the abdomen and your testicles rise slightly. (Try not to hold your breath, pull in your gut or tense your buttocks while doing the exercise.)

Hold the contraction as strongly and tightly as you can, for about 10 seconds.

Do these contractions 18 times a day...

● **Perform three contractions every morning while standing** (perhaps while shaving) and three every evening while standing (perhaps while brushing your teeth).

● **Perform three contractions every morning and three every evening while sitting,** perhaps at breakfast and again at dinner.

● **Perform three contractions every morning while lying** (before getting out of bed) and three in the evening (after getting in bed).

IF ONLY THEY WERE LOVE HANDLES!

Love handle, spare tire, beer belly, potbelly—whatever you call extra abdominal fat, you can't really call it sexy.

Guys over 60 with big bellies are more likely to have ED, say Brazilian researchers in the *Journal of Urology*. In fact, the scientists found that the men with the biggest waistlines were 20 times more likely to suffer from the problem than those with trim middles.

But men who *lose* weight (by cutting calories and increasing physical activity) are 30% more likely to reverse ED compared with overweight, inactive men, say Italian researchers in the *Journal of the American Medical Association*.

You can also tighten pelvic muscles rhythmically *during* sex to help maintain penile rigidity. For maximum benefit, "maintain the exercises for the rest of your life," says Dr. Dorey.

Also helpful: Slow, thrusting movements during sex are another way to generate higher pressure inside the penis and keep it more rigid.

ASIAN GINSENG PROVIDES PROVEN POTENCY

For thousands of years, Asian men have used local varieties of the energy-giving herb Asian ginseng—also called *panax ginseng,* Korean ginseng, Korean red ginseng and Chinese ginseng—to protect or restore potency. But, as one text on natural remedies puts it, "There are no studies to support this usage." Now there are, with the latest in the *Asian Journal of Andrology.* ("Andrology" is the study of men's health and sexuality.)

▍▶ *Breakthrough Study*

Doctors in the Sector of Sexual Medicine at Sao Paulo University in Brazil gave 60 men with ED either 3,000 milligrams (mg) a day of Korean red ginseng or a placebo.

After three months, the men taking ginseng had an average 22% increase in their scores on the International Index of Erectile Function. (Meanwhile, the men taking the placebo had an improvement of only 4%.) Two-thirds of the men on ginseng reported improved erections, with more "rigidity," "maintenance" and "penetration," say the doctors. "Korean red ginseng can be an effective alternative for treating male ED," they conclude.

In a similar study, conducted in Korea, men with ED receiving 2,700 mg of Asian ginseng a day for two months had a 27% improvement in erectile function.

"Asian ginseng is a safe, widely available alternative remedy that improves a man's ability to achieve and maintain an erection sufficient for intercourse, even in men with severe ED," says Amy Price, MD, an assistant professor in the Department of Family Medicine at the University of Virginia Health Sciences Center. "It's a reasonable, nonprescription treatment, especially for men with reservations about taking Viagra—because of availability, safety and cost." (Asian ginseng is a lot cheaper than Viagra, she points out. "A 500 milligram capsule costs about six cents, compared with ten dollars for a tablet of Viagra.")

Why it works: No one knows for sure, says Amanda McQuade Crawford, a medical herbalist based in Los Angeles. But, she adds, it is known that ginseng improves microcirculation in the penis and helps regulate the levels of male hormones—two effects that probably help counter ED.

Suggested intake: 2,500 to 3,000 mg a day, in three doses, says Crawford. If you're taking a liquid extract of ginseng, use 1 to 3 milliliters a day, or about ½ teaspoon, twice a day.

Ginseng is a tonic, with long-term positive effects that aren't dependent on daily use. Once you see a benefit from the herb, consider taking it three out of every four weeks rather than every day.

ⓘ For purity and effectiveness, try the powdered and encapsulated ginseng from Enzymatic Therapy, or the liquid extract from Herb Pharm, says Crawford. Both are available in retail stores and on-line.

Important: You may have read that ginseng is too stimulating an herb for long-term use, particularly for men with high blood pressure or heart disease. But, says Crawford, ginseng is generally safe. *However...*

Caution: If you're taking blood-thinning drugs such as warfarin, talk with your physician before taking ginseng, which may decrease the power of these medications. Men with uncontrolled blood pressure should avoid ginseng. Ditto for those suffering from chronic headaches or insomnia.

RED KWAO KRUA—MEN IN THAILAND LOVE THIS HERB

Its Latin name is *butea superba*. And this herb from Thailand—a vine with glorious flowers and a thick, reddish root that has traditionally been ground into a powder and used as an ingredient in sexual tonics—does a superb job of relieving ED.

▐▶ *Breakthrough Study*

Researchers at Chulalongkorn University in Bangkok studied 24 men with ED, aged 30 to 70, giving them 500 mg of *B. superba* twice a day for three months. *And after three months, the men taking B. superba were much happier...*

• **Sexual confidence.** At the start of the study, 80% of men taking the herb had "low confidence" about getting an erection during sex. By the end of the study, that number was reduced to 23%.

• **Hardness.** At the start of the study, 41% of the men never or almost never had an erection hard enough for penetration. After three months, only 18% of the herb takers had this problem.

• **Endurance.** Before taking the herb, 65% had difficulty maintaining an erection to the end of intercourse. The final number was 30%.

Overall, say the researchers, 82% of the men taking the herb showed "fair to excellent improvement" in ED.

Why it works: Erections are orchestrated by the *corpus cavernosum*—two wads of spongy tissue along the length of the penis that fill with blood. For the *corpus* to expand, several biochemical dominos have to fall—nitric oxide activates an enzyme that increases *cyclic guanosine monophospate* (cGMP), which relaxes the smooth muscles, allowing blood to flow into the penis, stiffening it. Viagra, Cialis and Levitra work by blocking *phosphodiesterase*—an enzyme that destroys cGMP. *Butea superba* may work the same way, say the researchers— "by increasing the relaxation capacity of the corpus cavernosum smooth muscles via phosphodiesterase inhibition."

The researchers also conducted blood tests to gauge the drug's safety. There was no negative change in any biochemical measurement, they report, adding that several men with heart disease and type 2 diabetes safely took the herb.

Also important: Laboratory studies show that *B. superba* also kills cancer cells; increases *acetylcholine,* a chemical that aids memory; and boosts sperm count. (It also stimulates the heck out of male rats. An extract of the herb triggered more mounting, less time between mounting and more ejaculations.)

ⓘ Kwaopet, a product with *butea superba* and other restorative herbs from Thailand, has been created under the supervision of Dr. Wichai Cherdshewasart, the researcher who conducted the study.

Suggested intake: Follow the dosage recommendation on the label. Talk to your doctor before taking *butea superba.*

☀ *www.butea-superba.net.* PhuketHerb Ltd., 369/22 Yoawarach Road, Taladyai Mueng Phuket, Thailand 83000 (66-76-218-212); e-mail: *info@phuketherb.com.*

GINKGO—AVOID ED WITH ANTIDEPRESSANTS

Talk about depressing! Taking antidepressant medications—particularly *serotonin selective reuptake inhibitors* (SSRIs) such as Celexa, Luvox, Paxil, Zoloft or Prozac—can increase the risk of ED by 70%! (SSRIs are also a common cause of orgasm difficulties—having no orgasm, a delayed orgasm or an unsatisfying orgasm.)

The herb ginkgo biloba—a circulation-boosting herb often taken to improve memory—may improve those odds.

▌▌▌➡ *Breakthrough Study*

Researchers at the University of California in San Francisco (UCSF) gave an average daily dose of 200 mg of ginkgo biloba extract to men with antidepressant-caused ED. After taking ginkgo, 76% of the men had more reliable erections (and more consistent orgasms). In another study, conducted by researchers in England, ginkgo produced "spectacular individual responses" in men with antidepressant-caused ED.

Why it works: Any number of factors might cause the improvement, say the UCSF researchers, including improved blood flow and positive changes in brain chemistry.

Suggested intake: 200 to 240 mg a day, in doses of 100 to 120 mg, twice a day.

🛈 Ginkgo biloba is widely available. Some brands with the suggested intake include NOW Gingko Biloba, 120 mg; Jarrow Formulas Ginkgo Biloba, 120 mg and Natrol Gingko Biloba, 120 mg.

Caution: Ginkgo biloba might boost the power of blood-thinning medications for heart disease, such as aspirin or warfarin, and of glucose-lowering oral medications for diabetes, such as metformin. Take ginkgo biloba only after a conversation with your doctor or pharmacist.

Also helpful: Other ideas you and your doctor might want to consider to counter sexual side effects from antidepressants, from Pam Rockwell, DO, assistant professor in the Department of Family Medicine at the University of Michigan Medical School: Don't take your daily antidepressant medication until *after* sex. Reduce the dosage. Switch to a different antidepressant, such as Wellbutrin.

POMEGRANATE JUICE— NATURE'S APHRODISIAC

"If the pomegranates flourish, there will I give thee my breasts."

That sexy passage from the Song of Solomon may in fact be prophetic. A study in the *International Journal of Impotence Research* shows that drinking pomegranate juice may help you overcome ED.

▌▌▌➡ *Breakthrough Study*

Doctors from the University of Southern California and The Male Clinic in Beverly Hills asked 61 men with ED to drink either pomegranate juice or a look-alike placebo drink every day for two months. Forty-seven of the men drinking pomegranate juice reported improved erections, nearly one-third more than the placebo group.

"These findings suggest that pomegranate juice is a nondrug way to alleviate ED," says Harin Padma-Nathan, MD, clinical professor of urology at USC, and one of the researchers who conducted the study. "Drinking pomegranate juice daily could be an important addition to a healthy diet in the management of this condition."

Why it works: Previous studies have shown that antioxidant-rich pomegranate juice improves blood flow—a crucial factor in overcoming ED.

Suggested intake: The men in the study drank 8 ounces a day, with or just after dinner.

ℹ️ The study used POM Wonderful pomegranate juice, which is widely available.

ACUPUNCTURE FOR MORE SEXUAL ENERGY

Acupuncture is an ancient healing system from China—the acupuncturist inserts tiny (and virtually painless) needles along one or more of the body's "meridians," or energy channels, restoring and balancing energy.

And acupuncture, it seems, can deliver more energy to where you might want it most.

⫸ *Breakthrough Study*

Doctors in Austria gave men with ED either acupuncture for ED or acupuncture for headaches (a placebo treatment). Seventeen men out of 20 receiving acupuncture ED showed improvement, compared to only two out of 20 in the placebo group. "Acupuncture can be an effective treatment option for ED," says Paul Engelhardt, MD, in the *International Journal of Impotence Research.*

☀️ *www.acupuncture.com:* scroll down the home page to "Find an Acupuncturist," where you can search a database of more than 30,000 acupuncture practitioners by zip code. Or contact Acufinder.com, 825 College Blvd., Suite 102-211, Oceanside, CA 92057 (760-630-3600).

THE MARLBORO MAN PROBABLY HAD ED

You've seen the classic sexy image, where a guy lights up a cigarette after sex and takes a deep, leisurely drag. *Well, that guy might not be having sex again anytime soon…*

What you may not know: In a study of nearly 5,000 men between the ages of 35 and 74, smokers who *didn't* have heart disease—in other words, basically healthy guys—had a 41% higher risk of ED than nonsmokers. And the more they smoked, the higher the risk, say researchers in the *American Journal of Epidemiology.* Those smoking up to 10 cigarettes a day had a 27% higher risk; those puffing away on 11 to 20 cigarettes a day, 45%; and those smoking more than a pack a day, 65% higher.

In other words, where there's smoke, there's a lot less fire.

Good news: Stopping smoking can help restore normal erections in less than 24 hours, say researchers from Lahey Hitchcock Medical Center in Burlington, MA.

YOHIMBE TO RESTORE ORGASMS

Sometimes a man can get an erection but can't have an orgasm, a problem known as *orgasmic dysfunction.* There are many possible causes, both physical (such as nerve damage or a drug side effect) and psychological (such as depression or severe stress).

Whatever the cause, *yohimbine*—the active ingredient of the herb *yohimbe,* the bark of an evergreen tree from West Africa and a traditional aphrodisiac—may help.

⫸ *Breakthrough Study*

Doctors in England gave 20 mg a day of yohimbine to 29 men with orgasmic dysfunction, allowing them to increase the dose if needed. Sixteen of the men achieved orgasm—including several men who subsequently fathered children. "Yohimbine is a useful treatment option in orgasmic dysfunction," say the doctors, in the *Asian Journal of Andrology.*

Red flag: Yohimbine is a potent herbal extract that stimulates the adrenal glands and

---

SIZE DOESN'T MATTER— EXCEPT TO YOU

If your partner is like 85% of women, she's pleased with the size of your penis.

If you're like 45% of men, you still want a bigger member.

That desire is particularly common among men with ED, say Drs. Kevin Wylie and Ian Eardley, urologists at St. James Hospital in Leeds, England, writing in *BJU International.* When the machinery isn't working properly, it's perfectly normal to question whether it was properly manufactured.

But if anxiety about your six inches (5.5 to 6.2 inches is the length of the average erect penis, and most men are average) becomes obsessive—if you think about penis size frequently and check it often—you may have what the doctors call "small penis syndrome." *Their advice...*

• Make an appointment with an understanding urologist. The doctor can reassure you that your penis is normal. (Unless you have a relatively rare condition called *micropenis*—a penis less than 2.75 inches when erect.)

• Stay away from penis-extending systems, such as Phallosan and Penistretcher. There is no scientific evidence they offer real benefits.

• Ditto for plastic surgery. Except in the case of a truly deformed penis, the techniques are unproven and may cause harm.

• If the visit with the urologist doesn't relieve your anxiety, and concern over a small penis continues to dominate your life, consider seeing a psychotherapist.

---

can cause rapid heart rate, high blood pressure, anxiety, dizziness and insomnia.

What to do: Use a low, safe dose of yohimbe (15 to 30 mg), in combination with other herbs that can improve sexual functioning, says Ray Sahelian, MD, author of *Natural Sex Boosters* (Square One Publishers).

 Passion Rx with Yohimbe, which Dr. Sahelian says can not only help with orgasmic dysfunction but also increase sex drive and overall sexual enjoyment.

Suggested intake: Follow the dosage recommendation on the label. However, says Dr. Sahelian, men with circulatory problems of any kind (high blood pressure, high cholesterol, heart disease, stroke, diabetes) should use a stimulating herb such as yohimbe only with the approval and supervision of a physician.

☀ *www.physicianformulas.com.*

USE L-CARNITINE WHEN VIAGRA FAILS

What should you do when Viagra doesn't *Viva?* You might try Viagra *and* L-carnitine, a vitaminlike nutrient that helps the body turn fat into energy.

▐▐▐▶ *Breakthrough Study*

Italian researchers from the University La Sapienza in Rome studied 40 men with ED and diabetes who had tried Viagra (*sildenafil*) at least eight times—without success. They divided the men into two groups. One group took Viagra again; one group took Viagra *and* daily doses of L-carnitine.

After 6 months, 68% of the men taking Viagra and L-carnitine had improved erections; only 23% of the Viagra-takers could say the same. Seventy-six of those taking the drug with the nutrient had "successful intercourse attempts," compared with 34% among the Viagra-only group.

What to do: If you've tried Viagra without success, talk to your doctor about adding L-carnitine to your regimen. (L-carnitine is considered very safe; none of the men in the Italian study reported significant side effects from the nutrient.)

Suggested intake: Two grams of L-carnitine daily.

🛈 The researchers used a form of L-carnitine called *propionyl-L-carnitine* (PLC), which is widely available.

BALDNESS

By the age of 50, more than 50% of men suffer from some degree of baldness—what doctors call *androgenetic alopecia,* or male pattern hair loss. And studies show that when men start to lose their hair, they often (not surprising) feel less attractive, old, depressed—and worried about going *completely* bald.

But research also shows that fewer than 25% of men actively pursue treatments for stopping, slowing or reversing hair loss—even though many men who are treated and experience some degree of success feel more attractive, with higher self-esteem.

What are your options if you want to slow or stop hair loss, or restore your hair?

Drugs can help. There's Propecia (*finasteride*), an oral medication. It works by blocking the action of 5AR (*5-alpha-reductase*), an enzyme that speeds the conversion of testosterone into DHT (*dihydrotestosterone*), the hormone that shrinks hair follicles. Problem is, Propecia also causes low libido, erectile dysfunction and/or delayed orgasms in about 2% of men who take it. (These problems usually reverse when a guy stops taking Propecia, but not always.)

There's also Rogaine (*minoxidil*), a topical treatment that probably works by speeding up hair growth and increasing the size of follicles. Hair replacement surgery is another possibility.

Those are reliable and reasonably safe options, used by many men. But if drugs or surgery don't match your style (or your budget), there are also drug-free treatments that scientific studies show can work to slow, stop or reverse hair loss.

LASER COMB—HALT THE HAIR LOSS

When you think of a *laser,* you probably think of a high-powered beam of light slicing through steel or deflecting a missile. But for more than 30 years, doctors around the world have used *low-level laser light* to speed wound healing and relieve pain, with more than 2,500 scientific studies showing low-level lasers work.

In the last decade, studies have found the low-level laser light can affect the *scalp,* helping men grow more hair. Now, even the government's Food and Drug Administration (FDA) thinks this drug-free baldness remedy is a good idea.

‖▶ *Breakthrough Study*

Dermatologists conducted clinical studies at four medical centers in the United States on 123 men aged 30 to 60 with varying degrees of hair loss, from mild to fairly advanced. They asked the men to brush their hair for 10 to 15 minutes, 3 times a week, for 26 weeks—either with a comb installed with a low-level laser light or a fake, look-alike comb with a nonlaser light.

After 26 weeks, the men using the laser comb had an *increase* of 19 hairs per square centimeter of scalp. The men using the fake laser had a *decrease* of 11 hairs per centimeter.

How it works: Low-level laser light stimulates *mitochondria,* energy-generating structures in every cell, including the cells of hair follicles, explains Matt Leavitt, DO, founder and medical director of Medical Hair Restoration and Advanced Dermatology, a company providing hair restoration in 40 cities across the United States. With more energy production, hair follicles function more normally—and are more likely to sprout hair.

The best candidate: "The earlier you are in the balding process, the better the laser comb will work to delay hair loss and restore hair," says Dr. Leavitt. In fact, he uses it himself, along with Propecia and Rogaine. "I started using the laser comb a year ago and notice more fullness in my hair," he says. But you have to comb every day, he adds, because if you stop daily use, restored hair falls out.

ℹ️ The comb used in the study was the HairMax LaserComb, and based on the research with the device the FDA approved it to "promote hair growth in males with androgenetic alopecia."

Caution: There are other laser comb products on the market, but they are not FDA-approved because no scientific research shows they work.

☀ *www.lasercomb.net* (800-963-4369). Lexington International LLC, 777 Yamato Road, Suite 105, Boca Raton, FL 33431. The HairMax Lasercomb is also widely available on the Internet and through retail outlets.

LOSE YOUR HEALTH, LOSE YOUR HAIR?

Male pattern hair loss—*androgenetic alopecia*—is *genetic* right? In other words, you're not to blame—but your dad, granddad and great-granddad sure are. *Or are they...*

Doctors in the Department of Public Health at the University of Oulu in Finland studied 245 63-year-olds, 58% of whom had extensive hair loss. Those with less hair also had less health. They were 43% more likely to have type 2 diabetes and 26% more likely to have high blood pressure. Is there a connection?

Maybe, says Paivi Hirsso, MD, PhD, the lead author of the study. It might be *insulin resistance.* This blood sugar disorder, common to both diabetes and high blood pressure, reduces circulation—possibly reducing the flow of oxygen and nutrients to hair follicles, triggering hair loss.

Dr. Hirsso isn't saying, however, that treating diabetes or high blood pressure will cure baldness. But he is advising men with hair loss to get a medical checkup to make sure they don't have undiagnosed (and therefore dangerously untreated) type 2 diabetes or high blood pressure.

PROCYANIDINS—WHY ADAM WASN'T BALD

Although the Bible says Adam lived to be 930 years old, there's no mention that he ever went bald. Maybe it was the apple he ate.

▶ *Breakthrough Studies*

In the 1990s, researchers in Japan examined about 1,000 plant extracts for their power to grow hair. One type of extract was particularly impressive, *procyanidins,* found in apples and grapes. In the laboratory, procyanidins more than doubled the growth of hair follicle cells in mice. And, say the researchers, procyanidins showed "remarkable" ability to switch hairs from the resting *telogen* phase to the growing *anagen* phase.

As their research developed, the scientists isolated two uniquely effective procyanidins, which they named B-2 and C-1. Topical application of these procyanidins on the backs of shaven mice triggered 70 to 80% hair regrowth.

In 2000, the researchers tested apple-derived procyanidins in people, treating 29 men with male pattern baldness with scalp applications of either B-2 or a placebo. After six months, the men getting B-2 had seven more hairs per 0.05 square centimeters of scalp, compared with no increase for the placebo group. "Procyanidin B-2 therapy shows potential as a safe and promising cure for male pattern baldness," say the researchers, in *Phytomedicine*.

A few years later, in 2005, the Japanese scientists duplicated these results in a study in which they treated 43 men with male pattern baldness for one year with either a topical formula containing apple procyanidins or a placebo. After six months, the procyanidin group had 3.3 more hairs per 0.5 square centimeters, while the placebo group lost an average of four hairs. "Procyanidin therapy shows potential hair-growing activity," say the researchers, in the *Journal of Cosmetic Dermatology*.

"Perhaps the old adage 'An apple a day keeps the doctor away' may change to 'An apple a day keeps the hair transplant surgeon away,'" says William Rassman, MD, founder of the New Hair Institute, in Los Angeles, CA.

How it works: Procyanidins may reduce the activity of an enzyme—protein kinase C —that limits the growth of hair cells.

ⓘ Revita shampoo, from DS Laboratories, contains high levels of procyanidins B-1 and C-2, along with a number of other natural ingredients intended to stimulate hair growth. It is widely available in retail stores and on the Internet. For more information, see *www.dslaboratories.com/revita*.

Also helpful: Two other topical products rich in apple procyanidins are Poly-GRO Procyanidin B-2 and Poly-GRO Ultimate. Order via the Internet at *www.applepoly.com,* by mail at Apple Poly, PO Box 732, Morrill NE 69358-0732 (888-277-5332).

SAW PALMETTO NOURISHES HAIR FOLLICLES

The herb saw palmetto (*Serona repens*) works like Propecia, blocking the enzyme 5AR, so that less testosterone is converted to follicle-shrinking DHT. Could saw palmetto help slow, stop or reverse hair loss? One study says so.

||||▶ *Breakthrough Study*

A team of doctors in Colorado asked 10 men between the ages of 23 and 64 with mild to moderate hair loss to take a supplement with 200 mg of saw palmetto and several other natural ingredients for six months. During the study, *all* the men said their hair loss stopped, and eight said it had reversed, with new hair that was somewhat thicker. At the end of the study, an independent team concluded that six of the 10 men had improvement, with hair loss slowed, stopped or reversed.

"This study establishes for the first time the effectiveness of natural 5AR inhibitors against androgenetic alopecia," say the researchers, in the *Journal of Alternative and Complementary Medicine*.

Suggested intake: 200 mg of saw palmetto extract a day.

ⓘ The researchers used the Revitalizing Oral Softgel supplement from HairGenesis.

Red flag: HairGenesis sells this supplement as part of a line of four hair-restoring products, including a topical serum, shampoo and conditioner, notes Paradi Mirmirani, MD, Department of Dermatology at Vallejo Medical Center, CA. However, she says, there are no scientific studies that show any of the other three products work. She also points out that buying all four HairGenesis products costs approximately $200 for a three-month supply—while saw palmetto supplements cost about $3 per month.

☀ You can buy the saw palmetto supplement from HairGenesis—without having to buy their entire line of hair-restoring products—at *www.hairgenesis.net,* or by calling 800-736-0729. Follow the dosage recommendation on the label.

ENLARGED PROSTATE

At least you're not alone. An enlarged or swollen prostate is *the* most common health problem among older men, hitting half of all guys in their 60s and nine out of 10 men in their 70s and 80s.

The good news is doctors call the disorder *benign prostatic hyperplasia* (BPH). And *benign* means what it says: BPH doesn't turn into prostate cancer or increase your risk.

The bad news is if you have BPH, the normally natural process of urinating can become difficult.

The prostate helps produce the semen that transports the sperm to their destination. But it's crowded down there. The prostate also hugs the urethra, the tube that channels semen and drains the bladder. So when the prostate swells, urination suffers.

The flow of urine might be hard to start…slow and weak after it gets going, with some stops and starts…and dribble at the end, with the sensation that your bladder isn't really empty. You might feel the need to urinate more often (including getting up at night) and feel a greater urgency when you have to go. As the swelling increases year after year, some men develop urinary tract infections and even kidney damage, as urine backs up.

What causes the prostate to enlarge as you age?

The main culprit is the same hormone that is responsible for triggering hair loss—DHT, or *dihydrotestosterone.* So it's not surprising that one of the main treatments is a drug that doubles as a baldness remedy (Propecia) and prostate treatment (Proscar)—*finasteride,* which works by inhibiting the action of an enzyme that converts testosterone into DHT.

You can also take a drug to relax the muscles around the prostate (a so-called *alpha blocker,* such as Flomax). You can try procedures that use microwaves, radio waves or lasers to shrink the gland. Or, for more advanced cases, there's surgery—*transurethral resection* of the prostate, or TURP, which slices off sections of the gland. Needless to say, none of these medical approaches are risk-free.

Surgery, for example, often produces *retrograde ejaculation*—semen shoots into the bladder instead of the urethra. A primary pleasure of life is put in reverse.

Enzyme inhibitors can also cause sexual difficulties, such as erectile dysfunction and/or low libido. And alpha blockers can make you less of an alpha male, triggering ejaculation problems. They can also cause headaches, stomachaches, low blood pressure and dizziness.

Given those side effects, it's not surprising that many men (particularly those with mild to moderate but still bothersome symptoms) opt for effective natural alternatives.

BETA-SITOSTEROL BEATS PROSTATE ENLARGEMENT

If you lived in Germany and saw a doctor for mild to moderate urinary symptoms from an enlarged prostate, you might get a prescription for Harzol—but it's not a drug! It's a natural medication that contains concentrated amounts of *beta-sitosterol*—a *phytosterol* (a cholesterol-like substance) found in many foods, such as pumpkin seeds, wheat germ and soy beans.

Beta-sitosterol probably works like Proscar, the prostate drug that blocks the action of an enzyme that turns testosterone into dihydrotestosterone (DHT).

⫸ *Breakthrough Study*

German doctors in the Department of Urology at the Ruhr-University of Bochum gave 200 men with BPH either 60 mg of beta-sitosterol a day or a placebo. After six months, the men taking the supplement had a 35% increase in the strength of their urine flow and a 54% decrease in the amount of dribbling at the end of urination. They also urinated less frequently (including at night) and had less sense of urgency when they needed to urinate. There was no change in the placebo group.

After 18 months, the men taking beta-sitosterol continued to have the same positive benefits—and 27 men with BPH in the placebo group who had started taking beta-sitosterol after the six months of the original study also experienced similar improvements.

Beta-sitosterol is effective in treating BPH, say the doctors, in *The Lancet,* one of the world's leading medical journals.

Suggested intake: 20 mg, three times a day, with meals.

ℹ In their study, the German doctors used the beta-sitosterol supplement Harzol. It is an ingredient in ModuProst, a widely available over-the-counter herbal and nutritional supplement. Follow the dosage recommendation on the label. (ModuProst also includes the phytosterols from herb saw palmetto, which is discussed below.)

There are many other beta-sitosterol products available, with brands including Natrol, Source Naturals, NOW and Swanson.

SAW PALMETTO INSTEAD OF PRESCRIPTIONS

Call it the Two Million Man March—a march away from the bathroom and to the supplement section of the drugstore, supermarket or health food store…to buy saw palmetto.

Two million is the number of men in the United States with BPH who take the herb, an extract from the berries of *serona repens,* an American shrub that looks like a miniature palm tree. They have plenty of pals in Europe, Asia, Africa and India, where a standardized extract of saw palmetto—a natural medicine called Permixon—is considered the best first treatment for BPH, before prescription drugs are tried.

Why is saw palmetto so popular? Because it works.

⫸ *Breakthrough Study*

Glenn S. Gerber, MD, an associate professor of surgery and urology in the Division of Urology at the University of Chicago Medical School, has conducted several of the more than 30 scientific studies on saw palmetto and BPH. Working with a European colleague, he recently analyzed all the research on Permixon and BPH, publishing his results in the *British Journal of Urology.*

He looked at more than two decades of studies on Permixon—including a six-month study involving more than 1,000 men that compared Permixon to Proscar (finasteride). The study found that Permixon worked just as well as Proscar, but didn't cause impotence or lowered libido, two possible sexual side effects of the drug. His analysis also showed that Permixon works as well as alpha-blockers such as Flomax—but doesn't cause the ejaculatory difficulties sometimes triggered by these drugs.

Dr. Gerber concluded that "Permixon significantly reduces the symptoms of BPH,

327

increases urinary flow, improves the quality of life and is well-tolerated." And not only does it reduce those symptoms, he says, it can also slow the progression of the disease.

How it works: Like beta-sitosterol (discussed above), saw palmetto may reduce DHT, a hormone that stimulates the prostate.

It might also decrease inflammation, another possible cause of BPH. And studies show that saw palmetto may help regulate the lifecycle of prostate cells, stopping them from multiplying.

Safety: Dr. Gerber notes that serious side effects with saw palmetto are "extremely uncommon." Occasionally, he says, you might experience some mild GI upset, a side effect you can probably prevent by taking the herb with a meal.

What to do: Have your BPH symptoms evaluated by a doctor—and discuss whether saw palmetto might be a possible first-line therapy for the treatment of your urinary symptoms. In other words, it may be worth trying before you turn to prescription drugs and other medical treatments.

Suggested dosage: The level of dosing used in many studies and recommended by Germany's authoritative Commission E on herbs is 320 mg daily, in one or two doses.

GREEN TEA AS A PROMISING REMEDY

Korean scientists divided male rats into two groups, injecting one group with prostate-enlarging testosterone, and one group with testosterone *and* catechins, the active ingredient in green tea. The prostates of the catechin rats grew by 20%, while the prostates of the noncatechins rates nearly *tripled* in size. The next step for the researchers is to do studies on people.

Dr. Gerber recommends Permixon because decades of studies show it works and it contains a standardized extract of saw palmetto—but it's not available in the United States.

Fortunately, there are many over-the-counter products with saw palmetto. Unfortunately, a study in the *Journal of Urology* showed that three brands contained only 20% of the dose advertised on the label!

To avoid a bogus product, use a brand of saw palmetto approved by www.ConsumerLab.com, an independent testing firm that verifies the reliability of the ingredients on the label of nutritional and herbal products. Those brands include Designs for Health, Herbalife, Nature's Bounty, New Chapter, NOW, Nutrilite, PhytoPharmica, Premier Value, Puritan's Pride, Source Naturals, Sundown, TerraVita, Vitamin Shoppe, Vitamin World, Vitasmart (Kmart) or Walgreens.

PYGEUM AFRICANUM— ANOTHER OPTION

African healers from Angola to Zimbabwe use the powdered bark of a tall evergreen tree (*pygeum africanum* to botanists; gwane, kirah and muchambati to locals) to treat urinary problems from BPH. A group of doctors in Minnesota think they might have the right idea.

⫸ *Breakthrough Study*

Scientists from the Minneapolis Veterans Affairs Center reviewed 18 studies on pygeum africanum for BPH, involving more than 1,500 men. Compared with men taking a placebo, men taking pygeum africanum were twice as likely to report a benefit, with 20% fewer episodes of nighttime urination and a 23% increase in urine flow. "Pygeum africanum may be a useful treatment option for men with lower urinary tract symptoms" from BPH, say the researchers, in the *American Journal of Medicine.*

Why it works: It reduces inflammation and strengthens the bladder.

Suggested dosage: The typical dose used in studies is 75 to 200 mg a day.

ⓘ Pygeum africanum is widely available, often in combination with saw palmetto.

NETTLE TO RELIEVE BPH

If your prostate is stinging you with the urinary symptoms of BPH, you might want to sting back…by taking a supplement of stinging nettle (*urtica dioica*).

⏩ *Breakthrough Study*

Doctors asked 558 men with BPH to take either stinging nettle or a placebo. After six months, 81% of the men taking the herb had improved urinary symptoms, compared with 16% taking the placebo.

By the end of the study, the nettle group also had a 40% average improvement in their International Prostate Symptom Score (indicating more complete emptying, decreased frequency of urination, less urgency, stronger flow and other positive changes), compared with an 8% improvement in the placebo group. And their prostate shrank by 9%, while the prostates of the placebo takers stayed the same size.

Stinging nettle has "beneficial effects in the treatment of symptomatic BPH," says Mohammad Reza Safarinejad, MD, the researcher who conducted the study, an associate editor of the *Urology Journal* and the director of the Department of Urology at the University of Medical Sciences in Iran. The study was published in the *Journal of Herbal Pharmacotherapy.*

How it works: Three ways, says Dr. Safarinejad. It blocks the action of a biochemical called "prostate growth factor"…it limits the generation of energy in prostate cells…and it alters how prostate-stimulating hormones attach to prostate cells.

Suggested dosage and product: There have been more than a dozen studies on stinging nettle using a daily dose of the natural medicine Bazoton, a standardized extract of 300 mg of stinging nettle (*Urticae radix*). However, Bazoton is not available in the United States. Instead, look for a stinging nettle product that contains at least 300 mg of the herb; they are widely available.

Also helpful: Several studies show that combining stinging nettle with saw palmetto is very effective. In a recent study, German doctors gave an herbal combination of 160 mg of saw palmetto and 120 mg of stinging nettle or Flomax to 140 men with BPH for 14 months. Thirty-three percent of the men taking the herb had an improvement in symptoms, compared to 28% of the men taking the drug.

Caution: The men in the Iranian study didn't have any side effects from taking stinging nettle, even after followup at 18 months. But, says Dr. Safarinejad, the herb may increase blood sugar levels and may boost the power of medications for blood thinning and lowering blood pressure. As with all herbal and nutritional supplements, discuss stinging nettle (or a stinging nettle/saw palmetto combination) with your doctor and/or pharmacist before taking the herb.

PROSTATITIS

Prostatitis is the most common reason for men under 50 to see a urologist, with 2 million office vists a year. In 5% of cases, the problem is *acute prostatitis,* a bacterial infection of the prostate. Antibiotics clear it up. But in 95% of cases, the problem is *chronic prostatitis* (also called *chronic pelvis pain syndrome,* or CP/CPPS). At some point in their lives, approximately 10% of all men will suffer the painful and debilitating symptoms of CP/CPPS.

You can have pain in the perineum (the muscles at the floor of the pelvis)...pain at the tip of the penis...pain in the testicles...pain in the bladder area...pain in the rectum. You can have pain when you urinate...pain during orgasm. And the pain can go on and on—usually for three months or more, either intermittently or nonstop. With all that pain, it's likely you'll lose sleep, your sex drive and your enjoyment of everyday life.

But even when a man has *chronic* prostatitis, urologists typically prescribe antibiotics, which rarely clear up the problem. (A new study shows that antibiotics are no more effective than a placebo in treating chronic prostatitis.) Now, cutting-edge medical experts understand that in many cases of chronic prostatitis, the prostate isn't the cause of the pain.

New thinking: "Prostatitis is a *neuromuscular* disorder," says David Wise, PhD, a former sufferer and clinical psychologist who treats men with the problem. "It is a kind of ongoing Charlie horse, or cramp in the pelvic muscles, that takes on a life of its own in a chronic cycle of tension, anxiety and pain." And, says Dr. Wise, drugs and surgery don't solve the problem—in fact, they might make it worse.

"The most commonly prescribed medications for chronic prostatitis are not consistently effective," agrees Jeannette Potts, MD, a urologist at the Cleveland Clinic's Glickman Urological Institute. That's why, she adds, nondrug therapies for chronic prostatitis are growing in popularity among patients—and gaining acceptance among doctors.

RELAXATION AND TRIGGER POINT THERAPY—THE STANFORD PROTOCOL

Two health-care professionals—Dr. Wise and Rodney Anderson, MD, a urologist and director of the Stanford Pelvic Pain Clinic at the Stanford University School of Medicine—have created a new treatment based on the latest understanding of the cause of chronic prostatitis. It's called the Stanford Protocol. And the amazing news for men who have suffered for years from the pain of prostatitis is that (unlike most medical treatments)...it actually works!

⫸ *Breakthrough Studies*

Drs. Wise, Anderson and their team of researchers studied 138 men with prostatitis—men for whom every other treatment had failed. They asked the men to undergo a combination of two types of nondrug therapy—*paradoxical relaxation therapy* (PRT) and *myofascial trigger point assessment and release therapy* (MFRT).

• **PRT** is a customized breathing/relaxation technique that shows a man with prostatitis how to break the habit of chronically tensing his pelvic muscles, and how to relax those muscles—even when he's in pain. (Hence, *paradoxical* relaxation.)

• **MFRT** is a type of physical therapy, in which a physical therapist (or a patient who has learned the method) locates knotted "trigger points" in muscles that can shoot pain into various areas of the pelvis—and then presses and stretches them until they release.

After one month of PRT and MFRT, 72% of the men said their prostatitis symptoms were either moderately or markedly improved, with less pain. In those with marked improvement, pain scores fell by an average of 70%. "MFRT combined with PRT represents an effective therapeutic approach for the management of chronic prostatitis, providing pain relief superior to that of traditional [drug] therapy," say Drs. Wise and Anderson, in the *Journal of Urology.*

In a subsequent study at Stanford, the doctors and their team treated 146 men with chronic prostatitis (average age, 42) with MFRT and PRT. Not only did the men's pain improve, but they also had significant reduction in some of the most bothersome symptoms of prostatitis, such as urinary problems (urgency and frequency), lower libido and erectile and ejaculatory dysfunction (painful and/or delayed ejaculation).

How it works: The Stanford Protocol consists of several steps. First, a urologist examines the patient and rules out any underlying disease that might be causing chronic prostatitis, such as prostate cancer. Once a serious disease is ruled out, the patient is trained in trigger point release, paradoxical relaxation and techniques for reducing anxiety, which worsens the disorder.

"I had chronic pelvic pain syndrome for over twenty-two years and I have been symp-

"I STRONGLY ADVISE AGAINST SURGERY"

For a desperate man—a man in pain for years with chronic prostatitis—surgery might seem like the only way out. And thousands of men with CP/CPPS have had painful parts removed—a bladder, pelvic nerves, even testicles! Unfortunately, relief is rarely the result.

"I have never seen a satisfactory surgical intervention in cases where there is no evidence of infection and no anatomical abnormality," says Dr. Anderson.

"I have seen patients who have undergone multiple surgeries in a vain attempt to eradicate their problem. But, in my experience, surgery often hurts the patient, complicating management of their condition, creating new pain and making it *more* difficult to treat the original pain. I strongly advise against surgery for prostatitis from chronic pelvis tension."

tom free for many years as the result of using the protocol we have developed at Stanford," says Dr. Wise.

An "immersion clinic" to learn The Stanford Protocol is available through a six-day program in northern California. To find out more about the program, you can reach Dr. Wise at 866-874-2225 or *ahip@sonic.net.* Or visit *www.pelvicpainhelp.com,* where you'll find extensive information about the Protocol and a current schedule for the six-day intensives. The National Center for Pelvic Pain, PO Box 54, Occidental, CA 95465.

Book: A Headache in the Pelvis: A New Understanding and Treatment for Prostatitis and Chronic Pelvic Pain Syndromes, by David Wise, PhD, and Rodney Anderson, MD (fifth edition). To order, call 800-852-4890.

QUERCETIN—82% GOT BETTER

For men with CP/CPPS and the urologists who treat them, "frustration with this disorder is very high," says Daniel Shoskes, MD, a urologist with the Division of Urology at the Harbor-UCLA Medical Center in Los Angeles.

That's because many of the medical treatments for the condition—antibiotics, alpha blockers (a blood pressure drug that widens arteries and relaxes muscles), anti-inflammatory medications, muscle relaxants, even surgery—often don't work.

Looking for an alternative, Dr. Shoskes and his colleagues decided to test *quercetin*—a compound found in red wine, onions and green tea. Quercetin, research shows, is a powerful antioxidant and helps to reduce inflammation—two features that might make it effective for battling the pain of CP/CPPS. Plus, earlier studies on quercetin and prostatitis showed the nutrient might work.

IIII➤ *Breakthrough Study*

Dr. Shoskes and his colleagues asked 28 men with CP/CPPS to take either quercetin or a placebo for one month. The men taking quercetin had a 38% decrease in pain and urinary problems—the placebo group, 7%.

In the second month of the study, the researchers gave 17 additional men with prostatitis a supplement containing quercetin and two enzymes (bromelain and papain) that boost quercetin's absorption and antioxidant power. Fourteen of the men had a significant reduction in prostatitis symptoms.

Therapy with quercetin provides significant symptomatic improvement in most men with chronic pelvic pain syndrome, says Dr. Shoskes. The therapy, he adds, is "inexpensive and safe."

ℹ️ Dr. Shoskes favors Prosta-Q—the combination of quercetin, bromelain and papain. "I use this product with my patients and I'm thrilled with the results," he says.

Suggested dosage: One 540-mg capsule, three times a day, with meals. "If three times a day is successful, you may be able to manage your symptoms long term with two or even one capsule per day," says Dr. Shoskes.

You may notice a benefit after a few days. However, says Dr. Shoskes, it may take as long as one month to see any reduction in symptoms. "But if Prosta-Q hasn't worked in six to eight weeks, it's unlikely to help you."

What do you do if Prosta-Q completely resolves your symptoms? "I recommend staying on a maintenance dose of one capsule per day for an additional two to three months," says Dr. Shoskes. You may find you can stop the product without symptoms reoccurring—or you might find you need to stay on either the full or the maintenance dose. "Some men have utilized a three-weeks-on/one-week-off regimen with success," he says.

Finally, Dr. Shoskes says if you decide to use Prosta-Q, don't use any other nutritional or herbal remedies for prostatitis. "There is no way of knowing how ingredients in other natural remedies will interact with Prosta-Q—it may interfere with the absorption of Prosta-Q or block its action in other ways."

☀️ Prosta-Q is manufactured by Farr Laboratories. You can order Prosta-Q on-line from Farr Laboratories at *www.farrlabs.com*, or by phone at 877-284-3976.

Caution: Don't take Prosta-Q with quinolone antibiotics (Trovan, Cipro, Levaquin, Noroxin, Floxin, etc.), because it can interfere with their action.

ACUPUNCTURE PINPOINTS THE PELVIC PROBLEM

CP/CPPS is a pain problem that's poorly understood, says Jillian Capodice, LAc. But, she adds, acupuncture is often used to treat painful, chronic conditions, understood or not. And it may work for men with CP/CPPS.

IIII➤ *Breakthrough Study*

Capodice and a team of researchers at Columbia University asked 10 men with CP/CPPS—men for whom at least one conventional medical treatment (such as antibiotics or anti-inflammatory drugs) had failed—to undergo acupuncture treatments twice a week for six weeks. Before the study, and six months to a year after the last acupuncture treatment, the men were asked about their symptoms. The results were remarkable.

On average, the men had 66% less pain, 75% fewer urinary symptoms and a 74% improvement in "quality of life."

"These findings," says Capodice, in the journal *Chinese Medicine,* "suggest that there is a potential therapeutic role of acupuncture in the treatment of CP/CPPS."

☀ To find an acupuncturist near you, Capodice recommends the Web site of the National Certification Commission for Acupuncture and Oriental Medicine, at *www.nccaom.org,* where you can search for certified acupuncturists by area code or zip code. "Look for a practitioner who specializes in urological or chronic pain problems," she says. "Ask your medical doctor and acupuncturist to coordinate their care so that they can implement the treatment plan that works best for you."

BIOFEEDBACK TAMES TENSE PELVIC MUSCLES

In biofeedback, you're hooked up to a machine that monitors a bodily function, such as heart rate, blood pressure or muscle tension. When the function is out of whack—heart racing, pressure spiking or muscles tensing—the machine gives you feedback, perhaps with a beep that sounds more rapidly or a light that flashes more frequently. When you directly *experience* the problem, you can *correct* the problem—and that goes for CP/CPPS.

▶ *Breakthrough Study*

A team of urologists and physical therapists in Holland asked 31 men with CP/CPPS to undergo a "pelvic floor biofeedback re-education program"—a series of biofeedback treatments that showed them when pelvic muscles were tense, and then showed them how to relax them. After the treatment, the men had a 66% decrease in tension in pelvic floor muscles—and a 52% decrease in pain and urinary problems.

Biofeedback leads to a significant improvement of symptoms in men with CP/CPPS, say the researchers, in the journal *European Urology.*

☀ To find a nearby biofeedback practitioner, please see the information on page 57.

MALE INFERTILITY

Fifteen percent of couples who try to have a baby can't. In 30 to 50% of those cases, it's the man's problem—and it's usually a problem with his sperm.

Sperm count might be low—way below the normal 20 million (yes, million) per milliliter. *Sperm morphology* (shape) might be abnormal—too long or too short. *Sperm motility* (action) might be impeded—instead of swimming vigorously forward, the sperm might be sluggish or even at full stop.

But new scientific research shows that there are plenty of natural ways for men to produce healthy sperm that can make the journey to the finish line.

VITAMIN C FOR CONCEPTION

Sperm are *cells*—with membranes that are easily damaged by oxidation (a kind of biological rust) triggered by factors such as stress, aging, chronic illness and pollutants. Vitamin C is a powerful *antioxidant*—it can shield sperm.

▶ *Breakthrough Study*

Doctors in Dubai gave 13 infertile men vitamin C for 2 months. Sperm count more than doubled…sperm motility nearly doubled…and

333

WANT HEALTHIER SPERM? HAVE MORE SEX!

Infertile men are often advised to cut back on sex to increase sperm count. Bad advice!

When you don't have regular sex, sperm accumulate in the epididymis, your testicular storage tank. While waiting for action, those sperm are *more* likely to incur DNA (genetic) damage—making it *less* likely they can fertilize an egg. A study conducted by Australian doctors with 42 men at a fertility clinic shows that daily ejaculation reduced DNA damage to the men's sperm by an average of 12%.

So, says David Greening, MD, the fertility specialist who led the study, if the fertility doc has told you that low sperm *quality* and not low sperm *count* is a probable cause of infertility—make sure you have daily sex! (Or, at least, ejaculate every day.)

sperm morphology (the total number of normal-shaped sperm) improved by 48%.

"Vitamin C supplementation in infertile men might have a place as an additional supplement to improve semen quality," say the researchers, in the *Journal of Medicinal Food*.

Suggested dosage: 1,000 mg, twice daily.

Other antioxidants work too: Researchers at the School of Public Health at the University of California, Berkeley, measured antioxidant intake and sperm quality in 97 healthy men. Higher intake of vitamin C was associated with higher sperm counts...higher intake of vitamin E with more motility...and higher intake of beta-carotene with more motility.

Writing in the *Archives of Andrology*, researchers in the Middle East asked 20 infertile men to take a daily supplement containing two antioxidants—400 mg of vitamin E and 225 micrograms (mcg) of selenium. After three months, the men had significantly improved sperm motility—while infertile men on vitamin B supplements showed no improvement.

Supplements of coenzyme Q10 (an antioxidant, they say, found in "remarkable levels" in semen) improved sperm count and motility. "We use coenzyme Q10 as an antioxidant treatment for reduced sperm motility and male infertility," says Giancarlo Balercia, MD, a specialist in male infertility at the University of Marche in Ancona, Italy.

L-CARNITINE AS FUEL FOR SPERM

Without L-carnitine, you'd run out of gas—this nutrient (synthesized in the body from two amino acids, three vitamins and one mineral) hauls fatty acids into the cell, where they're burned for energy. Sexy energy.

The highest levels of L-carnitine in the male body are found in the sperm and in the epididymis where sperm mature. Studies show men with the highest levels of L-carnitine have the most energetic sperm. And more energetic sperm are more likely to produce a pregnancy.

▶ *Breakthrough Study*

Doctors in China analyzed the results of several studies in which infertile men were treated with either L-carnitine or a placebo. The men taking L-carnitine had, on average, seven times higher sperm motility (activity); 11 times higher "forward sperm motility" (the sperm weren't just energetic—they moved); five times fewer abnormal sperm; and—the key statistic—partners with a four times higher pregnancy rate.

Suggested intake: In most of the studies on L-carnitine and infertility, men took 3 grams of L-carnitine daily, 1 gram with each meal.

Also helpful: In several fertility studies, men took both L-carnitine and L-acetylcarnitine, another form of the nutrient. "The combined use of L-carnitine and L-acetylcarnitine is more effective in improving fertility than either nutrient alone," says Michele De Rosa, MD, a professor of endocrinology at the University Federico in Naples, Italy. These studies used daily doses of two grams of L-carnitine and one gram of L-acetylcarnitine.

ℹ️ Supplements of L-carnitine and L-acetylcarnitine (also sold as acetyl-L-carnitine) are widely available, in many brands.

MODERN LIFE IS MURDER ON SPERM

Research shows that average "sperm density" (the amount of sperm in a milliliter of semen) has declined from 113 million in 1940 to 66 million in 1990—a decrease of 58%.

Why are sperm a semiendangered species? Pollutants, stressful lifestyle and shoddy diet are three likely suspects, says Steven Sinclair, ND, LAc, a naturopath and acupuncturist in Hagerstown, MD. He recommends the following for healthy sperm, in *Alternative Medicine Review...*

- **Nosh natural.** Synthetic estrogens—widely used in the livestock, poultry and dairy industries—may mangle sperm. Use organic dairy products and meats.
- Pesticides can be spermicides; again, emphasize organic foods.
- Eat more cell-strengthening omega-3 fatty acids, found in fish such as wild salmon and mackerel, and in leafy greens, flaxseed and flaxseed oil and walnuts.
- Stay away from hydrogenated oils, found in many baked goods and margarine—they've been shown to harm sperm.
- **Keep your cool.** Sperm need a cool environment to thrive—which is why the testicles are *outside* the body.

MOBILE PHONE, IMMOBILE SPERM

Cell phones work by emitting electromagnetic waves. Some fertility experts worry those waves might be drowning sperm.

Doctors from the Reproductive Research Center at the Cleveland Clinic divided 161 men undergoing infertility tests into four groups according to their level of cell phone use—no use, two hours a day, two to four hours a day and more than four hours a day.

The more time a man used his cell phone, the less healthy his sperm—with progressively decreasing sperm counts, poorer sperm shape (morphology) and lower levels of sperm activity (motility).

"Use of cell phones decrease the semen quality in men," say the researchers, in the journal *Fertility and Sterility.*

The researchers consider their findings preliminary. They don't know exactly *how* cell phones hurt sperm (maybe it's the waves...or the heat generated by the phone...or a combination of both) and are conducting further studies.

But if you and your partner are trying to conceive, try hanging up your cell phone (or use it a lot less, or keep it in your briefcase when it's on, rather than hooked to your belt or in your pocket)—until it's time to call family and friends with the good news.

- Don't wear tight-fitting pants, which can overheat sperm, says Dr. Sinclair.
- Ditto for tight underwear—prefer boxers to briefs.
- Avoid strenuous, overheating exercise—a brisk walk is better than an intense run.
- Stay out of hot tubs, and take showers instead of baths. Infertile men who stopped using hot baths and hot tubs had a fivefold improvement in sperm count, say researchers at the University of California, San Francisco.
- **Don't smoke.** On average, smokers have 19% fewer sperm than nonsmokers.

13

OSTEOPOROSIS
NEW WAYS TO BUILD STRONGER BONES

Odds are that it's going to be your mom or your wife or your girlfriend... or it could be you...

One out of every two women over 50 ends up with a broken bone—a fractured hip, a crushed vertebrae, a broken wrist—because her skeleton has been slowly but surely eroded by *osteoporosis,* the bone-thinning disease.

That's more than 1.5 million fractures a year...leading to 500,000 hospitalizations... and 180,000 new residents in nursing homes. In fact, of the women with osteoporosis who break a bone, one in five subsequently perishes as a result of the fracture—first bedridden, then weakened, and finally wasted.

No wonder two million Americans spend billions of dollars a year on *bisphosphonates* (Fosamax, Actonel, Boniva), drugs that build bone. But the drugs themselves are far from harmless.

You could end up with severe pain in your muscles, joints and bones (there are hundreds of reports about this problem, says the FDA)... double your risk of the irregular heart rhythm called *atrial fibrillation*...or even become one of the dozens of victims of the strange and gruesome condition called "jaw death," in which a chunk of the jaw bone decays and dies, usually after a routine dental procedure, such as an extraction. Perhaps it's not surprising that most people prescribed a bisphosphonate stop taking the drug within a year.

If you're a man reading this, worried about your spouse or mother or sister, think twice... about yourself. One in eight men over 50 has osteoporosis—and one in three die because of their fractures, a higher rate than the so-called weaker sex.

What to do?

Weak bones are not built in stone.

Bone is an active, living tissue, says Alan Gaby, MD, author of *Preventing and Reversing Osteoporosis* (Prima). Cells called *osteoclasts* break down bone. Cells called *osteoblasts* build new bone. This process of breaking down and building up is called *remodeling.* And scientific research shows that the right types of exercise, nutritional supplements and foods can remodel your skeleton, resulting in stronger, healthier bone and preventing, slowing, stopping (and even reversing) osteoporosis.

For the 10 million Americans with outright osteoporosis...for the 34 million more with osteopenia, thinning bones that put them at risk for the disease...here are the bone-protecting, bone-building breakthroughs that science says work best.

STRENGTH TRAINING BUILDS UP BONE

Bone remodels in response to so-called "repetitive stress"—for example, a right-handed tennis player has bigger, thicker bones in her right arm than in her left. Could strength training—the regular "stress" of lifting weights—build new bone in fracture-prone hips and spine? Yes, say scientists.

⫸ *Breakthrough Study*

Researchers at the University of Arizona followed a group of 167 healthy, postmenopausal women (average age of 56) for four years—some of them did strength training regularly during that time, and some didn't. When the study started, the researchers used the superaccurate DXA bone scan (dual energy x-ray absorptiometry) to measure the bone density of all the women. They took a second set of DXA scans four years later.

Those who strength trained regularly—two or three times a week, week after week, over four years—*gained* bone density. They had denser hipbones, denser spinal vertebrae and denser thigh bones.

Those who strength trained semi-regularly—one to two times a week—*maintained* bone density, but didn't gain any.

Those who didn't strength train—*lost* bone.

"Most of the postmenopausal women in our study either had osteopenia or osteoporosis when the study started," says Timothy G. Lohman, PhD, professor in the Department of Physiology at the University of Arizona and one of the authors of the study. "On average, the women who regularly lifted weights increased their bone mass anywhere from three to seven percent—enough to *reverse* osteopenia or osteoporosis."

What you may not know: "A postmenopausal woman can lose ten percent of bone in her fifties, which is what sets her up for fractures in her sixties or seventies," explains Dr. Lohman. "Our study shows that if you lift weights regularly in your fifties, you can *prevent* osteoporosis."

What they did: In a typical strength-training routine, you perform a "set" of exercises using six or more machines, doing two to three sets per session. On each machine, you use a weight that you can lift (or push or pull) about 10 to 12 times, until temporary muscular exhaustion sets in; at that point, you move on to the next machine in the set. You and your instructor determine the right amount of weight for each machine. (A qualified instructor is a must for learning how to lift weights correctly and safely.)

Newer approach: The exercisers in Dr. Lohman's study did things a little bit differently. On each machine, they used a weight they could lift *six to eight times*, until muscular exhaustion. In other words, they used *heavier* weights, with *fewer* repetitions. And they did two sets per session rather than three.

"We believe that doing fewer repetitions with heavier weights is critical—*critical*—to improving bone density with strength training," says Dr. Lohman.

Recommended: His advice is to go to a gym...work with an instructor to find the right weight for each machine, for six to eight repetitions...and then work out two to three times a week, doing two sets each time. (Dr. Lohman doesn't think that home strength-training routines can provide heavy enough weights to preserve or add bone.)

"As you gain in strength, you'll gradually increase the heaviness of the weight you can lift six to eight times at each machine, until you reach a plateau, usually somewhere after the first year of strength training," he says. "And that's fine—you don't have to keep increasing the heaviness of the weights to keep building or preserving bone."

Dr. Lohman says the three most important fracture-preventing exercises in the routine used in the study are…

- **Military press** (targeted bone: spinal vertebrae)

- **Smith squat** (targeted bones: hip, spinal vertebrae)

- **Leg press** (targeted bone: thigh)

Three other exercises, to complete the set, are:

- **Lat pull-down** (targeted bone: spinal vertebrae)

- **Seated row** (targeted bone: spinal vertebrae)

- **Back extension** (targeted bone: spinal vertebrae)

Important: All the women in the study took a daily supplement of 800 mg of calcium citrate. "After menopause, the effectiveness of exercise to increase bone mineral depends heavily on an adequate intake of calcium," says Katarina Borer, PhD, a professor in the Department of Movement Science at the University of Michigan. For more information on calcium and osteoporosis, see page 342 in this chapter.

Also helpful: Dr. Lohman urges you to get a DXA bone scan before you start strength training, and every year thereafter—and to do so at the *same* clinic or doctor's office each year, for the best year-to-year comparison. That way, you can see if strength training is working for you. The cost of a DXA scan is $100 to $250,

DON'T SMOKE YOUR SKELETON!

Smoking is bad for your lungs, bad for your heart and—you guessed it—bad for your bones, too…

Researchers looked at 86 studies on smoking and bone mass, involving more than 40,000 people, and found that a lifetime of smoking increases the risk of a hip fracture by 31% in women and 40% in men, and the risk of a spinal fracture by 13% in women and 32% in men. They also found that the more you smoke, the higher your risk—but that if you *stop* smoking your risk starts to reverse.

What you may not know: Secondhand smoke gives you second-rate bones. A study by a team of researchers from the Harvard School of Public Health found that premenopausal women who lived with one smoker *doubled* their risk of osteoporosis, while women who lived with two or more smokers *tripled* their risk.

and is covered by insurance if your doctor writes a prescription for it.

As for taking bone-protecting drugs—Dr. Lohman thinks that the more natural approach of using exercise and calcium is the way to go. "If you could 'bottle' the benefits of exercise, it would be the top-selling medication in the country," he says.

But, he adds, while most people respond to exercise, some don't. "If your yearly DXA shows that, even with regular exercise, your bone density is going down and you're at risk for a fracture, talk to your doctor about medication."

WALK BRISKLY TO PRESERVE BONE

For most people, regular exercise means *walking*. But how *much* walking does it take to protect your bones—particularly if you're a postmenopausal women at risk for osteoporosis? Surprisingly, scientists didn't know. Now they do.

⫸ *Breakthrough Study*

Researchers at the University of Michigan asked postmenopausal women to participate in 30 weeks of supervised walking—three miles a day, four days a week, at either a low- or high-intensity pace. At the start, in the middle and at the end of the study, the researchers measured the mineral content of the women's bones.

Result: *High-intensity walking* preserved bone mineral density in postmenopausal women, says Dr. Borer, one of the authors of the study. But what is high intensity, exactly?

Pace: Walking very briskly at a four-minute-per-mile pace, or a mile every 15 minutes.

Heart rate: Sustaining a heart rate above 82% of what exercise scientists call "age-specific maximum heart rate"—above 140 beats per minute for a 50-year-old, above 135 beats per minute for a 55-year-old, above 130 beats per minute for a 60-year-old, and above 127 beats per minute for a 65-year-old.

Caution: Be sure to get clearance from your doctor before beginning a vigorous exercise program.

☀ Heart-rate monitors for less than $50 are widely available from companies such as Oregon Scientific, Timex and Mio. For a wide selection, see *www.heartratemonitorsusa.com*, HRM USA, 36 Vincent Circle, Suite B, Warminster, PA 18974-1515, (800-403-8285, 215-259-2702 or fax 215-547-2551); e-mail *sales@hrm usainc.com*.

Instructions for taking your pulse and calculating your heartbeats per minute, from the National Emergency Medicine Association...

1. Turn the palm side of your hand face up.

2. Place your index and middle fingers of your opposite hand on your wrist, approximately 1 inch below the base of your hand, below your thumb.

3. Press your fingers down in the groove between your middle tendons and your outside bone. You should feel a throbbing—your pulse.

4. Count the number of beats for 10 seconds, then multiply this number by 6. This is your heartbeats per minute.

Helpful: If you want to walk faster, try out these tips from Patty C., personal trainer, marathon walking coach and founder of the Web site *www.thewalkingsite.com*:

• **Use good posture.** Walk tall, looking forward (not at the ground) and gazing about 20 feet ahead. Your chin should be level and your head up.

• **Keep your chest raised and your shoulders relaxed (down and back).**

• **Bend your arms in a slightly-less-than 90-degree angle.** Cup your hands gently. Swing your arms front to back (not side to side: your arms should not cross your body). Do not swing your elbows higher than your sternum (breast bone). Swing your arms faster and your feet will follow.

• **Resist the urge to elongate your stride.** To go faster, take smaller, faster steps.

• **Concentrate on landing on your heel,** rolling through the step and pushing off with your toes. Use the natural spring of your calf muscles to propel you forward.

• **As you walk, take deep, rhythmic breaths.**

MEN, WANT STRONG BONES? DON'T JUST WATCH SPORTS— PLAY THEM!

For 35 years, Swedish researchers at the University Hospital in Uppsala tracked the physical activity levels and bone health of more than 2,000 middle-aged men (aged 49 to 51). *At the end of the study, hips fractures had struck...*

• 20% of sedentary men,

• 13% of medium activity men, and

• 8% of highly active men.

The highly active men had answered yes to one or both of these questions: "Do you engage in any active recreational sports or heavy gardening for at least three hours every week?" and "Do you regularly engage in hard physical training or competitive sport?" The researchers also verified the men's physical fitness (or lack of it) with exercise tests when the men were 60, 70, 77 and 82. (Not that a man would ever exaggerate his level of physical fitness, of course.)

"Engaging in a high level of physical activity substantially reduces the risk of hip fractures—the most devastating of osteoporotic fractures—in men," says Karl Michaëlsson, MD, one of the authors of the study. His straightforward recommendation: "To reduce their risk of fractures, older men should increase their leisure physical activity."

HIGH-TECH "PASSIVE EXERCISE" THAT WORKS

Hear the words "passive exercise" and maybe you think of old-fashioned machines wiggling the bottoms of overweight people who'd rather not work out. But passive exercise—now called whole-body vibration—has entered the 21st century. Dozens of scientific studies show that high-tech whole-body vibration machines can increase muscle strength, help heal injuries, improve balance—and build bone.

▦▶ *Breakthrough Study*

Scientists at the Osteoporosis Research Center at Creighton University in Nebraska and the Department of Biomedical Engineering at the State University of New York studied 56 post-menopausal women for one year.

Half the women spent 10 minutes, twice a day, standing on a whole-body vibration machine that generated fast but low-level vibrations—a kind of slight shaking. The other half stood on placebo devices. At the beginning, throughout and at the end of the study, the researchers measured the women's bone mineral density (BMD). *After one year...*

• **Hips.** The vibration group had 2.2% more BMD in the hip joint than the placebo group.

• **Spine.** The vibration group had 1.5% more BMD in the spine than the placebo group.

• **High-risk women.** Thinner women are at higher risk for spinal fractures from osteoporosis. Thinner women in the vibration group had a 3.5% greater spinal BMD than thinner women in the placebo group.

"This nondrug approach can slow the decline of BMD after menopause, particularly in the spines of women with the greatest need for help," says Clinton T. Rubin, MD, one of the authors of the study.

He also points out that whole-body vibration may be the perfect "exercise" for the elderly—because regular exercise could increase the risk of a fall, causing the very problem (a broken bone) that it was trying to prevent.

How it works: The vibration applies positive stress to the bone, which responds by adding thickness and strength.

Problem: Whole-body vibration equipment for your home is extremely expensive. The cheapest home machine from Power Plate—the

340

leading manufacturer of whole-body vibration equipment—costs $2,500.

Solution: To find a local fitness or wellness facility near you that has a Power Plate, use the state-by-state "Plate Locator" at the Power Plate Web site, *www.powerplate.com*. Power Plate North America, Inc., 400 Skokie Blvd, Suite 105, Northbrook, IL 60062 (877-877-5283 or fax 847-509-6004).

BONE CELLS AND FAT CELLS—THE STRANGE BUT SIGNIFICANT CONNECTION

Inside of your bones is *bone marrow*—in a variety of colors. There's red marrow, where the body generates red blood cells. And then there's yellow marrow, where the body generates fat cells (adipocytes) and bone-building osteoblasts.

New finding: Scientists at the University of Georgia discovered that when there are *more* fat cells in the yellow marrow, there are *fewer* osteoblasts. In other words, fat-forming crowds out bone-forming!

Theory: Killing fat cells in the bone marrow would encourage the growth of osteoblasts—and help the body build more bone.

What to do: The scientists are testing natural products that kill those fat cells. Two successes so far are CLA (conjugated linoleic acid) and EGCG (green tea extract). (For more information on CLA and EGCG, see Chapter 14, "Overweight.")

Also helpful: Simply cutting intake of fat might also help. Researchers at Pennsylvania State University analyzed data on fat intake and bone mineral density in nearly 15,000 men and women. People who had the highest intake of saturated fat (found mostly in red meat) had the lowest bone mineral density, particularly in fracture-prone hips, and especially among men.

STRONTIUM CUTS FRACTURE RISK BY 49%

Calcium, calcium, calcium. That's the nutritional mantra for protecting your bones, right? Well, add another mineral to your bone-building incantation. Strontium, strontium, strontium.

⮞ *Breakthrough Study*

An international team of researchers (from America, France, Australia, Italy, Poland, England, Spain, Hungary, Germany, Denmark and Switzerland) gave 1,649 postmenopausal women with osteoporosis either daily strontium or a placebo for three years. Both groups also received calcium and vitamin D.

- **Fewer fractures.** The group taking strontium had a 49% lower risk of suffering a fracture in the first year of the study, and 41% over three years.

- **Denser bone.** After three years, those taking strontium had a 14% increase in bone mineral density (BMD) of the spine, and a 10% increase in BMD of the hip.

Strontium can reduce the risk of vertebral fractures rapidly, effectively, and safely among postmenopausal women, say the researchers, in the *New England Journal of Medicine*.

And they note that the decreased fracture rate is similar to that achieved by people taking a bisphosphonate such as *alendronate* (Fosamax) or *risedronate* (Actonel).

Also helpful: Other studies show that postmenopausal women with osteoporosis who take strontium have less back pain, better mood and better overall physical functioning and that women with osteopenia who take strontium lower their risk of fracture by 28%.

How it works: Strontium increases bone formation and decreases bone "resorption," or the breakdown of bone.

Recently, doctors in France performed bone biopsies on 133 postmenopausal women who had been receiving strontium for one to five years. *Compared with similar women who did not get strontium, their bones had…*

- **9% more minerals,**
- **38% more osteoblasts,** the cells that form bone,
- **18% more thickness and**
- **16% more connective fibers.**

"These changes may explain the decreased fracture rate among those who take strontium," say the doctors in the *Journal of Bone and Mineral Research.*

What to do: The studies used a form of the mineral called *strontium ranelate,* which is not available in the United States. But other forms of strontium, such as *strontium gluconate* and *strontium citrate,* have shown similar benefits, says Dr. Jacob Teitelbaum. He advises you to take the supplement in the morning on an empty stomach, and not at the same time as calcium, which can block its absorption.

Suggested intake: 680 mg daily.

Strontium-containing supplements include:

- Strontium Bone Maker from Doctor's Best
- Strontium Osteo-Complex from Nutricology/Allergy Research Group
- Strontium from Vitamin Research Products
- Strontium from Pure Encapsulations
- Strontium from Nutraceutical Sciences Institute (NSI)

These supplements are widely available through retail stores, Internet sites and catalogs.

CALCIUM AND VITAMIN D— PARTNERS IN PROTECTION

Bone is mostly calcium. Vitamin D helps calcium get into bone. Together, they're tough to beat for beating osteoporosis.

▶ *Breakthrough Study*

Australian researchers analyzed 29 studies on calcium, vitamin D and osteoporosis, involving nearly 64,000 people aged 50 and older, with an average age of 68. *They found…*

- **Fewer fractures.** A supplement containing calcium and vitamin D reduced fractures of all types by 12%.

Better: In studies where people took the supplement at least four out of every five days, or 80% of the time, the benefit was doubled— fracture risk was reduced by 24%.

- **Denser bone.** People who took a calcium and vitamin D supplement had a reduced rate of bone loss at the hip and the spine, compared with people who didn't take the nutrients.

"The efficacy of calcium and vitamin D supplements in reducing the risk of fractures later in life is comparable to more established preventive measures, such as aspirin, which is widely taken to reduce the risk of cardiovascular events such as heart attacks and strokes," says Benjamin Tang, MD, one of the authors of the study.

Important: "The results show the importance of starting supplements early in life, at around the age of 50, when bone mineral loss begins to accelerate," he adds.

"Calcium and vitamin D supplements are relatively cheap, but the impact they have on your health and well-being later in life is priceless," says Dr. Tang.

Also helpful: The researchers found the supplements were particularly effective in preventing fractures in those over 70, people with low dietary intake of calcium and thin people (who are at a higher risk for fractures).

Suggested intake: The most protective amount is a minimum of 1,200 mg of calcium and 800 IU of vitamin D. Supplements with this dosage are widely available.

TAKING FOSAMAX? KEEP TAKING CALCIUM AND VITAMIN D!

In all of the big scientific studies that showed bisphosphonates such as alendronate (Fosamax) worked to prevent fractures—people also took anywhere from 500 to 1,000 mg of supplemental calcium. That's why every official guideline for bisphosphonate therapy recommends people also take a calcium or calcium/vitamin D supplement with the drug. But that's not what's happening.

New study: Scientists at the Stanford Prevention Research Center looked at two national databases that included information on calcium intake and osteoporosis. They found that between 1994 and 2004...doctor visits for osteoporosis increased fourfold, from 1.3 to 5.8 million...the percentage of those visits in which bisphosphonates were prescribed increased from 14 to 81%...and the percentage of osteoporosis patients taking calcium fell from 43 to 23%. In fact, one of the databases showed that only 40% of osteoporosis patients had a calcium intake more than 1,200 mg a day.

"Even though the effectiveness of new osteoporosis medications depends on adequate calcium intake, calcium is being neglected as a component of osteoporosis management," say the researchers.

Don't make that mistake!

Smart idea: Ask your doctor to prescribe a calcium/vitamin D supplement.

Red flag: Calcium can interfere with the absorption of Fosamax. Wait at least 30 minutes after taking Fosamax to take a calcium/vitamin D supplement.

FOR STRONG BONES, DON'T FORGET THE FOOD!

You're remembering to take your calcium/vitamin D supplement every day—good for you! But you're not eating a couple of servings a day of calcium-rich foods, such as milk, cheese or yogurt—and that could be bad for you.

⏭ *Breakthrough Study*

Researchers at the Washington University School of Medicine in St. Louis studied 183 postmenopausal women, asking them to keep a detailed food and supplement dairy for one week. They also checked out the women's bone mineral density (BMD). And they measured urinary levels of "active estrogen metabolites," a known bone-building factor. *The results were surprising...*

● **Women who got 70% of their calcium from supplements** (the supplement group) had the lowest BMD. Their total daily intake of calcium was 1,030 mg.

● **Women who got 70% of their calcium from dairy products and other foods** (the diet group) had the medium BMD—even though their total daily intake of calcium of 830 mg was *lower* than that of the supplement group.

● **Women who got their calcium from food and supplements** (the diet plus supplement group) had the highest BMD. Their daily intake of calcium was 1,620 mg.

Obviously, a high intake of calcium from diet *and* supplements is your best strategy. But why did the diet group have stronger bones than the supplement group, even though their overall calcium intake was lower?

Theory: The diet group and the diet plus supplement group both had more active estrogen metabolites in their blood than the supplement group, says Reina Armamento-Villareal, MD, assistant professor of medicine in the

Division of Bone and Mineral Diseases and one of the authors of the study. Perhaps dietary calcium but not supplemental calcium generates those metabolites. Maybe dairy products boost the level of those metabolites in the body.

Another possible reason the supplement group had the lowest BMD is that many calcium supplements are poorly absorbed.

Smart idea: If you take a supplement with *calcium carbonate*, you must take it with a meal for maximum absorption, advises Dr. Armamento-Villareal. If you take a supplement with *calcium citrate*, you can take it anytime during the day.

Dairy products are the best dietary source of calcium. But if you're sensitive or allergic to dairy, consider drinking calcium-fortified orange juice, she says. Green leafy vegetables are also a decent source.

MAGNESIUM—THE SECRET BONE-BUILDER

Secret, because most people worried about losing bone don't give it a second thought, or even a third. But like calcium, magnesium plays a major role in forming bone—and maybe a major role in losing bone, if you don't get enough.

▌▌▌➤ *Breakthrough Study*

Scientists at the University of Tennessee analyzed diet and health data from more than 2,000 women and men, aged 70 to 79. The higher their intake of magnesium, from food and supplements, the higher their bone mineral density.

What to do: Chances are you're not getting enough magnesium. The government's recommended daily value for magnesium is 400 mg a day, but a survey conducted by the Centers for Disease Control and Prevention found that the average intake among Americans is only 290 mg. Fortunately, it's easy to increase your intake. *Foods rich in the mineral include...*

- **Nuts** (almonds, cashews and Brazil nuts)
- **Wheat** (whole wheat, wheat germ, wheat bran)
- **Whole grains** (millet, rye, brown rice, barley)
- **Soy products** (soybeans, tofu)
- **Dried fruit** (figs, apricots, dates, prunes, raisins)
- **Vegetables** (avocado, potato, sweet potato, beets, broccoli, cauliflower, carrot, celery, asparagus, green pepper, winter squash)
- **Greens and seaweed** (collard greens, dandelion greens, dulse, kelp)
- **Meat** (beef, chicken)

SOFT DRINKS = SOFT BONES

Danish scientists asked 11 healthy guys in their twenties to go on a low-calcium diet for two periods of 10 days each—drinking 80 ounces of skimmed milk a day during the first 10-day period, and drinking 80 ounces of Coca-Cola a day during the second.

Results: In just 10 days of Coke-drinking, the men's bone biochemistry took a turn for the worse, with higher levels of several biomarkers that signaled their bones would erode if they kept drinking Coke.

Warning: "The trend toward replacement of milk with cola and other soft drinks, which results in a low calcium intake, may negatively affect bone health," say the researchers, in the journal *Osteoporosis International*.

"Colas are among the worst foods imaginable for someone trying to prevent osteoporosis," adds Alan Gaby, MD, author of *Preventing and Reversing Osteoporosis* (Prima).

In other words, if you're drinking cola—can it.

Also helpful: A supplement can ensure you get enough magnesium. Look for a product that contains highly absorbable *magnesium citrate*, with a daily dosage of 300 to 400 mg.

VITAMIN K FOR FRACTURE PREVENTION

When Norwegian scientists discovered this important nutrient in 1929, they dubbed it *K* for *Koagulation*—the vitamin helps the liver manufacture proteins that control blood clotting.

Now, scientists know that vitamin K also aids in the formation of *osteocalcin*, a protein that helps calcium bind to bone. Which means the nutrient may help prevent or treat osteoporosis.

Breakthrough Studies

Researchers from the University of York in England analyzed data from 13 Japanese clinical trials that used large, pharmacological doses of vitamin K to treat osteoporosis. The vitamin reduced the rate of spinal fractures by 40% and hip fractures by 13%. (Vitamin K is the number one treatment for osteoporosis in Japan.) The results were reported in the *Archives of Internal Medicine*.

In another study, scientists at Harvard Medical School analyzed data on dietary vitamin K intake and bone health in more than 70,000 women. Those with the highest dietary intake of vitamin K had a 30% decreased risk of hip fracture compared with those with the lowest intake. Other studies show similar results for men.

What to do: For adults, the government's recommendation for daily vitamin K intake is 65 to 80 micrograms (mcg). That level is high enough to prevent outright vitamin K deficiency. But is it high enough to keep your bones healthy? That's a question nutritional scientists are asking but haven't yet answered, says Sarah L. Booth, PhD, director of the vitamin K laboratory at the Jean Mayer USDA Human Nutrition and Research Center on Aging at Tufts University. However, scientists *do* know how to maximize your intake of vitamin K. Follow your mother's advice and "eat your vegetables."

Green vegetables—leafy and otherwise—are some of the best sources of vitamin K in the diet. Vegetable oils are also rich in the nutrient. Top vegetables include kale (726 mcg per 100 grams), turnip greens (650 mcg), spinach (450 mcg), collard greens (440 mcg), Brussels sprouts (250 mcg), broccoli (147 mcg), cabbage (110 mcg), lettuce (75 mcg), asparagus (70 mcg), green beans (46 mcg) and green peas (33 mcg). Among vegetable oils, soybean (198 mcg) and olive oil (30 mcg) score highest.

Don't have a taste for kale and spinach? Don't worry, says Dr. Booth. One half cup of broccoli sautéed in olive oil gives you plenty of vitamin K. Or a lettuce salad with a teaspoon of salad dressing. And don't worry about cooking, either; it doesn't destroy the vitamin.

Recommended: "As an added insurance policy, you may want to supplement your diet with vitamin K," says Dr. Gaby.

Suggested intake: Dr. Gaby recommends 150 to 500 mcg a day.

Vitamin K supplements are widely available at many drug and health-food stores.

VITAMIN B IS FOR BONES

Homocysteine is an amino acid derived from the normal breakdown of *methionine*, a component of protein. What is *abnormal*, however, is a high blood level of homocysteine, a condition called *homocystinemia*, which has been linked to heart

A WARNING ABOUT VITAMIN K AND WARFARIN

Warfarin (Coumadin, Jantoven, Marevan and Waran) is a so-called blood-thinning medication given to people who have had or are likely to develop an artery-blocking blood clot. Reasons a doctor might prescribe warfarin include a heart attack, stroke, irregular heart rhythm (atrial fibrillation), artificial heart valve, blood clot in the leg (deep venous thrombosis) or a clot that traveled to the lung (pulmonary embolism). If you take warfarin, you should *not* take a supplement with vitamin K, which interferes with its action, and you *should* maintain a steady, daily intake of vitamin K-containing foods. How do you do that?

Smart idea: "Don't eat dark, leafy green vegetables," says Dr. Booth. Her research shows the amount of vitamin K in these foods can vary threefold, depending on where they're grown.

For example, a serving of spinach could contain 200 mcg of vitamin K...or 600. That's a huge difference in vitamin K intake for someone taking warfarin, she says.

Instead, she recommends eating three daily servings of vitamin K-rich foods with lower but dependable amounts of the nutrient. That could include ½ cup of broccoli, ½ cup of green peas and 6 ounces of tomato juice. Other good choices are lettuce and asparagus.

disease, stroke and Alzheimer's. Now scientists are showing that homocystinemia also plays a role in osteoporosis and broken bones—and that B vitamins can fix the problem.

⫸ *Breakthrough Study*

Researchers in Norway analyzed 13 years of health data from nearly 5,000 men and women, who were 65 to 67 years old when the data collection started, in 1992. They found women with the highest level of homocysteine had more than *double* the risk of a hip fracture than women with the lowest level. Men with a high homocysteine level had a 37% greater risk of a hip fracture.

"Our findings support the theory that homocysteine plays a role in osteoporotic fractures," says Clara Gram Gjesdal, MD, one of the authors of the study, which appeared in the *Journal of Mineral and Bone Research.*

What happens: Too much homocysteine can block bone mineralization and stop protein fibers from linking up and forming stronger bones.

What to do: High levels of homocysteine are caused by a low intake of folic acid, B-6 and B-12, three B vitamins that trigger the body to either excrete homocysteine or turn it back into methionine, explains Kilmer S. McCully, MD, author of *The Homocysteine Revolution* (McGraw-Hill). *His advice…*

● **Get enough dietary folic acid, B-6 and B-12.** You need a daily intake of 350 to 400 mcg of folic acid, 3 to 3.5 mg of B-6 and 5 to 15 mcg of B-12.

Problem: Most Americans get only 200 to 250 mcg of folic acid, and 1.1 to 1.3 mg a day of B-6. And Americans over 65 get only 1.3 to 1.5 mcg of B-12. They also absorb less of the vitamin, due to a decline in stomach acid and intrinsic factor, a protein that facilitates the digestion of B-12.

Solution: Emphasize vitamin-rich fruits and vegetables (six to ten daily servings), whole grains (two to three daily servings), fresh fish, dairy products and meats (one to two daily servings) and avoid processed foods, which are low in B vitamins.

Foods particularly rich in B-6 include bananas, beans, lentils, brown rice, fish, liver, poultry, meats, cauliflower, broccoli and kale.

Foods particularly rich in folic acid include fresh leafy green vegetables, beans, citrus fruits, brown rice and liver.

Recommended: Whole foods are the best way to get these three vitamins. But a multivitamin supplement provides insurance, says Dr. McCully. And if you're over 65, the supplement compensates for your decreased ability to absorb vitamins.

Suggested intake: The supplement should contain…

- 5–10 mg of vitamin B-6
- 400–1,000 mcg of folic acid
- 200–1,000 mcg of vitamin B-12

ℹ️ Reliable, nationally available multivitamins include Twin Labs, Solgar, Centrum, Carlson and Theragram.

Also helpful: Regular exercise lowers homocysteine and smoking increases it.

WALNUTS AND FLAXSEEDS PRESERVE YOUR BONES

Milk is the food most often touted for healthy bones. But maybe the last time you got milk you also got a stomachache—many people don't digest dairy very well. Are there other foods that might help build bone? Yes, say scientists.

▶ *Breakthrough Study*

Researchers from the Department of Nutritional Sciences at Pennsylvania State University asked 23 people to go on three different diets, eating each diet for six weeks—an "average American diet," with saturated fat from meat and full-fat dairy products; a diet rich in linoleic acid, a type of omega-6 fatty acid found in vegetable oils such as corn oil; and a diet rich in alpha-linolenic acid (ALA), a plant-derived omega-3 fatty acid similar to those found in fatty fish such as salmon and mackerel. (The researchers used walnuts, walnut oil and flaxseed oil to supply the ALA.)

WHAT YOU NEED TO KNOW (AND DO) ABOUT WEIGHT LOSS AND BONE LOSS

Just about every health expert says it's smart to lose weight. But there's a dark side to weight loss—*bone* loss. Study after study shows that when you slim your hips, you might slim your hipbones (and other bones) too. Well, scientists have figured out how to get rid of extra fat without risking a fracture.

New approach: If you want to lose weight without losing bone—cut calories and add exercise, say researchers in the Division of Geriatrics and Nutritional Sciences at Washington University School of Medicine, in St. Louis.

For one year, they studied 48 men and women, with an average age of 57, dividing them into two groups. One group cut calories to lose weight, eating 20% fewer daily calories than the amount needed to maintain weight. The other group stabilized their calorie intake at a maintenance level, while exercising enough to boost daily calorie burning by 20%.

After a year, both groups had lost roughly the same amount of weight—24 pounds for the low-calorie group, and 18 pounds for the exercise group.

But the low-calorie group also lost bone mineral density—about 2% at both the hip and the spine. The exercise group had no measurable loss.

"Exercise should be an important part of a weight-loss program, to offset the adverse effects of calorie-restriction on bone," says Dennis T. Villareal, MD, one of the authors of the study, published in the *Archives of Internal Medicine.*

Results: Compared with the average American diet, the ALA-rich diet lowered blood levels of *N-telopeptides* by 15%. Why is that important? Those are microscopic protein fibers that help build bone. Lower blood levels mean that less bone is being resorbed, or destroyed.

"Eating plant sources of omega-3 fatty acids may improve the health of your bones," says Rebecca L. Corwin, PhD, one of the authors of the study.

What to do: Consider including more walnuts, walnut oil and flaxseed oil in your diet. *The high-ALA diet used in the study included...*

- **1 ounce of walnuts a day.** The walnuts were from walnut granola, honey walnut butter, walnut pesto and as a snack.

- **1 tablespoon of walnut oil.** You can substitute walnut oil for other cooking oils.

- **1 tablespoon of flaxseed oil.** Flaxseed oil is not for cooking.

The oil has a rich, nutty flavor. Add it to yogurt or fruit smoothies; use it in (or as)

TEN PRUNES A DAY KEEPS OSTEOPOROSIS AWAY

Dried plums—known to scientists as *Prunus domestica,* and to the rest of us as *prunes*—are loaded with powerful natural compounds that fight cell-damaging oxidation and inflammation. Could they protect bones?

In a study conducted in 2002, postmenopausal women who ate 9 to 10 prunes a day for three months had big boosts in two biomarkers that indicate bone growth. A group that ate dried apples didn't have an increase.

In 2005, female rats that had eaten a bone-eroding diet were given diets rich in prunes, and bone mass returned. The animals had incurred a type of bone damage that scientists up to then thought was irreversible—but prunes reversed it, says Bahram H. Arjmandi, PhD, RD, a professor at Florida State University and the lead researcher on all the prune studies.

In 2006, Dr. Arjmandi and his colleagues showed that prunes prevent bone loss in male rats.

In 2007, a study showed that prunes strengthen the structure of bone in male and female laboratory animals. And in 2008, Dr. Arjmandi launched another study with postmenopausal women, who will eat nine or 10 prunes a day for one year. At the start of the study, the women had their bone density measured; similar measurements will be taken at the end of the study.

Of course, you don't have to wait until the study is concluded to begin snacking on prunes. After all, the proof is in the prune pudding. *Speaking of which...*

Try this: The California Dried Plum Board (which *insists* on calling prunes dried plums) offers the following ideas for putting more, uh, dried plums in your diet...

- Snack on dried plums.

- Sprinkle dried plums on oatmeal or ready-to-eat cereal, or into pancake batter as a complement to sliced bananas.

- Add chopped and pitted dried plums to apple butter, orange marmalade, peanut butter or low-fat cream cheese.

- Add halved and pitted dried plums to turkey or chicken salad.

- Sauté dried plums with sliced onions and apples, as an accompaniment to chicken or pork.

- Add chopped, pitted dried plums to muffin or quick bread batter.

- Soak pitted dried plums overnight in orange juice for a sauce to spoon over low-fat ice cream or frozen yogurt.

- Drink prune juice.

☀ Find dozens of dried plum recipes at *www.californiadriedplums.org.* California Dried Plum Board, 3840 Rosin Court, Suite 170, Sacramento, CA 95834 (916-565-6232 or fax 916-565-6237).

salad dressing; use it to flavor hot foods such as grains and breakfast cereals

SOY BUILDS POSTMENOPAUSAL BONE

Tofu or not tofu, that is the question—at least for postmenopausal women, who wonder if eating more soy foods might help build bone. By all means, bean your bones.

⫸ *Breakthrough Study*

Researchers at the Vanderbilt University School of Medicine analyzed five years of health data from approximately 75,000 women, aged 40 to 70.

Result: Women who ate the most soy foods had a 37% lower risk of a fracture than women who ate the least. And soy foods were even more protective for women in the decade right after menopause—with a 48% lower risk of fracture for those eating the most. (For women 10 years or more from the start of menopause, soy foods still decreased fracture risk by 29%.)

"It's wise for postmenopausal women to include soy foods in their diet to promote bone health," says Xiangliang Zhang, MD, the lead researcher on the study.

Why it works: Soy probably works by stimulating bone formation and slowing down the "resorption" or breakdown of bone, say the researchers. Isoflavones, for example, trigger bone-building cells called *osteoblasts* to generate a substance that snuffs bone-destroying cells called *osteoclasts*. Isoflavones also trigger production of a "growth factor" that tells osteoblasts to speed up bone building.

What to do: "There are many ways to add soy to your diet," says Nancy Chapman, RD, executive director of the Soyfoods Association of North America. Pour soy milk over your morning cereal. Snack on soy nuts. Sprinkle edamame—soybeans boiled whole (steam for five minutes) in their pods (remove from pods after cooking)—over your salad. Stir-fry tofu and add it to vegetable dishes; for best results, Chapman favors "firm" or "extra-firm" varieties. Try a meatless meal, substituting soy burgers for hamburgers or soy dogs for hot dogs. In fact, there's a nearly limitless variety of soy substitutes for meat, says Chapman, including soy patties, links and deli slices. And don't forget the soy cheese.

☀ For free soy recipes, visit *www.soyfoods. org.* Soyfoods Association of North America, 1050 17th Street NW, Suite 600, Washington, DC 20036 (202-659-3520); e-mail *info@soyfoods.org.*

Also helpful: In a study conducted by researchers at Case Western University in Cleveland, OH, 19 postmenopausal women (average age of 70) who took a daily soy isoflavone nutritional supplement for six months had a 37% decrease in urinary biomarkers of bone resorption and increases in bone mineral density in spinal vertebrae.

Suggested intake: 110 mg of soy isoflavones was the amount used in the study.

ⓘ Soy isoflavone supplements are widely available.

Caution: Women at high risk for breast cancer or diagnosed with breast cancer should not take supplements of soy isoflavones, as there is a theoretical risk that the phytoestrogens in soy might promote the disease or interfere with the action of anticancer drugs, such as tamoxifen.

14

OVERWEIGHT
EASY WAYS TO SHED THE POUNDS FOR GOOD

By now, the statistic about us Americans is almost as familiar as the fact that there are 50 states—from sea to shining sea, 65% of the citizenry are overweight, with an increased risk for chronic conditions such as arthritis, heart disease, Alzheimer's and many cancers.

You've heard the statistic. Odds are you're among the two out of three with weight you'd like to lose. But how? Take a drug and watch the pounds peel off? Fat chance.

New finding: "People taking anti-obesity drugs will only see modest weight loss and many will remain significantly overweight or obese."

That's the conclusion of a recent article in the *British Medical Journal* that reviewed 30 studies on the three most commonly prescribed weight-loss medications—*orlistat* (Xenical and Alli, its nonprescription cousin), *sibutramine* (Meridia) and *rimonabant* (Acomplia). The study found that most people who take the drugs lose only 5% of their total weight, if that. Not too encouraging.

A drug-free approach is the best way to weight loss, say top experts.

"If you want to lose weight and keep it off, you need to cut your calories and boost your physical activity," says Rena Wing, PhD, director of the Weight Control and Diabetes Research Center at Brown Medical School, in Rhode Island, and cofounder of the National Weight Control Registry, the largest ongoing study of long-term successful weight-loss maintenance.

But that doesn't mean you have to eat like a monk and run like a marathoner.

"Small changes are the key to weight-loss success," says James O. Hill, PhD, cofounder with Dr. Wing of the National Weight Control Registry and director of the Center for Human Nutrition at the University of Colorado. "You don't have to achieve your weight-loss goal right away. You just have to keep moving toward your goal, step by small step. The small changes are the way to get to—and sustain—the big change of permanent weight loss."

You'll find the best of those science-verified small steps—eating a bowl of soup, taking a 10-minute walk, using a nutritional supplement that prevents holiday weight gain—in this chapter.

WHAT "OVERWEIGHT" MEANS

Scientists use several terms to define weight levels, including *normal, overweight, obese* and *extremely obese*. Those levels are determined by *body mass index*, or BMI, a formula that divides weight by height. A BMI of 19 to 24.9 is *normal*, a BMI of 25 to 29.9 is *overweight*, a BMI of 30 to 39.9 is *obese* and a BMI of 40 or over is *extremely obese*.

So, for example, a 5'10" man is…

• **Normal** with a weight of 132 to 173 pounds,

• **Overweight** with a weight of 174 to 208 pounds,

• **Obese** with a weight of 209 to 277 pounds and

• **Extremely obese** with a weight of 278 pounds or more.

A 5'4" woman is…

• **Normal** with a weight of 110 to 144,

• **Overweight** with a weight of 145 to 173,

• **Obese** with a weight of 174 to 231 and

• **Extremely obese** with a weight of 232 pounds or more.

☀ An automatic BMI calculator and complete BMI tables are available at the Web site of the government's National Heart, Lung and Blood Institute, *www.nhlbisupport.com/bmi/bmicalc.htm*.

EAT A LOT OF FOOD, LOSE A LOT OF WEIGHT

You count them. You cut them. You hate them. You love them.

We're talking *calories*, of course—those tasty units of pure energy packed into every food. And you *need* that energy—to read this sentence, to take your next breath, even to digest the other calories you ate at lunch. Calories are the fuel of life.

But as you (and your waistline) may know all too well, calories aren't only crucial. They're also confusing.

Surprising: When scientists asked everyday eaters to guess the number of calories in a typical multicourse, restaurant meal, they underestimated. Not by 10%, 20% or even 30%—but by 38%.

Why are calories so challenging? And is there a way to get them working for weight loss instead of against it?

Well, say nutritional scientists, there is a simple secret to comprehending and conquering the calorie. It's the concept of *calorie density. A concept you can understand in one easy lesson…*

Compare two 100-calorie snacks—ten jellybeans and 2¾ cups of strawberries. That's right, they're *both* 100 calories.

Jellybeans, you see, have a very high calorie density—a little bit of food with lots of calories. Strawberries, on the other hand, aren't pure sugar. Their sweetness is diluted by no-calorie water and fiber. Strawberries have low calorie density—a lot of food with a little bit of calories.

Now imagine a 200-calorie snack of either the jellybeans or the strawberries. If you're a jellybean junky, you can probably polish off those bite-size candies in a minute or two. But 5½ cups of strawberries? Even if *Strawberry Fields Forever* is your favorite song, it's doubtful you could eat all that fruit in a single sitting. You'd stop after a while. You'd feel *satisfied*.

New approach: Weight-loss experts say that eating more foods like those strawberries—foods with low calorie density, filling foods that deliver a lot of eating pleasure for very few calories—is one of the best (if not *the* best) way to lose weight. And you don't have to count calories to do it!

▸ *Breakthrough Study*

Researchers in the Department of Nutritional Sciences at the Pennsylvania State University studied 71 overweight women, aged 22 to 60. Dieticians counseled the women in either one of two weight-loss strategies—how to reduce fat, or how to reduce fat *and* increase low calorie density foods, particularly fruits and vegetables.

Neither group, however, was told to cut a specific amount of fat or calories. In fact, they were told to *eat as much food as they wanted* —while following the strategy they had just learned.

Result: After one year, both groups had lost a lot of weight. But the lower calorie density group lost more—an average of 17.4 pounds, compared to 14.1 pounds for the fat-reducing-only group.

And the daily food and diet logs kept by both groups showed that those following the low calorie density strategy were happier. They ate a lot *more* food (by weight), and felt a lot *less* hungry day to day.

"Choosing foods that are low in calorie density helps to control hunger and is a healthy strategy for losing weight over the long term," says Barbara J. Rolls, PhD, who led the study and is the author of *The Volumetrics Eating Plan* (Harper), which features a diet based on low calorie density foods.

In another study, Dr. Rolls and her colleagues looked at calorie density and weight loss in 658 people with prehypertension and hypertension who had started to follow any one of three variations on a healthful, pressure-lowering diet. After six months, those with the largest reduction in calorie density lost 13 pounds, those with the middle-level reduction, 9 pounds and those with the smallest reduction, 5 pounds.

And in a study conducted with the government's Centers for Disease Control and Prevention, Dr. Rolls and her colleagues analyzed dietary data from more than 7,000 people. They found that those with low calorie density diets ate fewer calories a day (425 fewer for men, and 275 for women)—*but significantly more food* (14 ounces for men, 10.5 ounces for women). Calorie density and overweight was also a perfect match—people who weren't overweight had the diets lowest in calorie density; people who were overweight had the diets highest in calorie density.

Why it works: "Your body has many satiety systems that signal you've eaten enough, and low calorie density, high-volume foods activate most of them," says Dr. Rolls. *She explains…*

You're able to select a normal portion of food…you see a big, appetizing plate of food in front of you…you have more to eat—to smell, chew, taste and swallow, so you send more sensory satiety signals to the brain…a bigger volume of food fills your stomach…and the larger amount of food also stimulates satiety signals in the liver, pancreas, small intestine and large intestine as it moves through the digestive system.

What to do: It's easy, says Dr. Rolls. Simply choose more foods with high natural water content!

Trap: Drinking more water doesn't work, her research shows. It quenches thirst but doesn't satisfy hunger.

Best: The top foods are most fruits and vegetables, skim milk and broth-based soups.

On the second tier are cooked grains, breakfast cereals (served with low-fat 1% or fat-free milk), low-fat meats (including red meat, poultry and fish), legumes (dry beans, peas, chickpeas, lima beans, soybeans and lentils), salads, fat-free salad dressings and cottage cheese.

You'll also want to emphasize water-rich dishes, such as stews, casseroles, pasta with vegetables and fruit-based desserts.

"On the other hand," she says, "you'll have to be very careful about foods that are very low in water—high-fat foods such as potato chips, but also low-fat and fat-free foods that contain very little moisture, such as pretzels, crackers and fat-free cookies."

Fat, she explains, has more than twice as many calories per portion as either carbohydrate or protein. "So, if you cut fat you can lower the calorie density of a meal."

You can also combine the strategies. Increase the water and fiber content of foods, while lowering the fat content to get satisfying portions with few calories.

Dr. Rolls offers these tips for including low calorie density foods in your diet…

- **For fruits and veggies, think convenience.** Stock your kitchen with fruits and vegetables that keep well, such as onions, potatoes, carrots, apples, oranges and bananas…pack bite-size fruit or veggies in lunch bags for work, such as small apples, orange quarters, cherry tomatoes or baby carrots…buy ready-to-eat bagged veggies or veggies from the supermarket salad bar…use frozen fruit and skim milk to make appetite-satisfying smoothies.

- **Soup is super.** "The next time you feel hungry, try a large soothing bowl of broth-based soup," says Dr Rolls. "If you have it as a first course at lunch, it will be easier to eat fewer calories during lunch and you probably won't eat more at dinner. If you have it as a first course at dinner, you're likely to eat less at that meal, too."

New study: Research by Dr. Rolls and her colleagues found that eating *any* kind of low calorie density, broth-based vegetable soup before lunch—with the vegetables whole, or chunky, or chunky and pureed, or pureed—cut total calorie intake at lunch by 20% (with no jump in calories eaten at dinner).

- **H$_2$O is AOK.** "For a beverage, I recommend water, or noncaloric drinks such as diet soda," says Dr. Rolls. "If you drink low-fat or skim milk, continue to do so."

New study: Dr. Rolls and her colleagues served lunch to 44 people in her nutritional laboratory, once a week for six weeks, with a different 12-ounce drink each week (but no drink the first week)—water, diet cola, regular cola, orange juice or 1% milk. They found that when people drank the caloric beverage they didn't eat less—they just *added* those calories to the meal, consuming about 100 calories more than when drinking the noncaloric beverage. The moral of the study is, if you want to lose weight, no-cal beverages with a meal are the best choice.

- **Use sugar substitutes.** "They help reduce calorie intake and increase the amount of food you can eat," says Dr. Rolls. "Consider nonfat flavored yogurt. For eighty calories you can have a half cup of yogurt sweetened with sugar or a three-quarter cup of the same yogurt sweetened with aspartame."

- **Spice right.** "Add flavor without calories by using spices, herbs, garlic, vinegar, black pepper and lemon juice," she says.

- **Eat foods with irregular shapes.** "They produce a bigger volume because they don't pack down. Think of flaky or puffed cereals."

- **Snack on air-popped popcorn.** Three cups are 90 calories.

- **Desserts to diet for.** "Low-fat frozen yogurt and low-fat ice cream are low in calorie density when compared with other dessert choices," says Dr. Rolls.

☀ Dr. Rolls is the author of two books on low calorie density eating—*The Volumetrics Eating*

Plan (Harper) and coauthor *The Volumetrics Weight-Control Plan* (HarperTorch).

WEIGH YOURSELF DAILY, WEIGH 7 POUNDS LESS

Maybe you've heard diet experts counseling would-be weight-losers not to weigh themselves every morning. It's obsessive, depressing, self-defeating and focuses on short-term success (Lose 10 Pounds in One Week!) rather than the hard-won triumph of permanent weight loss. Those experts should weigh the issue more carefully.

▶ *Breakthrough Studies*

Researchers in the Department of Psychology at Drexel University conducted a one-year study on 3,000 people who had lost 30 pounds and kept it off for a year.

At the start of the study, 36% said they weighed themselves (self-weighing) at least once a day—and those who self-weighed the most had the lowest body mass index, and the highest scores on psychological tests measuring a rational, restrained approach to eating choices.

A year later, they found that changes in the rate of self-weighing after the start of the study—whether the participants self-weighed less or more during the year—matched the amount of weight regained.

● **Those who self-weighed less regained nine pounds.**

● **Those who self-weighed at the same rate regained four pounds.**

● **Those who self-weighed more regained two pounds.**

"Consistent self-weighing may help individuals maintain their successful weight loss by allowing them to catch weight gains before they escalate, and make behavior changes to prevent additional weight gain," says Meghan Butryn, PhD, who led the study.

More evidence: In a study of more than 4,600 women by researchers at the University of Michigan, those who self-weighed the most had the lowest BMI.

And at the University of Minnesota, scientists studied two groups—1,226 people in a weight-gain prevention program and 1,800 in a weight-loss program. Over two years, those who self-weighed the most had the *smallest weight gain* in the prevention program and the *largest weight loss* in the weight-loss program.

Researchers at Brown University Medical School studied 314 "successful losers" for 18 months. They found those with the highest rate of self-weighing had the most dietary restraint, were less likely to binge and were less likely to gain back weight. Daily weighing may be "an important aspect of weight-loss maintenance," they say.

What to do: "The most striking similarity among people who don't regain lost weight is that they have discovered a way to nip weight gain in the bud," says Anne M. Fletcher, MS, RD, author of *Thin for Life: 10 Keys to Success from People Who Have Lost Weight & Kept It Off* (Houghton Mifflin). "That is, they monitor their weight closely, and if they gain just a small amount, they *immediately* take it off." And nine out of 10 people she interviewed for her book on weight-maintenance monitored their weight not by checking the fit of their clothes or their image in the mirror—but by weighing themselves regularly.

Important: Since weight tends to fluctuate through the day, weigh yourself at one particular time each day.

Smart ideas: To nip weight gain in the bud, their strategies included one or more of the following—decrease snacking, decrease portion sizes, moderately increase exercise, eat more fruits and vegetables, give up sweets.

HOW MUCH WALKING PREVENTS WEIGHT GAIN?

If you want to *lose* weight, don't place your hopes on exercise.

Surprising: "Losing weight and keeping it off are very different," says James O. Hill, PhD, director of the Center for Human Nutrition at the University of Colorado and coauthor of *The Step Diet* (Workman). "Scientific studies on weight-loss show that adding exercise to dieting doesn't make much difference."

Why not? Run (or walk) the numbers, says Dr. Hill.

"You can reduce your dietary intake of calories by a thousand a day and lose one to two pounds a week," says Dr. Hill. "But if you're overweight and out of shape, you can't burn a thousand calories a day by exercising—in fact, you're lucky if you can burn a hundred calories a day."

But exercise is absolutely key to keeping weight *off* after you've lost it—because burning up 100 or 200 calories every day with exercise is the perfect strategy to prevent the creeping ounce-by-ounce return of the pounds. And Dr. Hill thinks there's a uniquely effective exercise for weight maintenance.

"It's walking. My colleagues and I have studied thousands of people who lost weight and kept it off, and walking is their number one activity. Nearly everyone can do it, and it doesn't take a special setting or special equipment."

And the best way to guarantee you'll walk enough every day is by using a pedometer—a small device hooked to your waistband that measures exactly how many steps you take. "A pedometer allows you to set a goal and then gives you instant feedback about how you're doing in reaching it."

Ten thousand steps a day is the number that's often recommended for weight control (and health). But is that the number of *steps* that *really* works? The latest research provides the answer.

▐▐▐➤ *Breakthrough Study*

A team of 14 researchers from the United States, Australia, Canada, France and Sweden analyzed data from more than 3,000 people (average age, 47) who had used a pedometer to prevent weight gain. *The steps-per-day that worked to keep pounds off…*

	AGE	STEPS PER DAY
MEN	Age 18 to 50	12,000
	Age 50 or over	11,000
WOMEN	Age 18 to 40	12,000
	Age 40 to 50	11,000
	Age 50 to 60	10,000
	Age 60 or over	8,000

Now you know how many steps to take. *If you want more proof that those steps will help you maintain weight—check out the results from these other studies...*

• **Fewer steps, fatter body.** A study from the University of Colorado found that obese people walk an average of 2,000 fewer steps a day than those of normal weight.

• **Put on a pedometer, burn 27% more calories.** If you use a pedometer with a daily step goal, you're likely to increase your daily steps by at least 2,100 a day and your calorie-burning physical activity by 27%, say researchers from Stanford University, in the *Journal of the American Medical Association*. They analyzed data from 26 pedometer studies, involving nearly 3,000 people.

"Much to my surprise, these little devices were shown to increase physical activity by about one mile of walking per day," says Dena Bravata, MD, MS, who led the study.

• **Smaller waist, thinner hips.** Researchers at the University of Tennessee studied 80 women with an average age of 50, giving them pedometers and recording their daily steps. Those who took the most steps had the lowest percentage of body fat, the lowest BMI, smaller waists and thinner hips.

• **A thousand more steps, 30% more likely to lose weight.** Italian researchers studied 36 overweight and obese men who had completed a nine-month weight-loss program,

asking them to use a pedometer to increase their physical activity. For every additional 1,000 steps the men walked, their likelihood of losing 10% or more of body weight increased by 30%.

What to do: Using a pedometer is easy, says Dr. Hill.

• **Spend $5 or more.** There are many pedometers out there. How do you know which ones accurately count steps and which don't? "The really cheap ones—under five dollars—aren't accurate," says Dr. Hill. "Those in the five-to-fifteen dollar range are decent. And those fifteen dollars and higher are very accurate."

The Digi-Walker from New-Lifestyles (starting at $16.95) is the brand recommended by Dixie Thompson, PhD, a pedometer researcher and professor of Exercise, Sports and Leisure Studies at the Center for Physical Activity and Health at the University of Tennessee. They are widely available.

www.new-lifestyles.com. New-Lifestyles, 5201 NE Maybrook Road, Lee's Summit, MO 64064 (816-373-9969 or fax 816-373-9929); e-mail *info@new-lifestyles.com.*

• **Setting your goal.** "First, if there is any question about your capacity to increase your steps, see your physician," says Harry Preuss, MD, a professor at George Washington University and coauthor of *The Natural Fat-Loss Pharmacy* (Broadway).

"When you start wearing the pedometer, do your usual daily routine and record the number of steps, every day for a week," says Dr. Preuss. "Your highest daily number for that week is your minimum. Your goal for the following week is to increase your minimum by five hundred steps. For example, if your minimum was four thousand the first week, your goal for the second week is forty-five hundred steps a day. Each following week, increase your steps by another five hundred, until you reach your target goal, such as ten thousand steps a day.

• **Reaching your goal.** Dr. Hill's top strategy for getting your daily steps—Go for a walk! A mile is approximately 2,100 to 2,600 steps, depending on the length of your stride. If you walk a mile in 20 minutes (3 miles an hour, which is a moderately fast, steady pace), you'll walk about 3,000 to 3,500 steps in 30 minutes.

Also try: To add steps throughout the day, he suggests you might...take two more 10-minute walks...at work, choose the entrance to the building farthest from your parking spot...get off a bus earlier and walk the extra blocks to your destination...walk around your living room during TV commercials...take the stairs rather than the escalator or elevator...start a walking club with friends or coworkers... empty wastebaskets every day...walk at the airport while waiting for your plane.

FOR MAXIMUM FAT LOSS, EXERCISE WITH A TUNA

Is there a way to boost the fat-burning, pounds-burning power of exercise? *Yes, take a tuna with you on your next walk...*

New finding: Australian researchers studied 75 overweight people, dividing them into four groups...

Group 1 exercised and took fish oil supplements (omega-3 fatty acids).

Group 2 exercised and took placebos.

Group 3 took fish oil supplements.

Group 4 took placebos.

After 12 weeks, only Group 1 (the people who exercised *and* took fish oil supplements) had lost a substantial amount of weight *and* body fat—4.4 pounds, of which 2.6 pounds was fat. (Dieters always lose some muscle, too—and many dieters lose more muscle than fat.)

"Combining regular exercise and fish oil supplements may be more effective than either approach alone," say the researchers, in the *American Journal of Clinical Nutrition.*

What happens: The researchers theorize that the omega-3 fatty acids in fish oil improve blood flow to exercising muscles, activating enzymes that allow muscles to more easily use fat as fuel.

What to do: The exercise/fish oil group walked briskly for 45 minutes, three days a week. They took 6 grams (6,000 mg) of fish oil a day, containing a combined total of 1.9 grams of the omega-3 fatty acids DHA (docosahexaenoic acid) and EPA (eicosapentaenoic acid).

THE HAZARDS OF MINDLESS EATING

Ahh, a cookie you can have a couple more of, because the label says low-fat. *Hold those hungry horses...*

Surprising: People eat an average of 28% *more* calories when they eat low-fat snacks than the regular variety, says Brian Wansink, PhD, director of the Cornell Food and Brand lab at Cornell University and author of *Mindless Eating: Why We Eat More Than We Think* (Bantam).

"People don't realize that low-fat foods are not always low-calorie foods," he says. (The fat is often replaced with sugar.) So while low-fat snacks are an average 11% lower in calories, people wrongly believe they are about 40% lower—and eat a lot more of them.

Breakthrough Study

Dr. Wansink and his colleagues held two holiday open-house parties. At one, they served chocolate candies labeled "Regular." At the other, they served candies labeled "Low-fat." The low-fat partygoers ate a third more chocolates—and 28% more calories.

What to do: "Stick with the regular version, but eat a little bit less," says Dr. Wansink. "It's better for both your diet and your taste buds."

Also helpful: Here are more ways to stop high-calorie "mindless eating," from breakthrough research by Dr. Wansink and the Cornell Food and Brand lab...

● **Listen to "internal," not "external" cues.** Why are the French thinner than Americans even though their diet is loaded with fatty foods? A new survey of people in Paris and Chicago shows that the French tend to stop eating based on internal clues (such as whether or not they feel full), while Americans tend to depend on external clues (such as whether their plate is empty or the TV show is over). And the more a person weighs, the more likely they are to pay attention to external clues, says Dr. Wansink.

Advice: Stop eating when you feel full, not when the plate is empty.

Keep those candy wrappers around. The researchers found that people ate only *half* as many mini-size Halloween candies when they kept the wrappers in plain sight rather than throwing them out right away. "Having a visual reminder of how much you eat keeps you honest and eating less," says Dr. Wansink.

Advice: Throw out those wrappers when you're sure you're done eating, not before.

● **Don't eat more fast food because it's "healthy."** People who ate at Subway restaurants—which makes healthy claims about their food—ate 131% more calories than when they ate at McDonald's, which doesn't make the same claims.

Advice: Most of the extra calories were in the side dishes. Try not to order as many.

If you're sad and eating a comfort food—check the calories on the label. Dr. Wansink and his colleagues showed people either a happy movie (*Sweet Home Alabama*) or a sad movie (*Love Story*). Those watching the sad movie ate 36% more buttered popcorn! In a follow-up study, they found that sad people with nutritional information about the comfort food they were eating ate much less.

Advice: "While each of us may look for a comfort food when we are either sad or happy, we are likely to eat more of it when we are sad," says Dr. Wansink. "Since nutritional information appears to influence how much people eat when they are in sad moods, those eating in a sad mood would serve themselves well by checking the nutritional information of the comfort foods they choose to indulge themselves with."

● **Make better food decisions.** Dr. Wansink's research shows that people *think* they make about 15 food decisions a day—but in reality they make more than 200! "The problem with making so many more food decisions than we are aware of," he says, "is that each of these small decisions is a point where a person can be unknowingly influenced by environmental cues."

Advice: "Rather than try to overly obsess about our food decisions, it's better to change the environment so it works for us rather than against us, making it easier to make decisions to eat less," he says. *His recommendations...*

● **Use smaller bowls.** Research shows you may eat 60% less.

● **Take the snack out of the package.** And put it in a bowl. You may eat 134 fewer calories, says a study.

● **Don't avoid your comfort food.** Just eat it in a smaller portion.

● **Use the rule of two.** Appetizer, drink, dessert—have *two*, not all three.

● Out of sight, out of stomach. People ate 23% less candy when it was in

CUT 201 CALORIES A DAY— EAT...MORE...SLOWLY

If you stop rushing through meals and take the time to savor your food—you may end up eating fewer calories...

New finding: "In 1972, scientists hypothesized that eating slowly would allow the body time to feel full and you would eat less," says Kathleen Melanson, PhD, RD, an associate professor in the Department of Nutrition and Food Sciences at the University of Rhode Island. "Since then, we've heard that idea over and over again, and it's become common knowledge. But no studies have been conducted to prove it."

To see if slow-calorie was low-calorie, Dr. Melanson studied 30 women in her nutrition laboratory, feeding them the same lunch on two days—a super-size portion of pasta, topped with tomato-vegetable sauce and grated Parmesan cheese, and a glass of water.

Before one of the lunches, the women were instructed...to...eat...slowly—to take small bites, chew each bite 15 to 20 times, and put down utensils between each bite.

At the other lunch, they were told to eat as fast as possible.

On both days, they were asked to eat until they felt comfortably full.

On the speed-eating day, the women ate an average of 646 calories in 9 minutes.

On the slow-food day, they ate 579 calories in 29 minutes.

"Add up that difference in calories over three meals, and that's about two hundred calories a day—a big difference," says Dr. Melanson. And she notes that the women said they enjoyed the meal more when eating slowly.

What to do: "Sit down and *savor* your food," counsels Dr. Melanson. "Put down the fork between bites, or sip water. Have a conversation while you're eating. Linger over your meal."

an opaque-covered candy dish rather than a see-through dish.

● Keep food at arm's length. They ate even less when that opaque dish was across the room rather than on the desk.

☀ You can find more information about mindless eating at the Web site of Dr. Wansink and the Cornell Food and Brand lab (plus a free "Mindless Eating" refrigerator magnet, and free copies of the newsletter "The Mindless Eater") at *www.mindlesseating.com*.

CLA PREVENTS HOLIDAY WEIGHT GAIN

Most of us gain only a pound or so over the holiday season. *Problem is, most of us never lose that pound again...*

Landmark study: Researchers at the National Institutes of Health studied 165 people over the holiday season and found most of them gained about a pound. (However, the overweight and obese gained an average of five pounds.) But when the researchers weighed them a year later—they hadn't lost the added weight!

"Although an average holiday weight gain of about a pound may seem unimportant, that weight was not lost over the remainder of the year," says Jack A. Yanovski, MD, PhD, who led the study.

"The cumulative effects of yearly weight gain during the fall and winter are likely to contribute to the substantial increase in body weight that frequently occurs during adulthood," say Dr. Yanovski and his colleagues, in the *New England Journal of Medicine.* "Promotion of weight stability during the fall and winter months may prove useful as a strategy to prevent age-related weight gain in the United States."

New approach: Well, researchers in the Department of Nutritional Sciences at the University of Wisconsin-Madison have found a startlingly simple and effective way to help prevent holiday weight gain—taking a supplement of CLA (conjugated linoleic acid).

▶ *Breakthrough Study*

CLA is a fatty acid (a component of fat) discovered in 1978 by researchers at the University of Wisconsin-Madison. Since then, thousands of cellular, animal and human studies have shown this unique nutrient can stymie cancer cells, stimulate a lackluster immune system, calm inflammation and lower cholesterol.

In 1997, scientists also discovered that CLA can flip a metabolic switch, telling the body to make less fat and build more muscle. Could CLA's fat-busting, muscle-making power prevail over pumpkin pie and Christmas cookies?

To find out, researchers asked 40 overweight men and women to take either CLA or a placebo for six months, from the beginning of August to the end of January.

Every month, the researchers weighed the participants and measured their levels of "fat mass" (fat) and "lean mass" (muscle and skeleton).

During the months of the study, the CLA group and the placebo group ate roughly the same amount of calories and had the same level of physical activity.

Result: During November and December, the placebo group gained 2.4 pounds, including 1.5 pounds of fat mass.

"Within the placebo group, holiday weight gain was significantly greater," says Andrea Buchholz, PhD, RD, one of the researchers conducting the study.

Meanwhile, by October the CLA group had already lost weight—1.7 pounds. On closer analysis, the researchers found they lost 2.2 pounds of fat and gained one-half pound of muscle. And they didn't gain *any* additional weight during the holidays.

"Despite no differences between the CLA and the placebo group with regards to calorie intake or physical activity throughout the study, the CLA group still managed to lose weight prior to the holiday season and didn't gain any weight over the holidays," says Dr. Buchholz.

To sum up this remarkable result, "CLA versus placebo prevented weight gain during the holiday season among overweight adults, and therefore may play a role in reducing the cumulative weight and fat gain that occurs with age," say the researchers.

More evidence: This study wasn't the first to find that CLA can help you lose weight and/or fat...

Swedish researchers studied 180 men and women for two years, with half of them taking CLA and half taking a placebo. The CLA group lost 4.5 pounds of fat and gained 1.5 pounds of muscle—without dieting or exercise. The placebo group had no change.

Researchers in Norway gave 47 overweight people either CLA or a placebo for three months. The CLA group lost four pounds of body fat; the placebo group didn't.

In another study from Sweden, 24 men who were "abdominally obese" took either CLA or a placebo for four weeks—and those taking the supplement lost a half-inch off their waistlines. The placebo men saw no difference.

And in a recent analysis of 18 studies on CLA and weight loss, researchers at the University of Wisconsin found that those who took the supplement lost nearly a pound of fat a month—compared to little or no change for those taking the placebo.

How it works: There are several ways CLA probably works to stymie fat, says Michael W. Pariza, PhD, the discoverer of the nutrient. It might stop dietary fat from entering fat cells.

It might kill fat cells as they're forming. And it might burn up fatty acids in muscle tissue.

Suggested intake: The study participants took 3.2 grams of CLA a day. Most 1,000 mg pills contain 800 mg of CLA; take four pills a day.

ℹ️ Most studies on weight loss use Tonalin CLA, a form that is a balanced combination of two CLA isomers. (Isomers are molecules with the same types of atoms but different structures. Some CLA products use only one isomer.) Tonalin CLA is an ingredient in many brands of CLA supplements, including Country Life, Doctor's Trust, GNC, Natrol, NOW, Puritan's Pride, Swanson and Vitamin World.

Caution: Some people may experience mild digestive side effects when they take CLA, such as stomachache, loose stools or nausea. If that happens, reduce the amount of CLA you're taking by half, says Jean-Michael Gaullier, MD, who conducted the two-year weight-loss study on the supplement. "If the side effects persist, stop completely for a few days and then start again, at full dosage. If, at that point, the problems don't disappear, you're not someone who can take CLA."

But the supplements have been studied on more than 6,000 people, and are generally very safe, says Dr. Buchholz. "We looked at effects on liver function, inflammation and insulin resistance and found no adverse effects," she says. "It looks as though there are very few risks in taking the mixed-form [two isomer] supplements—and lots to be gained."

Or lost.

THE VEGETARIAN ADVANTAGE

Here's a simple way to lose weight—eat more salad and less steak.

⫸ *Breakthrough Studies*

Led by Neal D. Barnard, MD, from the Department of Medicine at George Washington School of Medicine, a team of researchers studied 59 overweight postmenopausal women, with BMIs ranging from 26 (overweight) to 44 (extremely obese). They assigned the women to one of two weight-loss diets for 14 weeks.

One was a "vegan diet," with no animal foods, including milk—a diet of vegetables, fruits, grains and beans, with no added oils, avocados, olives, nuts, nut butters or seeds (and with a standard multivitamin to supply vitamin B-12, which is found mostly in meat). The new vegans were also encouraged to favor whole foods over processed foods.

The other diet was the National Cholesterol Education Program Step II Diet (NCEP)—a typical low-fat diet, with 30% of calories from fat, 15% from protein and 55% from carbohydrates.

Neither the vegan nor the NCEP dieters counted calories. And both groups were asked to stick with the same level of physical activity as when the study started.

Result: After 14 weeks, those on the vegan diet had lost an average of 13 pounds. Those on the standard low-fat diet lost eight pounds.

"The degree of weight loss for the vegan group was similar to that seen with low-calorie diets of about twelve hundred calories a day," says Dr. Barnard. "But the vegan group lost weight with no calorie cutting, no smaller portion sizes and no additional exercise."

However: Studies on weight-loss diets are often criticized because they don't last long enough. Sure, those 59 women lost weight after three months—but what about after one year, or even two?

Well, Dr. Barnard and his colleagues conducted a follow-up study on the two groups of women, checking their weight after one and then two years…

• **After one year**, the women in the vegan group had lost an average of 11 pounds. The NCEP group lost four pounds.

• **After two years**, the weight loss was seven pounds for the vegan group and two pounds for the NCEP dieters.

"As the rates of obesity rise, it is increasingly important to find diets that produce effective weight loss and that can *continue* to produce weight loss or weight-loss maintenance over the long term," says Dr. Barnard. "The vegan diet is one of those diets."

New finding: A recent study from England shows that *any* change away from meat eating can keep you from gaining weight. The researchers followed nearly 22,000 people over five years, dividing them into four groups—meat-eaters, fish-eaters, vegetarians and vegans. The average yearly weight gain of all the groups was just shy of a pound (14 ounces). But those who changed their diet *away* from meat eating had the smallest yearly weight gain, with the lowest among the vegans (eight ounces).

Why it works: In an article in the journal *Nutrition Reviews*, Dr. Barnard and his colleague Susan E. Berkow, PhD, CNS, review how vegetarian diets—that include not only fruits, vegetables, grains and beans, but also dairy products and eggs—help people lose weight.

They point out that 29 studies show that vegetarians weigh significantly less than non-vegetarians—10 to 28 pounds lower among men, and 6 to 23 pounds lower among women. Why? *Because the diet is…*

• **Lower in calories.** Anywhere from 5 to 22% lower than nonvegetarian diets, studies show.

• **Higher in fiber.** Thirty-six to 41% higher. Fiber helps fill you up at a meal so you eat less. It also slows digestion, delaying hunger.

• **Higher in carbohydrates.** Particularly from fruits, vegetables, legumes, nuts, whole-grain breads and cereals—allowing people to eat more food (by weight) but take in fewer calories.

• **Lower in fat.** Fat has more than double the calories of carbohydrates and protein.

Surprising: "There is scientific evidence that a vegan diet causes an increased calorie burn after meals, meaning plant-based foods are being used more efficiently as fuel for the body, as opposed to being stored as fat," says Dr. Barnard.

• **Lower in protein.** Studies show that people eating lower levels of protein are more likely to have lower BMIs. "All essential and nonessential amino acids [the building blocks of protein] can be supplied by plant sources," say Drs. Barnard and Berkow.

• **And easy to eat.** In Dr. Barnard's study of postmenopausal women, 75% of those on the vegan diet said it was "fairly," "moderately" or "extremely easy" to prepare. Nearly half said that staying on the diet required "only a little effort," "almost no effort" or "no effort at all." Ninety-three percent said the diet was "extremely good," "good" or "moderately good." Overall, the level of acceptance of the "seemingly austere low-fat vegan diet" was the same as that for the "more permissive" conventional low-fat diet, says Dr. Barnard.

"Our research reveals that people can enjoy unlimited portions of high-fiber foods such as fruits, vegetables and whole grains to achieve or maintain a healthy body weight without feeling hungry," says Dr. Berkow.

What to do: There are three easy steps to start a vegetarian diet, says Dr. Barnard.

• **Step 1.** "Think of three vegetarian meals that you already enjoy," he says. "Common ones are tofu and vegetable stir-fry, vegetable stew or pasta primavera."

• **Step 2.** "Think of three recipes that you prepare regularly that can be adapted to a vegetarian menu," he says. "For example, a favorite chili recipe can be made with all of the same ingredients—just replace the meat with beans or texturized vegetable protein. Instead of beef burritos, enjoy bean burritos using canned vegetarian refried beans. Instead of hamburgers, eat veggie burgers. Instead of grilled chicken sandwiches, enjoy grilled eggplant and roasted red peppers. You can also make many soups, stews and casseroles into vegetarian dishes, with a few simple changes."

• **Step 3.** "Check out some vegetarian cookbooks from the library and experiment with the recipes for a week or so until you find three new recipes that are delicious and easy to make. Just like that, with minimal changes to your menus, you will have nine vegetarian dinners.

"After that," he says, "coming up with vegetarian options for breakfast and lunch is easy. Try muffins with fruit spread or cereal for breakfast. For lunch, try sandwiches with spreads such as hummus or white bean pâté with lemon and garlic, or pasta salads or dinner leftovers."

☀ For a free Vegetarian Starter Kit from the Physicians Committee for Responsible Medicine (Dr. Barnard is the founder and president), call 202-686-2210, ext. 306, or e-mail *literature@ pcrm.org*. The kit is also available as a downloadable PDF at the Web site of the Physicians Committee for Responsible Medicine, *www. pcrm.org*. You can find a link to it on the Web site's home page.

Well-reviewed and popular books on vegetarianism and veganism include…

The New Becoming Vegetarian: The Essential Guide to a Healthy Vegetarian Diet by Brenda Davis, RD, and Vesanto Melina, MS, RD (Healthy Living Publications).

How to Cook Everything Vegetarian: Simple Meatless Recipes for Great Food by Mark Bitman (Wiley).

Veganomicon: The Ultimate Vegan Cookbook by Isa Chandra Moskowitz and Terry Hope Romero (Da Capo).

EAT HALF A GRAPEFRUIT, LOSE THREE POUNDS

The Grapefruit Diet is synonymous with fad diet—the kind of exotic regimen that dieticians and doctors unanimously declare *don't work* for long-term weight loss. But new research shows that the Grapefruit Diet— originated in the 1930s, and called for drinking eight ounces of unsweetened grapefruit juice before every meal, along with a calorie-restricted regimen—may have had something going for it. *Such as grapefruit…*

New finding: Researchers in the Department of Nutrition and Metabolic Research at the Scripps Clinic in California studied 91 obese people, dividing them into four groups, each with a different before-meal regimen…

1. Seven ounces of apple juice and placebo capsules

2. Seven ounces of apple juice and grapefruit extract capsules

3. Eight ounces of grapefruit juice and placebo capsules

4. Half a fresh grapefruit and placebo capsules

After three months…

Group 4 (fresh grapefruit) lost 3.5 pounds.

Group 3 (grapefruit juice) lost 3.3 pounds.

Group 2 (grapefruit capsules) lost 2.4 pounds.

Group 1 (apple juice) lost 0.7 pounds. Notice a trend?

"Although the mechanism of this weight loss is unknown, it would appear reasonable to include grapefruit in a weight-reduction diet," say the researchers.

Becoming Vegan by Brenda Davis, RD, and Vesanto Melina, MS, RD (Book Publishing Company).

SLIMMER THIGHS— WITHOUT EXERCISE

It's been described as looking like a cross between an orange peel, a bowl of cottage cheese and a lumpy mattress.

It's *cellulite*, that undesirable dimpling of the fatty tissue under the skin of the buttocks and thighs. An estimated 85 to 98% of women end up with some—and probably all of them wish they hadn't.

Nobody knows the cause of cellulite, although genes, hormones, lack of exercise and second-rate nutrition have been blamed.

A team of five Brazilian dermatologists was looking for a solution to the problem. *Sorry to say, they didn't find it.* But in the process of testing a caffeine-containing cream, they may have found an easy way for women to slim their thighs.

▊▊▶ *Breakthrough Study*

Led by Omar Lupi, MD, PhD, the doctors at the Federal University of Rio de Janeiro studied 99 women with cellulite. For 30 days, the women were asked to treat only *one* of their thighs with a cream containing 7% caffeine. They applied a half ounce of the cream twice a day, in the morning and evening, to the upper and lower thigh.

Result: After 30 days, 80% of the women had slimmer thighs. The new measurement was about two centimeters (0.8 inch) off the circumference.

"There is no cure for cellulite," say Dr. Lupi and his colleagues, who reported the results in the *Journal of Cosmetic Dermatology*. "But this

WEIGHT-LOSS SECRET— DON'T READ THE NEWSPAPER!

Or only read the front page, the sports section and the funnies…

New finding: Scientists at the Marshfield Clinic Research Foundation in Marshfield, WI, studied newspapers in 12 cities with populations over 400,000, including Los Angeles, Dallas, Detroit and Philadelphia. *Their exposé…*

- **The higher the average calorie count of the dessert recipes in the newspaper,** the higher the percentage of obese people in that city!

"These data are intriguing, and suggest that newspapers may play a greater role in preventing or promoting obesity than previously recognized," says Catherine A. McCarty, PhD, MPH, who led the study.

What to do: The calories in the desserts ranged from 180 to 600 per serving. If you cut out dessert recipes from the newspaper, cut out some calories too. A few substitution tricks from home baker Diana Baker Woodall, at *www.dianasdesserts.com…*

- **Whole milk.** For one cup of whole milk, substitute one-half cup evaporated milk plus one-half cup water, or one cup water, plus one-third cup nonfat evaporated dry milk powder. If a baking recipe calls for whole milk, you may be able to substitute a low-fat milk variety like skim, 1% or 2% fat. Be cautious about substituting skim milk in pudding, custard and sauce recipes. (These recipes rely on the dairy fat for added texture and flavor.) Baked items such as cakes and cookies can usually tolerate the use of low-fat milk.

- **Shortening.** For shortening, you can usually substitute cooking sprays such as PAM to prepare baking sheets and baking pans.

- **Sugar.** "I use Splenda Granular a lot in my baking—as I am a diabetic, and also a Weight Watcher who has lost seventy pounds," says Woodall. "It works great."

treatment can help women who want to look thinner."

☀ The researchers used the over-the-counter product Elancyl Chrono-Actif, from Galenic, a French company.

Latest development: A leading French consumer's magazine (similar to *Consumer Reports* in the United States) asked 200 women to test 10 different cellulite-reducing creams (20 women testing each cream), with another group of women using placebo creams. Only two of the creams worked, including Elancyl Chrono-Actif, which reduced thigh circumference by the same average amount as in Dr. Lupi's study—a little less than an inch.

"We have tested creams on three previous occasions and have never found them to be more effective than a thigh massage," the editor of the magazine told *The Independent*, a British newspaper. "This time, our test has come to the very conclusion that women want to hear. People have been astonished to find us giving the thumbs up."

☀ Elancyl Chrono-Actif is available at the "cosmetic surgery and anti-aging" Web site, *www.makemeheal.com*. Make Me Heal, 15452 Cabrito Road, Van Nuys, CA 91406 (866-363-4325).

MAINTAIN IN THE MEDITERRANEAN

Olive oil. Pasta. Avocados. Nuts. Hummus.

Sounds yummy. But after eating all those fatty or carbohydrate-rich foods, you'll have to go on a diet.

No, that *is* the diet.

⏩ *Breakthrough Studies*

Those foods are some of the staples of the Mediterranean diet—that sunny, southern European style of eating that emphasizes not only fresh fruits and vegetables (the centerpiece of any weight-loss plan) but also foods considered a waistline's worst nightmare, such as olive oil, at 120 calories per teaspoon.

Well, an international team of researchers from Spain and the United States recently conducted a three-year study of nearly 28,000 Spaniards—and found the good-tasting Mediterranean diet is your waistline's dream.

During those three years, about 7% of the study participants became obese. But those who ate a Mediterranean diet pattern—vegetables, fruits, legumes, nuts, fish, meats, whole grains and olive oil—had a 31% lower risk of becoming obese.

"Eating habits consistent with Mediterranean Diet patterns may be a useful part of efforts to combat obesity," says Michele Mendez, MD, who led the study.

Why it works: Possible factors include… high fiber…low calorie density foods…and less saturated fat (from meat and milk)…all factors that have been linked to weight loss, says Dr. Mendez.

However: "There are concerns that the added fat in this diet might cause obesity. But despite the high intake of fat from olive oil among those eating a Mediterranean diet, our study didn't show a link between olive oil consumption and either overweight or obesity."

Example: Cornell researchers studied diners in an Italian restaurant and found that people who soaked their bread in olive oil ate 23% less bread over the course of a meal.

More evidence: Spanish researchers studied 3,162 men and women and found those who ate the Mediterranean diet were 39% less likely to be obese.

Greek researchers studied 3,042 men and women and found those who ate a Mediterranean diet were 51% less likely to be obese.

Researchers at Harvard Medical School asked 61 overweight people to go on either a moderate-fat Mediterranean diet or a low-fat diet for 18 months. Those on the Mediterranean diet lost nine pounds and three inches off their waists, while those eating low-fat *gained* six pounds and one inch. (Because only 20% of the low-fat eaters were on the diet after 18 months, compared with 54% of the Mediterranean group!) "A moderate-fat, calorie-controlled Mediterranean-style diet offers an alternative to a low-fat diet, with superior long-term participation and consequent improvements in weight loss," say the researchers.

What to do: Here are tips to follow the Mediterranean diet, from the Mediterranean Foods Alliance…

• **Make olive oil your primary source of dietary fat.** (Substitute olive oil for butter.)

• **Incorporate an abundance of food from plant sources,** including fruits and vegetables, breads, grains, beans, nuts and seeds. (Snack on almonds instead of fat-free cookies. Spread avocado on a sandwich to replace the mayonnaise.)

• **Eat low to moderate amounts of fish and poultry weekly.**

• **Eat low to moderate amounts of cheese and yogurt daily.**

• **Drink a moderate amount of wine** (one to two glasses per day for men, one glass per day for women).

☀ You can find out more about the Mediterranean diet (including an easy-to-use Mediterranean diet pyramid and information about the "Med Mark" label to help you find

TOO MUCH SNACKING AT NIGHT? EAT CEREAL!

"In an informal survey at a weight-loss center, fifty percent of the patients said that after-dinner snacking was either a large or very large component of their weight problem," says Nikhil V. Dhurandhar, PhD, Department of Nutrition and Food Science at Wayne State University, in Detroit.

He and his colleagues may have found an unusual solution—eat breakfast after dinner!

New finding: Dr. Dhurandhar theorized that a bowl of ready-to-eat cereal—a predictable, healthy after-dinner snack—could replace high-fat, high-calorie snacks, cut calories and lead to weight loss. To test his idea, he studied 62 overweight people who said they snacked six or seven nights a week and that snacking was a big part of their weight problem. He divided them into two groups—cereal (CR) and no cereal (NC).

The CR group was asked to eat one cup of ready-to-eat cereal, in a two-third cup of low-fat milk or low-fat soymilk, at least 90 minutes after dinner. The NC group was asked not to make any changes in their diet.

After one month, those in the CR group who had eaten cereal at least five days a week had lost an average of 1.9 pounds. The NC group lost an average of 0.4 pounds.

The CR group also ate 396 fewer calories a day, compared to 23 fewer calories for the NC group. And they ate 104 fewer calories after dinner, while the NC group had increased their post-dinner calories by 86. "The simple addition of a structured evening snack of ready-to-eat cereal helped nighttime snackers lose weight," says Dr. Dhurandhar.

What to do: If you're a nighttime snacker, try eating a bowl of cereal about 90 minutes after dinner.

ℹ Kellogg's supplied the cereals, which were all 100 and 135 calories a bowl, and between one to two grams of fiber, such as Corn Flakes and Product 19.

Mediterranean diet foods in the supermarket) at the Web site of the Mediterranean Foods Alliance, *www.mediterraneanmark.org*. The Alliance is a division of Oldways, a nonprofit organization dedicated to traditional eating and sustainable agriculture. Oldways Preservation & Exchange Trust, 266 Beacon Street, Boston, MA 02116 (617-421-5500 or fax 617-421-5511).

Weight-loss books featuring a Mediterranean diet include...

The Advanced Mediterranean Diet: Lose Weight, Feel Better, Live Longer by Steven Paul Parker, MD (Vanguard Press).

The Mediterranean Prescription: Meal Plans and Recipes to Help You Stay Slim and Healthy for the Rest of Your Life by Angelo Acquista, MD (Ballantine).

The Miami Mediterranean Diet: Lose Weight and Lower Your Risk of Heart Disease with 300 Delicious Recipes by Michael Ozner, MD (Benbella Books, 2008).

The Sonoma Diet by Connie Gutterson, RD, PhD (Meredith).

TEN MINUTES TO A THINNER WAIST

If you're overweight and inactive, even 10 minutes a day of exercise can whittle your waistline...

New research: Scientists at the Pennington Biomedical Research Center at Louisiana State University studied 464 postmenopausal women who were overweight or obese, and inactive. They assigned them to one of four groups—190, 135 or 75 minutes a week of exercise, or no exercise.

Six months later, even the women exercising 75 minutes a week—that's *half* as much as the recommendation from the National Institutes of Health—were fitter. And *slimmer.*

Compared with the no-exercise group, their waists were an average of 1.2 inches smaller. They also had 2% less body fat and weighed one pound less. (The women who exercised 135 or 195 minutes were fitter than the 75-minute group, but they weren't any slimmer.)

Good news: "Exercise is an effective way to reduce waist circumference, even without substantial weight loss," says Timothy Church, MD, MPH, PhD, who led the study, published in the *Journal of the American Medical Association.* "And the reduction of waist size is of particular importance, because research links excess abdominal fat to an increased risk for insulin resistance, metabolic syndrome, diabetes and death from any cause.

"The major reason for not engaging in more activity is lack of time," continues Dr. Church. "The results of this study should be encouraging to sedentary adults who find it difficult to find the time for a hundred fifty minutes of activity per week, the public recommendation of the National Institutes of Health."

What to do: The women in the study exercised on a treadmill or stationary bicycle. But any regular increase in activity—from 10 minutes of brisk walking to 10 minutes of yard work or housework—will do the trick, says Steven N. Blair, PED (Doctor of Physical Education), a professor in the Department of Exercise Science at the University of South Carolina and a study researcher.

EGGS FOR BREAKFAST, LESS CALORIES AT LUNCH

You're awake. You're hungry. And you're trying to lose weight. What's the better choice for breakfast—eggs and toast, or a bagel and cream cheese?

ⅢⅢ➡ *Breakthrough Study*

To find out, a team of researchers (from Saint Louis University in Missouri, Wayne State University in Detroit and the Rochester Center for Obesity Research and Treatment in Michigan) studied 30 overweight and obese women.

They fed them two different breakfasts two weeks apart, one egg-based and the other bagel-based. The egg breakfast consisted of two scrambled eggs, two slices of toast, and one tablespoon of reduced-fat fruit spread. The bagel breakfast consisted of a 3.5-inch-diameter bagel, two tablespoons of cream cheese and three ounces of nonfat yogurt. The two breakfasts had similar calorie levels and even weighed about the same.

Afterward, the researchers measured how full the participants felt between breakfast and lunch (satiety)…the intensity of their post-breakfast food cravings…how many calories they ate for lunch (pasta with marinara sauce, and a dessert of sliced apples, with encouragement to eat as much as they wanted)…and how many calories they ate in the 24 hours after lunch.

Results: The bagel had egg on its face.

• **Fewer calories at lunch—and for the next 24 hours.** The egg group ate *686 fewer calories* at lunch than the bagel group. They also ate fewer calories that day…at breakfast the next day…*and* at lunch the next day.

• **More satisfaction after breakfast.** The egg group had a higher satiety rating 15 minutes after breakfast, 90 minutes later and 3 hours later.

• **Calmer cravings.** The egg group had fewer food cravings between breakfast and lunch.

How it works: "The nutrients in eggs responsible for promoting satiety, as well as the mechanism involved are unknown," say the researchers. It might be the protein. It might be that eggs balance blood sugar. Eggs might slow "gastric emptying"—the flow of food out of the stomach—thereby prolonging satiety.

But regardless of *why* it works, "the fact that an egg breakfast has greater satiety value compared to another breakfast of equal calories is an important finding that is potentially useful in weight management diets."

What to do: Have some scrambled eggs for breakfast! Or hard-boiled. Or poached. Or an omelet, quiche, crepe or soufflé. (But go easy on the cheese, bacon, butter and other high-cal accompaniments.) "Eggs are an integral and established part of breakfast in numerous cultures, and the satiating effect of eggs may be useful in reducing calorie intake, thereby promoting weight management," say the researchers.

For more information about the upside of eggs, including two books about how to enjoy more eggs in your diet, see page 214 in Chapter 9, "Heart Disease and Stroke."

LOW-CARB DIET, HIGH-SPEED WEIGHT LOSS

Study after study shows that diets with plenty of fruits and vegetables—high in fiber, low in fat, delivering lots of satisfying food for few calories—are among the most effective for losing and maintaining weight.

But if you want to lose weight a little bit *faster*—for a vacation at the beach or your daughter's wedding or just *because*—you might want to consider a low-carbohydrate, high-protein diet.

ⅢⅢ➡ *Breakthrough Study*

A team of scientists from the Radiant Research group in Chicago asked 86 people to go on either one of two diets for 12 weeks—a low-carbohydrate, high-protein diet or a low-fat, portion-controlled diet.

Result: After three months, those on the low-carb, high-protein diet lost 10.8 pounds, compared with 5.5 pounds for those on the low-fat diet. The low-carb dieters also lost twice as much body fat. (Dieters lose both fat and muscle.)

However: After one year, the amount of weight loss and fat loss "did not differ significantly," between the two groups, say the researchers, in the *American Journal of Clinical Nutrition*.

A low-carbohydrate diet "produced significantly greater losses of body weight and fat during an initial weight-loss period than did a traditional portion-controlled diet," says Kevin Maki, PhD, who led the study.

☀ The diet used in the study was similar to *The South Beach Diet* (Rodale), with an initial phase of carbohydrate restriction, and a second phase of adding slow-digesting carbohydrates such as fruits, vegetables, beans and whole grains. For more information, e-mail *questions @southbeachdiet.com* or visit the Web site *www. southbeachdiet.com*, or call 866-218-2681.

THREE WAYS TO CONTROL BINGE EATING

That night, Susan ate stew, a little bit of water mixed with all the leftovers in her refrigerator—the semi-stale pasta, the half can of refried beans, the wrinkled apple and the antique meat with a touch of mold. On other nights, she ate frozen food without defrosting it. Sometimes she ate food right out of the microwave, scalding her mouth. Sometimes she ate from the trash can.

Susan has *binge-eating disorder,* or BED.

What most people don't realize: There are three eating disorders listed in the DSM-IV, the manual used by psychiatrists and psychologists to officially define and diagnose mental disorders—anorexia, bulimia and BED.

Of the estimated 10 to 20 million people who suffer from eating disorders, *half* have BED—it's three times more common than the binging and purging of bulimia, and four times more common than the starvation of anorexia. In fact, one-third of obese people have BED.

Definition: According to the American Psychiatric Association, you have BED if for at least two days a week, you regularly eat much larger-than-normal amounts of food in two hours or less and feel a lack of control over your eating—you can't stop or limit the amount. You might also eat more rapidly than normal; eat until you feel uncomfortably full; eat when you're not hungry; eat alone because you're embarrassed by how much you're eating and feel disgusted, depressed or very guilty after eating.

Binge-eating disorder typically starts in a person's thirties. It's often triggered by (or recurs during) a major stressful event, such as divorce, chronic illness or retirement, explains Trisha Gura, PhD, author of *Lying in Weight: The Hidden Epidemic of Eating Disorders in Adult Women* (HarperCollins).

Like any serious mental disorder, BED requires professional help. But a recent study by researchers at the Yale University School of Medicine shows that there are three simple ways a person with BED might reduce binging and lose weight.

▐▐▐➡ *Breakthrough Study*

Led by Robin M. Masheb, PhD, researchers surveyed the food habits of 173 obese women and men with BED. *They found...*

• **Only 43% ate breakfast regularly;**

• **The 32% who ate three meals a day weighed significantly less than the 68% who didn't,** and had fewer binges and

• **Those who ate frequent meals *and* snacks also weighed less.**

"Eating more frequently, having breakfast and consuming three meals every day" may be important for people with BED, says Dr. Masheb.

☀ Support groups are one of the most effective ways to overcome an eating disorder, says Dr. Gura. "Meeting regularly with other people with binge-eating disorder is an effective way to overcome the problem. There is comfort in knowing that there are other people like you. It is much easier to talk to them about your problems. There is shared experience from which all can benefit. And there is mutual support."

To find a support group in your area, go to the "Treatment Referrals" section of *www.nationaleatingdisorders.org*, the Web site of the National Eating Disorders Association, the largest nonprofit organization dedicated to the elimination of eating disorders. National Eating Disorders Association, 603 Stewart Street, Suite 803, Seattle, WA 98101 (206-382-3587 or fax 206-829-8501); e-mail *info@nationaleatingdisorders.org*.

Dr. Gura's Web site, *www.trishagura.com*, offers up-to-date information about eating disorders and extensive lists of resources for help and treatment; e-mail *trisha@trishagura.com*.

HOW TO LOSE 100 POUNDS— WITHOUT GASTRIC BYPASS

You're not just 10, 30 or even 50 pounds overweight.

You're 80 or more pounds overweight— what experts call "extremely obese."

And if you also have high blood pressure and type 2 diabetes (common complications of extreme obesity), the standard medical recommendation is *gastric bypass surgery*. In this operation—performed more than 200,000 times a year in the United States—the surgeon uses staples or a plastic band to reduce the size of the stomach, which is then attached directly to the middle of the small intestine. Your stomach is a lot smaller, you feel fuller with less food and you lose weight. But you might also lose your life.

What most people don't know: Complications from gastric bypass surgery kill 0.5% of people in the hospital…1% of patients within 30 days…and 1.5% within a year. Nonfatal complications include vomiting and diarrhea, mineral deficiencies and the resulting bone loss and pain, infections, abscesses and leakage (of digestive fluid into the rest of the body)— and those complications strike 40% of people who've had gastric bypass surgery. That's a lot of misery for the sake of weight loss.

Fortunately, there's a scientifically verified way to overcome extreme obesity *without* surgery.

▶ *Breakthrough Study*

Led by James W. Anderson, MD, professor of medicine, researchers at the University of Kentucky treated 1,531 severely obese patients with a 12-week educational and nutritional program consisting of a calorie-restricted diet, regular physical activity and behavioral modification (learning new eating habits).

Results: After 30 weeks, the average weight loss for those who completed the 12-week program was 68 pounds for the women and 94 pounds for the men. (Many lost 50 pounds in 12 weeks.) Two hundred sixty-eight participants lost more than 100 pounds—an average of 128 pounds for women and 145 for men.

Many of the participants also lowered blood pressure, cholesterol levels, normalized blood sugar and cleared up sleep apnea—in fact, 66% were completely able to stop *all* medications!

After seven years, the participants who completed the program had maintained 59% of their weight loss. The 100-pound group had maintained 65% of their weight loss. (Considering 85% of people typically regain all the weight they lose on a diet, these are astounding results.)

They published the results in the *International Journal of Obesity*.

"Many extremely obese persons become frustrated and turn to surgery," says Dr. Anderson. "This study shows that they can participate in an intensive weight-loss program and go on to lose significant amounts of weight, sometimes over a hundred pounds. This program has much lower risks than surgery and can lead to similar long-term results."

Why it works: The key to the program is *meal replacements*—eating a structured, planned, nutritionally complete menu of prepackaged entrees, shakes and bars. "The extremely obese person can make a clean break from the eating habits of the past," says Dr. Anderson.

The people who participated in Dr. Anderson's study used the meal replacement and weight-loss program created by Health Management Resources (HMR), which has treated more than one million people in the last 25 years. Their programs are available at medical centers and weight-loss clinics across the country, and at-home, with optional phone support. You can locate an HMR program near you with their "Find a Program" feature on the home page of their Web site, *www.hmrprogram. com*. Health Management Resources, 59 Temple Place, Suite 704, Boston, MA 02111 (800-418-1367, 617-357-9876 or fax 617-357-9690).

How it works: The HMR approach includes three possible levels, depending on how fast you want to lose weight. For fastest weight loss, you eat five meal replacements (two entrees and three shakes or bars) a day. Or you can do that program with five meal replacements *and* an additional five servings a day of fruits and vegetables. Or the meal replacements, the fruits and vegetables *and* a healthy meal of your choice. At the same time, you're also learning how to identify and change the cues that cause you to overeat, and how to incorporate regular physical activity in your life.

15

SKIN PROBLEMS
SMART SOLUTIONS, FROM ADULT ACNE TO WRINKLES

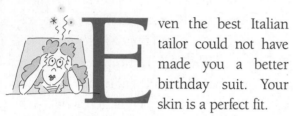 ven the best Italian tailor could not have made you a better birthday suit. Your skin is a perfect fit.

From the *epidermis,* the protective and waterproof topmost layer...to the mid-level *dermis,* packed with nerves that provide your sense of touch...to the insulating *subcutaneous* layer...the skin is also a miracle of feeling and functionality.

But like the finest clothing, your skin requires care—and sometimes repairs.

"The skin, important for both our appearance and well-being, needs special care to look and perform its best," says Joni Loughran, a cosmetologist in northern California and author of *Natural Skin Care* (North Atlantic).

Yet even with the best skin regimen possible—gentle cleansing, a daily sunscreen, and a dermis-friendly diet—your skin is going to get into some scrapes.

"*Everyone* has a skin condition," says Audrey Kunin, MD, a dermatologist and author of *The DERMAdoctor Skinstruction Manual* (Simon & Schuster). "It doesn't matter if it's your first case of acne or your first issue with crow's feet."

In this chapter, you'll find the top science-supported breakthroughs to help you cope with, care for and even cure those conditions.

FIRMER, YOUNGER SKIN— TRY A CHOCOLATE SHAKE!

Dermatologists call it *photoaging*—and they're not talking about the fact that you look a little older each year in your family "Season's Greetings" family photo.

No, *photoaging* is medical terminology— "photo" from the Greek "photos," meaning *light.* Meaning *sunlight.*

"The number one cause of aging skin is sun exposure," says Manjula S. Jegasothy, MD, a dermatologist at the Miami Skin Institute.

Check it out for yourself. Compare an area of skin that's regularly exposed to the sun (such as your face) to an area that's not (such as your backside). One is sun damaged; the other isn't.

On the cellular level, photoaging destroys collagen, the protein that gives skin its structure. It oxidizes skin-firming fats and skin-sustaining DNA. (*Oxidation* is the process that rusts metal and rots fruit, not exactly what you want happening to your complexion.) And it riles up melanocytes, pigment-producing cells.

On the mirror level, photoaging produces, well, aging—skin that's thinner, drier and rougher; skin that's wrinkled, reddened, mottled and veined.

How do you fight photoaging? With *photoprotection*, say dermatologists.

Photoprotection from the outside.

Example: A wide-brimmed hat.

Photoprotection from the inside, via foods loaded with the nutrients that can shield skin cells.

Example: Dark chocolate.

➤ Breakthrough Study

German researchers studied 24 women, aged 18 to 65, dividing them into two groups. Every day for 12 weeks, both groups drank a 3.4-ounce (100 milliliters) mixture of cocoa powder and water. But one group used a dark chocolate powder high in *flavanols,* an antioxidant; the other group used a low-flavanol powder.

Result: Dark chocolate was like a pair of dark glasses—*photoprotective…*

• **Less damage from UV radiation.** At the beginning of the study, after six weeks, and after 12 weeks, the researchers exposed a tiny patch of the participants' skin to "solar-simulated radiation" (the same type of sunburn- and wrinkle-producing ultraviolet rays beamed at you by Ol' Sol) and then measured reddening, a sign of sun damage.

(There are two types of ultraviolet radiation—UVB, which causes sunburn and increases your risk of skin cancer; and UVA, which penetrates more deeply, causes skin aging, such as wrinkles, leathery skin and sagging, and may play a role in skin cancer.)

After six weeks of drinking the cocoa, the high-flavanol group (HF) had 15% less reddening than at the beginning of the study; after 12 weeks, the reddening was 25% less.

However, the low-flavanol group (LF) didn't have any change in the degree of reddening—or in any other measurement of skin health and youthfulness. *But after 12 weeks, the HF group also had…*

• **11% thicker and 13% denser (firmer) skin,**

• **11% moister skin,**

• **28% less skin dehydration,**

• **30% less roughness,**

• **43% less flaking and**

• **100% better blood circulation in the skin.**

"The regular consumption of a beverage rich in cocoa flavanols can confer substantial photoprotection as well as help maintain skin health by improving skin structure and function," says Ulrike Heinrich, MD, who led the study, published in the *Journal of Nutrition.*

Why it works: The cocoa flavanols might neutralize oxidizing molecules called "free radicals"…absorb ultraviolet radiation…and cut inflammation, reducing redness.

What to do: If you ate dark chocolate to get the amount of flavanols used in the experiment, you'd need to eat 3½ ounces a day—nearly 400 calories worth! That's why the study used one tablespoon of *cocoa powder,* at about 200 calories. *You can mix it in water, no-fat or skim milk, or…*

"Add cocoa powder to all your favorite smoothies, protein drinks, coffee mixes, desserts—or anything else you can think of," says David Wolfe, MS, nutritionist and coauthor of *Naked Chocolate* (Sunfood Nutrition). "Just one or two spoonfuls can transform any recipe into a healthy chocolate treat. It even goes great on top of fresh fruit."

ℹ The flavanol-rich products below use the name "Cacao," another word for cocoa.

Raw Organic Cacao Powder, from Sunfood Nutrition, *www.sunfood.com;* call 800-205-2350, 619-596-7979.

Dagoba Organic Chocolate Cacao Powder, *www.artisanconfection.com;* Artisan Direct, 2000 Folsom Street, San Francisco, CA 94110 (866-237-0152, 415-626-7900 or fax 415-626-7991); e-mail *customercare@artisanconfection.com.*

MOTHER NATURE'S ANTIWRINKLE PILL

What do you get when you combine extracts from soy, tomatoes, white tea, grape seeds and fish...vitamins A and C and the mineral zinc... and the herb chamomile? Fewer wrinkles.

▐▐▐▶ *Breakthrough Study*

US researchers and scientists from the Department of Dermatology at the University of Copenhagen in Denmark studied 80 postmenopausal women, giving one group a nutritional supplement with the above ingredients, and the other group a placebo.

At the beginning of the study and after six months, the researchers took photos of the face and the upper part of the chest (décolletage) of the participants, evaluating their skin for health and youthfulness with a standard dermatological grading system. They also took an ultrasound of their skin. *After six months, the women taking the supplement had...*

Less noticeable wrinkles on their foreheads, around their eyes and around their mouths...less dark mottling...less sagging and loose skin...an improvement in dark circles under the eyes...and an improvement in overall appearance.

Eighty-two percent of the women who took the supplement said the overall appearance of their face had improved, with 84% saying their skin was smoother, 82% saying it was less dry, 71% saying fine lines and wrinkles had diminished and 59% saying spider veins had decreased. (Sixty-six percent also said they would recommend the supplement to a friend.)

"This novel dietary supplement provides improved condition, structure and firmness of the skin in postmenopausal women after six months," say the researchers, in the *European Journal of Clinical Nutrition.*

How it works: The fish extract supplies protein and carbohydrates that help support skin tissue...the soy extract stimulates the creation of collagen...the antioxidants in the tomato and white tea extracts, and vitamins C and E, fight the sun-sparked free radicals that cause skin aging...zinc renews aging skin cells...and chamomile calms and soothes. (Stress shows up on your skin.)

ⓘ The study used Imedeen Prime Renewal.

Suggested intake: Two tablets, twice a day.

☀ *www.imedeen.us.* You can order Imedeen Prime Renewal (and other Imedeen products) at this site, which also includes a state-by-state "Retail Locator" to find a store near you that sells Imedeen products. Ferrosan Inc., 515 N. Cedar Ridge Road, Suite 7J, Duncanville, TX 75116.

Imedeen Prime Renewal is also available at many Web sites, including *www.dermadoctor.com,* a dermatological superstore created by dermatologist Audrey Kunin, MD, where you can find products by brand and condition, plus a wealth of practical information from Dr. Kunin about everyday skin care and how to resolve skin conditions. Call 877-337-6237 or e-mail *service@dermadoctor.com* for more information.

LESS BRUISING AFTER A FACELIFT—WITH ARNICA

You've decided to have a facelift. You're looking forward to the change—to a refreshed and more youthful appearance. But you're *not* looking forward to the week or two following the facelift—to the bruising, the swelling and the pain.

Arnica might help.

New study: Led by Corey S. Maas, MD, a plastic surgeon and director of the Maas Clinic in San Francisco, doctors studied 29 plastic surgery patients having facelifts. Starting the day of the surgery, they treated them with either placebo pills or *Arnica montana,* a classic homeopathic remedy for bruising.

Using a new system of computer analysis of digital photos, the doctors found an "extremely significant" difference between the two groups. The patients taking Arnica had measurably smaller areas of bruising on the first and seventh days after surgery. And the bruises of the Arnica group started to improve the day after surgery, while bruising in the placebo group worsened through day five and then started to improve.

ℹ️ The Arnica product used in the study was SinEcch, from Alpine Pharmaceuticals.

"All my patients love SinEcch," says Kimberly Henry, MD, a plastic surgeon in Independence, MO. "Some have no swelling or bruising after their facelifts, which I find to be incredible."

Suggested dosage: The patients took 12 doses of SinEcch, with the first dose on the morning of surgery, and subsequent doses every eight hours for the next four days.

☀️ *www.alpinepharm.com.* Alpine Pharmaceuticals, 1940 Fourth Street, San Rafael, CA 94901 (866-846-8366).

LYCOPENE STOPS THE REDNESS

Like beta-carotene, its carrot-coloring orange cousin, lycopene is a "carotenoid"—a plant pigment, a color in Mother Nature's palette.

Lycopene, however, is *red,* tinting foods such as tomatoes, watermelon, guava and pink grapefruit. And red trumps red—lycopene might stop you from becoming redder, from sunburn, or from a lifetime of sun damage.

⎟⎟⎟➡ *Breakthrough Study*

Scientists in Germany divided people into three groups. One group took a daily supplement of synthetic lycopene; one group took a daily tomato extract; and one group drank a daily beverage containing extracts of lycopene and several other carotenoids (beta-carotene, lutein and zeaxanthin).

At the beginning of the study and after three months, the researchers aimed a "solar light simulator" at a small patch of the participants' skin, giving them a dose of sunburn-causing ultraviolet radiation.

Result: Compared to the reddening from UV radiation at the beginning of the study, three months later there was…25% less reddening in the synthetic lycopene group…38% less in the tomato extract group…and 48% less in the group drinking the beverage with a multicarotenoid extract.

"Dietary carotenoids may contribute to lifelong protection against harmful UV radiation," say the researchers.

Why it works: The colorful carotenoids absorb UV light, so your skin doesn't.

ℹ️ The tomato extract used in the study was Lyc-O-Mato. It is an ingredient in many lycopene supplements, including products from Healthy Origins, Natrol and Swanson.

The multicarotene extract in the beverage was Lyc-O-Guard; it hasn't yet hit the market.

If you're interested in a supplement containing lycopene, beta-carotene, lutein and zeaxanthin, try Multi Carotene from Puritan's Pride, Octa-Carotene from Nature's Plus or Multi-Carotene from PhysioLogics.

A DIET TO PREVENT SKIN CANCER (OR A RECURRENCE)

Skin cancer is the most common cancer in America—more common than lung, breast, prostate or colon, with 1.3 million people diagnosed yearly, and nearly 11,000 dying. And rates are rising 5% a year.

"But unlike other cancer epidemics, the cause isn't a mystery," says Dr. Kunin. "Blame the sun."

Ultraviolet rays from the sun damage the skin's DNA, she explains. "Normally, the skin's repair system literally cuts out damaged DNA, and replaces it with healthy code. But too much ultraviolet damage can overwhelm the system, leading to skin cancer."

Surprising: Eating the right *foods* might help stop skin cancer. Even help stop it from recurring.

▶ *Breakthrough Study*

Australian researchers analyzed diet and cancer data in 1,360 people, aged 25 to 75.

THE THREE TYPES OF SKIN CANCER

There are three types of sun-induced skin cancer.

- **Basal cell carcinoma (BCC).** This slow-growing skin cancer is the most common type, with 800,000 Americans diagnosed yearly. Called "basal" because it forms in the *basal* (basement) layer within the epidermis, it can grow large but rarely spreads to other parts of the body. At first, BCC looks like reddish, dry skin patches that don't heal. Later, it tends to become a flesh-colored bump. Usually, treatment is surgical removal, although smaller cancers may be treated topically with the drug *imiquimod* (Aldara).

- **Squamous cell carcinoma (SCC).** Affecting 200,000 Americans a year, this skin cancer spreads to other parts of the body in about 1% of cases, killing 2,000 people. SCC usually looks like a hard red bump, and is sometimes scaly or crusty. It is usually surgically removed.

- **Melanoma.** Seventy-four thousand Americans die of this cancer every year. "Early detection is key—melanoma is almost a hundred percent curable if detected early," says Dr. Kunin.

"Under certain conditions, moles can begin to change, a situation called *dysplasia*. While a dysplastic mole does not guarantee the formation of cancer, the more severe the dysplasia, the more it is of medical concern. Fortunately, moles don't change into melanoma overnight. Knowing four symptomatic warning signs—the ABCD's of melanoma—can save your life," she says. *They are...*

- Asymmetry. The mole is not completely even in appearance—one half doesn't look like the other half.
- Border. The margins should be even and smooth, without ratty or projecting edges.
- Color. Color should be uniform, not varied from one area to another.
- Diameter. The mole should not measure more than 6 millimeters across—the size of a pencil eraser.

Treatment of melanoma involves a biopsy with a full excision; if the mole is cancerous, the area is re-excised. "If the excision took care of the problem, the patient should have a complete skin examination every three months for five years," says Dr. Kunin.

Result: They found that those who ate the most red meat and fat were 83% more likely to develop *squamous cell carcinoma* (SCC)—and nearly *four times as likely* to develop SCC if they'd already had skin cancer. (For an explanation of the three main types of skin cancer, see the box on page 376.)

Eating more fruits and vegetables decreased risk by 54%—with most of the protection from green leafy vegetables. (People who ate the most green leafy vegetables had a 45% decreased risk.)

"A dietary pattern characterized by high meat and fat intakes increases SCC tumor risk, particularly in persons with a skin cancer history," say the researchers, in the *American Journal of Clinical Nutrition.*

Earlier, the same team analyzed data from 26 studies on skin cancer and diet—and found a link between intake of fat and risk for basal cell carcinoma (BCC).

What to do: There's strong evidence that high-fat diets put you at higher risk for many different types of cancer. If you want to avoid skin cancer—particularly if you want to avoid a recurrence—consider a diet that's lower in fat and goes easy on the meat.

For advice on vegetarian diets, see page 361 of Chapter 14, "Overweight."

For advice on increasing fruits and vegetables in your diet, see page 75 of Chapter 4, "Cancer."

STOP SKIN CANCER—WEAR SUNSCREEN IN THE CAR!

Americans have responded to the pleas of the American Cancer Society, the American Dermatological Association and the dermatologist downtown—and are using more sunscreen. Nearly 60 million tubes in a recent year, 13% more than the year before. *But...*

Are we applying sunscreen before we drive? We should.

⫸ *Breakthrough Study*

Led by Scott W. Fosko, MD, researchers at the Saint Louis University School of Medicine studied 898 people with skin cancer. They found a higher incidence of several types of melanomas on the *left* side of the body—74% of noninvasive melanomas and 70% of lentigo maligna melanomas.

"This finding supports our theory that drivers who spend more than the average amount of time in the car over the course of several years are more likely to develop skin cancers on the left side of the body, particularly skin cancers like lentigo maligna and basal cell carcinoma that develop gradually over time," he says.

After this first finding, Dr. Fosko and his team began asking skin cancer patients to fill out a questionnaire about driving habits.

"Our initial data shows that those individuals under 70 who consistently spent the most time per week driving a car were more likely to develop left-sided skin cancers," he says. "We're also finding that *all* drivers who occasionally drive with the windows open had a higher incidence of left-sided skin cancers."

What you may not know: Windshields typically block UVB and UVA rays, but side and rear windows are made from nonlaminated glass that is designed to block UVB only. Studies show that *tinting* automobile glass can help reduce UVA exposure, says Dr. Fosko.

☀ For more information on tinting automobile glass, and to find an installer of automobile tinting near you, visit the Web site *www.llumar.com.* CPFilms, Inc., LLumar Window Film, PO Box 5068, Martinsville, VA 24115

(800-255-8627 or fax 276-627-3032); e-mail *llumar@cpfilms.com.*

You can also find a "National Tint Shop Locator" at *www.autowindowtinting.com,* which provides lists of automobile window tinting shops by zip code.

What to do: When you're in the car, Dr. Fosko says to cover all exposed areas with a "broad spectrum" sunscreen (providing both UVA and UVB protection), with an SPF 15 or higher, and to wear protective, skin-covering clothing whenever possible.

Sound advice, and here's more—the most practical information about choosing and using a sunscreen to prevent skin cancer and skin aging, from the Skin Cancer Foundation...

● **How much sunscreen should I use?** One ounce with each application—about the amount that would fit in a shot glass.

Trap: Studies show that most people apply only half to a quarter of that amount.

● **When should I apply it?** Thirty minutes before sun exposure and every two hours after that—even if it's waterproof or sweatproof. Immediately reapply after swimming, toweling off or sweating a lot.

Trap: Don't believe the myth that most cancer-causing, skin-damaging sun exposure has *already* happened, when you were a teenager and younger. It's *men over 40* who spend the most time outdoors, and get the highest annual doses of UV rays.

● **What SPF should I use?** A sun protection factor of 15 or higher.

What it means: If it takes 20 minutes for unprotected skin to start turning red, using an SPF 15 sunscreen may prevent reddening 15 times longer—about five hours.

● **Which ingredients are best?** Look for "broad spectrum" protection against both UVB and UVA rays. You need at least three active ingredients—one to block UVB, one to block

shorter wavelength UVA and one to block the remaining UVA wavelengths.

● For UVB, look for PABA derivatives, salicylates or cinnamates (octyl methoxycinnamate and cinoxate).

● For shorter-length UVA, look for benzophenones (such as oxygenzone and sulisobenzone).

● For the remaining UVA wavelengths, look for avobenzone (Parsol 1789), titanium dioxide or zinc oxide.

● **What is the best sunscreen for everyday use and for beach or outdoor use?** For everyday use, an aftershave lotion or moisturizer that includes SPF 15 sunscreen is fine. If you work outside or are spending a lot of time outdoors, look for a "water-resistant" or "very water-resistant" variety. And wear those sunscreens on completely cloudy days—40% of UV radiation reaches you through the overcast.

Red flag: Products that combine sunscreen *and* insect repellant (there are about 20 on the market) may *not* be safe—the insect repellant may decrease the protection of the sunscreen, and the sunscreen may increase the absorption of the insect repellant, upping the risk of toxicity. (Canada has discontinued the sale of these products.)

Better: Use insect repellant (such as DEET) and sunscreen separately, applying the sunscreen 30 minutes before the repellant.

ⓘ For a list of sunscreens with the "Seal of Recommendation" from the Skin Cancer Foundation, visit *www.skincancer.org.* The Skin Cancer Foundation, 149 Madison Avenue, Suite 901, New York, NY 10016 (212-725-5176 or fax 212-725-5751); e-mail *info@skincancer.org.*

The American Dermatological Association (ADD) also grants its "Seal of Recognition" to sunscreen products meeting its criteria for skin protection. For more information, visit the Web site *www.add.org.*

THE THREE BEST WAYS TO STYMIE SKIN CANCER

What are the *best* ways to stop the sun from triggering skin cancer?

Surprising: The top three list does not include sunscreen, says a team of dermatologists from Switzerland, Denmark and the Mayo Clinic in the United States.

⫸ *Breakthrough Study*

Led by Stephan Lautenschlager, MD, a dermatologist at the Triemli Hospital in Zurich, the researchers reviewed more than 200 articles on sun protection—and concluded sunscreens are a *last* resort

"In a skin cancer prevention strategy, wearing sun protective clothes and a hat, and reducing sun exposure to a minimum should be preferred to sunscreens," says Dr. Lautenschlager.

His suggestions...

#1 Strategy: "**Completely avoid sun exposure.**" Fifty percent of the total daily ultraviolet dose reaches the earth between noon and 3:00 p.m., says Dr. Lautenschlager. "The best technique for reducing ultraviolet exposure is to avoid the sun, especially in the middle of the day."

#2 Strategy: "**Seek shade at times when disease-inducing wavelengths are relatively intense.**" Fog, haze, clouds, pollutants—they all reduce ultraviolet radiation, but not by much. "Shade alone reduces solar ultraviolet radiation by fifty to ninety-five percent," says Dr. Lautenschlager. "The amount of protection varies considerably between different shade settings, with a beach umbrella showing the least, and dense foliage the most protection."

☀ For UV-blocking sun parasols and umbrellas, visit the Web site *www.coolibar.com.* Coolibar, 2401 Edgewood Avenue South, Minneapolis, MN 55426 (800-926-6509 or fax 952-922-1455); e-mail *service@coolibar.com.*

#3 Strategy: "**Wear clothing protective against ultraviolet radiation penetration.**" Clothes are a reliable way to protect your skin, says Dr. Lautenschlager. But not all clothes are created equal—a light-colored cotton shirt has a paltry SPF10.

Clothes that increase protection: Tightly woven fibers; thicker fabrics; denim; wool; synthetic materials, such as polyester; dark colors; unbleached fabrics.

Clothes that offer low-level protection: Loosely woven fibers, thinner fabrics, cotton, linen, acetate, rayon, stretched textiles, light colors, bleached fabrics.

"Garments specifically manufactured to be ultraviolet protective provide excellent protection against the hazards of solar radiation," says Dr. Lautenschlager.

TOPICAL HERBS FOR SKIN CANCER—A VERY BAD IDEA

If you have skin cancer, *don't*—repeat, *don't*—treat it with topical herbal preparations.

Reason: "The removal of skin cancer by conventional methods is highly successful" and usually involves minimal damage to skin, says Shana McDaniel, MD, at the University of Vermont College of Medicine, in the *Archives of Dermatology.* "Nonetheless, some patients seek alternative, nonsurgical treatment for lesions that could be readily treated in a standard fashion."

These alternatives, she explains, are corrosive topical preparations called *escharotics* that destroy skin, producing a thick crust (eschar) and then a scar. Frederic E. Mohs (the founder of Mohs Micrographic Surgery, the modern form of skin cancer surgery) first used them in the 1930s as a "fixative" to prepare skin cancers for removal.

They were also popularized in the 1930s and '40s by Harry Hoxsey, whose cancer sanatoriums offered an herbal tonic for internal use and an escharotic paste for external cancers. The escharotics used by Mohs and Hoxsey were similar—a caustic preparation containing antimony sulfide, bloodroot and zinc chloride, says Dr. McDaniel.

"Interest in the use of escharotics as a treatment for skin disease fell out of favor with dermatologists, owing to the high level of effectiveness of conventional treatment for nonmelanoma skin cancer," she says. But over the last decade, there has been an Internet-sparked revival of the remedies.

"Recently, several of our patients elected to self-treat with escharotic agents that are available via the Internet and mail-order companies," she says.

None of them had any success…

• **Case 1.** A 47-year-old man with a basal cell carcinoma (BCC) on his right temple treated it with an herbal anticancer paste. The cancer "vanished." Several months later, a biopsy revealed that there was still a residual tumor, which was removed with standard surgery. *Product not to use:* Curaderm Cancer Cream.

• **Case 2.** A 52-year-old man had a biopsy of a lesion on the left side of his nose, and Mohs surgery was recommended. He decided to forgo the surgery and use an escharotic instead.

The lesion "vanished." When he next saw the doctor several years later, the lesion had returned—and had become an enormous BCC of the left nose, lips and cheek that surgery revealed had penetrated deep into his face. It required two surgeries to remove, with plastic surgery to repair the surgical wound. Eventually, the cancer spread to the lymph nodes and then to bone. *Product not to use:* Bloodroot (*Sanguinaria canadensis*).

Other products to avoid: Dr. McDaniel also urges people with skin cancer not to use Cansema from Alpha Omega Labs, or HerbVeil8 from Viable Herbal Solutions.

Warning: "Up to one million cases of nonmelanoma skin cancer will be diagnosed and treated in the United States this year," says Dr. McDaniel. "Natural and alternative treatments are increasingly used by patients for the treatment of skin cancer. Many of the natural remedies available both within the US and from overseas are wholly unregulated and are of unknown strength and purity."

"With escharotic therapy, there is no scientifically documented proof of efficacy, and likewise there is no proof of tissue selectivity. In fact, as evidenced from photographs on the escharotics Web sites…it is clear that escharotic agents in many cases damage and destroy normal tissue as well as diseased skin. The irony is that conventional allopathic medicine has an extraordinary and proven track record of successful treatment for skin cancer."

ⓘ "There is a line of clothing called Solumbra, made by Sun Precautions, that has an SPF rating of 30," says Jeanette Jacknin, MD, a dermatologist in private practice at the Physicians Skin Institute in Scottsdale, AZ, and author of *Smart Medicine for Your Skin* (Avery).

☀ *www.sunprecautions.com.* Sun Precautions, 2815 Wetmore Avenue, Everett, WA 98201 (800-882-7860, 425-303-8585 or fax 425-303-0836).

Also try: "Throw a packet of Rit Sun Guard Laundry Treatment UV Protectant in with your laundry and give your clothing an SPF 30 (compared to a mundane SPF 4)," says Dr. Kunin.

And don't forget your wide-brimmed hat! "Hats that really block the sun can protect most of your face," says Lawrence J. Green, MD, an assistant clinical professor of dermatology at George Washington School of Medicine and author of *The Dermatologist's Guide to Looking Younger* (Crossing Press).

#4 Strategy: **"Use topical sunscreens to specifically prevent or reduce ultraviolet-induced cellular damage to a minimum."** But don't use them as an excuse to stay out longer in the sun, warns Dr. Lautenschlager. (Two studies showed that people on vacation using high SPF sunscreens stayed out in the sun a lot longer than those not using sunscreen.)

"Sunscreens can, in general, be used only *in addition* to the more reliable measures of clothing protection, and reduction of ultraviolet exposure during peak hours of solar radiation," says Dr. Lautenschlager.

SKIN CANCER SELF EXAM—GET A HELPING HAND

Melanoma causes 73% of deaths from skin cancer. But studies also show that a regular *self-exam*—checking your skin for suspicious-looking moles—can catch the disease in its early, treatable stage, before the deadly spread. (Please see page 376 in this chapter for the ABCD's of skin self-exams—the four signs a mole might be melanoma.)

Now, scientists have found that asking a spouse to partner in your self-exam may produce a better level of protection.

▶ *Breakthrough Study*

"There is evidence to suggest that deaths from melanoma could be lowered by as much as sixty-three percent if people performed monthly skin self-examinations," says June K. Robinson, MD, a professor of clinical dermatology at the Northwestern University Feinberg School of Medicine. "However, routine skin self-exams may be even more important in people at high risk for skin cancer, such as those with a personal or family history of the disease." (People who've had a melanoma have an 11.4% chance of developing another one within the year.)

"Our study examined how involving a partner in skin self-exam affected the attitudes and behaviors of people with melanoma or atypical moles," she says.

Dr. Robinson studied 130 people with melanoma, dividing them into two groups. One group learned self-exams on their own; the other group learned with a spouse (or someone living in the same house for at least a year).

Results: "Our study showed that participants in the partner-learning group were significantly more likely to conduct self-exams at the four-month follow-up compared with those in the solo-learning group," says Dr. Robinson.

Why it works: "Having a partner assist in skin self-exams led to significantly more positive attitudes toward the importance of skin self-exams, and higher reports of confidence in the ability to perform the exams," says Dr. Robinson. And, she adds, "Participants with partners had significantly less concern about developing sun-damaged skin in the future than participants in the solo-learning group.

Bottom line: "People should be encouraged to utilize a partner when performing skin self-exams."

BEST MOISTURIZER FOR DRY, ITCHY SKIN

If you're over 65, it's likely you're among the 60 to 85% of people with dry skin. In fact, it may be dry, itchy, red, scaly *and* cracked.

You want relief! But what you don't want is the bother of reapplying moisturizer throughout the day. (Maybe you can't even figure out *which* moisturizer to use, since there are so many out there.)

Well, scientists have found the solution—a once-a-day moisturizing cream that works on the driest, itchiest skin.

Breakthrough Study

Researchers at the Crestwood Care Center in Chicago studied 15 older people (average age, 76) with dry, itchy skin, treating them for five days with a once-a-day moisturizer.

At the start of the study, six of the 15 had severely dry skin, with a "fish scale" appearance; eight had moderately dry skin, with "dandruff-like" flakes; and one had mildly dry skin, with minimal flaking.

Result: After five days, 11 of the 15 people in the study had *complete* resolution of their dry skin; the other four improved to mildly dry.

Ten people were scratching their itchy skin regularly at the start of the study; after five days, only four continued to scratch (those with mildly dry skin).

Seven people had mild redness at the start of the study; only three did at the end.

"Implementing a twenty-four-hour moisturizer was found to significantly decrease the symptoms of dry skin," says Dasie Wilson, RNC, who led the study.

The researchers used Sween 24, a cream from Colopast Corp.

Its primary ingredient is dimethicone, an "emollient" that keeps the skin hydrated, and smoothes and soothes skin. It's fragrance-free and lanolin-free. (Lanolin is a wool-based ingredient that can cause allergic reactions).

You can order the product at *www.sweenstore.com.* Coloplast Corp., Attn: Medical Customer Service, 200 South Sixth Street, Minneapolis, MN 55402 (800-533-0464); e-mail *usmedweb@coloplast.com.*

Also try: Bathe no more than once a day, using lukewarm water, says Wilson. When you take a bath, go easy on the washcloth. And use mild skin cleansers.

"Cleansing one time a day is all that is necessary for dry skin, and this is best done in the evening," says Loughran. "In the morning, splash the face with warm water or use warm facial compresses. Never use soap on dry skin, and avoid abrasive scrubs."

ROSACEA AND ACNE—TRY B VITAMINS, ZINC

Rosacea strikes 14 million Americans—in the face, with acne, redness, flushing, broken blood vessels and sensitive skin that can be dry, oily or both.

In adult acne, the pimples and other blemishes of adolescence persist or return. (Occasionally, people get acne for the first time as an adult.) Doctors have tried calming both problems with steroids and antibiotics.

"However, long-term use of these medications has drawbacks," says Neil M. Niren, MD, of the University of Pittsburgh Medical Center. "Steroids may induce numerous side effects, such as high blood pressure and osteoporosis. Overuse of antibiotics may contribute to the development of bacterial resistance, plus a whole host of nuisance side effects, such as diarrhea and yeast infection."

Is there a natural alternative to steroids and antibiotics? Yes, he says.

⫸ *Breakthrough Study*

Dr. Niren and his colleagues studied 198 people with rosacea and/or acne, giving them a supplement containing 750 milligrams (mg) of the B vitamin nicotinamide (a form of niacin), 25 mg of zinc, 1.5 mg copper and 500 micrograms (mcg) of the B vitamin folate.

After one month, they asked the study participants to rate their overall appearance, and to quantify whether or not they had fewer facial "lesions," such as pimples.

Result: Seventy-nine percent of people taking the supplement said their appearance had improved—that they were moderately better or much better.

Fifty-five percent reported either moderate (26 to 50%) or substantial (more than 50%) reduction in lesions.

And those percentages continued to go up during the next four weeks.

Another group of patients who got the nutritional supplement *and* oral antibiotics *didn't* show a greater improvement than those who got only the supplement.

"It appears that the addition of an oral antibiotic to a treatment regimen that includes

the nicotinamide and zinc supplement may not be necessary," says Dr. Niren.

"Nicotinamide and zinc tablets appear to be an effective oral therapy for the treatment of rosacea and acne when used alone or with other topical therapies, and should be considered a useful alternative approach to oral antibiotics," he says.

Why it works: Both nicotinamide and zinc are *anti-inflammatory*—they help control the overactive immune system that causes the symptoms of rosacea and acne. They can slow the movement of white blood cells…stop inflammation-causing mast cells from breaking down…fight the bacteria that causes acne (*Propionibacterium acnes*)…and decrease the production of facial (sebum). Folate is also anti-inflammatory. And since high levels of zinc can decrease cooper absorption, the supplement contains copper.

ℹ️ The study used the supplement Nicomide.

Suggested intake: One or two tablets a day.

What to do: Nicomide is a prescription product. Talk to your dermatologist about whether it's right for you.

HORSE CHESTNUT FOR VARICOSE VEINS

Aging, overweight, genes and standing all day as part of your job description are the main factors that can produce varicose veins, the blue, thick, twisty cords unattractively lashed to the legs of 20% of Americans (and an estimated 50% of those over 50).

What happens: Veins carry blood to the heart, and with each muscle-powered pump up from the legs, tiny valves shut to stop blood from flowing backward. If those valves weaken and fail, blood pools in your veins—and you have a *varicosity*.

You might not have any symptoms, or your heavy-feeling legs might ache, throb, burn, swell or cramp.

And varicosities can turn into a crisis, as ulcers form in venous tissue weakened by the constant pressure of stranded blood.

Short of injections that shut down the veins, or surgery to "strip" them out of the body, medical care doesn't offer much in the way of help, except compression hosiery, which most people won't wear because it's uncomfortable and ugly.

The good news—a supplement of horse chestnut seed extract works just as well as the hosiery.

⫸ *Breakthrough Study*

Researchers in England analyzed the six most rigorous studies on the use of horse chestnut seed extract (HCSE) for varicose veins.

Result: The supplement helped relieve leg pain, reduced swelling and improved the appearance of veins—just as effectively as compression stockings.

HCSE is a safe and effective treatment for varicose veins, say the researchers.

How it works: The active ingredient in HCSE is *aescin*—it strengthens veins, blocks enzymes (metabolic triggers) that play a role in forming varicose veins and calms vein-weakening inflammation.

Suggested intake: Look for a standardized supplement (it contains the therapeutic amount of aescin—50 to 75 mg per dose), taking 300 mg, twice a day.

ℹ HCSE supplements with that dosage are widely available, in retail stores, catalogs and on-line.

VITAMIN E—DON'T USE IT ON SCARS

Maybe you've heard the recommendation to slather vitamin E on a healing wound, as a way to reduce the size and improve the flexibility of a forming scar.

The recommendation for E gets an F from dermatologists.

⫸ *Breakthrough Study*

"Vitamin E has been tried for the treatment of every type of skin lesion imaginable," says James M. Spencer, MD, a clinical professor of medicine in the Department of Dermatology at the Mount Sinai School of Medicine, in New York. "People claim that it speeds wound healing and improves the cosmetic outcome of burns and other wounds. In fact, many people use vitamin E on a regular basis to improve the appearance of scars, and some doctors recommend applying topical vitamin E after skin surgery."

To find out if vitamin E *really* improves scars, Dr. Spencer and his colleagues studied 15 people who had their skin cancers surgically removed. The researchers asked them to treat each scar with two different lotions—1) a moisturizer or 2) a moisturizer mixed with vitamin E, covering half the scar with number 1 and the other half with number 2.

After one week, one month, and three months, the study participants and the researchers evaluated the scars for appearance, to see if the vitamin E side looked any better.

Result: In nine out of 10 cases, there was *no* difference in the appearance of the part of the scar treated with vitamin E—and in some cases the vitamin E side looked a lot worse!

Not only that—one out of three people developed a skin allergy (contact dermatitis) to vitamin E.

"There is no benefit to the cosmetic outcome of scars by applying vitamin E after skin surgery—and the application of topical vitamin E may actually be *detrimental* to the cosmetic appearance of a scar," says Dr. Spencer. "The use of topical vitamin E on surgical wounds should be discouraged."

And in a similar study at Harvard Medical School, dermatologists found that onion extract (Mederma)—another popular and supposedly scar-reducing natural product—didn't improve the appearance, redness or size of a scar.

Good news: Most new scars get better with time—smaller and less red—whether you treat them or not, says Dr. Spencer.

What to do: However, he says *there are a couple of smart ways to prevent or minimize scars...*

• **Moisten the wound.** A *wet* wound is best for scar-reducing healing, he says. Use an over-the-counter antibiotic ointment (preventing infection is also a must for effective healing) or a petroleum-based product such as Vaseline.

• **Cover the wound.** This is another key to effective healing, he says. "Hundreds of products are available. Choose one you find comfortable and easy to use, and keep the wound covered 24/7 until it's completely healed."

• **Don't pick.** A scab is dry—delaying wound healing and possibly creating a scar. Moistening and covering the wound should prevent a scab. But if one forms, don't tear it off—you can deepen the wound and worsen the eventual scar.

• **Massage.** After healing is complete, cover a scar with petroleum jelly and massage it gently but firmly with the tips of your fingers, for 10 minutes or so a day, for one to two months. "This will soften the scar," says Dr. Spencer.

CHRONIC HIVES? GET A PATCH TEST

Blame it on your mast cells.

These touchy members of your immune system congregate in the skin. When an allergen or other factor triggers them to release their histamine—a compound that turns tight, sturdy blood vessels into wide, fluid-dispersing sieves—the result is those itchy, red, warm bumps called *hives.* (Doctors call it *urticaria.*)

What are the triggers? *A minefield of the mundane...*

Heat can cause a hive. So can cold. So can foods, such as peanuts, strawberries, milk and citrus fruits. So can medications, such as antibiotics, aspirin and ibuprofen (Advil, Motrin). And exercise. And insect bites. And pressure on your skin. Even getting upset can set them off!

Fortunately, most cases of hives are *acute*—the hives come and go in about a day.

But sometimes hives are *chronic*—they come and go but also keep on coming, day after day and week after week.

And even with extensive tests, the trigger is *never* discovered in 95% of cases of chronic hives.

People with this misery-making condition ("overall quality of life is markedly reduced in chronic urticaria patients," says one study) usually depend on antihistamines to get them through the day. Some even take certain heartburn medications or antidepressants, which also block histamine.

Now, researchers at the University of Genoa in Italy think they've found a way to uncover the cause of about 40% of cases of chronic hives—and completely resolve the problem in every case the cause is discovered!

⫸ *Breakthrough Study*

To the dozen or so tests typically used for patients with chronic urticaria, the allergists decided to add the classic "patch test," in which 25 to 150 allergens are applied to the back in tiny patches, to test for skin allergy (contact dermatitis).

Much to their surprise—since none of the patients had a medical history of contact dermatitis—50 of 121 patients (40%) tested positive to one or more contact allergens.

"All patients with positive patch tests were prescribed appropriate avoidance measures for the sensitizing substances," says Giovanni Passalacqua, MD, in the *Journal of the American Academy of Dermatology.* "In all fifty patients, avoidance measures led to remission between ten days and one month.

"We suggest that patch tests be included among the diagnostic procedures for chronic urticaria, since they allow effective diagnosis and treatment of a relevant number of patients."

What to do: If you have chronic hives and your allergist or dermatologist hasn't figured out the cause, talk to the physician about a patch test.

If your doctor wants to read the article about patch tests and chronic urticaria, the citation is…

Laura Gerra, MD, et al.*, Journal of the American Academy of Dermatology* 56, no. 1 (January 2007): 88–90. You can also e-mail Dr. Passalacqua at *passalacqua@unige.it.*

EVENING PRIMROSE OIL FOR ECZEMA

Your dermatologist calls it "dermatitis" and subdivides the condition into nine different types, such as atopic dermatitis (the most common form), nummular dermatitis (round, coinlike patches) and hand dermatitis (affecting just the hands).

But a rash by any other name is still a rash, and this is the Mother of All Rashes—*eczema,* dry, red, rough, scaly and cracked skin, with severe itching.

Fifteen million Americans have it, about one-third of them adults, where the rash usually burrows into skin folds—the front of the wrist, the elbow, the back of the knees. Nobody knows the cause, but heredity is a big factor.

Eczema can't be cured. The goal of treatment is to calm outbreaks quickly and prevent flare-ups. What are your options?

Well, the medical mainstay is steroids, topical or oral. But regular use of steroid creams can thin skin—so badly that it bruises easily and even tears. And years of taking oral steroids can increase your risk of heart disease, osteoporosis and a host of other major health problems.

In recent years, doctors and patients have turned to a new and powerful class of drugs called "immunomodulators"—*tacrolimus* (Protopic) and *pimecrolimus* (Elidel), creams that calm inflamed skin by muting the immune system's response. They seemed like miracle medications—and 10 million people with eczema took them.

But in 2006, the FDA slapped its notorious "Black Box" warning on the drugs, after they were linked to dozens of cases of skin and blood cancer, and caused cancer in test animals.

But there's an option other than steroids and immunomodulators. Evening primrose oil, a rich source of the essential fatty acid GLA (*gamma-linolenic acid*), can quiet upset skin.

||||➡ *Breakthrough Study*

A team of Canadian and British dermatologists analyzed the results from 26 studies on eczema and evening primrose oil, involving more than 1,200 people.

They found daily supplements of evening primrose oil reliably improved dryness and relieved itching.

The supplements also lessened skin crusting, decreased swelling and redness and alleviated insomnia (because of discomfort).

And they were safe for long-term use, unlike most conventional drugs for eczema.

They also point out that people with eczema who use steroids *and* supplements of evening primrose oil did better than people who only took steroids—in some cases, reducing steroid dosages by 30%. (They also note that people taking the highest doses of oral steroids see the smallest gains from evening primrose oil, if any.)

Why it works: Evening primrose oil supplies GLA (gamma-linolenic acid), which is lower than normal in people with eczema. The researchers theorize that eczema is an EFA-deficiency—and that this nutritional lack damages the immune system and deprives the skin of essential structural elements.

ℹ The evening primrose oil used in the studies was Efamol.

Suggested intake: Dosages in studies where Efamol worked have ranged from two to sixteen 500 mg capsules a day, supplying anywhere from 80 to 640 mg of GLA. If you decide to use Efamol, discuss the dosage with your dermatologist or another qualified health practitioner.

Important: Don't expect instant results, say the researchers. Efamol takes four to eight weeks to work.

☀ Efamol is widely available in retail stores, catalogs and on the Internet, as a primary ingredient in many different brands of evening primrose oil supplements. It is manufactured in England. The distributor of Efamol in the United States is Emerson Ecologics Inc., 7 Commerce Drive, Bedford, NH 03110 (800-654-4432, 603-656-9778); *www.emersonecologics.com* or e-mail *cs@emersonecologics.com.*

NEWEST ECZEMA TREATMENT— MAKE OUT TO MOZART

You're upset—and so is your skin! People with atopic eczema (the most common kind, with an allergic component) know that stress can make the problem worse.

That's why Japanese doctors studied several different stress-relieving options for people with atopic eczema...

- **Laugh.** When 20 people with atopic eczema watched the humorous video *Modern Times*, featuring Charlie Chaplin, they had an increase in the level of an antibacterial protein. (The doctors measured the protein because skin infections are a common problem in people with atopic eczema.) "Viewing a humorous video...may be helpful in the treatment of skin infection of atopic eczema," say the doctors, in the *Journal of Psychosomatic Research.*

- **Cry.** Sixty people with atopic eczema and latex allergy watched a weather information video and then a sad movie (*Kramer vs. Kramer*). Forty-four of the 60 people cried while watching the movie—and, when "challenged" with exposure to latex right after the movie, had a less intense allergic reaction than normal. There was no crying during the weather information video—or lessening of allergic reactions to latex afterward.

- **Kiss.** Twenty-four people with atopic eczema kissed with spouses or lovers for 30 minutes while listening to soft music. Before and after kissing, researchers measured levels of white blood cells activated by allergic responses—and found they were far lower in the post-smooching period.

- **Listen to Mozart.** People with atopic eczema and latex allergy had less intense allergic reactions to latex after listening to Mozart—but not Beethoven. Roll over, Beethoven.

Also try: In a study of 161 patients with eczema conducted at Drexel University, a cream containing the herb chamomile prevented eczema flare-ups effectively as a cream containing 0.025% hydrocortisone. The cream is CamoCare Soothing Cream, which is widely available.

BEST WAYS TO PREVENT BEDSORES

It starts as a patch of reddened, itchy skin.

Later, it's a sore—blistered or scraped, surrounded by red and purple discoloring.

Soon, the skin gapes, revealing a craterous trauma to the tissue beneath.

Eventually, there's even deeper damage, to muscle and bone.

Those are the four stages of a bedsore, or pressure ulcer—a gradual and perhaps ghastly wound, usually on a hip, buttock or heel, caused by constant, circulation-robbing pressure on the skin of someone confined to a bed or wheelchair.

Sixty percent of bedsores happen in hospitals, which treat 2.5 million of them a year, at the cost of $11 billion. Many of them might have been prevented.

⏸▶ *Breakthrough Study*

A team of American and Canadian doctors analyzed 59 studies on bedsores to discover proven ways to prevent them.

They looked at studies investigating…support surfaces for beds and cushions for seats…regimens of repositioning…exercise…incontinence care…nutritional supplementation…and moisturizing dry skin.

They reported their results in the *Journal of the American Medical Association…*

• **Support surfaces.** "Specialized support surfaces (such as mattresses, beds and cushions) reduce or relieve the pressure that the patient's body weight exerts on skin and subcutaneous [under the skin] tissue as it presses against the surface of a bed or chair," says Madhuri Reddy, MD, who led the study.

Compared with regular hospital mattresses, the two most effective bed surfaces to prevent bedsores were…

• Specialized foam, convoluted or cubed rather than flat, and

• Specialized sheepskin, denser and thicker than regular sheepskin.

What to do: Pressure ulcers can develop quickly—within two to six hours! If you or a loved one is scheduled for hospitalization, or is a resident in an extended-care facility and has reduced mobility, talk to a doctor or nurse about arranging for the use of one of these support surfaces over the mattress.

☀ You can find specialty foam mattress overlays and sheepskins at *www.rehabmart.com*. RehabMart LLC, 150 Sagewood Drive, Winterville, GA 30683-1563 (800-827-8283, 706-213-1144 or fax 603-843-2144); e-mail: *info@rehabmart.com*.

You can also find extra-thick "medical sheepskin" at *www.sheepskinexperts.com* or by calling 800-558-6188. Click "Home Products" and then "New Zealand Sheepskin" to find the item. E-mail *info@sheepskinexperts.com*. The address of the retail store of this company is the Sheepskin Experts, Inc., 5931 Van Nuys Blvd., Van Nuys, CA 91401 (888-357-4308, 818-785-2799 or fax 818-989-8933).

• **Nutritional supplements.** "It appears that the use of nutritional supplements may be of benefit in the prevention of pressure ulcers," say the researchers.

What to do: The researchers cite a study that showed adding a protein-based nutritional supplement to the diet of older patients in a nursing home lowered their risk of developing pressure ulcers by 14%.

And in another study, a high-protein supplement that also contained nutrients known to help skin heal (the amino acid arginine, vitamin C and zinc) increased the healing of pressure ulcers—by nine points on the 1-to-17 "Pressure Ulcer Scale for Healing," compared with three points for those not taking the supplement.

☀ The high-protein product used to heal bedsores was Resource Arginaid Extra, from Novartis Medical Nutrition.

If you or a loved one is about to be hospitalized or is a resident in an extended-care facility and has reduced mobility, talk to a dietician about using this supplement, which is widely available at retail stores and on-line.

• **Moisturizing.** "Moisturizing skin is inexpensive and unlikely to be of harm, so it would be a reasonable strategy to implement to prevent pressure ulcers," says Dr. Reddy.

What to do: See page 382 in this chapter for a moisturizer that a scientific study shows can effectively and quickly relieve dry skin.

Red flags: Some of the leading risk factors for pressure ulcers, say the researchers, are being bed- or chair-bound; being unable to reposition without assistance; difficulty with walking or independent feeding; stroke; fecal incontinence; dry skin on the *sacrum*, the bony area at the base of the spine; and underweight.

GUMWEED FOR POISON IVY AND OAK

Allergists call it *contact dermatitis*—a rash from something you touch. And the most common form of contact dermatitis is a rash from contact with the oil (*urushiol*) in poison ivy and poison oak—with at least 10 million Americans a year failing to let be those leaves of three.

As anyone knows who has been "poisoned," the red, itchy, painful, oozing, blister-ridden rash is pure misery, and usually lasts anywhere from three to six weeks.

Now, two naturopathic physicians report they may have found a drug-free way to ease and shorten the misery.

▐▐▐▶ *Breakthrough Study*

The patient had been picking blackberries four days earlier—in a patch of poison oak!

Her rash was obviously from the plant, and the naturopaths started her on a cream of

---

BEDSORES HEAL FOUR TIMES FASTER—WITH HONEY

Before the days of hydrogels, collagen, silicone and other high-tech dressings for wounds, healers often used *honey,* whose sugary syrup stopped infection and moistened the wound (two musts for speedier healing). Newer studies show honey dressings can also reduce wound inflammation, pain and odor. And that they're good for bedsores.

New study: Turkish researchers treated 36 patients with advanced bedsores with either a standard or a honey dressing.

Good news: After five weeks, "Healing among those using a honey dressing was approximately four times the rate of healing" in the group using the standard dressing, say the researchers.

"The use of a honey dressing is effective and practical," they conclude.

What to do: If you or a loved one has developed a bedsore, talk to your doctor or nurse about using a honey dressing on the wound.

☀ For a sterilized honey dressing specially formulated for wound healing (MediHoney by Derma Sciences), visit the Web site, *www.woundcareshop.com.* Eagle Highland Pharmacy, 3850 Shore Drive, Suite 111, Indianapolis, IN 46254 (866-207-5909).

Calendula officianalis (marigold) and *Ocimum tenufolium* (holy basil), along with rhus tox 30C, a homeopathic remedy.

But the rash—which started on the left forearm and right upper inner arm—worsened, with new patches appearing on the lower legs, right forearm and above the pubic area.

The woman tried a friend's hydrocortisone cream, which didn't help. The physicians switched her to two other homeopathic remedies, which also didn't help.

Next, they treated her with an herbal tincture of a classic natural remedy for poison ivy and oak—jewelweed (*Impatiens capensis*). Again, no improvement.

So, a day later, they tried an herbal tincture from the herb gumweed (*Grindelia*), applying it directly to the rash—which *immediately* stopped the itching and weeping. Then, they mixed the tincture with the calendula cream. The woman applied the cream to the rash and covered it with cotton pads coated with the gumweed/calendula cream.

"Within forty-eight hours, the dried area grew and the weeping area shrank. Along with the total area of redness and inflammation, the weeping and the itching almost completely subsided," says Eric Yarnell, ND, RH, in the Department of Botanical Medicine at Bastyr University, and one of the physicians treating the woman. "Within one week, the entire affected areas were resolved."

The topical application of gumweed tincture is a "potentially valuable therapy" for poison oak and poison ivy, he says, in the *Journal of Alternative and Complementary Medicine.*

What to do: If you have poison oak or ivy, talk to your physician or other qualified health professional about using gumweed tincture. First, put the tincture directly on the affected area. Then, mix it with calendula cream. (Use 40 milliliters (ml) of tincture—about two tablespoons—to 60 (ml) of cream—about a quarter

cup.) Apply the gumweed/calendula cream. Keep the affected areas covered with cotton pads coated with gumweed/calendula cream, until the rash resolves.

 Calendula cream is widely available.

You can purchase gumweed tincture from *www.darcyfromtheforest.com,* the Web site of Darcy Williamson, an herbalist with 30 years experience. From the Forest, PO Box 4190, McCall, ID 83638 (208-634-8701); e-mail *fromtheforest@hotmail.com.*

www.greenbrierherbalist.com, the Web site of herbalist Sharon Moncrief. Greenbrier Herbalist, PO Box 175, Pipersville, PA 18947 (215-766-7716); e-mail *sharon@greenbrierherbalist.com.*

HERBAL CREAM FOR PSORIASIS

Normally, skin cells take about 30 days to migrate from the "south" to the "north"—from the deepest level of the skin, where they're born, to the skin surface, where they die.

But for the skin cells of the five to seven million Americans with psoriasis, the trip takes just three or four days, and the skin's surface becomes jammed with extra cells—a red, thick, dry overgrowth blanketed with silvery scales that can itch and burn, even crack and bleed.

Psoriasis usually happens in phases, flaring up and then quieting. It can inhabit a small patch of skin or disfiguring swatches.

There are several forms. Plaque psoriasis, the most common, can hit any part of the body. Other types hone in on the nails, or the scalp, or "inverse" areas such as the armpits, the groin and the skin under the breasts. And in 10 to 30% of those affected, psoriasis even jumps on the joints, causing the pain and swelling of arthritis.

Psoriasis is an *autoimmune disease*—infection-fighting cells mistakenly identify skin cells as "foreign" and attack them, triggering their rapid passage to the surface. Experts don't know what causes the disease, though they have identified factors that can spark flares, such as stress and infections.

Treatments depend on the severity and frequency of the flares, and include a range of powerful drugs, salves and coatings (including coal tar), along with light therapies, from ultraviolet radiation to lasers.

An herbal salve may offer a safe and effective alternative.

⫸ *Breakthrough Studies*

Researchers at the Dermatology and Cosmetic Center in Rochester, NY, studied 200 people with mild to moderate plaque psoriasis, dividing them into two groups. For 12 weeks, one group used a topical cream containing a highly concentrated extract of the Oregon Grape (*Mahonia aquifolium*), a coastal plant native to North and South America that was traditionally used to treat skin disorders. The other group used a placebo cream.

Result: Both groups had their plaques measured using the Psoriasis Area Severity Index, which grades for how red, thick and scaly plaques are, and how extensive. The Mahonia aquifolium group had an average decrease of 3.6 points on the index; the placebo group, 2.2.

The people with psoriasis also filled out questionnaires rating the quality of their everyday life—their mood, their sleep, their relationships. The scores of the Mahonia aquifolium group improved by 26 points; the placebo group by 15 points.

"Patients with mild to moderate psoriasis who were treated with the Mahonia aquifolium topical cream achieved a significantly greater improvement in the signs and symptoms of psoriasis compared with the control group," say the researchers, in the *American Journal of Therapeutics*.

"Because Mahonia aquifolium is a natural product with an excellent safety profile, it can be used for prolonged periods of time, and does not pose the same potential problems commonly associated with steroids," says Howard Donsky, MD, one of the researchers.

And in another scientific paper, Canadian researchers from Memorial University in Newfoundland summarized the results of three studies of Mahonia aquifolium involving 104 patients with psoriasis. In the first study, 39 people with psoriasis saw "statistically significant improvement" after four weeks. In the second study, 32 people with psoriasis treated half of their body with Mahonia aquifolium and the other half with *calcipotriene* (Dovonex cream), a standard treatment. After six months, 84% of those using Mahonia aquifolium rated the treatment "good to excellent"—and 64% said it was equal to or better than Dovonex. In the third study, 33 people with psoriasis treated half of their body with Mahonia aquifolium and the other half with a standard psoriasis cream—again, Mahonia aquifolium was as good or better.

Why it works: Laboratory studies show Mahonia aquifolium can stop the production of new skin cells, quiet inflammation and stop the "hyperproliferation" of the type of skin cell that forms the plaques of psoriasis.

ℹ The researchers studied Reliéva, which is available as a cream, lotion and shampoo.

☀ For more info and to order Reliéva, visit *www.relievaforpsoriasis.com*. Apollo Pharmaceutical Inc., 300 State Street East, Suite 222, Oldsmar, FL 34677 (866-772-2111, or fax 813-749-8855).

Also helpful: A recent study also shows Reliéva is effective in relieving the symptoms of eczema.

16

STRESS, INSOMNIA & FATIGUE
OVERCOMING THE OVERWHELMING

Seventy-five percent of Americans say they're assaulted by stress, with money and work the biggest battering rams…50% say their stress has skyrocketed over the past five years…and 33% say their stress is *extreme*.

Those are the, well, *stressful* results of a national survey conducted by the American Psychological Association (APA). "Stress in America continues to escalate and is affecting every aspect of people's lives," says Russ Newman, PhD, former director of the APA.

Energy levels are taking the biggest hit. The survey showed that fatigue and insomnia are the most common stress-caused problems. "People are *exhausted* from stress—worn out by it during the day and kept awake by it at night," says Kathleen Hall, PhD, director of the Stress Institute in Atlanta, GA, and author of *A Life in Balance* (AMACOM). How does stress do its dirty work?

Stress—feeling pressured, tense, troubled, even threatened—triggers your adrenal glands to release *adrenaline* and *cortisol*, so-called "stress hormones" that spike blood pressure, speed heartbeat and tense muscles. That's great if you're trying to escape a charging tiger. That's

not so great if the stress is inescapable, like the boss or the bills. Chronic stress causes or complicates nearly every disease, from heartburn to heart attacks. "Ninety percent of all health problems are stress-related," says Dr. Hall.

But while stress is a fact of life, feeling stressed isn't. Nearly 28% of Americans are managing their stress extremely well, says the APA survey. Want to join them?

"Using simple, effective strategies for stress reduction makes all the difference in managing stress," says Dr. Hall.

You might start by taking a unique anti-stress supplement that soothes your brain.

L-THEANINE—THE ESSENCE OF A SOOTHING CUP OF TEA

Camellia sinensis—the plant that gives us black and green tea—contains a rare amino acid called *L-theanine*. (The only other source is a species of mushroom.) And that unusual amino acid has the unusual talent of defusing stress.

▶ *Breakthrough Study*

Japanese researchers asked 12 people to take four stress-inducing tests in which they quickly tried to solve difficult math problems. The participants took L-theanine before the first test, and midway through the second. They took a placebo before the third test. They took nothing before the fourth.

Results: When the participants took L-theanine, they had lower heart rates and lower levels of stress-generated immune factors in their saliva. Theanine causes "antistress effects," say the researchers.

How it works: In a Japanese study of university students, L-theanine increased *alpha waves*, brain waves that gently rock the mind into a state of relaxed alertness. (In other words, you're calm but not drowsy.)

Suggested intake: 200 milligrams (mg), two to three times a day, recommend the research scientists, writing in *Alternative Medicine Review*.

ℹ️ Suntheanine is the patented form of L-theanine that the Japanese researchers used to reduce stress in the test-takers and induce alpha waves in the university students. It is an ingredient in many L-theanine supplements, which are widely available.

GUIDED IMAGERY—TAKE STRESS TO THE BEACH

The sun is shining. Your skin is warm. You can smell the salty air. The sound of waves is Mother Nature's lullaby. Yes, you are…at home, in your living room, *imagining* that you are at the beach. You are practicing *guided imagery*.

"Imagery is a flow of thoughts you can see, hear, feel, smell or taste," says Martin L. Rossman, MD, codirector of the Academy for Guided Imagery in Malibu, CA, and author of *Guided Imagery for Self-Healing* (New World Library). "An image is an inner representation of your experience or your fantasies."

In guided imagery, you choose images that help create a state of deep relaxation. It is a pow-

erful stress management technique, says Dr. Rossman. And that's not just his imagination.

▶ *Breakthrough Study*

Japanese scientists at Kyoto University studied 148 people who had practiced guided imagery at home for 20 minutes a day, for six to 14 months.

Result: Those who had been practicing the longest had the lowest stress levels and the most positive moods, say the researchers. In fact, those able to generate the most vivid images had the least stress.

"Stress reduction in healthy people is difficult using methods of conventional medicine," such as medications, say the researchers. "People producing specific images can relax their mind and body, thereby reducing stress and maintaining health."

What to do: The researchers found that a 20-minute, daily session of guided imagery decreased stress. *Here are Dr. Rossman's instructions for a stress-relieving session…*

Get comfortable, either lying face up on the bed or a carpeted floor, or sitting in a comfortable chair. Loosen any tight or restrictive clothing. Take a couple of deep breaths, releasing tension and discomfort in your body.

Then focus your awareness on your body, part by part, from the tips of your toes to the top of your head, allowing enough time for each area to relax—feet…calves…thighs…hips…pelvis…abdomen…chest…shoulders…neck…upper arms…elbows…forearms…wrists…hands…face…forehead…scalp.

Now, deepen this comfortable state by imagining yourself at the top of a stairway that has ten steps leading down from where you stand. When you are ready, begin to descend the staircase a step at a time, counting backward from ten to one as you go, allowing yourself to feel more deeply and comfortably relaxed with each step you descend.

At this point, says Dr. Rossman, you're ready for the guided imagery...

Imagine yourself in a very beautiful place. This might be somewhere you visited before or somewhere you make up in your imagination. Just let the image of the place come to you. It really doesn't matter what kind of place you imagine as long as it's beautiful, quiet, peaceful and serene. Let this be a special inner place for you—somewhere that you feel particularly at ease, a place where you feel secure and at one with your surroundings. Maybe you've had a place like this in your life. Somewhere you go to be quiet and reflective, somewhere special and healing for you. Or it could be a place you've seen in a movie or read about or just dreamed of. It could be a real place, like a meadow or a beach, or an imaginary place, like a soft cloud.

Let yourself explore whatever quiet imaginary place you go to, as if you were there now. Notice what you see there...what sounds you hear...even the smells and aromas that you sense there. Immerse yourself in the beauty, the feelings of peacefulness, of being secure and at ease.

As you explore this special inner place, find a spot that feels particularly good to be in, a spot where you feel especially calm, centered and at ease. Let this be your "power spot"—a place in which you draw from the deep sense of peacefulness you feel here, a place of healing and rest, and a place where you can explore and use the power of your imagination to best effect. Take some time to relax into the deep feelings of peacefulness, quiet and healing you can sense in this spot. Take as much time as you need.

When you're done with your session of guided imagery, says Dr. Rossman, all you need to do is recall the imaginary staircase you descended, imagine yourself at the bottom of the stairs and become more and more wide-awake, alert and aware of your surrounding as you ascend, step by step.

☀ Dr. Rossman sells the CD "Stress Relief Through Guided Imagery," as well as other guided imagery CDs at the Web site *www.thehealingmind.org*. The Healing Mind, 1341 South Eliseo Drive, Suite 350, Greenbrae, CA 94904; e-mail *info@thehealingmind.org*.

You can also get a free "Stress Buster" audio download at his Web site, with Dr. Rossman leading you through a brief session of stress-relieving guided imagery.

POST-TRAUMATIC STRESS— HEALING THE MEMORY

You see your buddy killed in battle. A hurricane destroys your house.

These are violent and terrifying events. Add to that list mugging, rape, kidnapping, child abuse, an earthquake, a car wreck, a plane crash—*any* ordeal that involves threatened or actual physical harm. All of them are traumatic. And all of them can trigger post-traumatic stress disorder, or PTSD.

You relive the trauma repeatedly, in upsetting memories, daytime flashbacks and nightmares. You startle easily. You go out of your way to avoid situations that remind you of the stressful trauma. And, if you are reminded (for example, by the smell of gasoline, if you've been in a car accident), you might panic—you're suddenly sweaty, shaky and short of breath, with your heart pounding like an inner alarm.

You might feel depressed. You might get angry at the slightest provocation. To numb your emotional discomfort, you might drink heavily or take drugs. And you might distance yourself from your loved ones, because intense feelings remind you of...the trauma.

Latest development: New research shows you also might get sick. People with PTSD have nearly double the risk of heart disease, along with more arthritis, skin problems, headaches, fatigue and digestive problems.

ⅢⅢ➡ *Breakthrough Studies*

PTSD is the disaster after the disaster. But there is PTSD relief. *In fact, say scientists, there is even PTSD prevention…*

Preventing PTSD: Sandro Galea, MD, and a team of researchers at the University of Michigan, School of Public Health, studied nearly 3,000 New Yorkers in the 30 months following the September 11, 2001, terrorist attacks. Levels of PTSD shot up from 2% to 14%. But there was a pattern to who got PTSD and who didn't. Those most likely to develop the disorder had the most *everyday* stress—with every additional stressor, such as money worries or marital difficulty, increasing the risk of PTSD by 91%.

To help prevent PTSD, Dr. Galea recommends "interventions to minimize ongoing stressors," such as getting emotional support from family and friends. To reduce everyday stress, you can also use the techniques in this chapter, such as mindfulness-based stress reduction (page 397), guided imagery (page 393) and repeating a mantram, also known as mantra (page 402).

Treating PTSD: Researchers in Wales analyzed results from 29 studies on psychological treatments for PTSD. They found that *trauma-focused cognitive behavioral therapy* (CBT) and *exposure therapy* were the most effective.

And in a study of 160 trauma victims who had received one of seven psychological treatments, CBT and exposure therapy were the most preferred, say researchers in the Department of Psychology at Trinity University in San Antonio, Texas.

- **Cognitive-behavioral therapy.** You learn to identify negative thoughts and behaviors triggered by the trauma, and replace them with thoughts and behaviors that help relieve PTSD.

Example: A soldier may feel guilty about decisions made during battle. CBT helps you understand that the traumatic event was not your fault. (For more information on cognitive therapy, see page 108 in Chapter 5, "Depression and Other Emotional Downers.")

- **Exposure therapy.** You're gradually and carefully exposed to scary thoughts, feelings, memories and real-life situations that remind you of the trauma, in a process known as *systematic desensitization*, explains Jeanne Segal, PhD, a psychologist, author of *Living Beyond Fear* (Ballantine) and editorial reviewer of *www.helpguide.com*, a Web site offering information on improving mental and physical health. Little by little, PTSD goes away.

What to do: You can find a cognitive therapist near you who specializes in trauma and/or exposure therapy through the "Find a Therapist" feature at *www.abct.org*, the Web site of the Association for Behavioral and Cognitive Therapy, or by calling 212-647-1890.

Latest development: Virtual reality enhanced exposure—wearing a virtual reality helmet (which positions two goggle-sized miniature computer monitor screens close to the eyes and small speakers close to the ears)—is used to re-create the experience of trauma. In a study of people being treated for PTSD after the World Trade Center attacks, virtual reality enhanced exposure improved PTSD symptoms by 53%, making it an "effective tool for enhancing exposure therapy," says JoAnn Difede, PhD, director of the Program for Anxiety and Traumatic Stress Studies, at Weill Cornell Medical College, in New York.

To find out more about virtual reality enhanced exposure for PTSD, visit *www. patss.com.* Program for Anxiety and Traumatic Stress Studies, Weill Medical College of Cornell University, 525 East 68th Street, Box 200, New York, NY 10065 (212-821-0783 or fax 212-821-0994).

● **EMDR (Eye movement desensitization and reprocessing).** There have been more than two dozen studies on treating PTSD with this unusual technique, with the American Psychiatric Association supporting its effectiveness, and the government's Department of Veteran Affairs saying it is "strongly recommended" for PTSD.

"Cognitive-behavioral therapy and EMDR are equally effective," say researchers who reviewed studies on both techniques, in the journal *Psychological Medicine.*

In EMDR, you visualize the traumatic event while moving your eyes rapidly back and forth. The theory is that it unlocks information processing systems in your brain that were "frozen" at the time of the trauma, explains Francine Shapiro, PhD, coauthor of *EMDR* (Basic Books). When those systems are "unfrozen," you can process memories of the trauma, draining them of their disturbing intensity. At the same time, you work to replace a trauma-caused negative belief about yourself with a positive belief.

What to do: To find a qualified EMDR therapist, use the "Find A Therapist" function on the home page of the Web site of the EMDRIA, the EMDR International Association, at *www. emdria.org.* EMDR International Association, 5806 Mesa Drive, Suite 360, Austin, Texas 78731 (866-451-5200, 512-451-5200 or fax 512-451-5256); e-mail *info@emdria.org.*

Or use the "Find an EMDR Clinician" function on the home page of the EMDR Institute, at *www.emdr.com,* or contact the EMDR Institute, Inc., PO Box 750, Watsonville,

CA 95077 (831-761-1040 or fax 831-761-1204); e-mail *inst@emdr.com.*

LEMON BALM—TURN OVER A NEW LEAF

What could be more relaxing than a warm cup of tea? Maybe a warm cup of lemon balm tea.

▶ *Breakthrough Study*

Psychologists in England subjected 18 people to an "Intensity Stressor Simulation." Four tasks were shown simultaneously on a four-way split computer screen. *Imagine you are there…*

● **Solving a math problem using an onscreen calculator,** with a new problem popping up right after you click "Done," while…

● **A high or low tone sounds every five seconds,** and you click a box labeled "Incoming Mail" at the high tone, while…

● **A small dot drifts to the edge of a ring of five concentric circles,** and you allow the dot to get as close as possible to the outermost edge before you click the reset button, while…

● **Four letters appear and disappear in a horizontal bar every four seconds,** and a single letter appears in a circle above the bar every 10 seconds and you click "Yes" or "No" to indicate if the single letter was in one of the four-letter groups, while…

A numerical counter in the center of the screen tallies an accumulating score, reflecting your accuracy and speed on the four tasks. (You probably felt stressed just *reading* about that device!)

The participants used the Intensity Stressor Simulator for 20 minutes on two days. One hour before each session they took either 300 or 600 mg of an extract of lemon balm (*Melissa officinalis*), or a placebo.

Result: Those taking the 600 mg dose had significantly less stress. After the test, they were more than twice as calm compared with those who took either 300 mg or the placebo.

Lemon balm can help prevent the negative change in mood associated with stress, says David O. Kennedy, PhD, in the Division of Psychology at the University of Northumbria in England. The 600-mg dose, he says "significantly improved calmness," which is "consistent with this herb's reputation as a calming agent." And he poses this question to his fellow scientists: Would taking lemon balm regularly be a safer alternative than taking prescription tranquilizers for coping with stress?

How it works: "The mechanisms of action are poorly understood," says Dr. Kennedy. In other words, just relax and enjoy the herb!

What to do: "Lemon balm makes a delightful-tasting tea you can drink simply for pleasure or for its calming effects," says David Winston, RH (AHG), a clinical herbalist and the coauthor of *Adaptogens: Herbs for Strength, Stamina, and Stress Relief* (Healing Arts). Winston notes that lemon balm is also effective for stress headaches and insomnia.

Suggested intake: To make lemon balm tea, use 1 to 2 teaspoons of dried leaf in an eight-ounce cup of hot water, steeping covered for 15 minutes. Drink two to three cups a day, says Winston. As a tincture, use 80 to 100 drops, four times a day, he says. In capsule form, the effective dose in the study was 600 mg.

Precaution: If you have Hashimoto thyroiditis or any other type of low thyroid (hypothyroid) condition, don't use lemon balm, says Winston—in large doses it can cut the production of thyroxin, a thyroid hormone.

Also helpful: In another study, Dr. Kennedy and his team found that sage—the herb, *salvia officinalis*—helped reduce stress in 30 people using the Intensity Stress Simulator, increasing

calmness, contentment and alertness. The effective daily dose was 300 mg of a dried extract, in capsule form.

MINDFULNESS-BASED STRESS REDUCTION

"The stress in our lives is now so great that more people are making the deliberate decision to understand it better and bring it under control," says Jon Kabat-Zinn, PhD, founding director of the Stress Reduction Clinic and the Center for Mindfulness at the University of Massachusetts Medical School and author of *Full Catastrophe Living* (Delta).

And one of the best ways to do that is with *mindfulness.* A difficult task in today's world of fast food and instant messaging.

"Mindfulness is moment-to-moment awareness," says Dr. Kabat-Zinn. "It is cultivated by purposefully paying attention to things we ordinarily never give a moment's thought to. Think of mindfulness as a lens—taking the scattered and reactive energies of your mind and focusing them into a coherent source of energy for living, for problem solving and for healing."

And for dealing more effectively with stress...

▶ *Breakthrough Studies*

Researchers from the Center for Mindfulness at the University of Massachusetts and from the University of Kentucky taught 174 people with stress-related problems to practice mindfulness meditation and the body-scan technique. (To learn more about the body-scan technique, see page 401.)

After eight weeks, participants had more mindfulness—and less stress. And the more time they had spent practicing mindfulness meditation, the *less* stressed they felt, says James

THE BREAKOUT PRINCIPLE— TURN STRESS INTO SUCCESS

If you're in a competitive environment of any kind—work, school, sports—you're probably *stressed*. Your heart pumps, you're more alert—and you're more efficient. And that's *good*. But *too much* stress can overload your system, hurting your performance—and eventually your health. How can you get to the finish line without crashing? By carefully *controlling* stress, says Herbert Benson, MD, associate professor of medicine at Harvard Medical School and director emeritus of the Benson-Henry Institute for Mind Body Medicine at Massachusetts General Hospital. And the best way to do that is with what he calls "The Breakout Principle."

▶ Breakthrough Study

Dr. Benson describes the four steps of The Breakout Principle in the *Harvard Business Review*:

1. Push yourself to the most productive stress level by grappling intently with the problem at hand—that means fact-gathering for the businessperson, demanding physical training for the athlete or studying for the student. Stress hormones are flooding your body!

2. As you find yourself flagging, do something relaxing *and* unrelated to the task at hand. Dr. Benson calls these unrelated activities "Breakout Triggers"—and there are a lot to choose. Listen to your favorite music. Do yoga or tai chi. Read poetry or look at a work of art. Take a long shower or soak in a hot tub. Walk, jog or bike. Do needlepoint. Go fishing or sit quietly in a garden. Pet a calm cat or dog.

   What happens: All of these activities trigger the release of body chemicals that counter stress hormones.

3. During a Breakout Trigger, your brain will quiet down. But brain activity will simultaneously and paradoxically *increase* in areas associated with attention, space-time concepts and decision-making, says Dr. Benson. You will have a sudden, creative insight...or improvement in athleticism...or vigorous rejuvenation—The Breakout!

4. Now you are in a "new-normal state," says Dr. Benson—and your improved performance will continue, maybe indefinitely.

☀ *The Breakout Principle* by Herbert Benson, MD, and William Proctor (Scribner).

Carmody, PhD, director of research for the Center for Mindfulness.

Seven Secrets of Mindfulness

There are several attitudes that form the basis of mindfulness practice, says Dr. Kabat-Zinn.

1. **Nonjudging.** "Become aware of the constant stream of judging and reacting to experiences that we are all normally caught up in," he says. "When practicing mindfulness, it is important to recognize this judging quality of mind and to intentionally assume the stance of an impartial witness by reminding yourself to just observe it."

2. **Patience.** "Understand and accept the fact that sometimes things must unfold in their own time," he says. "Why rush through some moments to get to other 'better' ones? After all, each is your life in this moment."

3. **Beginner's mind.** "Too often we let our thinking and beliefs about what we 'know' prevent us from seeing things as they really are," he says. "To see the richness of the present moment, cultivate a 'beginner's mind'—a mind that is willing to see everything as if for the first time."

   Example: The next time you see somebody who is familiar to you, ask yourself if you are seeing this person with fresh eyes, as he or she really is, or if you are only seeing the reflection of your own thoughts about this person.

4. **Trust.** "If at any time something doesn't feel right to you, why not honor your feelings?" asks Dr. Kabat-Zinn. "Why should you discount them or write them off as invalid because some authority or some group of people think or say differently?"

5. **Non-striving.** Meditation is different from other human activities because it's a form of *non-doing*, says Dr. Kabat-Zinn.

   Trap: "If you sit down to meditate and you think, 'I am going to get relaxed', then you have introduced an idea in your mind of where you should be, and along with it comes the notion that you are not okay right now," he says.

   Better: "In meditation, the best way to achieve goals is to back off from striving for results and instead start focusing carefully on seeing and accepting things as they are, moment by moment."

6. **Acceptance.** "Acceptance means seeing things as they actually are in the present. We often waste a lot of energy denying and resisting what is already fact. In meditation, we cultivate acceptance by taking each moment as it comes and being with it fully, as it is."

7. **Letting go.** "When you start paying attention to your inner experience, you rapidly discover that there are certain thoughts, feelings and situations that the mind seems to want to hold on to," says Dr. Kabat-Zinn. "Instead, just let your experience be what it is and practice observing it from moment to moment."

Practicing Mindfulness Meditation

To prepare for meditation, assume a comfortable posture lying on your back or sitting, says Dr. Kabat-Zinn. If you're sitting, keep your spine straight and let your shoulders drop. Close your eyes, if that feels comfortable.

"The easiest and most effective way to begin practicing mindfulness as a formal meditation practice is to simply focus your attention on your breathing and see what happens as you attempt to keep it there," says Dr. Kabat-Zinn.

"There are a number of different places in the body where breath can be observed," he continues. "Obviously, one is the nostrils—focus on the feeling of the breath as it flows past the nostrils. Another is the chest as it expands and contracts. Another is the belly, which moves in and out with each breath if it is relaxed.

"No matter what location you choose, be aware of the sensations that accompany your breathing at that particular place and hold them in the forefront of your awareness from moment to moment. Doing this, *feel* the air as it flows in and out past the nostrils. Or *feel* the movement of the muscles associated with breathing. Or *feel* the belly as it moves in and out.

"Paying attention to your breathing means just paying attention. Nothing more. It doesn't mean you should 'push' or force your breath, or try to make it deeper or change its pattern or rhythm. There is no need to control it. Simply be aware of the *feeling* of each breath in, and each breath out. When you notice that your mind has wandered off the breath, notice what it was that took you away and then gently bring your attention back to the feeling of the breath coming in and out.

"In the stress clinic," adds Dr. Kabat-Zinn, "we generally focus on the feelings of the breath in the belly because doing so tends to be particularly relaxing and calming. This is a valuable way of reestablishing your inner calmness and balance in the face of emotional upset or when you have a lot on your mind.

"Practice this exercise for fifteen minutes at a convenient time every day, whether you feel like it or not, for one week, and see how it feels to incorporate a meditation practice into your life. Be aware of how it feels to spend some time each day just being with your breath without having to do anything."

☀ To locate a class in mindfulness-based stress reduction in your area, visit the Web site of the Center for Mindfulness in Medicine, Health Care, and Society, of the University of Massachusetts Medical School, at *www. umassmed.edu/cfm*, which includes a state-by-state directory of instructors and classes.

For mindfulness-based CDs and tapes from Dr. Kabat-Zinn, PhD, see the Web site *www.mindfulnesstapes.com*. Stress Reduction Tapes, PO Box 547, Lexington, MA 02420.

Best-selling books by Jon Kabat-Zinn on mindfulness-based stress reduction, in meditation and daily life are *Full Catastrophe Living: Using the Wisdom of Your Body and Mind to Face Stress, Pain and Illness* (Delta), and *Wherever You Go, There You Are: Mindfulness Meditation in Everyday Life* (Hyperion).

ENERGY HEALING— CALMING YOUR BIO-FIELD

Here's a far-out theory of stress relief…

There is a universal energy field. Yogis call it *prana*…practitioners of Traditional Chinese Medicine, *chi*…Polynesian healers, *mana*… Native Americans, *wakan*…and intrigued Western scientists, the *bio-field*.

If you tune in to the energy field—and it's easy to do it, once you learn how—you can transmit that energy to another human being. If you're on the receiving end of the transmission, you feel relaxed, nourished, energized—and a whole lot less stressed.

So says a very nonmystical group, the scientists in the Division of Neuroscience and Psychological Medicine at Imperial College, in London.

▌▌▌➡ *Breakthrough Studies*

To create "acute stress," the UK scientists asked 33 medical students to solve difficult math problems quickly. Before the stress, half of the students received 10 minutes of *Johrie*, an energy healing technique; the other half didn't.

After the acute stress was over, the scientists found that those receiving Johrie had moods that were more positive and less anxious, and had slightly lower levels of cortisol, a stress-generated hormone.

The same team of scientists also studied 48 students scheduled to take exams in two months. In the weeks before the exams, the students received stress reduction training (guided imagery), Johrei treatments or sessions with a fake biofeedback machine that they were told reduced stress.

As exams approached, the group given the fake biofeedback had changes in levels of immune cells that signaled increased levels of stress, such as fewer health-protecting "natural killer cells." Those who learned self-hypnosis or received Johrei had far fewer immune changes.

Energy healing may reduce stress, say the scientists, in *Brain Research Bulletin*.

And in other studies on energy healing, scientists at the Center for Frontier Medicine in Biofield Science, at the University of Arizona, found that Johrei treatments decreased negative emotional states and increased positive emotions in 236 healthy people; and decreased stress and depression in 12 substance abusers.

☀ If you want to find someone trained in energy healing—or learn it yourself—consider the following four options…

1. **Johrei.** This form of energy healing originated in Japan and is taught by the Johrei Foundation (*www.johreifoundation.org*), which

has centers in 17 American cities, including their national headquarters in the Los Angeles area. Phone 310-318-6054 or e-mail *johrei@johreifoundation.org.*

2. **Quantum-Touch.** Anyone can quickly learn this simple but effective form of hands-on energy healing, which uses focused attention and deep breathing, says Richard Gordon, author of *Quantum-Touch: The Power to Heal* (North Atlantic Books). His Web site, *www. quantumtouch.com,* has a state-by-state directory of practitioners. Quantum-Touch, PO Box 512, San Luis Obispo, CA 93406 (888-424-0041 or fax 805-781-9237); e-mail *mail@ quantumtouch.com.*

3. **Therapeutic Touch.** This form of energy healing developed in 1972 by Dolores Krieger, PhD, RN, is widely used in hospitals. The practitioner first *centers* herself… then *accesses* the person being treated, by holding her hands two to six inches away from this person's energy field…then *clears and balances* the field. You can find a state-by-state list of certified practitioners at the Web site *www.therapeutictouch.org.* NH-PAI, Inc., Box 419, Craryville, NY 12521 (877) 32NHPAI, 518-325-1185 or fax 509-693-3537); e-mail *nhpai@therapeutic-touch. org.* See also *Accepting Your Power to Heal: The Personal Practice of Therapeutic Touch* by Dolores Krieger (Bear & Company).

THE BODY-SCAN TECHNIQUE

"In the Stress Reduction Clinic at the University of Massachusetts, we ask people to practice the body scan once a day for at least four weeks," says Dr. Kabat-Zinn, PhD. (For more information on mindfulness and mindfulness-based stress reduction, see pages 397 to 401 in this chapter.) "It is the first daily mindfulness practice that our patients engage in. For many people, it brings them to their first experience of well-being in meditation." *Here are Dr. Kabat-Zinn's instructions for practicing the body scan…*

The idea in scanning your body is actually to *feel* each region you focus on and linger there with your mind right *on* it and *in* it. Breathe in *to* and out *from* each region a few times and then let go of it in your mind's eye as your attention moves to the next region. It helps if you can feel or imagine that the tension in your body and the feelings of fatigue associated with it are *flowing out* on each out-breath and that, on each in-breath, you are breathing in energy, vitality and relaxation.

To start, lie down on your back in a comfortable place, such as a foam pad on the floor or your bed. Make sure that you will be warm enough—you might want to cover yourself with a blanket.

Allow your eyes gently to close. (If you have trouble staying awake, try doing the body scan with your eyes open.)

Start with the toes of the left foot and slowly move up the foot and left leg to the pelvis, feeling the sensations as you go and paying attention to the breath, directing it in and out from the different regions. From the pelvis, go to the toes of the right foot and move up the right leg back to the pelvis. From there, move up through the torso, through the low back and abdomen, the upper back and chest and the shoulders.

Then go to the fingers of both hands and move up simultaneously in both arms, returning to the shoulders. Then move through the neck and throat, finally all the regions of the face, the back of the head and the top of the head.

End by breathing through an imaginary "hole" in the very top of the head, as if you were a whale with a blowhole. Let your breathing move through the entire body from one end to the other, as if it were flowing in through the top of the head and out through the toes, and then in through the toes and out through the top of the head.

4. **Reiki.** "Reiki is a technique for stress reduction and relaxation that also promotes healing," says William Lee Rand, a Reiki therapist. "It is administered by 'laying on hands' and is based on the idea that an unseen 'life force energy' flows through us. If one's 'life force energy' is low, then we are more likely to feel stress or get sick, and if it is high, we are more capable of being happy and healthy." The International Center for Reiki Training, 21421 Hilltop Street, Unit #28, Southfield, MI 48033 (800-332-8112 or fax 248-948-9534); e-mail *center@reiki. org* or visit *www.reiki.org*. A top-selling guide to this technique is *Essential Reiki* by Diane Stein (Crossing Press).

MANTRAM—ANOTHER WORD FOR STRESS RELIEF

Could simply repeating a peaceful-sounding sacred or holy word or phrase—a *mantram* (or what is also known as *mantra*)—create more peace in your life? *Yes, yes, yes, say scientists…*

"Silent, frequent repetition of a mantram—a word or phrase with spiritual significance—may reduce stress," says Jill E. Bormann, PhD, RN, in the Veterans Administration San Diego Healthcare System, in California.

▐▐▐▶ *Breakthrough Study*

"To test the usefulness of mantram repetition, we offered it to a highly stressed group—forty-two hospital workers," says Dr. Bormann. Those who used the mantram regularly experienced significantly less stress—and less anxiety and anger, with an improved quality of life and greater spiritual well-being.

"Stress-related symptoms such as anxiety, obsessive thoughts and insomnia are frequently treated with medication, psychotherapy or a wide variety of cognitive-behavioral stress man-

STRESS DRIVING YOU NUTS? EAT MORE PISTACHIOS!

That's the nutty but smart advice from nutritional scientists at Pennsylvania State University.

The scientists conducted a study in which participants ate a heart-healthy diet for one month—with one group eating no pistachios; one group eating 1.5 ounces a day (about a handful, or one-third cup); and one group eating three ounces a day (about two handfuls, or two-thirds cup).

At the end of the month, the scientists stressed the participants with a math test. Then they measured their *peripheral vascular resistance*—whether their arteries were tight or loose.

Those who had been eating three ounces of pistachios a day had the most relaxed arteries—a sure sign their bodies were coping better with the stress.

The researchers theorize that high levels of healthy monounsaturated fats and antioxidants are doing the trick. Favor raw, unsalted nuts that aren't dyed. Look for a bright green kernel with a white creamy shell, says Tanya Zuckerbrot, RD, a registered dietician and author of *The F-Factor Diet* (Perigee).

agement techniques," says Dr. Bormann. "Such approaches may be effective, but medications may have side effects, and other therapies are time-consuming to implement." Instead, she says, "frequent, silent mantram repetition could be used for managing stress."

What to do: To choose a mantram, try a time-tested "spiritual phrase drawn from faith traditions," says Dr. Bormann. Examples are "Glory be to God," or "My God and my All" from the Christian tradition; "Shalom" from the Jewish tradition; "Om Mani Padme Hum" from the Buddhist tradition; "Om Shanti" from the Hindu tradition; "Allahu Akbar" from Islam—

or the name of God from any tradition. (If you don't have a religious or spiritual preference, you could use a phrase like, "Sweet harmony" or "Take it easy"—but Dr. Bormann's studies show they don't work nearly as well.)

Once you've chosen your mantram, repeat it silently to yourself as much as possible, particularly when you're *not* under a lot of stress, says Dr. Bormann. While walking. Washing the dishes. Falling asleep. (If other thoughts pop up, "passively disregard" them, she says—don't resist them; just easily return to the mantram.) Then, when you're experiencing stress or stress-caused emotions, such as anxiety or anger, repeat the mantram again, to keep yourself centered, calm and focused.

"As a stress-management technique, mantram repetition is portable, invisible and non-toxic," says Dr. Bormann.

She also advises using the mantram to help you slow down your thinking process. "Slowing down—focusing on one task at a time, as a guard against hurry, time pressure and to help you prioritize activities—supports the practice of silently repeating the mantram to evoke a calm and balanced mental state."

☀ The instructional text used in her study was *The Mantram Handbook* by Eknath Easwaran (Nilgiri Press). "This is a universal and nonsectarian presentation that is suitable for most people," says Dr. Bormann.

HOSPITAL-PROVEN STRESS RELIEF

Imagine the most stressful job in the world...

If you're careless for a second you can kill somebody—or yourself. You switch shifts constantly, working 7 a.m. to 3 p.m. one week and 11 p.m. to 7 a.m. the next. (When you're off work, it's hard to fall asleep, stay asleep, get enough sleep or even know *when* to sleep.) You have to lift and pull heavy, awkward objects. You clean dirty people—who then swear at you because they're in pain. The job?

Nursing.

Nurses are so stressed that scientists consider them perfect "subjects" for testing stress-relief techniques. Here are a few that definitely work. And if they work for a nurse, chances are they'll work for you.

➤ Breakthrough Studies

• **Massage.** Researchers in Australia studied 60 hospital nurses; half received a 15-minute

TO BEAT STRESS, GO FISHING (FOR SALMON)

To relax when you're under stress, you can look at fish swimming in an aquarium. *Or eat a couple of them...*

New study: Australian researchers studied 30 employees at a university who had high scores on a psychological test called the "Perceived Stress Scale." They divided them into several groups, one of which took daily supplements containing 1.5 grams of DHA (docosahexaenoic acid), an omega-3 fatty acid found in fatty fish such as salmon, tuna and mackerel.

After six weeks, the level of perceived stress in the DHA group had fallen by 25%.

How it works: DHA cuts the level of stress-generated hormones that tax your system, says Joanne Bradbury, of the Australian Centre for Complementary Medicine, Education and Research. With less of those hormones in your bloodstream, you feel less stressed.

What to do: Eat fatty fish such as salmon or mackerel two or more times a week, or take fish oil supplements. The Nordic Naturals brand used in many scientific studies has proven the value of fish oil; their DHA supplement contains 450 mg of DHA per capsule.

YOU'RE A PERFECTIONIST— AND PERFECTLY STRESSED

Researchers in Switzerland found that 50 middle-aged male perfectionists secreted more of a stress hormone during public speaking than their nonperfectionist counterparts. They also felt more fatigued and irritable.

"Perfectionists set exceptionally high standards for themselves and are intensely critical when they do not reach them," says Michael D. Yapko, PhD, a clinical psychologist in private practice in Solana Beach, CA, and author of *Breaking the Patterns of Depression* (Main Street Books).

Helpful: "You can't be perfect even if you want to be, but you could be *really* good," says Dr. Yapko. "Define success in realistic terms, taking human factors into account. The laws of human nature *do* apply to you, believe it or not."

back massage once a week and half didn't. Five weeks later, the massaged nurses had less psychological stress—while stress levels of non-massaged nurses went up.

To help you find a licensed massage therapist near you, the American Massage Therapy Association (AMTA) provides this Web site, *www.findamassagetherapist.org.* AMTA, 500 Davis Street, Suite 900, Evanston, IL 60201-4695 (877-905-2700, 847-864-0123 or fax 847-864-1178); e-mail *info@amtamassage.org* or visit *www.amtamassage.org.*

• **Aromatherapy.** During their 12-hour shifts, nurses in an intensive care unit dabbed themselves with drops of lavender or clary sage essential oils. They experienced decreased stress levels, say researchers in the School of Nursing at the University of Texas.

Arlys Naturals, *www.arlysnaturals.com,* sells a wide variety of lavender essential oils and a high-quality clary sage essential oil. Contact 877-502-7597, 954-523-9513 or fax 954-767-8973; e-mail *susan@arlysnaturals.com.*

• **Mindfulness-based stress reduction.** Sixteen nurses and nurses' aides practiced mindfulness-based stress reduction for one month and experienced less stress—they had less physical fatigue, mental weariness and emotional negativity, and felt more relaxed and satisfied. Mindfulness-based stress reduction is a promising method for managing stress, say researchers at the University of Toronto.

See page 397 in this chapter for information on mindfulness-based stress reduction, plus a source for ordering mindfulness tapes for home use, a list of books on mindfulness and how to find a mindfulness instructor near you.

• **Assertiveness training.** Twenty-five nurses took a 70-minute course in "assertiveness training." After the course, they experienced less job stress and less mental stress, say Japanese researchers.

What to do: "Assertion means caring for yourself," says Virginia Williams, PhD, coauthor of *Lifeskills* (Times). "You ask for what you want and need—or you say no to the requests of others, when to say yes would keep you from what you want or need."

To ask for what you want, says Dr. Williams, simply request that another person engage in a specific behavior. "Avoid vague requests," she says. Instead of saying, 'Please do your fair share of work,' try 'Please take Linda to her seven o'clock dance rehearsal at the gym.'"

You should say no if you're the type of person who routinely overextends yourself on behalf of others, and ends up exhausted and resentful, says Dr. Williams. Begin with a restatement of what the person has asked you to do—"You want me to chair the Public Safety Committee next year"—and then communicate an explicit no—"Sorry, but no. I don't want to chair the Public Safety Committee next year."

• **Social support.** Researchers looked at stress levels among 263 nurses and found that those who had the most "social support" from their coworkers had the lowest level of stress.

What to do: Social support includes your spouse, family, friends, coworkers, coreligionists and people in other types of affiliate groups. "Supportive relationships buffer the effects of stress," says Beverly A. Potter, PhD, a psychologist and author of *Overcoming Job Burnout* (Ronin). To help build those relationships, she recommends you show interest in others, give compliments and ask for advice.

• **Stretching.** Researchers in China taught stretching techniques to 17 nurses. One month later, the nurses said they felt much less stress.

What to do: A quick and simple stretch for tense shoulders, from certified personal trainer Vicki R. Pierson...

"Sit comfortably with your back straight, your shoulders relaxed and your arms at your sides. Slowly begin rolling your shoulders in a circular, backward motion. Keep the movement isolated to your shoulders, and keep your arms relaxed. Roll your shoulders back ten times, then begin rolling them forward ten times. Make the largest circles you can, and feel the full range of motion as your shoulders move."

☀ The book *Stretching* by Bob Anderson (Shelter Publications) and Anderson's DVD by the same name.

INSOMNIA

D iabetes. High blood pressure. Heart disease. Stroke. Depression. Overweight. What do those diseases and conditions have to do with insomnia? More than you might think.

Every one of those health problems (and many others) are partly caused or greatly complicated by insomnia, says a new report from the government's Centers for Disease Control and Prevention (CDC). In fact, research shows that health costs for people with insomnia are *three times higher* than for normal sleepers.

And there are a *lot* of insomniacs. The CDC estimates that 70 million Americans have difficulty falling asleep, wake up repeatedly throughout the night, or wake up too early and can't get back to sleep. For 30 million, those problems are chronic.

To stop the tossing and turning, many Americans turn to the doctor—and the doctor's prescription pad.

"Sleeping pills don't cure insomnia," says Gregg D. Jacobs, PhD, an insomnia specialist in the Sleep Disorders Center of the Beth Israel Deaconess Medical Center in Boston, assistant professor of psychiatry at Harvard Medical School and author of *Say Goodnight to Insomnia* (Henry Holt). Sleeping pills, he says, can have serious side effects...are only moderately effective...stop working once you stop taking them...and can lead to physical or psychological dependency.

Instead, Dr. Jacobs and many other sleep experts favor drug-free approaches to solving the problem.

LAVENDER—THE SCENT OF SLEEP

Lavender is a clean and relaxing scent found in soaps, shampoos, perfumes, potpourris, candles, bath beads—just about anything fragrant with a price tag on it. Lavender can also sweeten your dreams.

⫸ *Breakthrough Studies*

Researchers at the University of Southampton in England studied 10 people with insomnia. For one week, they had no treatment; for another, they slept in a bedroom with an aromatherapy diffuser that dispensed the scent of lavender into the air. (Aromatherapy is the technique of healing with essential oils; a diffuser is a device that releases the scent of essential oil into the air.) At the end of each of the two weeks, they filled out a questionnaire indicating the severity of their insomnia over the past week.

Result: After the treatment with lavender, their insomnia improved by 50%—they got to sleep faster, woke up less often and had less daytime fatigue.

Lavender oil may be an effective treatment for insomnia, say the researchers, in the *Journal of Alternative and Complementary Medicine.*

Other studies show why insomniacs fall in love with—and asleep with—lavender.

Fall asleep faster: In a Korean study, 42 college students with insomnia feel asleep faster and slept deeper after "lavender fragrance treatment."

Sleep more soundly: In a Japanese study, hospital patients in an intensive care unit slept more soundly after a hot bath containing lavender essential oil.

Less restlessness: In a UK study reported in *The Lancet*, one of the world's top medical journals, residents of a nursing home fell asleep faster and were less restless during sleep when lavender oil was dispensed during the night.

What to do: Lavender can help lull you to sleep in many different ways, says Barbara Close, an aromatherapist and author of *Aromatherapy: The A-to-Z Guide to Healing with Essential Oils* (Dell). "Lavender essential oil may be diffused to relieve insomnia and help you get a good night's sleep. You can also place a few drops on your pillow. Or add a few drops to a warm, before-bed bath.

ⓘ For top-quality lavender oils and a wide selection of aromatherapy diffusers, visit Arlys Naturals at *www.arlysnaturals.com.*

EXERCISE—WALK BRISKLY INTO DREAMLAND

Consider the phrase "dead tired." That's exactly how sleeping pills might make you feel. Researchers at the University of California in San Diego analyzed data from more than one million people and found that those who took more than 30 sleeping pills a month *were at three times the risk of dying,* while those who took between 1 and 29 pills had a 50 to 80% higher death risk.

Is there an alternative to "big sleep" relief for insomnia? Rather than six feet under, try two feet over and over.

⫸ *Breakthrough Studies*

"Sleeping pills have a number of adverse effects," says Shawn Youngstedt, PhD, an expert on exercise and insomnia in the Department of Exercise Science at the University of South Carolina. "Other treatments such as cognitive-behavioral therapy are more effective than sleeping pills but difficult and costly to deliver. By contrast, exercise could be a healthy, safe, inexpensive and simple means of improving sleep." *Here's the scientific proof…*

• **Half-mile to the Land of Nod.** Researchers in the Sleep Disorder Center at the University of Arizona studied more than 700 men and women with insomnia and other sleep problems and found that those who slept deepest and longest also exercised—and not necessarily a lot. Even a daily walk of one-third to one-half mile at a normal pace improved sleep!

AFTERNOON SLEEPINESS? GET MORE NOONTIME LIGHT

Nodding out at 3:00 p.m.? Maybe you need a noontime pick-me-up...of light.

New study: Japanese scientists studied 16 people who had typical mid-afternoon sleepiness, dividing them into three groups. One group napped for 20 minutes at 12:45 p.m. One group worked from 12:40 to 1:10 p.m. near windows exposing them to natural, bright light. One group stayed in dim light during that time.

The bright light group had the lowest levels of mid-afternoon sleepiness. "Brief exposure to natural bright light may decrease afternoon sleepiness," say the researchers, in the journal *Sleep*.

What to do: At lunch, find a sunny place to eat or go for a 30-minute walk outdoors.

● **Falling asleep, staying asleep.** Japanese researchers analyzed health data from more than 3,000 people and found that exercising regularly protected people from insomnia.

● **Deeper sleep over 50.** In a study published in the *Journal of the American Medical Association*, researchers from Stanford University asked 43 insomniacs aged 50 to 76 years old to start exercising—brisk walking or low-impact aerobics, for 30 to 40 minutes, four days a week. After four months, an insomnia questionnaire showed that their sleep had improved by 38%—they were falling asleep faster, and sleeping longer without waking up. Meanwhile, another group of older insomniacs who hadn't exercised showed no improvement.

Older adults with sleep complaints can improve sleep quality with regular exercise, say the researchers.

How exercise works: There are many ways exercise can work to beat insomnia, says Dr. Youngstedt. It can reduce anxiety and relieve depression, common causes of insomnia. By raising body temperature, it helps regulate the internal thermostat that plays a big role in whether you fall asleep and stay asleep. And it can normalize circadian rhythms—your body's ability to match its sleep-wake cycle with nature's cycle of night and daylight.

What to do: "Do twenty to thirty minutes of exercise, at least three days a week," says Kathleen Hall, PhD, director of the Stress Institute in Atlanta and author of *A Life in Balance* (AMACOM). To stick with exercise, she recommends varying your routine. "Rent or buy DVDs of new types of exercise, such as Pilates, yoga, tai chi or aerobics." Or if you're bored, "put your treadmill in your television room, jump on for twenty minutes and watch your favorite show at the same time."

Caution: Don't exercise strenuously too close to bedtime, as it can interfere with sleep.

MELATONIN—INSOMNIA RELIEF FOR SENIORS

In the core of your brain is the *pineal gland*, a pea-sized structure that secretes *melatonin*, the hormone that triggers sleepiness. Melatonin levels drop in your twenties and continue to fall as you age. That's one reason why older people are so prone to sleepless nights. And why melatonin supplements can help clear up the problem.

▶ *Breakthrough Study*

French doctors gave either 2 mg a day of extended-release melatonin or a placebo to 170 insomniacs aged 55 and older.

Result: After three weeks, the quality of sleep of those taking melatonin was 27% better than the placebo group, and their morning alertness was 57% better.

Prolonged-release melatonin increases the "restorative value of sleep," in people 55 and older, say the doctors, in the *Journal of Sleep Research*.

What most people don't realize: For melatonin to be maximally effective, you need to take *the right dose* at *the right time*, says Michael Terman, PhD, a professor in the Department of Psychiatry at Columbia University and director of clinical chronobiology at the New York State Psychiatric Institute.

"Melatonin is almost always taken in immediate-release formulations at high levels—hundreds or even thousands of times higher than the pineal gland produces," he explains. These supplements create high blood levels that diminish quickly—not ideal if your goal is seven to eight hours of restful sleep.

Another problem is *when* to take melatonin. "The supplements only work if you take them before the pineal gland starts producing melatonin at night," says Dr. Terman. "If you follow the conventional routine of taking the supplement one-half hour before you want to go to sleep, it may not work, because your pineal gland is already producing melatonin."

What to do: Dr. Terman recommends finding a very low-dose melatonin supplement and taking it about four to five hours before your usual bedtime.

ℹ️ Life Extension sells a 300-microgram (mcg) time-release capsule. You could also purchase a 1 mg melatonin tablet, cut it in quarters, and take one quarter-tablet, says Dr. Terman.

Good news: Taking a small amount of melatonin a few hours before bedtime is not only effective for older people with insomnia, says Dr. Terman. It can also help the millions of insomniacs, old and young, who find themselves wide awake at midnight or 1:00 a.m.- and then struggle to get out of bed and function at 7:00 a.m. in the morning, when it's time to go to work.

SHIFT WORK—MINIMIZE THE DISRUPTION

"Shift workers experience poorer sleep quality, shorter sleep and more difficulty falling asleep and staying asleep than regular day workers," says Dr. Gregg D. Jacob, an insomnia specialist. Now scientists know why.

⫸ *Breakthrough Study*

Researchers in Argentina studied 683 men—437 day workers and 246 workers on rotating shifts. The shift workers had 9% lower blood levels of *serotonin* (5HT), a brain chemical that helps regulate sleep. They also had 18% lower levels of 5HIAA, a serotonin-related body chemical.

Better: If you have to work shifts, ask your supervisor to move your shifts *forward*—for example, from the 11 p.m.–7 a.m. shift, to the 7 a.m.–3 p.m. shift, to the 3 p.m.–11 p.m. shift, et cetera. Dutch researchers at Maastricht University studied more than 700 shift workers and found those with backward-moving shifts had a *three times higher* need for postshift recovery time, and triple the health problems of those with forward-moving shifts.

Also helpful: *Here are other ways to help keep shift work from ruining your sleep, says Dr. Jacobs…*

● **Maintain the same sleep-wake schedule** on each of your days off.

● **Wear sunglasses when leaving work in the morning,** to prevent sunlight from causing your body temperature and alertness to rise (both counterproductive to falling asleep).

● **Don't let anything interrupt your sleep**—light, doorbells, telephones, street noise or people. Use earplugs and an eyeshade, and place rugs on wooden floors to deaden footsteps.

IMAGERY—GUIDE YOURSELF TO DREAMLAND

Want to get some shut-eye? Shut your eyes and imagine you're falling asleep.

⊪▶ *Breakthrough Study*

Brazilian researchers studied 24 insomniacs, teaching 12 of them *imagery rehearsal therapy* —using guided imagery to relax, to shed worries and imagine drifting off to sleep.

"Imagery rehearsal therapy was associated with improvement in insomnia severity, sleep quality, sleep disturbance and worries about sleep," says Dr. Yara Molen, of the Federal University of São Paolo. Total time of sleep increased by 30 minutes, compared with the group not practicing guided imagery.

What to do: Use the guided imagery "induction" on page 393 of this chapter, from Dr. Martin Rossman.

When you get to your "Power Spot," says Dr. Rossman, "imagine yourself sleeping safely through the night and awakening refreshed and energetic."

ℹ You can purchase an audio CD with guided imagery for insomnia—*Natural, Restful Sleep*—at Dr. Rossman's Web site, *www.the healingmind.org*. The Healing Mind, 1341 South Eliseo Drive, Suite 350, Greenbrae, CA 94904; e-mail *info@thehealingmind.org*.

HIGH-GI CARBS— SNOOZE FOOD

The glycemic index (GI) is a measurement nutritionists and doctors use to indicate how quickly carbohydrates turn into blood sugar (glucose)—high-GI carbs such as instant white rice turn into glucose quickly; low-GI carbs such as brown rice, slowly. Health experts say a diet emphasizing low-GI carbs is good for you—helping prevent or slow type 2 diabetes, heart disease and obesity—while too many high-GI carbs are bad.

Surprising: If you have trouble falling asleep at night, you might want to consider eating a dinner that emphasizes fast-digesting, high-GI carbs.

⊪▶ *Breakthrough Study*

Australian researchers at the University of Sydney studied healthy men, feeding them four different ways on four different days.

1. A heaping bowl of jasmine rice and steamed tomatoes, with a glycemic index of 104 (very high), 4 hours before bedtime.
2. The same meal, 1 hour before bedtime.
3. A heaping bowl of long-grain white rice and steamed tomatoes, with a glycemic index of 50 (reasonably low), 4 hours before bedtime.
4. The same meal, 1 hour before bedtime.

Result: When the men ate the high-GI jasmine rice four hours before bedtime, they fell asleep 49% faster than when they ate the low-GI rice four hours before bedtime.

When the men ate the high-GI rice four hours before bedtime, they fell asleep 38% faster than when they ate it one hour before.

In other words, eating the high-GI meal four hours before bedtime was a real snoozer!

"A simple manipulation of food intake can significantly improve sleep onset," say the researchers, in the *American Journal of Clinical Nutrition*. High-GI meals, they add, could be a "convenient, inexpensive and noninvasive therapy for treating difficulty with sleep initiation [falling asleep]."

How it works: Fast-digesting carbohydrates increase blood levels of tryptophan, an amino acid that increases serotonin, a brain chemical that helps regulate sleep.

NIGHT OWLS AREN'T WISE

If you have insomnia and you're a "night owl"—a person who tends to stay up late at night—your symptoms are likely to be worse than those of a "morning person" with insomnia, says Jason C. Ong, PhD, in the Department of Psychiatry and Behavior Sciences at Stanford School of Medicine, in California. He and his colleagues surveyed 312 people with insomnia and found the night owls had the most disturbed sleep habits and the most daytime fatigue. Being a night owl "may perpetuate insomnia," he says. Consider being an earlier bird!

What to do: "Eat low-GI foods throughout the day, but if you have insomnia, enjoy a high-carbohydrate, low-protein, high-glycemic index meal about four hours before bed," says Chin Moi Chow, PhD, who led the study. (Don't follow this advice, she adds, if you have type 2 diabetes, heart disease or are overweight. Stick with low-GI foods—and use exercise to help clear up insomnia. For more on exercise and insomnia, see page 406.)

Other high-GI foods include instant rice and rice cakes; mashed potatoes, baked white potatoes and French fries; white bread and white bagel; watermelon; breakfast cereals, such as Corn Flakes, Rice Krispies and Cheerios; and parsnips and rutabagas.

Preparing jasmine rice: Use 2½ cups of jasmine rice—a fragrant rice with a nutty aroma from Thailand—to three cups of water, instruct the experts at *www.templeofthai.com*, who say the rice is "the center of any Thai meal." Cover the pot with a lid and place over medium to medium-high heat. Bring to a boil. Reduce heat to low. Simmer, covered, for 10 minutes, or until water has evaporated completely. Turn off the burner and allow rice to sit, covered, for five minutes. Serve hot or at room temperature. Serves 2 to 3.

JET LAG—TRICK THOSE TIME ZONES

Jet lag is a drag—on your energy and your mood, on the enjoyment of a vacation or the success of a business trip. And the more time zones you cross, the longer the sleep-disturbing lag, particularly if you're flying east, says Charmane Eastman, PhD, of the Biological Rhythms Research Laboratory in the Psychology Department of Rush University Medical Center in Chicago. You are "lagged" because your circadian rhythms—the inner clocks that align your system with the local light-dark cycle—are lagging behind the cycle at the new location.

Surprising: You can "phase advance" your circadian rhythms to the new time zone before you leave on your trip, says Dr. Eastman.

⫸ *Breakthrough Study*

Several studies by Dr. Eastman and her colleagues show that three techniques can help you phase advance your circadian rhythms for flights going east. (There are complex reasons—the advanced calculus of chronobiology—as to why the technique doesn't work for the western-bound.)

1. Altering the sleep-wake cycle in the direction of the new time zone.

2. Exposure to bright light immediately upon waking, using a light box.

3. Taking a daily supplement of melatonin, the circadian-controlling hormone.

"Our findings are very practical," says Dr. Eastman. "Go to bed one hour earlier each night and wake up about one hour earlier each morning, always staying in bed at least eight hours. So, for example, if you typically go to bed at 11:00 p.m. and wake up at 7:00 a.m., you would go to bed at 10:00 p.m. and wake up at 6:00 a.m. the first night of the program, at 9:00 p.m. and 5:00 a.m. the second night, et cetera.

"Every morning, as soon as you wake up, use a light box for one to two hours.

"And take 0.5 milligrams of melatonin every evening.

"The more days you follow this procedure, the less jet lag you will have on landing—and the sooner you will adjust and feel *no* jet lag. If you do this for the number of days equivalent to the number of time zones you will cross, you will be *completely* adjusted to the new time zone *before* you fly."

Don't want to go to all that trouble to prevent jet lag? "Even following the schedule for two or three days before flying will reduce the jet lag you experience upon arrival at your destination," she says.

☀ The Center for Environmental Therapeutics (*www.cet.org*) sells a light box proven safe and effective in studies to adjust circadian rhythms to treat sleep disorders, the Day-Light, from Uplift Technologies. You can order the light box at the CET site, or call the company directly at 800-387-0896 x105.

For more information on the use of a light box, see page 99 in Chapter 5, "Depression."

FATIGUE

"During my years of practicing medicine, I've heard more complaints about fatigue than any other condition," says Leigh Erin Connealy, MD, medical director of the South Coast Medical Center for New Medicine, in Tustin, CA. "So many patients have told me that they have been to doctor after doctor, only to be told there's nothing wrong with them—and nothing to do for fatigue but try to 'get a little more sleep' or 'take it easy.' "

But you *can* do something about fatigue, says Dr. Connealy. You can maximize energy-giving whole foods in your diet, such as fruits, vegetables, lean proteins and good fats from nuts. You can spend some time every day in an enjoyable physical activity such as walking, even if it's for only 10 or 15 minutes. You can stop and take a deep breath. You can spend time in rejuvenating natural environments, such as parks. You can get adequate rest at night.

And, she says, you can take nutritional supplements that nourish the *mitochondria*, the energy-generating structures in every cell.

You might want to start with Coenzyme Q10.

COENZYME Q10—THE CELLULAR ENERGIZER

"The mitochondria are the energy factories of the cell, the system that keeps all the other systems running," says Erika Schwartz, MD, coauthor of *Natural Energy* (Putnam). "Most cells contain from five hundred to two thousand mitochondria—and every organ system contains millions. In order for the mitochondria to make energy, they need raw materials—and one of those materials is Coenzyme Q10, a biochemical sparkplug found in every cell in the body. Without enough CoQ10, your mitochondria can't make energy."

And extra CoQ10, might be the natural energy boost mitochondria needs.

▪▪▪▶ *Breakthrough Study*

As part of a government-sponsored "Overcome Fatigue" research program, Japanese scientists studied 17 healthy people, giving them either supplements of Coenzyme Q10 or a placebo for eight days. After eight days, the researchers asked the study participants to pedal a stationary bicycle for two hours, followed by a four-hour rest, and then two more hours of pedaling—240 minutes of pedaling in all. After 30 minutes and 210 minutes of pedaling, the bicyclists were asked to pedal as fast as they could—at "maximum velocity"—for 10 seconds.

Result: Researchers compared the maximum velocity levels of the CoQ10 and the placebo group at 30 minutes and at 210 minutes. Compared with the placebo group, those taking CoQ10 achieved higher levels of maximum velocity during the 210-minute session. In other words, they were less worn out by hours of biking.

They also recovered faster after each session of maximum velocity, returning more quickly to their normal, sustained pace of cycling than did the placebo group.

And when asked to quantify how fatigued they felt after 240 minutes of cycling, those taking CoQ10 were much less fatigued than the placebo group.

Supplements of Coenzyme Q10 lessened fatigue and improved physical performance, say the researchers, in the journal *Nutrition*.

Suggested intake: The researchers gave the study participants either 100 or 300 mg of CoQ10—but only the 300-mg dose worked to block fatigue. However, everyday doses don't have to be that high, say energy experts.

For those who are fatigued and stressed out, Dr. Schwartz recommends 180 mg of CoQ10 a day, in three divided doses—60 mg with breakfast, 60 mg with lunch, and 60 mg with dinner.

Jacob Teitelbaum, MD, author of *From Fatigued to Fantastic!* (Avery), recommends 100 to 200 mg of CoQ10 a day. To improve absorption, he says to take the supplement with a meal that contains oil, such as butter, olive oil or salad dressing.

ⓘ "CoQ10 is available in many different forms," says Dr. Schwartz. She recommends soft gel capsules for maximum absorption.

EXERCISE—LOW INTENSITY, HIGH RESULTS

"Too often we believe that exercise will leave us worn out—especially when we are already feeling fatigued," says Tim Puetz, PhD, at the Exercise Psychology Laboratory of the University of Georgia. Instead, believe in exercise.

▸ Breakthrough Study

Dr. Puetz and his colleagues studied 36 healthy but persistently fatigued people, dividing them into three activity groups...

1. Twenty minutes of low-intensity exercise on an exercise bike, three days a week, for six weeks. (Low-intensity exercise is like a leisurely, easy walk.)

2. Twenty minutes of moderate-intensity exercise on an exercise bike, three days a week, for six weeks. (Moderate-intensity exercise is like a fast-paced walk, with hills.)

3. No exercise.

Result: The *low*-intensity exercisers decreased their fatigue levels by 65%—compared to 49% for the *moderate*-intensity group! (The nonexercisers were still fatigued at the end of the study.)

Why was low intensity better than moderate intensity? "It could be that moderate-intensity exercise is too much for people who are already fatigued," says Patrick O'Connor, PhD, who helped conduct the study.

"A lot of people are stressed and not sleeping enough," he continues. "Exercise—even low-intensity exercise—is a way for people to feel more energetic."

Why it works: It wasn't fitness. In the study, improvements in energy and fatigue *weren't* matched to increases in aerobic fitness—to extra heart, lung and/or muscle power.

Exercise probably acts directly on the brain and central nervous system to relieve fatigue and increase energy, says Dr. Puetz. "What this means is that in every workout, a single step is not just a step closer to a healthier, less fatigued body, but to a healthier mind."

What to do: Walk at an easy, leisurely pace for at least 20 minutes, three times a week.

Important: Exercise can also *prevent* fatigue. An analysis by Dr. Puetz of 12 studies on exercise and fatigue showed that active people were 39% less likely to be fatigued than inactive people.

GINSENG FOR MENTAL FATIGUE

Fatigue is physical *and* mental—you sit at your desk and work for hours, and your mind eventually wants to call it quits. (Heck, even a half hour of doing taxes can wilt your neurons.) The herb ginseng can help.

▌▌▌▶ *Breakthrough Study*

Researchers in the Human Cognitive Neuroscience Unit at Northumbria University in England asked 30 people to take a 10-minute test of challenging mental exercises—six times in a row! That same day, they also took either 200 or 400 mg of Asian ginseng, or a placebo.

Result: Those taking the 200-mg dose did better on the mental test *and* had significantly reduced mental fatigue, compared with those taking 400 mg or the placebo.

"Asian ginseng can improve performance and reduce feelings of mental fatigue during sustained mental activity," say the researchers, in the *Journal of Psychopharmacology.*

Suggested intake: The effective dose in the study was 200 mg a day.

ℹ️ Not all ginseng products are reliable, says Amanda McQuade Crawford, a medical herbalist based in Los Angeles. For purity and effectiveness, she recommends ginseng from Enzymatic Therapies. It is available in retail stores and on-line.

Caution: If you're taking blood-thinning drugs such as warfarin, talk with your physician before taking ginseng, which may decrease the power of these medications, says Crawford.

ARE YOU TIRED, FATIGUED OR EXHAUSTED?

There's a difference, says Karin Olson, PhD, a researcher from the University of Alberta.

Dr. Olson studied fatigue in different groups of people—shift workers, long distance runners, depressed people, those with chronic fatigue syndrome, people being currently treated for cancer and cancer survivors. "The kind of fatigue experienced by people with cancer is different from the feeling that you or I have at the end of a busy week," she says. To help clarify the different types of fatigue and what they mean for health, she created three definitions and descriptions of energy levels.

1. **Tired:** You still have a fair bit of energy. You sometimes feel forgetful and impatient. You experience heaviness or weakness in your muscles after work, but it's cleared up by rest.

2. **Fatigue:** You're anxious, have difficulty concentrating, difficulty sleeping, less physical stamina than you used to and avoid social situations you once enjoyed.

3. **Exhaustion:** Your loss of energy is sudden. You're confused, almost as if you have dementia. You're emotionally numb. You have difficulty staying awake. Your withdrawal from social activities is complete.

"If you have a sudden onset of fatigue that's not normal for you, see a doctor," says Dr. Olson. Exhaustion is a medical condition requiring immediate attention.

413

CARNITINE—AN ENERGY PILL FOR 100-YEAR-OLDS

The good news is you've lived a century. The bad news is you're feeling a little worn out. (Who can blame you?) Try taking the supplement L-carnitine.

New study: Italian researchers in the aptly named Department of Senescence at the University of Catania in Italy divided 66 centenarians "with onset of fatigue after even slight physical activity" into two groups. One group received daily 2-gram supplements of L-carnitine, and the other group, a placebo.

Result: Those who took the nutrient had five times less physical fatigue, three times less mental fatigue and twelve times less overall "severity of fatigue," say the researchers.

Why it works: Carnitine ushers fatty acids into the mitochondria, the energy-producing structures in every cell, explains Dr. Erika Schwartz. "Without those fatty acids, energy production will stall. It's as simple as that."

Dr. Schwartz recommends carnitine supplements (in the form of either L-carnitine or acetyl-L-carnitine) not only for centenarians but also for anybody who is fatigued. "I have seen the positive effect of carnitine supplementation in hundreds of patients who look and feel reinvigorated within weeks of starting." If you wake up tired every morning, she suggests 2.5 grams a day—1 gram with breakfast, 500 mg with lunch and 1 gram with dinner.

❶ L-carnitine and acetyl-L-carnitine supplements are widely available. "Stick to reputable, well-known brands," says Dr. Schwartz.

D-RIBOSE—A MIRACLE FOR CHRONIC FATIGUE

"Chronic fatigue syndrome is a group of symptoms associated with severe, almost unrelenting fatigue," explains Dr. Jacob Teitelbaum.

Not only are you fatigued all the time. Your sleep is lousy. You ache all over. Your short-term memory is tattered. Your concentration is wandering around lost somewhere east of your cerebellum. When you try to exercise, you feel even worse. And you're one among an estimated six million Americans with the same problem (which may be related to a similar condition, *fibromyalgia*).

Chronic fatigue syndrome (CFS) is a complex disease that requires informed medical care, says Dr. Teitelbaum. But his new research shows that one, simple, self-care action—taking the nutritional supplement D-ribose—can help reduce the fatigue and other symptoms of CFS. Almost immediately.

▶ *Breakthrough Study*

D-ribose is a sugar used by the mitochondria—the tiny energy factory in every cell—to make ATP (adenosine triphosphate), the fundamental fuel that powers the body. Studies show that D-ribose supplements help people with heart disease function better and exercise more, and athletes recover faster after intense exercise. So Dr. Teitelbaum and his colleagues decided to see if it could boost energy levels in 36 people with chronic fatigue syndrome (CFS) and fibromyalgia—people who had been wearied by the disease for an average of seven years. They took 5 grams of D-ribose, three times a day, every day, for 25 days.

Result: Sixty-six percent—23 of the 36 people with CFS or fibromyalgia taking the supplement—had more energy, better sleep, more mental alertness, less pain and more well-being, says Dr. Teitelbaum. On average, the increase in energy was 45%.

"This is very dramatic for a single nutrient," says Dr. Teitelbaum.

"Several of the patients participating in the study contacted me to tell me about the relief they found with ribose therapy. They talked about the profound joy they felt when they were able to begin living normal, active lives, sometimes after years of fatigue, pain and suffering."

"One patient, an elementary teacher, wrote, 'I had so much fatigue and pain I thought I was going to have to quit teaching. When I take ribose, I feel like a huge weight is being lifted from my chest, and I'm ready to take on those kids again!' "

Suggested intake: 5 grams (1 teaspoon), three times a day.

ⓘ The study used powdered D-ribose from Valen Labs. *Its patented D-ribose formulation, Bioenergy Ribose, is available in many brands, including...*

• **Corvalen** from Bioenergy Life Science, Inc. (866-267-8253 or visit *www.bioenergy.com*)

• **NSI Bioenergy Ribose** from Nutraceutical Sciences Institute (available in retail and on-line stores)

• **Best D-Ribose** from Doctor's Best (available in retail and on-line stores)

• **PoweRibose** from Dexter Sport Science (available in retail and on-line stores)

• **Bioenergy Ribose** from NutraBio.com (call 888-688-7224 or visit *www.nutrabio.com*)

BURNOUT—WHEN YOU FEEL "WORKED OVER"

Do one or more of the following sentences sound like you...

• **You're irritable and snap at people at work.**

• **You're bored and frustrated at work,** and find it hard to concentrate.

• **You have trouble sleeping** because you're worried about work.

• **Your performance at work is subpar**—in fact, your attitude is "Why bother?"

• **You don't have much to look forward to at work,** and you don't like going.

Those are all descriptions of *burnout*, says Dr. Beverly Potter. "Burnout is a motivational

CHOCOLATE—THE PERFECT PICK-ME-UP FOR CFS

The severe fatigue of chronic fatigue syndrome (CFS) might be reduced by *chocolate*. Or so say newly converted researchers from the University of Hull in England...

New study: They studied 10 people with CFS, feeding five people dark chocolate for eight weeks, while the other five ate milk chocolate dyed brown. While eating dark chocolate, fatigue levels fell by 23%. While eating the sugary milk chocolate, they rose by 12%.

Remarkably, two people who were so fatigued they couldn't work were able to return to work after starting to eat dark chocolate, say the researchers—and they've continued to eat it since!

How it works: Dark chocolate contains high levels of *polyphenols*, explains Steve Atkin, MD, one of the researchers who conducted the study. These natural substances increase several crucial brain chemicals, including serotonin, which helps regulate energy levels.

What to do: To get a hefty dose of polyphenols, look for dark chocolate containing 70 to 85% cocoa solids, which supplies 150 calories and a minimum amount of fat and sugar in 1 ounce of chocolate, says Roger Corder, MD, an expert in polyphenols and health.

Suggested intake: The study participants ate 45 grams a day of dark chocolate—about 1½ ounces.

ⓘ Widely available brands of dark chocolate include Scharffen Berger, Dagoba, Green & Black's and many others.

problem where enthusiasm dies and working becomes meaningless drudgery."

If you're a service provider who constantly has to deliver compassion, such as a nurse or counselor…if you make life-and-death decisions, such as airplane pilot or heart surgeon…if you're a manager, under pressure to lead and succeed…if you work under demanding time schedules, such as a journalist…if your job requires exacting attention, such as an air traffic controller…or detail work, such as a proofreader…you can burn out.

But no one is immune from job burnout, says Dr. Potter. "Any person, in any profession, at any level can become a candidate for job burnout."

Fortunately, psychologists who specialize in work have figured out a few ways to prevent and treat the problem.

⫸ *Breakthrough Studies*

Take control. Researchers from the Department of Psychology at Pennsylvania State University studied 196 workers and found that more autonomy on your job—personal control over what you do and how you have to behave—is key to preventing the "emotional exhaustion" of burnout. They report their findings in the journal *Applied Psychology*.

Lack of control might mean too much work, too little opportunity to manage your own assignments, too little freedom of movement or lack of career mobility, says Barbara Bailey Reinhold, PhD, author of *Toxic Work: How to Overcome Stress, Overload, and Burnout and Revitalize Your Career* (Plume).

"More control means more responsibility," she says. "Ask yourself if you're willing to take that on." If the answer is yes, strategize about how to do it. *You could…*

1. Set new performance goals with your manager and ask for necessary training.

2. Volunteer for new projects and negotiate for the desired amount of autonomy.

3. Suggest task forces and work teams to get jobs done more collaboratively.

"Think about your situation, and then talk about it with a few well-chosen people," says Dr. Reinhold. "The only thing *not* to do is sit by, feeling controlled, eroding your mental and physical health."

● **Maximize your vacation.** Vacations help you relax and refresh. But Austrian scientists who studied 109 white-collar employees discovered that some vacations were *more* effective in reducing work strain. *They included…*

- plenty of free time for yourself
- warmer and sunnier locations
- a lot of exercise during the vacation
- plenty of sleep
- making new friends.

17

WOMEN'S HEALTH
IT'S TIME TO TAKE CARE OF YOURSELF

Talk to women doctors who emphasize drug-free healing—to natural-minded MDs, naturopathic doctors and doctors of oriental medicine—and they're seemingly unanimous about the most important step a woman can take to get healthy and stay healthy. And it's *not* taking a vitamin, an herb or a walk. No, it's taking the step toward trust—in you!

"Each woman needs to determine for herself the best path to reaching health and wholeness," says Misha Cohen, OMD, LAc, a doctor of oriental medicine, a research specialist in integrative medicine at the Institute for Health and Aging at the University of California and coauthor of *The Chinese Way to Healing: Many Paths to Wholeness* (Perigee). "She needs to be informed about her options by caring and competent providers—and then she needs to choose the approach that is best for *her*."

"Women need to be their own 'primary-care givers,'" says Holly Lucille, ND, RN, a nationally recognized naturopathic physician, in private practice at Healing Within Health Care in Los Angeles and author of *Creating and Maintaining Balance: A Woman's Guide to Safe, Natural Hormone Health* (Impakt Health). "She

needs to remember that the doctor is working *for* her, and not give away her power to the medical establishment.

"Often, when I'm lecturing, a woman will raise her hand and say something like, 'I'm on Fosamax for my bones, what do you think about it?' And I reply, 'What do *you* think about it? Why are you on it?' And the woman says, 'Because my doctor told me to take it.' This is a dismissal by a woman of her own power. If doctors 'knew best,' we'd all be in lot better health than we are!"

"Most women are trained to look outside themselves for answers," says Christiane Northrup, MD, author of *Women's Bodies, Women's Wisdom* (Bantam). "We live in a society in which so-called experts challenge and subordinate our own judgment—in which our ability to heal or stay healthy without constant outside help is not honored, encouraged or even recognized. In the end, only the connection with your inner guidance and emotions is reliable."

And, say these doctors, as you connect to your inner guidance, also connect with the natural wisdom of your *body*.

"In general, it's always best to treat any health problem with the most natural method—because that's the method that promotes the body's natural capacity to heal," says Judith Stanton, MD, at the California Healing Institute, in Albany, CA.

And while these doctors agree that medications are often necessary to heal "acute" situations, such as intense pain or a raging infection, they think that drugs (and surgery) are far from ideal for long-term healing.

"Drugs or surgery may provide symptomatic relief, but they do not stimulate a cure, and they can make the situation worse," says Dr. Lucille. "On the other hand, natural remedies such as nutritional supplements, herbs and exercise stimulate healing from the inside out. They empower a woman to take responsibility for her health."

In this chapter, you'll find a range of suggestions and ideas about drug-free remedies that you can choose in your pursuit of health and healing.

MENOPAUSAL SYMPTOMS

In July 2002, the results from the Women's Health Initiative (WHI)—the largest study ever conducted on the effects of hormone replacement therapy (HRT)—changed forever the way women think about menopause.

The multimillion dollar, 15-year project—sponsored by the National Institutes of Health and involving more than 16,000 healthy, postmenopausal women—was halted early when it became clear that women taking HRT faced an increased risk of breast cancer and other problems.

The study also found that HRT—taking a daily dose of synthetic estrogen and progesterone, the sexual and reproductive hormones that dwindle with menopause—does *not* prevent heart disease as doctors had thought but actually *increases* the risk for heart attack and stroke.

Overall, the study found that HRT increases the risk of breast cancer by 26%...coronary heart disease by 29%...and stroke by 41% percent. It also *doubled* the risk of an artery-clogging blood clot.

Latest development: Increased risk of cancer—both breast and lung cancer—persisted for two years *after* women stopped HRT, surprising scientists.

Problem: Forty-two million American women are menopausal, with an estimated 1.5 million more reaching menopause every year—and about 85% of them experience symptoms such as hot flashes, night sweats, vaginal dryness, painful intercourse, poor sleep and mood swings.

HRT can ease those symptoms. HRT can be deadly. Are there any other options? Quite a few. But the most effective natural option is an herb you may have heard doesn't work...

THE TRUTH ABOUT BLACK COHOSH AND MENOPAUSE

Wrong *form* of black cohosh. Wrong *dose* of black cohosh.

Unfortunately, that's what was used in a major study sponsored by the National Institutes of Health to find out if the herb black cohosh (*Cimicifuga racemosa*) really works to reduce hot flashes and night sweats in menopausal women, says Francis Brinker, ND, a naturopathic doctor, clinical assistant professor at the Program of Integrative Medicine at the University of Arizona College of Medicine and author of *Complex Herbs—Complete Medicines* (Eclectic Medical Publishers).

The one-year study, involving 351 women who were perimenopausal (approaching menopause, with at least one missed period in the past 12 months) or menopausal (no menstrual cycle in the past 12 months), concluded "Black cohosh…shows little potential as an important therapy for relief" of hot flashes and night sweats.

But, says Dr. Brinker, rather than using the extract of black cohosh proven effective in dozens of other studies, the researchers used an entirely different type of extract (much higher in ethanol), at a 20 to 40 times higher dosage.

"When you increase ethanol in an herbal extract, you increase the amount of resinous components from the herb and decrease the amount of water-soluble components," says Dr. Brinker. "Well, the active components of black cohosh are not known. So by changing the composition of the extract you could easily change the herb's activity in the body—and its effectiveness.

"As for dosage—you would think that a dosage that was twenty to forty times higher would be *more* effective, but that's not how pharmacology works. Sometimes a small dose works, but a larger dose has the *opposite* effect.

"The form of an herb matters and the dose of an herb matters—and sometimes you can give the wrong form and the wrong dose and make the herb ineffective."

What form of black cohosh *is* effective?

Other studies provide the answer, says Dr. Brinker.

▌▌▌➡ *Breakthrough Studies*

Recently, Chinese doctors studied 244 menopausal women for three months, giving them a black cohosh extract or a tibolone, a synthetic steroid with estrogen-like effects. (Tibolone is used in 70 countries to treat the symptoms of menopause, but has not been approved by the FDA for use in the United States.)

After three months, the women taking the black cohosh extract had an average 68% drop in their "Kupperman Score," a standard measurement of menopausal symptoms.

That means after taking black cohosh extract they had fewer and less intense hot flashes…fewer and less intense night sweats… slept better…were less nervous and irritable… were less depressed…and their concentration improved.

Tibolone produced similar benefits. But it also produced vaginal bleeding, breast pain and abdominal pain.

"The benefit-risk balance for black cohosh extract was significantly superior to tibolone," say the researchers.

"The efficacy of black cohosh extract is as good as tibolone for the treatment of menopausal complaints, even for moderate to severe symptoms. Black cohosh extract is clearly superior regarding the safety profile.

"Black cohosh is an excellent option for treatment of menopausal complaints," they conclude.

ℹ️ This study uses the form and dosage of black cohosh extract that, as Dr. Brinker points out, has been tested successfully in more than 90 scientific studies—Remifemin, from Enzymatic Therapy.

Suggested intake: Follow the dosage recommendation on the label—one tablet in the morning and one in evening, with water.

Important: There are reports from Australia that black cohosh may harm the liver, and both the European Medicines Agency and Health Canada issued warnings about a link between the herb and liver damage. Should you be concerned?

There is "no compelling case for concern or for not using this herb," says Tori Hudson, ND, a professor of gynecology at the National College of Naturopathic Medicine, director of A Woman's Time clinic in Portland, OR, and author of *The Women's Encyclopedia of Natural Medicine* (McGraw-Hill).

In a recent review of the safety and effectiveness of black cohosh in the journal *Alternative and Complementary Therapy*, Dr. Hudson points out that reports linking black cohosh and liver problems have serious flaws; and that the government's National Institutes of Health (NIH) concluded that there was "inadequate evidence" to link black cohosh to liver problems. (The NIH also said that there is "no competent evidence" to support concerns about the safety of black cohosh for women with breast cancer, says Dr. Hudson.)

There is only one caution for people taking black cohosh, says Dr. Hudson—if you're taking the chemotherapeutic drug *cisplatin*, don't take the herb. An animal study shows that black cohosh might shield cancer cells from the drug.

"Standardized extracts of black cohosh continue to be one of the most reliable herbal approaches to treating a wide array of perimenopausal and menopausal symptoms," says Dr. Hudson. "You should expect results within four weeks. In my experience, approximately eighty-five percent of women will gain a benefit, and maybe fifty percent will experience complete amelioration of their hot flashes and night sweats."

She also points out that you can use the herb safely and effectively *with* hormonal therapy, perhaps allowing your doctor to lower the dose of HRT.

For menopausal women, "black cohosh is our most well-researched and important botanical therapy to date," she concludes.

Also helpful for mood changes: Researchers in the Department of Obstetrics and Gynecology at the College of Medicine of the University of Illinois reviewed studies testing various herbs and herbal combinations for sadness, depression and anxiety in perimenopausal and postmenopausal women. The most effective herbs —black cohosh and St. John's wort.

THE HERB THAT RESETS YOUR THERMOSTAT

Scientists don't know exactly what causes hot flashes, the intense burst of body heat that regularly and uncomfortably roasts eight out of 10 menopausal women.

But they do know that ebbing estrogen plays a role, perhaps by lowering levels of key neurotransmitters, brain chemicals that (among many other duties) control the body's thermostat.

Black cohosh may help your brain reset your body's temperature at "normal."

New thinking: For many years, doctors theorized that black cohosh extract reduced hot flashes because it contained *phytoestrogens*—estrogen-like plant compounds. But black cohosh "does not appear to be estrogenic whatsoever," say researchers at the University of Illinois in Chicago, who analyzed the estrogenic properties of the herb.

Now, that same team of researchers, led by Z. Jim Wang, PhD, has discovered the way that black cohosh might work. *Dr. Wang explains…*

Your brain has opiate receptors—chemical sensors that respond to opiates such as morphine and endorphins. When the opiates attach to their receptors, they trigger key brain functions, such as the regulation of pain, appetite and body temperature.

"We found that elements in black cohosh extract bind to the 'mu' opiate receptor," says Dr. Wang. "This particular opiate receptor system affects several aspects of female reproductive neuroendocrinology, such as the levels of sex hormones and neurotransmitters that are important for temperature regulation."

In other words, black cohosh might work in your brain to correct the drop in neurotransmitters that disrupts your personal thermostat. Cool!

☀ To learn more about Remifemin and purchase the product, visit the Web site, *www.remifemin.com*. The site also includes a "Where to Buy" feature to locate stores that sell Remifemin. Remifemin, Enzymatic Therapy, Inc., 825 Challenger Drive, Green Bay, WI 54311 (800-783-2286 or fax 920-469-4444); e-mail *michele@remifemin.com*.

To find more black cohosh supplements with the formulations used in clinical studies showing the herb's effectiveness, and also herbal supplements containing both black cohosh and St. John's wort (Woman's Passage Menopause Support), see the Web site, *www.vitanica.com*. Vitanica, PO Box 1285, Sherwood, OR 97140 (800-572-4712, 503-692-5085 or fax 503-692-5685); e-mail *inquiries@vitanica.com*.

WALK AWAY FROM POSTMENOPAUSAL STRESS

For many women, menopause magnifies emotional turmoil and mood swings—the sense of feeling stressed intensifies…anxiety heightens …and sad moods deepen.

Exercise might help you ride out (or walk out) the hormonal storm.

⫸ *Breakthrough Studies*

For eight years, researchers at Temple University studied 380 women living in Philadelphia; their average age was 42 when the study began. Every two years, the women reported their level of physical activity. And about every 10 months, they reported their level of stress, anxiety and depression.

After eight years, 20% of the women were menopausal (no periods), and 18% were perimenopausal (intermittent periods).

And at the end of the study, the researchers categorized the women into three levels of physical activity…

1. The top-level exercisers, who walked at a moderately fast pace (four miles an hour, or one mile every 15 minutes) for at least 90 minutes, five days a week.
2. The mid-level exercisers, who walked at a moderately fast pace for 40 minutes, five days a week.
3. The low-level exercisers, who walked 15 minutes, about five days a week.

• **Less stress, anxiety and depression.** Among the menopausal women, those who exercised the *most* had the *lowest* levels of perceived stress, anxiety and depression. On the other hand, those who exercised the *least* had the *highest* levels of perceived stress, anxiety and depression.

"Physical activity can help throughout the menopause transition and afterward," says Deborah B. Nelson, PhD, the study leader. "If you stick to a moderate-paced walking schedule, it can lower the risk of stress, anxiety and depression. It is one way for aging women to stay mentally healthy."

• **Fewer hot flashes and night sweats.** In another study, researchers at Pennsylvania State University looked at 164 sedentary postmenopausal women (average age, 49). Compared with women who didn't exercise, those who started walking regularly (30 minutes, three times a week) or attending yoga class (90 minutes, twice a week) not only had more positive moods but also fewer hot flashes and night sweats.

"Fitness could be one way to reduce menopausal symptoms," says Steriani Elavsky, PhD, who led the study.

• **Lower risk of heart disease and stroke.** "Regular physical exercise is a good way to not only decrease postmenopausal symptoms but also to reduce the risk of cardiovascular disease, the leading cause of death of American women," says Michael Brown, PhD, of Temple University.

He came to that conclusion after studying 48 nonexercising postmenopausal women, 21 who were on hormone replacement therapy (HRT) and 27 who weren't. After exercising three times a week for six months, the women had an 11 to 18% drop in the level of a bio-chemical that signals *oxidative stress*—the interior rust that corrodes arteries and is a major risk factor for heart disease and stroke.

"Exercise was able to reduce oxidative stress levels in these women, regardless of whether or not they were using estrogen replacement," says Dr. Brown. "Given the controversy with hormone replacement therapy, postmenopausal women can now use aerobic exercise to lower chemical stress levels, thus reducing another risk factor for chronic disease."

What to do: "No one is too old to begin an exercise program," says Dr. Brown. "But it is imperative to consult your physician first. And

CAN BEES TAKE THE STING OUT OF MENOPAUSE?

To turn an everyday infant into a queen, worker bees feed it nonstop helpings of a food called *royal jelly*.

Bee pollen is, of course, the breakfast, lunch and dinner of far-flying, hardworking bees.

Perga is "bee bread," a fermented mixture of pollen and honey that the industrious insects munch on in the hive.

Combined in one supplement, these bee products have generated some buzz about menopause relief...

New study: Researchers in Bulgaria studied 55 healthy women who had recently become menopausal women, with moderate to severe symptoms; they asked them to take a supplement containing the bee products.

After three months, the women had a 62% drop in their Kupperman Score (see page 419)—they had fewer and less intense hot flashes, fewer and less intense night sweats, they slept better, were less nervous and irritable, were less depressed and their concentration improved.

"The sixteen-point decrease in the Kupperman Score is especially impressive," says Nikolai Manassiev, MD, a study researcher. "This is similar to the ten- to nineteen-point decrease that has been reported to occur with estrogen patches and gels."

Why it works: The supplement is rich in *flavonoids* and *lignans*, two *phytoestrogens*—

plant compounds with a chemical structure similar to estrogen. But while the phytoestrogens bind to the estrogen receptor—helping to protect bones, heart and brain—they also *block* the body's own hormone, helping decrease the risk of cancer, say scientists who have studied the supplement.

It is also a concentrated source of amino acids, the building blocks of protein, which help nourish and regenerate cells, and stimulate the secretion of growth hormone, which can help control hot flashes, say the scientists. And it contains phytosterols, plant compounds similar to cholesterol, which help synthesize hormones. And a rich source of enzymes, compounds that spark biochemical reactions.

ℹ️ The researchers studied the product *Melbrosia*.

Suggested intake: The women took two capsules a day for two weeks, and one capsule a day for the next 10 weeks.

The manufacturer's scientific advisers recommend taking three capsules a day for the first 10 days, two capsules a day for the next 10 days, and one capsule a day thereafter. Take the capsules at mealtime, with a glass of water.

☀️ Manufactured in Austria by Melbrosin, Melbrosia is widely available in the United States. Order on-line at *www.melbrosin.at* or for questions, e-mail *office@melbrosin.at*.

Caution: If you have a pollen allergy, don't take Melbrosia.

it is important to start slow and build your program to your comfort level."

For a gradual walking program, see page 355 in Chapter 14, "Overweight."

BIO-IDENTICAL HORMONES— ARE THEY SAFER?

Suzanne Somers takes them—and says they turn menopause into the "sexy years." A doctor's book claims they're a "miracle" for menopause. Another physician says it will turn you into a "Natural Superwoman." What's behind all that ballyhoo?

Bio-identical hormones.

One hormone that is *not* "bio-identical" is the estrogen in the estrogen replacement (Premarin) that's been on the market for more than 30 years—it's derived from the urine of pregnant mares.

But when the Women's Health Initiative study showed that hormone replacement therapy (HRT) with "conjugated equine estrogens" and synthetic progesterone increased the risk of heart disease, stroke and breast cancer, many women started looking for alternatives to reduce the symptoms of menopause.

"Bio-identical hormone replacement therapy [BHRT] is one treatment that is currently gaining interest and popularity among both consumers and health care practitioners," says Jessica J. Curcio, ND, in the Women's Integrative Medicine Department, at the Southwest College of Naturopathic Medicine, in Tempe, AZ.

BHRT uses synthetically created versions of *human* estrogens—a combination of *estriol* (a hormone that is elevated during pregnancy), along with *estradiol* or *estrone*. A bio-identical form of progesterone is sometimes included.

And many women do consider them safe. In one survey, 71% said that BHRT have fewer risks than HRT—or no risks at all. And 62%

said they were just as or more effective than HRT for managing menopausal symptoms.

Studies show BHRT *can* work just like HRT to reduce hot flashes, improve mood and ease vaginal dryness. *But they may not be any safer...*

Red flag: "The current data available on estriol, the major hormone component in BHRT, does not demonstrate that BHRT is safer than traditional HRT with regard to cardiovascular risks," says Dr. Curcio, in the medical journal *Treatments in Endocrinology.*

She points to a study showing that 61% more women taking estriol had increased levels of C-reactive protein, compared with women taking a placebo. C-reactive protein is an immune component linked to the artery-clogging blood clots and ruptured arterial plaque that can cause a heart attack or stroke. "It has been identified as an independent risk factor for cardiovascular disease in postmenopausal women," says Dr. Curcio.

Recommendation: "With the results from the WHI trial, caution is warranted regarding the oral use of estradiol," she says.

In other words, both HRT and BHRT might put your heart at risk. Consider that risk when discussing BHRT with your doctor.

HOMEOPATHY FOR HOT FLASHES

Hundreds of women were happier—in France and Italy, in Morocco and Tunisia, in Poland and Bulgaria, in Portugal and Brazil. Why?

They were having fewer hot flashes. Their hot flashes were less intense and bothersome. In fact, many of them were *cured* of hot flashes.

And they weren't taking risky hormones. Instead, they took a homeopathic preparation.

IIII▶ *Breakthrough Study*

"Hot flashes are sudden sensations of intense heat, mainly affecting the upper part of the body, and lasting for one to five minutes on average," says Marie-France Bordet, MD, of France. "They may be accompanied by facial redness, perspiration that is sometimes heavy, heart palpitations, anxiety, irritability and night sweating."

HRT is the main medical treatment for hot flashes, but drug-caused disease is a "major issue," she says. Her proposed alternative is to treat hot flashes with homeopathy.

Dr. Bordet and a team of French researchers looked at five months of records from 99 doctors in eight countries, all of whom included homeopathy among their treatment options. During those five months, the doctors used homeopathy to treat 438 women with menopausal symptoms.

Result: "At the first visit, eighty-nine percent of patients suffered from daily hot flashes," says Dr. Bordet. "This percentage was reduced to thirty-nine percent by the final visit."

The patients also rated their daily discomfort from menopausal symptoms—it fell by an average of 59%. And sleep disturbances fell by an average of 61%.

The results, say the researchers, "suggest that homeopathic treatment is effective for hot flashes."

How homeopathy works: "Homeopathic medicine is a natural pharmaceutical science," says Dana Ullman, MPH, a homeopath in Berkeley, CA, author of *The Homeopathic Revolution* (North Atlantic) and other books on homeopathy, and founder and director of the Homeopathic Educational Services, *www. homeopathic.com.*

"The homeopathic practitioner seeks to find a substance that in large doses would cause similar symptoms to those the sick person is experiencing. When the match is made, the substance is then given in very small, safe doses, often with dramatic effects." He compares the process (known to homeopaths as the "law of similars") to the use of small amounts of infection-causing substances in vaccines, and to the use of very small doses of allergens to cure allergies.

ⓘ The five homeopathic medicines that were the most effective in relieving hot flashes...

Lachesis mutus, 9c (the number indicates concentration)

Belladonna, 15c

Sepia officinalis, 9c

Sulphur, 9c

Sanguinaria canadensis, 15c

Homeopathic medicines are widely available from health stores and the Internet.

☀ To find a homeopathic practitioner near you, visit the Web site of the North American Society of Homeopaths (NASH), *www.homeo pathy.org*, which includes an extensive state-by-state registry of members certified by NASH.

NASH, PO Box 450039, Sunrise, FL 33345-0039 (206-720-7000 or fax 208-248-1942); e-mail *NashInfo@homeopathy.org.* In Canada, contact NASH, 9 Bantry Avenue, Richmond Hill, ONT L4B 4J4 (905-886-1060).

RECHARGE YOUR LIBIDO WITH L-ARGININE

Forty-three percent of American women report some type of sexual problem—lack of interest in sex...inability to have an orgasm...pain during sex...lack of sexual pleasure...anxiety about sex...or trouble lubricating.

Among perimenopausal and menopausal women, the most common of these problems—caused by the drop in sexual and reproductive hormones—is painful intercourse and a decrease in sexual desire.

Now there's a natural way to help you feel sexy again.

⫸ *Breakthrough Study*

A team of researchers from Rutgers University, Stanford University School of Medicine and the University of Hawaii studied 108 women (ages 22 to 73) with sexual problems (lack of sexual desire or trouble getting aroused).

Fifty-nine of the women were premenopausal (regular periods), 20 were perimenopausal (irregular periods, leading up to menopause) and 29 were postmenopausal (no periods for at least a year, age 50 or older).

The researchers divided them into two groups. For one month, one group took an herbal and nutritional supplement containing L-arginine (an amino acid), the herbs Korean red ginseng (*Panax ginseng*), ginkgo biloba and damiana leaf (*Turnera aphrodisiaca*), vitamins A, C, E, B-6, B-12, biotin, folate, niacin, pantothenic acid, riboflavin and thiamin, and the minerals calcium, iron and zinc. The other group took a placebo.

At the beginning and end of the study, the women filled out the "Female Sexual Function Index," which quantifies sexual desire, frequency of sex and other indicators of sexual participation and satisfaction.

Result: After four weeks…

• **More desire and satisfaction for postmenopausal women.** Fifty percent of postmenopausal women taking the supplement had increased sexual desire, compared to 8% for the placebo group. Fifty percent had increased satisfaction with their sexual relationship; placebo, 31%.

• **More lubrication, sensation and sex for perimenopausal women.** Eighty-six percent of perimenopausal women taking the supplement had increased frequency of intercourse, compared to 17% for the placebo group. Seventy-nine percent had increased satisfaction with their sexual relationship; placebo, 33%. Seventy-one percent had increased clitoral sensation; placebo, 33%. Sixty-four percent had less vaginal dryness; placebo, 17%.

"There was a greater effect in the perimenopausal women on physical attributes such as vaginal dryness, frequency of sex and clitoral sensation," say the researchers. "It is possible that this is the stage of life when these attributes are most at issue because of the rapid changes or decrease in hormone-supported functions. At some point during late menopause, the decrease in ovarian hormones may become a more overwhelming factor."

• **More overall satisfaction for premenopausal women.** Seventy-two percent of premenopausal women taking the supplement had increased intensity of sexual desire, compared to 47% for the placebo group. Sixty percent had increased frequency of sexual desire; placebo, 38%. Sixty-eight percent had increased overall satisfaction with their sex life; placebo, 35%. Fifty-six percent had increased frequency of intercourse; placebo, 26%.

And in an earlier study of 77 women with sexual problems, among women who took the supplement 74% had more satisfaction with their sex life…71% had higher levels of sexual desire…53% had more clitoral sensation when stimulated…and 47% had greater frequency of orgasms.

"Since this supplement has been shown to exhibit no estrogen activity, it may be a desirable alternative to hormone therapy for sexual concerns," says Beverly Whipple, PhD, RN, professor emeritus at Rutgers University, past-president of the American Association of Sexuality Educators, Counselors and Therapists and a study researcher.

"This is an increasingly important issue as we now have a higher population of menopausal women than ever before," Dr. Whipple continues. "This is the only supplement of its kind that has clinically proven results."

How it works: The amino acid L-arginine converts into nitric oxide (NO), the body's signaling molecule for starting and maintaining the engorgement of sexual organs with blood…ginseng may assist in the conversion of L-arginine to NO…ginkgo biloba improves the microcirculation involved in sexual arousal …damiana reduces anxiety…and the range of vitamins and minerals support general health, a must for normal sexual desire and function.

ℹ️ The researchers studied ArginMax for Women.

Recommendation: "With no negative side effects reported, the supplement is clearly an option for some women," says Mary Lake Polan, MD, PhD, MPH, the chair of the Department of Gynecology and Obstetrics at the Stanford School of Medicine and a study researcher.

"Women who suffer from sexual dysfunction should first talk to their doctor before taking a nutritional supplement. There may be a physical reason a woman is experiencing pelvic pain or vaginal dryness, for example, and both of these problems can be treated medically. Or there may be a relationship issue. But ArginMax does give women more choices."

Suggested intake: Follow the dosage recommendation on the label, which are six capsules daily.

☀ You can buy ArginMax for Women at the Web site *www.arginmax.com.* The Daily Wellness Company, 1946 Young Street, Suite 390, Honolulu, HI 96826 (888-866-0826); e-mail *dwcservice@dailywellness.com.* ArginMax for Women is also available in retail stores, on-line and from catalogs.

FOUR DRUG-FREE WAYS TO MINIMIZE MENO-MISERY

Can herbs and other drug-free treatments really reduce the symptoms of menopause?

New finding: Yes, says a new study in the journal *Family Practice.* Researchers in England looked at 45 menopausal women, dividing them into two groups—those who were treated by a trained medical herbalist and those who weren't. (The herbal treatments included dietary and lifestyle advice.) After six months, those seeing the herbalist had fewer hot flashes and night sweats, less anxiety and depression and higher levels of sexual desire.

Here are four herbal and dietary treatments for menopause that scientific studies are finding might work.

▶ *Breakthrough Studies*

• **Flaxseed.** "Hot flashes are a bothersome issue for women experiencing menopause," says Sandhya Pruthi, MD, of the Mayo Clinic. "We hope to find more effective nonhormonal options to assist women—and flaxseed looks promising."

In her study of the food, 29 women used 40 grams (four tablespoons) of crushed flaxseed a day, mixing two tablespoons into cereal, juice, fruit or yogurt, twice a day.

After six weeks, their frequency of hot flashes decreased 50% and the intensity decreased by 57%. The women also said they had improvements in sweating and chills (both of which can accompany hot flashes), in mood and in joint or muscle pain (common problems in menopause).

"We are quite pleased with the improvements noted by these women in their quality of life," says Dr. Pruthi. "Not only does flaxseed seem to alleviate hot flashes, but it appears to have overall health and psychological benefits as well."

• **Hops extract.** Hops are famous for the preparation of beer. They might also brew up some menopausal relief.

Researchers in Belgium studied 67 postmenopausal women, dividing them into two groups—one received a supplement of hops extract standardized to contain high levels of 8-prenylnaringenin (a phytoestrogen, a plant compound similar to estrogen). The other group took a placebo. After three months, those taking the hops extract had fewer hot flashes and other symptoms of menopause. Hops extract "may provide an attractive addition to the alternative treatments available for relief of hot flashes and other menopausal discomforts," say the researchers.

Supplements with hops extracts are widely available.

• **Pycnogenol.** This extract from pine bark, rich in antioxidants, treats many different conditions, including heart disease and diabetes. In a study by researchers in Taiwan and Germany, 155 perimenopausal women took either pycnogenol or a placebo for six months.

Compared with those taking the placebo, those taking the extract saw a significant improvement in hot flashes and night sweats, depressed mood, memory and concentration, anxiety, sexual satisfaction and sleep problems.

"There is a shift away from the use of hormone replacement therapy due to side effects, and in its absence women are searching for safe and natural options to help manage their symptoms," says Peter Rohdewald, MD, the study's lead researcher. "This study investigating pycnogenol as a natural alternative is very encouraging."

The researchers used 200 milligrams (mg) a day of pycnogenol. The widely available extract is found in hundreds of supplements.

• **Soy isoflavone extract.** Soybeans are rich in a compound called *isoflavones*, which are phytoestrogens. Researchers at Harvard Medical School studied 247 menopausal women, asking them to take either an isoflavone-rich soy extract or a placebo. After three months, hot flashes were reduced by 52% in those taking soy, compared to 39% in the placebo group.

The study used an extract rich in *daidzein*, a soy isoflavone found in the soybean germ.

"The chemical structure of this compound is very similar to that of our own estrogen, allowing it to act as a regulatory mechanism if the body's natural levels of estrogen decrease," says Hope Ricciotti, MD, in the Department of Obstetrics and Gynecology, a study researcher.

The researchers used the supplement Effisoy. For more information or to purchase the product, visit *www.effisoy.com*. FermaHealth, Lincoln Executive Center III, 3245 146th Place SE, Suite 220, Bellevue, WA 98007 (866-834-3334, 425-747-1995 or fax 425-747-4504); e-mail *Customerservice@effisoy.com*.

Red flag: "Soy phytoestrogens are seen by some as an alternative to estrogen therapy to treat postmenopausal symptoms," say scientists at the government's Agency for Healthcare Research and Quality, who recently reviewed 21 studies using soy or soy isoflavones for hot flashes and night sweats, and found the results "inconsistent." However, they say, "the estrogenic effect of soy in potentially promoting tumor recurrence raises concern for its use by breast cancer survivors."

"Soy may help some people with hot flashes, but the question is, at what risk," adds Kaayla T. Daniel, PhD, CNN, author of *The Whole Soy Story: The Dark Side of America's Favorite Health Food* (New Trends Publishing). She points out that research shows soy isoflavones might not only increase the risk of breast cancer but also damage the thyroid; and that the Israeli Health Ministry, the French Food Agency and the Institute of Risk Assessment in Germany have all recommended women not take soy isoflavone supplements.

What to do: If you're considering a soy iso-flavone supplement—particularly if you have a personal or family history of breast cancer—talk to your doctor about the risks and benefits.

Seventy-five million women called in sick. Not all at once, of course. But that's the estimated number of missed workdays a year because of *dysmenorrhea*—the crampy abdominal and pelvic pain that starts right before menstruation and lasts one to three days, with nausea and fatigue sometimes hitching a ride. Some estimates say nine out of 10 premenopausal women deal with the problem; in one study, 42% of young women had severe cramps, 33% moderate and 25% mild.

And up to 20% of premenopausal women also suffer from *premenstrual syndrome* (PMS), a cluster of symptoms including depression, irritability, mood swings, fatigue, abdominal cramping, breast tenderness and headaches—symptoms that descend in the days or even weeks before menstruation.

Painkillers such as ibuprofen (Advil) are often used to treat menstrual cramps. PMS is treated with drugs such as oral contraceptives and antidepressants. Drug-free remedies can also work.

MASSAGE YOUR ANKLES, RELIEVE YOUR CRAMPS

What do your ankles have to do with your menstrual cramps?

Well, say acupuncturists (the practitioners of Traditional Chinese Medicine who treat health problems by inserting tiny, painless needles into *acupoints*), there is a universal life force or energy called *chi* that moves through your body along channels called *meridians*.

The *spleen meridian* (SP) starts at the big toe and runs up the inside of the leg, passes through the spleen and then the heart, and ends at the tongue.

And on the inside of the ankle, three finger-widths above the anklebone, lies Acupoint SP6—Sanyinjiao, or Three Yin Crossing. And if you have menstrual cramps, it can do you a lot of good.

▶ *Breakthrough Study*

Taiwanese researchers studied young women with menstrual cramps. For two menstrual cycles, during the worst of the cramping, the women received *acupressure* on SP6—pressing and massaging the acupoint.

"Acupoint SP6 was selected because it is the acupoint of choice in women's health problems, and is easy for women to locate and apply pressure to without medical assistance," says Chung-Hey Chen, PhD, RN, who led the study.

During the first cycle, a trained nurse gave the acupressure treatment; during the second cycle, the women received instructions and treated themselves.

Result: On average, menstrual pain decreased 40% after the acupressure treatment by the nurse, and 37% after self-treatment.

Eighty-nine percent of the women said the technique was "more than moderately helpful" in relieving pain, and 94% said they were "more than moderately satisfied" with acupressure in treating menstrual cramps.

"Acupressure is an effective and safe form of therapy" for menstrual cramps, say the researchers. "Acupressure at SP6 is cost-free and easy to learn."

What to do: Use the SP6 point whenever you're suffering from menstrual cramps.

The researchers instructed the study participants to press SP6 with the thumb for six seconds and release for two seconds...for five minutes on each leg, repeating four times (five minutes on the left leg, five minutes on the right, five minutes on the left, five minutes on the right)...for a total acupressure treatment of 20 minutes.

Helpful: How can you make sure you've found the SP6 point? "The accuracy of the acupoint was confirmed if the participant felt a slight ache, dull pain, tingling and/or an electrical sensation," says Dr. Chen. "This feeling is what acupuncturists describe as the 'de chi' sensation, which means that the chi has been accessed."

AROMATHERAPY MASSAGE FOR MENSTRUAL CRAMPS

Menstrual cramps don't get enough respect.

"Despite frequent occurrence and severity, menstrual cramps are not acknowledged as a serious problem," says Jane Buckle, PhD, RN, author of *Clinical Aromatherapy: Essential Oils in Practice* (Churchill Livingstone). In fact, she says, the "intra-uterine pressure" of a woman in the midst of an extremely severe menstrual cramp is *greater* than that of a woman in labor!

Seventy percent of women use drugs to treat the pain—"analgesics, sedatives, antispasmodics, prostaglandin inhibitors, uterine contraction inhibitors, nonsteroidal anti-inflammatory drugs, vasopressin antagonists and medication to stop ovulation," adds Dr. Buckle.

But scientific reviews, she says, show that "none of these therapies are particularly effective. Many conventional drugs have side effects or their main effects do not last long."

Well, Dr. Buckle and a team of researchers in Korea have studied a new and gentle way to provide pain relief from menstrual cramps—

WHY CHAMOMILE CALMS CRAMPS

Chamomile is a classic home remedy for menstrual cramps. *Now scientists think they may know why...*

New study: Researchers in England asked seven women to drink five cups of chamomile tea daily, for two weeks. They discovered the women had higher urinary levels of *glycine*, an amino acid shown to relieve muscle spasms.

This may explain why the tea appears to be helpful in relieving menstrual cramps, says Elaine Holmes, PhD, of the Imperial College London, in the *Journal of Agricultural and Food Chemistry*. She also notes that the glycine levels remained high two weeks after the women stopped drinking the tea.

What to do: Drink several cups a day to enjoy chamomile's "age-old use to soothe menstrual cramps," says Michael Castleman, author of *The New Healing Herbs* (Rodale).

receiving a massage with the essential oils of aromatherapy.

▮▮▶ *Breakthrough Studies*

"Aromatherapy is the therapeutic use of essential oils from plants," explains Dr. Buckle. "Essential oils can be absorbed into the body via the skin or the olfactory system. Aromatherapy is thought to be particularly effective against menstrual cramps."

To find out, Dr. Buckle studied 67 college students with moderate to severe cramps, dividing them into three groups.

On the first and second days of their period, Group 1 received a 15-minute abdominal massage using lavender, clary sage and rose essential oils, in a base of almond oil. Group 2 received the same massage just with the almond oil. Group 3 didn't receive any treatment.

Result: Group 1—those receiving the aromatherapy massages—had a decrease of pain of

29% on the first day of their period, and 56% the second day.

There was no change in Group 2, and an insignificant 7% drop in Group 3.

"Aromatherapy using topically applied lavender, clary sage and rose is effective in decreasing menstrual cramps," says Dr. Buckle. "Because there are no side effects, aromatherapy can be regarded as a safe, simple, cost-effective and viable method of care, suitable for all persons."

How it works: "The essential oil of this lavender (*Lavandula angustifolia*) is thought to be an antispasmodic," says Dr. Buckle. "It may also be useful as a sedative and to alleviate pain.

"Clary sage also has many good antispasmodic properties, and may have functions similar to estrogen, such as normalizing the menstrual cycle and strengthening the uterus.

"Rose is thought to be the 'women's essential oil,' as it has great affinity for the uterus and can help regulate the menstrual cycle."

These three essential oils together provide a synergistic blend in treating the pain of menstrual cramps, says Dr. Buckle.

"Different methods are used to deliver aromatherapy, such as diffusers, baths, massage and compresses. Massage is believed to be an effective way to improve blood and lymph circulation, and to reduce stress and ease stiff muscles."

What to do: The massage mixture contains two drops of lavender (*Lavandula officinalis*), one drop of clary sage (*Salvia sclarea*) and one drop of rose (*Rosa centifolia*) in two ounces of almond oil.

Dr. Buckle's instructions for the massage…

"A fifteen-minute abdominal massage, beginning with effleurage strokes (smooth, soothing strokes with the fingertips or the palm) in the shape of a flat diamond, working clockwise with a pressure of four on a scale of zero to ten, where zero is no pressure and ten is crushing pressure. The masseur's left hand was placed on the right hand, and both hands were placed on the right lower abdomen. The stroke went to the ribs and then across the abdomen to the left lower abdomen. This was followed by a gentle kneading at the left and right of the waist, and then stroking across the abdomen.

"Following this, the effleurage flat diamond stroke began again. The strokes were slow, smooth and continuous."

Note: A cushion was placed under the person's knees to keep the abdomen relaxed.

☀ Arlys Naturals, *www.arlysnaturals.com*, sells a wide variety of high-quality essential oils, including lavender, clary sage and rose. Contact 877-502-7597, 954-523-9513 or fax 954-767-8973; e-mail *susan@arlysnaturals.com*.

Books: *Aromatherapy Massage* by Claire Maxwell-Hudson (DK Publishing) and *The Illustrated Guide to Massage and Aromatherapy* by Catherine Stuart (Southwater).

FOR MENSTRUAL RELIEF, HEAT BEATS TYLENOL

What's the best way to counter menstrual cramps—taking 1,000 mg of acetaminophen (Tylenol) or cuddling up continuously inside a low-level heat wrap?

It's better to be hot and not bothered.

▐▐▐➡ *Breakthrough Study*

A team of researchers studied 81 women with menstrual cramps, dividing them into two groups. On the first day of their period, one group took 1,000 mg of acetaminophen and the other wore a heat wrap that generated eight hours of continuous low-level heat, at 102°F.

Result: Those wearing the heat wrap had 13% less pain during the eight hours of wearing the wrap. They also had 10% less cramping and tightness. And there was "significantly decreased fatigue and fewer mood swings," say the researchers, in the *Journal of Reproductive Medicine*.

"Continuous low-level topical heat therapy was superior to acetaminophen for the treatment" of menstrual cramps, they conclude.

And in an earlier study, the same type of heat wrap was as effective as ibuprofen (Advil) in providing pain relief from cramps.

"Of importance, the heat therapy is a nondrug treatment that will be useful for women who have adverse effects" from taking painkillers, say the researchers, in the journal *Obstetrics & Gynecology*.

How it works: The heat increases circulation, which delivers oxygen and nutrients to cramping muscles.

ℹ️ The researchers studied Menstrual Cramp Relief, from ThermaCare HeatWraps—a very thin "Menstrual Patch" worn under clothing and covering the lower abdomen. The heated discs in the patch contain iron, salt, sodium thiosulfate, water and activated charcoal, which react with the air to create heat.

☀️ To learn more about the ThermaCare HeatWrap, visit *www.thermacare.com*, where you can also search for nearby stores that carry the product.

SKIM MILK PREVENTS PMS

The statistics show that menstruation can be a vicious cycle…

Eighty-five to 95% of premenopausal women have some sort of physical or emotional discomfort during the *luteal phase* of the menstrual cycle—the time between ovulation and the onset of bleeding.

About 10 to 20% have premenstrual syndrome, or PMS—a combination of life-disturbing symptoms that can include depression, irritability, fatigue, abdominal cramping, breast tenderness and headaches.

And 5 to 8% have severe premenstrual depression, a condition called *premenstrual dysphoric disorder*, or PDD.

Landmark study: A decade ago, the Premenstrual Syndrome Study Group at Columbia University in New York found that supplementing the diet with 1,200 mg of calcium carbonate could help reduce PMS symptoms by nearly 50%.

A team of researchers from the University of Massachusetts, Harvard Medical School and the University of Iowa wanted to find out if high intakes of calcium could *prevent* PMS. And whether getting plenty of calcium *and* vitamin D—which boosts calcium absorption—could aid PMS prevention.

⫸ *Breakthrough Study*

The researchers analyzed 10 years of diet and health data from 3,025 women aged 27 to 44 who didn't have PMS when the study began. Over the 10 years, 1,057 women developed PMS; 1,968 women didn't.

Result: Women with the highest dietary intake of calcium at the beginning of the study were 30% less likely to develop PMS than women with the lowest intake. Women with the highest dietary intake of vitamin D were 41% less likely to develop PMS.

The researchers also found that those who drank the most skim and low-fat milk had the lowest risk of developing PMS.

"A high intake of calcium and vitamin D may reduce the risk of PMS," conclude researchers.

How it works: The symptoms of PMS may be caused by a calcium and vitamin D deficiency, which disrupts the body's hormonal system.

What to do: The amount of calcium and vitamin D that might prevent PMS is 1,200 mg of calcium and 400 IU of vitamin D—"the amount in four servings per day of skim or low-fat milk, fortified orange juice or low-fat dairy foods such as yogurt," say the researchers.

"The finding that frequent milk intake is protective against PMS is consistent with our results for calcium and vitamin D," they add. "Each serving of fortified milk contains approximately 300 mg of calcium and 100 IU of vitamin D—four, eight-ounce servings per day would provide women with approximately the amount of calcium and vitamin D from food sources at which we saw a significantly lower risk of PMS." (The researchers don't know why whole milk didn't show the same effect.)

COMMON PROBLEMS, UNIQUE SOLUTIONS

CHASTEBERRY EASES BREAST PAIN

At some point in their lives, 50 to 80% of women experience breast pain, or what doctors call *mastalgia*. The most common type is *cyclical mastalgia*—changing hormones in the two weeks before your period also change breast tissue, which becomes tender and inflamed.

"The lack of reliable remedies for mastalgia can lead to severe impact" on a woman's quality of life, says Amtul R. Carmichael, MD, a breast specialist in England, writing in the journal *Evidence-Based Complementary and Alternative Medicine.*

Well, try relying on an extract from the fruit of the chasteberry tree (*Vitex agnus-castus*).

||||➡ *Breakthrough Study*

Chasteberry "has been used in the treatment of many conditions of women's health, such as menstrual disorders, premenstrual syndrome, infertility, menopause and disrupted lactation," says Dr. Carmichael. *And studies show it also works for cyclical mastalgia…*

● **For 50% of women, an end to severe pain.** Researchers in the Czech Republic gave women with cyclical mastalgia either a tincture of chasteberry or a placebo. Those taking the herb had 57% more pain relief, with more than 70% of the participants benefiting. In fact, half the women taking chasteberry no longer had *any* severe pain during their menstrual cycle; and in another quarter of the women, the number of days with severe pain was cut by 80%. Chasteberry is effective, say the researchers, in the journal *Breast*.

● **For women with PMDD and breast pain—relief.** Researchers in Turkey studied 41 women with premenstrual dysphoric disorder (PMDD), a severe form of PMS dominated by depression. They divided them into two groups—one took fluoxetine (Prozac); the other chasteberry. Fifty-eight percent of those taking chasteberry saw a reduction in mastalgia, which wasn't reduced by Prozac. (Prozac, however, improved psychological symptoms, while chasteberry did not.)

● **Relief of breast pain—and irritability, mood swings, headaches and bloating.** Researchers in Germany studied 160 women with PMS, including breast pain, dividing them into two groups—for three menstrual cycles, one group took a daily supplement of chasteberry, while the other took a placebo. Fifty-two percent of the women in the chasteberry group had a reduction of breast pain, compared to 24% in the placebo group. Half the women who took chasteberry also had a more than 50% reduction in many of the other symptoms of

PMS. Chasteberry "is an effective treatment for women with the premenstrual syndrome," say the researchers.

Chasteberry "is safe, effective and efficient in the treatment of cyclical mastalgia," concludes Dr. Carmichael.

How it works: Chasteberry cuts the production of the hormone prolactin, which increases after ovulation, explains Dr. Carmichael. "Some women respond to the stimulation of *prolactin* release with a hypersection of this hormone, resulting in stimulation to the mammary gland, leading to cyclic mastalgia. The ability of chasteberry to lower the prolactin level in women with cyclical mastalgia has been shown in clinical and laboratory studies."

ⓘ In Germany, where chasteberry is approved as a treatment for cyclical mastalgia, you can find a range of standardized and science-tested products, such as Femicur, Agnolyt, Agnucaston and Mastodynon—none of which are available in the United States. Although there is no single active ingredient in chasteberry, look for a standardized extract, perhaps at 0.5% agnuside or 0.6% aucubin, two active components.

Suggested intake: Use either 40 drops per day of a tincture or 175 mg per day of a standardized extract, says Dr. Hudson, who calls chasteberry "the single most important plant for the treatment of premenstrual syndrome."

Also helpful: In a study in the *Breast Journal*, 111 women with breast pain and breast cysts who took a daily iodine supplement had a "clinically significant reduction in overall pain" after three months. "I have prescribed iodine supplements for women with breast pain for years with excellent results, usually within only two weeks," says Christiane Northrup, MD, author of *Women's Bodies, Women's Wisdom* (Bantam). "The iodine decreases the ability of estrogen to adhere to estrogen receptors in the breast." Talk to your doctor about whether iodine is right for you.

BETTER BRAIN POWER WITH MORE IRON

One out of five women in America has *iron-deficiency anemia*. Twice as many may be iron-deficient (your lab tests don't show outright anemia, but you do have lower-than-normal blood levels of iron). Why is there such a widespread iron shortage?

Because of heavy periods (blood is rich in iron)...or diets low in the mineral...or an iron-sapping pregnancy.

The practical result—you no longer have enough iron in your body to create sufficient *hemoglobin*, a protein that rides piggyback on red blood cells, delivering oxygen throughout the body. And when your cells are gasping for oxygen, you feel tired. Really tired.

Now, scientists from the Department of Nutritional Sciences at Pennsylvania State University have discovered that if you have iron-deficiency anemia, or even just iron deficiency—your brain might feel bushed, too.

▐▐▐▶ *Breakthrough Study*

Iron deficiency is "the most prevalent single nutrient deficiency," says Laura E. Murray-Kolb, PhD. Studies show that low levels of iron can cause fatigue, weaken the immune system, upset temperature regulation and, in children, lower scores on intelligence and educational achievement tests. Could a lack of iron also ambush adult brains?

To find out, Dr. Murray-Kolb and her colleagues studied 149 women between the ages of 18 and 35—42 were iron sufficient, 73 were iron deficient but not anemic, and 34 had iron-deficiency anemia.

They gave all the women a series of computer-based tests to measure their "cognitive ability"—their ability to be attentive, to remember and to learn. The tests measured mental speed and accuracy in response to visual stimuli...short-term memory of lists and groupings...and the time it took to learn complex mental tasks.

The iron-sufficient women performed the best; the iron-deficient anemic women performed the worst; the iron-deficient women were in between.

The women with low iron levels were then treated with iron supplements. After about four months, the iron levels of most women normalized.

And when those newly iron-sufficient women retook the mental tests, their attention, learning, and memory skills improved significantly—five to seven times higher!

Why it works: Less iron in the brain may change levels of the neurotransmitter dopamine, which affects memory, learning and attention.

Trap: "Throughout the day, most people will be required to attend to various situations, to remember and even to learn certain information," say the researchers. "In some situations, multitasking is expected and may be required. If a person has a deficit in attention, memory or learning accuracy because she has a depletion of essential body iron pools, that person's ability to interact with the world at large will be lessened."

Solution: "This study," they conclude, "challenges the traditionally held viewpoint that iron deficiency does not have functional consequences until it has reached the level of anemia. Given these findings, better iron status surveillance practices are encouraged to identify people who may be at risk of cognitive defects."

In other words, see your doctor to find out if you're iron deficient (not just anemic), which involves blood tests measuring a number of factors, including hemoglobin and iron levels. If you're iron deficient, discuss treating the problem with an iron supplement.

Suggested intake: The women were given slow-release iron supplements of 160 mg ferrous sulfate, with 60 mg of elemental iron.

ℹ️ Iron supplements are widely available.

Important: Good dietary sources of iron include red meat, beans, iron-fortified breakfast cereals, leafy greens, nuts and dried fruit. Also, try a tablespoon of iron-rich blackstrap molasses, twice a day, says Dr. Lucille.

EXERCISE PREVENTS UTERINE FIBROIDS

Fifty percent of women develop uterine fibroids, or *myomas*, noncancerous growths that take root in the muscular lining of the uterus.

They can be small as seeds or large as bowling balls, but in many cases, they're quiet enough to be undetectable.

Sometimes, however, fibroids make their presence known via unpleasant symptoms, such as heavy menstrual bleeding or, in 30% of cases, abnormal bleeding *between* periods. They can also cause urinary incontinence, painful intercourse or pelvic pain, with a feeling of pressure, congestion, bloating and heaviness.

Those symptoms are often troublesome enough to require the removal of the myomas —and often of the entire uterus. Fibroids are the number one reason for hysterectomies, with 600,000 performed in the United States every year. "Uterine fibroids are *the* most common indication for major surgery in women," says Dr. Hudson. That's because there are few other ways to treat them.

Clearly, *preventing* fibroids is the priority. One more reason to go for a walk...

FLAVONOIDS FOR CHRONIC PELVIC PAIN

Chronic pelvic pain is a complex condition, with many possible causes, including endometriosis (growth of uterine tissue outside the uterus), uterine fibroids (noncancerous growths in the uterus) and interstitial cystitis (chronic bladder infection).

In many cases, however, the cause of the pain is never found. It simply persists—mild or severe, intermittent or steady, day after day.

If you have chronic pelvic pain that lasts six months or longer, see your doctor.

But you might also help yourself—with a supplement of *flavonoids*, plant compounds found in citrus fruits.

New study: Doctors from the Department of Obstetrics and Gynecology at Akdeniz University in Turkey studied 20 women who had chronic pelvic pain without a diagnosed cause.

For six months, 10 of the women took a flavonoid supplement that can tone and strengthen veins, and has successfully treated varicose veins and hemorrhoids. The other 10 women took a placebo. After six months, the two groups switched, with the placebo group taking the flavonoids and vice versa.

For both groups, by the third month of taking flavonoids "the frequency and severity of pelvic symptoms began to decrease" say the doctors. By the end of six months, pain scores were "significantly less."

Improving "venous tone" may restore pelvic circulation and relieve pelvic symptoms, say the researchers, in the journal *Clinical and Experimental Obstetrics and Gynecology*.

ℹ️ The type of flavonoid used in this study was *micronized purified flavonoid fraction*, or MPFF, a specially processed flavonoid derived from citrus rinds. It is very similar to an over-the-counter flavonoid product *diosmin*.

☀️ Diosmin is an ingredient in the following supplements, which are available in retail stores, on the Internet or in catalogs—Diosmin from Baywood; Diosmin-HMC from Thorne Research; and Ultra DiosVein Diosmin/Hesperidin from Swanson. Follow the dosage recommendation on the label.

▸ *Breakthrough Study*

A team of researchers at the National Institutes of Health and George Washington University Medical Center analyzed data from nearly 1,200 women, aged 35 to 49, who participated in the government's Uterine Fibroid Study.

They found that women with the highest level of physical activity were 40% less likely to develop fibroids than women with the lowest level.

"Regular exercise might help prevent fibroids," they conclude.

Why it works: One theory is that estrogen goads the growth of fibroids. "Physical activity has been reported to be protective for breast cancer, another hormonally related tumor," say the researchers. "Several mechanisms have been proposed that might explain the protective effect of exercise. Those mechanisms might also be applicable to fibroid development." In particular, exercise might reduce fibroid-fueling sex hormones and insulin, they say.

Good news: "Women have little control of other factors known to affect fibroids," say the researchers, "but exercise is a modifiable practice [that is, *you* can decide to do it], and also has other positive effects on women's health."

What to do: The protective level in the study was four hours of moderate exercise a week.

For an easy way to develop a lifelong walking program, see page 355 in Chapter 14, "Overweight."

STOP RECURRENT UTI WITH CRANBERRY EXTRACT

You have the symptoms of a bladder infection (also called a urinary tract infection, or UTI)—burning on urination, blood in the urine and fever. See a doctor, get a urine culture taken and, if it's positive, take an antibiotic. (Neglecting the problem could lead to a kidney infection, which can permanently damage your kidneys and even spread to your bloodstream, which is a life-threatening condition.)

But 25% of women who get one bladder infection get another. And maybe another. And another after that. Treating a bladder infection with an antibiotic can kill off friendly bacteria in your body, causing all kinds of other problems, from yeast infections to digestive upset; treating *recurrent* infections with antibiotics increases the risk of all those side effects.

The classic cure for UTIs—cranberries—can break the cycle.

Scottish researchers recently analyzed 10 rigorous studies on using cranberry juice or cranberry extracts to stop UTIs. They found regular use of cranberry lowered the risk of UTIs by 45%—and were particularly effective in stopping recurrent UTIs in women.

For the best results in resisting recurrence, get the best form of cranberry.

|||⮞ *Breakthrough Study*

Escherichia coli are the bacteria that cause bladder infections. They have little attachments that allow them to hang from bladder walls. Cranberries are rich in two natural compounds called *phenolics*—fructose and proanthocyanidins—that reduce the size of those attachments. The bacteria can't get a foothold and bladder infections don't start.

In fact, new research shows that the proanthocyanidins in cranberries are structured in a unique way that stymies the bacteria. And that they may change the shape of the bacteria from rods to spheres, so that they bounce off bladder walls.

That's why researchers at Helios Integrated Medicine clinic in Boulder, CO, decided to test a cranberry extract particularly rich in proanthocyanidins—containing 25%, whereas supplements with dried cranberries typically contain 0.5%, and supplements from dried juices range from 3 to 7%.

The researchers studied 12 women, aged 25 to 70, who had an average of six bladder infections a year. The women took one capsule of the extract, twice a day.

Result: After three months, not one of the women had a UTI.

And after two years, the eight women who had continued to take the extract still hadn't had another UTI!

"A cranberry preparation with a high phenolic content may completely prevent UTIs in women who are subject to recurrent infections," say the researchers, in the journal *Phytomedicine*.

"Not one of the women developed a UTI during the twelve weeks of treatment," the researchers add. "This is in contrast with their history of an infection every two months. Further, those women who continued to take a cranberry product remained free from infections two years later. It is a remarkable finding."

Suggested intake: Two hundred milligrams, twice a day.

ⓘ The high-proanthocyanidins extract used in the study was Women's Cranberry Supreme, from GNC.

Also helpful: If you'd rather use cranberry juice, mix 16 ounces of unsweetened cranberry juice and 16 ounces of water and drink it throughout the day, says Dr. Lucille.

A NEW REMEDY FOR INTERSTITIAL CYSTITIS

Interstitial cystitis (IC)—also called painful bladder syndrome (PBS), or chronic pelvic pain syndrome (CPPS)—is a chronic inflammation of the bladder. You feel like you have to go to the bathroom all the time. And you *do* go to the bathroom a lot—as much as 60 times a day (and night), passing only small amounts each time. And you *hurt*, usually in the "suprapubic" area, above the genitals. (Sex is also painful.) But tests show you *don't* have a bladder infection.

In the United States, an estimated one million women suffer from IC.

Doctors don't know the cause and they don't have a cure.

But one doctor—Theoharis C. Theoharides, PhD, MD, a professor of pharmacology, internal medicine and biochemistry, at Tufts University, in Boston—thinks he may have discovered a drug-free way to get IC under control.

▶ *Breakthrough Study*

Dr. Theoharides observed that the bladder walls of people with IC contained a large number of *mast cells,* the immune cells that spark allergic reactions and inflammation. (About 60% of people with IC also have an allergy.) Earlier, other researchers had found defects in the protective *glycosaminoglycan* (GAG) layer of the bladder walls in people with IC.

"A dietary supplement was formulated to include natural molecules that could replenish the GAG and reduce inflammation," says Dr. Theoharides. Then he tested it.

He asked 37 women with IC who had "failed all forms of therapy" (which can include various medications, pain-reducing devices and even surgery to remove damaged sections of the bladder) to take the supplement.

Result: After six months, their IC symptoms had decreased by 58%...another measure of IC severity, the "problem index," had decreased by 59%...and a "global assessment scale" of IC (10 being worst, 1 being best) fell from 9.0 to 4.3.

"The treatment of IC presents a unique challenge for clinicians, since the cause of the disease is not known," says Dr. Theoharides. "These results are very promising."

And in a second study of 269 women with IC, the global assessment scale was reduced from 7.4 to 3.7.

How it works: Here are the ingredients in the formula and their mechanisms of action...

Chondroitin sulfate is a major component of the protective GAG layer of the bladder. And it stops the release of enzymes that damage the bladder. *Sodium hyaluronate* is also found in the GAG layer. "It is essential in the rebuilding process," says Dr. Theoharides. *Glucosamine sulfate* is another building block of the GAG layer. *Quercetin* is a compound extracted from the saphora plant. It stops the activation of mast cells. "It is added to relieve pain and discomfort," says Dr. Theoharides. *Rutin*, another extract from the saphora plant, also quiets inflammation, and it improves the absorption of quercetin. *Olive kernel extract*, a potent antioxidant, helps repair damaged tissues. It also improves the absorption of chondroitin sulfate, quercetin and sodium hyaluronate.

🛈 The researcher used the supplement Cystoprotek.

Suggested intake: Dr. Theoharides recommends that people with heartburn, irritable bowel syndrome or a sensitive stomach start their regimen slowly—on the first and second days of taking the supplement, take one capsule a day, with a full meal; on days three to seven, take one capsule twice a day, with a full meal.

Then go on the regular schedule, which is two capsules twice a day, with a full meal. "If your symptoms are severe, you may increase the

Bottom Line's Breakthroughs in Drug-Free Healing

dosage up to three capsules, three times a day with a meal, for the first three months," says Dr. Theoharides. "Then you may slowly reduce the dosage to two capsules twice a day, with a meal."

☀ For more information about Cystoprotek, or to purchase the supplement, visit the Web site *www.cysto-protek.com.* Alaven Pharmaceutical LLC, 2260 Northwest Parkway, Suite D, Marietta, GA 30067 (888-317-0001 or fax 770-916-3900); e-mail *cystoprotek@alavenpharm.com.*

BORIC ACID FOR PERSISTENT VAGINITIS

At some time in their lives, 75% of women end up with a vaginal yeast infection, or *vulvovaginitis candidiasis.* Symptoms can include a watery or thick white discharge, burning, redness and swelling of the vaginal area; pain during urination and pain or discomfort during sex.

Between 40 and 50% of women with a first case of vaginitis have one or two more. And 5 to 7%—approximately three million women—have recurrent infections.

The bad news—the number of recurrent infections is expected to grow, as yeast fungi continue to mutate and resist currently available antifungal medications.

The good news is there may be a natural way out: boric acid vaginal suppositories.

||||▶ *Breakthrough Study*

Researchers in the Department of Endocrinology and Metabolism at the All India Institute of Medical Sciences in New Delhi studied 112 women with vaginal yeast infections, dividing them into two groups. One group took a single dose of the standard antiyeast oral medication *fluconazole* (Diflucan); the other used boric acid vaginal suppositories.

Sixty-four percent of those treated with the suppository were cured, compared to 29% with fluconazole.

Recommendation: "Nothing impresses me more than the success rate of boric acid suppositories for the treatment of candidia vulvovaginal infections," says Dr. Hudson.

She cites another study, in the *Journal of Reproductive Medicine,* in which women with chronic resistant yeast infections who had "failed extensive and prolonged conventional therapy" were treated with 600 mg boric acid vaginal suppositories twice a day for two to four weeks. Ninety-eight percent of the women were cured!

"Clinical effectiveness doesn't really get any better than this," she concludes.

Caution: "The only downside I have observed is that if the tissue has been irritated enough by the infection, burning can occur when the boric acid passes over this tissue," says Dr. Hudson. "Using vitamin E oil or lanolin or even Vaseline on the external genitalia to protect the tissue from the boric acid seems to avert any significant discomfort."

What to do: For an acute, first- or second-time infection, Dr. Hudson recommends 600 mg vaginal suppositories, twice a day, for three to seven days.

For recurrent infections, 600 mg vaginal suppositories twice a day, for two to four weeks.

For preventing recurrence, 600 mg vaginal suppositories, four days per month during menses, for four consecutive months.

ⓘ Yeast Arrest by Vitanica. Follow the usage instructions accompanying the product.

☀ Yeast Arrest is available on-line from many sources.

KEGELS WORK— IF YOU DO THEM RIGHT

For many women, urinary incontinence—any involuntary leakage of urine—is an embarrassing condition that's all too real.

Ninety percent of cases are *stress urinary incontinence* (SUI)—incontinence when you're coughing or sneezing or laughing or lifting something heavy. Thirty to 50% of women experience it now and then.

Unfortunately, the problem can become increasingly common with age, with a loss of tone in the bladder and urethra—one in six women between the ages of 40 and 65 has SUI.

The typical recommendations are take a drug, have surgery or wear diapers.

But those therapies should be *last* resorts, not first-line care, says Kathryn Burgio, PhD, director of the continence program at the University of Alabama at Birmingham.

The first resort is *Kegel exercises* to strengthen the *pubococcygeous* (PC) muscle, which you already tighten automatically when you squeeze your urethra and stop the flow of urine.

▐▐▐➡ *Breakthrough Study*

Researchers in Australia recently analyzed 24 studies on using Kegel exercises—or what they call "pelvic floor muscle training" (PFMT)—for urinary incontinence.

They found the exercises *cured* women of SUI in 73% of cases, and vastly improved the situation in 97% of cases.

There is strong evidence for the effectiveness of PFMT for the treatment of stress urinary incontinence, they conclude, in the journal *BMC Women's Health*.

Problem: Many doctors and their patients think Kegels *don't* work to cure USI.

Solution: "That's because Kegels usually aren't taught properly," says Dr. Burgio. *Here's her advice on how to do them right…*

"First, you need to know where the muscles are," she says. "You can locate them by

---

ARE YOU SURE IT'S A YEAST INFECTION?

"Everything that itches isn't a yeast infection," says Susan Hoffstetter, PhD, assistant professor of obstetrics, gynecology and women's health at Saint Louis University School of Medicine.

"People keep treating themselves with over-the-counter medicines for yeast infections, or they call the doctor to get a prescription for medicine over and over again."

New thinking: But, she says, three out of four times they're treating a problem they don't have!

Dr. Hoffstetter analyzed the medical records of more than 150 new patients at her clinic, the SLUCare Vulvar and Vaginal Disease Clinic, which specializes in women with recurrent vaginitis. All of these women thought they had vaginitis. Only 26% did.

Yes, the women had itching and a vaginal discharge. But, says Dr. Hoffstetter, that could also indicate an inflammation, dry skin tissues or a sexually transmitted disease (STD). "Their symptoms didn't correlate with the clinical evidence of a yeast infection," she says. And they needed a treatment for the problem they actually *had*, not the one they *thought* they had.

Recommendation: If you think you have a yeast infection, call your doctor or a woman's health nurse practitioner for an appointment, says Dr. Hoffstetter. The health professional will do a pelvic exam to detect swelling and unhealthy discharge, and may take a swab to get a specimen for a lab test, or to examine under a microscope, to see if yeast is the true culprit.

"If you treat yourself and it never goes away, you shouldn't continue to treat yourself," says Dr. Hoffstetter. "The optimal strategy is to get evaluated."

stopping or slowing the stream of urine the next time you go to the bathroom. The muscles you use to do that are the pelvic floor muscles. Another way to identify them is to tighten the same muscles that you use to stop yourself from passing gas in public. You can also find them by tightening the vaginal muscles.

"Several times a day, squeeze the muscles and hold the contraction for ten seconds," she says. "At first, you may not be able to hold for very long, but don't worry. Start by holding for a count of three—one Mississippi, two Mississippi, three Mississippi—then let go. Over time, build up to a count of ten.

"You may have a tendency to contract your abdominal muscles by mistake," she continues. "Breathing normally and regularly while doing the Kegels will help you keep those muscles relaxed. You can also put one hand over your abdomen to double-check that you're not tightening the muscles there.

"When you're doing Kegels correctly, you'll feel a lifting sensation in the area of your vagina or a pulling sensation in your rectum," she says.

What's the right amount to cure incontinence? "Do forty-five Kegels a day," she says. "It's best to do them fifteen times in a row, three times a day."

Trap: "The most common error is that people simply forget to do them," she says. "The best way to remember to do your Kegels is to pick a few activities that you do every day—such as taking a shower, brushing your teeth—and do the exercise during those activities.

"Exercising your pelvic floor muscles can reduce incontinence, but to get the most out of Kegels, you need to *use* them. Remember to squeeze the muscles right before and during those activities that cause leakage, such as coughing and sneezing. This helps to close the opening to the bladder and prevent urine loss."

And don't be discouraged! "At first, you'll have to concentrate quite a bit," says Dr. Burgio. "But after they become a habit, you'll start doing Kegels automatically."

Good news: You should see improvement after eight weeks of exercises, she says.

☀ If you'd like to find a nearby practitioner with expertise in incontinence—a urogynecologist, nurse practitioner or physical therapist—visit the Web site of the American Urogynecological Society, *www.mypelvichealth. org*, and click "Find A Provider" on the home page. 2025 M Street NW, Suite 800, Washington, DC 20036 (202-367-1167; fax: 202-367-2167); e-mail *info@augs.org*.

INFERTILITY

Six million American women—10% of the reproductive-age population—want to have a baby but can't, not even after six months to a year of unprotected sex. Why are they infertile? Well, it could be that eggs don't mature properly...ovaries are pocked with tiny cysts...abnormal growths crowd the lining of the uterus...cervical mucous is too thick...fallopian tubes are damaged...endometrial tissue blocks the entrance to the uterus...their partner has too few or weak sperm.

In other words, a lot can go wrong with our reproductive machinery! To improve their odds of having a baby, many women turn to modern medicine—from medications that multiply eggs, to in vitro fertilization. And medical care to overcome fertility can work—more than one million babies are the evidence. But there's more help for hopeful women and their partners.

"High-tech medicine isn't the only answer," says Jorge E. Chavarro, MD, ScD, of the Harvard School of Public Health and coauthor of *The*

Fertility Diet (McGraw-Hill). "These medical approaches aren't perfect. They lead to a viable pregnancy only about one-quarter of the time. They are time consuming and invasive. They can have unwanted side effects. Many couples would rather not turn to technology for something as intimate and personal as conceiving a child. Others can't afford it."

Another option to up your odds of having a baby—eat for two *before* you're pregnant...

THE FERTILITY DIET

"Ovulatory problems are a common cause of infertility in women, and contribute to between eighteen and thirty percent of all cases of infertility," says Dr. Chavarro.

He explains that three hormones—lutenizing hormone (LH), follicle-stimulating hormone (FSH) and estrogen—trigger ovulation, the maturation and release of an egg from the ovary. But ovulation depends on those hormones being "just right"—not too high or too low, and released with impeccable timing. *Lifestyle can help those hormones behave...*

"Making the right dietary choices and including the right amount of physical activity in your daily life may make a large difference in your probability of becoming fertile, if you are experiencing problems with ovulation," he says.

▌▌▶ *Breakthrough Study*

Dr. Chavarro analyzed earlier studies on diet and lifestyle factors and ovulatory-caused infertility, compiling a list of factors that increased the odds of getting pregnant.

They included eating more monounsaturated fats (found in olive oil and avocados) and less trans fats (found in processed baked goods), taking a daily multivitamin, getting enough iron, eating more whole grains and fiber, eating more vegetable protein and less red meat, eating

more whole-fat dairy products, maintaining normal weight and exercising regularly.

Then he and his colleagues matched those "fertility factors" with eight years of diet and health data from more than 17,000 married women as they tried to become pregnant or became pregnant.

Result: "We analyzed what happens if you follow, one, two, three, four or more different factors," says Dr. Chavarro.

"What we found was that, as women started following more of these recommendations, their risk of infertility dropped substantially for every one of the dietary and lifestyle strategies undertaken.

"In fact, we found a *sixfold difference* in ovulatory infertility risk between the women following five or more dietary and lifestyle habits and those following none."

What to do: Here are 10 key recommendations from Dr. Chavarro, based on the research...

1. "Avoid trans fats, the artery-clogging fats found in many commercially prepared products and fast foods."

2. "Use more unsaturated vegetable oils, such as olive oil or canola oil."

3. "Eat more vegetable protein, such as beans and nuts, and less animal protein."

4. "Choose whole grains and other sources of carbohydrates that have lower, slower effects on blood sugar and insulin, rather than highly refined carbohydrates that quickly boost blood sugar and insulin."

5. "Drink a glass of whole milk or have a small dish of ice cream or full-fat yogurt every day; temporarily trade in skim milk and low- or no-fat dairy products such as cottage cheese and frozen yogurt for their full-fat cousins."

6. "Take a multivitamin that contains folic acid and other B vitamins."

7. "Get plenty of iron from fruits, vegetables, beans and supplements, but not from red meat."

8. "Beverages matter—water is great; coffee, tea and alcohol are okay in moderation; leave sugared sodas unopened."

9. "Aim for a healthy weight. If you are overweight, losing between five and ten percent of your weight can jump-start ovulation."

10. "If you aren't physically active, start a daily exercise plan. If you already exercise, pick up the pace of your workouts. But don't overdo it, especially if you are quite lean—too much exercise can work against conception."

"These ten tips work on many levels," says Dr. Chavarro. "They are simple. They don't have side effects. They are available to everyone, not just those with good health insurance. Best of all, they are every bit as good for your long-term health—and your partner's—as they are for improving infertility. And they can be used on their own, or as a booster for assisted reproduction technologies."

However: "Keep in mind," he says, "that diet, exercise and other self-help approaches can't beat a blocked fallopian tube or the condition known as *azoospermia*—fewer or inactive sperm in the semen."

☀ *The Fertility Diet* by Jorge E. Chavarro, MD, ScD, Walter C. Willett, MD, DrPH, and Patrick J. Skerrett (McGraw-Hill).

ACUPUNCTURE IMPROVES IN VITRO FERTILIZATION

You take fertility medications to stimulate the production of eggs in the ovaries. You undergo a minor surgical procedure under local anesthesia, in which a hollow needle is inserted into the pelvic cavity and the eggs are retrieved.

Your partner contributes his sperm. The eggs and sperm are combined in a laboratory dish, which is placed in an incubator for fertilization. A few days later, the two-to-four cell embryo is inserted into your uterus, via a catheter.

This stressful and expensive procedure (around $12,000) is called *in vitro fertilization*, or IVF, and it's a common option for infertile couples, with 120,000 performed in the United States yearly.

Problem: More often than not, IVF doesn't work!

The "live birth rate" for each attempt at IVF is 30 to 35% for women under age 35…25% for women 35 to 37…15 to 20% for women 38 to 40…and 6 to 10% for women over 40.

Needles can improve those numbers. And we're not talking about another injection or operation. We're talking about acupuncture—a healing technique from Traditional Chinese Medicine (TCM), in which tiny, painless needles are inserted into acupoints in order to balance chi, the body's fundamental energy.

▐▐▐▶ *Breakthrough Study*

Researchers at the Center for Integrative Medicine at the University of Maryland School of Medicine analyzed seven studies on acupuncture and IVF, involving 1,366 women.

Result: They found that adding acupuncture to IVF improved the odds of pregnancy by 65%, ongoing pregnancy by 87% and live birth by 91%.

"This review suggests that acupuncture given with embryo transfer improves rates of pregnancy and live birth among women undergoing in vitro fertilization," says Eric Manheimer, MS, the study leader.

How it works: There are four ways that acupuncture might improve IVF outcomes, says Belinda Anderson, PhD, LAc, of the Pacific College of Oriental Medicine. It might…help

GET A BEAD ON BIRTH CONTROL

From Alesse to Zovia, many of the medications for birth control can breed health problems. Possible side effects listed on the package insert of one oral contraceptive include acne, gallbladder disease, hair loss and heart attack—and that's just four out of the 70 items on the list!

Devices such as diaphragms and IUDs, while generally safe and effective, also have downsides—for example, diaphragm use can trigger chronic bladder infections, and an IUD can cause spotting and severe cramping.

Are there drug-free, device-free ways to stay baby-free?

Yes, the Ovulation Method and the Symptothermal Method—methods for determining fertile days of your menstrual cycle when you need to avoid unprotected intercourse.

Problem: While those methods are effective, they're difficult to learn and complex to use. The Symptothermal Method, for example, requires that you monitor (among other signs) cervical secretions, basal body temperature, breast tenderness and libido. It's not surprising that less than 1% of women in the US use "fertility-awareness" as their birth control.

Solution: The Standard Days Method—simply keep count of the days of your menstrual cycle, and avoid unprotected intercourse on days eight through 19, the "fertile window" when you're most likely to become pregnant.

The Study: Research shows that the failure rate among women using the Standard Days Method is 4.8%—fewer than five women out of 100 using the method for one year will get pregnant in the first year of use. That's *more* effective than the correct and consistent use of spermicides or a diaphragm, and only a little less effective than the correct and regular use of a condom.

How it works: The Standard Days Method makes use of a simple device called CycleBeads—a string of beads that lets you track your cycle. Day by day during the month, you simply move a rubber ring over a series of color-coded beads, with each bead representing a day of your cycle. All the *white* beads mark the days when you're likely to get pregnant if you have unprotected sex. All the *brown* beads mark the days when you are not likely to get pregnant.

"Most people who use the Standard Days Method do so because it is natural and has no side effects," says Victoria H. Jennings, PhD, director of the Institute of Reproductive Health at Georgetown University and inventor of CycleBeads.

You can purchase CycleBeads and find out more about them at *www.cyclebeads.com* or e-mail *info@cyclebeads.com*.

However: If you have more than one cycle a year that is less than 26 days or more than 32 days, CycleBeads won't work for you. (Approximately 20% of women have cycles outside this range.) If you can answer yes to these two questions—"Do your periods usually come about once a month?" and "Do your periods usually come when you expect them?"—it's likely the beads and you are a match. Using the beads themselves also provides a simple method for quickly identifying whether your cycle is shorter than 26 or longer than 32 days—if it is, you should stop using them. You can take a self-screening test at *www.cyclebeads.com* to find out if CycleBeads are right for you.

Also helpful: "Evidence shows that 20% of women are unsuccessful in their attempts to *get* pregnant simply because they do not know on which days pregnancy is most likely. Knowing exactly when she is fertile is critical to a woman who wants to achieve a pregnancy," says Dr. Jennings.

regulate hormones…increase blood flow to the uterus and ovaries…reduce inflammation…and reduce stress, anxiety and depression.

What to do: Many of these studies involved two sessions of acupuncture on the day of the embryo transfer, one immediately before the transfer and one immediately after.

However: "Realistically, most acupuncturists are not part of the staff of the IVF center, so they can't give the treatments in this manner," says

Khim Choong, MS, LAc, RN, an acupuncturist specializing in infertility, at Los Gatos Oriental Medicine, in California.

If that's the case, she suggests a series of twice-weekly acupuncture treatments, in the four weeks before the transfer. "This will help increase the thickness of the uterine lining, increasing the likelihood of a successful pregnancy," says Choong.

She also recommends that an infertile woman work with a practitioner of TCM to improve her health comprehensively, not only through acupuncture, but also herbal treatments, diet and other lifestyle changes. "I've had patients who were considered to be 'low responders,' producing few eggs when their ovaries are stimulated—and even these women can conceive when they commit to getting themselves healthier," says Choong.

☀ To find an acupuncturist near you, visit the Web site of the National Certification Commission for Acupuncture and Oriental Medicine, *www.nccaom.org*, where you can search for certified acupuncturists by area code or zip code.

THE BABY SUPPLEMENT

"Vitamins and minerals play a major role in fertility function, and using nutritional supplements as a first step in treatment could improve key factors essential to fertility," says Lynn Westphal, MD, of the Stanford Fertility and Reproductive Medicine Center.

"Herbs have been used for the treatment of infertility since at least two hundred AD, and herbal products also have the potential to add to existing treatment options," she adds.

The challenge for physicians and their patients, she says, has been a lack of scientific evidence about *which* nutrients and herbs are

the most effective...what levels are safe...and what combinations are safe.

Dr. Westphal may have answered some of those questions.

▶ *Breakthrough Study*

Based on scientific studies on various herbs and nutrients for fertility, Dr. Westphal and her colleagues formulated a supplement containing the herb chasteberry (*Vitex agnus-castus*), green tea catechins, the amino acid L-arginine, vitamins B-6, B-12, C, E and folate, and the minerals iron, magnesium, zinc and selenium.

Next, they studied 93 women, aged 24 to 42, who had tried unsuccessfully to conceive for six to 36 months, dividing them into two groups. For three months, one group took the supplement and the other a placebo.

Result: Thirty-two percent (17 of 53) of the women in the supplement group became pregnant, compared to 10% in the placebo group (four of 40).

"It surprised us when nutritional and herbal supplementation worked as well as it did," says Dr. Westphal. "Supplementation may play an important role in optimizing fertility health, leading to improved conception rates, and could provide an effective alternative or addition to conventional fertility therapies, particularly in cases of menstrual irregularity or unexplained infertility."

How it works: Dr. Westphal explains—the herb chasteberry supports good hormone balance and normal ovulation by increasing levels of luteinizing hormone and progesterone...the amino acid L-arginine helps improve circulation to the reproductive organs, which may help the development of eggs and also embryo implantation...the antioxidants vitamin E, selenium and green tea catechins reduce oxidative damage to the reproductive organs...studies have shown that vitamins B-6, B-12 and the minerals iron, zinc and magnesium can improve female fertility...and folic acid assists in the reduction of neural tube birth defects.

ℹ The doctors studied Fertility Blend.

Suggested intake: Follow the dosage recommendation on the label—three capsules a day.

☀ You can purchase FertilityBlend and read more about the supplement at *www.fertility blend.com*. The Daily Wellness Company, 1946 Young Street, Suite 390, Honolulu, HI 96826 (866-222-9862); e-mail *dwcservice@dailywell ness.com*.

LOW-CARB DIET FOR PCOS

Ten percent of American women have polycystic ovary syndrome (PCOS)—and it's the number one cause of infertility. And no wonder.

Periods are irregular or stop...your body produces high levels of *androgens*, male hormones such as testosterone, with the outward signs of coarse hair on the face and chest, male pattern baldness and acne...the egg-producing ovaries are prickly with tiny cysts...50% of women with PCOS are overweight (itself a risk factor for infertility)...and most suffer from blood sugar problems.

In fact, *insulin resistance*—the refusal of muscle and fat cells to heed the call of the hormone that tells them to absorb blood sugar—is a common feature of the disease. High insulin levels trigger the production of more androgens, and block the production of *sex hormone binding globulin*, which helps keep testosterone in check.

That's why doctors at the Duke University Medical Center in Durham, NC, decided to see if a very low-carbohydrate diet might help

regulate blood sugar and insulin levels, thereby easing the symptoms of PCOS.

▐▐▶ *Breakthrough Study*

The researchers studied five women with PCOS. All of them were overweight, with a body mass index of 27 or higher. (For example, a 5'4" woman with a BMI of 27 would weigh 157 pounds.)

At an initial group meeting, the women were instructed how and why to eat a very low-carbohydrate diet, limiting their carbohydrate intake to less than 20 grams a day. They continued to meet for one hour every other week for the next six months, receiving further instruction and encouragement.

Results: After six months, the women lost an average of 12% of their weight...their testosterone dropped by 22%...their insulin levels dropped by 54% (a sign of less insulin resistance)...and their blood pressure dropped significantly. Also, there was a greater balance in two of the hormones that regulate menstruation.

The symptoms of PCOS also decreased, with more regular periods, less body hair and more balanced emotions.

Best of all, two of the 11 women became pregnant—"despite previous infertility problems," says John C. Mavropoulos, MPH, of the Duke University Medical Center.

"The results were quite dramatic, he says. "This magnitude of weight loss, with the resolution of PCOS symptoms, is a desirable effect in any intervention."

What to do: The study participants followed the "Induction Phase" of the Atkins Diet. *The diet includes...*

• **Animal foods.** Unlimited consumption of animal foods (meat, chicken, turkey, other fowl, fish, shellfish).

• **Cheese.** Four ounces of prepared and two ounces of fresh cheeses a day.

- **Eggs.** Unlimited eggs.
- **Salad vegetables.** Two cupfuls a day of salad vegetables such as alfalfa sprouts, arugula, bok choy, celery, chickory, chives, cucumber, daikon, endive, escarole, fennel, jicama, lettuce, mushrooms, parsley, peppers, radicchio, radishes, romaine and sorrel.
- **Low-carbohydrate vegetables.** One cupful a day of low-carbohydrate vegetables, such as artichoke hearts, asparagus, bamboo shoots, bean sprouts, broccoli, Brussels sprouts, cabbage, cauliflower, chard, collard greens, dandelion greens, eggplant, heart of palm, kale, kohlrabi, leeks, okra, onion, pumpkin, rhubarb, sauerkraut, scallions, snow peas, spaghetti squash, spinach, string or wax beans, summer squash, tomato, turnips, water chestnuts and zucchini.
- **Water.** Six, eight-ounce glasses of water a day. Abstain from alcohol and caffeine.
- **Daily multivitamin.**

Caution: The Induction Phase of the Atkins Diet is designed to last for two weeks; the women stayed on it for 24 weeks. Talk to your doctor or a nutritionist about whether an extended very low-carbohydrate diet is a good strategy for you.

☀ *Dr. Atkins New Diet Revolution* by Robert C. Atkins (Avon).

FOR A SMARTER BABY, TAKE OMEGA-3

To form, brain cells need the essential fatty acid DHA (docosahexaenoic acid), an omega-3 fatty acid found mainly in fish oil. Scientists in Norway theorized that pregnant women who got more DHA in their diets might have smarter babies.

To find out, they studied 262 pregnant women, dividing them into two groups. From the 18th week of pregnancy until three months after delivery, one group took cod liver oil (10 milliliters a day, or about two teaspoons); the other took the same amount of corn oil.

Four years later, 76 of the children had IQ tests, 41 from the cod liver oil group, and 35 from the corn oil group.

On average, the DHA kids had IQs that were 4.1 points higher.

"Our study shows that four-year-old children have higher mental processing scores [the basis of the IQ test] when the mothers are supplemented with omega-3 fatty acids during pregnancy and lactation," say the researchers, in *Pediatrics*, the journal of the American Academy of Pediatrics. "The maternal intake of DHA during pregnancy appears to be important for mental development measured at four years of age."

What to do: Talk to your pediatrician about whether cod liver oil or a supplement of omega-3 fatty acids is right for you. The cod liver oil contained 1,183 mg of DHA and 803 mg of EPA (eicosapentaenoic acid), another fatty acid found in fish oil.

INDEX